Beyond Pleasure and Pain

Beyond Pleasure and Pain

How Motivation Works

E. TORY HIGGINS

Columbia University

OXFORD
UNIVERSITY PRESS

2/17/12
ww
$ 69.95

OXFORD
UNIVERSITY PRESS

Published in the United States of America by Oxford University Press, Inc.,
198 Madison Avenue, New York, NY, 10016
United States of America

Oxford University Press, Inc. publishes works that further Oxford University's objective of excellence in
research, scholarship, and education

Oxford is a registered trade mark of Oxford University Press in the UK and in certain other countries

Library of Congress Cataloging-in-Publication Data

Higgins, E. Tory (Edward Tory), 1946-
  Beyond pleasure and pain : how motivation works / E. Tory Higgins.
    p. cm. — (Oxford series in social cognition and social neuroscience)
  Includes bibliographical references and index.
  ISBN 978-0-19-976582-9 (hbk) 1. Motivation (Psychology) I. Title. II. Series.
  BF503.H53 2011
  153.8—dc22   2011010642

3 5 7 9 10 8 6 4 2
Typeset in Minion
Printed on acid-free paper
Printed in the United States of America

To Robin and Kayla
The Bookends of My Life

CONTENTS

PREFACE

When did I begin this book? In pondering this question, I realized that there was more than one answer to this question. This book is about how motivation works and, especially, how motivation is *beyond pleasure and pain*. In everyday life, the notion that motivation is about maximizing pleasure and minimizing pain—about the hedonic properties of objects and events in the world—is often translated into trying to manage others' motivation through "carrots and sticks." When I think back, the first time that I can remember learning that there was another way to manage others' motivation was a story that my mother, Aggie Higgins, told me. As a nutritionist, she tried to motivate poor pregnant women to eat extra food during pregnancy to make up for their current nutritional deficits.

Did she use some form of pleasant "carrot," such as praise, or some form of painful "stick," such as guilt or blame, to motivate her clients? No. Her method was something that I, as a 10-year-old, could fully appreciate only many years later. What she did was to go home with her clients and talk to their families. The families she worked with in Montreal were typically quite large, which meant that usually the family already had one or more children, in addition to the husband. My mother's method was to involve both the husband and the children. She asked them to set an extra plate on the table for the "soon-to-be-born" child and to help out by filling that plate with extra food that the mother would eat as a proxy for the child. The "soon-to-be-born" child was treated as already having a place at the table and needing to eat along with everyone else.

What this method did was to create a new reality or truth for the family about what the "soon-to-be-born" child needed—extra food. It involved everyone in being effective at establishing this new reality about the child. What this method also did was to give the family some control over what happened to the child even before it was born. It involved everyone in being effective at managing what happened. It was not about motivating through pleasure and pain. Rather, it was about motivating through *truth* and *control* working together so that the entire family, including the "soon-to-be-born" child, would "go in the right direction." This was my first exposure to a different approach to what motivation is and how it can be used to motivate others—an approach that emphasizes motives other than just pleasure and pain. Needless to say, this was just one of many lessons on motivation that I received from my mother while I was growing up. Thanks Mom!

Over 20 years later, there was another period that contributed to the story of this book. It was a time when I became depressed. I could not understand what was happening to me, as I was no longer motivated to pursue goals. I was not interested in accomplishing anything. Before this event, I thought I had a pretty good understanding of what motivated people. But I knew now that I didn't have a clue about how motivation works. I decided that if I were ever to work again as a psychologist, I would study motivation and try to understand what I was experiencing and where it came from. Thanks to an exceptionally talented therapist, Brian Shaw, I did recover and I did begin to study motivation.

My goal was to understand better the difference between the psychology of depression and the psychology of anxiety. This led to the development of Self-Discrepancy Theory in the mid-1980s (a theory about how failure to attain hopes and aspirations produces depression, whereas failure to meet duties and obligations produces anxiety), which later gave birth to Regulatory Focus Theory in the mid-1990s (a theory about the differences in how goals are pursued, problems are solved, and decisions are made when people have promotion concerns with advancement versus prevention concerns with security). What these two theories have in common is an emphasis on the *different ways* that people approach pleasure and avoid pain. To understand the difference between depression and anxiety, for example, it is necessary to go beyond pleasure and pain because both depression and anxiety are painful. It is not the pain that matters; it is the different ways in which depressed people and anxious people are ineffective. Depressed people are ineffective in attaining their aspirations (their ideals), in attaining what they want to accomplish. In contrast, anxious people are ineffective in maintaining their responsibilities (their oughts), in maintaining the security they want.

Self-Discrepancy Theory and Regulatory Focus Theory were the grandparent and parent of Regulatory Fit Theory (a theory about how people engage more strongly and "feel right" about what they are doing when the manner of their goal pursuit sustains their orientation toward the goal). This book would not have happened without Regulatory Fit Theory because it was research testing this theory that discovered how the value of something does not depend on its hedonic properties alone. What also matters is how strongly people engage in their pursuit of something. And people are more strongly engaged when *how* they pursue a goal *fits* their goal orientation, such as eagerly pursuing an ideal aspiration or vigilantly pursuing an ought responsibility. Rather than pleasure and pain, often *it's the fit that counts*.

Because this book would not exist without Self-Discrepancy Theory, Regulatory Focus Theory, and Regulatory Fit Theory, the collaborations with those colleagues who helped me develop and test these theories is another compelling answer to when I began this book. Their contributions to these theories were critical. I cannot mention all those who contributed, but I do need to give special thanks to Kirsten Appelt, Tamar Avnet, Amy Taylor Bianco, Jenny Boldero, Miguel Brendl, Joel Brockner, Joe Cesario, Ellen Crowe, Baruch Eitam, Jens Forster, Becca Franks, Tony Freitas, Heidi Grant, Ruth Klein, Lorraine Idson, Angela Lee, John Levine, Nira Liberman, Marlene Moretti, Dan Molden, Jill Paine, Michel Pham, Jason Plaks, Abel Rodriguez, Chris Roney, Abby Scholer, James Shah, Steen Sehnert, Scott Spiegel, Tim Strauman, Orit Tykocinski, Elizabeth Van Hook, Shu Zhang, and Canny Zou.

I also need to thank those colleagues with whom I worked to develop and test Regulatory Mode Theory. This theory is also an important part of this book. It distinguishes between when people are motivated simply to move from place to place ("Just Do It") and when people are motivated to compare and critically evaluate different options ("Do It Right"). The former is a control motivation and the latter is a truth motivation. Neither motivation is about pleasure and pain. Moreover, how these motivations work *together* effectively provides a key example of how motivation works beyond pleasure and pain. In addition to some of the colleagues above who also contributed to Regulatory Mode Theory, I need to thank especially Arie Kruglanski (the co-creator of Regulatory Mode Theory), Lucia Mannetti, and Antonio Pierro.

The next answer to when I began this book is when Walter Mischel began prompting me (should I say nudging?) to write it. Walter and I have been colleagues together in the Department of Psychology at Columbia for over 20 years, and we have been friends for much longer. About 10 years ago, I began to envision a Motivation Science Center at Columbia. More generally, I began to envision the emergence of motivation science as a major intellectual force in science, and beyond science to the humanities as well, just as cognitive science and neuroscience had achieved before. (This is not to suggest that motivation science is independent of cognitive science and neuroscience, but the emphasis is different.) Walter told me that it was fine to devote time to Center activities but there was something I should do that was even more important; specifically, to write my own book on motivation science. He argued that I needed to convey my answers to how motivation works. What exactly was this science of motivation that I believed so strongly everyone should know about? It took a few years for me to follow Walter's sage advice, but I did eventually begin writing this book on motivation. Thanks Walter!

Once I started the book I soon realized that I did not know what the book was actually about. What were the takeaway messages? Who was the audience? I have an operating style of choosing titles for articles or chapters before I write them in order to identify the gist of my message and to set constraints on what

I will cover. Following this style, I began to create working titles for the book. For over two years, I kept changing the title. The patient audience who heard each new title, which I announced with great enthusiasm every time, was my wife Robin. Time after time she managed to be supportive, without fully sharing my enthusiasm. Given that time after time I abandoned the new title for a newer title, her not-fully-enthusiastic response was appropriate. Indeed, for many months it was not even clear that I would end up writing a book at all, given that I still did not know what the book was really about. Finally a point came that I did know what I wanted to say and Robin became convinced that the book was going to happen. From the first title to that point, Robin was always the great listener, advisor, and booster. She gave me the help I needed. Thanks Robin!

I also received exceptional support from my family. By "family," I refer not only to my nuclear family and relatives but also to my professional family. I have written that developing and testing theories is a "family affair." Writing this book was also a family affair. The members of my lab over the years are an essential part of the story of this book. I have mentioned many of them already, but I need also to thank all those other Honors and Supervised Individual Research undergraduates, postbacs, doctoral students, and postdoctoral students whom I have not mentioned by name who were part of the history of my lab over the past 25 years.

Then there are those who read chapters of the book at different stages of its development and gave me invaluable feedback about how to improve it. It is customary in a Preface to say something about how those who gave comments and suggestions are not responsible for any mistakes or errors or false ideas in the book. I have always found that a little annoying; of course they are not responsible for that. But are they responsible for making the book better? Instead of saying they are not to blame, how about giving them credit? With gratitude, I thank Joel Brockner, Ran Hassin, Ean Higgins, Harvey Hornstein, Eric Schoenberg, Ed Smith, Peter White, and Mark Zanna, who gave me thoughtful comments and suggestions on different chapters at different stages that changed the book for the better. For providing feedback on the *entire* book, improving both the ideas and how to express them, I am especially grateful to Bill Green, Jennifer Jonas, Arie Kruglanski, John Levine, Walter Mischel, Diane Ruble, and Yaacov Trope. I fully appreciate how much the final product owes to their insights and critical feedback.

Marion Osmun also gave feedback on the entire book. She was chosen by Catherine Carlin from Oxford University Press to provide professional feedback on both the writing and the entire structure and organization of the book. I learned a lot from her feedback, paid close attention to her comments, and approached the book differently from that point on. I am indebted and very thankful to her. I am also very thankful to Catherine, who not only recommended Marion to work on the book but was also an early enthusiastic backer for my writing the book and was unfailingly supportive when I most needed it. Thanks Catherine and Marion! I am also grateful to Ran Hassin as a Series Editor at Oxford University Press for his early support of this project. The final stages of production would not have been possible without the tireless help of Tracy O'Hara and the support of Joan Bossert. Thanks Ran, Tracy, and Joan!

There are two editors of my book whom I need to single out for special thanks. They also gave me feedback on every chapter of the book. The first person deserving special thanks as editor is my daughter Kayla Higgins. She was the first person to read and comment on every chapter in the first phase of writing this book. Her feedback was invaluable because I needed to know whether the chapters communicated to someone without a background in psychology. She told me, paragraph by paragraph, sentence by sentence, when they did or did not communicate. Over time, I got better at communicating, thanks to her. Thanks Kayla!

The second person deserving special thanks as editor is my wife Robin. She was the last person to read and comment on every chapter of the book. Robin had provided feedback on chapters at earlier stages of the project, but I asked her to go through every chapter one more time at the very end when I thought the book was finished. I asked her because I knew she wanted the book to be as good as it could be and would push me one last time when I needed to be pushed. This was a very important final stage, and I made many changes based on Robin's comments that I believe improved the book significantly. So once again, thanks Robin!

In my writing the chapters of this book, Kayla and Robin were my bookends. They are my bookends as well in the chapters of my adult life. I dedicate this book to them.

PART ONE

Introduction and Background

1

Motivation Beyond Pleasure and Pain

Let me begin at the beginning—the Genesis story of Adam and Eve in the Garden of Eden as told in the Bible. I believe that what the story tells us about the motivations of Adam and Eve at genesis is still relevant today for understanding what humans want. The story is as follows:

> And out of the ground made the Lord God to grow every tree that is pleasant to the sight, and good for food; the tree of life also in the midst of the garden, and the tree of knowledge of good and evil . . . And the Lord God commanded the man, saying, Of every tree of the garden thou mayest freely eat: But of the tree of the knowledge of good and evil, thou shalt not eat of it: for in the day that thou eatest thereof thou shalt surely die. (Genesis 2: 8–9, 16–17 [King James version])

Adam and Eve were blessed by God in being placed in the Garden of Eden—not only a paradise but *the* original paradise. The story clearly tells us that this was a place of all pleasure and no pain, a place in which grew "every tree that is pleasant to the sight, and good for food." Moreover, in the midst of the garden was the *tree of life*. This is important because Adam and Eve knew, from God's command, that they could eat the fruit of every tree in the garden except the *tree of knowledge*. This meant that they had permission to eat the fruit from the *tree of life*, and thus they could have a life of all pleasure and no pain *forever*. All they had to do was stay in the Garden of Eden and enjoy the fruit of the *tree of life* and the other abundant pleasures in this paradise.

But, as we all know, this is not what Adam and Eve chose to do. They chose instead to eat the forbidden fruit from the *tree of knowledge*. And it is precisely because this fruit was explicitly forbidden by God's command that there is no ambiguity about whether or not Adam and Eve freely chose to eat the fruit from the tree of knowledge. It was not an accident. What could possibly motivate them to make this choice when, by making it, they would "surely die," or at minimum be banished from paradise, losing an everlasting life of pleasure and no pain? If what people really want is to maximize pleasure and minimize pain, Adam and Eve would never have made this choice.

I believe that this story is telling us that there is more to human motivation than maximizing pleasure and minimizing pain. What else is there? The answer lies in why Adam and Eve would want to eat the fruit of the tree of knowledge. It is no accident, I believe, that it is, in fact, the tree of *knowledge*, the tree of *truth*. I believe that a central motivation of humans is to *establish what's real*, to distinguish between truth and falsehood, between reality and fantasy. This motivation for the truth can be as important to humans as life itself.

But this is not the end of what the Genesis story teaches us. The tree of knowledge is not just any knowledge—it is the *"tree of the knowledge of good and evil."* This means that eating the fruit of this tree also satisfies another central human motivation, the motivation to *manage what happens*, the motivation to control our lives. Only when humans have the knowledge of what is good and what is evil can they make *choices* based on competing preferences, choices that distinguish between different options that can vary in their hedonic and moral attributes; only then can they control their lives.

Importantly, Adam and Eve's life in the Garden of Eden has little need for truth or control because everything is provided for them in this paradise; whatever benefits and pleasures they enjoy are not due to their being effective in obtaining them. Thus, Adam and Eve cannot really be effective at having truth or control *unless* they eat from the tree of the knowledge of good and evil. And, significantly, this one tree *combines* the motivation for truth with the motivation for control. It is an example of the importance of *motivations working together* to direct life choices.

What is God's role in all this? It is no coincidence, I believe, that God is represented in the Bible as being both omniscient (possessing all *truth*) and omnipotent (possessing all power or *control*)—the same truth and control found in the tree of the knowledge of good and evil. Some critics have wondered why God would have created such a situation for Adam and Eve given that He would have foreseen their choice (truth) and could have changed their fate (control).

Some Christian theologians have asked, why would God set the conditions that would lead Adam and Eve to make a choice whose consequence was expulsion from paradise? One answer is that God knew the truth about what it meant to be truly human. God understood that, in order to be human, Adam and Eve had to disobey His command and eat from the tree of the knowledge of good and evil. Knowing what humans would really want and would need to choose in order to be truly effective, God set the necessary conditions for Adam and Eve to make their choice and leave the Garden of Eden in order that they could begin to experience a truly *human* life.

This Genesis story captures two major themes of this book. First, to understand human motivation it is necessary to go beyond pleasure and pain and appreciate the significance for human motivation of people wanting to be effective at establishing what's real (truth) and managing what happens (control). Second, it is important to recognize that these motivations do not function in isolation. They work together, and often the relations between and among them tell the story about what motivation is and how it functions. I believe that the significance of these relations among motivations—*how motivations work together*—has received insufficient attention in the literature.

FOUR EXPERIMENTS ON MOTIVATION

To provide a hint of where this book will take us, let me describe four experiments for you to ponder. For each study, I will begin with a description of the design and procedure—what the different experimental conditions were for the participants. After each study, I will ask you to predict what the results of the study would be or should be if people were motivated to maximize pleasure and minimize pain.

The "Eating a Worm" Study[1]

The participants in this study were told that they would perform a task and their physiological reactions to it would be measured. In one condition, they were shown three tasks: a neutral task of discriminating the weights of different small objects; a negative, disgusting task of eating a dead worm with a fork; and a negative scary task that involved shocking oneself. Some of the participants were told that they had been assigned to eat the worm and were seated in front of that task. They were read a statement reminding them that they were free, without penalty, to leave the study at any time. Only a few participants chose to leave the study.

While waiting for the worm-eating task to begin, they filled out a questionnaire asking them about the type of person they were, with options that included

"I am a brave person" and "I deserve to suffer." The experimenter then explained to the participants that a mistake had been made and they would not be eating the dead worm. Now that the worm task was eliminated, the participants were free to choose which of the remaining tasks they wanted to do. They could choose between the weight discrimination task and the shock task that involved giving themselves painful electric shocks.

If people are motivated to maximize pleasure and minimize pain, which task would they choose to do? The answer is obvious—the participants would choose the discrimination task rather than the shock task. Indeed, among those participants who were not originally assigned to the "worm-eating" task, 0% chose the shock task. However, among those participants who were originally assigned to the "worm-eating" task, 50% chose to give themselves painful electric shocks rather than do the weight discrimination. What is going on here? The answer will be given later in this chapter, but first another study to ponder.

The "Rat Race" Study[2]

During a training phase, rats had to pull either a heavy weight or a light weight to obtain a small amount of food. The rats were equally successful in attaining the food in the two weight conditions. They obtained the food on every trial (100% reinforcement) so that the benefits of their effort were the same in both conditions. But the effort costs were greater for the rats that had to pull the heavier weight to attain the food. Greater effort for the same benefit—welcome to the "rat race." Then in the test phase, which took place a day after the training phase was finished, the same food was offered, but the weight was removed so the rats could run freely. The value of the food that had been established during the training phase was now measured during this test phase by how fast the rats ran to the food, how fast they ate it, and how much they ate.

If rats, like humans, are motivated to maximize pleasure and minimize pain, which rats would value the food more? The answer is again obvious. Given the benefits/costs or pleasure/pain ratio for attaining the food during training, one would expect that the food would be valued more by the rats who had been trained in the light weight condition because they received the same food benefits with less effort costs. However, the *opposite* was found: the food was valued *more* by the rats that had been trained in the *heavy weight* condition. What is happening here?

The "Make Learning Fun" Study[3]

Undergraduates were given a paired-associate learning task to work on. In this task, they had to learn the association between a novel nonsense word, such as

"Bleemus," and its unusual definition, "the act of trying to start one's car when the engine is already running." These novel associations, inspired by Sniglets but not quite as funny,[4] were chosen to allow there to be different instructions to the participants. For the "high importance" instructions, the participants were told to be serious while learning the material because the paired associates were definitions of new words being created by linguists. For the "high fun" instructions, the participants were told to have fun while learning the somewhat amusing material. There were also "low fun" instructions (i.e., a forewarning that the task was tedious) and "low importance" instructions (i.e., introducing the task as just a pilot study) that were combined with the "high fun" and "high importance" instructions to create the following four types of instructions about how to learn the material: to learn it as "high importance and low fun," or as "high importance and high fun," or as "high fun and low importance," or as "low fun and low importance."

If humans are motivated to maximize pleasure and minimize pain, which participants should perform best on this task? Your answer could depend on whether you think high importance, compared to low importance, is relatively positive or relatively negative. Let's assume for this prediction that high importance (e.g., interesting) is more positive than low importance (e.g., boring). What would you then predict based on the assumption that humans want to maximize pleasure and minimize pain? You would predict that the participants in the "high importance and high fun" condition would perform best. But this is not what the study found: it found that participants who received "high importance and *low fun*" instructions learned the paired associates *better* than those who received "high importance and *high fun*" instructions. That is, adding "high fun" instructions *hurt* performance, and this was true despite the fact that participants did report having more fun under "high fun" instructions than "low fun" instructions. Why did this happen?

The "Eager vs. Vigilant Decision Making" Study[5]

Undergraduates at Columbia University were given the choice of deciding whether they preferred a Columbia coffee mug or an inexpensive pen. The manner in which they made this decision was manipulated by giving them different instructions prior to making their choice. Half of them were told to think about what they would gain by choosing the mug and what they would gain by choosing the pen—an *eager* manner of choosing that ensures advancement. The other half were told to think about what they would lose by not choosing the mug or what they would lose by not choosing the pen—a *vigilant* manner of choosing that ensures against making mistakes. This manner of making a choice did not influence their choice—almost all of them preferred the Columbia coffee mug over the pen.[6] After choosing the mug as their preferred option, the participants were given the opportunity to buy it with their own money. A measure taken at the beginning of the experimental session indicated that some of the participants had especially strong concerns with accomplishments and advancement (what we call a predominant "promotion" focus) whereas other participants had especially strong concerns with safety and security (what we call a predominant "prevention" focus). The study found that this personality difference by itself did not affect how much participants were willing to pay to buy the chosen mug.

If humans are motivated to maximize pleasure and minimize pain, which participants should value the chosen mug more as reflected in how much they were willing to pay to buy it? Your answer could depend on whether you think making a decision in an eager manner is a more positive experience than making a decision in a vigilant manner. If like most people you think that this is so, then you would predict that the participants who made their choice eagerly would offer to pay more to buy the mug than those who made their choice vigilantly. However, you might instead think that the manner of decision making is irrelevant; what are relevant are the hedonic properties of the chosen mug. Given that almost everyone chose the exact same mug, this predicts that it does not matter whether the decision was made in an eager or vigilant manner. If you made the latter prediction, then you are correct! In fact, as with the personality difference between predominant promotion and predominant prevention focus, how the choice was made (i.e., whether in an eager or vigilant manner) had *no* effect on what was offered to buy the mug.

However, this is not all that was found in this study. What was found to have a major effect was the *relation* between personality and manner of decision making. Predominant promotion participants who made their decision eagerly and predominant prevention participants who made their decision vigilantly offered much more money to buy the mug than predominant promotion participants who made their decision vigilantly and predominant prevention participants who made their decision eagerly—almost 70% more money for the exact same mug! Why?

WHAT WAS GOING ON IN THE STUDIES

It is time now to reveal the answers to what was going on in these four studies.

The "Eating a Worm" Study

Among those participants in this study who were originally assigned to the "worm-eating" task, 50% chose to give themselves painful electric shocks rather than do the weight discrimination task. Why did this happen? Among the participants who were assigned the "worm-eating" task, almost all of them chose to remain in the study. When asked on the questionnaire why they chose to remain in the study and do the "worm-eating" task, many of them decided that they must be a brave person or a person who deserved to suffer. When subsequently given a choice between the weight discrimination task and the shock task, they wanted to create *consistency* between their belief about themselves (i.e., "I am brave" or "I deserve to suffer") and their choice between the shock task and the weight discrimination task. They wanted consistency to establish what was real about themselves (truth). To do so, they needed to choose the task in which they would shock themselves. Thus, they chose to do something that they would normally never do just for the sake of consistency.

The results of this study illustrate how the motive to establish a coherent reality (truth) can trump the hedonic motive of avoiding pain. Later in the book, I will provide other compelling examples of the importance of truth motivation to humans. I will discuss the different ways in which people go about establishing what's real, including fulfilling their uniquely human desire to share reality with others, as reflected in our wanting others to believe what we believe and feel about the world the way we feel about the world. I will discuss how influential models of motivation, such as the classic subjective utility and expectancy-value models in psychology and economics, have failed to appreciate the significance of truth motivation in the choices that people make and in their commitment to them.

The "Rat Race" Study

By how fast the rats ran to the food, how much of the food they ate, and how fast they ate it, the rats in the high-costs condition (the heavy weight) showed that they valued the food more than the rats in the low-costs condition (the light weight). What is going on here? During the training phase, the weight that has to be pulled to reach the goal functions like an interfering force. This force needs to be opposed in order to get to the goal. Opposing an interfering force during goal pursuit strengthens engagement in the goal-pursuit activity. Stronger engagement intensifies the force of attraction toward the goal, which enhances the value of the goal object—in this case the food. I will be describing the results of other studies in this book that show the importance of strength of engagement in motivation.[7] Compared to the overwhelming attention that pleasure and pain have received as determinants of the value of things, strength of engagement has been overlooked as a determinant of how much we value things in our lives. This critical factor provides another example of how we need to go beyond pleasure and pain to understand more fully how motivation works.

The "Make Learning Fun" Study

Parents, teachers, and the creators of children's coloring storybooks all know that children's interest in learning will be enhanced if fun is added to the activity. After all, research on classical conditioning emphasizes that associating a positive experience with an activity would make that activity more positive. So shouldn't performance on the paired-associate learning task be enhanced by adding fun to it?

The answer is "yes," *if* individuals initially believe that paired-associate learning is more of a fun type of activity than it is an important type of activity, because then a fun manner of doing the activity would fit the participants' prior belief that this kind of activity is fun. But that is not the case for this kind of activity. Learning, especially when it seems to relate to intelligence, is thought to be more an important than a fun type of activity. This means that in this study a fun manner of doing the activity was a *non-fit* with the participants' prior belief that this kind of activity is important rather than fun, and this non-fit hurt their performance. What this and other studies have found is that what matters is not the orientation toward the activity in itself (i.e., a fun activity; an important activity) nor the manner in which the activity is engaged (enjoyable manner; serious manner) but, instead, the relation between the orientation and the manner. *It's the fit that counts.* When there is a fit between individuals' prior orientation toward an activity and the manner of carrying out the activity, engagement in the activity is strengthened, which can enhance performance. When there is a non-fit, as when an activity is thought to be important but the manner of engagement is enjoyable rather than serious, then engagement is weakened, which can hurt performance. This is what happened in the "make learning fun" study. I will later describe other studies on fit and non-fit and will discuss how to use the principles of regulatory fit to manage motivation more effectively and avoid the pitfalls of adding positives, like bonus incentives, when they do more harm than good.

The "Eager vs. Vigilant Decision Making" Study

Predominant promotion participants who eagerly chose a Columbia coffee mug over an inexpensive pen, and predominant prevention participants who vigilantly made the same choice, subsequently offered much more of their own money to buy the mug than predominant promotion participants who vigilantly chose the same mug and predominant prevention participants who eagerly did so. Given that the participants in these different conditions chose the same mug with the same hedonic properties, it is mysterious why the mug would be valued so much more in the former two conditions than the latter two.

What is going on? If you guessed, "It's the fit that counts," then you're right: once again, there is a fit effect. For predominant promotion individuals, pursuing goals in an eager manner fits their orientation and strengthens engagement in what they are doing—likewise for predominant prevention individuals who pursue goals in a vigilant manner. Vigilance is a non-fit for promotion and eagerness is a non-fit for prevention, and non-fit weakens engagement. Stronger engagement intensifies attraction toward a valued chosen object.

BEYOND THE HEDONIC PRINCIPLE

The findings of these four studies, like the story of Adam and Eve in the Garden of Eden, illustrate that the answer to what motivates people is beyond just pleasure and pain. The purpose of this book is to describe what psychologists have learned, especially in the past few decades, about how motivation works beyond pleasure and pain. You might be asking yourself whether such a book is really necessary: do we really believe that motivation is basically about maximizing pleasure and minimizing pain?

I cannot, of course, answer for each reader, but most of us still try to motivate ourselves and others as if we do believe this. In particular, we still resort to using incentives—the carrot and the stick—as our main tool of motivation. For example, a British diplomat on BBC News was recently quoted as saying that the solution to a political settlement with the moderate Taliban in Afghanistan was "the right combination of carrot and stick." As another example, consider the answer that Warren Buffett, the legendary investor, gave when answering a question at the Columbia Business School about how to manage heads of financial institutions who are running risks that they shouldn't be running. He said that in rewarding CEOs at the top we've been better at the carrots than the sticks: "but I think, I think that some more sticks are called for."

These examples illustrate the pervasive belief that incentives—different forms of "carrots" as pleasant rewards and "sticks" as painful punishments—should be used to motivate people to do what we want them to do. This belief derives from the conviction that people's actions and decisions are motivated by their wanting to approach pleasure and avoid pain—the *hedonic principle* of motivation that was recognized at least as long ago as the time of the ancient Greeks. Since then, there have been changes in the kinds of "carrots" we use to reward (or promise) people to get them to do what we want them to do, and in the kinds of "sticks" we use to punish (or threaten) people to get them to stop doing what we don't want them to do. In contemporary society, we use fewer material incentives like food, shelter, and corporal punishment, and use more social incentives like praise and blame. We understand that people are motivated not only by biological needs but also by the need for achievement or the need for social recognition. But this new understanding about what motivates people is simply translated into new kinds of incentives to get people to do what we want and not to do what we don't want.

I am not suggesting that the hedonic principle of approaching pleasure and avoiding pain has been the only motivational factor that has received attention traditionally. It has been recognized for a long time, for instance, that the strength of people's commitment to a decision depends not only on their beliefs about the pleasure or pain the decision will produce but also on their beliefs about the *likelihood* that these hedonic outcomes will actually occur. Indeed, both subjective utility theory and expectancy-value theory include likelihood as a critical part of motivational commitment. Yet these theories still emphasize hedonic outcomes. The likelihood part simply increases (for high likelihood) or decreases (for low likelihood) the motivational force associated with a hedonic outcome. For example, if you enjoy taking a walk on a sunny day, then you are likely to choose to take a walk rather than stay home. But the strength of this preference will be greater if the likelihood that it will be sunny is 90% rather than 50%. Notice that although likelihood is added as a factor, this is still fundamentally a story about hedonic outcome—about enjoying taking walks on a sunny day. Hedonic outcome is the only motivational force in these models. However, as I shall discuss, likelihood has its own separate motivational force. It is *not* the case that hedonic outcome is simply made stronger or weaker by likelihood.[8]

Thus, many people, including academic scholars, still believe that motivation is about maximizing pleasure and minimizing pain, and they are not familiar with the new ideas and discoveries in motivation science that this book describes. These new ideas and discoveries are significant in what they reveal about managing motivation more effectively and enhancing well-being.

Still, writing a book on motivation is a daunting task. Motivation is a topic that has received thoughtful attention for hundreds of years from thousands of eminent scholars. It is also a topic in which we all believe we have some expertise, whether or not we are formal scholars in the area. Even young children have to figure out what motivates their caretakers' actions towards them in order to get what they need from those caretakers. Managing others' motives is pervasive in human societies, from parents and children managing one another, to teachers and students, coaches and athletes, business supervisors and employees, military officers and subordinates, politicians and citizens. In fact, humans spend much of their lives managing others' motives and having their motives managed by others. We also spend much of our lives trying to manage our own motives. To carry out all of this managing of motives, we spend time trying to infer and understand our motives and those of others, as well as to establish a shared reality with others about our motives. Given that we spend so much time managing, comprehending, and sharing the motives of ourselves and others, in a real sense we *are* all experts in motivation.

What, then, can I add to all this scholarship and expertise? In brief, I plan to integrate what is now known about motivation into a new conceptual framework that can be used to re-address basic motivational issues in everyday life. Yes, people have expertise in motivation, but in most cases the expertise is applied rather than theoretical. By understanding motivation within a broader, more conceptual framework, people can apply their expertise in motivation even more effectively, whether they be parents, teachers, coaches, business supervisors, military officers, or politicians (or their children, students, athletes, employees, subordinates, or citizens).

At the outset, I do want to make clear what I mean by going beyond pleasure and pain. To begin with, I want to make clear what the traditional claim means that pleasure and pain are what really motivate people. The general motivational question that I am trying to answer is, "What is it that people want and don't want?" I am using the term "want" advisedly. To avoid tautological reasoning, I need a general terminology for motivation that does not presume, by definition, what motivation is all about. The term "want" is ideal in this regard because it captures in everyday language a wide variety of relevant meanings of motivation: to have or feel need of, to be necessary (require); to wish or demand the presence of; to desire to come, go, or be; to have a strong desire for or inclination to (i.e., to like); to fail to possess (lack); to hunt or seek in order to seize.[9]

Now if "pleasure and pain" were defined as "want and don't want," then they would become, *by definition*, the answer to "What do people want and don't want?" This would not be useful because it would serve to eliminate alternative viewpoints right from the beginning simply by defining "pleasure and pain" so broadly. What is needed, then, is a more precise definition of "pleasure" and "pain." The *Oxford English Dictionary* (1971) defines pleasure as the sensation that is induced by the experience or anticipation of what is felt to be desirable, with an emphasis on sensuous enjoyment. And it defines pain as physical or bodily suffering, an unpleasant or agonizing sensation. Thus, pleasure and pain are, respectively, *desired and undesired feelings or sensations* (including anticipatory feelings or sensations).

The traditional viewpoint, then, is that motivation is about people approaching desired feelings or sensations (pleasure) and avoiding undesired feelings or sensations (pain). Why is it necessary to provide an alternative viewpoint that goes "beyond pleasure and pain"? First, pleasure and pain refer to only one kind of outcome of goal pursuit—hedonic experience. There are outcomes other than hedonic experience that people care about; in particular, they want to be successful at what they do even if they have to suffer to make it happen.

Second, although hedonic experience contributes to how intensely people value things in the world, it is not the only mechanism that contributes to value intensity; in particular, how strongly people engage in goal pursuits affects how intensely they value the objects and activities associated with those goal pursuits. Third, even when motivation is about pleasure and pain, there is more than one way to approach pleasure and avoid pain, such as doing so with promotion concerns with accomplishment and advancement or with prevention concerns with safety and security. And the distinct motivational systems underlying the different ways people approach pleasure and avoid pain each have their own separate effects on thoughts, feelings, and behavior. For example, success (pleasure) or failure (pain) in the promotion system produces cheerful or dejected feelings (e.g., feeling "happy" or "sad"), whereas success or failure in the prevention system produces quiescent or agitated feelings (e.g., feeling "calm" or "worried"). Fourth, motivation is not just about having desired outcomes, such as having pleasure and not having pain. People also want to manage what happens in their lives (control), and they want to distinguish what's true in the world from what's false, to establish what's real (truth). Finally, and importantly, the different ways of being effective do not function in isolation from one another. Much of motivation concerns the relations among the different ways to be effective—how they work together. One example of this is that, often, it is the *fit* that counts.

Thus, I believe that the best answer to the question of what it is that people want is that they *want to be effective*. People want to be effective at having desired outcomes (value), but they also want to be effective at establishing what's real (truth) and at managing what happens (control). Precisely what I mean by this will become clearer as the book continues. But here a caveat is needed to avoid misunderstanding. I am not claiming that wanting to be effective encompasses *all* of motivation. After all, motivation to see a sunset is not, one hopes, just to succeed at something ("I think that I am watching the most beautiful sunset that anyone has ever seen"); it is simply to enjoy a wonder of nature. For humans at least, anticipating the experience of some sensual pleasure in the future—be it watching a sunset, drinking a great red wine, or taking a warm bath, to name a few such pleasures—can influence choices in the present. When people engage in these and similar activities solely for the sensual experience they afford, then the motivation involved cannot reasonably be considered as just wanting to be effective.

Nonetheless, I believe that wanting to be effective is generally what motivates people, with pleasure and pain typically functioning as feedback signals of success (pleasure) and failure (pain) at being effective. For example, failure in having enough food or enough water produces painful feedback signals of hunger and thirst. Working to get the needed food or water is not about wanting future pleasure—it is about being effective in satisfying current bodily needs. I will expand on this point throughout the book. I will also point out that even for the hedonic activities I just mentioned (e.g., drinking a great red wine), there can be components of wanting to be effective that go beyond just wanting a pleasant experience.

Thus, while wanting to be effective is *not* the whole story of motivation, what this book shows is that it is much more of the story than people appreciate. Indeed, I believe that it is the major part of the story of how motivation works when it also includes how value, truth, and control effectiveness *work together*. I believe that this story needs to be described more fully than it has been in the past.

In this book, I review and integrate research and ideas from the scientific literature that provides this alternative viewpoint on motivation. I attempt to present an original perspective on what motivation is and how it works. I propose ways of thinking about motivation, conceptual distinctions, and underlying mechanisms that are new and have inspired recent research, including my own work on *regulatory focus* (promotion vs. prevention), *regulatory fit*, and *strength of engagement*.

I believe that those who are concerned with motivating themselves or others, or are the target of others motivating them, need to know about the motivation science discoveries of the past few decades. It is not simply that the hedonic story—the notion that approaching pleasure and avoiding pain is how motivation works—is incomplete and needs to be augmented. It can also be wrong. Often belief in this story leads to attempts to motivate that are counterproductive, that impede rather than support success.

Although the emphasis in this book is on the research and ideas from recent decades that tell the story of how value, truth, and control effectiveness work and work together, I also review classic ideas and research from earlier periods. I believe that a historical context is needed to appreciate the contribution of recent discoveries, and that there are historical precursors of current ideas that should be acknowledged and appreciated. Whether I am reviewing classic work or more recent work, I want the book to be comprehensible to readers *without* a background in psychology. As the book proceeds, I attempt to provide the necessary conceptual and empirical background in such a way that the new picture of motivation slowly unfolds. This story is new even to most academic psychologists and, thus, I make as few assumptions as possible regarding what the reader already knows about motivation. At the same time, I am challenging a dominant viewpoint—the hedonic principle—and this means that it takes an effort to develop an understanding of and appreciation for the new viewpoint being proposed. I believe that the journey and the destination will make the effort well worthwhile.

The next chapter revisits in more detail the questions of "What do people really want?" and "What does it mean to be motivated?" that underlie, ultimately, the general question of "What is motivation?" The answers from various viewpoints provide a historical background on the topic of motivation, and my own proposed answers serve as the foundation and framework for the subsequent chapters.

Chapter 3 describes how value effectiveness, truth effectiveness, and control effectiveness are distinct from maximizing pleasure and minimizing pain and, importantly, are distinct from one another. The subsequent chapters then describe concepts and research findings that are relevant for understanding how each of these ways of being effective functions psychologically—value effectiveness (Chapter 4), truth effectiveness (Chapter 5), and control effectiveness (Chapter 6). The next chapters concern how these distinct motivations *work together*: value–truth relations (Chapter 7), value–control relations (Chapter 8), and truth–control relations (Chapter 9).

In Chapter 10, I put all the effectiveness elements—value, truth, and control—together within an *organization* of motivations. I describe how these different ways of being effective support one another, how an impact on one element can spread to influence each of the other elements, how they can receive differential emphasis or significance, and how working together as a whole, they are more important and more meaningful than when they work as independent elements.

This book, then, reflects my personal way of organizing and reviewing the motivation science literature as it relates to my overall "value, truth, and control" framework and to my ideas about what motivation is and how it works. This book is not intended to be a textbook in the usual sense because it emphasizes knowledge that goes beyond the classic pleasure and pain story and because it offers my personal perspective on motivation. As such, I hope that it will inspire readers to think differently about motivation, to try different ways to motivate themselves and others, and to carry out new research—both basic and applied. To assist in this last goal, I use the ideas that have been reviewed and developed in this book to address, in the final chapters, some longstanding issues in psychology: What are the motivational underpinnings of personality differences and cultural differences (Chapter 11)? What are the best ways to manage motives effectively (Chapter 12)? What is the "good life" and how does motivation contribute to well-being (Chapter 13)? It is my hope that you will find the ideas in this book both challenging and useful.

2

What *is* Motivation?

Each of us has a general idea of the difference between what people are like when they are motivated and what they are like when they are not. Each of us also has a general idea of what motivates people. However, we don't all have the *same* ideas. And the ideas we have about motivation usually remain tacit and thus are not critically evaluated. Indeed, most of us try to manage others' motives, as well as our own motives, without an explicit awareness of our assumptions about what motivation is or how it works. We just get on with "motivating" without thinking a lot about what exactly we are doing. This makes sense in many cases because managing motives can proceed, and reap benefits, without the need to be explicit about our motivational assumptions. But I cannot proceed to write a book about motivation without taking a stand on what I think motivation is and how it works, and I must be precise about my starting assumptions. In this chapter, I will present different positions on what it means to be motivated and what it is that people want, along with my own preferred answers to these questions.

WHAT DOES IT MEAN TO BE MOTIVATED?

Years ago I taught a class in motivation for the Columbia Business School's Senior Executive Program. The students taking the class were generally high-level executives who spent much of their time managing their subordinates' motives. They could be thought of as applied motivation experts who had some professional knowledge about motivation as part of their executive training in business. I began the class by asking them what they thought it meant to be motivated. The most common answer was that it meant to have high energy or to be willing to expend high energy (effort) in the pursuit of goals. This answer reflects the most influential conception among professional scientists and laypersons alike—the conception of motivation as *energy* (to be directed). Let's begin with this proposal.

Motivation as All-Purpose Energy (To Be Directed)

The notion of motivation as all-purpose energy that can then be directed brings different images to mind. One image is igniting the fuel in your car and then guiding the car to a destination. Another image is putting a battery in a battery-powered toy, like the Energizer Bunny, or turning the key in a windup toy, and then directing the toy to some destination. These images treat motivation as energy that can be created within some object—by putting in fuel or a battery or winding a spring—and this energy provides the power that can be directed toward some destination. From this viewpoint, it does not matter where the energy comes from—fuel, battery, wound spring—as long as it provides power that can be directed. It is *all-purpose energy*. For example, once the fuel is in the car and is ignited, the car can go forwards or backwards, to the left or to the right, for short or long distances to any destination until the energy is depleted.

When the senior executives in my course offered "energy (to be directed)" as the answer to what is motivation, I think they had something very much like these examples in mind. I don't mean to say that they treated their subordinates as objects to be manipulated rather than as human beings. Instead, when they thought of energizing their subordinates, it was with very human incentives like social recognition and praise. What I am saying is that they believed that they needed to use the appropriate incentives and work conditions to get their subordinates "energized," "fired up," and then the subordinates could be directed to the destination or goal that management wanted. There is a long history of eminent scholars in psychology and other disciplines who, like these senior executives, have treated—and still treat—motivation as all-purpose energy.

SUPPORT FOR MOTIVATION AS "ALL-PURPOSE ENERGY (TO BE DIRECTED)"

In the first half of the 20th century, there were three highly influential schools of thought in psychology—the psychodynamic school, the learning or conditioning school, and the Gestalt school. Although these schools differed from each other in critical ways, they all viewed motivation as all-purpose energy to be directed. For Sigmund Freud, the father of the psychodynamic school, there is an underlying quantitative, finite amount of *instinctual energy*, "drive cathexis" or "libido," that can be used in different kinds of activities.[1] This energy powers our life pursuits. Freud made the additional assumption that this energy inherently seeks to discharge or release, which is associated with his classic "hydraulic" notion of undischarged drives overflowing the "reservoir," producing anger and aggressive behavior. Freud's notion of general psychic energy powering life pursuits was shared by many influential thinkers in the psychodynamic movement, such as Alfred Adler, Carl Jung, and Harry Sullivan.

In the 1940s and 1950s, Clark Hull developed his neobehaviorism theory. In this theory, the essential motivational construct was the concept of drive, which is an energizer. Hull proposed that the level of drive is the sum total of all the drives, including those that are not relevant to a current task, such as trying to win a prize by solving anagrams after receiving instructions from a sexually attractive experimenter. Each drive combines with all the others to produce an undifferentiated amount of drive—a pooled energy source.[2]

This Hullian concept of *drive as a pooled energy source* was widely accepted among other learning theorists. As stated by Hilgard and Marquis in their classic book on conditioning and learning: "The motivation of behavior comes about through the existence of conditions (drive-establishing operations) which release energy originating in the organism's metabolic processes. *This energy, in and of itself, is directionless and may serve any of a variety of motivational objectives*" (my italics).[3] In the same book, Hilgard and Marquis go on to say that "it is important to distinguish between the guidance and the energetics of behavior. The term *motive* should, we think, be reserved for the latter function" (their italics).[4] Similarly, Donald Hebb, a pioneer of behavioral neuroscience, said: "drive is an energizer, but not a guide; an engine, but not a steering gear."[5]

Kurt Lewin, a central member of the Gestalt family of thinkers (and the father of experimental social psychology), offered a different version of motivation as "energy (to be directed)." He proposed that a person's need or goal (e.g., to become a professional artist), or a person's quasi-need or subordinate goal (e.g., to buy a book to prepare for the art school entrance exam), translates into a *goal intention* that corresponds to a *system in tension* within the person. The system in tension involves a force acting upon the person, producing a tendency to locomote or move toward the goal. When the goal is reached (i.e., the need is satisfied), then the tension is released.[6] Thus, by giving someone a goal, you can create a system in tension, a force, within that person for movement toward the goal.[7]

Conceptualizing motivation as general, all-purpose energy to be directed or guided or shaped also has etymological roots. According to the *Oxford English Dictionary*, the etymology of *motive* (the root of "motivation") includes an early Anglo-Norman term *motif*, which can be translated as "drive." Any answer to a basic question that receives this amount of support from both formal scientists and expert applied motivation scientists (including the *Oxford English Dictionary*) is likely to possess some usefulness as well as some truth.

My Critique

What I like about the notion of motivation as energy is that it naturally connects the idea of being motivated to actors' putting effort into what they are doing, and putting out effort is certainly part of what it means to be motivated. Perhaps this was also a central part of what my Senior Executive Program students had in mind when they thought that motivation was energy (to be directed). It is certainly true that our bodies, for example, need energy to do what they do, and that blood delivers the fuel that releases the needed energy in our cells. There is also evidence that when a task is perceived as doable but difficult, more effort is allocated to the task, and this is reflected in the heart pumping blood more strongly (i.e., increased blood pressure). There is a connection, then, between being motivated to allocate more effort (i.e., being in this sense more strongly motivated) and releasing more energy to do the task. This is why the expressions of "getting fired up" and "being energized" are reasonable descriptions of someone being highly motivated. Moreover, when it comes to bodies, the notion that the energy is all-purpose makes sense because the process and the nature of the energy that is released in different parts of the body to deal with different tasks are basically the same.

But there are also aspects of the notion that I don't like. For one thing, motivation is not all about the energy needed to perform some task. Motivation, for example, is also about how strongly individuals are engaged in what they are doing, and the amount of effort and energy individuals expend in what they are doing is not the same thing as how strongly they are engaged. This is evident when individuals are "in flow" or "in the zone," where engagement steadily increases to the point of complete absorption while the effort expended remains the same or even decreases.[8]

But what I most dislike about the notion of motivation as all-purpose energy (to be directed) is the *all-purpose* idea. I think it has gotten us all into trouble. The idea is that if you can get someone energized—no matter *what* the source of the energy—then this energy can be directed or guided toward some destination or desired performance. If company managers, for example, want to motivate other employees, then they can use any type of incentive, any type of "carrot" or "stick," that energizes them, and this energy can be directed toward their goal. If you want to get employees to be more safety conscious, for instance, then offer a reward bonus for increased safety-related behavior. The reward bonus will, indeed, get the employees "energized," but it could also give them a promotion focus because a reward bonus is a gain that relates to promotion concerns with advancement. If your goal is more safety-related behaviors, then you want the employees to have prevention focus concerns with safety and security rather than promotion focus concerns with accomplishment and advancement. The "energizing" strategy of offering a reward bonus could be counterproductive—a point I return to in Chapter 12 on "managing motives effectively."

What is not being considered in the "all-purpose energy" notion is the importance of the relation or fit between the source of the energy and the recipient of that energy, the vessel into which that energy is being poured. We don't put "general, all-purpose fuel" in a car. We put some particular type of fuel in a particular kind of car. And I know from bitter experience that putting unleaded gasoline fuel in a car with a diesel engine will stop the car in its tracks.[9] And putting any kind of petroleum fuel in the Energizer Bunny would not be a great idea either. There needs to be a fit between the source of motivation and the recipient of motivation. For example, the task performance of prevention-focused individuals is better if their vigilance is increased (e.g., thinking about what they need to do to avoid failure on the task) than if their eagerness is increased (e.g., thinking about how they will succeed on the task).[10]

There is another problem with the *all-purpose* energy notion: it is a quantitative rather than a qualitative notion of what it means to be motivated. Hull, for example, was explicit in saying every source of drive combines quantitatively with all the other sources to produce a pooled energy source of undifferentiated drive. I sometimes wonder whether this non-qualitative conception of motivation relates to the curious tendency of proponents of the all-purpose energizer notion to use non-human metaphors. This tendency is found not only in the traditional notion of shaping behavior through "the carrot or the stick," where *either* one will do the trick, but also in Freud's hydraulic reservoir metaphor, Hebb's engine metaphor, Lewin's metaphor of the recipient being a mass point in a field of forces, and in my personal favorite from John Watson, the founder of behaviorism, that good parenting is like hammering molten metal into whatever shape is desired.

From the all-purpose energizer viewpoint, it does not matter whether energy is created by a positive carrot incentive or a negative stick incentive, as long as the resultant energy can be directed toward the desired destination. But beginning in the second half of the 20th century, there was increasing evidence of the need to distinguish between positive and negative sources of motives—evidence that the *quality* of the source of motivation *does* make a difference. It does make a difference whether the incentive is a carrot or a stick. It does make a difference if you motivate through hope versus fear. Indeed, as we will see later in the book, even the type of carrot (i.e., the type of reward) makes a difference.

Suffice it to say that failing to distinguish among qualitatively different types of motive sources is not useful. Even if you could identify some commonality across different sources of motivation, this would not mean that they could simply be combined to function as an all-purpose energy. For example, when people think an activity is important they are more motivated to do it, and they are also more motivated to do an activity that they think is fun. However, as evident from the results of the *"make learning fun" study* described in Chapter 1, *adding fun* to an activity that people consider to be important (e.g., learning new words) *hurts* rather helps performance.[11]

Motivation as Approaching or Avoiding Something

A second longstanding viewpoint on what it means to be motivated relates to another etymology of the word "motive." According to the *Oxford English Dictionary*, the Latin term *motivum* can be translated as "that which moves or initiates motion"—motivation as movement. The movement in this case can be understood as the classic movements of approach and avoidance. This conceptualization has the distinct advantage of being easily related to what is perhaps the best-known principle of motivation—the *hedonic principle* that people are motivated to *approach pleasure and avoid pain.*

SUPPORT FOR MOTIVATION AS "APPROACHING OR AVOIDING SOMETHING"

There is an obvious advantage to having an answer to the question "What does it mean to be motivated?" (to approach or avoid something) that can be easily combined with an answer to another question, "What do people really want?" (to approach pleasure and avoid pain). Indeed, the psychological literature typically combines these two answers in the form of models that describe the motivation to move toward desired end-states and to move away from undesired end-states. Again, there is a long history of such models, from animal learning/biological models[12] to control models[13] to dynamic models.[14]

But one can have a notion of motivation as approaching or avoiding something without associating it with the hedonic principle of pleasure and pain. The cybernetic model of Norbert Wiener[15] and the TOTE model of George Miller, Eugene Galanter, and Karl Pribram,[16] which were precursors to many subsequent approach–avoidance models, made no claims about pleasure and pain *per se.* These early models conceptualized approaching or avoiding something not in terms of movement in relation to anticipated pleasure or anticipated pain, but simply in terms of movement in relation to reference points.[17]

Let's consider Miller, Galanter, and Pribram's example of hammering a nail into a board of wood. The current state of the nail is compared to the reference point of the nail ending up flush to the wood. If there is a discrepancy between the current state of the nail and its "flush" end-state as the reference point (i.e., if the nail "sticks up"), then action is taken to reduce the "sticking-up" condition of the nail: the nail is struck with the hammer to reduce the discrepancy by moving the nail toward the wood surface. It is true that when a person is doing the hammering, the human actor might represent the "flush" end-state of the nail as a desired end-state and experience pleasure from reducing the discrepancy. But a machine could be doing the hammering with no such representation or experience.

MY CRITIQUE

I like that this notion of what it means to be motivated—to approach or avoid something—can be easily combined with the answer to the question of what people really want (i.e., to maximize pleasure and minimize pain) to provide an overall answer to what is motivation. Motivation is to approach pleasure and avoid pain. *Voilà*, the hedonic principle! This is a definite advantage. I also like the fact that, once again, it has support from the *Oxford English Dictionary* with its root meaning of "to move." Moreover, the notion that what it means to be motivated is to approach some things and avoid other things naturally connects to the notion of being attracted toward some things and repulsed by other things, which is basic to the psychological experience of value. And value is a big part of motivation. This is all reasonable and useful.

But there are other aspects of the notion of motivation as approaching or avoiding something that I don't like. Just how seriously should we take the core concept of *movement* that underlies this notion? Consider, for example, the control theory of Charles Carver and Michael Scheier,[18] a highly influential reference point theory for human self-regulation that was inspired by the control process models of scholars such as Miller, Pribram, and Gallanter and, especially, William Powers.[19] In this theory, there are two self-regulatory systems. One has a desired end-state as the reference point that is discrepancy-reducing, and the system attempts to move the current self state as close as possible to the desired end-state. The other self-regulatory system has an undesired end-state as the reference point that is discrepancy-amplifying, and the system attempts to move the current self state as far away as possible from the undesired end-state.

Now if one takes seriously the concept of movement, then negative reference point regulation must be less stable and more open-ended than positive reference point regulation because it would involve an ever-increasing deviation from the negative reference point with no specific end-state to approach. There would be no obvious "stop" signal. As end-states, there would be an asymmetry between a positive approach goal that provides a "stop" signal by having a clearly defined end-state and a negative goal of moving away without an end-state to provide a "stop" signal.[20]

Carver and Scheier recognize and comment on this asymmetry.[21] But is there a different way to think about self-regulation in relation to desired and undesired end-states that removes this asymmetry created by the movement metaphor? One solution is to distinguish between two distinct functions of goals. Goals are not just end-states; they are also standards that individuals use to evaluate their current state—how well am I doing now relative to where I want to end up? People are motivated by whether their current state does or does not match their goal as a reference point.[22] Conceptualized in this way, self-regulation in relation to either a positive or a negative reference point involves matches and mismatches. Self-regulation in relation to a negative reference point is no longer open-ended. Rather than attempting to "move away" from a negative reference value, self-regulation in relation to a negative reference point would involve attempts to minimize matches to the negative reference value. From this perspective, self-regulation would not differ in principle from self-regulation in relation to a positive reference point.[23]

Another problem with the movement notion is that motivation need not produce movement at all. Often the adaptive response for someone who is highly motivated is *not to move at all*—to inhibit or suppress movement. Take fear, for example. Someone in a state of fear can fight (approach the source of danger to remove it) or flee (avoid the source of danger by removing oneself). These movements are consistent with the approach–avoidance viewpoint. But someone in a state of fear can also freeze. Freezing is *not* moving. Moreover, it is often a very strong motivational condition, such as extreme danger, that produces this *non*-movement.

Motivation as Preferences Directing Choices

I believe that what it means to be motivated is *to have preferences directing choices*. This is the kind of answer that might be found in classic economics, although an economist is more likely to say "preferences as revealed in choices." These phrases are not exactly the same, however.

For economists, "preferences as revealed in choices" is about *utility*, one of their key concepts. It is assumed that when individuals choose among a set of alternatives, they will choose the alternative that has the highest utility for them—that alternative with the best benefits-to-costs (or gains-to-losses) ratio of *outcomes* (decision utility).[24] In contrast to this position, I do not assume that the preferences that direct choices are all about outcomes. Actors, whether humans or other animals, also have preferences for *how* they go about pursuing goals that are separate from their preferences for the different outcomes of their goal pursuits.[25] To illustrate such *strategic* preferences, let us now consider more fully the difference between having a promotion orientation versus a prevention orientation.

As I mentioned earlier, individuals with a promotion orientation are concerned with accomplishments and advancement, whereas individuals with a prevention orientation are concerned with safety and security. According to regulatory focus theory,[26] the same goal, such as having a good marriage, can be experienced in promotion as a hope or aspiration (something you want ideally to happen) or experienced in prevention as a duty or responsibility (something you believe you ought to or must make happen). In promotion, goal pursuit is about change from a current satisfactory state to something better (changing from "0" to "+1"); it is about gains. In prevention, goal pursuit is about stopping change from a satisfactory current state to something unsatisfactory (stopping change from "0" to "−1"); it is about non-losses. Given the nature of promotion concerns, the natural preference is for *eager, enthusiastic* strategies that support advancement, that support change from "0" to "+1." Given the nature of prevention concerns, the natural preference is for *vigilant, careful* strategies that support maintenance of a satisfactory state, that stop change from "0" to "−1." Thus, even when the same outcome is desired, such as having a good marriage, individuals with a promotion versus a prevention orientation can have different *preferred strategies* for attaining that outcome—a preference for eager versus vigilant strategies, respectively.[27]

These *strategic preferences* can have a major impact on *how* goals are pursued, which in turn can influence what choice is made independent of the outcomes that are associated with the choice alternatives. Thus, preferences directing choices are not just about utility and outcomes as described in classic economics: it is broader than that. The final choices that are made reflect preferences at multiple levels—outcome preferences and strategic preferences, as well as tactical preferences.[28] They involve *motivations working together*. It is this organization of motives that I wish to emphasize by the expression "preferences directing choices." Such an organization of motives implies that what it means to be motivated is always an integration of preferences from different regulatory levels whose resultant state directs a choice. This organization of preferences varies not only in strength (quantity) but also in quality, as I discuss more fully in Chapter 10.

The notion of motivation as "preferences directing choices" has another advantage as well. Preferences can be revealed only when there is a range of possible responses over which an individual has some control; that is, when an individual could have behaved in a different way.[29] Thus, motivation is about preferences under conditions of choice, where the preferences actually direct the choice. From this perspective, humans are not the only animal that has motivation. At the same time, this perspective would *not* consider energy-driven and moving windup toys to be motivated. It is those *making choices while using such toys* who are motivated. Whereas windup toys can be "energized" and "approach" things, they do not have preferences directing choices. Thus, the notion of motivation as "preferences directing choices" has the advantage of conceptualizing motivation in a way that reasonably includes humans and other animals while excluding things like windup toys.

WHAT DO PEOPLE REALLY WANT?

I have proposed that what it means to be motivated is to have preferences that direct choices. This answer provides a beginning for understanding motivation, but it is not sufficient. It is also necessary to know where the preferences that direct choices come from. What is it that people want that underlies their preferences? What does a motivated person really want? There is more than one reasonable answer to the question. That said, I do believe that some answers are better than others. In my review of possible answers, I will restrict myself to the strongest ones (as defined by historical precedence and consensus).

People Want to Survive

Thanks to Charles Darwin, we all appreciate that "survival of the fittest" is a biological imperative.[30] If so, then "to survive" must be what we really want. But, actually, biologists consider the phrase "survival of the fittest" to be a metaphor and prefer the phrase "natural selection," which does not emphasize "survival" in the same way.[31] Moreover, it should be noted that "survival" in the phrase "survival of the fittest" is not very helpful because survival is the outcome and what we want to know is the motivation (i.e., what people really want) that leads to this outcome. That is, we want to know which motivation makes a person the "fittest" to survive. Indeed, those individuals who want, above all else, to survive personally need not be the fittest to survive. For example, those whose predominant motive is personal survival may not be more likely to reproduce (i.e., natural selection), or even to survive personally, than those who have other predominant motives, such as the motive to work with others to achieve common goals (e.g., a cooperative motive) or the motive to do better than others (e.g., a competitive motive).

SUPPORT FOR "SURVIVAL" BEING WHAT PEOPLE REALLY WANT

Although an evolutionary argument *per se* does not require that "survival" be the answer to what people really want, the notion that moment to moment an individual wants to survive, preferring "to stay alive" rather than "to die," is powerful. So powerful, in fact, that in the early 20th century it dominated theories of what humans and other animals wanted, and it remains influential. The specific form it took in psychology was to translate "survival" into satisfying basic biological needs—those biological needs considered necessary for the preservation of an individual and species. Satisfaction of biological needs was thought to be so central to motivation that even the value or desirability of something, such as the value of food or water or social interaction, was conceptualized in terms of the extent to which it was instrumental in satisfying a biological need. Psychologists with theoretical perspectives ranging from behavioristic to Gestalt to psychodynamic proposed that the value of something—how much one wants something—comes from the extent to which it satisfies some need.

In the classic version of the notion that the value or desirability of something derives from need satisfaction, behavior is directed toward the removal of tissue deficits (e.g., to satisfy hunger or thirst). Drives were manifest in behavior, had physiological correlates, and naturally gave rise to human desires.[32] A striking illustration of this source of value is provided in the classic experimental psychology textbook of Robert Woodworth and Harold Schlosberg.[33] If one feeds an animal for a few days on a diet that is deficient in vitamin B, one creates a biological need for this vitamin. If one then offers the animal a choice between a meal that is rich in vitamin B and one that lacks vitamin B, the animal will choose the vitamin B-rich meal.

For humans, there is another motivational implication related to "survival" as the answer to what a motivated person really wants. Only humans are aware of their own mortality, and such awareness has been said to create a terror about the inevitability of death that humans are motivated to resolve above all other motives. According to *terror management theory*,[34] it is basic to human motivation. It relates not only to wanting to satisfy the biological necessities of life, such as hunger and thirst, but also to wanting to enhance self-esteem and pursue a meaningful life, with a goal of living on after death by leaving a legacy as, say, a famous scientist or public servant.

MY CRITIQUE

Do humans and other animals want water when they are thirsty and food when they are hungry? Are they willing to fight to live rather than die? Yes. There is little question, then, that some sense of wanting to survive, such as wanting to satisfy basic biological needs, is part of what people really want. Like most, if not all, readers of this book, I like the notion that people want to survive. But like it as much as we do, it is not clear how useful it is as an answer by itself. It is compelling, but is it sufficient?

I believe that it is not sufficient because it does not give enough attention to people's life experiences. The "survival" answer to what a motivated person really wants refers to life versus death, to satisfying biological needs or not. This answer is silent on how people's life experiences affect what they want. Strictly speaking, the "survival" answer would predict motivational force to be a direct function of the extent to which something satisfies biological needs, the extent to which it contributes to survival. But this is not the case. For example, people will choose to eat "junk food" snacks that they know have no nutritional value and are unhealthy for them. What these snacks do have is a sweet flavor that they like.

More generally, what is critical to motivation—to preferences that direct choices—is whether a person does or does not experience that something matters.[35] Consider the common refrain that people often don't appreciate something (i.e., don't value it) until they don't have it anymore—"Sometimes you don't know what you want until you've lost it." But whatever this "it" might be, such as physical health, it had survival importance before it was lost and not just after it was lost. Thus, the motivational significance of something is not a direct function of its actual importance for survival but of *experiencing it as important*. The general point is that because some needs are generally being satisfied, without it being necessary to pay much attention to them or make them a priority, the experience of wanting the needs to be satisfied is weak and motivational efforts are directed elsewhere. In terms of preferences, satisfaction of these needs is *not* directing choices. When suddenly the need is not being satisfied, *then* people experience their attraction to it. Only *then* do they value it highly and make choices on that basis. Given this, it is not useful to argue that what motivates people is wanting to survive. This answer does not explain most people's moment-to-moment preferences that direct their everyday choices.

The key point is that something that *actually* satisfies a need does *not* direct choices for that reason alone. There are many biological functions, including at the cellular level, that are critical to survival, but while they function properly they do not determine our preferences that direct our choices. Critical biological functions, like breathing, can be taken for granted and not be appreciated, and while they are not being appreciated they are not directing our choices despite their survival value. Again, it is experiencing their importance that is essential for motivation, essential for creating preferences that direct choices. This point is developed further in the next section, which provides an alternative, experiential answer to what people really want.

People Want to Maximize Pleasure and Minimize Pain

The most common answer historically to the question of what people want is that they want to maximize pleasure and minimize pain. Indeed, the American Declaration of Independence states that "We hold these truths to be self-evident," that all people are endowed with "unalienable Rights," including "the pursuit of Happiness." That is, because maximizing pleasure and minimizing pain is so obviously basic to human motivation, it is "self-evident" that humans have an "unalienable right" to do so through their pursuit of happiness.

SUPPORT FOR "MAXIMIZING PLEASURE" BEING WHAT
PEOPLE REALLY WANT

The obvious importance to human motivation of maximizing pleasure and minimizing pain has been recognized for centuries, going back (at least) to Greek discussions of the hedonic principle. The term *hedonic*, which derives from the Greek term for "sweet," means relating to or characterized by plea-sure.[36] Jeremy Bentham, the highly influential 18th-century English philoso-pher, argued that pleasure and pain dictated what people do.[37] For Bentham, even the value or utility of something was based on its relation to maximizing pleasure. For example, he defined utility as "that principle which approves or disapproves of every action whatsoever, according to the tendency which it appears to have to augment or diminish the happiness of the party whose interest is in question."[38]

Within psychology in the first half of the 20th century, Freud described moti-vation as a *hedonism of the future*.[39] It might seem from the title of his book, *Beyond the Pleasure Principle*, that his theory of motivation went beyond the notion that people are motivated to seek pleasure. But actually, the title refers to Freud's proposal that people are not only motivated to seek pleasure, such as the desire for immediate gratification that is associated with the "Id" or pleasure principle, but they are also motivated to avoid pain. According to Freud's notion of the "Ego" or reality principle, people are motivated to avoid punishments from violations of normative or "Superego" demands. For Freud, then, behavior and other psychical activities were driven by anticipations of pleasure to be approached (wishes) *and* anticipations of pain to be avoided (fears). One reason that my book is entitled *Beyond Pleasure and Pain* is to distinguish my view-point on motivation from Freud's hedonic emphasis on pleasure and pain.

In his field theory, Lewin described how children learn to produce or suppress their behaviors from the "prospect" of reward or punishment, respec-tively.[40] Later, the influential learning and conditioning psychologist Orval Hobart Mowrer (1960) also proposed that the fundamental principle underly-ing motivated learning was approaching hoped-for end-states and avoiding feared end-states.[41] In his model of achievement motivation, John Atkinson, a giant figure in personality psychology, also proposed a basic distinction between self-regulation in relation to *hope of success* and self-regulation in relation to *fear of failure*.[42] And in their classic paper on prospect theory, the Nobel Prize-winning cognitive psychologists Daniel Kahneman and Amos Tversky distinguished between mentally considering the possibility of experiencing pleasure (gains) and mentally considering the possibility of experiencing pain (losses).[43] Closing out the century in 1999, a book edited by Kahneman and two other distinguished psychologists, Ed Diener and Norbert Schwarz, contained over two dozen papers by world-renowned psychologists and economists whose purpose was to set "the foundations of hedonic psychology."[44]

MY CRITIQUE

There is little question that maximizing pleasure and minimizing pain are at least part of the answer to what people really want. There are sensual pleasure experiences, such as sweet drinks or warm baths, that are clearly motivating. Moreover, the motivation for pleasure, such as sweetness, is so important that it can even trump the motivation to satisfy basic biological needs. It has been known for over half a century that animals will choose on the basis of hedonic experiences independent of any biological need being satisfied.[45] There are early studies, for example, showing that animals not only prefer sweet water with saccharin to regular water, but they also prefer sweet food to a physiologically better food, such as a food that is more beneficial for an animal given its vitamin deficiency.[46]

There are also classic studies by James Old and Peter Milner showing that rats will work to press a bar that activates the pleasure area in the brain but does not satisfy any biological need.[47] In the original and follow-up studies, metallic electrodes were implanted in certain regions of the lateral hypothalamus, causing some rats to push the lever up to 5,000 times an hour, even to the point of collapsing. In a T-maze, with both arms baited with food mash, rats would stop at a point halfway down the runway to self-stimulate by pushing the lever, never going to the food at all. Some mother rats even abandoned their newborn pups—despite the biological imperative of mothers' caring for their young—in order to press the lever thousands of times per hour.

There is also evidence from classical conditioning studies that animals will learn to value the conditioned cues themselves despite their satisfying no biological need. For instance, such studies have found that pigeons would make eating-like pecks at light cues that were previously associated with an edible reward and would make drinking-like pecks at the same light cues if they had been previously associated with a liquid reward, even though the light cues themselves satisfied neither hunger nor thirst.[48] Indeed, the motivational force of physiological needs can be, and historically has been, re-conceptualized in terms of maximizing pleasure and minimizing pain. Being thirsty or hungry is a painful state, and the motivation to drink or eat can be re-conceptualized in terms of wanting to reduce these painful experiences rather than to satisfy physiological needs.

So did the Greeks have it right? Is maximizing pleasure the answer to what people really want? I do believe that it is part of the answer, and a significant part given that pleasure can override biological needs in directing choices, which contradicts a purely survival perspective on motivation. But I also believe that maximizing pleasure is only *part* of the answer, and given this, there is a problem with its being anointed for centuries as being *the* answer. It has dominated thinking about motivation for far too long. It has taken attention away from other basic motivational principles that are independent of pleasure and pain *per se*.[49] In Chapter 1, I briefly discussed some of these other principles, such as regulatory focus, regulatory fit, and strength of engagement, and I will consider these and other principles more fully as the book proceeds. Here, let me provide just a couple of examples.

The first example is addiction. It is commonly believed that addictive behaviors, such as smoking opium or tobacco, gambling, drinking alcohol, and so on, are fundamentally motivated by a search for pleasure, by the pleasant "high" or "kick" that the activity provides. But many experts in the area of addiction, and by experts I mean both scientists and addicts themselves, call this belief a myth. William S. Burroughs, the famous American novelist and opiate addict, is quoted as saying, "Junk is not a kick. It is a way of life."[50] Similarly, Lance Dodes, an addiction treatment expert, states: "No addiction is fundamentally motivated by a search for pleasure. On the contrary, addictions are compulsively driven whether they lead to pleasure or not."[51] Indeed, during the intoxication stage of addiction to drugs, addicts use more of the substance than would be necessary if they only wanted to experience the intoxicating effects. Moreover, there are phases of addiction where the motivation to engage in the addictive activity increases even though the pleasure experienced from engagement in the activity decreases.

Kent Berridge and Terry Robinson, experts in the neuroscience of addiction, provide critical insight into these phenomena by distinguishing psychologically between brain systems related to "liking" and those related to "wanting." Specifically, they distinguish between pleasure/pain (hedonic) feelings related to "liking" something, and incentive motivations related to "wanting" something.[52] I will discuss more fully what it means to "want" something beyond pleasure seeking in the next section of this chapter. The point here is simply that the "wanting" motivation to engage in the addictive activity can steadily *increase* even while the hedonic "liking" of the addictive activity *decreases*.

The second example is also a well-known human phenomenon—engagement in life-threatening activities that often involve hardship and even intense suffering. Almost 30 years before Tenzing Norgay (from Nepal) and Edmund Hillary (from New Zealand) climbed Mount Everest on May 29, 1953, British mountain climber George Mallory (in 1924) attempted to do so, despite knowing the extreme dangers and hardships involved in such a climb. In fact, he and his climbing partner Andrew Irvine disappeared on the way to the summit. Before he left on this dangerous venture, he was asked why he wanted to climb Mount Everest. His famous answer was, "Because it's there." Thus, it is not just survival or just pleasure that people want: it's also succeeding at something—in this case succeeding at something that is extremely challenging.

George Mallory was not the first to engage in an extreme sport activity. And he was certainly not the last: now we can even watch televised programs of people engaging in extreme sports, such as the "X Games." Unlike the athletes in the X Games, however, most of those who engage in extreme sports are not participating in competitions where they might earn fame and glory. Instead, they are competing against environmental obstacles and challenges. The sports are considered extreme precisely because the environmental weather, such as a sudden storm, and terrain conditions are inherently uncontrollable and need to be dealt with on the spot. "Survival" and "pleasure" would *not* be the answers given by the athletes for why they choose to engage in these sports, which makes sense given that these sports are often both dangerous and grueling. Moreover, such athletes also consider the "adrenaline junkie" label to be just a stereotype. Instead, they say they are motivated by developing their physical or mental competence and discipline, by testing their ability to master difficult environments—answers often equivalent to "Because it's there."

A famous paraglider pilot, Bob Drury, is quoted as saying, "We do these things not to escape life, but to prevent life escaping us."[53] That is, people engage in life-threatening activities not because they have some "death wish" but because they experience what it means to be alive when they are dealing with extreme challenges. The danger associated with many extreme sports is not itself the critical motivating factor for these athletes; rather, it is the challenge of overcoming extraordinary obstacles and difficulties. Danger just happens to be associated with such extreme challenges. Eric Brymer, an expert on what people experience when engaging in extreme sports, sees direct parallels between this experience and those in non-dangerous activities such as meditation.[54]

The examples of engaging in addictive activities and extreme sports suggest that there is more to what people really want than "survival" and "pleasure." In addiction, the intensity of "wanting" to engage in an addictive activity need not parallel the intensity of "liking" for the activity. In extreme sports, both "survival" and "pleasure" can be risked for the sake of an activity that is extremely difficult and challenging. What, then, is the motivation underlying these activities? What is it that people really want?

People Want To Be Effective in Life Pursuits

When I say that "to be effective in life pursuits" is my preferred answer to what people really want, I am not suggesting that this answer originated with me. Far from it: there is a long history of great scholars within and outside of psychology who have argued for this answer. It is not possible to review the full history of those who have taken this position. Instead, I will give some historical highlights that will help to clarify what I mean by being effective in life pursuits.

KEYNES AND MOTIVATION AS THE URGE TO ACTION

In his magnum opus, *General Theory of Employment, Interest, and Money* (1936/1951), John Maynard Keynes, the renowned British economist, made the following statement:

> Even apart from the instability due to speculation, there is the instability due to the characteristic of human nature that a large proportion of our positive activities depend on spontaneous optimism rather than on a mathematical expectation, whether moral or hedonistic or economic. Most, probably, of our decisions to do something positive, the full consequences of which will be drawn out over many days to come, can only be taken as a result of animal spirits—of a spontaneous urge to action rather than inaction, and not as the outcome of a weighted average of quantitative benefits multiplied by quantitative probabilities. Enterprise only pretends to itself to be mainly actuated by the statements in its own prospectus, however candid and sincere . . . Thus if the animal spirits are dimmed and the spontaneous optimism falters, leaving us to depend on nothing but a mathematical expectation, enterprise will fade and die.[55]

Here is Keynes, the father of modern economics, making a profound statement about human motivation that other economists—and other social scientists—have not taken seriously enough. Most social scientists continue to take for granted that it *is* expected utility—"the outcome of a weighted average of quantitative benefits multiplied by quantitative probabilities"—that defines what people really want and underlies the preferences revealed in their choices. What about the alternative that Keynes is identifying? What about "animal spirits"? What about the "spontaneous urge to action rather than inaction"? Keynes is saying that this urge is critical to motivation.

WOODWORTH AND MOTIVATION AS DIRECTED ACTIVITY

Around the same time that Keynes was thinking about motivation as the urge to action, Robert Woodworth, the psychologist who coined the term *drive*,[56] was coming to a similar conclusion. This is evident in the following quote from his 1940 book, *Psychology*:

> To some thinkers on these matters it appears self-evident that dealing with the environment occurs only in the service of the organic needs for food, etc. They say that the muscles and sense organs have evolved simply as tools for the better securing of food and other organic necessities, and for reproducing the race. Only the organic needs, on this view, are entitled to rank as primary drives; all activity dealing with the environment is secondary. The facts of evolution do not compel us to adopt this view, for motility and responsiveness to the environment are present way down to the bottom of the scale of animal life. There is no more reason for saying that the muscles exist for the purpose of obtaining food than for saying that food is needed to supply energy for the muscles . . . What we find in the young animal is activity directed toward the environment, along with the organic needs, and with no sign that one is more primitive and unlearned than the other. It is safe to assume dealing with environment as a primitive characteristic of the organism.[57]

This was a radical statement for an experimental psychologist to be making at the height of behaviorism and neobehaviorism in America—when motivation was about biological need satisfaction and pleasure "stamping in" behavior.[58] Woodworth is suggesting that rather than action being in the service of attaining food to eat and water to drink, which is the traditional viewpoint, perhaps eating food and drinking water are in the service of taking action. Similarly, driving cars is not in the service of attaining gasoline to burn, but, instead, burning gasoline is in the service of driving cars. Combining the statements of Keynes and Woodworth into a single message, we are being told that there is something inherently valuable, inherently motivating, about taking action. It need not be in the service of expected outcomes from taking the action, such as satisfying a biological need or producing pleasure. What people really want is to take action—period. The message is that to experience living fully, rather than just being alive, we need to take action. Which is what extreme sport athletes do, and indeed what drug addicts do, despite the risks and dangers in doing so.

Generally speaking, I think that this is a useful message about motivation—that what matters is taking action itself. But by itself, it is not sufficient. What is this action taking itself all about? What is it, actually, that is motivating?

Fortunately, others also asked themselves these questions and provided some useful answers to them. Once again, I will restrict my review to a few such answers that have influenced psychological thinking about motivation.

HEBB AND MOTIVATION AS OPTIMAL STIMULATION

In his 1955 paper "Drives and the C. N. S. (Conceptual Nervous System),"[59] Donald Hebb takes the reader on a journey along the different paths of his thinking across a quarter century, from 1930 to 1955. He divides his journey into two periods. During the first, 20-year period, Hebb became convinced that there was more to motivated action than could be understood in terms of drives, even if one included a drive related to our curiosity about things in the world and our investigations and manipulations of them. Hebb had been a teacher, and in the late 1920s he was appointed headmaster of a troubled school in a Montreal suburb (at the same time working as a part-time graduate student at McGill University). His pedagogical experimenting to improve the school provided the kind of evidence that convinced him that something was missing in psychological theories of motivation.[60] In the experiment, the pupils in the school, who ranged from 6 to 15 years of age, were suddenly told by the teachers that they didn't have to work anymore if they didn't want to. Moreover, if they interfered with other students' work in the classroom, they would be *punished* by being sent outside to *play* in the playground.

Hebb found that after just a couple of days of these new conditions, *all* of the students chose to work quietly in the classroom. He concluded that "the human liking for work is not a rare phenomenon, but general."[61] He argued that the human need for intellectual activity, such as the riddles, puzzles, and puzzle-like games (e.g., chess, bridge) that we devise just to create problems to solve, is a highly significant fact about human motivation. Hebb's answer, around 1945, as to what such actions say about human motivation was *self-motivating brain cells*: "any organized process in the brain is a motivated process, inevitably, inescapably; that the human brain is built to be active, and that as long as it is supplied with adequate nutrition will continue to be active. Brain activity is what determines behavior, and so the only behavioral problem becomes that of accounting for *in*activity" [italics in the original].[62]

This, too, was a radical statement to be making about what motivates behavior. Hebb, like Woodworth, was saying that rather than food and other nutritional needs being the motivational driving force, they were simply supplying the energy for self-motivated action. For Hebb, there were self-motivated brain cells that were built to be active.

For a while, Hebb was happy with this answer. But then, in the second part of his intellectual journey as a scientist, along came an experiment on sensory deprivation that he conducted with McGill college students.[63] The participants were paid a substantial amount of money to do almost nothing for hour after hour. They could see nothing and they could hear and touch very little. Their primary needs, such as food and water, were satisfied and they were free from pain. Given the high payment they received, as well as the opportunity to contribute to science, one would expect them to be highly motivated to remain in these conditions for a long time. And they were quite happy for several hours. But then they became increasingly unhappy and chose to leave the experiment.

The results of this study caused a problem for Hebb. The problem was not that the students chose to leave the experiment despite their receiving strong rewards for participation and having all their primary needs satisfied. That finding *is* a problem for a drive theorist who believes that what people want is to satisfy their biological needs. But Hebb was *not* a drive theorist. The problem for him was that there was nothing about the sensory deprivation conditions that would stop the participants' thought processes, and these organized brain processes should have been self-motivating. That is, the results were a problem for his notion of *self-motivating brain cells*.

Hebb's solution was a new answer to what people really want—*optimal stimulation*. Basically, the idea here is that too little stimulation disrupts motivation, which was what happened in the sensory deprivation study, and too much stimulation also disrupts motivation, which is what happens, for example, when people are in a high state of fear. Stimulation that is in between these conditions—not too low and not too high—is optimal.[64] Thus, when people's current state of stimulation is not high enough, they create their own problems to solve, engage in games and puzzles, and take other kinds of action in order to reach an optimal level of brain activity—independent of physiological need satisfaction or hedonic pleasure *per se*.

Note that Hebb's revised answer to what people want continues to take the position, like Woodworth's position, that people take action not to satisfy their biological needs or to experience hedonic pleasure but because of something inherent in the action itself. Specifically, action is motivating in itself because it is stimulating. We would refrain from taking stimulating actions only when we have already reached an optimal level of stimulation. What Hebb's new answer adds is the idea that brain activity by itself (i.e., *self-motivating brain cells*) is no longer considered a sufficient source of stimulation. As evident in the deprivation studies, taking action is also needed for sufficient stimulation. This new idea could be called *self-motivating action*.

WHITE AND MOTIVATION AS HAVING AN EFFECT ON THE ENVIRONMENT

The idea of "optimal stimulation" is one kind of answer to why taking action is motivating. Let me turn now to a different kind of answer that was proposed by the clinical psychologist Robert W. White in his highly influential 1959 paper, "Motivation reconsidered: the concept of competence."[65] In this paper, White integrated and synthesized the findings and ideas of his contemporaries across different areas of psychology, including child development, animal behavior, personality, and psychoanalytic ego psychology. He argued that something important was left out when psychologists made drives the motivating force for the behaviors of humans and other animals, with the drive theories of Freud and Hull being his prime examples. As an alternative answer to what motivates humans and other animals, White proposed *competence*: "an organism's capacity to interact effectively with its environment."[66]

When considering humans and other mammals, White gave special emphasis to the role of learning in the capacity for effective interaction with the environment. He inferred that motivation must be involved in the directed and persistent behaviors that lead to learning. He argued that the motivation needed to attain such competence could not derive solely from drives as the sources of energy.[67] White reviews evidence for animals being strongly motivated by the opportunity to be active, as when rats choose to run around and around in a wheel; the opportunity to manipulate objects, as when monkeys choose to try over and over again to solve a mechanical problem; and the opportunity to explore the environment, as when monkeys work to open a window that would allow them to look out and see what is happening in the entrance room of the laboratory—without any of these activities being related to satisfying some organic need.

White also points out that although it is true that people seek rest at the end of the day, rest is not the objective during most of the day. Indeed, even when the primary biological needs have been met, humans remain active and up to something. When children's major needs are met, for example, they spend their time actively watching objects and events around them. They want to have *an effect upon the environment*, deal with it and change it. White mentions the work of two pioneers in the study of children's play, Karl Groos[68] and Jean Piaget,[69] who observed that children have a joy in being the producer of effects, especially something dramatic, such as making a clatter or jumping up and down in puddles, and they have a special interest in objects that they can affect by their own movements.

As Piaget himself noted, "Indeed, when the child looks for the sake of looking, handles for the sake of handling, moves his arms and hands (and in the next stage shakes hanging objects and his toys) he is doing actions which are an end in themselves, as are all practice games, and which do not form part of any series of actions imposed by someone else or from outside. They no more have an external aim than the later motor exercises such as throwing stones into a pond, making water spurt from a tap, jumping, and so on, which are always considered to be games."[70] In his landmark book *The Origins of Intelligence in Children,* Piaget describes the sensorimotor learning that occurs during the first few months of life. He argues that the actions of infants, such as their sucking after a meal when they are no longer hungry, are not motivated by pleasure or biological needs but by the motivation to exercise the action, to be effective in making it function.[71]

White summarizes this line of argument as follows: "The ever-present, ever-primary feature of motivation is the tendency to deal with the environment."[72] He is not, however, arguing that motivation is only about having an effect on the environment. He explicitly states that he does not want to "down-grade the drives." He proposes instead to bring together all the phenomena just described under the general heading of competence. He says: "The concept of competence . . . emphasizes dealing with the environment, and it belongs in the trend away from drive *orthodoxy* but it is not intended to supplant, or even to subsume, such dynamic forces as hunger, sex, aggression, and fear, which everyone knows to be of huge importance in animal and human nature" [italics in the original].[73]

Referring to the dictionary, he points out the broad range of meanings associated with "competence"—fitness or ability, capability, capacity, efficiency, proficiency, and skill. He concludes that the motivational aspect of competence needs its own name, and proposes that the name be *effectance*. Effectance motivation is not a deficit motive like hunger or thirst; there are no consummatory acts (e.g., eating; escaping from danger). Satisfaction lies in the *arousal and maintaining of activity* rather than reduction: "Because there is no consummatory climax, satisfaction has to be seen as lying in a considerable series of transactions, in a trend of behavior rather than a goal that is achieved. It is difficult to make the word 'satisfaction' have this connotation, and we shall do well to replace it by 'feeling of efficacy' when attempting to indicate the subjective and affective side of effectance."[74] Importantly, according to White, there are still organic needs that can capture the "energies" of the motivational system, but, between episodes of homeostatic crises, effectance motivation occupies the waking time. Thus, White separates effectance motivation from drive reduction, need satisfaction, and consummatory climax. For him, effectance is an important character in the story of motivation that deserves higher billing, but it is not the whole story: there are still the drives.

White's motivational concepts of competence, effectance motivation, and feeling of efficacy were influenced by the work of many psychologists before him, and they have influenced the work of many psychologists since. I will now consider two theories that themselves have been highly influential in both understanding and applying motivation as it relates to effectiveness.

BANDURA AND MOTIVATION AS PERCEIVED SELF-EFFICACY

Albert Bandura, a pioneer in social-cognitive learning, has proposed that *perceived self-efficacy* is central to human effectiveness. He proposes that our judgments of our capabilities, our thoughts about our ability to manage events in our lives, influence our dealings with the environment: "Perceived self-efficacy is concerned with judgments of how well one can execute courses of action required to deal with prospective situations."[75] For example, when people look at recipes while planning a meal, they look at the ingredients and instructions for how to make each dish not only to decide whether they would like to eat it but also to decide whether they are capable of actually executing it. People want to be efficacious. Their choices of which courses of action to pursue, how long to pursue them, how much effort to expend on them, and whether to persist or not when confronting obstacles, are all influenced by their self-efficacy judgments (whether these judgments are correct or not).

In self-efficacy theory, self-referent thoughts, rather than being global, are particular to the specific situational circumstances of specific activities. According to Bandura, our interest in engaging in an activity can grow from the satisfaction we experience when our performance accomplishments engender perceived self-efficacy. Importantly, the satisfaction need not come from perceiving an increase in self-efficacy; it can come simply from *verifying* or *substantiating* an existing self-efficacy without any new skills being acquired in the activity engagement. When acquiring a new competency, self-efficacy can also be experienced prior to acquisition by setting subgoal standards that mark progress along the way and provide a sense of growing self-efficacy. It should also be noted that perceived self-efficacy can even influence hedonic experiences themselves. For example, people who believe that they have efficacy in coping with pain can withstand more pain (e.g., keep their hand in ice-cold water for a longer period).[76]

Although Bandura's theory of self-efficacy is related to White's motivational concepts of competence, effectance motivation, and feeling of efficacy, there are important differences that should be highlighted. First, White's effectance motivation—the motivational aspect of competence—is a general motivation to initiate or maintain activity and to have an effect upon and change the environment. Bandura's perceived self-efficacy, in contrast, is much more contextualized. He gives the example of how someone's perceived self-efficacy in public speaking can vary depending on what the audience is like and what the format of the presentation is.[77] Second, while being more contextualized, perceived self-efficacy is broader in its range of applicability. White's discussion of effectance motivation restricts its range of applicability to conditions when organic needs are not capturing the energies of the motivational system—that is, when the motivational system is not concerned with meeting the primary biological needs. In contrast, perceived self-efficacy would also influence decisions about how to meet organic needs, such as whether or how to hunt a particular animal for food (e.g., in a hunter-gatherer society). Bandura considers self-efficacy judgments to be involved in regulating all types of performance except for habitual, highly routinized behavior patterns.

DECI AND RYAN AND MOTIVATION AS SELF-DETERMINATION

Another highly influential theory of competence and effectiveness is self-determination theory, developed by the motivation scientists Edward Deci and Richard Ryan.[78] According to Deci and Ryan, the starting point for self-determination theory is "the postulate that humans are active, growth-oriented organisms who are naturally inclined toward integration of their psychic elements into a unified sense of self and integration of themselves into larger social structures . . . it is part of the adaptive design of the human organism to engage interesting activities, to exercise capacities, to pursue connectedness in social groups."[79]

Self-determination theory states that to understand human motivation it is necessary to consider the innate psychological needs for competence and autonomy. Following White, *competence* refers to the need to feel effective and to have control in relation to our environment (effectance motivation). *Autonomy* refers to the need to self-endorse our own actions and to *experience volition*, with the opposite of autonomy being excessive external control. Autonomy as the experience of volition is notable. Volition has two related meanings: (1) an act of making a choice or decision and (2) the power of choosing or determining.[80] Self-determination theory—not surprisingly, given its name—is especially concerned with the second meaning.

I believe that the most distinctive contribution of self-determination theory concerns the need for autonomy, and thus I will concentrate on this aspect of the theory. A critical feature of self-determination theory is its proposal that self-regulation in society varies in relative autonomy along the following continuum of *internalization*: first, there is the lowest-autonomy condition where individuals are *externally controlled*, such as acting out of hope for tangible reward or fear of punishment for disobeying some rule (the classic "carrot and stick" administered by others); at the next level, individuals are *introjected*, as when they follow social norms in order to feel pride or avoid guilt (the inner state version of the "carrot and stick" producing internal conflicts); at the next level is *identification*, when individuals consciously recognize and accept the underlying value of some activity (i.e., identify with the activity); and finally there is *integration*, the highest-autonomy level of internalization, where the value of an activity is well assimilated with other values and aspects of the self to create a coherent, harmonious whole.[81]

Engaging in activities can also be intrinsically motivated (i.e., an end in itself), as when people freely engage in activities they find interesting, novel, or challenging. *Intrinsic* motivation is considered to involve the highest level of autonomy and self-determination. Indeed, according to self-determination theory, motivation is not intrinsic unless there is perceived autonomy. Finally, when there is neither extrinsic nor intrinsic motivation there is *amotivation*, which is a state where people lack the intention to do anything. Even externally controlled extrinsic motivation involves the *intention* to do something (e.g., in response to a carrot or stick). According to self-determination theory, a condition of amotivation is likely to occur when people lack a sense of efficacy or control over making something happen or not happen, as when they feel helpless because their actions have no effect on what happens to them.

I have now reviewed influential ideas within and outside of psychology suggesting that *to be effective in life pursuits* is what people really want. Although the term "effective" is not precisely the one that has been used in prior discussions of this motivation, it clearly relates to previous terms such as "effectance" and "efficacy." I prefer "effective" because it is a more common term in everyday language. In addition, its formal dictionary definitions capture best what I have in mind, and what others have said, about this motivation[82]: (a) *having the power of acting upon something*; (b) *that part of a force that is instrumental in producing a result*; (c) *executing or accomplishing a notable effect*; (d) *fit for work or service.*

More broadly, I have also discussed three answers to the question, "What do people really want?" Each of these three answers—"to survive," "to maximize pleasure," and "to be effective in life pursuits"—tells us something important about motivation and has supporting evidence. My reasons for preferring the answer "to be effective in life pursuits" will become clearer as the book proceeds. Here, let me note just a couple of reasons. First, people will choose to endure pain and risk their biological health in order to meet challenges. This shows how the motivation to be effective—wanting to succeed at something—can trump hedonic and survival concerns. Second, if what it means to be motivated is to have preferences that direct choices, I believe that wanting to be effective in life pursuits provides the best answer to what determines people's preferences moment to moment in everyday life. Being effective is about wanting to be successful at something and making choices in order to be successful, and thus it generally involves preferences directing choices. This view about what it means to be motivated and what it is that people really want provides an answer to the general question with which this chapter began: *What is motivation?*

MOTIVATION IS DIRECTING CHOICES IN ORDER TO BE EFFECTIVE

I am not suggesting that "directing choices in order to be effective" is the only reasonable perspective on what is motivation. In fact, there are reasonable alternatives that have been around for a very long time because they capture important insights about what motivation is and how it works. Let me consider two major alternative perspectives—the "approaching pleasure and avoiding pain" perspective and the "directing energy in order to survive" perspective— and consider how they answer the main questions about motivation raised in this chapter.

Approaching Pleasure and Avoiding Pain

As discussed earlier, the hedonic principle underlies both the accepted notion that people prefer pleasure to pain, which is generally true, and the common assumption that a good way to motivate someone is the promise of reward (the "carrot") or the threat of punishment (the "stick"), which is not necessarily true but can be true. The hedonic principle is an elegant overall answer to the general question of what is motivation because it effortlessly combines an answer to "What does it mean to be motivated?"—to approach or avoid something— with an answer to "What do people really want?"—to maximize pleasure and minimize pain. Motivation, according to this principle, is thus "approaching pleasure and avoiding pain."

My preferred view that motivation is "directing choices in order to be effective" does not contradict the hedonic principle. One way people can be effective is to have pleasure rather than pain. And their choices will be directed by their preference for pleasure over pain. However, people's preferences are not based only on the hedonic outcomes they anticipate. There are other kinds of outcomes, such as knowing the truth about something (even when the truth hurts). In addition, anticipated outcomes, whether hedonic or not, are not the only sources of preferences that direct choices. People also prefer to do something in a particular *way*, such as pursuing goals in an eager way rather than a vigilant way, and these *strategic preferences* also direct choices. And it is not as if some way of doing things, such as being eager rather than vigilant, is more motivating because it is more pleasant. Indeed, if a person has prevention concerns, behaving in an eager manner has been shown to *reduce* motivation.[83]

Beyond these considerations, citing pleasure and pain as the determinants of people's choices can overemphasize the motivational force of the hedonic consequences of self-regulatory success in the future. The basic function of pleasure and pain is to provide *feedback* about self-regulatory success and failure. For example, a thirsty animal gets unpleasant "thirsty" feedback that motivates seeking a liquid to drink that will reduce the thirst. What the animal wants is just to reduce the thirst; it is not looking to experience the future pleasant feedback signal of success from drinking the needed liquid. In addition, during the goal-pursuit process itself the animal manages what happens (control effectiveness), and once it drinks the liquid it has the desired result of no longer being thirsty (value effectiveness).

Characterizing all these motives as just wanting a future pleasant feedback signal is not reasonable. At worst, it is a teleological error (i.e., a logical fallacy) because it implies that a future event caused a past event. Yes, thanks to the feedback signal, there are hedonic experiences involved in this goal pursuit, and they are part of the motivational story. But it is misleading to treat them as *the* story. And for nonhuman animals that are not self-conscious of their own future self experiences, it is especially misleading to suggest that their choices in the present are determined by the pleasant feedback signals they will experience in the future from successful self-regulation.

Another limitation of the hedonic principle is that it fails to distinguish among different kinds of motivational experiences that relate to different ways of being effective. There is not a single success experience of pleasure and a single failure experience of pain; there are many different kinds of success and failure experiences. For example, if a goal pursuit is successful, individuals with a promotion focus and individuals with a prevention focus will both feel proud and satisfied, which are feelings of being effective at having what's desired, but, in addition, the promotion-focused individuals will feel happy while the prevention-focused individuals will feel relaxed.[84] For successful promotion- and prevention-focused individuals, characterizing those positive feelings that are the same (proud and satisfied) and those positive feelings that are different (happy vs. relaxed) as simply *pleasant* feelings does not capture the fact that these feelings are different because the motivational states that underlie them are different.[85]

There are other positive feelings as well that are not just pleasant. Both promotion- and prevention-focused individuals will "feel right" about what they are doing if the strategic manner of their goal pursuit fits their focus, where an eager manner fits promotion and a vigilant manner fits prevention.[86] Feeling right about what you are doing is an experience of success in managing what happens (control effectiveness). It is *not* the same as just feeling pleasure.[87]

The distinct positive feelings that are associated with a particular self-regulatory system provide feedback that the system is regulating effectively. Each system also has distinct negative feelings that signal that it is not regulating effectively. For example, people feel hungry when they have not had enough to eat and feel thirsty when they have not had enough to drink. People feel sad or discouraged when their promotion system fails, and they feel nervous and tense when their prevention system fails.[88] It has been suggested that the primary function of affective experiences is to signal or provide feedback about self-regulatory success or failure—that some self-regulatory system is working or not working.[89]

Thus, rather than people doing things only for the sake of "happiness" or "life satisfaction," which is a hedonic motivational story, they often do things in order to experience value, truth, or control effectiveness. The motivational instigator is not to feel good but to be effective, and when we are effective we receive a "success" feedback signal that happens to feel good. The motivation is to be effective in our life pursuits, and we use feedback signals to manage these goal pursuits. Just because these feedback signals can be pleasant or painful, and we prefer pleasure over pain, does not mean that they instigated the goal pursuits.

I believe that the hedonic principle receives more credit than it deserves for what motivates someone to do something. Indeed, placing too much emphasis on the hedonic principle, as when people blithely use "carrot and stick" incentives, can guide motivation in the wrong direction, as I discuss more fully in Chapter 12. It is true that when people succeed in their goal pursuits they experience pleasure, and when they fail they experience pain. But it does not follow from this that these hedonic outcomes motivated the goal pursuits to begin with. Was it really pleasure and pain that people wanted? I believe that people really want to be effective, and it is this motivation that generally initiates goal pursuits. Pleasure and pain function as highly useful feedback signals about whether the goal pursuit has been effective or not. And, as feedback signals, pleasure and pain are an important part of the motivational system. But this does not make them the initiator of motivation.

Earlier I described classical conditioning studies that found that pigeons will make eating-like pecks at light cues that were previously associated with an edible reward and drinking-like pecks at the same light cues when they were previously associated with a liquid reward, despite the fact that the light cues themselves do not satisfy hunger or thirst. I mentioned these studies as evidence against physiological needs, or survival, being a sufficient answer to what is really wanted. I concluded that these studies show that experience matters. I also implied that they support the pleasure and pain answer to what is really wanted. On that final implication, I could have been giving pleasure and pain too much credit. Yes, experience matters. But the experience could be one of being effective and not hedonic experience. Were the pigeons really pecking for the sake of pleasure or were they pecking to be successful at something that they had learned to do? From a Piagetian perspective, was the pecking of the pigeons like the non-nutritive sucking of infants who want to exercise that function? Upon reflection, the latter alternative seems a stronger possibility.[90]

Again, I am not claiming that "directing choices in order to be effective" encompasses *all* of motivation. There *are* experiences of pleasure (e.g., watching a sunset) and pain that motivate people beyond their implications for being effective. But what generally motivates people is the desire to be effective, with pleasure and pain typically functioning as feedback signals of success and failure at being effective.

Directing Energy in Order to Survive

The "directed energy" answer to what it means to be motivated can be combined with the "survival" answer to what people really want. From this perspective, motivation is "directing energy in order to survive." This answer to what is motivation also has a long history, especially within psychology in the first half of the 20th century, and it is implicitly held by some current evolutionary perspectives on motivation.

It is true that energy is expended in goal-pursuit activities. It is also true that activities can be pursued in order to satisfy biological needs of survival. Thus, people can choose to invest their energy more in one activity than in another as a function of each activity's contribution to satisfying biological needs of survival. In short, people can direct choices of energy investment in order to be successful at survival. This alternative, then, is certainly part of the story of motivation. But again it is not the whole story because not all of our choices are directed by biological survival needs. People can make choices that are directed by motives that *decrease* rather than increase their chances of survival, such as thrill-seeking activities and addictions.

In addition, it is *not* the case that stronger motivation necessarily means investing more energy, or that more energy is the key to success at survival or at any other objective. Regardless of how much effort people would be *willing* to invest in order to be successful at something, they will invest only the amount of energy that is actually *required* to ensure success.[91] Given this, the amount of energy that is invested in doing something does not directly reflect the strength of motivation to succeed at it. And, most important of all, there is no all-purpose energy that can simply be directed to attain any goal. Success in goal pursuit depends on making strategic and tactical choices that *work together effectively* with one's goal orientation. Success is not about the amount of energy that is invested; it is about the right organization of motives.

The underlying assumption of this book is that, generally speaking, motivation is *directing choices in order to be effective*. In the next chapter, I will be discussing the three ways in which people want to be effective—*value*, *truth*, and *control*. I will compare and contrast them as well as describe briefly the relations among them. I will then devote a chapter to each way of being effective.

It is important to know about each one in its own right because each is critical to motivation. But the three different ways of being effective do not operate just as separate dimensions of effectiveness: it is the *relations* among them as they *work together* that is a central theme of this book. Thus, in later chapters, I will discuss the significance of specific pairs of relations—between value and truth, value and control, and truth and control—and then consider the structural organization among all three ways of being effective: *value, truth, and control working together.*

3

Value, Truth, and Control

Ways of Being Effective

I believe that people want to be effective in their life pursuits. My discussion in Chapter 2 as to why I believe this was based on the insights of eminent scholars and scientists such as Keynes, Woodworth, Hebb, White, Piaget, Bandura, and Deci and Ryan. I believe that they have provided convincing reasons for why "being effective" is the best answer to the question of what is it that people want. So convincing, in fact, that I wish to *broaden* the conception of being effective to cover even more of motivation than has been highlighted in previous proposals. To do so, I need to be clear what I mean by success or failure in being effective.

My concept of "success" and "failure" in being effective is broader than previous theoretical proposals. For example, I would include motives to satisfy hunger, thirst, or other primary biological or survival needs because individuals can be effective or ineffective in meeting these needs, whereas the theory of effectance motivation excluded such motives. Similarly, I would include within effectiveness (i.e., within competence) motives for relatedness or belongingness because someone can succeed (gain social acceptance) or fail (incur social rejection) to meet this need and such success or failure also contributes to feelings of being effective. This is in contrast to self-determination theory, which treats motives for relatedness or belongingness as separate from competence.[1] In addition, I would include ways of being effective that do not require conscious attention to our personal competencies or capabilities, in contrast to self-efficacy theory, which is restricted to this kind of reflective self-consciousness. After all, reflective self-consciousness is not a necessary condition for humans or non-human animals to want to be effective and emotionally react to success and failure in doing so.

It is true that the language of "success" and "failure" has been typically used more in the domain of performance than in other domains. In the domain of decision making, for example, the terms usually used are "good" or "bad" choices rather than "success" or "failure." But decision making, like other domains, involves some purpose, goal, or need that is either met/satisfied (success) or not met/satisfied (failure) by the choice that is made. Making a "good" choice is being effective (a "success") and making a "bad" choice is being ineffective (a "failure").

Some people might argue that the motivation to be effective, when defined in this way, is really the same as the classic hedonic principle, with success being pleasure and failure being pain. I disagree with this argument. Indeed, equating success/failure to pleasure/pain has been a problem for motivation science—whether it occurs in economics, psychology, or any other discipline. It overgeneralizes what are the specific sensation experiences of pleasure and pain. Marathon runners will endure pain in the service of trying to succeed, even when they stand to gain no material or social rewards for success (e.g., cash prizes; media attention) but just a feeling of efficacy. Ballet dancers will practice staying *en pointe* for long periods despite it being very painful. And we can all think of many other examples beyond marathon runners and ballet dancers. As Hebb pointed out, most of us, if not all of us, will engage sometimes in game-like activities on our own, with no social or material rewards, just to challenge ourselves and test our competence, even when we find the activity frustratingly difficult. In such cases, it is all about engaging in an activity that tests our effectiveness, independent of whether our sensation experiences during the activity itself are pleasant or unpleasant. Thus, the motivation to be effective should not be confused with the hedonic motivation to approach pleasure and avoid pain. I will return to this point throughout this chapter.

I should also make two additional points clear from the start. First, as in self-efficacy theory and self-determination theory, I do not mean to associate the notion of wanting to be effective with just personal, individual success. Success in being effective can also include communal success, collective success, or cooperative success—in short, "our" success from what "we" did, and not just "my" success from what "I" did. Second, the motivation to be effective is not limited to short-term outcomes. Humans, especially, are time travelers who make plans for success that are far ahead in the future, even years in the future.[2] Actions along the way can include many short-term failures that are unpleasant without undermining the long-term motivation to succeed in the future. Short-term obstacles can be experienced as unpleasant adversities, but this experience can actually increase motivation when people treat these obstacles as interfering forces to be opposed, because opposing them will strengthen engagement in what they are doing.[3] In addition, the same performance outcome can be experienced by one person as a "failure" and decrease that person's motivation, but be experienced by another person as a phase in the learning process and increase that person's subsequent motivation[4]—as captured in everyday maxims like "mistakes are gifts," "mistakes are learning opportunities."

What I have in mind, then, concerning the motive to be effective is quite broad. However, it is not as broad as the most general dictionary meaning of the terms "succeed" and "fail."[5] The terms "failure" and "to fail," for example, apply not only to living things but to machinery, as with "failure" meaning "breaking down" or "to fail" meaning "to become deficient." As I discussed in Chapter 2 when addressing the question of what it means to be motivated, machines do not have preferences directing choices, and I would not include their performance as part of what I mean by wanting to be effective. The key is the term "wanting." I restrict "wanting" to preferences directing choices. This rules out machinery as being motivated to be effective.[6]

DISTINGUISHING AMONG VALUE, TRUTH, AND CONTROL EFFECTIVENESS

Now that I have introduced my perspective on the nature and boundary conditions of the motivation to be effective, it is time to describe more fully the three different ways of being effective—value, truth, and control—that together constitute what it means for people to want to be effective in their life pursuits.

Value Effectiveness

By "value effectiveness" I mean actors being successful in ending with the outcomes they desire. Value effectiveness is about success with respect to outcomes, about the consequences of goal pursuit—success in ending with benefits versus costs, pleasure versus pain, biological needs satisfied versus unsatisfied. This includes cases where we use another person to succeed (a proxy agent) and cases where we collaborate with others on a joint project to succeed (collective or communal "we" effectiveness). Simply put, *value effectiveness is being successful in having what's desired*. It should be emphasized that what matters for value effectiveness is ending with the desired outcomes and not how this ending came about, whether through a proxy, through collaboration with others, or through our own actions.

Value effectiveness was emphasized by drive theories and the hedonic principle. For drive theories, it was the value derived from the benefits of satisfying primary biological needs, such as reducing hunger (e.g., finding food) or reducing fear (e.g., escaping danger). For the hedonic principle, it was the value derived from the benefits of making something pleasant happen or something painful not happen. *Goal* theories have also emphasized value effectiveness.[7] Indeed, they often include goal pursuit as part of the very definition of "motivation," with motivation constituting forces within us that are goal-directed or purposive.[8] Woodworth, once again, said it clearly: "What persists, in purposive behavior, is the tendency towards some end or goal. The purposeful person wants something he has not yet got, and is striving towards some future result."[9] In social psychology at least, a major influence on this conceptualization of motivation was Lewin's work on goal-directed action and goal striving within a field of forces where positive value relates to a force of attraction and negative valence relates to a force of repulsion.[10] It is possible to conceptualize goal pursuit very broadly, including unconscious goal pursuit and biologically driven goal pursuit, with value effectiveness deriving from wanting our goal-directed pursuits to end with successful outcomes.

Given the historical emphasis in psychology on the desired states associated with need satisfaction and hedonic states, I should highlight again that value effectiveness is not restricted to being successful in having a desired biological state or having a desired hedonic state. To take an earlier example, there is value from succeeding in a challenging task, such as finding the solution to some puzzle, even if no biological needs are satisfied and the success is not rewarded in any way (e.g., a prize; praise by others). And this is true even for task activities that are frustrating while they are being worked on. Yes, there is a pleasant "success" signal at the end. But the pleasant experience of this feedback signal need not be what motivated the choice to do the task to begin with. It can be the anticipation of having the desired result—of being effective in finding the solution.

I do need to add a caveat, however. Humans are different from other animals in the extent to which they are aware of their experiences and can time travel to the future and anticipate those experiences. Thus, unlike other animals, humans can anticipate that by being successful in the future they will receive a success feedback signal that will be pleasant. This conscious awareness and ability to time travel could motivate humans to make a choice in the present that they anticipate will produce a pleasant feedback signal in the future. I believe that this, in fact, can influence our choices in the present. It *is* a factor underlying our preferences that directs our choices. But I do not believe that it is a factor for other animals or that it is *the* major factor for humans. Wanting to be effective is the major determinant of our choices. It is not that we want a success feedback signal because the signal itself is a pleasant experience. What we want is success feedback *signaling* that we have been effective. And when it comes to choosing activities like searching for and finding a solution to a puzzle, the effectiveness that is experienced is likely to derive not only from value effectiveness but also from truth effectiveness and control effectiveness.

Truth Effectiveness

By "truth effectiveness" I mean actors being successful in knowing what is real. The root meaning of "truth" (as well as "trust") relates to "true"; "truth" is the quality of being "true." Something being "true" means being in accordance with an actual state of affairs, being consistent with the facts; conforming to or agreeing with an essential reality; being that which is the case, representing things as they are—in brief, knowing what's real, what's reality.[11] "True" also relates to accuracy; to being correct, right, and legitimate; to being genuine, honest, and faithful. It is contrasted with being imaginary, spurious, counterfeit.[12] Thus, *truth effectiveness is being successful in establishing what's real.* Value effectiveness—having desired results—is critical for humans and other animals. But so is truth effectiveness—knowing what's real in the world, representing things as they are. Without truth effectiveness we would bump into walls, we would live in a world that William James referred to as "one great blooming, buzzing confusion."[13]

Young children, and some troubled adults, find it difficult to distinguish reality from fantasy. Children sometimes fear what is lurking under their bed or hiding in their closet, and some adults have paranoid delusions. I will discuss later in more detail the difficulties that *all* of us can have in distinguishing what is real from what is imagined or mentally constructed. And it is evident from religious and political differences in belief systems that what is reality to one group is mere illusion or delusion to another. But what is clear is that each individual, and each group, is strongly motivated to know what is real—to attain truth effectiveness. This plays out in a myriad of ways, including in concerns with accuracy, or about what is correct or incorrect, right or wrong, legitimate or illegitimate, honest or deceitful, genuine or fraudulent. The different ways that people establish reality are the focus of Chapter 5.

Is truth just another kind of beneficial outcome? If so, wouldn't it be more parsimonious (à la Occam's razor) to have just value effectiveness as one variable and treat truth as a special case of value effectiveness? The answer is that truth is *not* just another kind of outcome. It has a relation to *all* outcomes. Motivation for goal pursuit depends not only on the anticipated benefits and costs of success but also on the reality of the goal pursuit. Is it realistic to anticipate that I will succeed? And if I do succeed, are the anticipated benefits from success realistic or just imagined outcomes? And what is the correct way, the accurate way, to even define what counts as a successful or unsuccessful outcome of a goal pursuit? These truth effectiveness questions can be applied to *all* goal-pursuit outcomes.

This is not to say that people cannot treat truth, such as learning something or knowing something, as a goal, as a valued end-state that they pursue. They can. And when they do treat truth as a goal, such as a learning goal, then when the learning has been achieved, the knowledge that has been learned constitutes having what's desired; it has value effectiveness. But even then there could be additional truth questions about whether the anticipated benefits from having this desired knowledge are realistic.

I also want to highlight the difference between truth effectiveness and the hedonic principle. As we all know, the truth can be painful, and yet people often seek it out even when they believe it will be painful. When something pleasant but unexpected happens to people, they often want to know why it happened. Others will tell them to just enjoy it and not worry about why it happened, yet they still want to know why. The movie "The Truman Show" clearly illustrates this.

The central character in the movie, Truman, is living the perfect hedonic life. His life is all pleasure and no pain, with one exception: he is anxious about being on the water because he believes his father drowned in a boating accident. In fact, unknown to him, his entire life is a reality TV show that began airing at his birth. He is the star in a continually running TV show and everyone else he knows are actors playing their roles. Where he lives is just a huge TV studio. Close to his 30th birthday, he finally discovers that his life is a fake. Despite everyone reassuring him and despite his perfect hedonic life, Truman willingly takes on pain and hardship. He even risks actual death by sailing across the water he fears because he needs to follow up his discovery and seek the truth. He finds a door and leaves the constructed reality of perfect hedonism for an uncertain real world—and leaves as the hero of the movie.

The movie "The Matrix" provides another compelling example. In the movie, there is a future where the reality perceived by humans is actually a *simulated* reality—the Matrix—that provides people with a hedonically positive life to pacify them. Morpheus, the leader of the rebels, gives the character Neo a choice between a blue pill that will keep him in this comfortable simulated reality or a red pill that offers only the truth. Morpheus tells Neo, "All I'm offering is the truth, nothing more." Neo chooses the red pill—and again is the hero of the movie. Neo's motivation, like Truman's, is truth effectiveness, which trumps just hedonic pleasure. As a final example, remember the decision of Adam and Eve to eat from the *tree of knowledge* and lose an everlasting life of pleasure and no pain.

Control Effectiveness

By "control effectiveness," I mean actors experiencing success at managing what is required (procedures, competencies, resources) to make something happen (or not happen). Having control relates to exercising direction or restraint upon action; to having power or authority to guide or manage; to having influence over something.[14] *Control effectiveness is being successful in managing what happens.* Whereas value effectiveness relates to outcomes (benefits vs. costs) and truth effectiveness relates to reality (real vs. illusion), control effectiveness relates to *strength* (strong vs. weak influence over something). It is very general. People can have strong versus weak muscles, eyesight, intellect, character, arguments, willpower, teamwork, and so on. Managers, leaders, administrators can be strong or weak.

While high control effectiveness increases the likelihood of beneficial outcomes, it is separate from outcomes, as reflected in maxims such as "It's not whether you win or lose, it's how you play the game." In victory or defeat, you play with skill and courage—with strength. Indeed, control effectiveness, like truth effectiveness, can trump value effectiveness. Consider, for example, a study with rats that learned that by pressing a lever they could make a food pellet fall into a food tray where they could eat it. In one experimental condition, a food dish was placed in the cage, which meant that the rats could obtain the same food pellets for free (i.e., without having to work for them). On occasion a rat would accidentally push the free food dish in front of the food tray. Despite the fact that they could effortlessly attain the food from the free food dish in front of them, the rats actually pushed the food dish *out of the way* (not eating from it), and then pressed the lever to make a food pellet fall into the food tray where they ate it.[15] Such behavior is about control effectiveness and not just about value effectiveness. If it was just about value effectiveness the rats would eat from the free food dish, thereby maximizing the benefits/costs ratio given that it would be the same beneficial food for less cost in effort.

There is also evidence that when people work together on a joint project, they often take disproportionate credit for the outcome—even when the joint project has a *bad* outcome.[16] Taking credit enhances their control effectiveness, and this can trump the value effectiveness concerns with acknowledging a failed outcome. As has often been noted, individuals, and not just Frank Sinatra, care about doing something "my way," even if this reduces outcome value. Witness the classic response of adolescents to a parent who wants to help them avoid making the same painful mistake the parent made when growing up: "Let me make my own mistakes!" It's not about pleasure and pain—it's about control effectiveness.

Is control just another kind of beneficial outcome, and thus shouldn't it be treated as just a type of value effectiveness? No, as for truth, control is *not* just another kind of outcome because it is relevant to *all* outcomes. What you end up with is one thing; how you got there is another thing. Before you can have the value effectiveness of success in reaching a desired end-state, you need to carry things out that get you there. Control effectiveness is about the levels of competence, self-efficacy, personal causation, and autonomy that are experienced along the way while carrying out the goal-pursuit process, before there are any desired results at the end. It is not the same as value effectiveness because individuals who in the end are equally successful in making happen what they wanted to happen can have very different experiences of competence, self-efficacy, and autonomy along the way. It is also not the same as truth effectiveness because our perceptions or beliefs about our success in competence, self-efficacy, or autonomy (i.e., our control effectiveness) can themselves be evaluated in terms of how realistic they are (i.e., in terms of their truth effectiveness). The motive for control effectiveness is sufficiently strong that it can occasionally trump both truth effectiveness and value effectiveness, as when people defend beliefs regarding their personal strengths (or the strengths of a group with which they identify) despite evidence that shows those beliefs are untrue and non-beneficial.

As a further illustration of the difference between control effectiveness and value effectiveness, consider the following thought experiment offered by Robert Nozick in his book *Anarchy, State and Utopia*.[17] He asks us to imagine that an inventor has devised an experience machine that could give us whatever desirable or pleasurable experiences we could possibly want. If you choose to get into this machine, your pleasant experiences will be fully convincing; you would not be able to tell that they were not real. The inventor promises that for the rest of your life in the machine you will have a fully convincing experience of a life that is better than whatever would have happened to you outside the machine—that is, your value effectiveness within the machine is guaranteed to be better than your value effectiveness outside the machine. For example, whatever your salary would be outside the machine, it will be experienced as higher within the machine; you will marry a more attractive wife or husband; your children will be better behaved; your career promotions will occur sooner; all your life-pursuit outcomes will be experienced as happening better within the machine than outside the machine.

The point of the thought experiment is that most people choose *not* to get into the machine, which does not make sense if hedonic experience, or value effectiveness more generally, is the only effectiveness people care about. One reason for this choice could be the desire for truth effectiveness to the extent that people consider what would happen inside the machine to be an illusion rather than reality, inauthentic rather than authentic. At the moment of making their choice, they prefer a future of reality to a future of illusion, even though they know that what would happen to them if they entered the machine would be experienced as real. However, at least as important, I believe, is knowing that they would lack control effectiveness inside the machine. They would experience a life of successful outcomes—value effectiveness. But when making their choice whether or not to enter the machine, they know that these future outcomes would occur because of the *inventor's* control effectiveness rather than *their own*. Independent of their actions, the inventor's programming would always *improve* the outcomes, making *better* outcomes *non-contingent* with their actions. Thus, they know when making their choice that the better outcomes that will occur inside the machine would not reflect *their* competencies and effectance (even though they recognize that, once inside the machine, they will no longer know that).

Returning again to "The Matrix," just before Morpheus asks Neo to choose between the blue pill and the red bill, he asks, "Do you believe in fate, Neo?" Neo answers "No!" "Why not?" asks Morpheus. Neo replies, "Because I don't like the idea that I'm not in control of my life." For Neo it's about truth and control. It is certainly *not* about maximizing pleasure and minimizing pain. I believe that what Nozick's thought experiment and Neo's answer illustrate is that people generally prefer to give up the option of greater hedonic value with little or no control and prefer instead the option of lesser hedonic value with greater control.

There is also evidence from the landmark research by Charles Osgood, George Suci, and Percy Tannenbaum, described in *The Measurement of Meaning*, which suggests that control motivation differs from both value and truth motivation.[18] The participants in the studies were asked to make judgments of people and objects for dozens of different adjectives. The researchers discovered that two major dimensions that participants used to distinguish among different kinds of people and objects were evaluation (how beneficial or harmful a person or object was) and potency (how potent or impotent a person or object was). The adjective scales that were used to measure the evaluation dimension were mostly two kinds: one set of scales relating to value (e.g., positive vs. negative; pleasurable vs. painful; beautiful vs. ugly; kind vs. cruel), and another set of scales relating to truth (e.g., true vs. false; believing vs. skeptical; wise vs. foolish; meaningful vs. meaningless).[19] Given that the evaluation dimension captures both the good versus bad of value *and* the good versus bad of truth, it is not surprising that these scales were found to be especially important for distinguishing among different kinds of people and objects. But the research also found that the evaluation dimension containing both value and truth was psychologically distinct from the potency dimension whose scales related to control (e.g., strong vs. weak; vigorous vs. feeble; potent vs. impotent; tough vs. fragile).

I want to be explicit about the difference between control effectiveness and value effectiveness with regard to the process of pursuing goals. The psychological literature sometimes makes a distinction between process and outcome that can be confusing in the context of the present discussion. It might sound like the process of pursuing a goal is just about control effectiveness and the final outcomes or consequences of pursuing a goal are just about value effectiveness. But this is not the case. As I mentioned earlier, there are aspects of the process of pursuing a goal than can also involve desired results and thus relate to value effectiveness. There are both benefits and costs that can be experienced while a goal is being pursued, and these benefits and costs are part of "having desired results." However, while a goal is being pursued, people are also managing to make things happen. Thus, the process of goal pursuit involves *both* value and control effectiveness. Indeed, when we look around while walking to a destination, there can also be truth effectiveness from exploring our surroundings. Given that all three ways of being effective can be involved while pursuing a goal, whereas there is only value effectiveness once the goal is attained, it is not surprising that we all resonate to another well-known expression: "It's the journey, not the destination."

A final comment. The literature on goal pursuit also distinguishes between means and ends. Traditionally, it is the ends that are considered to be the source of the motivation to engage in the activities that are the means to the ends (e.g., rats pressing a lever in order to attain food). Yes it is recognized that people can be *intrinsically* motivated to engage in some activities that are means to an end, but this is because the means have become ends in themselves. The motivation is still about ends. This highlights the extent to which value (i.e., desired results) has dominated thinking about what motivates people. But even when people engage in an activity that is a means to an end (i.e., extrinsically motivated) rather than an end in itself, one should not conclude that value, i.e., wanting the desired endstate, is the only source of motivation to engage in that activity. Engaging in an activity that is a means to an end constitutes managing what happens, and thus control effectiveness is an additional source of motivation to engage in that activity. There has been insufficient attention in the motivational literature to individuals' wanting control effectiveness, and how this motivation impacts their choices among, and experiences of, different activities that function as means.

THREE VEXING QUESTIONS ABOUT EFFECTIVENESS

Later in this chapter I will provide additional examples of why it is both useful and necessary to distinguish among the three ways of being effective, but first I want to address a few important, even vexing, questions about the motivation to be effective overall.

Question 1: Don't People Sometimes Choose to *Give Up Their Control* to Others?

Yes, people *do* sometimes prefer that someone else make a choice for them. In fact, there are cultural differences in this regard, as demonstrated in a study that compared Anglo-American and Asian-American children on the effects of making their own personal choice versus having their choice made for them by someone else.[20] Elementary school children were shown six piles of word puzzles—anagrams—that were sorted into different categories (e.g., animals; food), and one of the categories was selected for them to work on. Then they were shown six markers of different colors and one marker was selected for them to work with. The critical variable was who made the selection. By random assignment, some of the children were allowed to make their own choice of both which category to work on and which marker to work with ("It's your choice"), whereas other children had both these choices made for them by their mother ("It's what your mom wants"). The study measured both the children's performance on the anagrams and the length of time they spent voluntarily doing anagrams when they were later given a free-play period to do whatever they wanted. For the Anglo-American children, both the performance and free-play time on the anagrams was higher when they made the choices than when their mother made the choices. However, for the Asian-American children it was the exact opposite—both performance and free-play time was higher when their mother made the choices than when they made the choices.

These results show that individuals need not experience a reduction in motivation when someone else is responsible for their choice of an activity. Younger American children (prior to 7 years old) also experience motivation to do an activity as stronger when a significant other (e.g., a parent) makes the choice for them rather than when they make their own choice.[21] As children grow up in America, they learn to want to make their own choices rather than to have them made for them. But it is clear from this research with younger children and older Asian-American children that reducing personal choice need not reduce motivation to engage in an activity. Beyond these examples, we all know that there are times when we prefer, we choose, to have trusted others make choices for us rather than make our own choices—times when we want *less* control effectiveness.

Is this not a problem for my proposal that motivation is wanting to be effective? Well, actually, my proposal is that people want success with respect to value, control, and truth. Let us begin with control, because this is the dimension most obviously affected by having someone else choose for oneself. When someone else makes a choice for you, does that not reduce your control? Not necessarily; I believe that it depends on how you experience the choice. If it is experienced as another person's choice, as in the case of the inventor and his programming in the Nozick thought experiment, instead of your own choice, then it *is* likely to reduce a sense of control. But if it is experienced as "*our* choice," then it is unlikely to reduce a sense of control and could even increase it.[22]

When parents make choices for their children, it is more likely that the children would experience the choice as "our choice"—a collective or communal choice—than when some strange adult makes the choice. Indeed, there was another condition in the cross-cultural study in which it was the experimenter who made the choice for the children rather than the children themselves or their mother.[23] For the Asian-American children, both the performance and free-play time on the anagrams was *lower* in this "experimenter-chooses" condition than in the personal choice condition. Thus, when someone else is making a choice for you, your *relationship* with that person is critical. If a parent versus a stranger chooses for a young child, it is much more likely that the child will experience the choice in a collective or communal manner—as "our choice." And it need not be only a parent: it could be a romantic partner, a close friend, a colleague, a roommate, and so on.

Your sense of control is also sustained if *you* choose to have someone else make a choice for you. After all, the other person is functioning as your instrument, your tool. In discussing "proxy control," Bandura says that people "are not averse to relinquishing control over events that affect their lives in order to free themselves of the performance demands and hazards that the exercise of control entails."[24] In such cases, you still have some control in the fact that *you* choose to use someone else as your proxy agent, *and* you have greater value from the fact that the benefits that accrue to you come at less cost.

But what about the case when someone else not close to you decides to choose for you—that is, someone whose choice would not be experienced as "our choice"? This is like the experimenter-chooses condition in the cross-cultural study. This was a low-control condition in that study and is likely to be a low-control condition generally speaking. But it is not necessarily a low-*effectiveness* condition overall, because value and truth must also be considered. As for proxy control, value could still increase from a reduction in the costs of your goal pursuit. My guess is this is precisely why people are willing at times to have someone else make choices for them—it provides benefits with low costs.

For all of this to happen, however, it is important that you trust the decision-making skills of the person who is making the choice for you. Yes, *trust* or *truth* is an important part of the story. I believe that trust is a critical factor in the phenomenon of people being willing to give up control to others. This is another reason why people typically would be more willing to have someone close to them make choices for them than to have a total stranger play this role. It is not only about experiencing the choice as "our choice" but also about trusting the choice. In fact, sometimes people trust a close other to make a *better* choice than they would make, as when they know that the other person, such as a parent, has more expertise in the choice domain. They could even trust a total stranger if they believed that the stranger's greater expertise in some domains would result in making better choices than they could make. Those expert choices would be higher in trust. Thus, even in the cases where there is a reduction in control from giving up one's choices to others, this decrease could be more than compensated for by increases in both truth (more accurate or realistic choice) and value (more beneficial choice). That is, one's overall effectiveness could be even higher because control is just one way of being effective.

Question 2: Doesn't Wanting to Be Effective Sometimes *Undermine Motivation?*

Let's begin by considering the implications of a prototypic study where engaging in an activity in order to attain a reward undermined subsequent interest in that activity.[25] In this study, all the children who participated liked to draw and were competent in drawing prior to the experimental session. The children in the "instrumental reward" condition received multicolored felt-tipped pens and drawing paper, had the opportunity to draw freely, and were promised (and later received) an award for helping out an adult by drawing pictures. Compared to children in the control condition, who were neither promised nor received an award, these children spent much less time drawing in a subsequent free-play situation where they could either draw or engage in alternative activities.

From the perspective of self-determination theory, the children in the "instrumental reward" condition were extrinsically motivated (probably, externally controlled) when they were drawing, whereas the children in the control condition were intrinsically motivated. The results of this study, and others like it, would be explained in terms of a reduction in intrinsic motivation in the "instrumental reward" condition that reduced motivation to do the activity again. Doesn't this mean that wanting to have the desired results of the award (i.e., value effectiveness) undermined interest in the drawing activity? And doesn't this confirm that motivation was *reduced* by wanting value effectiveness rather than enhanced? Not necessarily.

Although it is reasonable to infer that the children's experience of autonomy was reduced in the "instrumental reward" condition, they can still have effectance motivation and perceived self-efficacy regarding their competence in drawing pictures. Moreover, the fact that they were successful in drawing pictures for which they received a desired award could result in that reward having greater value to them than to the children in the control condition. But then why wasn't there evidence that the value of the reward itself increased in the "instrumental reward" condition? The simple answer: *it was never measured.*

To measure how the different conditions affected value generally, the study needed to include a measure of the value of the award itself—that is, how the children in the "instrumental reward" condition felt about the award. But this value was never measured in this study or in other similar studies. This is an important omission if we want to draw a general conclusion about the experience of effectiveness for individuals who engage in an activity as a means to an end. The common interpretation is that such extrinsic or exogenous motivation undermines the experience of effectiveness; that it is a bad thing that should be avoided if possible. But intrinsic motivation is not the only kind of effectiveness that is positively motivating to people. Consider the common example of people who work at a job just for the sake of its rewards (salary; health benefits; retirement benefits). The job is just a means to an end, not an end in itself. But is this a problem? Although they are not intrinsically motivated, they still have a sense of control from effectance motivation and perceived self-efficacy that is associated with the goal-pursuit process, and they have value from benefiting themselves and their family. Indeed, the value of the job's benefits to them and their family could increase because of the effort, or even sacrifice, made for their sake.[26]

Question 3: Don't People Sometimes Have a *Fear of Success*?

Yes, some people do fear success. In her influential Harvard doctoral dissertation, Matina Horner proposed that some women's achievement motivation was reduced by their fear of success.[27] The "fear of success" concept was appealing to many because it provided an explanation for an oft-noted difference between men and women with regard to their motive to succeed. Subsequent research, however, found that men can also experience fear of success. In any case, whether experienced by men or women, the central question is what motivation underlies individuals' fear of success. Do such individuals prefer to fail?

To answer this question, one must consider what it is about success that is being feared. I believe that what are feared are the implications or consequences of the success. There is evidence, for example, that attractive women fear that others will reject them for being too attractive and thus too different from the others. The underlying motivation is fear of failure (i.e., fear of rejection) rather than fear of success.[28] More generally, one's success can imply that one is different from, better than, others. Just being distinctive or standing out can be a problem in many cultures—"The nail that stands out gets pounded down."[29]

There are individuals in any culture who don't want the attention, recognition, and scrutiny that success might bring. Being superior to others can be even more of a problem. Let's say that you are better at a task than your older siblings or revered parents or friends. You may not want to succeed at that task because it could adversely change the nature of your relationships, threatening closeness and belongingness.[30] Another potential consequence of success is that expectations for your future performance (your own expectations and others' expectations for you) could change such that you will have to match or exceed your performance from then on—a pressure or demand on you that you would prefer not to have. More complex dynamics include success being inconsistent with your strongly held self-beliefs (e.g., "I deserve to fail"; "I am a loser"),[31] or signaling the end of life pursuits (e.g., "There is nothing left to do, nowhere to climb"; "I have come to the end of my journey"), or requiring that you change your goals or become a different person (e.g., "If I succeed, I won't be the same person, I will change somehow") or set constraints on your options for the future (e.g., "If I succeed, I will have to continue on that path").

These "fears of success," and others like them, are anticipations of negative consequences from succeeding. It is not a preference to be ineffective in the world but a preference to be effective in ways that will not have these anticipated costs. It is not a preference for failure over success but a concern that the consequences of a "success" will involve failure in valued areas such as maintaining closeness and belongingness with significant others, or failure in truth by being forced to change beliefs that are strongly held, or failure in control by having to meet others' new demands on oneself. Indeed, to avoid such failures in value, truth, and control effectiveness, people often devise strategies to reduce the "success," such as when individuals are self-effacing and underplay success ("No big deal"; "It is nothing"; "Just dumb luck"; "God was smiling"; "a lucky break").

WHY IT IS USEFUL TO DISTINGUISH AMONG VALUE, TRUTH, AND CONTROL

My purpose in this section of the chapter is to provide some examples of why it is useful, and even necessary, to distinguish among value, truth, and control. One way it is useful is to help clarify what kinds of motivation have been emphasized in prior theories of motivation. For example, it clarifies how drive theorists like Hull in the 1940s differ from competence theorists like White in the 1950s. Drive theorists emphasized value effectiveness, such as having biological needs satisfied. In contrast, White emphasized control effectiveness, such as learning how to have an effect on things in the world. He explicitly distinguished between his effectance motivation (control effectiveness) and drive reduction motivation (value effectiveness), but without suggesting that there is an overarching motivation to be effective in life pursuits that includes *both* control and value effectiveness. Moreover, neither he nor Hull discussed the third way of being effective—*truth* effectiveness. As we will see in Chapter 5, truth effectiveness received substantial attention from social psychologists, especially in the late 1950s and 60s.

The distinction among value, truth, and control effectiveness is also useful in highlighting differences in motivational experiences. Experiences of value success and failure are different from experiences of truth success and failure or control success and failure. Value experiences include feeling happy and encouraged from promotion success and feeling calm and relaxed from prevention success; feeling sad and discouraged from promotion failure and feeling nervous and tense from prevention failure.[32] Value experiences also include feeling hungry or thirsty from failures in food-related or water-related regulation.

There are also distinct feeling experiences associated with truth success and failure and control success and failure. When people succeed at truth (i.e., when they have established what's real) they feel confident and sure, and when they fail they feel confused and doubtful. These are feelings that people can have, for example, when they are traveling somewhere and either know where they are going or have gotten lost. Truth failure can also make people feel shock and surprise when something happens that is unexpected, as happens during a magic show.[33]

When control succeeds people feel vigorous, capable, and efficacious (i.e., have the power to produce an effect), and when control fails they feel powerless, helpless, and incompetent. When practicing a sport, for example, athletes can have "on" days when it seems that there is nothing they can't do, and they can have "off" days when it seems they can't do anything. It is important to note that the feelings from control are not determined by outcomes. While playing a game, for example, athletes can or cannot feel vigorous, capable, and efficacious independent of whether they win or lose (having a "strong game" and still lose; having a "weak game" but win). And the unpleasant feeling of helplessness does not derive from negative outcomes but from a feeling that the outcomes—positive or negative—are independent of one's actions (i.e., non-contingent) and that your fate is out of your hands.

These distinct feelings that people experience when they succeed or fail in value, truth, and control illustrate the significance of the three effectiveness dimensions at the micro level of analysis, at the level of the individual. Generally speaking, this book is directed at this level. But it is also possible to consider the significance of these dimensions at the macro level of analysis, at the level of social institutions. Historically, three institutions that have dominated people's lives in the West are the Monarchy (aristocracy; nobility), the Church, and the Military. At various historical periods in the development of states and nations there have been different alliances or realignments among these dimensions that reflect different forms of political organization.[34] One way to think about the shifting relations among these institutions is in terms of the effectiveness they provide.

Although each institution can involve all three ways of being effective, the dominant function of the Monarchy is to provide value (benefits vs. costs; pleasure vs. pain), the dominant function of the Church is to provide truth (reality vs. illusion; right vs. wrong), and the dominant function of the Military is to provide control (strength vs. weakness; potent vs. impotent). This is not to say that a ruler or ruling class cannot be effective in all three ways by heading all three institutions. Consider, for example, the prince-bishops in the 4th century and afterwards who took on the roles of secular manager (Monarchy), bishop (Church), and commander of the troops of their city (Military). The more typical situation is different people heading the different institutions, and this produces conflicts and alliances, with resulting variation in which institutions ultimately dominate. This variability continues to this day, with government and business now included in the Monarchy-value role, academia and the media now included in the Church-truth role, and the police now included in the Military-control role.

At both the macro and micro levels of analysis, there are also different combinations of effectiveness. Returning to the micro level, what do the different relations among two or all three dimensions of effectiveness yield motivationally? What happens when value, truth, and control combine with one another? These questions will be addressed in more detail in the subsequent chapters of the book. Here I only wish to illustrate the significance of considering these relations among ways of being effective because it matters how motivations *work together*.

As just one example, consider the *value–truth relation*. I believe that when people perceive something as providing them with both value *and* truth, their *commitment* to it strengthens. Commitment means to pledge or bind oneself to some particular course of action. For such a pledge to occur, the action must be seen as worthwhile, as being worth it, and this requires that it be perceived as having value. Commitment also includes the concept of putting one's trust in something.[35] Thus, there needs also to be truth. Value alone is not enough.

It is often necessary to induce commitment in others as well. When leaders and managers talk about motivating others, whether they are in business, education, sports, the armed forces, or some other domain, they often emphasize the importance of their workers, students, athletes, or soldiers, respectively, being committed to their goal pursuits. There is not a single all-purpose tool, such as introducing incentives (carrots or sticks), that can increase commitment in goal pursuits. Rather, a distinct type of effectiveness relation—a specific way in which motivations work together effectively—is involved in creating commitment. Incentives could be used effectively to increase value, but that would not be enough to yield commitment. For commitment there must also be trust (truth).

Again, motivations working together are what matter. And to know how motivations work together, distinctions need to be made among different types of effectiveness dimensions (i.e., value, truth, control). We need to go beyond pleasure and pain (e.g., motivational "carrots" and "sticks") to understand what motivation is and how it works. As an example, consider the well-known passage from the U.S. Declaration of Independence:

> IN CONGRESS, JULY 4, 1776—The unanimous Declaration of the thirteen united States of America
>
> We hold these truths to be self-evident, that all men are created equal, that they are endowed by their Creator with certain unalienable Rights, that among these are Life, Liberty and the pursuit of Happiness.

Short but powerful. The intention of this message from Congress was to gather support from American colonists in their fight for independence from Britain. How was the message constructed to garner support? What did the colonists need to hear that would motivate them to support independence? What did the declaration emphasize to justify independence? I believe that the declaration made reference to all three ways of being effective. But what was emphasized, especially, was not value but *truth*. Declaring independence was the right decision that deserved support because the reasons for it were simply expressions of the truth.

From the very beginning of the declaration we are told that it was *unanimous*. By being *unanimous*, the decision and the reasons for it are presented as *objective* and not subjective. Thus, the subsequent statement of beliefs is not an expression of opinion; it is an expression of fact. This point is then immediately reaffirmed by referring to the beliefs as "truths" that are "self-evident." But when it comes to truth, nothing is left to chance. Just to be sure, we are told that the to-be-declared "Rights" are endowed to humans "by their Creator." They are *literally* "God-given" truths, "God-given" rights. And, because they are God-given, they are "unalienable."

The power of perceived truth to motivate others to support an advocated position is well known in the persuasion literature. Indeed, many theories of what makes a message persuasive argue that the strongest motive of message recipients is *wanting to be accurate*. Thus people will be convinced and support what a message advocates if they believe that it is telling the truth.[36] Few messages, in just a few words, have made a stronger claim to be telling the truth than the Declaration of Independence.

Moreover, the rights that the Declaration of Independence claims are unalienable are, in addition to life itself, the right to have control—"Liberty"—and the right to have value—"the pursuit of Happiness." We cannot have control without having liberty or freedom, and, to have the right to liberty, we must support the decision of Congress to be independent of British governance. We cannot have value without having the right to pursue happiness, and, to have that right, we must support independence. And all of this is self-evident, God-given, and clearly the whole truth and nothing but the truth.[37]

WAYS OF BEING EFFECTIVE IN RELATION TO OTHER MOTIVATIONS

When I discussed in Chapter 2 different answers to the question "What do people really want?" there was one answer that I mentioned only in passing but that has often been suggested in the literature—*belongingness*. Within the rubric of belongingness I include attachment, relatedness, affiliation, and love. Not only has belongingness often been included among human's basic needs,[38] it has also been considered to be central or fundamental to human motivation.[39] Why have I so far largely overlooked something so important? Why have I chosen "wanting to be effective" as the answer to what people want rather than "belongingness"?

In fact, these two answers are not in conflict. I believe that belongingness *is* as important as everyone thinks it is precisely because it is critical to the success of all three ways of being effective. More than anything else in the world, it is other people who give us desired results—*value*. The feeling that we belong, are loved by others, are accepted by others who want to be with us is central to our feeling joy and peace; and the feeling that we don't belong, are hated by others, are rejected by others who do not want to be with us is central to our feeling depressed and anxious. In addition, more than anything else in the world, it is other people whom we can cooperate with or use as our agents to make things happen—*control*. Finally, more than anything else in the world, it is other people who teach us what is correct, what is right, and what is real, and with whom we create shared realities about the world—*truth*. And putting all this together, it is other people, more than anything else in the world, who support (or hinder) our being effective. Precisely because of its essential role in all three ways of being effective, belongingness does play a fundamental role in human motivation.

In contrast, some other motives as exemplified in certain activities can have a more complex relationship with wanting to be effective. I previously mentioned the example of watching a sunset. Other examples, for me at least, would be tasting a dark chocolate truffle, drinking a great red wine, or having a warm bath.

As emphasized earlier, when people engage in these and similar activities solely for the sensual experience they afford, then the motivation involved cannot reasonably be considered as just wanting to be effective.[40] I do want to be clear, however, that even for these activities there can be components of wanting to be effective. When wine enthusiasts drink a great red wine, for example, all three ways of being effective are likely to be involved, in addition to the purely sensual experience. Effort and resources will have been expended in the pursuit of attaining the wine, and such strong engagement in the wine attainment process will heighten the value of having what's desired. When researching and selecting the wine, and when critically evaluating its bouquet and flavors in comparison to previously experienced wines, one will experience the truth of establishing what's real. And during the entire process of finding, buying, opening, airing, smelling, and tasting the wine, one will experience the control of managing what happens. For wine experts, who are precisely the persons who most appreciate the sensual experience of drinking wines, these motives to be effective are a *big part* of the wine-tasting activity. Indeed, even the sensual experience can be effectively used as a *tool* to critically evaluate the wine. A formal wine tasting can become a way to be effective, accompanied, sadly, with only moments of simple sensual pleasure.

As another example to clarify the distinction between effectiveness and sensual experience, consider the activity of taking a warm bath. People will take a warm bath for a variety of reasons. It can be simply instrumental, such as an alternative to showering as a way to get clean, or as a method for reducing stress, or as a treatment for sore muscles. The motivation in these cases would be wanting to be effective. But, yes, sometimes people take a warm bath simply to enjoy its sensuous pleasure. When this is the motive, it is not just effectiveness. Notably, there is still control from all the acts that must be managed to make the warm bath happen the way you like it, some value from having what's desired, and perhaps even some truth from knowing about and correctly predicting how it will feel. *But* there is the sensuous experience itself, which is a hedonic motive. And, thus, it bears repeating: wanting to be effective is *not* the whole story of motivation.

On the other hand, people want so much to be effective in their lives that they have to be *reminded* to take some time away from being effective to enjoy the sensuous pleasures. In the bestselling book *A 6th Bowl of Chicken Soup for the Soul,* a line from a poem by Leon Hansen says, "Just be sure that seeking pleasure isn't all you ever do." Hansen need not worry. That won't happen. People cannot even take a warm bath without saying, "I needed that!," which instantly makes it more about effectiveness than sensory pleasure. Instead, it is more likely that being effective is all that we ever do, in the ways I've just described and will now explore in greater depth.

PART TWO

Ways of Being Effective

4

Value

Having Desired Results

The more an object or activity has value to us, the more we prefer it over alternative objects or activities. We want to have the object or do the activity. But what gives an object or activity its value? *Where does value come from?* This chapter considers several mechanisms that confer value on something. Some of these mechanisms, such as need satisfaction or hedonic experience, are well known to be desired results that would confer value. Other mechanisms, as we will see, are less well known and even surprising. I begin with a glimpse of one of these surprising mechanisms.

As in Chapter 1, I want you to predict the results of a study from its design and procedure. But this time you can use any theoretical perspective or personal insight, be it the hedonic principle or another viewpoint, to make your prediction. The participants in this study were initially asked to perform an activity, and they were told that if their performance was good enough they would receive a reward. Indeed, all of the participants were told after completing this activity that they had done well enough to receive the reward. Before leaving the room for several minutes, the experimenter told the participants that they could spend their time doing any of the activities that were available in the room, which included doing again the activity they had just completed or, instead, playing computer games or reading magazines. This was the *open period*. The study examined the participants' interest in doing the completed activity again rather than the alternative activities, which measured how much they valued the completed activity. These parts of the experimental procedure were the same for everyone.

Other parts of the procedure varied. The original activity to be performed prior to the open period differed among the participants. At the beginning of the study, they were randomly assigned to perform initially either a "Shoot-the-Moon" activity or a "Financial Duties" activity. "Shoot-the-Moon" is a game where the player manipulates a pair of parallel metal rails in order to slowly force a steel ball as far as possible up an inclined plane. The object of the game is to get the ball to travel up the inclined plane as far as possible. Underneath the rails are holes that the ball falls into. The further the player gets the ball to travel before it falls through the rails and into a hole, the more points he or she earns. In the "Financial Duties" task, each participant plays the role of a student advisor who rates the financial standing of other students based on their management of three types of financial transactions—checking accounts, savings accounts, and credit card payments.

In addition to the manipulation of which activity participants were given initially to perform, there were two other experimental manipulations. First, the participants were told to think of the reward they could receive either as an *enjoyable reward* "like a prize you win at a carnival" or as a *serious reward* "like the salary you receive at work." Second, the participants had the open period introduced to them either as an *enjoyable "free time" period* or as a *serious "time management" period*.

What do you predict that the participants in these different experimental conditions did during the open period? Who chose to spend more time on the just-completed activity rather than doing the alternative activities of playing computer games or reading magazines? If you took a traditional instrumental conditioning perspective, you might predict that the participants in every condition would want to do more of the completed activity because they had been rewarded for doing it (i.e., as Thorndike famously said, "pleasure stamps in"[1]). If you took an intrinsic versus extrinsic motivation perspective, you might predict the *opposite*: that the participants in every condition would *not* want to do more of the completed activity because they had been promised a reward for doing the activity (i.e., an external reward for doing an activity undermines intrinsic motivation to do it[2]). If you took a classical conditioning perspective, you might predict that participants in the enjoyable surrounding situation condition (i.e., enjoyable reward plus enjoyable open period) would want to do the completed activity more than participants in the serious surrounding situation condition (i.e., serious reward plus serious open period) because an enjoyable surrounding situation (vs. a serious surrounding situation) is likely to result in experiencing more pleasant feelings while doing the activity, and these pleasant experiences would become associated with the activity.

These are all reasonable predictions to make. But perhaps you remembered what happened in two of the studies that I described in Chapter 1 and you predicted instead that sometimes *it's the fit that counts*. Indeed, there was a fit effect in this study rather than the effects predicted by the alternative theoretical perspectives just mentioned. "Shoot-the-Moon" is a fun task, for which an enjoyable surrounding situation is a fit and a serious surrounding situation is a non-fit. The opposite is true for the "Financial Duties" task because it is an important task rather than a fun task. When doing this important activity, a serious surrounding situation is a fit and an enjoyable surrounding situation is a non-fit. The study found that participants with a fit (vs. a non-fit) were more interested in doing the completed activity again during the open period.

What was surprising in this study was what happened for the "Financial Duties" activity. Making the surrounding situation more enjoyable *reduced* rather than enhanced subsequent interest in doing that activity again. Moreover, adding a contingent reward for performance neither generally increased nor generally decreased subsequent interest in the completed activity. It was the fit between the nature of the reward (enjoyable or serious) and the activity (important or fun) that mattered. As we will see repeatedly in this book, the mechanism of fit makes a significant contribution to value—a contribution that has been overlooked by traditional answers to where value comes from.

In Chapter 3, I described the results of a classic study[3] in which children who liked to draw were promised an award for helping out an adult by drawing pictures. This study found that the children in this instrumental reward condition later spent less time drawing in an open period than other children. Drawing pictures for these children would be a fun task, but receiving an award from an adult for drawing would be a serious surrounding situation. This would be a non-fit that would decrease interest in doing more of the task during the open period. However, what the "Shoot-the-Moon" results show is that introducing an extrinsic, instrumental reward need not undermine interest in an intrinsically fun task *if* a fit is created by making the reward an enjoyable surrounding situation rather than a serious one. What this suggests is that there are factors that affect the value of things in the world that go beyond those that have been considered in the traditional literature.

Centuries ago, the question of where value comes from was central to many scholars. For example, an entire branch of classical and modern philosophy was concerned with understanding the sources of one kind of value—moral or ethical value. Gordon Allport, a founding father of personality psychology, suggested that value priorities were the "dominating force in life."[4] In contrast, the concept of "value" *per se* receives relatively little explicit attention in the current psychological literature, and the references that do appear are generally restricted to discussions of people's shared beliefs about desirable objectives or procedures, such as social or cultural values like "freedom" or "honesty."

The major exception to this general neglect is the emphasis given to "value" within value–likelihood models (the subjective expected utility model; the expectancy–value model), which I discuss in Chapter 7.

Instead of the concept of "value" *per se*, psychologists' concern with the motivational role of value is often addressed in terms of other concepts, such as "commitment," "goal," "norm," and "attitude." In social psychology, for example, a central component of the concept of attitudes is "evaluation,"[5] which certainly relates to the concept of value. However, the emphasis in the attitude literature is more on the implications of there being an evaluative dimension of attitudes, such as what evaluating something as good or bad means for predicting behavior, rather than on examining where the "goodness" or the "badness" itself comes from. In contrast, examining where "goodness" and "badness" come from is the central purpose of this chapter.

The Oxford and Webster dictionaries provide very similar answers to what is meant by something having "value" to someone:[6] (1) that amount of some commodity or medium of exchange that is considered to be a fair return or equivalent for something else; (2) the material or monetary worth of something, its marketable price. The primary definitions of value refer to equivalence to something in exchange, such as some material, commodity, or service, but especially equivalence in money—*the value of something as its monetary worth or marketable price*. This is an operational definition that is useful as a dependent measure in research on value, but it does not tell us what confers value on something to begin with. What exactly is the source of the "value" that people are willing to exchange money for? These definitions of "value" are about what happens when something *has* value rather than about *what gives* something value. Primarily, they tell us that if something has value, then it can be exchanged for something else that is considered equivalent (i.e., a fair exchange). They do not tell us where value comes from.

Thus, neither the dictionary nor the current psychological literature provides an answer to the question of where value comes from despite the importance of this question to understanding motivation. However, there are partial answers regarding mechanisms that could underlie value that can be gathered together from the historical literature. This chapter reviews this traditional literature and then goes beyond it to provide an overall answer to where value comes from.

WHAT MAKES SOMETHING HAVE POSITIVE OR NEGATIVE VALUE?

The major mechanisms that have been proposed traditionally as underlying value are value from need satisfaction; value from shared beliefs about desirable objectives and procedures; value from relating our current selves to personal standards; value from making evaluative inferences; and value from hedonic experience. I begin by reviewing each of these mechanisms because they provide an answer to the initial question of what makes something have positive or negative value (value direction). However, these mechanisms alone do not answer the further question of what determines *how* positive or *how* negative something is. In the subsequent section, I will discuss another motivational mechanism that has received insufficient attention as a contributor to *value intensity*—strength of engagement. I will describe research showing that factors, such as regulatory fit, that influence how strongly people engage in what they are doing can intensify how positive or how negative something is independent of the mechanisms that determine whether something is positive or negative.

Value From Need Satisfaction

At the turn of the 20th century, psychologists with theoretical perspectives ranging from behavioristic to Gestalt to psychodynamic proposed that value comes from need satisfaction. Specifically, something has positive value if it contributes to satisfying physical needs or reduces drives or deficiencies; that is, if it increases an individual's survival in the world. If it does the opposite, then it has negative value. This perspective on value as relating to something's usefulness in satisfying needs includes what an object or activity affords, such as a chair affording sitting.[7] Of course, these psychologists were not the first to suggest that value derives from need satisfaction, from usefulness. The eminent 18th-century Scottish philosopher and pioneer of modern economics Adam Smith argued that a prime example of something with high value was water.[8]

In the classic version of the viewpoint that value derives from need satisfaction, behavior is directed toward controlling deficits of specific substances in the body. Value derives from homeostatic responses to tissue deficits and physiological equilibrium.[9] Drives were manifest in behavior, had physiological correlates, and naturally gave rise to human desires.[10] Earlier in the book, I gave the striking example of an animal deficient in vitamin B choosing a vitamin B-rich meal over an alternative meal.

A broader version of the need satisfaction viewpoint is reflected in social-psychological research that used operant or classical conditioning to change attitudes. In one study, for example, participants talked to the experimenter. While they were talking, the experimenter casually responded positively to one set of linguistic forms the participants used, such as plural nouns, with approving head movements or expressions like "mm-hmmm" and did not respond or responded negatively to different linguistic forms the participants used, such as singular nouns. These responses of the experimenter did or did not satisfy the participants' need for approval, respectively.[11] The study found that over time, independent of the participants' awareness of what was happening, the approved linguistic forms were produced more frequently than the forms that were not approved—as if those linguistic forms had increased in value. Although such studies could involve other factors, Alice Eagly and Shelly Chaiken carefully reviewed this literature in their landmark book *The Psychology of Attitudes* and concluded that the traditional conditioning account, which involves need satisfaction, is reasonable as an explanation for the change in value found in such studies.[12]

The attitude literature in social psychology sometimes takes a need satisfaction viewpoint in others ways as well. For example, there is evidence that repeated exposure to a stimulus can increase liking for it,[13] which could be because repeated exposure to something makes it familiar in a way that satisfies the need for security. Studies finding that messages can be effective by appealing to people's fears[14] can also be considered as relating generally to value from need satisfaction in that anxiety reduction is likely to be involved. As another example, the literature on "message matching" finds that messages are more persuasive when their topic is matched to some aspect of the message recipient's motivational needs, such as the need to affirm a desired identity or the need to maintain a social relationship.[15] These findings could also reflect a need satisfaction mechanism in value creation.

Finally, I should mention again the work by Deci and Ryan on intrinsic versus extrinsic motivation.[16] Their self-determination theory emphasizes people's need for autonomy. When the conditions involved in doing an activity support autonomy or self-determination, interest in doing the activity increases. In contrast, when the conditions hinder or disrupt autonomy, interest is undermined. Studies showing such effects again reflect a need satisfaction mechanism in value creation.

Value From People's Shared Beliefs About Desirable Objectives and Procedures

An important feature of the need satisfaction viewpoint is that value can occur at the biological system level without any need for reflection or beliefs or even conscious experience. In addition, the viewpoint does not restrict the notion of value to humans; indeed, it was largely developed from research on non-human animals. A very different answer to where value comes from has neither of these features—it involves a kind of sharing of beliefs that is unique to humans. It relates to the common use of the term "value" in the psychological literature: value comes from people's *shared beliefs* about which ends or objectives are generally desirable (and which are undesirable), and which means or procedures for attaining these ends are generally desirable (and which are undesirable). This is typically the meaning of value when people talk about the values that they hold, such as "freedom" or "equality" having positive value.

Although these values are personal in the sense of being internalized, they are acquired within a social context and are shared with others. They are not idiosyncratic. In a clear statement of this viewpoint, Milton Rokeach, a pioneer theorist and researcher on the nature of human values, describes values as "shared prescriptive or proscriptive beliefs about ideal modes of behavior and end-states of existence."[17] Similarly, Robert Merton, a giant figure in sociology, noted that: "Every social group invariably couples its cultural objectives with regulations, rooted in the mores or institutions, of allowable procedures for moving toward these objectives." The cultural objectives are the "things worth striving for"—what has outcome value in the culture. The "allowable procedures" concern the acceptable ways to strive for the worthwhile things—what has process value in the culture.[18]

Thus, this alternative viewpoint on where value comes from concerns shared beliefs about both desired objectives (or end-states) and desired procedures (or means) for attaining and maintaining the objectives. It includes *norms* about what goals are worth pursuing and what moral principles or standards of conduct one should live by. As captured in the concept of "procedural justice,"[19] for example, people in many societies value the fairness of decision-making procedures independent of decision outcomes. Given that the importance of shared cultural or socialized values is what makes humans a unique kind of animal, it is not surprising that these values have received special attention in the literature on the psychology of values.[20]

These shared beliefs about desired (and undesired) states of existence concern both the outcomes of goal pursuit, such as "social justice," "freedom," and "social recognition," and the processes of goal pursuit, such as "honesty," "logic," and "obedience." Value from shared beliefs about what is desirable relates value to some *standard of excellence*. Kurt Lewin noted the special nature of such values. He said that such values influence behavior differently than do goals. For example, people do not attempt to "reach" the value of fairness even though it guides their behavior. He pointed out that such values function to define an activity's valence in a given situation (i.e., its motivational direction), to define whether it has positive valence (attraction) or negative valence (repulsion).[21] It functions as a standard rather than as a goal. But shared beliefs are not the only kind of standard of excellence that is a source of value. I consider next the impact of other kinds of standards.

Value From Relating Ourselves to Standards

The mechanism of value creation from shared beliefs about what is desirable (and undesirable) provides a complement to value creation from need satisfaction because it concerns the social construction of values and the role of socialization rather than biological nature. The "sharing" can be considered at more than one level of analysis—at both the broader community or societal level, where the values apply to people in general, and at the more interpersonal level, where significant others apply values to a specific person. Values from shared beliefs at the broader societal level are usually treated as social values or social standards. In contrast, values shared at the interpersonal level with significant others are usually treated as personal standards.

VALUE FROM RELATING OURSELVES TO PERSONAL STANDARDS

Historically, cybernetic and control process models have treated personal standards in terms of the relation between a current state of the self and some end-state functioning as a standard of reference. The value of the current self state depends on the extent to which it approaches a personally desired end-state or avoids a personally undesired end-state functioning as a standard or reference point.[22] For human motivation, the desired and undesired end-states that function as reference points or guides for self-regulation are typically acquired from interactions with others.

Developmentally, children learn about their caretakers' hopes and aspirations for them (their ideals) or about what their caretakers believe are their duties and responsibilities (oughts). Ideals relate to the promotion system that is concerned with accomplishments and advancement, and oughts relate to the prevention system that is concerned with safety and security. According to self-discrepancy theory, when children become capable of having their own perspective or standpoint on ideals and oughts, they can adopt their caretakers' ideals and oughts for them as their own. In this way, they create a *shared reality* about desired end-states, which are identified *self-guides*. An actual-self attribute that is congruent with (matches) an ideal or ought self-guide has positive value (it is a desired result), whereas an actual-self attribute that is discrepant from (mismatches) an ideal or ought self-guide has negative value (it is an undesired result).[23]

This viewpoint that value derives from relating ourselves to personal standards involves two different kinds of value. The person's ideal and ought standards of excellence are shared beliefs with significant others about which end-states are desired (positive value) and which are undesired (negative value). It is simply that the social sharing is with a significant other rather than with the larger community. But in addition to this, the actual-self states that are congruent with or discrepant from the ideal and ought self-guides themselves have positive or negative value, respectively. It is this second aspect of the proposal that uniquely characterizes this viewpoint—that is, the notion that the value of our actual or current self depends on its *relation* (match or mismatch) to our personal self-guides functioning as standards. It introduces the notion of value from monitoring our success or failure in meeting our personal self-guides—value from the answer to "how am I doing?"[24] Monitoring the relation of our actual self to our personal self-guides (typically shared with significant others) is an important determinant of how we value ourselves. For example, if our actual self is discrepant from the type of person we aspire to be (an actual–ideal discrepancy), then we feel disappointed in ourselves.[25]

VALUE FROM COMPARING AND ASSOCIATING OURSELVES WITH OTHERS AS STANDARDS

The viewpoint that value derives from relating ourselves to some standard is also found in the literature on social comparison. Comparing yourself to an acquaintance on some personal attribute that matters to you, such as the ability to carry out a lively conversation, will produce a positive self-evaluation when the other person possesses less of the desirable attribute than you, but a negative self-evaluation when the other person possesses more of the desirable attribute than you.[26] Direct value from social comparison (i.e., positive vs. negative self-evaluation) also occurs for standards represented by the attributes of those who function as positive and negative reference groups, such as the negative value of comparing your lifestyle to the lifestyle of the "rich and famous."[27]

It has also been noted that positive value created by matching standards can be achieved through indirect means as well. For example, people who are made to feel insecure or uncertain about whether they have the kind of identity they want to possess, such as desiring to be recognized as a rock musician, will engage in activities or present themselves in ways that are associated with being that kind of person, such as dressing like a rock star—*symbolic self-completion*.[28] They will also form relationships with other people who possess an attribute, such as exceptional musical ability, that they do not have but want to have. In this way they can possess the attribute by association—*basking in reflected glory*.[29] People whose personal identity fails to meet their standards of excellence will also act to enhance the value of the groups to which they belong in order to possess a *positive social identity* that does meet their standards, as when fans support their local sports club as much as they can.[30]

Note that, as for value from personal standards, there are two different kinds of value involved in comparing and associating ourselves with others as standards. The value of the others as standards typically derives from shared beliefs—our beliefs that we share with our community or significant others about the attributes we value in others. These valuable others are then used as standards of excellence to establish *our own value* by comparing or associating ourselves with them.

Value From Evaluative Inferences

When people speak of their lives as having value or not having value, it typically has to do with the kind of value that comes from the self-evaluative processes just described—monitoring our current actual self in relation to our personal self-guides or other standards of excellence. But value can come from other types of evaluative processes as well. These processes are different because they require an inference to identify the value. The value created from monitoring matches or mismatches in relation to self-guides, for example, does not require an inference to create value. An actual-self congruency with ideals and oughts *is* good. An actual-self discrepancy with ideals and oughts *is* bad. But there are times when people infer what the value of some activity or object is to them— value from evaluative inferences.

THE BEMIAN MODEL OF EVALUATIVE INFERENCES

Perhaps the most influential theory about evaluative inferences was postulated by the social psychologist Daryl Bem in his theory of self-perception.[31] A basic assumption of this theory is that people function like behavioral scientists engaged in hypothesis testing.[32] The critical proposal is that people make inferences about themselves in the same way that an uninterested outside observer would make inferences about them—based solely on observable evidence. They observe their own behavior and test hypotheses about its meaning or significance.

When we engage in an activity, for example, we could infer that we chose to do so because we value that activity. In Bem's terms, which he adapted from the work of legendary radical behaviorist B. F. Skinner,[33] people can hypothesize that the force to do an activity comes from within themselves and the behavior is emitted spontaneously (called a "tact"). An alternative hypothesis is that the behavior was demanded by the situation (called a "mand"); that is, it was elicited by outside forces or pressures. If there is strong support for the second hypothesis, as when we are promised a nice reward for doing a behavior, then we are less likely to infer that we chose to do the activity because we value it. Rather, we did it to attain the reward.

Classic studies on how the perceived value of an activity can be bolstered or undermined by such inferential processes provide some support for this Bemian viewpoint on how people make evaluative inferences.[34] But how people make evaluative inferences is not restricted to Bem's constraint that the evidence for the inference must be *publicly* observable. People also use their inner thoughts and feelings about something as evidence to infer its value. Indeed, they use their thoughts and feelings about something to draw evaluative inferences even more than they use their behaviors.[35] For example, rather than first deciding that a political candidate has desirable qualities and then feeling positive toward that candidate, people often first notice that they have positive feelings toward a candidate and then infer that they must feel this way because of the desirable qualities of the candidate—"If I feel this way just from seeing a photo of him, he must really be great." Such feelings can be erroneous, as when the weather puts us in a good mood but we infer that it is our life that is good, thereby feeling more satisfied with our life generally on sunny days than rainy days.[36]

And the evidence for drawing an inference is not restricted to thoughts or feelings about something. People also use similarities between one person and another person to draw evaluative inferences. For example, they will infer the value to them of a job candidate from the value of a previously known employee to whom the candidate is similar in some way.[37] This can produce erroneous inferences because the similarity could concern an irrelevant attribute such as a person's first name or birth date.

It should also be noted that the Bemian logic used to make an evaluative inference is relatively simple: the likelihood that we will make an evaluative inference about people (including ourselves) based on their behavior decreases the more we believe that their behavior was driven by situational forces. However, more complex kinds of logical reasoning can be used in evaluative inferences.[38]

For example, the reasoning behind making inferences regarding ethical value can be very complex, and it becomes more complex during human development. Of special interest historically is the reasoning postulated to underlie ethical value.[39] Philosophers from Aristotle to Immanuel Kant and Karl Marx have proposed that determinations of what is morally good or bad should be based, and to some extent *are* based, on logical reflection using criteria of justice that are provided by religious and political authorities.[40] Psychological research has found that people actually use multiple criteria to infer the ethical value of some action and engage in trade-offs among these criteria.[41] In some cases the judgment about ethical value derives from evaluative inferences combined with shared beliefs about desirable objectives and procedures.

THE ROLE OF CONTEXT IN EVALUATIVE INFERENCES

It should be emphasized that people do not infer the value of something in a vacuum. They do so in relation to whatever standards are currently available or accessible to them. And this varies not only by chronic factors such as individuals' personal self-guides but also as a function of the current context. The current context plays a critical role in evaluative inferences by providing different standards and frames of reference. Indeed, evaluative inferences are always contextualized either because the current situation provides a standard or frame of reference or it activates a particular stored standard or frame of reference, thereby making it more accessible than alternatives (i.e., contextual priming).

With regard to situationally provided standards or frames of reference, the value of something can be assimilated toward or contrasted away from the current context, as when a house table wine will taste better if it is drunk with other house wines than with *grand cru* wines.[42] The value of something can also vary depending on which mental account the context suggests is appropriate for calculating its value. For example, an option for an upgraded car radio/CD player can be perceived as more valuable (i.e., as worth it) when considered as part of the "getting a car" mental account than when considered as part of the "buying something to play music" mental account.[43] The value of some event can also vary in intensity when the context suggests that something else could have occurred—*counterfactual reasoning*. For example, when people miss a plane after getting stuck in traffic, the negative value of the event is worse if they reached the gate just 1 minute after the plane's departure (they can easily imagine how they might have caught the plane if the circumstances were just a little different) than if they reached the gate 40 minutes after the plane's departure (they think there was no way that they could have caught the plane).[44]

Value From Hedonic Experience

It is notable that value from hedonic experience is not explicitly mentioned in the dictionary definitions of value that I listed earlier. In philosophy, support for a value from hedonic experience viewpoint has a checkered history, especially with respect to ethical or moral value. Generally speaking, the dominant philosophical viewpoint has been more compatible with the value from evaluative inference viewpoint than the value from experience viewpoint, with specific emphasis on using reason and reflection to create an objective basis for determining what is good or bad.[45]

The tension between a reason-based and an experiential account of ethical value is captured in Plato's (4th century BC/1949) myth, described in *Timaeus*, of the gods' creation of human heads filled with reason. Because the heads alone could not move around in the world, the gods were forced to add bodies to the heads to permit movement. Emotions resided in the bodies. The moral of the story was that people were left with heads (i.e., reason) that must struggle with their passionate bodies to get them to behave ethically (and rationally). This moral was well accepted by most influential philosophers (e.g., Aristotle, Kant) and is embodied in Freud's classic conflict between the reasonable Ego and the passionate Id.[46] For centuries emotions have been connected with desires, desires with the potential for sin, and reason with the defense against sin.[47]

Plato's myth can be interpreted in another way, however. After all, the gods are *not* crazy, and they knew that the heads alone could take no action (i.e., move). The problem of bridging the gap between knowing and doing has been well understood by mere mortal psychologists as well. Edwin Guthrie, the "practical behaviorist," once made a joke on this point at the expense of Edward Tolman, one of the founders of cognitive psychology. Tolman's influential theory of behavior emphasized hypotheses and expectations, and Guthrie joked that Tolman's rats would never leave the start box to get to the goal because they would be "buried deep in thought." Reason alone does not motivate taking action. Something else must provide the motivation, bridge the gap from thought to action by making it worthwhile to take action. Adding bodies that can have experiential feelings provides the value that makes taking action worthwhile. It was the gods' inspired solution (i.e., god-like) for how to bridge the gap.

From this perspective, Plato's myth is not a sad tale about how, by adding emotional bodies, reason must now defend against passion. Instead, it is a happy tale about how value from experiential feelings can now bridge the gap from thought to action. It sends a message that value derives from experiential feelings: *value from experience is critical*. I will return to this point later after reviewing the different kinds of value from experience that have been proposed in the literature. Here I will simply add that, although somewhat in the minority, there have certainly been highly distinguished philosophers, including Jeremy Bentham, David Hume, and Adam Smith, who have argued that hedonic experience is critical to ethical value.[48]

I previously reviewed some evidence that animals are motivated by more than just satisfying biological needs, that they will choose on the basis of value experiences independent of any biological need being satisfied. For example, animals prefer sweet water with saccharin to regular water even though the saccharin has no physiological benefit, and they will even prefer sweet food to food that is physiologically better for them.[49] What such studies show is that there is something else creating value in these animals beyond actual biological need satisfaction. A star candidate suggested in the literature is value from hedonic pleasure.

Jeremy Bentham made an influential and explicit early statement on the importance of hedonic experiences to both ethical and non-ethical value:[50] "Nature has placed mankind under the governance of two sovereign masters, *pain* and *pleasure*. It is for them alone to point out what we ought to do, as well as to determine what we shall do. On the one hand the standard of right and wrong, on the other the chain of causes and effects, are fastened to their throne."

Interest in the role of hedonic experiences in value has continued over the centuries.[51] Daniel Kahneman, a founder of behavioral economics, has pointed out that "utility," the economic concept of value, has had two different meanings historically. One meaning is like one of the primary dictionary definitions described earlier—an operational definition where utility is inferred from observed choices (i.e., revealed in behavior). Kahneman refers to this concept as "decision utility." The second meaning reflects Bentham's perspective on utility as experiences of pleasure and pain and is called "experienced utility" by Kahneman. Kahneman argues that the best way to measure actual experienced utility is by moment-based methods where experienced utility of an episode is derived from real-time measures of the pleasure and pain that an individual experienced during that episode. He also proposes that people use their memory of pleasure and pain experiences to evaluate past episodes retrospectively, which he calls "remembered utility."[52]

For example, there is evidence that remembered pain is less influenced by the duration of the pain episode than by the "peak-end" rule, which is the average of the most intense level of pain over the episode and the level of pain at the end of the episode.[53] This indicates that the remembered pain is not an accurate reflection of the actual experienced pain, but that people use what they remember to make choices, such as whether or not to go to the dentist for a toothache. That is, decisions concerning the value of things (decision utility) can be determined more by retrospective value experiences based on memory (remembered utility) than by what pleasures or pains were actually experienced at the time of the episode (experienced utility). Of course, remembered utility *is* the subjective hedonic experience at the time the decision is being made. And the role of remembered hedonic experiences is not restricted to humans: animals' remembered emotional responses also play a critical role in their learning and performance.[54]

HEDONIC EXPERIENCE IN EMOTIONS

In the voluminous literature on emotions and affect, it is hedonic experience that has received the most attention. Early on, Benedict de Spinoza, the great 17th-century Dutch philosopher, proposed that all emotions can be reduced to some form of pleasure and pain.[55] Since then it has been suggested that the primary function of pleasant and painful emotional experiences is to signal or provide feedback about self-regulatory success or failure.[56] Although differing in several respects, the two best-known models of emotional experiences, the appraisal and circumplex models, as well as other influential models, universally agree in proposing a basic dimension that distinguishes between pleasant and painful emotions.[57] The bulk of research in social psychology that is concerned with value experiences has also emphasized hedonic experiences, such as the basic distinctions in the attitude literature between good and bad moods or between liking and disliking something.[58] Influential theories and findings in decision science have also emphasized basic hedonic experiences, such as the pleasure of gains and the pain of losses or the pleasure of hope and the pain of fear.[59]

This is not to say that there have been no theories and research in these literatures that have distinguished among types of pleasant experiences and types of painful experiences. Self-discrepancy theory, for example, distinguishes between the pleasure experience of actual-self congruencies with ideals (e.g., feeling happy) versus oughts (e.g., feeling calm), and between the pain experience of actual-self discrepancies with ideals (e.g., feeling sad) versus oughts (e.g., feeling nervous).[60] The emotion and affect literature also distinguishes among different types of pleasure and pain based upon the activation level of the experience (i.e., intensity), the target of the emotion (e.g., reaction to events vs. to agents), and other factors.[61] But such distinctions within pleasure and within pain do not in themselves challenge the historical predominance of hedonic experience in theories of value experience.

HEDONIC EXPERIENCE AS SELF-REGULATORY FEEDBACK
VERSUS SENSUOUS FEELINGS

I distinguished in Chapter 2 between pleasure and pain as *sensuous* experiences and pleasure and pain as *feedback* that a self-regulatory system is or is not working effectively. For example, people feel hungry when they have not had enough to eat, feel thirsty when they have not had enough to drink, feel sad or discouraged when their promotion system fails, and feel nervous and tense when their prevention system fails. These pain experiences *signal* different kinds of self-regulatory failure, different kinds of current states that are undesirable and need to be dealt with. It is possible, then, for pleasure and pain to contribute to the value experience of something by signaling success or failure to be effective. It is not necessary to impute additional sensuous experiences unrelated to being effective in order for hedonic experiences to contribute to value experiences of what is desirable and undesirable. They can do so, as with sunsets or warm baths, but it is not necessary that they do so. Their role in signaling success or failure to be effective is sufficient.

There is an issue that I should address at this point. It concerns the meaning of "hedonic" as "sweet" and the evidence of animals preferring sweet water with saccharin over regular water even though the saccharin has no physiological benefit. Doesn't this preference mean that it is the sensuous pleasant feeling that is motivating? Not necessarily, because the sweet taste can be functioning, once again, as a signal of self-regulatory success. Simply put, sweet relates to glucose, glucose relates to energy, and energy increases the likelihood of self-regulatory success. Sweetness, then, functions as a signal of self-regulatory effectiveness, and saccharin gives this signal even though it offers no physiological benefit.

Because the signal of effectiveness and the physiological benefit can be decoupled, errors can occur. Paul Rozin, a renowned expert on the cultural and biological determinants of human food choice, makes the point that sweetness is just a clue about a food's potential benefit:

> In fact, there is good evidence, over a wide range of animals including humans, for a system that regulates energy intake. Although we still don't know how it works, we have a great deal of evidence that it exists. The energy regulation system is complemented by an innate ability to sense and prefer two characteristics associated in nature with high energy density. These two characteristics are sweet taste and fatty texture. So, at a minimum, we seem to be born with a system that indicates our energy deficit and with some clues about what things in the environment are likely to satisfy this deficit.[62]

Thus, animals, including humans, can learn that sweet-tasting things have self-regulatory benefits when consumed. They can be consumed for the sake of self-regulatory effectiveness and not for the sake of sensual pleasure. When animals deprived of vitamin B choose to eat vitamin B-enriched food, this choice need not be made in order to experience a pleasant feeling. Indeed, it is unlikely in this case. Healthy people drink unpleasant medicinal liquids that they believe will prolong their lives without experiencing any pleasure from the medicines. These actions are in the service of some biological need rather than to approach pleasant feelings or avoid painful feelings. When people learn that eating some highly pleasant foods constitutes a self-regulatory failure (i.e., it makes them fat), they will switch to less pleasant foods, even unpleasant foods, to achieve self-regulatory success (i.e., staying thin).

This is not to say that pleasure and pain experiences are not important in self-regulation. They are important. But their importance can derive from their function as signals of self-regulatory success and failure rather than as sensuous feelings to be approached as desired end-states or avoided as undesired end-states.

Hedonic experience and the other four mechanisms that I have just reviewed—that is, value from need satisfaction, from shared beliefs about desirable objectives and procedures, from relating our current selves to personal standards, and from making evaluative inferences—have been discussed in the traditional literature and their contributions to making something positive or negative are generally well known. But there is another mechanism that is less well known that contributes to *how* positive or *how* negative something is rather than whether something is positive or is negative. How this mechanism works and creates value can be quite surprising and, in some cases, counterintuitive.

STRENGTH OF ENGAGEMENT AS A VALUE INTENSIFIER

Common sayings or maxims provide a clue that the contribution of experience to value is not restricted to the pains and pleasures of goal pursuit outcomes: "It is not enough to do good; one must do it in the right way," "What counts is not whether you win or lose, but how you play the game," "The ends don't justify the means," and "Never good through evil." What these maxims are saying is that there is something else about the process of goal pursuit, about *how* goals are pursued, that contributes to value experience beyond hedonic experience. This extra something has been usually understood in terms of moral or ethical factors. Indeed, the shared beliefs about desirable and undesirable procedures, the prescriptive norms and self-guides about how we ought to behave, could be conceptualized as going beyond hedonic experiences in assigning positive or negative value to different choices. This is, in fact, an important part of the story of value effectiveness because these shared beliefs significantly determine whether something has positive or negative valence—value direction—as well as contributing to value intensity. But it is not the whole story. What if we stick to our experiences as a source of value? Is it moral or ethical experiences that account for there being something about *how* goals are pursued that contributes to value experience beyond hedonic experience? Or might there be something else about the goal-pursuit process that contributes to value experience beyond hedonic experience that need not even involve moral or ethical considerations?

The answer is "yes": there are process factors that can *strengthen engagement*, which then intensifies our positive or negative reactions to something. Figure 4.1 provides an overall illustration of what *regulatory engagement theory* proposes as contributors to value experience.[63] Hedonic experience is one contributing factor, but there are other factors as well, including those that contribute to value experience through their impact on engagement strength. In discussing this proposal, I begin with the value experience itself on the far right side of Figure 4.1. What exactly is the nature of this value experience?

In thinking about this issue I was inspired by Kurt Lewin's early discussion of valence.[64] For Lewin, value related to *force*, which has direction and intensity. But for him the forces on a person's life space were analogous to natural physical forces on objects rather than to something that a person experiences. I nonetheless believe that Lewin's concept of "force" can be extended to personal experiences that have direction and intensity. Experiencing something as having positive value corresponds to experiencing a force of attraction toward it, and experiencing something as having negative value corresponds to experiencing a force of repulsion from it. Value experiences vary in intensity. The experience of a force of attraction toward something can be relatively weak or strong (low

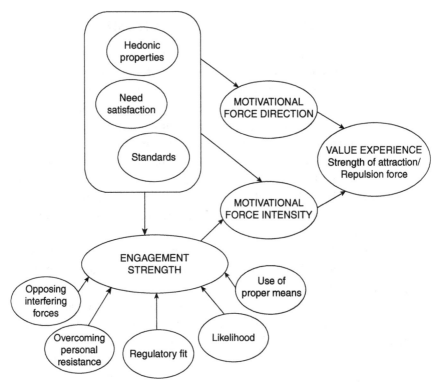

Figure 4.1 Illustration of the relations among variables that contribute to the value experience

or high positive value), and the experience of a force of repulsion from some-thing can be relatively weak or strong (low or high negative value).

Now let us turn to the factor of engagement strength, shown on the bottom left of Figure 4.1. The state of being engaged is to be involved, occupied, and interested in something. Strong engagement is to concentrate on something, to be absorbed or engrossed with it.[65] Historically, strong engagement relates to the notion that people can be involved in, interested in, and attentive to some-thing *separate from whether it is pleasant or unpleasant*. What makes us attend to things also invests them with value, and events that are interesting could be positively or negatively valued. Both Daniel Berlyne and George Mandler, two of psychology's greatest contributors to understanding value experiences, dis-tinguished "interesting" from pleasing or pleasant.[66] Strength of engagement alone does not make something attractive or repulsive; that is, it does not have direction. Instead, strength of engagement contributes to *how* positively or *how* negatively something is experienced by intensifying our value reaction— intensifying the force of attraction toward something or intensifying the force of repulsion away from something.

As illustrated in Figure 4.1, value-creation mechanisms such as need satisfaction, hedonic experience, and standards of different kinds all contribute to the direction of the motivational force, to whether the value force is positive attraction or negative repulsion. These mechanisms also contribute to the intensity of the motivational force, to how attractive or how repulsive something is. In contrast, strength of engagement, as illustrated in Figure 4.1, contributes only to the intensity of the value experience. However, this contribution can be highly significant, as we will see. In the following sections I review the factors that contribute to the intensity of the value experience through their impact on engagement strength—regulatory fit, use of proper means, opposing interfering forces, and overcoming personal resistance. I should note that I will postpone until Chapter 7 my discussion of the contribution of perceived likelihood to engagement strength and value intensification (see Fig. 4.1) in order to present more fully there the many ways that value and likelihood work together to affect commitment.

Regulatory Fit

Regulatory fit theory proposes that people experience *regulatory fit* when their goal orientation is sustained (vs. disrupted) by the manner in which they pursue the goal. For example, some students working to attain an "A" in a course are oriented toward the "A" as an accomplishment or an aspiration, as a grade that they ideally want to attain (a promotion focus). Others are oriented toward the "A" as a responsibility or as security, as a grade that they believe they ought to attain (a prevention focus). As a way to attain the "A," some students read material beyond what has been assigned (an eager strategy) whereas others are careful to make sure all course requirements are fulfilled (a vigilant strategy). Pursuing the goal of attaining an "A" with an eager strategy sustains a promotion focus (a fit), whereas pursuing it with a vigilant strategy disrupts a promotion focus (a non-fit). In contrast, pursuing the goal of attaining an "A" with a vigilant strategy sustains a prevention focus (a fit), whereas pursuing it with an eager strategy disrupts a prevention focus (a non-fit). According to regulatory fit theory,[67] engagement in a goal-pursuit activity is strengthened when regulatory fit sustains the goal orientation, and it is weakened when non-fit disrupts the goal orientation.

EVIDENCE THAT REGULATORY FIT STRENGTHENS ENGAGEMENT
According to regulatory fit theory, then, actors' strength of engagement in a task activity should be greater under conditions of fit than non-fit. The results of several studies support this prediction.[68] Some studies measured participants' predominant promotion or prevention orientation, whereas other studies

situationally induced a promotion or prevention orientation in the participants. Strength of engagement while working on an anagram task was measured either in terms of persistence on the task (as measured by time spent working on each anagram) or in terms of exertion on the task (as measured by arm pressure while working).[69]

In some studies, the participants worked on several different anagrams during the experimental session and separate measures were taken of their engagement strength when solving green-colored anagrams that added points to the total score (*eager anagram strategy*) and their engagement strength when solving red-colored anagrams that stopped points from being subtracted from the total score (*vigilant anagram strategy*). Given the classic "goal looms larger" effect, engagement strength should generally increase from the first anagram to the final anagram. What was of interest was how this increase in engagement strength might differ for eager versus vigilant responses as a function of the participants' promotion or prevention focus. For both the persistence and the exertion measures of engagement strength, these studies found that when the participants had a promotion focus, engagement strength increased over time more for the eager responses (fit) than for the vigilant responses (non-fit). In contrast, when the participants had a prevention focus, engagement strength increased over time more for the vigilant responses (fit) than for the eager responses (non-fit). As one might expect from the finding that fit yielded greater engagement strength in the task activity, there was also evidence that the participants solved more anagrams when there was fit between their promotion or prevention orientation and their eager or vigilant anagram strategy than when there was non-fit.

How Strengthening Engagement From Regulatory Fit Intensifies Value

Importantly, the effect of regulatory fit on engagement strength can also influence the intensity of a value experience. An example of this is provided by the "Columbia coffee mug and inexpensive pen" study that I discussed in Chapter 1—the "eager versus vigilant" decision-making study.[70] What this study found was that participants in the regulatory fit conditions (i.e., those with a predominant promotion orientation/eager decision-making manner; and those with a predominant prevention orientation/vigilant decision-making manner) offered almost 70% more money to buy the mug than did participants in the regulatory non-fit conditions (predominant promotion/vigilant decision-making manner; predominant prevention/eager decision-making manner). Although the hedonic properties of the mug itself were the same in the fit and non-fit conditions and the outcome of successful goal pursuit was the same (i.e., owning the mug), the experienced value of the mug was not the same. The experienced intensity of its attractiveness was clearly greater in the fit than the non-fit conditions.

Regulatory Fit as Motivations Working Together

Regulatory fit experiences differ fundamentally from hedonic and ethical experiences because they arise from a different aspect of self-regulation—the *relation* between actors' orientation to goal pursuit (e.g., promotion vs. prevention) and their manner of goal pursuit (e.g., eager vs. vigilant). This relation between orientation *value* (e.g., promotion value vs. prevention value) and manner of control (e.g., eager control vs. vigilant control) demonstrates a central theme of this book: *the significance of motivations working together*. In Chapter 8, I will discuss in more detail the nature and consequences of regulatory fit as a *value–control relation* and provide additional evidence that *it's the fit that counts*.

Fit experiences occur during the process of goal pursuit as a function of the relation between goal-pursuit orientation as value and goal-pursuit manner as control. The fit experiences that occur during this process are independent of the ultimate outcomes or consequences of the goal pursuit (both ethical and non-ethical). This is not to say that hedonic and ethical experiences cannot arise as well during the process of goal pursuit, but they do so in relation to additional, separate goals that are or are not attained. For hedonic experiences the other goals could be to have fun during the goal-pursuit process or to expend as little effort as possible. For ethical experiences the other goals could be to pursue the goal in a way that would meet with others' approval or gratitude. Unlike hedonic and ethical experiences, fit is not an experience of attaining some other goal that yields positive outcomes.

The difference between hedonic and ethical experiences on the one hand and the fit experience on the other is captured in what counts as a justification for how someone chooses to pursue a goal. To reasonably justify how a goal is pursued, there needs to be some (anticipated) positive outcomes from choosing that manner of goal pursuit. Thus, it seems reasonable to justify one's choice of goal-pursuit strategy by referring either to a hedonic outcome such as "It was fun to do it that way" or to an ethical outcome such as "It was the socially proper way to do it." In contrast, because regulatory fit is not about outcomes, it does not seem reasonable to justify the manner of goal pursuit by referring to there being a fit, such as "It was the way to do it that happened to fit my motivational state at the time." Fit is not an outcome; it is a manner of goal pursuit that sustains a goal orientation.

Engagement Strength From Fit as an Intensifier
of Positive *and* Negative Value Experiences

Regulatory fit strengthens engagement in what one is doing, and strengthened engagement intensifies value experiences. In the case of a positive value target, such as the Columbia mug, stronger engagement intensifies the experience of attraction. If the value target were negative, then strengthened engagement from regulatory fit would intensify the experience of repulsion.[71]

A study on the effectiveness of a persuasive message illustrates how evaluative intensification can occur in both positive and negative directions.[72] The study tested the persuasiveness of an *identical* message as a function of whether participants responded positively or negatively to the message. Regulatory fit or non-fit states were induced in participants prior to their receiving the message. In the first phase of the experimental session, they were asked to list either two promotion goals (i.e., list two of their personal hopes or aspirations) or two prevention goals (i.e., list two of their duties or obligations). They then listed for each of their goals either eager means of pursuit (i.e., strategies they could use to make everything go right) or vigilant means (i.e., strategies they could use to avoid anything going wrong). Promotion goals with eager means and prevention goals with vigilant means were the regulatory fit conditions. The manipulation of regulatory fit did *not* affect the participants' hedonic mood. But for those participants who subsequently had a positive reaction to the message, attitudes were more *positive* in the fit than non-fit conditions (i.e., increased attraction), whereas for those who had a negative reaction to the message, attitudes were more *negative* in the fit than the non-fit conditions (i.e., increased repulsion).

Use of Proper Means

The mechanisms contributing to the experience of value direction that are illustrated in Figure 4.1 do not include the moral or ethical experiences of approval and disapproval. I did not include them because I believe that there is a bigger story regarding moral or ethical experiences that concerns the more general phenomenon of *people doing things in the proper way*—even when this does not involve, strictly speaking, moral or ethical behaviors. For example, in choosing between a coffee mug and a pen, a person might believe that the proper or right way to make this choice would be to list the positive and negative properties of the mug, then list the positive and negative properties of the pen, look over each list, and then make the choice.

Making the choice in this way or in some other way would not traditionally be considered a moral or ethical issue. But it does involve our doing something in a proper or right way, and this can strengthen engagement in what we are doing. This stronger engagement in turn can intensify our attraction toward our ultimate choice—independent of the inherent properties of that choice. This would have broad implications for value because any decision could be made in a right way or a wrong way (i.e., not just moral or ethical decisions of approval or disapproval). And whether it was a right or wrong way would affect the value not only of the decision-making process itself but of other things as well, such as intensifying the value of the coffee mug that doesn't elicit moral approval or disapproval.

Recent studies have investigated the possibility that doing things in the right or proper way can have an impact on value intensity by increasing engagement strength. There is some suggestive evidence in the social psychological literature that making a decision in a proper way might increase strength of involvement in the decision. For example, there is evidence that fair procedures within groups produce more active group helping behavior.[73] If making a decision in a proper way increases engagement strength, does this intensify attraction to the decision that is made?

To investigate this question, Columbia undergraduates were again asked to express their preference between a Columbia coffee mug and an inexpensive pen. As in our other mug and pen studies, we were only concerned with those participants who made the *same* choice—overwhelmingly the coffee mug. In one study,[74] before the participants actually made their choice, they were randomly assigned to two different conditions that varied in what was emphasized about the decision. One condition emphasized the "Right Way"; it began with the title, "Making Your Decision in the RIGHT WAY!," and then continued as follows: "You need to make your decision in the *right way*. The right way to make a decision is to think about which choice has the better consequences. Think of the positive and negative consequences of choosing the mug. Think of the positive and negative consequences of choosing the pen. Please write down your thoughts on the lines below." The second condition emphasized the "Best Choice"; it began with the title, "The BEST CHOICE!," and then continued as follows: "The *best choice* is the choice with the better consequences. Think of the positive and negative consequences of owning the mug. Think of the positive and negative consequences of owning the pen. Please write down your thoughts on the lines below."

Note that in both conditions the specific behaviors requested of the participants were exactly the same: "Think of the positive and negative consequences of choosing the mug. Think of the positive and negative consequences of owning the pen. Please write down your thoughts on the lines below." All that varied was whether those behaviors were perceived by the participants as making their decision in the right way or as leading to the best future outcomes. After considering the two options and expressing their preference for the mug, the participants were given the opportunity to buy the mug. The primary dependent measure was how much money they offered to buy the mug. The study found that the participants in the "Right Way" condition offered substantially more money to buy the same chosen mug than participants in the "Best Choice" condition.

This study also asked participants how much they agreed with three cultural maxims concerning the importance of pursuing goals in a proper way: "The end does not justify the means"; "What counts is not whether you win or lose, but how you play the game."; and (reverse coded) "To do it this way or that, it does not matter; results are all that count." An index of "strength of belief in the importance of pursuing goals in a proper way" was computed by combining these three items. The more strongly individuals agreed with such maxims, the more strongly they should engage in the decision-making process when they are behaving in the proper way, and thus the stronger the predicted effect on value experience should be. Indeed, for those participants who had weak beliefs in the importance of pursuing goals in a proper way, there was no significant difference between the "Right Way" condition and the "Best Choice" condition in the money offered to buy the mug. But for those participants who had strong beliefs in the importance of pursuing goals in a proper way, the money offered to buy the mug was much higher in the "Right Way" condition than the "Best Choice" condition—$6.35 in the "Right Way" condition versus $2.61 in the "Best Choice" condition.

The findings from this research are consistent with the idea that pursuing goals in the right or proper way strengthens engagement in what we are doing, which intensifies attraction toward a positive value target.[75] James March, a major figure in organizational decision making, has proposed that pursuing goals in an appropriate or proper way has its own relation to value creation, separate from just hedonic outcomes (rational instrumentality).[76] The findings from these studies support his proposal in a novel manner by showing that the chosen object itself can increase in monetary value when the decision is made in a proper way.

Not only does pursuing goals in a proper way affect how we value ourselves, such as whether we see ourselves as being an ethical person whom we and others approve, but it also affects *how we value other things* in the world. It increases both our attraction to and repulsion from the things around us. Thus, in addition to regulatory fit as a source of engagement strength, there is evidence that pursuing goals in a right or proper way can strengthen engagement and intensify attraction toward a positive value target. I believe that there are at least two other general sources that can strengthen engagement and thereby contribute to value experiences by increasing value intensity—*opposing interfering forces* and *overcoming personal resistance*. Because both sources are clear examples of managing to make something happen that would otherwise not happen (i.e., control), I will also discuss them as *value–control relations* in Chapter 8.

Opposing Interfering Forces

Robert Woodworth had something insightful to say over half a century ago about opposing interfering forces. He said that a central characteristic of people and other animals is that they exert opposition or resistance to environmental forces on them in order to maintain a degree of independence. They resist wind that is trying to blow them over and gravity that is trying to make them fall. They have an active give-and-take relation with the environment, and value "springs from the individual's ability to deal effectively with some phase of the environment."[77] Kurt Lewin had a similar insight. He described how children's opposition to adult prohibitions that would interfere with their free movement increases the value of their activity, and he argued that such value creation from overcoming interference was of fundamental psychological significance.[78] I consider next a more modern version of this insight—value creation from reactance.

VALUE CREATION FROM REACTANCE

In the area of social psychology, the best-known examples of value creation from opposition to interfering forces are found in studies testing reactance theory, which was developed by Jack Brehm, a major contributor to understanding value and effort.[79] Reactance theory concerns people's belief that they can significantly control their own destiny, that they are free to act, believe, or feel as they see fit. It states that people will react so as to protect a freedom that is important to them when it is threatened with elimination or to restore it when it is actually eliminated.

In an early study by Brehm and his colleagues that tested the impact of reactance on value, participants listened to a taped selection from each of four different phonograph records and then ranked them according to how much they liked them.[80] They were told that they would receive one complimentary record when the actual records arrived the next day. When the participants returned to pick up their complimentary record, half of them learned that their third-ranked record was not included in the shipment and was thus eliminated from the original choice set. The participants were then asked to rate again the attractiveness of all of the original records. One might think that the attractiveness of the third-ranked record, which had been eliminated as an actual choice in the shipment, would decrease on this second ranking in order to protect the participants' feelings—why let yourself want something that you can't have? But, in fact, its attractiveness increased for the participants. According to reactance theory, the underlying mechanism for value creation in this and similar studies is a motivation to restore a freedom that has been eliminated (or threatened with elimination).

Reactance is not only produced by reducing options as in the Brehm studies, but, as Lewin noted,[81] it can also occur from the prohibitions and recommendations from others. For instance, warning labels on violent television programs, designed to *decrease* interest, often backfire and *increase* interest in watching the programs.[82] Recommendations, even in their innocuous forms, can create interfering forces to be opposed. A recent study, for example, provides a clear illustration of how this can unfold.[83] Participants were presented with a choice between four granola bars, one of which was the most attractive option. The decision was important to the participants because they would have an opportunity to take home their chosen granola bar (i.e., real stakes). When an expert recommended *against* the most attractive granola bar, they were *more* likely to choose it and were more confident in the value of their choice. Notably, the expert's recommendation against their preferred choice did result in these participants experiencing the decision *process* as being more difficult and unsatisfying, but, nonetheless, they chose their preferred option and valued *it* more.[84]

In addition to reactance, what else might be going on here? This study illustrates how an outside factor in goal pursuit—in this case, an expert's recommendation functioning like an interfering force—can produce a *negative experience* of the goal-pursuit activity itself but still result in the value target becoming *more attractive* because it strengthens engagement through opposing the recommendation, thereby intensifying the value target's positivity. It highlights the importance of distinguishing between the actor's personal experience of the goal-pursuit activity itself and the value that is created for the goal object.

VALUE CREATION FROM OPPOSING AN OBSTACLE OR INTERRUPTION
The elimination of a choice alternative and the resultant pressure to make a selection from an impoverished option set can be conceptualized as an obstacle to participants' preferred course of action. The participants could oppose this interfering force, which would strengthen their engagement in what they were doing. Given that the eliminated option was a positive option to begin with and its elimination makes it salient as an object, stronger engagement would intensify its attractiveness. When individuals oppose interfering forces, they oppose something that would hinder, impede, or obstruct a preferred state or course of action. They oppose a choice situation that would force them to select from an impoverished set of alternatives. This opposition can create value by strengthening engagement.

Thus, an obstacle or interference during goal pursuit can have two *opposite* hedonic effects: (a) it can make the goal-pursuit activity itself unpleasant and (b) it can intensify attraction toward the goal object by strengthening engagement from opposing the interference. And we have seen this phenomenon before—the "rat race" study.[85] In that study, some rats had to pull a heavy weight to obtain a small amount of food. This heavy weight functioned as an interfering force and it had to be opposed in order to attain the food, which is what the rats did. Pulling the heavy weight would have made the goal-pursuit activity itself unpleasant but, compared to the light weight, it increased the value of the food (as measured by how fast the rats ran to the food, how much of the food they ate, and how quickly they ate it).

Opposition to interfering forces also occurs when a task is interrupted before completion—the so-called *Zeigarnik* effect.[86] Consistent with the notion that opposing goal interruption as an interfering force would strengthen engagement and thereby intensify goal value, such interruption has been found to increase the attractiveness of the interrupted task.[87] In a study demonstrating this effect,[88] participants who were watching an entertaining movie had their movie watching interrupted at an exciting point by a projector breakdown. A confederate of the experimenter posed as an electrician and provided different information about whether the interruption was or was not just temporary. Once again, one might think that if the participants thought the movie was unlikely to resume, they would protect their feelings by downgrading its attractiveness—the "sour grapes" phenomenon. But, once again, the *opposite* happened. When participants believed that the movie was unlikely to resume (i.e., their goal was blocked), they valued the movie more. The interruption strengthened engagement with the movie as a value object (i.e., caused the participants to think more about it), which intensified their attraction toward the movie.

Value Creation From Opposing a Distraction

In the studies just cited, a goal pursuit is blocked or interrupted. There are other times when a goal pursuit continues but it is interfered with by a distracting event in the environment. The distraction itself can be a positive event that tempts us away from carrying on with our current activity, or it can be a negative event that we have to deal with while we keep on working. Both kinds of distractions have become common in our daily lives. Can opposing such distractions also create value?

Let me begin with the classic case of resisting temptation. In studies on resisting temptation, the participants' goal is to concentrate on some focal activity and resist paying attention to an attractive but peripheral object in the situation that they are tempted to engage, such as children having to resist playing with a fun clown toy that is present near them while they work on a focal task.[89] The literature suggests that resistance to temptation is stronger when individuals are vigilant against the tempting distraction than when they try to pursue the focal activity eagerly. If greater resistance to temptation creates value through strengthening engagement, then individuals who are vigilant in this situation should later value the focal activity more than those who are eager in this situation. This is precisely what has been found.[90]

But distracting circumstances can also be unpleasant. With unpleasant distractions, like a loud background noise, the challenge is to work on the focal task while dealing with an adversity rather than resisting a temptation. Despite the fact that the distraction itself produces unpleasant feelings, opposing it as an interference should also strengthen engagement, which can intensify attraction toward a positive task object. This possibility provides a new perspective on what happens when people have to deal with adversity.

Thus far, I have described people's responses to interfering forces as if they always oppose the interference, thereby strengthening engagement in the focal activity. But people do not always oppose an interference: sometimes they give up, and this would weaken engagement. More generally, people can have different responses to difficulty. One way of dealing with difficulty is to represent it as something interfering with the goal pursuit that must be overcome in order to succeed on the focal task—responding to the difficulty as opposing an interfering force. This response to difficulty should strengthen engagement in the focal task activity (i.e., *increase concentration*), which would increase attraction toward a positive goal object. But another possible response to difficulty is to represent the adversity as an aversive nuisance that produces unpleasant feelings that must be coped with—responding to difficulty as *coping with a nuisance*. By taking attention away from the focal task in order to cope with the unpleasant feelings created by the nuisance, this response to difficulty should weaken engagement (i.e., *divide attention*), which would *decrease* attraction toward a positive goal object. Some recent studies provide evidence that supports both of these predictions.[91]

In all of the studies, participants worked in the presence of an aversive background noise to solve enough anagrams to receive an attractive prize. All participants succeeded in winning the prize and the value of this prize was measured. In one study, participants were randomly assigned to two different background noises: a tape of dentist drills and a tape of spoken words. Both background noises are aversive, but only the "words" directly interfere with the task of solving verbal anagrams. Thus, it was expected that the participants would oppose the interfering "words" but cope with the nuisance "drills." In another study, all participants heard the *same* aversive sound but it was experimentally presented as either an *interference to oppose* or a *nuisance to cope with*.

Because these studies were examining what happens to the value of a goal object when people respond to difficulty in different ways (i.e., by opposing vs. coping), the predictions require that the participants perceive their situation as being difficult. There were two predictions. The first prediction was that for those participants who opposed the background noise as an interfering force, the more the noise was a difficult interference they had to oppose, the more they would have to concentrate, thereby strengthening engagement in the focal task and *increasing* the value of the prize. The second prediction was that for those participants who coped with the unpleasant feelings produced by the background noise, the more difficult it was to cope with the unpleasant feelings produced by the noise, the more their attention would be divided, thereby weakening engagement in the focal task and *decreasing* the value of the prize. The results of the studies supported both of these predictions.[92]

What this research highlights is that adversities, although unpleasant, do not necessarily make positive things in life less positive. Adversities can have this diminishing effect when people deal with them by disengaging from what they are doing in order to cope with the unpleasant feelings produced by the adversities. Such disengagement would decrease the positivity of positive things. But if people instead oppose adversities as interfering forces and concentrate even more on what they are doing (i.e., strengthen their engagement), then dealing with adversities can actually make positive things in life even more positive. This means that the difficulties in our lives can have very different value effects depending on how we deal with them.

THE ROLE OF DIFFICULTY IN VALUE CREATION

There are many kinds of forces that interfere with goal pursuit by increasing the difficulty or adversity that is encountered in the goal pursuit. Some tasks (the Sunday *New York Times* crossword puzzle) are more difficult than others (the Monday *New York Times* crossword puzzle). Sometimes the conditions under which one engages in a task are more difficult than others (e.g., writing an article to the strains of a jackhammer vs. Bach). Sometimes physical barriers are encountered (e.g., the stairs have to be taken to one's favorite shop because the elevator is broken). Although the sources of difficulty vary, all have the potential to strengthen or weaken engagement. The studies on "effort" and "adversity" that I have reviewed can be conceptualized more broadly as studies about *difficulty* as an interfering force. Lewin described a force that impedes or obstructs locomotion or progress to a goal as a "barrier" or "difficulty."[93] The "difficulty" can be an actual physical object blocking progress, such as a bench blocking a child's path toward obtaining a toy, or it can be an authority figure's prohibition of some act, or it can be the complexity of some task, and so on. As Lewin points out, psychologically such a difficulty, be it physical or social, constitutes a barrier; that is, an interfering force.

We have seen that difficulty does not necessarily strengthen engagement. It depends on how individuals deal with the difficulty. If individuals oppose difficulty or adversity, engagement is strengthened. If, however, difficulty or adversity results in individuals deciding not to initiate action in the first place or to give up during the goal pursuit or to divide their attention, engagement will be weakened.[94] Thus, I would not predict a simple monotonic positive relation between difficulty and engagement strength. It is possible that the relation between difficulty and engagement strength is bell-shaped, with increasing difficulty initially strengthening engagement until it reaches a point of such high difficulty that engagement weakens. Indeed, this kind of bell-shaped curve has been found for the relation between perceived difficulty and effort allocation.[95]

But even this "bell-shaped" hypothesis overlooks what it is about difficulty that determines engagement strength. It is not the difficulty *per se* but the opposition to it that is critical. As we have seen, people may cope with the unpleasant feelings produced by a difficulty and thereby divide their attention rather than oppose the difficulty as an interference and concentrate more. It is opposing difficulty as an interfering force that strengthens engagement, and the amount of opposition can vary for several reasons. For example, as Brehm has pointed out, the effort that people put into a task depends in part on how much effort is actually required to achieve their goal.[96] Thus, different individuals with varying abilities will expend different amounts of effort when engaging in a task as a function of the amount of effort they need to expend in order to achieve success. Again, it is not the effort *per se* that is critical; it is strengthening engagement from opposing interfering forces by increasing one's attention to what one is doing.

Overcoming Personal Resistance

Strengthening engagement from opposition to interfering forces occurs when individuals want to do something and yet experience a situational barrier or interruption or distraction when trying to do it. But there are also times when barriers spring from within, when individuals themselves initially resist doing something because it is aversive in some way. This is especially true when goal pursuit involves some unavoidable unpleasantness or has some real costs associated with it. Even when an obstacle is situational, the real challenge can be to overcome one's own personal resistance in order to engage in some pursuit. When people know that some aversiveness is inevitable if they engage in a particular goal pursuit, they naturally resist pursuing the goal initially. In such cases, people must overcome their own personal resistance in order to proceed with the activity. They must take action despite not wanting to do so.

CONDITIONS OF COGNITIVE DISSONANCE AS OVERCOMING PERSONAL RESISTANCE

When people overcome their own personal resistance and freely choose to pursue a goal that they know has unpleasant aspects, it strengthens engagement. These are precisely the conditions that increase commitment to goal pursuit and create value, according to Philip Brickman, a major contributor to understanding the relation between value and commitment.[97] Moreover, as

Brickman was the first to recognize, these are also precisely the conditions that underlie many prominent studies testing *cognitive dissonance theory.*[98]

According to Leon Festinger, the creator of this highly influential theory and a father of modern social psychology, the cognitions x and y are in a dissonant relation to one another if not-x would follow from y. According to this definition, then, the situational conditions in which people overcome personal resistance produce a state of dissonance because the belief that doing something is aversive, y, predicts the decision *not* to do it (not-x), but instead people overcome their resistance and do it anyhow. Instead of y and not-x occurring together (i.e., not doing something aversive), which would make sense and should happen, y and x occur together (i.e., doing something aversive). Dissonance theory concerns people's motivation to reduce such states of dissonance in order to achieve cognitive consistency and make sense of the world, and it considers the different ways that such dissonance reduction can occur.[99]

Of special relevance to this chapter are the experimental conditions under which inducing dissonance subsequently changes the value of something. Consider a classic study inspired by the phenomenon of a fraternity becoming more attractive to its new members *after* these pledges have suffered through the initiation "hazing" period of humiliating and painful ordeals. Shouldn't painful discipline from others decrease attraction? The fact that typically the *opposite* happens—attraction increases—is what makes the phenomenon so intriguing.

In the experimental study of this phenomenon,[100] undergraduate female volunteers had to undergo a severely negative initiation, a mildly negative initiation, or no initiation to become a member of a group. The group they wanted to join was one that would be discussing the psychology of sex. In the severe initiation condition, the participants had to read 12 obscene words to an experimenter. In the mild initiation condition, the participants read five words that were related to sex but were not obscene. Participants in the no initiation condition were the control group.

After undergoing the severe, mild, or no initiation, the participants listened to a discussion by the group they would be joining, and then they rated the group participants and the discussion (on scales such as dull/interesting; intelligent/unintelligent). As indicated by the ratings of the control group, the group participants and discussion were generally perceived as mildly to moderately positive. The study found that the group participants and discussion were rated *more* positively in the *severe* initiation condition than in the mild initiation condition (with the latter being the same as the control condition). That is, an *unpleasant* initiation experience to join the group had intensified *attraction* to the group.

According to cognitive dissonance theory, people would be more motivated to justify or make sense of why they agreed to do something severely aversive than if they had agreed to do something that was only mildly aversive. (If they didn't have to do anything, as in the control condition, then there is nothing to justify.) They can justify what they did by convincing themselves that it was worth it; in this case, worth it because the group participants and their discussion were so attractive.

However, in addition to this justification mechanism proposed by dissonance theory, the situational conditions involved in such studies might create value in another way. It would be natural for the participants in the severe initiation condition to be more resistant to carrying out the initiation than participants in the mild initiation condition. Nonetheless, they overcame their stronger personal resistance and did it anyhow, which would have strengthened their engagement in the discussion group. This strengthened engagement would intensify their attraction to the discussion group, as reflected in their ratings of the group participants and discussion. To return to the original real-life example, I am suggesting that fraternity pledges don't look forward to the initiation ordeals that they will have to face and they naturally resist doing them. But they overcome this personal resistance and by their doing so, their engagement with the fraternity is strengthened, and this intensifies their attraction toward it.

DIFFICULTY AS A SOURCE OF PERSONAL RESISTANCE TO BE OVERCOME

I discussed earlier how difficulty can be conceptualized as a barrier or interfering force that, if opposed, can strengthen engagement. But difficulty is not only an interfering force: it is *also* an aversive property of a situation, and dealing with it would naturally be resisted. Difficulty, then, can also contribute to strengthening engagement by inducing a personal resistance that has to be overcome to initiate and continue a goal pursuit. When goal pursuit is difficult, as when it requires high effort to succeed, there are high costs associated with the goal pursuit. Doing something despite these high costs imposed by difficulty involves overcoming resistance to doing something aversive. Great figures in psychology, including William James, Sigmund Freud, Kurt Lewin, and Jean Piaget, have recognized that overcoming one's own resistance is a special kind of agentic experience that relates to psychological commitment and "will."[101]

Engagement in an activity is strengthened when people, and other animals, knowingly face difficult and even painful circumstances in order to do it and continue with it, and the stronger engagement intensifies the value of that activity. Consider, for example, an intriguing program of research with rats that was inspired by dissonance theory.[102] In these studies, rats needed to run up an inclined runway in order to get a food reward. They were successful in obtaining the food on every trial (100% reinforcement). The incline was either

25 degrees (low effort) or 50 degrees (high effort). The measure of the value to the rats of getting a particular food reward was the number of trials it took to extinguish the rats' behavior, which would reveal that the more valuable the (now missing) food was to the rats the longer they would continue to try to attain it, despite failure to do so on each trial. Importantly, during the extinction trials *the incline remained the same as during the training*, and all the rats went from 100% reward to 0% reward.

It is evident that the benefits/costs ratio, or pleasure/pain ratio, is superior for the 25-degree incline than the 50-degree incline. Given this, we would expect that the food would have higher value (i.e., higher utility) for the 25-degree incline than the 50-degree incline. But the study found the *opposite*: the number of trials to extinction was *greater* for the 50-degree incline than the 25-degree incline. Moreover, despite the higher incline continuing to be more difficult during extinction, the average running time of the rats during the extinction trials was *faster* for the 50-degree incline than the 25-degree incline.

The cognitive dissonance explanation for these findings was that the rats added positivity to the food (i.e., consonant cognitions) in order to *justify* their decision to perform an aversive, high-effort activity (i.e., make sense of their decision). In addition to this justification explanation,[103] the conditions of these studies suggest an alternative possibility. Engagement strength could have been increased in two possible ways. One possibility is that opposition to interfering forces was involved: when the rats actually run up the incline, the 50-degree incline functions as an interfering force that needs to be opposed to get to the food. The other possibility is that overcoming personal resistance is involved. At the beginning of each trial, the 50-degree incline functions as an aversive cost producing personal resistance that must be overcome to initiate the goal pursuit. The strengthened engagement from either of these two possible sources would intensify the attractiveness of the food.[104]

Creating value from overcoming difficulty might also explain the otherwise puzzling phenomenon of very young animals becoming increasingly attached to an object to which they are initially attracted, including an inanimate object, even when they receive *pain* from it while interacting with it.[105] There would be a natural resistance to receiving pain, but this must be overcome in order to continue to be close to the attractive object. A history of overcoming this resistance would increase the value of the object, as reflected in the animal's becoming increasingly attached to it. Of course, increased attachment will occur under such circumstances only if the animal persists in making contact with the object despite the pain received.

This last example raises a general point that applies equally to the previous examples of value creation from overcoming personal resistance: *difficulty will not increase value if it makes someone give up*. Resistance to difficulty must be overcome in order to increase value. An especially interesting example of increased attachment value when an animal does *not* give up in the face of increased difficulty has been described by Eckhard Hess, a pioneer of ethology, in his "law of effort."[106] Ducklings had to climb over hurdles or up an inclined plane in order to follow the imprinting object. Hess found that strength of imprinting was positively correlated with the effort exerted by the ducklings in following the imprinting object. It is also notable that when animals were given meprobamate, a muscle relaxant that reduces muscular tension, then the strength of imprinting was no longer related to exerted effort. This is consistent with the notion that it is the *experience* of engagement strength that contributes to the value experience.

Some Clarifications

In my discussion of both opposition to interfering forces and overcoming personal resistance, several of my examples of positive value creation from strengthening engagement involve increasing effort. But I want to emphasize that I am *not* suggesting that greater effort generally increases attraction to something. If one were to predict a main effect, it would be more reasonable to predict that greater effort decreases attraction to something. After all, if the same benefit from some activity or outcome requires a greater effort, as for the rats running up a steeper incline to obtain the same reward, then the greater cost of the higher effort should reduce value according to the classic benefit/cost ratio perspective. Indeed, the same research program with rats running up an incline to attain food also reported that when a separate group of rats was given a direct choice between a high-difficulty and low-difficulty path to the food, they chose the low-difficulty path.[107] This is not surprising because rats are far from being stupid animals. In the actual study, however, the rats given the high-difficulty path did not have the option of taking the low-difficulty path instead. To pursue the positive goal of attaining the food they had to oppose the interfering force and overcome their personal resistance. What this highlights is an important point—*effort can have two opposite effects on value*. Effort can decrease value through the hedonic experience of costs, but it can also increase value through strengthening engagement as long as the value target remains positive and is pursued.

I should also note that opposing interfering forces and overcoming personal resistance as two sources of engagement strength differ in an important way from regulatory fit and doing things in the proper way as two other sources of engagement strength. Specifically, the latter two sources are likely to be associated with pleasant feelings during goal pursuit, whereas the former sources are more likely to be associated with unpleasant feelings. In regulatory fit, people could "feel right" about what they are doing, and when using proper means they could feel good about themselves (i.e., self-approval)—both pleasant feelings. Might such pleasant feelings during goal pursuit account for the value effects, such as adding positivity to the value target? The answer is "no" because stronger engagement from regulatory fit can intensify *negative* value as well as positive value, as when regulatory fit intensifies negative reactions to an unconvincing persuasive message and makes the message less persuasive rather than more so.

What matters about all of these sources is not the valence state they induce within the actor pursuing a goal, but their effect in strengthening engagement, which then intensifies whatever the reaction to a value target happens to be—whether that reaction is positive or negative. This is especially obvious in the examples I have presented concerning opposition to interfering forces and overcoming personal resistance. Here, people typically have unpleasant experiences during the goal-pursuit activity, such as the unpleasant state of tension described in the cognitive dissonance literature, but a positive-value target increases in attraction. Why? Because these sources strengthen engagement, which intensifies the experience of attraction toward the positive-value target. Again, it is not what a source does to the feelings of actors themselves that matters, but simply its effect on engagement strength, which then functions as an intensifier of positive or negative reactions when engagement is strengthened and as a "deintensifier" of positive or negative reactions when engagement is weakened.

CONCLUDING REMARKS

Changing engagement strength provides two different ways to enhance well-being. When something is attractive, *strengthening* engagement will make it *more* attractive. When something is repulsive, *weakening* engagement will make it *less* repulsive. These alternative routes have significant implications for people controlling their value experiences. Consider different motivational disorders, for example. Sometimes people find things too repulsive, as with phobias, and weakening engagement would be beneficial. Other times people find things not attractive enough, as with depression, and strengthening engagement would be beneficial. And still other times people find things too attractive, as with addictions (or mania), and *weakening* engagement would again be beneficial. Recognizing the contribution of engagement strength to value intensity can provide a route for value effectiveness that does not depend on changing value direction.

To summarize the take-away message of this chapter, which is illustrated in Figure 4.1, I propose that value comes from the experience of attraction or repulsion, which has both direction and intensity. Importantly, there are sources of engagement strength that contribute to the intensity of the value experience that are separate from the sources that contribute to value direction. Whereas sources of value direction, such as hedonic experience, can also contribute to value intensity (both directly and indirectly through engagement strength), sources of engagement strength just intensify the value that has been established by the value direction sources.

There are several different sources of value direction, including hedonic experience, need satisfaction, shared beliefs about desired objectives and procedures (social standards), relating our actual selves to some standard (personal standards), and contextualized evaluative inferences. There are also several different sources of engagement strength, including regulatory fit, pursuing goals in a proper way, opposing interfering forces, and overcoming personal resistance. Thus, value—having desired results—can be created by multiple factors that determine not only whether something is desired or undesired but also how much it is desired or undesired. And the sources of *how much* something is desired or undesired can be different from the sources of *whether* something is desired or undesired.

In addition, the effects of engagement-strength sources on our own feelings are different from their effects on how much we value something else. Indeed, something that strengthens our engagement in what we are doing can create unpleasant feelings in us while at the same time making something else more attractive. Thus, having desired results in the sense of valuing the positive things in our lives does not require that our goal-pursuit activities themselves give us pleasure while we do them. What matters is that when we pursue desired results, we are strongly engaged in the goal-pursuit process—even if the process itself is unpleasant (e.g., demanding or difficult). I will return to the more general question of what creates "the good life" and high well-being in Chapter 13.

5

Truth

Establishing What's Real

Is it real? This is a question that everyone asks at one point or another,[1] and it is not an easy question to answer. Young children, and adults as well, can find it difficult to distinguish between what is real and what is illusion or imagination. Indeed, when the question of what's real concerns a past event in our lives, all of us can have difficulty distinguishing reality from unreality. Let me give some examples.

People find it hard to distinguish between an event they personally experienced and one they simply imagined, as when they confuse what another person actually said with what they only imagined that person said.[2] Even when they definitely did experience an event and did not just imagine it, they find it hard to distinguish later between what precisely they saw happen and how what they saw was characterized by someone else. For instance, after people have seen a car collision, they are more likely to remember that they saw broken glass at the scene of the accident if another person describes the collision as a "smash" versus a "hit"—a potentially serious problem with eyewitness testimony in court.[3] And even when people themselves characterize something they observed, they find it hard later to distinguish between what they originally observed and what they said about it. For example, if we observe the behaviors of another person and then later describe what we observed to a friend of that person, our natural tendency is to describe that person's behaviors in a relatively positive manner. And when we subsequently try to recall the original behaviors, we recall them as being more positive than what we actually observed—a phenomenon called the "Saying-is-Believing" effect.[4]

People not only treat something as being real that is actually not real, but they also treat something as not being real that is actually real. In an early study on distinguishing imagination and perception, for instance, participants were asked to imagine a common object like a banana while they looked at a screen. Unbeknownst to them, the experimenter slowly raised from a subliminal level to a level above threshold an actual perceptual stimulus of the imagined object. Many of the participants mistook the real stimulus for their imagined object and incorporated features of the real stimulus, such as its orientation, into their report of their imagined object. When the participants were told that a real stimulus had appeared on the screen, they often did not believe it.[5]

In these ways, and in a myriad of others,[6] people have a difficult time knowing what's real and what's not real. And yet it is very important, even essential, for people to distinguish reality from unreality. *Our survival depends upon it.* There are cognitive mechanisms that can be used to help solve this problem.[7] But even with the availability of such cognitive tools, differentiating reality from unreality is not straightforward. Segal, an expert on the relation between imagination and perception, describes the problem as follows: "Thus we all perceive, we all image, we all hallucinate; there is no difference in the cognitive experiences of the schizophrenic, the hallucinating drug addict, and the college student in this regard. What varies are the patterns of past experience, individual differences, contextual probabilities, expectancies and biases that each one brings to the task, a process that passes as judgment."[8] This chapter is concerned with what people do as they search for the truth and establish what's real.

People want to be effective in finding the truth, at establishing what's real. Like value, truth is an experience. When we fail to establish truth, we feel confused and bewildered. William James described beliefs as resulting from a *reality check* on thoughts. He described believing as being an emotional experience of consent; that is, we decide that what had been just a thought before is now taken as truth.[9] Generally speaking, people prefer the stability and solidity of truth over the agitation and contradictions of doubt. This means that when less accurate knowledge of something provides a stronger experience of success at establishing what's real than more accurate knowledge (i.e., more supported by facts or evidence), people will sacrifice the more accurate knowledge in order to experience truth effectiveness. This is the power behind political and religious ideologies, or pet theories, and it is what makes the striving for truth so tricky. Not only are we motivated to be accurate, but we also want to experience ourselves as accurate. We want to experience ourselves as being successful in having understandings, beliefs, and knowledge that are the truth, that represent what is real. This additional motive of wanting to experience our inner-state representations of the world as being the truth is uniquely human.

The motive to establish what's real is so strong that, generally speaking, the default is to treat something as real rather than as imaginary or as an open question. In this sense the world is not the "buzzing confusion" described by William James,[10] because we treat actual confusion as if it were not. This default—that whatever we are experiencing and thinking *is* reality—is so strong that it is difficult for us to appreciate that other persons can have different perceptions, thoughts, and feelings about the same thing. Indeed, it takes years for children to come to this appreciation.[11] And even when children, around 3 years of age, can appreciate that individuals' perceptions and desires can vary, they still treat beliefs as real rather than considering the possibility that they could be false.

Consider the following example. As part of a study, a child is told a story about candy being taken out of a candy box and being replaced with pencils, and later the candy box is given to a child character in the story. The child in the study is then asked, "What will this child believe is in the candy box? How will the child react when the candy box is opened and there are pencils inside?" Whereas 4-year-olds understand that the child character will have the false belief that there is candy in the box and will be surprised or disappointed to find pencils instead, 3-year-olds will say that the character knew there were pencils inside and thus will be neither surprised nor disappointed. The 3-year-olds answer the questions in terms of what *they* know to be real and assume the character will know the same reality rather than have a false belief.[12]

A critical part of development is to learn that what is self-evident as being real can, in fact, be a false belief. Only slowly do we learn this fact as we grow up. And it depends on learning that our perceptions, feelings, and beliefs about something can be different from those of other people, and that it is others who can have the truth. Solomon Asch, a founding father of experimental social psychology, described the process as follows: "That shape looming in the distance has to me the vivid appearance of a monster, but to my neighbor it is simply the branch of a tree. Without the social check, this experience might remain that of a monster unaccountably changing into a tree; with my neighbor next to me it becomes a lesson in the difference between reality and appearance."[13]

Lee Ross, who has made landmark contributions to understanding person perception, has described a human worldview called *naïve realism*. Naïve realism is people's tendency to assume that what they perceive, believe, or prefer directly reflects objective reality, that their thoughts and feelings are a dispassionate and essentially unmediated apprehension of what is real.[14] That is, people assume that their own experiences and beliefs can be, and deserve to be, treated as real. As Ross and his colleagues point out, this can cause serious problems between persons, as well as between groups. After all, if someone else has been exposed to the same information about something as I have, but that person disagrees with my experience or belief about it, then that person (or group) *must* be irrational, ignorant, motivationally biased, or simply lying. My experiences and beliefs are simply *the* truth—*the whole truth and nothing but the truth.*

What this means is that human development where children become capable of understanding that there can be false beliefs is, apparently, applied more to other people than to ourselves. It remains difficult for us to give up the notion that *our* experiences and beliefs about things in the world *are* what's real. Yes, I have learned that others can hold false beliefs, but I don't hold false beliefs. *My* response to a situation simply reflects the reality of that situation, whereas *your* reaction might reflect some personality bias you have rather than what's real in the situation.[15]

But it is not only about my believing that I know the truth and, if you disagree with me, deciding that you hold false and biased beliefs. It is also the case that, as Asch noted, we learn that social verification or agreement from others is very important in our establishing what's real. That is, people are highly motivated to reach a *shared reality* with others. Moreover, people who have power over another person are usually highly motivated to help that person reach a shared reality with them, such as parents helping their child to reach a shared reality with them or politicians "helping" voters to have a shared reality with them. This was a major theme in George Orwell's classic 1949 book *1984*, where in the dreaded torture chamber Room 101, rebels are forced to believe in the realness of a false reality. The torturer and executioner O'Brien says to the rebel Winston:

> "You believe that reality is something objective, external, existing in its own right. You also believe that the nature of reality is self-evident. When you delude yourself into thinking that you see something, you assume that everyone else sees the same thing as you. But I tell you, Winston, that reality is not external. Reality exists in the human mind, and nowhere else. Not in the individual mind, which can make mistakes, and in any case soon perishes: only in the mind of the Party, which is collective and immortal. Whatever the Party holds to be the truth, is truth. It is impossible to see reality except by looking through the eyes of the Party."

How then do people strive for truth, establish what's real? What makes something real? What establishes reality? In my review of the answers to these questions, my emphasis will be more on the different motivational factors that underlie establishing reality rather than on the cognitive mechanisms.[16] An example of a motivational factor would be deciding something is real because other people with whom one wants a shared reality treat it as real.[17] An example of a cognitive mechanism would be to treat the memory as real (rather than imagined) to the extent that detailed perceptual information, as well as time and place information, was recollected.[18] Sometimes both motivational and cognitive mechanisms are involved when people seek the truth, as when they question *what* happened and *why* it happened, such as "Did I pass or fail the test?," and, if I failed, "Why did I fail?" People are motivated to find answers to *what* happened and *why* it happened, and cognitive processes are involved in finding such answers. However, my interest here is less in the cognitive mechanisms involved in questioning than in the motivational determinants and consequences of people's search for answers to their questions.

I begin with the questions of "what happened" and "why did it happen" because as two major sources of establishing what's real they have been central to the issue of truth and reality over the past half-century. Following this, I discuss how reality is established from cognitive consistency. Next, I consider how different truth-seeking strategies are used to establish reality by different individuals and in different situations. Finally, I describe the roles of social reality and shared reality in establishing what's real.

ESTABLISHING REALITY FROM JUDGING "WHAT?"

In a pioneering paper, Philip Brickman wondered why social psychologists, with all of their attention to attributional processes (i.e., to why something happened), had not considered how people judge whether something is real or not. His answer was that social psychologists simply assume that people would try to explain why something happened only for events that they already think are real; the question of how people know that the events are real to begin with is simply passed over.[19] But both the "what" and the "why" questions are part of establishing what is real. People need to believe that what happened was real, not imaginary, and then they want the truth about why this real thing happened. And there can be several different levels of this reality checking and truth seeking.

Consider a mother who wakes up due to a crying-like sound in the middle of the night. She might ask herself a series of questions:

"Is that something crying or am I still dreaming?"
"Are my ears playing tricks on me?"
"Is it a cry that I am hearing or just the wind?"
"Is that cry from my cat or from my child?"
"Why is my child crying?"

Each step of the way the mother is motivated to find the truth, to determine what is real and not real. This kind of questioning is not academic. It is not idle curiosity. It is dead serious. The mother wants to know the truth, to know what is *really* happening. Only then can she have the answers she needs to make a decision about whether to take some action or not and about what action to take if necessary. She wants to be successful in finding the correct answers—she wants to establish what's real.

To begin with, how do we know whether something is real or not? The answer to this question is especially important within human societies when it concerns what other people say or do. It can be critical to figure out whether someone is genuine versus faking, honest versus deceitful, telling the truth versus lying. It is important especially to humans because we recognize the difference between what people say and do and the *inner states* that underlie these observable behaviors. inner states such as their thoughts, feelings, and attitudes. We want to know the truth about those *inner states* and not just the truth about the behaviors.[20] Thus, one criterion that people use to decide whether someone's statements or actions are real is whether they can identify an inner state in that person that corresponds to the behavior—the criterion of *internal correspondence*. When people perceive no correspondence, they do not treat the behavior as real.[21]

If people are motivated to know what's real, and if questioning is in the service of learning what's real, then when they become suspicious about something, their questioning should increase. Indeed, this is the case. There is evidence that when people become suspicious of the inner motives underlying someone's behavior, such that the behavior no longer seems genuine, they engage in more active and thoughtful attributional analyses, deliberating about questions of plausible causes for the behavior.[22]

What should be noted here is that people in these cases are not questioning whether an event occurred but whether it is the type of event that it seems to be—something definitely did happen, but exactly *what* kind of something is it? The mother may decide that it is not a question of whether there was actually a crying-like sound as opposed to her just dreaming it or her ears simply playing tricks on her. She might be certain that there *was* really a crying-like sound. The mother initially recognized the crying-like sound as being a cry from some living thing—either her cat or her child. What she is now questioning is whether this recognition was real. Was it really a cry from some living thing? For the mother it really matters whether the crying-like sound was made by the wind or was made by her cat or her child. Similarly, when we see what is clearly a friendly-appearing behavior we don't question this appearance; rather, we question whether the person who produced the behavior is being genuinely friendly or is just faking.

Thus, for people generally, it matters *what* someone's behavior really means, and what it really means depends on the inner states of the person that led to its production. To find an answer to this concern, the first question people ask is whether the person intended to produce the behavior and its consequences or whether they were just accidental.[23] There are descriptions of attributional processes in the social-psychological literature that begin with a behavior being categorized as "X," such as "aggressive," and then discuss how people decide whether to attribute the cause of the behavior to the actor's character—that is, the actor is "X" (e.g., "aggressive")—or to attribute the cause of the behavior to situational circumstances.[24] But if the behavior was actually caused by the situational circumstances, then the person was not in full control of the behavior, and thus the behavior and its consequences were *not* intended. And for many behaviors, such as "aggressive" behavior, this means that the conditions for categorizing the behavior as "X" were *not met* to begin with. That is, the fact that the behavior was "aggressive" cannot be treated as a given, as something that's real. This is because for many behavioral categories (e.g., aggressive, kind, helpful, rude, competitive) the *intentions* of the actor are *essential* to the definition of the category; that is, if the aggressive-appearing behavior was not produced by an aggressive intent, then it should not be categorized as an "aggressive" behavior to begin with.

What this means is that the first step of questioning the inner states that led to producing a behavior is critical for establishing what's real. I should note that the questioning need not be, and is typically not, done consciously. In addition, people usually take for granted that a person intended to do what he or she just did, with the exceptions proving the rule—the extreme cases of individuals being too young, too emotional, too crazy, too drunk, too ill, and so on, to know or control what they did. Nonetheless, this first step of inferring intentionality cannot be ignored; it is a crucial part of the early process of establishing what's real.

Once intentionality is inferred (consciously or unconsciously), what comes next? Several person-perception models describe the judgmental process as involving a sequence of processing stages that begin with initial low-level steps that are largely automatic or unconscious and proceed to higher-level steps that are more controlled or conscious.[25] For example, there can be two steps in getting from seeing someone's change in mouth expression to categorizing the expression as "friendly." The first step involves treating the expression as a real "smile" (i.e., where the expression and its consequences on the viewer were intended), and the second step involves treating the "smile" as a "friendly" behavior. In his seminal contribution to the attribution literature, Yaacov Trope describes how the situation surrounding the production of a behavior, such as observing someone "smiling" when he or she greets another person at an airport versus observing someone smile after receiving a flattering compliment, can be essential for the interpretation that leads to identifying the behavior, such as identifying the first smile as "friendly" versus the second smile as "embarrassed." But people need not be aware, and often are not aware, of the influence of the situation on this early identification process.[26]

Judging "What" for Something That is Ambiguous or Vague

Although it often seems straightforward to decide what something is, it is far from being so. There are several ways in which it can be difficult. The input information is often vague or ambiguous. For example, we can be uncertain whether to characterize one person's behavior as persistent or stubborn or another person's behavior as confident or conceited. From an evaluative standpoint, the behavior cannot be positive and negative at the same time. Choice of behavioral category will determine whether the behavior is perceived as positive (persistent) or negative (stubborn). The evidence from just the behavior itself is insufficient to choose between the alternative categories. In these cases, a choice will often occur not because there is more evidence in the behavior itself for one option versus the other option but because one construct stored in long-term memory (e.g., "stubborn") happens to be more accessible (i.e., has a higher likelihood of being activated for use) than the other construct stored in memory ("persistent").

There is substantial evidence that the prior accessibility of alternative constructs in stored memory—*before the input is even received*—can influence how an input is categorized. That is, the prior accessibility of alternative constructs can determine the judgment of "what" something is independent of the properties of the input.[27] But people do not experience their judgment as being due to the accessibility of the construct. Instead, they experience their judgment as being *about* the properties of the input: "I judged the behavior as being stubborn because its properties fit that category."[28] The judgment of stubborn, for example, establishes that the person's behavior is *really* and *truly* stubborn. And this occurs despite the fact that this judgment of stubborn, instead of persistent, resulted from the "stubborn" construct having higher *prior* accessibility than the "persistent" construct, rather than from the actual properties of the behavior being more stubborn than persistent.

A judgment of "stubborn" as a negative evaluation, versus a judgment of "persistent" as positive, can have motivational consequences. For example, it could influence how much the perceiver likes the person who behaved this way. In one study in which participants were asked to judge the behaviors of a target person, the construct "stubborn" was made more accessible in memory than the construct "persistent" by having the participants incidentally exposed several minutes earlier to the word "stubborn" in a separate and unrelated situation—a *priming* manipulation. Only later in a new situation did they read about the ambiguous behaviors of the target person. Not only did the earlier unobtrusive priming, which they were not even aware of later, make it more likely that they would judge the target person's ambiguous behaviors as being stubborn rather than persistent, but it also resulted in the target person being evaluated more negatively as a person, and increasingly so over time.[29] *Accessibility from priming* established what was real about this person, independent of the person's actual behaviors.

Research on priming and accessibility demonstrates how answering the "what" question can establish what's real for people and have real consequences even when the answer goes beyond the facts. The facts in many of these studies are that what is happening is unclear—it is ambiguous or vague. Generally speaking, however, people do not want to keep things unclear because they experience this as a failure to find the truth. They prefer to have a clear answer to "what" something is, and they use whichever construct is most accessible to provide this answer despite its ignoring the facts to some extent. Like the phenomenon of naïve realism, this preference is another example of people wanting to experience effectiveness in establishing what's real.

Judging "What" for Something That Belongs to More Than One Category

Even when the evidence about something is factually clear, it can still be difficult to judge "what" it is because it belongs to more than one category at the same time. One version of this problem is that all things belong to different categories at different levels of abstraction. Roger Brown, a founder of the area of psycholinguistics, addressed this issue in his famous paper, "How shall a thing be called?"[30] He used the example of calling the same observed object "a tarnished 1952 dime," "a dime," "a coin," "money," "a metal object," "a thing." The properties of the object clearly permit each of these judgments to be made. Each of these categories would be accepted as being true of the target, and there is no conflict among them—*they can all be true.* Nonetheless, under different conditions one or the other category will be chosen as the answer to "what" the object is. And, once again, the choice will depend on factors that are independent of the object's factual properties, such as which level of abstraction is most useful given the perceiver's current goal. For instance, if I am organizing my coin collection and deciding what to keep and what to throw out, then "a tarnished 1952 dime" might be the best level of identification, but if I am trying to find something to twist the head of a screw, then "coin" might be the best level. Notably, whatever category level is chosen, it establishes what's real about that thing at that moment in time.[31]

Things can also belong to more than one category at the same level of abstraction. For example, each person belongs to more than one social category, such as an Asian female dentist who is "an Asian" and "a female" and "a dentist."[32] Once again, independent of the stimulus properties of the target, the relative accessibility of these different categories could determine which of them is used to judge the target, as could their relative usefulness for the perceiver's current goal pursuit. But once a category is chosen, the reality of the target is established with respect to that category, and it is the implications of that category that will have motivational significance. Regarding stereotypical responses, for example, people who respect Asians for their professional dedication might feel good when they discover that their dentist is an "Asian," whereas people who disrespect females' mechanical skills might feel bad when they discover that their dentist is a "female." The answer to "what" establishes what's real about this dentist and this reality has emotional and motivational effects.

In sum, it can be difficult to establish "what" something is, to find the truth about something. But the motivation to do so is strong because "what" something is has implications for making subsequent decisions about what action to take or choices to make. In this way, it can support having desired results, support value effectiveness. But learning about "what" the world is like does not have to support value effectiveness *per se* in order for people to want to do it. Independent of the potential utility of what is learned for taking action, people still want to establish what's real about the world they live in. Learning something and using what is learned are separate—the classic distinction between *learning* and *performance*. Let us consider this important distinction in more detail.

Knowing "What" from Observational and Latent Learning

In an early demonstration of the distinction between learning and performance, young children observed someone—the model—hit a Bobo clown, an inflatable plastic doll. They also observed that the model was either subsequently rewarded or subsequently punished for hitting the clown. Later the children were left alone with the clown. The children who had earlier observed the model being rewarded for hitting the clown were more likely to hit it than the children who had observed the model being punished for hitting the doll.[33] But when the children who had observed the punished model were told that they would receive a reward for showing what they had seen the model do with the clown, they were also able to copy the model's actions of hitting the doll. These children had also learned "what" could be done with a Bobo clown (i.e., it could be hit), but they would not use this knowledge to direct their behavior when they thought they would be punished for doing so.

Before discussing in more detail what motivates such *observational learning*, let me first describe another example of learning "what" things are in the world: *latent learning*.[34] This concept refers to people (or non-human animals) learning something that is not rewarded, is not immediately expressed, and may not even be available to consciousness, but later, when the knowledge becomes useful, the learning is revealed in behavior. Perhaps the best-known study on latent learning is an early animal experiment conducted by Edward Tolman and C. H. Honzik.[35]

The maze-learning behavior of rats was observed over a two-week period. One group of rats always found food at the end of the maze on the learning trial that took place each day. Another group of rats found no food at the end of the maze for the first 10 days, but they did find food on the 11th day. By the end of the first 10 days, the always-rewarded first group learned to run the maze much better than the second group. But after the 11th day, the maze-running ability of the second group quickly caught up to the first group, and by the next day the second group performed almost as well as the first group. What was clear was that the second group was learning about the maze during the first 10 days despite receiving no reward and not using what they had learned in their maze-running behavior.

There are everyday examples of latent and observational learning in children's behavior as well. One example, which comes as an unpleasant surprise to parents, is a young child suddenly swearing in public despite never having been rewarded for swearing; or, for that matter, never having seen anyone rewarded for swearing. As another example from firsthand experience, one evening at home I watched my 4-year-old daughter Kayla, totally unprompted, walk up to adults eating appetizers before dinner and ask them politely what they would like to drink—from out of nowhere, the perfect hostess taking orders.

What motivation, then, accounts for latent and observational learning? Not surprisingly, there were attempts to explain such learning in terms of value, such as Hull's "anticipatory goal reaction,"[36] where even an empty goal box was assumed to be rewarding to some extent. I believe, however, that observational and latent learning reflects the motivation to establish what's real, to learn "what" is happening in the world. And this *truth* motivation is found in non-human animals as well as humans. Observational and latent learning is not just in the service of value motivation. Rather, these types of learning derive from truth motivation in its own right. Once again, they illustrate how motivation is not just about pleasure and pain. Pleasure and pain in the form of incentives can be important for what is or is not performed, but there is motivation beyond them when it comes to learning—that is, wanting to establish what's real.

ESTABLISHING REALITY FROM ASKING "WHY?"

In their search for what is real, people often do not stop at the step of identifying or categorizing what they observe—deciding "what" something is. They often want to proceed with additional questions whose answers tell them more about *inner states*, such as why another person behaved a particular way. This next step of going from "what" people do to "why" they do it is the kind of truth seeking that has received the most attention in the social psychological literature. It concerns the process of drawing inferences about other individuals' feelings, thoughts, or personality, including trying to understand our own feelings or personality.[37] People want especially to know the truth about those inner states of someone that are stable over time, such as that person's abilities or attitudes, because this knowledge will allow them to make more accurate predictions about what that person is likely to do in the future—seeking in the present to know what will be real about that person in the future.[38]

I emphasized previously that a remarkable fact about humans is that they are *time travelers*.[39] They think about the future. This includes daydreaming and fantasizing about the future. But what people do most often is plan for the future, and they want the future they are planning for to be real. They want their predictions about it—about what they and others will do in the future—to be real. This requires knowing in the present what will remain stable about themselves or others over time.

Inferring Distinctive Versus Stable Traits About Someone

I should note that the social psychological literature has sometimes suggested that people are only interested in the "why" answer about someone's behavior that tells them how that person is different from others. It has been suggested that if someone does something that most other people would do under the same circumstances (i.e., what the "average" or "normal" person would do), such as being friendly at a party, then no judgment about that person's stable predispositions will be made.[40] According to this perspective, it is as if people are clinicians who want to know only what is *distinctive* about other people—to discover their unique personalities. But if instead people want to predict what someone will do in the future, then what they want to know is what is invariant or *stable* about that person's behavior over time, regardless of whether other people would also behave that way in the same situation.

Let me clarify this point. If it is only distinctive personality traits that people will infer about others, then they will infer a trait such as "friendly" for less than half of the individuals in the population, given that it must be different from the "average person." In fact, however, there are many traits that people think *most* people possess (i.e., over 50% of people), including both positive traits like being warm, outgoing, intelligent, and friendly and negative traits like being greedy, conceited, aggressive, and stubborn.[41] Moreover, they also predict that a person in a present situation who displays a trait-related behavior, such as behaving now in a friendly manner, is likely to show the same behavior in the future, despite the fact that most other people would behave the same way in the present situation.[42] Thus, it is not the case that people just want to know about someone's distinctive personality; what people want to know is what is stable about someone in order to establish what will be real about that person in the future—regardless of whether it is something that most other people would also do in the future.

I am not suggesting that people never want to know what is distinctive about someone's traits. When might this motivation be stronger or weaker? From the perspective of establishing what's real, we should want *really* to know the familiar people in our lives, such as our friends, family, and coworkers, because it would be useful to know what makes them "special" beyond what can be predicted from just knowing what most people are like. In fact, studies have found that inferences about *distinctively* stable attributes, such as someone's personality or particular goals, beliefs, or attitudes, are more frequent when others are familiar and significant to us.[43]

But it is also important to recognize that when people want to know what's happening or predict what will happen regarding someone's actions, the emphasis is not always on that person's stable traits. There can be as much or more emphasis on the role of the situation, including social situational forces such as social norms and role obligations that predict what individuals will do in the future.

Situational Explanations in Answering "Why"

In addition to learning how individuals' inner states affect what they do, people learn how different kinds of situations press for different kinds of behaviors for people generally. And they use this knowledge to predict future reality, such as learning about the social norms of behavior for a party versus a funeral. They learn as well that there are ethnic, cultural, and personality type differences in determining which kinds of behaviors are likely in which kinds of situations, such as learning that someone with an authoritarian personality will be dominant when interacting with a status inferior but will be submissive when interacting with a status superior. They also learn that different categories of people like different kinds of things, so that when a member of that category chooses to do something, such as a young child choosing to play with a toy, it establishes a reality about the toy being fun for children to play with (the situation) rather than a reality about what the child is like as an individual (the person). People want to know what's real for all of these different kinds of situational information and not just information about individuals' stable traits.

There are also cultural and developmental differences in the extent to which individuals explain others' actions in terms of the actors' stable traits or situational forces.[44] As an example of a development difference, 4- to 5-year-olds, 9-year-olds, and adults in one study selected an item from an array of food options (e.g., possible desserts) and then watched other people of the same age either agree (high consensus) or disagree (low consensus) with the actors' choice. When asked why an actor liked the chosen object best, the participants in all age groups used the consensus information: they explained the actor's choice more in terms of the qualities of the chosen object (situational force) rather than the actor's stable characteristics when there was high (vs. low) consensus about the choice. However, there was also an overall developmental difference in which kind of explanation was generally preferred: the 4- to 5-year-olds made stronger situational attributions than either the 9-year-olds or the adults.

What does this developmental difference show? It is possible that social-life-phase differences in *truth motivation* underlie this difference in attributional emphasis. For very young children, it is truth about someone's social category that matters and not his or her unique personal predispositions. What matters for them is to learn how members of a social category behave: caretakers behave in a certain way, playmates behave in a certain way, and so on. It is not especially useful to make fine distinctions within social categories. Young children, then, would perceive homogeneity within social categories, with every member of a social category having the same preferences. This creates an inference of high consensus within each social category, which produces stronger situational attributions. This object is preferred by everyone in that person's social category. Therefore, choosing that object reflects the qualities of that object and not the characteristics of that person.

I should note that this emphasis of the 4- to 5-year-olds need not be seen as reflecting a cognitive immaturity. Adults in non-Western cultures also emphasize social role and status obligations and other situational forces over individual independence, which is reflected in their giving greater attributional weight to situational forces than to actors' stable predispositions. It is in Western cultures that older children and adults learn to emphasize individual independence over social interdependence in a manner that becomes reflected in their attributional weights.[45] What varies is what kind of information matters, what truth is worth seeking out and establishing.

In sum, people want explanations for what happens in their lives. They want to understand the underlying causes of what they observe, the underlying reality of it. When they are trying to understand the actions of other people, they want to understand the human inner states that determine such actions. The forces producing these inner states include not only actors' personal stable traits (whether distinctive or not) but also the social norms and rules that are associated with different settings and apply to everyone as a function of his or her role, status, or social category membership. These are the realities that people want to know about in order to be effective in finding the truth.

People also want their different kinds of knowledge to work together, to form a coherent whole. They want present knowledge to be organized with past knowledge in a meaningful way. They want a past and present reality that makes sense together. They want the elements of what they already know to be *consistent* not only with one another but also with what is currently happening.

ESTABLISHING REALITY FROM COGNITIVE CONSISTENCY

You already have some idea of the motivational power of cognitive consistency from the "Eating a Worm" study described in Chapter 1. To be consistent with their own explanations when answering a questionnaire of why they had agreed earlier to eat a worm—explanations such as "I am a brave person" or "I deserve to suffer"—participants in this study freely chose to do a painful shock task rather than a neutral weight discrimination task.[46] Once they had established a reality about themselves while answering the questionnaire, they wanted to maintain this reality.

In his introductory chapter to a landmark book in social psychology, *Theories of Cognitive Consistency: A Sourcebook* (1968), Theodore Newcomb described the remarkable emergence of scientific attention to cognitive consistency motives:

> Often in the history of science, when the time is ripe, a large number of similar theories are put forward contemporaneously by researchers who have little if any direct contact with one another. So it was a decade or so ago when at least a half dozen of what we shall call "cognitive consistency" theories appeared more or less independently in the psychological litera-ture. They were proposed under different names, such as balance, congru-ity, symmetry, dissonance, but all had in common the notion that the person behaves in a way that maximizes the internal consistency of his cognitive system; and, by extension, that groups behave in ways that max-imize the internal consistency of their interpersonal relations.[47]

It is not possible in this chapter to review fully the conceptual and empirical contributions of the various different theories of cognitive consistency.[48] Instead,

I will illustrate how cognitive consistency motives can establish reality by considering the two cognitive consistency theories that have been the most influential—Fritz Heider's balance theory and, especially, Leon Festinger's cognitive dissonance theory.

Heider's Balance Theory

The classic condition in this theory[49] involves the relations among three cognitive elements, such as "me," "my friend," and "my enemy": the relation between "me" and "my friend," the relation between "me" and "my enemy," and the relation between "my friend" and "my enemy." Together, these relations form a triangle pattern. There are two types of relations between elements: *sentiment* relations and *unit* relations. Sentiment relations can be positive or negative— *like* or *dislike*, respectively. Unit relations can also be positive or negative—*associated* or *disassociated*, respectively. For example, the relation between "me" and "my friend" is positive with respect to both sentiment and unit (i.e., I like my friend and we spend time together), whereas the relation between "me" and "my enemy" is negative with respect to both sentiment and unit (i.e., I dislike my enemy and we stay away from each other).

Together, the three relations that constitute a triangle pattern can be in balance or imbalance. According to the theory, the pattern is in *balance* when the multiplication product of all three valenced relations is positive, and it is in *imbalance* when the multiplication product is negative. In my example, given that the relation between "me" and "my friend" is positive and the relation between "me" and "my enemy" is negative, the product of these first two relations is negative (i.e., multiplying the first relation ["+" sign] with the second relation ["–" sign] yields a negative product), and thus the third relation between "my friend" and "my enemy" would have to be negative in order to achieve balance overall (i.e., multiplying the negative product of the first two relations with a negative third relation ["–" sign] yields a positive product, or balance, for all three relations).

Psychologically, it makes sense to me, it is consistent, that my friend dislikes and keeps away from my enemy—I experience balance among these facts about the world. But what if I were to learn instead that "my friend" and "my enemy" have become friends? Now I experience imbalance (the multiplicative product is now negative: multiplying the first relation ["+" sign] with the second relation ["–" sign] again yields a negative product, but now multiplying this negative product and the third relation ["+" sign] yields a negative product, or imbalance, for all three relations). This pattern of facts about the world does not make sense to me; it is inconsistent that my friend would like my enemy and they would spend time together. When there is imbalance there is a problem. The world represented by this pattern of relations does not seem real to me.

In a thoughtful analysis of Heider's balance theory, Robert Abelson, who made major contributions on the interface of social and cognitive psychology, gave the following insightful comment:[50]

> Heider wrote as though with two minds on whether imbalanced triads produce intrinsic discomfort, or rather serve as a warning of potential situational trouble or a signal of possible existing trouble. The former view of imbalance as intrinsic discomfort derives from the Gestaltist view of perceptual imperatives. By analogy with the way in which the structure of the perceptual field may virtually compel a particular perceptual experience, so the structure of the cognitive field (so to speak) might virtually compel a particular cognitive result. Since certain perceptual structures, such as circles and straight lines, are good figures with imperative properties, by analogy there must be so-called conceptual good figures . . . The alternative theoretical grounding for the balance principle is motivational rather than perceptual.

I prefer the latter, motivational grounding for the balance principle. An imbalance signals that some part of our understanding of a pattern of relations does not accurately represent reality, which is a problem for truth effectiveness. Either my friend does not really like my enemy, or my enemy could become my friend if given a chance, or my friend is really my enemy or soon will become so. The imbalance gives me pause to rethink what I really know about each part of the pattern. What insight or new information could help me to establish a new reality that makes sense, a new representation that can help me experience the truth about my world? Perhaps my friend is only pretending to like my enemy for some ulterior motive, such as to function like a spy for me. Soon my friend will reveal the pretense and dissolve that relationship. Now that makes sense: my friend does not really like my enemy and that relationship will not last. Alternatively, perhaps I should rethink what my enemy is really like. The fact that my friend could like and become friends with my enemy suggests that there is something about my enemy that I must have overlooked. What is now clear is that I should give my enemy a second chance because we could become friends rather than enemies. That's surprising but it makes sense; my enemy could be my friend in the future because my enemy has likable qualities that I have overlooked.[51]

As illustrated in this example, searching for cognitive balance can establish a new reality—a new present reality and a new future reality. It is common, especially, for people to want a reality that makes sense to them, that is cognitively consistent, when it comes to interpersonal relationships. Consider, for example, when two persons you know get married and you admire one of them but have no respect for the other. You would find it difficult to understand how these two people got married (an imbalance). In such cases, people often conceive of a future reality where the pattern will become balanced: "There is no way that the marriage will last. They'll be divorced within a year." We thus transform the present reality to make it balanced because this future reality implies that the couple is actually incompatible, which creates a negative unit relation between the couple in the present.

It is important to emphasize that the motive to resolve an imbalanced reality is not a hedonic motive to reduce a painful condition. The motive is truth and not value. Indeed, Heider explicitly notes that the tension produced by imbalance can have a pleasing effect and that balance can be unpleasantly boring. Thus, it is not the hedonic nature of imbalance (vs. balance) that is critical to the experience. Rather, imbalance is the feeling that things "do not add up"[52]; that is, they are so difficult to understand as to be confusing. Importantly, even when imbalance is hedonically pleasing, feeling that things "do not add up" is an experience about reality that motivates changing an element in the imbalanced pattern in order to re-establish a reality that makes sense.

The motive to establish a reality that is balanced occurs even when people are not themselves one of the elements in the pattern. In one study,[53] for example, different participants were given different stories to read about a young couple. Each story, depending on what information was contained in the beginning, required a different ending in order for all the elements of the story to be in balance—whether the couple in the end got married or not. In one story, for instance, the woman wanted to have children but the man did not. Here "woman" has a positive sentiment relation to "having children," and "man" has a negative sentiment relation to "having children." To create balance among all of the elements (a positive multiplicative product overall), the third remaining relation between "man" and "woman" must be negative, a "–" sign. This means that the future reality of this couple, the ending of the story, must be that they did not get married (i.e., a disassociation unit).

In half of the conditions of the study, this story ended with the couple not getting married, which created balance, and in half of the conditions the story ended with the couple getting married, which created imbalance. Later, all participants were asked to recall the story they had read as accurately as they could. Many of the participants in the imbalanced story condition distorted the original information in their reproductions in order to create a new story that was now balanced. For example, some participants wrote that the man also wanted to have children. Moreover, when they were asked to indicate how confident they were that their reproduction of each part of the story was correct, they were *most confident* about the part they had *distorted* in order to produce balance. This illustrates how strong the need for a coherent reality can be.

Festinger's Cognitive Dissonance Theory

I briefly discussed this theory in Chapter 4 for the case where people resist doing something they don't want to do, such as suffering a hazing initiation to join a fraternity, but overcome their resistance and do it anyhow—with the surprising outcome that their attraction to the fraternity increases despite the pain of their hazing experience. Although this dissonance paradigm can be conceptualized in terms of value, the theory of cognitive dissonance itself was conceptualized by Festinger in terms of *truth*, in terms of establishing what's real. According to Festinger (1957), "the human organism tries to establish internal harmony, consistency, or congruity among his opinions, attitudes, knowledge, and values."[54] When people fail to do so, they experience dissonance, which gives rise to pressures to reduce that dissonance. Importantly, he states: "In short, I am proposing that dissonance, that is, the existence of nonfitting relations among cognitions, is a motivating factor in its own right."[55]

There are other well-known dissonance paradigms that clearly concern establishing truth more than having desired outcomes (value). One of the best known of these paradigms is "expectancy disconfirmation," and the classic study was described by Festinger and his colleagues in their book *When Prophecy Fails*.[56] The study was inspired by a headline they saw in the local newspaper: "Prophecy from planet Clarion call to city: flee that flood." A group of people believed that alien beings from planet Clarion would arrive on earth on a specific date and take them away on a flying saucer, thereby saving them from the great flood that would then end the world. In preparation for leaving the earth, the group members had made sacrifices, including quitting jobs and giving away money and possessions. Festinger and his colleagues believed that the date would come and go without any flying saucer, and this would create dissonance in the group members because the belief for which they had sacrificed would be disconfirmed by what actually happened. The question of the study was how the group members would resolve their dissonance in order to make sense of what happened. How would they establish what's real?

One possible way that the group members could resolve their dissonance and make sense of what happened would be to establish some new reality. This solution would involve creating new truths that are consistent with their previous beliefs and actions. In fact, the group members did make new judgments about the present and new predictions about the future that were consistent with their original belief, with the disconfirming event being treated like a bump in the road. After disconfirmation, for example, there was a sharp increase in the frequency with which group members decided that other people who telephoned them or visited their group were *actually spacemen*. They tried to get orders and messages from the "spacemen" for a future reality that would be consistent with their original beliefs. One of the leaders of the group even suggested that it was their true beliefs—*the light of truth*—that had spared their area while cataclysms *were* happening elsewhere.

Although the case described in *When Prophecy Fails* is unusual, people do often experience discomfort when their expectancies are disconfirmed, and they try to make sense of what happened by changing beliefs and adding new beliefs in order to make the whole set of beliefs consistent. This is a common phenomenon. Another related phenomenon is the dissonance that people experience after they make a decision between closely matched competing options that each have advantages and disadvantages. Whichever option is chosen, its disadvantages or costs and the advantages or benefits of the foregone option create dissonance, and people attempt to make sense of it all by changing and adding beliefs. Festinger points out that very few decisions are clear-cut, with one option all black and another all white. When a decision has been taken, "some dissonance is almost unavoidably created between the cognition of the action taken and those opinions or knowledge which tend to point to a different action."[57]

Consider the case of buying a car and choosing between a domestic model and a foreign model. There are benefits and costs of each option that concern different issues, such as "green" issues, "national loyalty" issues, service issues, and so on. Once the difficult choice is made, such as choosing the foreign model, there are costs of the chosen option, such as more expensive service, and forsaken benefits of the non-chosen option, such as supporting domestic workers. Each option creates dissonance. To establish a reality that has overall consistency, people will do cognitive work such as noting that it is not so much the expense of servicing a car that matters but the high reliability of a car that makes servicing less frequent, with this foreign model having higher reliability. They could also remind themselves that all cars, whether foreign or domestic, are really international products of many nations. Another cognitive tactic is to assign greater weight to a car attribute, such as increasing the importance of having good mileage (with the foreign model getting more miles to the gallon than the domestic model), which both increases the benefits of the chosen option ("green" and saving money) and the costs of the forgone option (anti-"green" and wasting money). This will make the chosen option even better and the forsaken option even worse—the *spreading* effect.[58] A new reality is created where things now begin to make perfect sense.[59]

If people are motivated to establish a new reality when they have dissonant cognitions, then this motivation should occur especially when the dissonant cognitions are accessible or activated rather than simply being available in long-term memory.[60] In a study that illustrates this point, another classic dissonance paradigm was used, the "forbidden-toy paradigm,"[61] and the accessibility of the relevant cognitions was manipulated.[62] As in the original study that used this paradigm, children were forbidden to play with a very attractive toy and had to resist the temptation to play with it while the experimenter was out of the room. Before leaving the room, the experimenter gave the children a threat about playing with the forbidden toy that was either quite mild (i.e., the experimenter would be a bit annoyed at them) or severe (i.e., the experimenter would be very angry and have to do something about it).

Almost all the children chose not to play with the forbidden toy while the experimenter was away. In the mild threat condition, there was dissonance between the children knowing they very much wanted to play with this great toy and knowing they were not playing with it even though, if they did, the experimenter would be only a bit annoyed. This is the standard dissonance condition. There was little, if any, dissonance in the severe threat condition because not playing with the toy was consistent with knowing that the children would be punished if they did play with it. To resolve dissonance in the mild threat condition, children derogated the toy to make it less attractive, thereby justifying the decision not to play with it.

This study added a condition that, while the experimenter was away, drew attention to both the forbidden toy and the threat associated with playing with it. Specifically, a white sticker with a black cross was placed on the side of the forbidden toy to remind the children that the experimenter would be "a little annoyed" (mild threat) or "very angry and upset" (severe threat) if they played with the forbidden toy. The presence of the sticker made the mildness or the severity of the threat highly accessible. In the mild threat dissonance condition, the study found that the proportion of children who later derogated the forbidden toy was much greater when the sticker was there than when it was not.[63] These results support the idea that it is having two incompatible cognitions accessible at the same time—"I am not playing with this attractive toy" and "The adult would be only a bit annoyed if I did play with this toy"—that creates the experience that something does not make sense. And this truth problem motivates a justification process that will establish a new reality—"I am not playing with this toy because it is not so attractive."

As reflected in these examples, the cognitive dissonance phenomena that have received the most attention are ones in which a person's action is inconsistent with one or more of that person's beliefs, which then motivates a process of justifying that action. But there is a higher-level version of dissonance as well. A society can act in ways that are inconsistent with its dominant ideology, which motivates the members of the society to justify those actions. For example, a central belief in a society's dominant ideology can be, "The economic system is fair," and yet members of the society could observe that there are wide disparities in wealth, even among members who are working full-time.

Together with his colleagues, John Jost, a major contributor to political psychology, has investigated how people justify such inconsistencies between societal ideologies and societal actions.[64] An especially powerful example is when people who are disadvantaged by a societal system justify its legitimacy, or "buy into" a system that works against their personal interests. Indeed, cognitive dissonance theory would predict that it is precisely those who are being disadvantaged by the current system who would have the strongest psychological need to justify the status quo because they are experiencing the most inconsistency from the cognitions "I am working hard to support my society" and "My society is not supporting me." In support of this prediction, there is evidence that lower-income Americans are *more* likely than higher-income Americans to support limitations on the rights of citizens to criticize the government and are *more* likely to believe that it is necessary to have large differences in salary in order to promote higher motivation and effort.[65]

In all of my discussion of people's motivation for cognitive consistency, have I not overlooked something? Don't individuals often welcome inconsistency, as when they curiously explore new things and become fascinated with puzzles to solve? Is this not a problem for the idea that people are motivated to resolve inconsistencies?[66] Yes, people can be motivated to approach inconsistencies and can find them fascinating (as Heider noted when saying that imbalance can be pleasing), but this does *not* contradict the proposal that people are seeking the truth, that they are motivated to establish reality. Curious exploration, puzzle solving, and so on are all in the service of increasing people's knowledge of the truth, of determining what is real. They enjoy working on such puzzles not for the inconsistency but for the truth success from resolving the inconsistency.

Thus far, my review of how people establish what's real has emphasized mechanisms that people generally use. However, there are also individual differences in preferred ways to establish reality. And even the same individual can use different strategies for establishing what's real in different situations. The next section considers such variability across persons and situations in the strategies that people use when seeking the truth.

USING DIFFERENT STRATEGIES OF TRUTH SEEKING TO ESTABLISH WHAT'S REAL

People spend much of their lives acquiring knowledge about the world around them, including about themselves as part of that world. Generally speaking, people generate hypotheses about some aspect of the world, such as the hypothesis that it is not raining outside, and then seek out evidence that is consistent or inconsistent with the hypothesis, such as opening a window and checking that there are no raindrops falling from the sky (consistent). But how exactly the knowledge acquisition process plays out, such as when the evidence-seeking process is terminated, depends on a person's motivational state. And this motivational state could reflect someone's personality (i.e., a chronic predisposition to be in that state), or it could be induced by the situation the person is in. In a landmark contribution to understanding motivated cognition, Arie Kruglanski has proposed a *theory of lay epistemics* that describes motivational factors that underlie the process of acquiring knowledge.[67]

Need for Closure in Establishing What's Real

According to the theory of lay epistemics, there are two separate motivational dimensions underlying knowledge acquisition: (1) need for closure versus need to avoid closure, and (2) specific closure versus nonspecific closure. When people have a motivational need for specific closure, they have a strong preference for a particular answer to their hypothesis question, such as wanting evidence that it is not raining outside because they don't want to get wet. When people have a motivational need for nonspecific closure, they simply want an answer—*any* answer—that provides a definite answer to their hypothesis question. In the rain example, evidence that there are either raindrops falling or no raindrops falling would satisfy their need for a definite answer.

People can also want to avoid closure. In the case of a need to avoid a specific closure, there is a specific answer to the hypothesis question that is not wanted, such as not wanting to see raindrops falling. Another example would be not wanting evidence that you failed an exam because of your low ability in the subject area. In the case of a need to avoid nonspecific closure, people want to keep the hypothesis question open and not have an answer; they do not look outside to see whether there are raindrops falling, or they continually check different weather reports to find some evidence consistent with the "rain" answer and other evidence consistent with the "no rain" answer.

What the rain examples demonstrate is that these different epistemic motivations influence how the knowledge acquisition process unfolds. The difference between the need for nonspecific closure and the need to avoid nonspecific closure is especially interesting. It involves a difference, respectively, between wanting *any* answer to the hypothesis question and wanting *no* answer at all. Situations can induce one or the other of these motivational states, as when time pressure to complete a judgment quickly induces a need for nonspecific closure where any answer will do or, alternatively, when apprehension that others will criticize the validity of the answer, whatever it is, induces a need to avoid nonspecific closure where no answer is best.[68]

I should note that people in a state of needing nonspecific closure, which is often referred to simply as "a need for closure," and people in a state of needing to avoid nonspecific closure, which is often referred to simply as "a need to avoid closure," can both be seeking the truth and wanting to establish what's real. Generally speaking, both can be engaging in the process of acquiring knowledge. But because their need states differ, their strategies for *how* to go about establishing what's real are different. What this highlights is that different epistemic concerns can create preferences for different ways of establishing reality. For example, there is evidence that when people have a need to avoid closure on some issue, as when they are afraid they will be held accountable later for any decision that they make, they will engage *more* in formal attributional and hypothesis-testing logic to generate multiple competing hypotheses, and then exhaustively search for confirming and disconfirming evidence for each.[69] If, instead, people have a need for closure, as when there is pressure to make a quick decision, these extensive processes will be simplified and narrowed.

Individuals with a need for closure have an urgent need to find closure on what is real, and once they have found it, once they believe they know what is real, they want to maintain it and make it permanent. These reality motives express themselves in two different strategies of truth seeking—*seizing* and *freezing*. The urgency motive produces seizing, and the permanence motive produces freezing. Studies of the "primacy effect" in impression formation provide evidence for both strategies. The primacy effect in impression formation refers to the tendency for people to base their impression of another person more on information presented early in a sequence than on information presented late.[70] Several studies have found that this primacy effect is especially strong for individuals with a need for closure.[71] These individuals seize on the first information they can use to form an impression of someone (i.e., establish a reality), and then maintain that impression (i.e., freeze on that reality) despite receiving later additional information with new implications.

In contrast, individuals with a need to avoid closure want to keep searching for the truth, remain open to alternative conclusions. An especially compelling illustration of this is evidence that the "priming effect" on impression formation is weaker for individuals with a need to avoid closure. The priming effect in impression formation, which I mentioned earlier in this chapter, refers to the tendency for people to characterize another person's behaviors, such as an ambiguous set of behaviors that could be characterized as either adventurous or reckless, in terms of whichever category has been made highly accessible to them by recent priming, such as priming "adventurous" versus "reckless" in a prior situation.[72] There is evidence that when individuals have a need to avoid closure, either as a personality predisposition or situationally induced, this priming effect on impression formation is reduced and even eliminated.[73] This is an impressive motivational effect of the need to avoid closure given the usual strength of the "priming effect." The strategy for establishing what's real for individuals with a need to avoid closure is to avoid jumping to conclusions.

Uncertainty/Certainty Orientations in Establishing What's Real

The strategic differences between individuals with a need for closure when acquiring knowledge and those with a need to avoid closure in this process result from the former seeking and accepting evidence more readily to attain the desired condition of having a clear answer while the latter keep the alternatives open to attain the desired condition of judgmental noncommitment.[74] This is one way in which individuals can vary in their truth-seeking strategies. Another individual difference in truth-seeking strategies has been discovered by Richard Sorrentino, a leading figure in the area of personality, and it has to do with uncertainty versus certainty orientations.[75]

Generally speaking, all people want ultimately to experience a sense of certainty about the world in which they live, to establish a reality that they feel confident about. I should note in this regard that individuals with a need to avoid closure do not necessarily have the goal of creating ambiguity or lack of certainty. They could have the goal of being as accurate as possible, wanting a truth-seeking process that can be fully justified to others and is beyond reproach, and these motives could produce a hypothesis-testing strategy that ends up with ambiguity as its product. The end-state of judgmental noncommitment would reflect the truth about a truly complex or ambiguous reality, and the individuals would feel confident or certain that there is no single (or simple) answer. Indeed, this is precisely the condition of many scientists when they are asked to make judgments on the frontiers of science. On these frontiers, the actual evidence is often complex and could be used to support more than one answer and, thus, an accurate answer would be judgmental noncommitment. Moreover, given the true ambiguity of the evidence, a strong commitment to any one particular answer is likely to be roundly criticized by other scientists. Being certain about the ambiguity, and thus noncommitted to any one answer, is a reasonable approach to take in such cases.

In studying people's search for a sense of certainty about the world, Sorrentino and his colleagues distinguish between *uncertainty-oriented* and *certainty-oriented* individuals. Both orientations have costs and benefits of seeking new information or sticking with old information. One way of thinking about these different trade-offs is in terms of how parents socialize their children concerning the best way to handle the uncertainty in the world that we all naturally face while we build confidence in the reality we establish:[76] (1) the best way to handle the uncertainty in the world is *to learn everything you can to master it*—learn more, explore the unknown; attain new knowledge; and/or (2) the best way is *to stick to a few guiding principles and ignore the mass of confusion*—avoid confusion, ambiguity; maintain consistency; maintain established knowledge.

The first parental lesson would socialize children to become *uncertainty-oriented* as a strategy to handle uncertainty and build confidence in what's real. The second parental lesson would socialize children to become *certainty-oriented* as a different strategy to handle uncertainty and build confidence in what's real. These socialized orientations can be considered independent in that both strategies could be used to handle uncertainty and build confidence in what's real, but often—within an individual or within a culture—one or the other strategy is emphasized.

Having an uncertainty strategy versus a certainty strategy influences how information about the world is processed and remembered. For example, in one study participants first read one of four brief descriptions of "Bob" that created an initial impression that he was either a friendly or an unfriendly person and that he was either intelligent or unintelligent.[77] After receiving one of these descriptions, all of the participants were given new, additional information about other behaviors of Bob. Some of these new behaviors were consistent with the initial impression (half of the new behaviors), some were inconsistent (a quarter of the new behaviors), and some were irrelevant (a quarter of the new behaviors)—all mixed up together. Later, the participants were asked to recall as many of these behaviors as they could.

The behaviors that were congruent with the initial impression were better recalled by the certainty-strategy participants than the uncertainty-strategy participants, whereas the incongruent behaviors were better recalled by the uncertainty-strategy participants than the certainty-strategy participants. In this way, individuals with an uncertainty strategy can establish a new reality by taking subsequent inconsistent information into account, and individuals with a certainty strategy can maintain the reality they have already established by paying attention to subsequent consistent evidence.

Regulatory Focus and Regulatory Mode Strategies in Establishing What's Real

The strategic differences relating to closure or to uncertainty/certainty orientations both directly concern motivational differences in truth seeking. There are other motivational differences that don't themselves directly relate to truth seeking but nonetheless create strategic differences in how reality is established. One example is the difference in orientation between individuals with promotion and those with prevention concerns that I have discussed previously. This difference is associated with differences in strategic preferences, with promotion individuals preferring eager goal-pursuit strategies and prevention individuals preferring vigilant goal-pursuit strategies. This difference in strategic preferences, in turn, influences truth-seeking tactics. For example, individuals with a promotion focus consider more explanations for why something happened and, more generally, generate more alternatives when hypothesis testing than do individuals with a prevention focus.

As an illustration of this regulatory focus difference, participants in one study performed an object-naming task in which they received a booklet with four pictures, each on a separate page. Each picture was of a familiar object presented at an unusual angle, making it difficult to recognize.[78] The task was to guess what the object was in each picture, and participants were told that they could list as many or as few answers as they wanted. It was not clear to participants viewing the pictures what were the right hypotheses. Generating more alternatives would increase the likelihood of finding a correct hypothesis—an information gain that would be a benefit for a promotion focus. However, generating more alternatives would also increase the likelihood of including a wrong hypothesis—an information loss that would be a cost to a prevention focus. Given this, promotion-focused participants should eagerly generate more alternatives, whereas prevention-focused participants should vigilantly avoid generating too many alternatives. This is what was found, with promotion-focused participants generating more hypotheses about what the object was in each picture than prevention-focused participants.[79]

Another difference in motivational orientation that creates strategic differences in how reality is established is the difference that *regulatory mode theory* describes between individuals with a locomotion orientation and individuals with an assessment orientation.[80] When people self-regulate, they decide what they want that they don't currently have. They then figure out what they need to do to get what they want, and then they do it. Two key functions of self-regulation are captured in this conception. First, people *assess* both the different goals to pursue and the different means to pursue them. Second, people *locomote* or "move" from their current state in pursuit of some alternative goal-pursuit state.

Assessment is the aspect of self-regulation that is concerned with critically evaluating entities or states in relation to alternatives, such as critically evaluating alternative goals or alternative means, in order to judge relative quality. Individuals with strong assessment concerns want to compare all options and search for new possibilities before making a decision, even if that process takes time and delays the decision. They relate past and future actions to critical standards. They want to choose the option that has the best attributes overall compared to the alternative options. They want to make the correct choice. They want to "get it right."

By contrast, the locomotion mode is the aspect of self-regulation that is concerned with movement from state to state. Individuals with strong locomotion concerns want to take action, to get started, even if that means not considering all the options fully. Once the task is initiated, they want to maintain it and complete it without undue disruptions or delays. They want to make steady progress. They want to "just do it."

This difference between assessment and locomotion in self-regulatory concerns produces different decision-making strategies, different preferences for how to seek information to find the truth, such as seeking information about which option is the best choice. This differential preference in truth-seeking strategies is illustrated in a study in which participants chose one book-light from a set of book-lights.[81] Either a locomotion orientation or an assessment orientation was experimentally induced at the beginning of the experiment. Afterward, different strategies for choosing among the book-lights were experimentally manipulated. Half of the locomotion participants and half of the assessment participants were given a *progressive elimination strategy*—move steadily from one book-light attribute to another and for each attribute at each step eliminate the worst alternative until only one alternative remains. The other half of the participants were given a *full evaluation strategy*—compare together all of the alternatives for all of the attributes and then choose the one with the best attributes overall. The progressive elimination strategy allows for steady movement toward the goal (a strategy that fits locomotion), but, by eliminating an alternative at each step, it increasingly reduces the number of comparisons for an attribute as the process continues (a strategy that does not fit assessment). In contrast, the full evaluation strategy allows for all possible comparisons of alternatives and attributes to be made (a strategy that fits assessment), but there is no progress in reducing options until the one final decision is made at the end (a strategy that does not fit locomotion).

The different book-lights were presented so that one was clearly the best choice, and all participants made that choice by the end of the decision process. In this way, the study examined participants' preferred strategy for establishing reality (i.e., establishing the right choice) rather than simply which option was chosen. The measure of which truth-seeking strategy fit their orientation was the money the participants offered to buy the book-light they chose (a regulatory fit effect on value creation described in Chapter 4). The study found that the participants offered much more of their own money to buy the same chosen book-light in the fit conditions where strategic preferences for how to establish reality were met (assessment/"full evaluation"; locomotion/"progressive elimination") than in the non-fit conditions where strategic preferences for how to establish reality were not met (assessment/"progressive elimination"; locomotion/"full evaluation"). Thus, when participants could establish the reality of which book-light was the best choice using the truth-seeking strategy that fit their regulatory mode concerns, they felt right about their choice and valued it more than when they had to use a truth-seeking strategy that did not fit their orientation.[82]

"Head" Versus "Heart" Strategies

Thus far I have discussed different motivational orientations and concerns that can produce different strategies for establishing what's real. The literature has also considered different procedures for establishing reality. Within social and personality psychology, a wide variety of dual-process or *dual-system* models have been proposed that distinguish between two manners of establishing reality, and, especially, the reality that relates to evaluating something:[83] (1) in a manner that relies on spontaneous feelings about and associations to something (the "heart" or "gut") versus (2) in a manner that relies on reflection and propositional reasoning (the "head").

The output evaluation in the former might be "I can't explain it, but my heart (gut) tells me that this is what I have to do," whereas in the latter it might be "I don't feel good about it, but I have concluded from the evidence that this is what I have to do." The "heart" manner of establishing reality is often described as using an unconscious, uncontrolled, and almost effortless process to produce the output (i.e., the reality), whereas the "head" manner of establishing reality uses a conscious, controlled, and effortful process.[84]

Most relevant to this chapter are models that describe the "heart," in contrast to the "head," as not assigning truth values, as not considering accuracy.[85] What this means is that, for the "heart," propositional reasoning is not used to assign truth values in a formal, logical manner. Importantly, this does not mean that an output from the "heart" system will not be treated as real, will not establish a reality. Indeed, reality is often established in this way, as is reflected in the following quote from Blaise Pascal, the brilliant French mathematician, physicist, and philosopher: "The heart has its reasons, of which reason knows nothing."

Not only is reality often established through the "heart" system, but there is even evidence that evaluations based on feelings or unconscious processing can be *more* accurate than evaluations based on reasons or conscious processing.[86] For example, in one study[87] participants evaluated two different types of posters before choosing one to take home. Those participants who were told to think about their reasons for choosing a poster ended up choosing a different type of poster than those without these instructions. Three weeks later, those partici-pants in the "reasons" (or "head") condition were *less* satisfied with their decision than the other participants.

This study demonstrates how *not* thinking of reasons can sometimes yield *greater* long-term satisfaction with one's choice. This is not to say, however, that thinking of reasons is always costly: each way of establishing reality can have both costs and benefits under different conditions. Such trade-offs are recog-nized in a new theory of self-regulation that provides an especially compelling version of the "heart" versus "head" distinction. With his students and col-leagues, Fritz Strack, a major contributor to understanding the interrelations between cognition and affect, has developed a theory that distinguishes between the experiential or impulsive determinants of judgments and decisions (related to associative processing) versus the informational or reflective determinants (related to propositional processing).[88]

Importantly, Strack proposes that judgments and decisions are influenced by both systems functioning in parallel rather than the systems being mutually exclusive (with one or the other dominating at any point). Consider, for exam-ple, Strack's compelling example of the Muller-Lyer illusion.[89] In this perceptual illusion, arrowheads are added to the ends of two lines. For Line A, the arrow-heads spread inward at both ends (like the sharp head of a real arrow). For Line B, the arrowheads spread outwards at both ends (like the feathered end of a real arrow). Even though Line A is actually slightly longer than Line B, Line B appears to be longer than Line A. It is a powerful illusion, so powerful that even after people measure each line with a ruler, and discover that Line A is actually longer than Line B, Line B still appears longer than Line A. When explicitly asked after measuring the lines which line is longer, people will answer from the reflective system that Line A *is* longer than Line B, but, at the same time, they will report from the experiential system that Line B *looks* longer than Line A. This is a striking example of the reflective and experiential systems of judgment giving opposite answers in parallel.

Earlier I discussed what people do when they experience cognitive disso-nance from incompatible cognitions, such as "I freely chose to do X; I knew that choosing X would have negative consequences." Specifically, people try to jus-tify or make sense of what they did by finding reasons for it, and this uses the reflection system. Given this, the change in attitude toward X that is found in dissonance studies (i.e., a more positive attitude toward X) should involve a change in the reflection system. This would mean that a propositional measure of attitude in which people are asked to make a conscious, explicit judgment about X should show the more positive attitude toward X. This would be like asking people to make an explicit judgment about which line *is* longer in the Muller-Lyer illusion. But what if what was measured instead was the attitude toward X according to the experiential system? Because that system was *not* used in the dissonance justification process, there need not be any attitude change within *that* system. Indeed, there is evidence that dissonance resolution can cause attitude change on an explicit, propositional measure while *at the same time* showing no attitude change on an unconscious, associationistic measure.[90] Not only does this demonstrate the importance of distinguishing between the experiential and reflective systems, but it also sheds light on the justification mechanism of dissonance resolution by highlighting its reflective, propositional nature.

A final comment on "heart" versus "head." Because these are two manners of establishing reality, they can provide different answers to what's real, and this can produce conflicts within a person. An example of this occurred in my life one morning when I was responsible for bringing my daughter Kayla to her school bus stop. She was only 5 years old at the time. All morning I kept pestering her to get ready to leave for the bus. Over and over I said, "Kayla, we're going to be late!" After we finally left home and were walking up the hill toward the bus stop, Kayla told me that she wasn't going to give me a goodbye kiss that day. When I asked her why, she expressed aloud an internal dialogue that was going on: "My heart tells me that I am so angry at Daddy that I don't want to kiss him goodbye today. But my head tells me that I do want to kiss him goodbye because, if I don't, I will feel bad later . . . But my heart tells me, I don't care, I'm angry . . . But my head says, Daddy was trying to get me to school on time . . ." And so it went all the way up the long hill, with me just an observer to her heart–head battle. Happily for me, at the top of the hill Kayla turned to me and said, "My head won!," and gave me a goodbye kiss.

Different Strategies for Establishing What's Real About Ourselves

When people entertain an hypothesis or question about what type of person they are, such as "Am I a friendly person?," how do they go about testing the hypothesis? Do they seek a conclusion that enhances or defends a positive view of themselves (self-enhancement)? Do they seek a conclusion that supports what they already believe about themselves (self-verification)? Do they seek a conclusion that would motivate changing themselves in a positive direction (self-improvement)? Or do they simply seek whichever conclusion is best supported by the available evidence (diagnostic accuracy)?

What the literature shows is that each of these strategies that people use for establishing what's real about themselves can occur depending on different conditions.[91] The strategy that has been emphasized the most, and is treated as the default strategy, is the one for self-enhancement. Indeed, in the literature, it is considered surprising when people use a strategy other than self-enhancement.

I believe that this historical bias in our literature reflects most psychologists' strong acceptance of the hedonic principle as the dominant motivational principle—the underlying assumption that people approach pleasure and avoid pain by enhancing or defending a positive view of ourselves. What is clear, however, is that self-enhancement is *not* the only way that people establish what's real about themselves. This fact suggests not only that we are motivated by more than pleasure and pain but also that we are motivated by ways of being effective other than just having desired results (value). The strategy of diagnostic accuracy and the strategy of self-verification, for example, are more about establishing what's real (truth) than about having desired results.

I begin with the work of Trope, who, in addition to his work on attributional processes, has been a leading contributor to understanding the cognitive mechanisms that underlie judgment and decision making. He has demonstrated that accuracy motivation, like wanting to predict correctly what will happen in the future, can compete with or even trump hedonic motivation, such that people use the strategy of *diagnostic accuracy* rather than that of self-enhancement. Trope emphasizes that the outcomes of people processing information about themselves must be distinguished from what motivated those outcomes. Yes, there are biases and errors in how people process information about themselves; and, yes, those biases and errors can support positive self-views. However, this does not necessarily mean that those biases and errors are strategies (conscious or unconscious) in the service of a motivation to enhance or defend positive self-views.

People's motivation can be to attain a veridical assessment of themselves—a positive or negative self-assessment—but they use information-processing tactics in their truth-seeking process that end up producing non-veridical, positive-self conclusions.[92] For example, once a hypothesis or question like "Am I a friendly person?" is considered, it primes stored episodic information that matches the construct "friendly." This "friendly"-matching information then becomes accessible, and it provides evidence consistent with drawing a "friendly" conclusion.[93] People's motivation can be to have a correct or veridical self-belief, but the principles of knowledge activation create a processing bias that yields a biased positive conclusion about themselves.[94]

Given such biases produced by knowledge activation principles themselves, it is important to use other methods to test whether people prefer the strategy of diagnostic accuracy or the strategy of self-enhancement. As Trope points out, it is important to examine not only people's cognitive processing but also their actions in the environment. Do they act in a self-enhancing manner or in a manner to attain veridical assessment of their competencies? Do they choose tasks, expend effort on a chosen task, persist or not in the face of difficulty, in order to confirm their unrealistically high self-regard or in order to attain a realistic assessment of their strengths and weaknesses?

In one study that addresses this question,[95] Trope investigated participants' choice between achievement tasks that varied in how diagnostic they were for success versus failure. If participants have a self-enhancement motivation, then they would prefer a task where success is diagnostic of possessing a desirable ability and where failure is *not* diagnostic of lacking that ability. That is, this is a good task for attaining a positive self-view because they win if they happen to succeed on the task and don't lose if they happen to fail. If, on the other hand, participants have a veridical self-assessment motivation, then they would prefer a task where *both* success and failure are diagnostic—the more diagnosticity the better. The study found that the participants preferred a task that was diagnostic for *both* success and failure. This is not to say that people would never sacrifice veridical self-assessment for the sake of self-enhancement. What these results do show is that veridical self-assessment can trump self-enhancement.

As a second case of when the motivation to experience accuracy or predictability can compete with hedonic motivation, let us now consider the work of Bill Swann, a leading expert in the field of self and identity. Swann proposed that people are motivated to confirm their self-views in order to support their general perception that the world is predictable and their knowledge of it is accurate.[96] He and his colleagues have provided evidence that people are motivated to verify their beliefs about themselves even when those beliefs concern undesirable personal attributes.[97] In one study,[98] for example, participants were selected who held self-views either that their sociability and social competence were both high (favorable self-view) or that they were both low (unfavorable self-view). After arriving at the study, each of these *target* participants filled out personality questionnaires that were then ostensibly given to other "participants" who evaluated the target participant. After a suitable delay, each target participant received feedback from the other "participants." One of the other "participants" rated the target participant as being high on both sociability and social competence and the other "participant" rated the target as being low on both.

The target participant was then given the opportunity to interact with one of these other "participants." This decision was made either in a hurry with little time for self-reflection or in a leisurely way with enough time for self-reflection. All target participants chose the "participant" with a favorable impression of them when there was little time for self-reflection—consistent with their using a self-enhancement strategy. But when there was time for self-reflection, those target participants with unfavorable self-views were much more likely than target participants with favorable self-views to avoid the "participant" who had a favorable view of them—consistent with their using a self-verification strategy rather than a self-enhancement strategy. Indeed, from a hedonic motivation perspective, target participants with an unfavorable self-view should be especially motivated to interact with someone who could help support a *new, more favorable* view of themselves. And yet, this is *not* what happened when there was time for self-reflection.

There are different mechanisms that could contribute to people using a self-verification strategy. One potential contributor could be that self-views are supported by a person's significant others. This includes negative self-views. A person could have acquired a negative self-view from a significant other to begin with, such as a parent who thought a child had certain limitations or weaknesses that the child should, realistically, know about. In such cases, the child's negative self-view would be a shared reality with the parent, and it would be defended because of its function in maintaining that significant relationship.[99] Similarly, in his discussion of people's search for perceived accuracy,[100] Swann discusses how individuals construct accuracy by negotiating their identities with other people, which would be a co-constructed shared reality. The role of such shared reality in establishing what's real is considered next.

ESTABLISHING REALITY FROM SOCIAL REALITY AND SHARED REALITY

In his *social comparison theory*, Leon Festinger discussed how physical reality can often be ambiguous and difficult to grasp, and when it is, people initiate social comparison processes in which they depend on others' judgments to construct a *social reality*.[101] Festinger also proposed that physical reality takes precedence over social reality. As we shall see, however, that is not always the case. The motivation to establish a shared reality with others can trump physical reality. This is illustrated in a classic study by Asch,[102] which shows that individuals can be motivated to treat something as real, to accept something as the truth, even though the physical evidence contradicts their decision.

In this study, college students were seated together in a classroom in groups of seven to nine individuals. Two white cardboards were placed on the blackboard in front of them. On the left cardboard was a single vertical black line that functioned as the standard. On the right cardboard were three vertical black lines that differed in length, numbered 1, 2, and 3. One of these lines was the same length as the standard line on the left cardboard. The students were told to select the line from the right cardboard that was the same length as the standard line on the left cardboard. They were to state their judgment by naming the number of the line. The students were then asked to announce their judgment in turn, beginning with the student seated at one end of the table.

They performed this task 12 times. Notably, they were explicitly instructed: "Please be as accurate as possible."

The key property of the experiment was that only one student in each group was an actual naïve participant. All the other students in each group were cooperating with the experimenter, called "confederates," and they gave the same predetermined judgment on each trial. The naïve participants were acquaintances of the confederates and were recruited by them for the study. The naïve participants arrived for the study with their confederate acquaintances and joined the other group members waiting to be seated. Importantly, the confederates took their seats so that the naïve participant was seated toward one end of the table (usually one seat from the end) and the confederate who began the series of judgments was seated at the other end of the table. This ensured that the confederates would announce their unanimous judgment before the naïve participant's turn. On the first two trials, and on three other trials, their unanimous judgment was the correct answer. On the remaining seven trials (the conflict trials) they unanimously gave an incorrect answer. Asch described this situation as follows: "Two opposing forces acted upon the single subject: one from a clearly perceived relation and another from a compact majority."[103] "A person is in a situation in which he makes judgments about relatively simple matters of fact. At the same time he is with a group in which others, equal to himself, share in the task of making the same discriminations."[104]

What happened? The naïve participants typically appeared perplexed and bewildered when those trials began in which the other group members announced unanimous, incorrect judgments; the naïve participants often fidgeted in their seats and changed their head position to look at the lines from different angles. On the conflict trials, about 40% of the naïve participants always made judgments that corresponded to the clearly perceived relation and not the unanimous, incorrect judgment made by the other group members. However, most naïve participants made judgments agreeing with the group's incorrect judgment on some of the conflict trials, and some made judgments agreeing with the group's incorrect judgment on every conflict trial.

Overall, then, most naïve participants in this study, at least some of the time, announced judgments that agreed with the group's unanimous judgment rather than the clearly perceived reality. The psychological literature usually describes this phenomenon in a manner that is critical of those who went along with the group's judgment on conflict trials, typically characterizing them as "conformists" with "weak character." Asch, however, interpreted what happened quite differently.[105] He described the naïve participants as searching for the truth, as trying to make sense of the situation. As mentioned early in this chapter, people learn that their perceptions and beliefs can be false and that the perceptions and beliefs of others can be more accurate than theirs. To reiterate Asch's comment, it is the social check provided by our neighbors that helps us to see a looming shape as just the branch of a tree rather than as a monster.

In Asch's study, many naïve participants began to doubt their perceptions, with thoughts like, "I doubt that so many people could be wrong and I alone right." Some became persuaded that the "voice of the group is right," that it *was* the truth. They wanted their judgment to be the truth, and thus they chose to agree with the unanimous group judgment. It was not about weakness of character, but about truth and respect for the apparently honest judgments of others who were providing evidence about the truth. After all, do we want to conclude that 4-year-old children have *weakness of character* when they finally learn to relax at bedtime because they now understand that their parents are right—the monster they believe is in their room is *not* real? As Asch put it, without the social check they would still be scared by the monster.

Asch also describes another motive of the naïve participants for treating the unanimous judgment of the group as real: longing to be in agreement with the group. This motive has more to do with maintaining social bonds by sharing the same reality as other members of the group. Although not just seeking the truth, this motive is also not properly characterized as "weak character." It is another motivation behind people treating something as real even when it is not.[106]

A compelling illustration of this shared reality motive is provided in an early study—and one of my favorite social psychology studies—by another pioneer of experimental social psychology, Muzafer Sherif.[107] Sherif had participants in a completely dark room estimate the movement of a point of light that, although actually stationary, perceptually appeared to move in different directions and amounts to different participants (the *autokinetic effect*). When individuals were brought together in a group and each gave independent estimates of the direction and amount of the light's movement, their initial judgments were typically quite disparate. However, Sherif found that over several trials the group members slowly abandoned their initially disparate judgments and converged on a mutually shared estimate of the light's direction and amount of movement—a *social norm* for that group regarding the light's movement. And the social norm was not given by the stationary light because different groups converged on different mutually shared estimates—different social norms for the light's movement. This is like different language communities converging on different social norms for what to call the furry animal that barks and fetches things—*dog* or *chien*, for example. The judgment of what name to assign the animal is not given in that animal's properties.

Subsequent research found that the arbitrary social norm created by a group was maintained even when the original members of a group were replaced, one at a time, by new participants who were themselves later steadily replaced—ultimately over several generations of groups who maintained the social norm for the group.[108] Moreover, Sherif also found that the social norm that was created in each group continued to determine the individual judgments of the group members even when they made their judgments of the light away from the group, *alone by themselves*. This is again like language norms for what to call something. In sum, the participants in each group constructed a shared reality about the direction and amount of the light's movement that did not reflect the reality that the light was stationary but that, nonetheless, was treated as real by new generations of group members and by individual group members when alone by themselves. This is a striking example of how a social reality, a shared reality, can trump people's initial perceptual experience of a physical reality.

Effects of Descriptive and Prescriptive Norms on Establishing What's Real

Sherif's study on group construction of a social norm was the first experimental examination of this critical process. But the importance of social norms to establishing what's real (and to manage what happens) had been recognized previously by eminent sociologists such as Emile Durkheim and Max Weber.[109] In addition, since Sherif's pioneering work in the 1930s, the concept of social norm has been developed further by both sociologists and social psychologists.[110] The role of social norms in establishing what's real has been highlighted recently in a couple of ways.

An important type of social norm are cultural rules about how group members *should* behave in a particular domain. Whereas the social norms that were constructed in Sherif's study were *descriptive* of what *is* real about the world (i.e., a group consensus about how the light was actually moving), social rules about how people ought to behave are prescriptive or *injunctive* social norms about what reality *should* be established.[111] Injunctive social norms can differ across cultures for a particular domain. There are stronger norms in China than in the United States, for example, that interpersonal animosity should be minimized when resolving a conflict, and that rewards should be allocated among group members according to equality (vs. equity). If norms establish what's real, then their impact should be greater for individuals who are especially motivated to establish what's real. Individuals with a high need for closure are strongly motivated in this way, and thus, they should be most likely to follow the social norms of their surrounding culture. This is precisely what recent research has found regarding the difference between China and the United States in terms of conflict resolution and reward allocation.[112]

An injunctive social norm is a prescription about how people *should* behave that results in approval when followed and disapproval when not followed.

Injunctive norms establish which behaviors are socially right in which situations for which people (as a function of their social role, identity, status, or position). In contrast, a descriptive norm provides information about how other people *are* behaving in some life domain (i.e., what people typically do in a particular situation). Robert Cialdini, a preeminent figure in the area of social influence and persuasion,[113] has noted that sociologists and social psychologists have paid much more attention to the influence of injunctive norms on social behavior than the influence of descriptive norms. And overlooking the power of descriptive norms can be problematic. Indeed, he has shown how a persuasive message can backfire when it uses injunctive norms to influence message recipients without recognizing that a descriptive norm is also being communicated.[114]

Cialdini, for example, describes how public service messages naturally try to mobilize action against a problem by showing how serious the problem has become, such as showing how common it has become for people to litter in public spaces. A famous example of such a message is the "Iron Eyes Cody" television spot in which an American Indian warrior and elder, while paddling his canoe down a river, sees garbage littering the highways and witnesses a car passenger throwing garbage out the window that splatters on the roadside. The message ends with a tear running down his cheek. Cialdini notes that this public service spot not only includes an injunctive norm message that "people should not litter," which is the intended message, but it unintentionally also includes a descriptive norm message that "many people litter." Both kinds of norms are motivating. The viewers want to do what is approved (injunctive norm), but they also want to do what other people do (descriptive norm). These messages establish two different kinds of reality that create opposing forces on behavior, which undermines the effectiveness of the message.

What is needed instead are messages in which the realities established by the injunctive and descriptive norms work in the *same* direction. For example, in one study[115] participants found a handbill on their car windshield that they could or could not drop into the environment around them. The environment around them was either clean or already littered. In addition, the participants either did or did not see someone (a confederate of the experimenter) drop trash into the clean or littered environment. The condition of seeing someone drop trash into an already littered environment replicates the descriptive norm communicated in the "Iron Eyes Cody" television spot. Contrary to the goal of that television spot, the amount of littering that occurred in this condition was the *highest* of all four conditions. That is, the descriptive norm, "people litter here," was the reality that people acted on.

Importantly, the least amount of littering occurred in the condition where participants saw someone litter in a clean environment. The message in this condition is that "most people do *not* litter here" (because it was clean before). Especially because just one person litters, it draws attention to the fact that, prior to what this person just did, other people did not litter; that is, it draws attention to the descriptive norm of *not* littering. In addition, watching some-one litter a clean environment is likely to produce a negative evaluation of that person—that he or she *should not* have done that—which brings the injunctive and descriptive norms into alignment.

This last study highlights something that probably also occurred in Sherif's studies—establishing what is real from a descriptive norm creates pressure for a corresponding injunctive norm that people *should* treat as real. If this is a place where people do not litter (descriptive norm), then this is a place where I and others should not litter (injunctive norm). If the group agrees that this light is moving in a specific way (descriptive norm), then I *should* say that this light is moving in that way (injunctive norm). If something is established as real, then it should be treated as real. Social norms, then, help to define reality, to establish what's real, and this defined reality affects people's judgments and decisions. Indeed, for several decades the field of symbolic interactionism has been directed by the following primary rule: "If men define situations as real, they are real in their consequences."[116]

The Role of Epistemic Authority in Establishing What's Real: The Milgram Study

Social norms are influential because social agreement establishes what's real. The more other people there are who agree with one another, the more we will rely on this consensus as a source of establishing what's real. When we rely on a source to establish what's real, that source has *epistemic authority*.[117] Social norms are a major source of epistemic authority, but social status and expertise are other sources as well.[118]

A striking illustration of the influential power of social status, expertise, and trustworthiness—all working together—was provided by Stanley Milgram in his highly publicized research on what he called "obedience to authority."[119] Participants volunteered to help out in what they believed was research directed by a professor at Yale University on ways to improve teaching and learning through the use of punishment. Supposedly on the basis of random assign-ment, the participants were assigned the role of "teacher." In this role, they tested the effects of punishment on learning by delivering electric shocks to someone in the role of "learner" whenever that "learner" made a mistake on the task. Unbeknownst to the participant "teacher," the "learner" was actually a confederate of the experimenter and received no electric shock.

The shock intensity received by the learner supposedly increased as more and more mistakes were made during the learning period. At some point the shock intensity rose to a clearly painful level, and the learner loudly complained and asked for the experiment to end. The teacher was told by the experimenter that it was necessary for the experiment to continue for the sake of the research, and that although the shocks may be painful, they caused no permanent tissue damage. Despite the obvious painful outcries and protests of the learner, many participants continued in their role of teacher and delivered what they believed to be increasingly painful shocks.

Milgram's findings are typically characterized as reflecting something negative about the character of those teacher participants who continued to deliver painful shocks to the learner—characterizations such as "weak" and "compliant," or worse, such as "immoral," with parallels made to the Nazi SS and Gestapo units. Milgram himself characterized them as "obedient," which means *submissive* to the command of authority, *willing to obey*. Its close associated meanings are *docile* and *tractable*, which mean easily managed or controlled. Milgram said that they "were seen to knuckle under to the demands of authority."[120]

I believe that to characterize these participants as "weak" (or worse) is unjust to the participants and incorrect as an explanation for their behavior. The confederate learner in this research did not actually suffer, but many of the participant teachers *did* actually suffer. Many displayed signs of extreme stress. They suffered from thinking that they were hurting the learners and would clearly have preferred that the experimenter end the study. I believe that the behavior of the participant teachers was *not* a reflection of a trait of "obedience" but, instead, reflected the psychological situation—*the definition of reality*—that had been created for them by the experimenter prior to the study and that continued to be emphasized throughout the study itself. Let me now describe how this definition of reality was constructed.

The individuals who later became the participant teachers in the study were male adults from the New Haven, Connecticut, community, where Yale University is located. These individuals responded to a local newspaper "Public Announcement" declaring that people were needed "to help us complete a scientific study of memory and learning. The study is being done at Yale University." The announcement explicitly said that factory workers, clerks, construction workers, city employees, and so on were wanted and that college students could not be used. If they met the qualifications, respondents were asked to mail a coupon to Professor Stanley Milgram, Department of Psychology, Yale University, affirming their desire "to take part in this study of memory and learning."

This method of recruitment established the reality of respondents committing themselves to *wanting to help out* in an important and prestigious scientific study supervised by a professor of psychology that could increase understanding of how people learn. The other participants would be people like themselves from the community. When they arrived for the study they were introduced to a 47-year-old man who ostensibly was another volunteer like them but was actually a confederate working with the experimenter. The experimenter himself was formally dressed in a gray lab technician's coat to look like a professional research scientist. He had a serious and somewhat stern demeanor. Titles, clothes, and trappings—*powerful symbols of high status and expertise.*[121] The participants were shown a book on the teaching–learning process and were given the following information:[122]

> But actually, we know very little about the effect of punishment on learning, because almost no truly scientific studies have been made of it in human beings. For instance, we don't know how much punishment is best for learning.

Overall, then, everything was set up and staged, from the announcement to the experimental setting itself, to impress participants with the high social status and expertise of the experimenter and the social significance of the research itself—*the need to help out in this important scientific study on learning.* The experimenter was someone with high epistemic authority. Participants had embraced the role of "helper" when they first responded to the announcement, and their commitment to that role would only increase after arriving for the experiment.

Importantly, the participants believed that by random assignment they could have been either the teacher or the learner in the study (although, in fact, each participant always became the teacher and the confederate always became the learner). They were willing to take either position in order to fulfill their "helper" role, and they understood that this was true for the other volunteer as well. They were both "helpers" in the study. Thus, when the participants began to suffer from believing that their fellow "helper," the learner, was suffering, they would naturally want the study to end. But the experimenter, with his high epistemic authority, re-established the social reality that the participants and their fellow "helper" needed to continue with the study or the benefits of the scientific research on learning would be lost. The participants were willing to continue suffering, along with the other "helper," in order to fulfill their role as "helper"—a role that they and their fellow "helper" had freely chosen when replying to the announcement.

According to Milgram, the teacher participants no longer perceived themselves as being responsible for what happened to the "learner." They had *cast off responsibility* and become "thoughtless agents of action."[123] I disagree totally with this characterization. It is clear from how much the participants suffered that they felt responsibility for what was happening. And, most important, they took responsibility for fulfilling the role of "helper" in this important scientific study on learning. Indeed, it was precisely the conflict between their *taking responsibility* for this role and their *feeling responsible* for the pain inflicted on the other "helper" that made them suffer so much. It was their high sense of responsibility that made the participants suffer. To characterize these participants as being "thoughtless," as casting off their responsibility in docile obedience to authority, as Milgram did, is both inaccurate and insulting.

What this research demonstrates, then, is that epistemic authority from high status and expertise can establish what's real for others. Milgram's findings are not about people wanting to quit the study but being too weak to do so when an authority commands obedience. Rather, his findings are about people wanting to be helpful, being told by an epistemic authority that to be helpful means to continue with the important scientific research, and their being willing to do so despite both them and the other "helper" having to suffer. Hannah Arendt, the famous political philosopher, referred to the phenomenon of people acting from commonplace motives when they do terrible things, such as the atrocities of Eichmann in Nazi Germany, as the "banality of evil."[124] The banality can be commonplace submissiveness or poor judgment, as Milgram and Arendt suggest. But I believe that the "teacher" participants had admirable motives rather than negative traits. I believe that they wanted to be helpful and were willing to suffer for it.[125]

If I am correct in this belief, it makes Milgram's findings even *more* troubling for *all of us*. Even when our motives are *admirable*, our actions can be *mistaken* and *harmful*. I think about the epistemic authority of parents, teachers, police and military officers, politicians, and business executives. They may try to fulfill their role responsibly, but in embracing their responsibility, rather than casting it off, they can behave in ways that are harmful. They can make mistakes and the resulting suffering can be significant. It is this effect of epistemic authority from high status and expertise that most concerns me: when it establishes a reality for well-intentioned roles that plays out in actions that hurt others. It is a commonplace effect that we cannot afford to ignore by explaining negative actions in terms of negative traits. Just because we know that our intentions are positive, we cannot afford to ignore the possibility that we could be hurting others by taking for granted the social reality that epistemic authorities have established. The usual interpretation of Milgram's findings allows the conclusion that all will be well if people only embrace their responsibilities to others. Wouldn't that be nice! Instead, what we need to recognize is that even when we embrace our responsibilities to others and have only positive intentions, we can still inflict pain if we fail to establish what's real beyond what epistemic authorities define for us.

The powerful influence that epistemic authority from high status and expertise can have on people begins early. From the perspective of young children, their parents (or other caretakers) have enormous epistemic authority from their status and expertise. As children develop and enter other social settings, they treat additional significant others as epistemic authorities in certain knowledge domains, such as friends, coaches, and teachers. They also gradually treat themselves as an epistemic authority, such as acquiring knowledge about their own preferences, strengths, and weaknesses.[126]

There are cultural and individual differences in how much epistemic authority is assigned to self or to different significant others. In addition, how much is assigned can be more or less adaptive. Some people may assign too much epistemic authority to their parents and remain overly dependent on them. Other people, such as those with avoidant attachment, assign themselves too much epistemic authority—"compulsive self reliance."[127] Research on adult attachment has found that individuals with secure attachment generally trust other people more than do individuals with anxious and avoidant attachment,[128] and thus they endow them with more epistemic authority. Usually it is the benefits of secure attachment that are emphasized in the literature. But there are potential costs as well if endowing others with more epistemic authority means that we fail to establish what's real beyond what they define for us.

The Role of Shared Reality in Establishing What's Real: Social Communication

What is striking about Sherif's findings is that a norm about what's real can be socially constructed *without a basis in physical reality*, and this norm will still have real consequences—*it will be treated as real*. Upon reflection, however, we should not be surprised that people are motivated to treat as real something that is a social or shared reality rather than a fact of nature. The willingness to do so underlies a necessary condition of human culture—using language to communicate with others about our inner states.

Communication through language plays a critical role in human societies. It requires, among other things, that members of a linguistic community agree on what words to use to name different things. As I mentioned earlier, one linguistic community agrees to assign the name *dog* to the furry animal that barks and fetches things, whereas another linguistic community agrees to call it *chien*. There is no reality that dictates which of these sounds is the right name for this animal. But each linguistic community agrees to use a particular name—a social norm that is maintained across generations and is used by individual members when they are alone by themselves. It is also notable that the members of each linguistic community experience the sounds that they use as being somehow better at representing the animal, as reflecting reality better. To many English speakers, for example, *dog* seems to suit the characteristics of the animal, whereas *chien* seems inappropriate if not strange.[129]

Linguistic communities, then, are motivated to create a shared reality about the names of different things. But the motive to create a shared reality about things in the world goes beyond social norms about the names of things. The motive to share reality is one of the most important goals of communication more generally.[130] And when people have this goal, they are motivated to describe something in a manner that matches their audience's beliefs or attitudes about it.

In an early study on this phenomenon, mentioned earlier in this chapter,[131] college student participants, who were in the role of communicators, were asked to describe a target person, Donald, based on a short essay that described his behaviors. The behaviors described in the essay were evaluatively ambiguous. That is, they could be labeled either positively or negatively, such as in one case being labeled either as "stubborn" or as "persistent" or in another case being labeled either as "adventurous" or as "reckless." For instance, the stubborn/persistent description was as follows: "Once Donald makes up his mind to do something it is as good as done, no matter how long it might take or how difficult the going might be. Only rarely does he change his mind even when it might well be better if he did."

The participants were given a referential communication task. They were told to describe the target person (without mentioning his name) to an audience who knew him and would try, based on the participants' message, to identify him from among a set of other possible persons. After being told in an offhand manner that their audience either liked or disliked the target, the participants produced their message for their audience. What this and dozens of other studies found is that communicators tune their message to suit the attitude of their audience, a phenomenon called "audience tuning." That is, communicators produce evaluatively positive messages when they believe that their audience likes the target person, and they produce evaluatively negative messages for an audience who dislikes the target. These messages are *not* accurate descriptions of the information the communicators were given about the target. An accurate description would have retained the ambiguous tone of the information. Instead, the information is distorted, biased in an evaluative direction that matches the audience's attitude toward the target. The communicators create *a new truth* about the target that allows them to share reality with their audience.

But this is not all that happened in this and other studies. Later, the participants were asked to recall as accurately as they could (i.e., word for word) the information about Donald's behaviors that was contained in the essay they had received. The study found that the evaluative tone of the communicators' own memory for the original essay information matched the evaluative tone of their previous message. That is, their recall reproductions were distorted to be more positive when they had tuned their message positively toward their audience and were distorted to be more negative when they had tuned their message negatively. And this memory bias was even greater when the recall took place weeks after message production than when it took place in the same session as the message production. In sum, participants ended up believing and remembering what they *said* rather than what they originally learned about the target, a phenomenon called the "Saying-is-Believing" effect.[132]

Thus, communicating with a shared reality goal can lead to treating the audience-tuned message as the truth about that topic—treating it as real—even though the message biases the actual facts about that topic. Before discussing further the implications of this conclusion, I need to address a potential problem with it. Is it not possible that the effect of the message tuning on memory was due to the stored representation of the message influencing the reconstructive memory process? If so, this would involve a cognitive mechanism of information reconstruction and inference rather than the motivational mechanism of shared reality. Such a cognitive mechanism would produce the "Saying-is-Believing" effect when the communication goal is something other than a shared reality goal, as long as the message tuning to the audience's attitude remains just as strong.

This is not the case, however. When the communication goal, for example, is entertainment (e.g., it would be fun to exaggerate or caricaturize the target to suit the audience's attitude) or instrumental (e.g., tune toward the audience in order to make the audience like and later reward the communicator), the amount of message tuning to the audience's attitude is just as strong but the "Saying-is-Believing" effect *disappears*.[133] What matters is whether the motive for the message tuning is to establish what's real, to establish the truth. Indeed, the instructions to "exaggerate" in the entertainment goal condition clearly indicate that the target person description in the message should *not* be treated as real, and the motive in the instrumental goal condition is clearly about value—getting the reward—rather than about truth. Thus, both of these goal conditions are explicitly *not* about the truth.

It is also assumed that the "Saying-is-Believing" effect occurs not simply because a message is created that happens to agree with the audience's attitude, but because people want to share reality with that particular audience. If this is the case, then the "Saying-is-Believing" effect should depend on who the audience is. After all, people do not regard just anyone to be an appropriate partner with whom to share reality. Research on both social comparison processes and group-anchored knowledge indicates that people regard others as more appropriate partners with whom to share reality when they perceive them as being similar to them or trustworthy than when they lack such qualities.[134] An audience that is or is not in the communicator's in-group would be particularly important in this regard. In fact, there is clear evidence that the audience's group membership does matter. When the audience belonged to the communicators' in-group, as in the original studies, then the "Saying-is-Believing" effect was found. But when the audience belonged to an out-group, as when communicators were German students and their audience was German-speaking but Turkish, the audience tuning still occurred but the "Saying-is-Believing" effect disappeared.[135]

Treating audience-tuned messages as saying something real about the world around us, even when it is distorted to suit the audience, has important implications for the construction of cultural knowledge. Because communicating to others with a shared reality goal is ubiquitous in human interactions, it is potentially a very important mechanism underlying the construction of culturally shared memories and evaluations of the world around us—a basic mechanism for constructing social, cultural, and political beliefs.[136] Rather than remembering topic information as originally given, communicators will remember the information as represented in their messages that were tuned to take the viewpoint of their audience into account. Such social tuning toward audiences, then, can create within a community a shared but biased perspective on the world. And because this process occurs not only for individuals as the topic of the message but also for groups as the topic of the message,[137] it could also contribute to the development of community-shared stereotypical beliefs about other groups.

The Nature of Human's Strong Motivation to Share Reality

The motive to share reality is a powerful force on all of us to accept what others believe and to persuade others to accept our beliefs. I was struck by the power of this motive when my very young daughter Kayla was with her friend Joey and they were arguing over what was the right name for a wooden toy that was near the front door. Kayla called it a "porcupine" and Joey called it a "skunk." They argued back and forth. As the argument continued, the tone of the conversation became more and more desperate, with heartfelt entreaties to agree on the name. Finally Kayla said to Joey, "Agree with me, *please*." Of course, she could have just agreed with Joey to establish a shared reality, but this was an object in her own home and she needed him to verify her past belief about it.

Why is the motive to establish a shared truth, a shared reality, so powerful? When we developed shared reality theory, Curtis Hardin and I concluded that it is nothing less than the motive to transform a subjective experience of uncertain reality into an experience of *objective reality*.[138] Indeed, the words "subjective" and "objective" reflect a basic distinction between two kinds of knowledge that reflects the critical role of shared reality.[139] "Subjective" refers to solipsistic experiences that are known only to the mind of an individual. In contrast, "objective" refers to "things" or "realities" that are known to exist independently of an individual and, importantly, can also be observed by other individuals. Within science, something is not considered to be objective until it can be verified by other scientists, once again highlighting the critical role of something being socially shared to be considered real.

Curtis and I adopted a statistical metaphor to describe how shared reality contributes to experiencing something as real. When our experience is shared by others, it functions to establish *reliability*, to ensure that our experience is not random or capricious. As mentioned earlier, when an independent other shares our experience it becomes objective knowledge and thus it functions to establish *validity*. Because another person shares our experience, the experience is broader than just our particular datum, and thus it also functions to establish *generality*. As in science, then, shared reality plays a critical role in making us accept our experiences as real because then they are reliable, valid, and general.

To live in an objective world, therefore, it is necessary to have our beliefs and feelings shared by others. This is why participants in Asch's study felt so uncomfortable when no one else shared their judgment about the lines on the two white cardboards. As illustrated by the case of Admiral Byrd (1938), the pioneering American polar explorer who decided to spend six months alone at an Antarctic weather station, total removal of options for social sharing can produce not only severe depression but also hallucinations and surreal fantasies.

The motivation to have others share our preferences and feelings is so strong that we will often think that most other people agree with us even when they do not—a *false consensus*.[140] In an illustration of this phenomenon, participants were asked, ostensibly as part of a study on communication techniques, to walk around a campus for 30 minutes wearing a large sandwich-board saying, "EAT AT JOE'S." It was made clear to the participants that they were free to participate or not, but that the experimenter would appreciate their helping him out with the research project. Some participants agreed to wear the sign and others refused to do so. The participants were also asked to estimate the probable decisions of other students to participate in the same study. Only 40% of the participants refused to wear the sign, but they predicted that two-thirds of the other students would also refuse to wear the sign. Other studies have also found that people's predictions of the commonness of preferences and habits are biased toward their own preferences and habits.[141]

Thus, people will perceive consensus when no consensus exits. Such false consensus supports their experience of having a shared reality with others. It should be noted, however, that people do not always need a majority of others to agree with them in order to experience a shared reality. When individuals believe they have strong evidence for a belief, such as the strong physical evidence of the length of the lines in the Asch study, then remaining in the minority can be sufficient as long as social verification is received from someone else. In another version of the Asch study, for example, one of the students cooperating with the experimenter always gave the correct answer. This one person, then, could function as a "partner" to the naïve participant by making the same judgment as what the naïve participant believed (i.e., the correct answer). Even with this partner, the naïve participant's judgment was still clearly in the minority among the group members (two in a group of seven to nine students). Nonetheless, when the naïve participants had a partner, there was a dramatic decrease in the frequency of naïve participants agreeing with the majority's incorrect judgment on the conflict trials—only one-third as many incorrect judgments. There was no longer any naïve participant who went along with the majority all the time, and all naïve participants joined with their partner against the majority on most of the critical trials.[142]

The basic motive, then, is to have a shared reality with another person and not necessarily to be in the majority. And what people want to share with another person is not just their behaviors but, especially, their thoughts, feelings, and attitudes, their goals and standards—their *inner states*. This is because they recognize—and only humans have such recognition—that the actions and decisions of others, as well as their own actions and decisions, are directed by such inner states. Thus it is these inner states that need to be comprehended, managed, and shared.[143] Other animals will pay attention to what other animals are looking at,[144] but only humans, including very young children, share their knowledge with one another, including creating joint attention and deliberate teaching.[145] We have all seen young boys or girls discover something interesting about something they are playing with and then gleefully share their new knowledge with their parent or playmate—*children as teachers of others*. This is not something that non-humans do. For humans, it is how we make our inner states real. And when another person does share our reality about our inner states, then what we are thinking and feeling becomes real.

The importance of social and shared reality to humans in establishing what's real is also evident in the way that people turn to others when they are uncertain about their beliefs. The Sherif light studies provide one kind of evidence for this, as did the increase in talking to others that followed the disconfirmed expectancy in *When Prophecy Fails*. In a study directly examining this motive to turn to others to establish a shared reality,[146] participants were given informational support for a target proposition (about why a boy should be allowed to enter elementary school early) that created either a strong or weak initial belief in the proposition. Later the participants were all given new information that clearly did not support the proposition. This new information would easily overwhelm a weak initial belief, but it would create ambiguity for those with a strong initial belief. This ambiguity or uncertainty about the truth was predicted to create a motive among those with a strong initial belief to turn to others as a source of reality. After receiving the new information, the participants were asked to give their final opinion about whether or not to support the proposition, but before doing so, they were given an additional opportunity to look at the opinion of another participant in the study. Among those with a strong initial belief, 65% turned to this additional social information, whereas only 30% of those with a weak initial belief did so.

Before ending this discussion of the role of shared reality in establishing what's real, I would like to return full circle to my earlier discussion about the shift from 3-year-olds' to 4-year-olds' understanding that people, including themselves, can hold false beliefs. What the literature shows is that this development in understanding is speeded up *if young children have a sibling.*[147] It does not matter if their sibling is older or younger, which indicates that the developmental facilitation does not derive simply from direct instruction of an older sibling to a younger sibling. What might account for this intriguing social facilitation of a critical change in children's "theory of mind" from a child having a sibling?

Perhaps a difference in viewpoint between the siblings is what matters most.[148] It could be like the difference described by Asch between one's seeing a monster in the woods and one's neighbor seeing a tree branch. When there is a difference in viewpoint, the siblings need to negotiate a shared reality with each other—like the "porcupine" versus "skunk" negotiation that my daughter Kayla had with her friend. This negotiation means that the initial belief of one or the other partner, or both, will be recognized as false. Interestingly, games of pretense can also facilitate the development of understanding "false beliefs"—as long as they involve taking different perspectives that need negotiation to create a shared reality.[149] What is critical is that siblings cooperate in constructing a shared reality.

In sum, what this chapter has shown is that people use different ways to establish what's real, to distinguish between what's true or false, what's right or wrong. We establish what's real by questioning *what* happened and *why* it happened. We create and maintain cognitive consistency among our different beliefs and feelings, and between our beliefs or feelings and our behaviors. As a function of chronic personality predispositions or situational forces, we use different strategies for seeking the truth and for accepting the truth. Finally, we use social reality and shared reality to create the experience of an objective truth, especially when reality is unclear, and we do so even when the truth we create is not supported by physical evidence or the facts.[150] The motivation to establish what's real can facilitate approaching pleasure and avoiding pain, which I discuss in Chapter 7, but it is itself separate from hedonic motivation. And as a separate motivation to experience success in seeking the truth, it can trump hedonic motivation. This is true as well for the motivation to successfully manage what happens—*control effectiveness*—which I discuss in the next chapter.

6

Control

Managing What Happens

In Homer's epic story, *The Odyssey*, the hero Odysseus faced constant challenges in his voyage to return home with his men after the Trojan War. The story is clearly *not* about value effectiveness. Odysseus did not experience success in having desired results at the end. Not one of his followers survived the voyage, and he himself was in bad shape. What the story of Odysseus is about is control, about managing what is needed to make something happen and, especially in this story, make *not* happen.

Take, for example, the episode of the Sirens. The Sirens were enchantresses who lived on a rocky island and used their music and voices to lure mariners toward them, where they would be shipwrecked on the rocks. Homer used this episode to illustrate the human challenge of struggling with an irresistible but deadly desire—the prototypic case of *self-control*. To manage his sailors' temptation, Odysseus had their ears stuffed with wax so they could not hear the music. Odysseus could have controlled his own temptation with the same tactic, but he was curious; he wanted to hear the Sirens' song. As it turned out, the Sirens' words were even more enticing than their beautiful voices because those words promised to give great wisdom to whoever came to the Sirens. How could Odysseus manage this irresistible temptation for knowledge—his motivation for truth effectiveness—when he knew that failure to resist would be disastrous? The solution was to have his followers lash him to the mast of the ship and to tie him even more securely when he pleaded to be set free to go to the Sirens. This tactic worked, but Odysseus was nearly driven mad by his temptation.

When people are *effective at control*, they manage what is required, such as managing procedures, competencies, and resources, to make something happen or not happen. Having control relates to exercising direction or restraint upon action, to having power or authority to guide or manage. Control is distinct from value and truth. Whereas value relates to having desired (vs. undesired) results or outcomes, and truth relates to establishing what's real or right (vs. illusion or wrong), control relates to having a strong versus weak influence over something.

The challenge of the Sirens is about resisting temptation. And both temptation and the consequence of failing to resist it are extreme in this story. But in milder forms, resisting temptation is something that we all do often in order to carry out our plans for future goals. Of all the forms of control effectiveness, how humans succeed or fail at resisting temptation has historically received the most attention, not only in the psychological literature but in other writing as well. Its significance, for example, is recognized in the Lord's Prayer: "And lead us not into temptation." For this reason, I begin this chapter with a review of major psychological perspectives on resisting temptation. I then review another significant self-control issue—controlling inner states like unwanted feelings and thoughts. Finally, I review the central functions that need to be controlled more generally in order to manage what happens in goal pursuit—selection, commitment, and feedback.

RESISTING TEMPTATION

In the literature, there are two well-known examples of self-control problems involving resistance to temptation. The first is from Freud, who first suggested that controlling conflicts between inner motivational forces was the major psychological problem that people faced.[1] The most fundamental conflict was between the motivational forces of the Id and those of the Superego (also called the Ego Ideal). The motivational forces of the Id relate to instinctual wishes and desires, such as those for sex, aggression, and egoistic self-satisfaction. They are primitive and impulsive forces that follow the program of the pleasure principle. In contrast, the motivational forces of the Superego are learned (i.e., internalized) demands and prohibitions, such as societal norms, prescriptions, and rules.[2]

In one of his last books, *Civilization and Its Discontents*, Freud describes how civilization demands that individuals curb their personal pleasures, causing civilized people to live a life of guilt and frustration. The development of civilization imposes restrictions on freedom. For Freud, a concrete example of this is toilet training, where the anal eroticism of young children must be controlled through their learning the rules of civilized defecation. Children must resist the temptation to defecate whenever and wherever they wish. This conflict between the Id's impulses to uncontrolled defecation and the Superego's restrictions on this act can produce guilt and frustration, and the resolution of this conflict illustrates the importance of effective control—the experiences of success and failure in managing when and where defecation does and does not happen.

The second classic example of a self-control problem involving resistance to temptation is from Walter Mischel, the dominant figure in the area of personality in the past half-century. Whereas Freud's problem concerned individuals suppressing wished-for acts that were forbidden by others, Mischel's problem concerned individuals tolerating self-imposed delays of something they wanted now. Mischel considers such *delay of gratification* (i.e., being willing to wait for something) to be a basic human task that is at the core of what is typically meant by *willpower*. And given humans' ability to time-travel into distant periods, the waiting period for a future want, such as attaining a college degree, can be several years. Thus something wanted now, such as getting a full-time job, marrying, and starting a family, might have to be delayed for a very long time.

The task Mischel selected to study delay of gratification was brilliantly simple.[3] Preschoolers were brought into a room one at a time, seated at a table, and shown two objects, such as a marshmallow or a pretzel. It was known from pretesting that although the test child liked both of the objects, one of them was clearly preferred, such as the marshmallow. To attain the preferred object, the child had to wait alone with the two objects on the table until the experimenter returned to the room. At any time the child could ring a bell to signal the experimenter to return. But the child knew that by ringing the bell, it would be the less preferred object, the pretzel, that he or she would have to eat rather than the more preferred object, the marshmallow. To eat the preferred marshmallow, then, the child must resist the impulse to ring the bell and have immediate gratification by eating the pretzel.

Preschoolers' performance on Mischel's "marshmallow test"[4] was found to predict school-related competencies many years later, which according to Mischel reflected significant continuity in self-control aspects of personality.[5] Most germane to this chapter, however, are Mischel's findings regarding which of the strategies the children used to succeed or fail in delaying gratification. From a traditional incentives perspective, the best strategy should be to think about the preferred object, the marshmallow, that will be attained by waiting. Thinking about the marshmallow's yummy properties and how delicious it will be to eat should make the marshmallow even more desirable as a reward, which should increase the child's motivation to wait to receive it as a reward. In fact, this incentive strategy makes it *more* difficult to wait.[6] Apparently, thinking about eating increases the motivation to *eat something now* rather than wait, which makes delaying gratification more difficult.

Effective Temptation-Resisting Strategies

MENTAL TRANSFORMATION

What does work for children as a strategy for delaying gratification is to mentally transform the objects you can eat into objects you cannot eat, such as mentally transforming the pretzel into a thin brown log or the marshmallow into a white fluffy cloud. It has been suggested by Mischel that this strategy works more generally because the concrete "hot" objects have been mentally transformed into abstract "cool" objects.[7]

The power of this mental transformation strategy has been demonstrated in other studies as well.[8] In some studies, while the children waited they were shown color pictures of the tempting objects rather than the actual objects, or they faced the actual objects but were asked to think of them as color pictures. Delay of gratification (i.e., how long the children were willing to wait) also increased in these conditions. Impressively, there is also evidence of the opposite effect of mental transformation. In another condition the children were shown pictures of the objects but they were instructed to think of them not as pictures but as the actual objects. Delay of gratification *decreased* in this condition. These findings demonstrate that mental transformations have a powerful effect on the ability to resist temptation: representing the tempting object in terms of its actual properties makes it more difficult to resist temptation, but representing it in terms of something other than its actual properties, such as imagining it as just a picture, makes it easier to resist temptation.

DISTRACTION

Another strategy for resisting temptation is distraction, which was a common strategy that children used successfully in the marshmallow test. The children avoided looking at the objects by covering their eyes or by resting their heads on their arms. They also distracted themselves from the unpleasant waiting activity by engaging in more pleasant alternative activities, such as singing or talking to themselves or trying to sleep.

Sound familiar? Yes, distraction is also commonly used by adults to resist temptation. And this includes basic techniques like not looking at the tempting object, such as a dessert or snack. Some societies also introduce normative attention-related strategies to resist temptation, such as having rules about what women must wear in order to conceal tempting parts of their bodies. Removing tempting objects from view is, indeed, effective. For example, when the objects in the marshmallow test were removed from sight, children were able to wait much longer than when the objects could be seen.[9]

VERBALIZING OUTCOME CONTINGENCIES

Another strategy that children used to delay gratification in the marshmallow test was explicitly reminding themselves about the outcome contingencies involved in the control situation. For example, some children reminded themselves, "If I wait, I get the marshmallow. If I hit the bell, I get the pretzel." There is evidence that children are more successful in delaying gratification not only when they spontaneously use this strategy but also when they are instructed to use it.[10]

This strategy reflects a *value–control* relation. Contingencies involve propositions about goal–means relations, about which actions will effectively result in having what one desires. It is notable that the literature on socialization reports that children's moral development (i.e., their self-control) is enhanced by parents who use *induction techniques*. These techniques refer to parent–child interactions in which parents communicate explicitly to a child their rules and reasons for responding as they do to what the child does. In other words, induction techniques also involve clear statements and explanations of outcome contingencies for the child to internalize.[11]

WHEN ATTENDING TO A TEMPTATION CAN BE A TEMPTATION-RESISTING STRATEGY

In Mischel's "marshmallow" studies, thinking about the yummy marshmallow that would be attained by waiting was not an effective strategy for the children because it made it more difficult to resist eating something, even if it was the less-preferred pretzel. Recent studies, however, have found that there are some conditions—at least for adults—in which paying attention to a temptation can enhance self-control.[12] One such condition is having a prevention focus when exposed to a temptation. Generally speaking, it is easier to resist temptation when individuals have a prevention goal orientation than a promotion goal orientation, because prevention goals are experienced as necessities whereas promotion goals are not.[13] Moreover, the vigilance required to resist some temptations is a regulatory fit with a prevention focus but a non-fit with a promotion focus. For example, when working on math problems, promotion-focused individuals performed worse when they were exposed to attractive and distracting video clips than when the video clips were not present, whereas prevention-focused individuals actually enjoyed the math problems more and performed better when the distracting video clips were present than when they were not present.[14]

There is another surprising effect regarding resistance to temptation. Sometimes the best way to achieve a goal and to resist a temptation that would undermine that goal is to begin by paying attention to the temptation itself. When a preferred goal (e.g., dieting) is clearly a priority over a temptation (e.g., some fattening snack), then exposure to the temptation will activate the goal with its higher priority, which in turn will override the temptation.[15] But for this to work there needs to be already-established associations not only between the temptation and the preferred goal, but also between the temptation and the resolve to oppose this temptation for the sake of the preferred goal. Under these conditions, exposure to the temptation will automatically activate the resolve to oppose it.[16]

As one example, women who were concerned about their weight were initially exposed in a waiting room to stimuli related to their preferred goal of dieting (e.g., *Shape* magazine; dieting flyers), or stimuli related to tempting fattening foods (e.g., *Chocolatier* magazine; cookies), or neither of these types of stimuli (e.g., magazines on geography and the economy).[17] Next the participants were given a task that surreptitiously measured the accessibility of their diet goal. Then they were given a choice between two gifts—a chocolate bar or an apple—that measured behaviorally whether their diet goal had been activated. Finally, the participants reported their intention to avoid eating specific tempting fattening foods in the future, such as French fries, pizza, cake, and so on.

The study found that the diet goal was activated more strongly among the participants who were exposed to stimuli related to either dieting or tempting fattening foods (both diet-related stimuli), as compared to the participants who were exposed to neither of these diet-related stimuli. This was indicated by the diet goal being more accessible for participants exposed to diet-related stimuli than participants not exposed to diet-related stimuli. In addition, the participants exposed to diet-related stimuli chose the healthy apple almost twice as often as the participants who were not exposed. But in addition, and most important, plans to resist specific tempting fattening foods in the near future were much stronger among those participants who had been exposed in the waiting room to stimuli related to tempting foods than among the other participants, including those who had been exposed to stimuli directly related to dieting.

These findings suggest that for individuals who have the goal of dieting, direct activation of this goal is less effective than presenting tempting foods that will activate not only the goal of dieting but also the resolve to abstain from these foods. In fact, these conditions are more likely to be established for people who are more effective self-regulators in a particular domain, such as the domain of dieting. Indeed, the participants in the above study were specifically selected to have had experience already in restricting their dietary intake and to be concerned about what they ate. Thus, they were likely to meet the conditions of having specific plans to abstain from tempting fattening foods by associating that abstinence with their general goal of dieting.

COUNTERACTIVE CONTROL

The uniquely human ability to time-travel also has implications for resisting temptation. People can anticipate that when they are faced with a future choice between a tempting alternative and the alternative that they actually prefer, they will fail to resist temptation and end up without their preferred outcome. For example, they can know that the long-term benefits of having a medical checkup in the future would clearly outweigh the short-term discomfort costs of the checkup, but they anticipate that when the time comes to actually make an appointment for the checkup, they will be unable to resist the temptation to avoid the checkup costs. What can they do in the present to control this anticipated failure to resist temptation in the future?

One solution is to institute counteractive control mechanisms to deal with the influence of the short-term costs.[18] For example, people sometimes use the tactic of promising another person that they will make a checkup appointment by the end of the month, which creates a social pressure to carry through with their promise. This tactic enlists value effectiveness by creating a future social penalty for failure to keep the promise.[19] Thus, the counteractive control mechanism represents another *value–control relation*.

Another counteractive control mechanism is to boost the value of the preferred alternative in the present to make the preference for it over the tempting alternative even greater in the future. How might such boosting be done? Once again, the irony is that thinking about the temptation ahead of time can be the answer. Specifically, an effective tactic is to think in the present about the future temptations that need to be resisted. Thinking about them in the present can produce a counteractive response now of increasing the value of the preferred alternative, *before* the actual temptation needs to be resisted.

In one study examining the effectiveness of this counteractive response strategy,[20] undergraduate nursing students, one week before their midterm exam, were asked to imagine themselves in a pleasant social situation and think about their "sociable" selves. For these students, engaging in sociable activities rather than studying the last few days before the exam was tempting, but their preference was to get good grades by studying for the exam. After imagining their "sociable" selves, these students valued studying now *more* than did a comparison group of other students who had not thought about their "sociable" selves. In addition, the increased value of studying now predicted better performance on the exam one week later.

Construal Level

Another strategy for resisting temptation is to change how the temptation and the preferred alternative are represented or construed.[21] It is not uncommon for the temptation, such as a sweet dessert, to be construed at a low concrete level, while the preferred alternative, such as a "healthy diet," is construed at a high abstract level. Construal level theory[22] proposes that high-level construals capture more of the essential and primary features of a stimulus, whereas low-level construals capture more peripheral and secondary features. Thus, it should be easier to resist a secondary temptation for a primary goal when the conflict situation is construed at a higher level because then the primary motive would receive greater weight than the secondary motive. Indeed, resisting temptation has been found to be easier when people ask themselves *why* they are doing an activity (a high-level abstract construal) rather than *how* they are doing it (a low-level concrete construal).[23]

The Role of Self-Regulatory "Resources" in Resisting Temptation

Roy Baumeister, a major contributor to understanding the psychology of self-control and, especially, self-control failures, conceptualizes self-regulatory processes in terms of *strength*.[24] Temptations, such as an impulse to consume alcohol after watching a beer commercial, vary in strength. The motives to resist the temptation, such as the motive to remain "on the wagon," also vary in strength. If a temptation is weak, then resisting it will be relatively easy and will not require a high level of strength from the resisting motive. However, if a temptation is strong, then the resisting motive must be strong to be successful.

Baumeister proposes that self-regulatory strength overall is a limited resource. Thus, if people have had to use some of their self-regulatory strength on an initial task, they will have fewer self-regulatory resources available for the subsequent task. If the subsequent task requires resisting a strong temptation, for example, then the depletion of resources during the initial task would leave insufficient strength to resist the subsequent temptation, thus causing a self-control failure.

In one study demonstrating this "limited resource" phenomenon,[25] participants in an initial task either had to perform a resource-depleting task of making many different consumer choices within and between different product categories or had to spend an equal amount of time on a less-demanding task of writing about their reactions to different advertisements. The next task was the "cold pressor" self-control task, where participants were to try to submerge their arm in near-freezing water for as long as possible, which requires resisting the natural tendency to remove their arm from the frigid water. The study found that participants who had initially performed the more demanding "consumer choice" task were less able to resist removing their arm from the frigid water than those who had initially performed the less-demanding writing task. This study shows that when people have used some of their self-regulatory strength on an initial task, they will have less self-regulatory resources available for a subsequent self-control task.[26]

If self-control failures occur because of insufficient resources for a task, then increasing resources should reduce this problem. Indeed, there is evidence that the negative impact of an initial self-control task on a subsequent task is reduced by giving people a lemonade drink sweetened with sugar before they begin the two tasks, where the glucose in the sugar provides energy for brain activity.[27] Finally, I should note that conceptualizing self-control in terms of strength and resources, as will*power*, is consistent with my proposal that control effectiveness is related to the dimension of strength.

Resistance to temptation is a type of self-control in which people try to suppress doing what they are tempted to do in the service of some other competing motivational force, such as a personal desire to attain a future outcome that will be forgone if they engage in the temptation. There is another type of self-control in which people try to manage inner states that they *do not want* rather than trying to resist doing something they are tempted (i.e.,want) to do. This type of self-control has also received substantial attention in the psychological literature.

CONTROLLING UNWANTED (AND WANTED) INNER STATES

Once again, I begin with Freud. For Freud, the prototypic case of unwanted inner states is the anxiety or guilt that people feel when they have forbidden thoughts, feelings, or desires about another person. And his prime example was the anxiety and guilt that very young boys (between 3 and 5 years of age) experienced when they desired to kill their father in order to possess their mother— the *Oedipus complex*. Controlling these desires, by ultimately identifying with the father, wanting to be like him and possess *him* (i.e., identification), was considered to be critical to male gender development in particular and, more significantly, to the development of a Superego and conscience.

Notably, the unwanted feelings and desires associated with the Oedipus complex are *not* temptations resisted by the Superego; rather, it is the *resolution* of these unwanted inner states, through repressing the Oedipus complex, that contributes to the *formation* of the Superego.[28] In other words, until the resolution occurs, *there is no Superego*. Freud describes a boy's resolution of the Oedipus complex as follows: "The child's parents, and especially his father, were perceived as the obstacle to a realization of his Oedipus wishes; so his infantile ego fortified itself for the carrying out of the repression by erecting this same obstacle within itself. It borrowed strength to do this, so to speak, from the father, and this loan was an extraordinarily momentous act."[29]

From a psychoanalytic perspective, the case of controlling the unwanted feelings and desires associated with the Oedipus complex (and its female analog) has special significance to human development. From this perspective, controlling Oedipal-like feelings and desires through repression—keeping them unconscious—is considered to be a continuing self-control task of all well-functioning adults. It should be emphasized that the purpose of this repression is to keep the feelings and desires from consciousness because, if conscious, they would make people feel extremely anxious and guilty. Thus, the self-control task is not the same as resistance to temptation. It is not that some other higher-priority goal, such as "love thy parents," is trying to resist the interfering temptations of killing one parent to bed the other. Rather, unwanted feelings and desires are being controlled through the mechanism of repression.

Oedipal-like feelings and desires are not the only unwanted inner states that people are motivated to control, and repression to keep them unconscious is not the only mechanism for controlling unwanted inner states. Indeed, inner states need not even be unpleasant to be unwanted, as when people are distracted from their focal task by pleasant extraneous thoughts, such as daydreaming, and try to exert control and bring their attention back to the focal task. The psychological literature has mostly studied mechanisms for controlling unpleasant inner states (i.e., for controlling or coping with psychological problems). It has even been suggested that regulating negative feelings may be more important to overall quality of life than regulating positive feelings.[30] Nonetheless, because many models of self-control describe mechanisms that attempt to increase wanted inner states as well as decrease unwanted inner states, and both kinds of mechanisms are part of the general story of control effectiveness, my review will not be restricted just to mechanisms that control unwanted inner states. Consistent with the past literature, however, the issue of how people regulate unwanted inner states will be emphasized in my review.

Self-Control and Affect Regulation Strategies

VERBALIZATION VERSUS REPRESSION

A major concern of clinicians and non-clinicians alike is finding ways to control the suffering that comes from experiencing affective disorders such as depression and anxiety, in both their relatively mild and severe forms. The mild forms of these unpleasant emotions are ubiquitous in people's everyday lives. But even the severe forms (i.e., severe enough to disrupt normal functioning) are alarmingly common: over 20% of the population will suffer from depression or anxiety disorders at least once during their lifetime. It is beyond the scope of this chapter to discuss clinical treatments for the severe forms of these unwanted emotions, but it is useful to consider a few examples of mechanisms that people use to control the less severe forms.

One of the most common mechanisms is repression. However, despite its common use, repression is not generally considered to be an effective strategy.[31] One possible reason for this is that repression reduces guilt as well as anxiety, and guilt has been found to contribute positively to self-control.[32] Instead of repression, processing and working through negative emotions has been found to be effective.[33] One version of this is people talking or writing about past stressful emotional events. In one study,[34] for example, first-year undergraduates during the first semester wrote for three consecutive days either about their most basic thoughts and emotions on coming to college for the first time or about some object or event in an objective manner. Consistent with the instructions, participants in the former condition rated their essays as being more emotional and personal than those in the latter condition. Compared to the participants who wrote on neutral topics, those participants who had written emotionally and personally about their difficulties in college improved their grades more from the first to the second semester, and, in the two months following the essay writing, visited the health center less.

The adjustment benefits from verbalizing about emotionally stressful events rather than repressing thoughts about them have been explained in terms of what happens when people write or talk about traumatic experiences.[35] First, an organized and coherent explanation or story is constructed about the trauma. Second, labeling the emotions associated with the trauma helps individuals to integrate them into their general understanding of the traumatic event.[36]

It is important, however, to recognize that trying to get to the bottom of things, asking "Why?" questions, is not always beneficial. When individuals go over and over in their mind about why something happened, trying incessantly to make sense of what happened, it can have psychological costs. There is evidence that *rumination* as a method of coping with emotionally stressful events can actually intensify the negative affect, making things worse rather than better.[37] What is it about rumination that is counterproductive as a form of "verbalization"? For one thing, asking questions and not getting answers is a problem. There is evidence, for example, that the benefits of verbalizing traumatic experiences occur when the talking or writing actually produces insights and causal explanations for what happened.[38] Just verbalizing does not do it. And it is precisely those individuals who do not arrive at an explanation, who do not find insight, who are most likely to go on and on thinking about what happened (i.e., ruminate). Thus, trying to find the truth is not in itself beneficial. What matters is feeling that one has been successful at finding the truth (i.e., experiencing truth effectiveness).

DISTANCING

What might we do when searching for an explanation to "Why?" that would help us to find an answer but not intensify the negative affect? A mechanism that has been recently suggested is to *distance ourselves* when thinking about a past traumatic event in our lives while still allowing ourselves to consider what happened and why it happened, rather than repressing or removing attention from the event.[39] A tactic for distancing ourselves is to take a *third-person perspective*, to step back and imagine watching the traumatic event as if it were happening to us again and we were watching it from a distance as we would watch a video.

As an example of how this tactic can be effective, undergraduates in one study[40] were asked to recall an interpersonal experience that made them feel overwhelming anger and hostility. Some participants were told to use the self-distancing tactic. Other participants were told to relive the time and place of the event and experience it as if it were happening all over again—the *self-immersion* tactic. In each of these conditions, participants were asked to think about either *what* they emotionally experienced at the time or *why* they felt the way they did. After thinking about the past event again, those participants who used the self-distancing tactic combined with the "Why?" questioning felt significantly less anger than the participants in the other three conditions. A follow-up study showed that the self-distancing plus "Why?" questioning was effective because it tended to produce insights about what happened and to make sense of it. In other words, once again, it was effective when it was associated with the experience of increased truth effectiveness—truth working together with control as partners.[41]

AFFECT REGULATION BEYOND HEDONIC MOTIVATION

Managing moods and emotions—affect regulation—is not restricted to extreme feelings. People manage their mild and moderate feelings as well, such as trying to keep a good mood or get over a bad mood. Moreover, affect regulation is not just about trying to reduce painful feelings and to increase pleasant feelings. It is more complicated and nuanced than that. Generally speaking, people use a variety of methods to maintain or alter both the *intensity* and the *duration* of their feelings.[42] They do not try simply to maximize the intensity and duration of their positive feelings and minimize the intensity and duration of their negative feelings; that is, affect regulation is beyond just controlling pleasure and pain.

Sometimes people want their positive feelings to be mild rather than intense, as when they want to feel peaceful and serene. At other times they want to maintain rather than reduce their negative feelings, as when they feel contemplative and sad on a day of remembrance for a loved one who has passed away. Sometimes affect regulation is not about having pleasant rather than painful feelings (i.e., feeling *good* rather than *bad*) but instead is about having *whatever feeling is suitable* to the demands of the situation (i.e., feeling *right*).[43] It is more appropriate to feel sad rather than happy at a funeral, for example. This illustrates in yet another way how motivation goes beyond the hedonic principle of maximizing pleasure and minimizing pain.

People regulate their feelings for a couple of major reasons. First, different feelings have different *experiential qualities* and, at a given time, people might prefer to experience some particular feeling state rather than another, just as they prefer the taste of one kind of wine over another depending on what kind of food they are eating (i.e., wine–food pairings). Second, different feelings constitute different kinds of *motivational forces* that can be used to serve specific goals. This is why some people want to maintain their sadness when remembering a lost loved one because it helps them re-experience how much that person meant to them. Sometimes people want to stay angry in order to fortify their resolve to stand up to someone they want to confront, such as a female employee who believes she has been mistreated by her boss because of her gender.[44]

There are also times when people want to *reduce* their current happy mood if they believe that a more neutral mood would be more appropriate to an upcoming situation. As one example of this, participants in one study[45] were first exposed to either cheerful music or depressing music while they waited for the experimental session to begin. This music put them into either a happy mood or a sad mood, respectively. There were two parts of the experimental session that were supposedly unrelated. In the first part, the participants made judgments of newspaper stories. They were told to select which stories they would most like to read because there was not enough time to read all the stories. From the story headlines it was clear that some were cheerful, some were sad, and some were neutral. Before making their selections, the participants were told that in the second part of the session they would work with another participant, and they were given some background information about their future partner. Embedded among the partner's autobiographical answers to various questions was the partner's answer to the question, "How are you feeling right now?" In one condition, the answer revealed that the partner was in a neutral mood. The study found that when expecting soon to meet a partner who was in a neutral mood, the participants chose to read sad news stories more when their current mood was happy than when it was sad; that is, they wanted to *reduce their happy mood* to match the neutral mood of their future partner.

Emotion-Focused and Problem-Solving Strategies for Coping with Stress

One of the most important and best-studied issues in affect regulation concerns how people cope with the stress in their lives and, especially, with their stress-related negative emotions. Richard Lazarus, who pioneered the study of this issue, introduced a basic distinction between emotion-focused and problem-focused coping.[46] *Emotion-focused coping* is when people use tactics to reduce the stress-related negative emotions themselves. *Problem-focused coping* is when people use tactics to solve the problem that caused them to feel the negative emotions in the first place. Generally speaking, using problem-focused strategies is associated with less emotional distress than using emotion-focused strategies.[47] And using emotion-focused coping can actually interfere with higher-order goals that require resisting temptation,[48] as when people gratify or indulge in immediate pleasures like eating chocolates as a coping strategy to reduce their negative mood.

However, the relative effectiveness of these strategies also depends on the controllability of the stressor. There is evidence, for example, that children do better if they can generate several problem-focused strategies when dealing with stressors that they believe they can change or control, such as problems with a homework assignment (controllable stressors), but *not* if they generate such strategies to deal with stressors that they do not believe they can change or control, such as a poor grade on a final exam (uncontrollable stressors).[49] This highlights a more general point about adjustment to stressors: individuals experience less distress overall when they *flexibly* adopt different strategies for the demands of different situations.[50] Once again, there is a need to match the strategy to the situation.

When distinguishing between emotion-focused and problem-focused coping, Lazarus emphasized the actions that people actually took in problem-focused coping to solve the problem underlying their current emotional stress. However, because people are time-travelers, they want to control not only their current feelings but also the feelings they expect to have in the future (i.e., their future reality). Thus, they frequently plan how to avoid a stress-creating problem in the future. Indeed, it is often the case that people cannot go back and undo a problem and thus they plan ways to avoid similar problems in the future.[51]

Diversionary and Engagement Strategies
of Affect Regulation

Affect-regulation strategies can be roughly organized into two sets of strategies.[52] One set, *diversionary* strategies, includes distraction (getting your mind off your negative feelings and the problematic situation that produced them), suppression (keeping yourself from expressing the negative feelings), and self-reward (providing yourself with pleasurable activities). What is common among these strategies is that people are disengaging from the feelings and thoughts associated with their suffering and the situation that produced it.

In contrast, the second set, *engagement* strategies, do just the opposite. These include cognitive reappraisal, in which people search for deeper meaning or a positive interpretation of the problematic situation, such as the proverbial finding of the "silver lining" in the dark cloud. And a cognitive reappraisal strategy, such as searching for a positive interpretation, can be used before a stressful event happens, such as days before giving a professional speech, to reduce the anxiety from anticipating the event.[53] There is evidence that cognitive reappraisal as an engagement strategy can be more effective in regulating feelings than suppression as a disengagement strategy. Cognitive reappraisal has broad applicability as a mechanism to control both emotional experience and expression, whereas suppression as a control mechanism can have both physical and mental costs.[54]

A well-known type of engagement strategy is venting. The idea of venting as a beneficial mechanism to relieve distress is, once again, associated with Freud and the particular form of venting called "catharsis." But the idea actually originated with Freud's mentor and friend, Dr. Joseph Breuer, and Dr. Breuer's patient "Anna." Anna was the classic example of a patient suffering from *hysteria*, which means that her symptoms, such as losing the feeling in her hands and feet, appeared to be physical but actually were not. Breuer and Freud wrote a book on hysteria where they claimed that every hysteria has its root in a traumatic past experience that has strong feelings associated with it. The trauma-related feelings are being expressed indirectly in the hysterical symptoms. If a patient can be helped to understand the true meaning of the symptoms, through the use of hypnosis for example, then the trauma-related feelings can be directly expressed in a manner that is appropriate to what actually happened in the traumatic past event. It was Breuer who called this process "catharsis," from the Greek word for cleansing or purging. He proposed that in the cleansing catharsis process, the emotional infection that could not be expressed previously would finally be released and the hysteria symptoms would disappear or drain away.

Many people believe that venting one's feelings, especially anger, *is* beneficial. The metaphor is that if anger is "bottled up" and not expressed, it will continue to build up until it explodes in a destructive manner. The solution is to "let the steam out," to get the anger out of one's system. However, beginning in the 1970s, psychologists advised against using venting as a mechanism for dealing with anger in particular. If anything, psychologists said, venting will make people even more angry and aggressive.[55] A common example of this is people complaining over something that happened to them and feeling even angrier after they have vented. Costs of venting have been found for other negative feelings as well. In contrast, venting positive feelings can be an effective way to enhance positive feelings.[56]

One way to think about these effects is to conceptualize venting, generally speaking, as an intensifier.[57] Venting increases engagement strength in relation to the target object or event. If the emotional reaction to a target is negative, then venting will intensify its negativity. If the emotional reaction to a target is positive, then venting will intensify its positivity. This would be consistent with my discussion in Chapter 4 of the effects of engagement strength on value.

But where does that leave Anna and catharsis? The results of studies on venting have led psychologists to reject not only venting but the notion of catharsis itself as a useful tool for regulating negative affect. Still, when conclusions about catharsis are made based on venting studies that do not concern hysteria, something important is being overlooked. Specifically, what is being overlooked in cases like Anna's is that she presented with debilitating symptoms, such as losing feeling in her limbs, that were themselves *non-affective*. Her problem was that she was *not* trying to reduce her negative feelings about what happened in the past. Indeed, a central assumption about patients suffering from hysteria is that they are *not* in touch with their feelings at all. It could well be that helping them to release their heretofore unrecognized feelings, to have them become aware of their negative past and their feelings associated with it, *is* a helpful *first* step. For the second step, now that the feelings are out in the open, some mechanism other than venting might be more helpful. Additional venting at this point might in fact be more costly than beneficial, and some other mechanism, such as cognitive reappraisal, would be better. This would relate to the earlier discussion of how expressing feelings when combined with new understanding—control and truth working together—can be beneficial. And to be fair to Freud and Breuer, another part of the overall catharsis cure was the intellectual insight that was expected to follow the catharsis. Such *insight* could certainly involve cognitive reappraisal and, once again, involve control and truth working together as partners.

Another very common engagement strategy is to seek support from other people. There is substantial evidence that, generally speaking, spending time with other people, having many friends and intimates, is positively associated with indicators of well-being.[58] With respect to affect regulation *per se*, what is important is to choose the right social relationship given one's current condition or problem. As I discussed with respect to problem-focused versus emotion-focused coping, the effectiveness of an affect-regulation strategy can be greater under some conditions than others. This appears to be the case for social support as well, with specific types of social support being more beneficial for particular kinds of stress.[59] For example, sometimes people just need to be comforted to reduce their negative feelings, and at other times they need good advice to solve a problem.

There is also evidence from the pioneering work of Niall Bolger that social support can be more effective when it is *invisible* rather than when it is visible. For example, female undergraduates in one study[60] expected a stressful speech task in which their performance would be evaluated by graduate teaching assistants. A confederate peer provided support after the participant gave a practice talk. The support involved the confederate providing information, always in a warm manner, that was a useful tip for public speaking. In the visible support condition, the confederate addressed the participant and gave her the tip directly. In the invisible support condition the confederate addressed the experimenter and the participant overheard it; that is, the participant was aware of the confederate's action but the supportive nature of the action was sufficiently subtle that the participant did not interpret it as support directed at her.

The support was found to be beneficial in reducing the participant's distress feelings *only* when it was invisible. In contrast, visible support, despite the confederate being perceived as warm and supportive by the participant, left the support recipient no better off, or even worse off, than receiving no support at all. Why is this? Additional data indicated that for the social support to be beneficial to the recipient, it was critical that the supportive confederate not appear to view the recipient as weak and needy. When the support was invisible it was less likely to be seen by the support recipient as a sign that this other person (the confederate) saw her as weak and needy. These findings indicate that seeking social support as a mechanism for controlling distress can be a tricky matter because its benefits depend on how the support is actually given and how it is perceived.[61] What could be important is that the supporters and the recipients agree about what the recipients can do for themselves versus what help they actually need to receive from the supporters. In other words, what might be critical is for supporters and recipients to have a *shared reality* about what direct help is *really* needed—yet another *truth–control relation*.

Thus far I have discussed mechanisms of control effectiveness with respect to resisting temptation and controlling unwanted (and wanted) inner states. These forms of control effectiveness have received substantial attention in the psychological literature precisely because they concern psychological problems that need to be solved. They are the "squeaky wheels" of control effectiveness—the classic issues of self-control. But control effectiveness is not restricted to managing problems of self-control. Indeed, it is mostly about successfully managing all of the different functions required to pursue goals. It is beyond the scope of this chapter to review all of these functions in detail.[62] I will, however, describe three central functions—*selection, commitment,* and *feedback*—in order to provide a broader picture of what control effectiveness is all about and to set the stage for later discussions of value–control relations (Chapter 8) and truth–control relations (Chapter 9).

MANAGING GOAL PURSUIT

Selection

Effective management of what happens during goal pursuit (control effectiveness) requires making different selections during different phases of the goal-pursuit process. Heinz Heckhausen and Peter Gollwitzer, pioneering figures in understanding self-regulation, have described some of these different selections in their Rubicon Model of self-regulation.[63] Expanding on Lewin's earlier distinction between a "goal setting" phase that determines which goals a person will choose to pursue and a "goal striving" phase of taking action directed toward attaining the selected goals,[64] the Rubicon Model distinguishes *within* goal setting between a preactional *deliberation* phase and a preactional *implementation* phase.

THE DELIBERATION PHASE

The first preactional phase is the deliberation phase. This is when goals are selected. People deliberate over which of their many different wishes and needs they prefer to pursue; only a few at most can be pursued simultaneously. There are individual differences in the relative strength of the different competing wishes or needs that contribute to which of them are selected.[65] There are situational or conditional factors as well, such as greater opportunities to fulfill some wishes than others or greater temporal urgency to satisfy some needs than others. This deliberation phase involves assessing and comparing both the desirability and the feasibility of different wishes or needs in order to construct goal preferences.

However, identifying which wishes or needs are preferred is not sufficient to create commitment. According to the Rubicon Model, the preferred wish or need must be transformed into an *intention*. There must be sufficient resolve to create a feeling of *determination* to fulfill the wish. This is part of the commitment story and I will discuss it in more detail later in this chapter.

In the Rubicon Model, what is emphasized most for the deliberation phase is selection of and commitment to a particular goal to pursue. However, because the same basic goal, such as being committed to graduating from college, can be associated with different reference points and different orientations, goal selection involves not only selecting which goal to pursue but also selecting a *reference point* and an *orientation* for the selected goal. Regarding reference point, the fundamental distinction is between a desired end-state as reference point versus an undesired end-state as reference point; for example, someone could represent the goal of graduating from college as either approaching the desired end-state of graduating from college or avoiding the undesired end-state of not graduating from college.[66] Regarding orientation, a goal can also involve different orientations; for example, someone could represent the same desired end-state of graduating from college as either a promotion-related accomplishment (an ideal) or a prevention-related responsibility (an ought).[67]

These reference point and orientation selections need not be as systematic as assessing and comparing the desirability and feasibility of different wishes during the deliberation phase (as described in the Rubicon Model). However, these selections can be purposeful. And they matter because they have significant downstream effects when the goal pursuit is actually carried out (i.e., effects during and after the actional phase). For example, individuals who pursue avoidance goals rather than approach goals have been found to perform worse, feel less competent, report more physical illness symptoms, and generally have lower subjective well-being.[68]

For orientation selection, pursuing the same goal with a promotion versus a prevention orientation affects the strategies we prefer to use during the goal pursuit (e.g., eager versus vigilant), as well as how we feel when the pursuit succeeds (e.g., happy versus relaxed) or fails (e.g., sad versus nervous).[69] And the strategies we use have an impact on control effectiveness. For example, people will be better able to shield the goal they selected in the deliberation phase from competing goals in subsequent phases if their initial orientation to that goal is prevention rather than promotion because prevention increases the sense of obligation or commitment to the goal intention.[70]

As another example of the importance of orientation selection for control effectiveness, participants in one study[71] were given the same goal of drawing four different pictures by connecting the numbered dots in each picture. Some participants had a predominant promotion orientation to goals, whereas others had a predominant prevention orientation. The study found that the promotion-oriented participants sacrificed their accuracy in connecting the dots (e.g., missing some dots) for the sake of completing each picture faster, whereas prevention-oriented participants sacrificed speed of completing the picture in order not to miss connecting any dots. Moreover, this impact of orientation selection on effectiveness in speed versus accuracy became greater and greater as the participants progressed from the first picture to the last picture.

THE IMPLEMENTATION PHASE

The second preactional phase is the implementation phase. This phase involves *planning*. Unless there is nothing else going on and a single step is all that is required to carry out the goal intention, planning is critical for successful goal pursuit. And rarely is there nothing else going on and a single step is all that is needed. Planning is obviously required for a goal like graduating from college, but it is warranted for mundane activities like making breakfast or brushing one's teeth as well. Not only does planning typically take place over many steps, but it also takes place at different levels of self-regulation—at the strategic, tactical, and behavioral levels.[72] During the implementation phase, strategies, tactics, and specific behavioral intentions need to be planned.

Implementation planning involves selecting those strategies, tactics, and behaviors to be initiated, executed, and terminated during the goal-pursuit process. Such planning requires addressing questions of *when* to start acting, *where* to act, *how* to act, and *how long* to act.[73] The strategies selected play an especially important role in the goal-pursuit process because they serve as the link between the goal and the tactics or behavior. This strategic level reflects the general plans or means for goal pursuit, such as strategic eagerness or strategic vigilance.

Planning occurs not only at the level of the selected goal with its reference point and orientation but also at the strategic and tactical levels. For goal-pursuit management to be effective and efficient, the different levels need to work together.[74] This is especially true for the goal and strategic levels. A regulatory fit between strategic manner of goal pursuit and goal orientation, such as eager pursuit of a promotion goal orientation, strengthens individuals' engagement in the goal pursuit and makes them "feel right" about what they are doing. In contrast, a non-fit, such as vigilant pursuit of a promotion goal orientation, weakens individuals' engagement in the goal pursuit and makes them "feel wrong" about what they are doing. There are clear advantages for people to select an implementation strategy that fits their goal orientation.

I discussed earlier how once a goal has been established, implementation planning requires addressing questions of *when* to start acting, *where* to act, *how* to act, and *how long* to act. Research by Gollwitzer and his colleagues has shown that having people answer the *when*, *where*, and *how* questions during the preactional implementation phase increases the effectiveness of the subsequent goal pursuit (the actional phase).[75] In one demonstration that regulatory fit can increase commitment to such implementation plans,[76] participants with either a predominant promotion focus or a predominant prevention focus were asked to write a report on how they would spend their upcoming Saturday and to turn it in by a certain deadline. If they met the deadline they would receive a cash payment. Before they left the lab, all participants were asked to imagine certain implementation steps that they might take in writing the report—steps in which they simulated *when*, *where*, and *how* they would do the report.

The simulation instructions framed the implementation strategies to be used as either eager ways or vigilant ways for carrying out the *when*, *where*, and *how* steps. For example, the eager framing of the *when* step told participants to imagine a good, convenient time when they would be able to write their report, and the vigilant framing of the *when* step told participants to imagine bad, inconvenient times during which they should avoid writing their report.

Whether the implementation strategies themselves were framed as eager steps or as vigilant steps had no independent effect on participants' success in turning in their reports. However, regulatory fit had a big effect. When predominant-promotion participants took eager steps and predominant-prevention participants took vigilant steps (the fit conditions), they were almost 50% more likely to turn in their reports than when predominant-promotion participants took vigilant steps and predominant-prevention participants took eager steps (the non-fit conditions).

Another demonstration of how control effectiveness depends on strategic selection that fits a person's orientation comes from research on *defensive pessimism*. Together with her students and colleagues, Nancy Cantor, a major contributor to understanding the role of strategies and tactics in motivation, has identified different strategies that people use to cope with goal pursuit when there is the possibility of failing.[77] Individuals who are defensive pessimists "expect the worst" when entering a new situation, even though in the past they have performed as well as individuals with a more optimistic outlook.[78] However, when defensive pessimists adopt a negative outlook for anticipated events they have *better* outcomes than when they adopt a positive outlook.[79] Whereas reflecting on the possibility of failure in an upcoming task can hurt the performance of optimists, it facilitates the preparation of defensive pessimists, which helps them perform better.[80]

Defensive pessimists are successful at prevention and use the possibility of future failure as an effective tactic to maintain their strategic vigilance: "If I'm not careful and don't do what's necessary, then I could fail." There is evidence that the ability of defensive pessimists to harness their vigilance and perform well can be disrupted when other people try to get them to adopt a more positive outlook, such as drawing their attention to the inconsistency between their negative forecast and the fact they have performed so well in the past.[81] This disruption of their strategic vigilance undermines their success—yet another example of when adding pleasure to something can hurt motivation. Because of such harmful effects, students who are defensive pessimists actively avoid those friends who, prior to an upcoming test, try to motivate them by telling them how well they have done in the past.[82]

My discussion of selection of strategies would be incomplete without noting that the selection can occur without conscious planning. Implementation planning by answering *when*, *where*, and *how* questions is conscious. But the strategic preferences that individuals have with particular goal orientations, like promotion-oriented individuals' preference for eager strategies, need not be conscious and typically are not.[83] In addition, there are stored associations between goals and means such that the activation of a goal will activate an associated means unconsciously.[84] With his students and colleagues, John Bargh, a pioneer in relating the principles of automaticity to the area of motivation,[85] has provided powerful demonstrations of how priming a goal-related construct at one point in time can unconsciously influence how a task is carried out later.

In one of Bargh's studies,[86] participants took part in two supposedly unrelated tasks. During the first task of constructing grammatically correct sentences, the participants were exposed to various words. For half of the participants, some of these words were related to cooperation (e.g., "helpful," "support," "share"), whereas for the other participants they were always neutral regarding cooperation ("salad," "mountain," "zebra"). Next they participated in a resource-management game in which they played the role of a fisherman who, along with one other fisherman, was licensed to fish a small lake with a limited stock of fish (100). They knew that all their profits from all their catches would be lost if the number of fish in the lake got too low (70). They fished for several seasons, always caught the same amount (15 fish), and decided each time how much of their catch to keep for themselves and how much to return to the lake to help restock it.

The participants were given no instructions for how to play this game. The study found that a tactic that served cooperation (i.e., returning fish to restock the lake) was higher for those participants in the "cooperation" priming condition, although they were completely unaware that "cooperation" had been primed earlier. Subsequent research has shown that even when a goal is carried out unconsciously, the strategies and tactics that are used can be flexible to the changing demands of current conditions.[87]

In sum, managing goal pursuit effectively requires several different kinds of selection during the preactional deliberation and implementation phases. It requires selecting not only a goal but also a reference point and an orientation for the selected goal. It also requires selecting goal-pursuit strategies that fit the goal orientation. And the selections can be unconscious as well as conscious. Such selections are difficult because cases where one selection is inherently better than another are rare. Most often, the benefits and costs of any selection vary depending on the relations of that selection to what else is selected, as illustrated by the effects of regulatory fit and non-fit. In the end, it is how the selections *work together* that is critical.[88]

Creating Commitment

For effective control, selecting a wish during the deliberation phase is not sufficient. Only when there is a feeling of determination to fulfill the wish will the wish be transformed into a goal intention—goal commitment. As noted, this transition from simply deliberating to having a determined *commitment* to a goal—called "crossing the Rubicon" in Heckhausen and Gollwitzer's model—is critical for effective goal pursuit. Where does this feeling of determination to pursue a goal come from?

The standard answer is that it comes from the *utility of a goal pursuit*, to which two factors contribute—the subjective *value* of successful goal pursuit and the subjective or perceived *likelihood* of successful goal pursuit. Commitment to pursuing a goal will be stronger when the subjective value of success is high (vs. low). It will also be stronger when people perceive a high (vs. low) likelihood of success. This is consistent with the beneficial effects of perceived self-efficacy on commitment[89] because when people believe they are competent (vs. not competent) to perform the actions needed in a goal pursuit, they will also perceive that success is more likely. In the Rubicon Model, goal commitment during the deliberation phase was also postulated to depend on both its desirability and feasibility.

In the classic utility model of goal pursuit, commitment derives from a multiplicative function of these two factors—the *value* × *likelihood function*.[90] The function is multiplicative because it is assumed that there will be no commitment to the goal pursuit if the value of the goal is zero, no matter how high is the likelihood of success, and that there will be no commitment if the likelihood of success is zero, no matter how high is the value of the goal. More generally, the multiplicative function reflects the assumption that the contribution that a higher likelihood of success makes to increasing commitment to a goal pursuit matters more for a high-value goal than a low-value goal.

Consider, for example, commitment to the goal of winning a cash prize from a lottery. Imagine that in one case the likelihood of winning is 1 out of 10, and in another case the likelihood is 1 out of 1,000. Now imagine that the cash prize to be won is either $5,000 or $5. You can get a free ticket for the lottery, but you have to walk 30 minutes to pick it up. Generally speaking, most people would be more willing (i.e., determined) to walk the 30 minutes to get the ticket when there is a 1 out of 10 chance of winning than only a 1 out of 1,000 chance of winning. The question is whether this effect on commitment from the difference in likelihood of winning is different when the cash prize is $5,000 than $5. Most people would answer in the affirmative. If the cash prize is $5, I don't care all that much whether my chance of winning is 1 out of 10 or 1 out of 1,000. But if the cash prize is $5,000, then I care a lot whether my chance of winning is 1 out of 10 or 1 out of 1,000. The fact that the increase in commitment from the difference in likelihood of winning is greater when the value of the prize is greater means that the value–likelihood function is multiplicative (i.e., a difference in differences).

COMMITMENT FROM "VALUE × LIKELIHOOD" IN PROMOTION VERSUS PREVENTION

The multiplicative "value × likelihood" function makes intuitive sense. It would seem to answer the question of where commitment to a goal pursuit comes from. However, although the "value × likelihood" function is an important part of the story of commitment, it is not the whole story. It is not enough to know just the subjective value of goal success, such as knowing that winning $5,000 matters much more to me than winning $5, and just the subjective likelihood of success, such as knowing that a 1 out of 10 likelihood of winning matters much more to me than a 1 out of 1,000 likelihood of winning. It is also necessary to know what goal *orientation* is involved in the goal pursuit. For example, the "value × likelihood" function works differently for a promotion than a prevention orientation.

When people pursue the goal of winning money in a lottery, they are likely to have a promotion orientation, given that they typically see winning the lottery as gaining money that would advance them forward from their current, generally satisfactory, state. But some lottery players may currently be in a negative, unsatisfactory state and might see winning as a way of getting out of danger and finding security. These lottery players would have a prevention orientation. More generally, there are many goal pursuits where most, if not all, people would have a prevention orientation. When parents take care of their very young children, for example, they often have a prevention orientation, as when a mother firmly holds her child's hand while crossing a busy street.

But does goal orientation really matter for something so basic as the value × likelihood utility function? This function describes a positive multiplicative function in that the effect of higher likelihood of success on increasing commitment is greater as the value of success increases. The question is whether this positive multiplicative function operates in basically the same way regardless of whether people's goal orientation is promotion or prevention. There is evidence that, in fact, *it does not*.

In one study,[91] for example, college participants were asked to imagine that they were deciding whether to take a course in their major. They were given information about the purported value of doing well in the course and the likelihood of doing well in the course. This information was experimentally varied. The value of doing well in the course was established by telling the participants that the percentage of previous majors who were *accepted into their honor society* after receiving a grade of "B" or higher in the course was either 95% (high value of receiving a "B" or higher) or 51% (low value of receiving a "B" or higher). The likelihood of doing well in the course was established by telling participants that the percentage of previous majors who actually received a "B" or higher in the course was either 75% (high likelihood of receiving a "B" or higher) or 25% (low likelihood of receiving of "B" or higher). After reading the information, the participants' commitment to taking the course was measured. Personality differences in chronic strength of promotion orientation and of prevention orientation were also measured.

The first finding was that the strength of participants' promotion orientation moderated the positive value × likelihood function. Consistent with promotion being associated with a maximization goal,[92] the predicted effect of higher likelihood having a greater effect on commitment as value increased was stronger for participants with a stronger promotion orientation. This means that *strength of promotion orientation* matters for the *magnitude* of the predicted value × likelihood effect; that is, the magnitude of the effect predicted by the classic utility model is greater for strong-promotion than for weak-promotion individuals.

The study also found an *opposite* multiplicative function for participants with a stronger prevention orientation. For them, the multiplicative value × likelihood effect was *not* a positive function; it was a *negative* function. Rather than higher likelihood having a greater effect on commitment as value increased, the impact of higher likelihood on commitment actually *decreased* as value increased. Specifically, participants' commitment to taking the course was generally greater when the likelihood of getting a good grade was higher (75% vs. 25%), but for prevention-focused students this effect of higher likelihood was *weaker* when the course had *higher value*. And this same *negative* value × likelihood effect was found for prevention-focused students in another study. In this study, students provided their own subjective judgments of the value and the likelihood of their doing well on a task, and their commitment to the task was measured by their actual performance on the task.[93]

Why is there a *negative* value × likelihood function for individuals with a prevention focus? It is not due to something about their socialization when growing up, because the same negative function was found when a prevention orientation was experimentally induced by framing the value and likelihood information in prevention language rather than in promotion language.[94] So what is happening here?

Think of the motivational state of a mother with the goal of safely leading her young son across a busy street. The safety of her son is an absolute. His life is priceless to her. She *must* get him across the street safely. Her commitment to this goal is not going to vary as a function of the likelihood that she will succeed: I don't think a mother would say "Hmm . . . The traffic is very busy and erratic today. The likelihood that I will succeed in getting my son across the street safely is lower than usual. It makes me feel less committed today to trying to get my son across the street safely." For prevention goals, like safety, the more valuable the goal, the more people feel that they *must* attain it, *regardless of the likelihood of success.*

People are determined to pursue a high-value prevention goal even when the likelihood of success is small because pursuing the goal is a *necessity*. For the mother, getting her son across the street safely is just such a necessity. For prevention goals, then, as the value of the goal increases to a high level, differences in likelihood have less and less effect on commitment to goal attainment. This reversal of the multiplicative "value × likelihood" effect when there is a strong prevention orientation provides a striking example of the need to go beyond standard hedonic models in trying to understand how motivation works.

Commitment from "Value × Likelihood" in Strong Locomotion

It is not only regulatory-focus orientation (promotion vs. prevention) that alters how the "value × likelihood" utility function actually works. In Chapter 5, I discussed the difference between an assessment goal orientation and a loco-motion goal orientation.[95] Whereas individuals with a strong assessment orien-tation critically evaluate options among goals and the alternative ways to attain them, individuals with a strong locomotion orientation want to initiate action, to get started, even if that means not considering all the options fully. Individuals with a strong locomotion orientation are much more concerned about oppor-tunities to initiate and sustain movement than about maximizing value. They are motivated to change for the sake of change itself because it means movement,[96] and they will commit to change even when it might produce costs rather than benefits—a motivation very different from classic hedonic motivation.

This suggests that the "value × likelihood" function would work differently for individuals with a strong locomotion orientation. And, indeed, there is evi-dence that it does. High locomotors have been found to be relatively sensitive to differences in likelihood and relatively insensitive to differences in value. They are relatively insensitive to differences in value because it is change itself that is motivating rather than the benefits or costs that change can produce as outcomes. They are relatively sensitive to differences in likelihood because low likelihood is associated with difficulties, with obstacles or barriers that will disrupt smooth movement, whereas high likelihood is associated with easy and uninterrupted movement.[97]

Strength of Commitment as a Function of
the Goal-Pursuit Process

Effective control depends on having strong commitment. We have seen that strong commitment depends not only on the value and likelihood of successful goal pursuit but also on goal orientation. Strength of commitment also varies as a function of the goal-pursuit process itself. To illustrate the effects of the goal-pursuit process, I will consider two related motivational phenomena that Lewin and his colleagues were the first to study systematically—the "goal looms larger" effect and the "resumption of an interrupted task."[98]

Let's begin with the "goal looms larger" effect, where people's motivation to carry out the steps needed to reach a goal becomes stronger and stronger as they get closer to the goal. You might think that this effect can be explained by the value × likelihood function because as people get closer and closer to the goal they naturally believe that their likelihood of success is getting higher and higher. However, there is evidence that the "goal looms larger" effect is found even when the perceived likelihood of success is controlled by giving feedback throughout the goal-pursuit trials that explicitly maintains the same likelihood of ultimate success.[99] Indeed, because participants can be overconfident when they begin a task and the overconfidence slowly dissipates, the increased motivation as participants move toward the final trials of the task could even co-occur with decreased perceived likelihood of success on the task.

I believe that the motivational mechanism that produces the "goal looms larger" effect on commitment is the value of discrepancy-reducing steps rather than either the likelihood of success or the value of success.[100] As we continue with a goal pursuit that has a completion indicator (place or time), each step that we take reduces the *distance to completion* (distance in space or time). Thus, as we go along, each step *reduces the distance* to a greater extent. If you imagine 10 steps, for instance, the very first step reduces the remaining distance by 10%, but the very last step reduces the remaining distance by 100%. This increases commitment to perform each step more and more as we go along and get closer to completion of the goal-pursuit process.

If the mechanism underlying the "goal looms larger" effect is increased commitment to perform each step as we get closer to completion, then the strategic motivations involved in each step should increase in strength as we get closer to completion. And this increase in strategic motivation should be *specific to the strategies* that fit participants' goal orientation. In fact, there is evidence from several studies[101] that for participants with a promotion goal orientation, the "goal looms larger" effect is found for strategic eager responses that increase in strength (but not vigilant responses), whereas for participants with a prevention goal orientation, the "goal looms larger" effect is found for strategic vigilant responses that increase in strength (but not eager responses).

Let us now consider the second commitment phenomenon from Lewin and his colleagues—"resumption of an interrupted task." This refers to the fact that people, generally speaking, are strongly motivated to resume a task whose completion was interrupted rather than to begin a new task. From the perspective of the "value × likelihood" model, whether people choose to resume an interrupted task or instead choose to do a new task would depend on the value × likelihood utilities of the two options. Whichever has the greater utility would be chosen. But this is not always the case. For example, preference for the interrupted task is found even when the interruption involves failing to complete one item among a series of items from the exact same task. Even though the task is the same, people prefer to resume the item that was interrupted rather than start a new item from the same task.[102]

I believe that commitment to a goal pursuit that is interrupted, as reflected in resuming it rather than starting something new, derives not from the value or the likelihood of success in the goal pursuit but from motives concerning the goal-pursuit process itself. The original task that was interrupted represents where participants began, and not resuming the task means that there would be a missing step in the goal-pursuit process—a missing step along the way. Once again, the motivation is about *completion*. In this case it is about sustaining a course of action that has begun rather than switching to something new. If this is true, then the preference for resuming the interrupted task should be especially strong for individuals with a prevention goal orientation because their goal-process preference is maintenance of the status quo as long as it is satisfactory. Individuals with a promotion goal orientation, on the other hand, have a goal-process preference for advancement, for making progress.

In a study that tested these predictions,[103] prevention-oriented participants were much more likely than promotion-oriented participants to resume the interrupted activity rather than start a new one. In fact, more than half of the promotion-oriented participants preferred to start a new activity if they had to resume the interrupted activity from the very beginning. In contrast, 70% of the prevention-oriented participants still wanted to resume the interrupted activity, even when that meant redoing the part they had completed before the interruption.

In sum, the classic "value × likelihood" model, where commitment to goal pursuit derives from the positive multiplicative function of the subjective value of goal-pursuit success and the subjective likelihood of success, is an important part of the story of commitment, but it is not the whole story. Strength of commitment also varies as a function of the goal orientation of the goal pursuit, as well as other characteristics of the goal-pursuit process. In Chapter 7, I will discuss other ways that value and likelihood, and value and truth more generally, work together to create the commitment that is essential to effective control.

Sustaining Commitment

I turn now to the more specific issue of commitment management. For effective control, it is not enough to create strong commitment. Commitment must remain strong. *How is commitment sustained over time?* One answer has been discussed already—by planning *where*, *when*, and *how* the goal intention is implemented. We next consider some other answers.

GOAL SHIELDING

As I discussed earlier, competing goals have an inhibitory connection to one another. Given this, then activating or priming a competing goal, even if done unconsciously (i.e., subliminally), should reduce commitment to the focal goal. This is, in fact, the case.[104] Therefore, it is important for people to shield their focal goal from competing goals during goal pursuit. Evidence indicates that one way to accomplish this is to keep the focal goal activated, such as by reminding ourselves of its importance, in order to inhibit other goals competing with it.[105]

Other goal-shielding tactics include using selective attention to avoid activating a competing goal; biasing the processing of input information so that only focal goal-relevant information is encoded; or making a social commitment to other people to pursue the goal.[106] Yet a further shielding tactic would be to take a prevention orientation toward the goal, such as treating it as a personal duty or obligation, thereby experiencing the goal as a necessity.[107] A goal selected in the deliberation phase that is treated as a necessity would be shielded more effectively in subsequent phases.

SETTING A DIFFICULT GOAL

Inspired by the pioneering work of Edwin Locke, there is substantial evidence that performance can be enhanced by setting a difficult goal rather than an easy goal, such as my setting a weekly goal for writing this book at 15 pages rather than just 5 pages.[108] It is possible that setting a difficult goal is effective because it is another strategy for sustaining commitment. Generally speaking, the more difficult a task is, the more time and effort must be continually expended in order to succeed at it. With an easy goal of 5 pages a week, for example, I could begin on Monday and reach the goal by Wednesday and then stop for the rest of the week. With a difficult goal of 15 pages a week, I would have to work on the book almost every day of the week. Setting a difficult task, then, will sustain commitment to the goal pursuit. Perhaps this is why high-need achievers prefer a difficult task over an easy task.[109] However, selection of a difficult task has not only the downside of increasing the anticipated and actual likelihood of failure, but also the downside that the completion point may seem so far away that the motivational benefits from the "goal looms larger" effect will be lost.

MANIPULATING STRUCTURAL CHARACTERISTICS

Just as the connection between goals can be either facilitative or inhibitory, so can the connection between a goal and a means for attaining that goal. Given this, another strategy for strengthening commitment to a goal pursuit would be to strengthen the connection or association between a goal and a means for attaining it. Indeed, there is evidence that strengthening the goal–means connection by subliminal priming of both a goal and its means of attainment results in strengthening commitment to pursuing the goal more than priming just the means alone.[110]

There can also be competing means to the same goal, and they too, like competing goals, inhibit each other. Given this, commitment to carrying out a means activity in pursuit of a goal should be higher when there is only one means to the goal—*means uniqueness*—rather than multiple competing means. This prediction was tested in a study in which participants generated a goal and listed either just the focal means activity for attaining that goal or the focal means activity plus one additional means for attaining that goal. The study found that participants were more committed to the focal means activity when it was the only means for attaining the goal (i.e., it had means uniqueness).[111]

Making the Goal Pursuit Itself More Interesting

Thus far, I have emphasized properties of a goal (e.g., its value, its type of orientation, its shielding) that increase commitment to its pursuit. But commitment to pursuing a goal can wane during the actional phase of goal pursuit. The value of the goal, the expectancy of attaining it, the goal shielding, and so on are not always sufficient to maintain commitment throughout the goal-pursuit process, especially when interest in the goal-pursuit activity was low to begin with and the reasons for doing it were never that strong.

What happens if the goal is not that high in importance and the goal activity itself is quite boring? How do you stop yourself from quitting? Something else is needed to keep going. Carol Sansone, a renowned expert on the self-regulation of motivation, has found that people often use strategies to make the process of the goal pursuit, the goal activity itself, *more interesting*. For example, people will change the context in which the goal activity occurs, such as playing background music or doing the activity with another person.[112]

In sum, sustaining commitment to a goal pursuit is critical for effectively managing what happens (control effectiveness). There are various other factors that contribute to sustaining commitment beyond the "value × likelihood" function. These include goal shielding, goal setting, goal structure characteristics, and interest in the goal-pursuit process itself. These different factors are an important part of the story of commitment.

A Final Note on the Downside of Sustaining Commitment Too Long

With all of the emphasis on factors that create and sustain commitment for effective control, it is easy to overlook the fact that strong commitment has a downside as well. Single-minded, tenacious goal pursuit can be a problem. As one example, there can be *overcommitment* that produces *opportunity costs*, where the blind pursuit of a single goal results in forgoing the pursuit of other goals that could have even greater benefits. There can also be the *sunk-cost effect* of continuing to invest resources in a goal pursuit that is failing (i.e., "throwing good money after bad").[113]

Thus, people need to temper commitment to a goal pursuit with a willingness to be open to new options as they arise—both new goals and new means.[114] After all, the initial selection of the currently pursued goal occurred at one point in time in the past, sometimes the distant past, and things could have changed since then. People need to be willing to update, to *re-deliberate* about currently available options. Mechanisms that support such *flexibility* have received less empirical attention than mechanisms to increase commitment.[115]

Feedback

Effective control also requires receiving feedback about the goal pursuit. Feedback involves two stages of evaluating the goal pursuit activity—one while it is still ongoing ("How am I doing?") and the other after it is completed ("How did I do?"). People can evaluate themselves or be evaluated by someone else, as when a boss evaluates an employee. Models of self-regulation have paid most attention to self-evaluative feedback, which I will also mostly emphasize. I begin with the work of Carver and Scheier, whom I briefly mentioned in Chapter 2, because they have offered the most-developed and best-known model of self-regulatory feedback. I will describe their model for approaching goals or desired reference values (e.g., finding a better job), although the model also considers avoiding anti-goals or undesired reference values (e.g., avoiding being fired). I will also compare and contrast the proposals of their model to those I have made in *self-discrepancy theory*.

CARVER AND SCHEIER'S FEEDBACK CONTROL MODEL
Carver and Scheier's model proposes that there are two layers of managing what happens through feedback that keep a person on track during goal pursuit.[116] Both layers of feedback originate within the person. The first layer concerns goal attainment or maintenance and consists of an *input*, a *reference value*, a *comparison*, and an *output*.[117] The *input* is information about the present condition, the current state. This current state is *compared* to the *reference value* provided by the goal or desired end-state. If a discrepancy between the input (current state) and reference value (desired end-state) is detected in this comparison, then there is an error signal and an *output* of taking action to reduce (or eliminate) the discrepancy.

The second layer of feedback involves *affect* and provides the degree of urgency behind the action to reduce a detected discrepancy. This second layer functions simultaneously with the first layer and it monitors or checks on how well the first process is doing in its goal attainment or maintenance. Specifically, the input for the second layer of feedback is the *rate of discrepancy reduction over time*. There is a *rate criterion* that determines what affect occurs. When the rate of progress is above this criterion (doing well), positive affect occurs; when the rate of progress is below this criterion (not doing well enough), negative affect occurs.[118]

There is no assumption in Carver and Schier's feedback control model that people think about the significance of the affect that occurs from being above or below the rate criterion. Instead, the model proposes that the significance of the affect is intrinsic or inherent to the rate of progress being above or below the criterion. In other words, having an "above criterion" rate of progress in discrepancy reduction *is* positive affect, and having a "below criterion" rate of progress in discrepancy reduction *is* negative affect. This proposal of the feedback control model complements a proposal that I have made in *self-discrepancy theory* regarding the nature of affect.[119] Again, no additional inferential processes are postulated. Instead, it is assumed that affective experiences are the *direct experience* of specific relations within distinct self-regulatory systems. For example, when people experience a match between their current state and one of their ideal self-guides (a hope or aspiration), this experience of promotion success *is* feeling happy; and when there is a mismatch to their ideal self-guides, this experience of promotion failure *is* feeling sad. In contrast, when people experience a match between their current state and one of their ought self-guides (a duty or obligation), this experience of prevention success *is* feeling calm; and when there is a mismatch to their ought self-guides, this experience of prevention failure *is* feeling nervous.[120]

There is another aspect of Carver and Scheier's feedback control model worth noting. This is the idea that not only can the rate criterion change slowly over time as a function of experience, but it can also be influenced by the goal orientation that a person takes to the action, such as whether an individual has a promotion orientation or a prevention orientation. I agree with this position and would go further to suggest that goal orientation can influence whether the rate criterion is even the factor that determines what counts as "success" or "failure" in goal pursuit.

In Carver and Scheier's feedback control model, rate criterion concerns the rate of progress in discrepancy reduction. If people have made progress in their goal pursuit, it means that over a period of time they have managed to get closer to their goal than they were initially—*the current discrepancy is less than the initial discrepancy*. This certainly matters to individuals with a promotion orientation toward their goal pursuit. It is unclear, however, whether *progress per se* matters in the same way to individuals with a prevention orientation or a locomotion orientation. What matters for individuals with a prevention orientation is to meet their duties and obligations, to do what they ought to do. Anything less is unacceptable. Strictly speaking, there is no experience of progress. If you consider following the Ten Commandments to be a duty and obligation, something you ought to do, then you will not feel good about your rapid progress in moving from meeting six of them last week to meeting eight of them this week. Meeting all ten is necessary for control to be successful. Anything less is a failure that makes people feel agitated.

For individuals with strong locomotion concerns, what counts as successful control is also different. For them it is not about making progress by being closer now than before to the desired goal. In fact, it is not about a desired goal or end-state at all. It is about a change in state, about movement from an earlier state to a different state. And it is about the quality of the movement itself, whether it is smooth and uninterrupted—independent of the speed of discrepancy reduction. The path might not even be direct to the goal and thus progress might be minimal, but the control is successful as long as the movement continues undisrupted.

Thus, for individuals with a strong locomotion or a strong prevention orientation, the rate criterion is not the critical determinant of what counts as "success" or "failure." What this means is that people can evaluate their current state in terms of where they began (their initial state as reference point), or in terms of where they want to end up (their desired end-state as reference point), or in terms of how much progress they have made in reducing the discrepancy between where they are and where they want to be (both their initial state and desired end-state as reference points).[121] As Carver and Scheier's model suggests, individuals with a promotion orientation would evaluate their progress using both their initial state and desired end-state as reference points. But individuals with a prevention orientation would emphasize more the desired end-state as the reference point (the necessity to be there), and individuals with a locomotion orientation would emphasize more the initial state as the reference point (to move away from).

EFFECTS OF AFFECT ON SELF-REGULATION

In Carver and Scheier's feedback control model, as well as in self-discrepancy theory, monitoring the relation between our current state and our goal creates affective experiences. What is the impact of these affective experiences on self-regulation? In the feedback control model, the function of the affect is a sensed rate of progress regarding the goal-pursuit action that produces changes in rate of action to satisfy the rate criterion. For example, the model predicts that *positive affect*, which signals exceeding the criterion rate of progress, will produce *coasting*—easing back and slowing down to return to the criterion. Affect also influences the priority that is given to this goal pursuit versus alternative goal pursuits, such as *negative affect* signaling the need for *greater investment* in the focal goal.[122]

Affective experiences have other effects as well on self-regulation. In self-discrepancy theory, for example, affective experiences are pleasant or painful experiences that motivate taking action. The hedonic experiences are specifically tied to the process of self-evaluation, with each goal also functioning as a self-evaluative standard, and meeting or failing to meet that standard produces positive or negative self-evaluations, respectively.[123] There are two ways that a current discrepancy produces motivation to take action to reduce the discrepancy: taking action to meet the standard in order to remove the pain from the *present* negative self-evaluation, and taking action in order to attain the anticipated pleasure from a *future* positive self-evaluation.

Consistent with the emphasis in the psychological literature, I have emphasized thus far the feedback system involving self-evaluation regarding "How am I doing?" But people can also experience feedback about how they are doing from others, including feedback associated with the viewpoints of significant others. In addition, rather than self-evaluative feedback about the current state of affairs producing feelings as described in the above models, feelings themselves can provide feedback about the current state of affairs. Let us now consider some of these additional feedback mechanisms and functions.

Success and Failure Feedback from Significant Others

When considering the affective consequences of success and failure feedback, we must keep in mind that it is not only individuals' personal viewpoint or standpoint on success and failure that matters to them. The ideal goals or ought goals that significant others have for an individual can also matter. Following a long history of psychodynamic concepts,[124] self-discrepancy theory distinguishes among three types of goals: (a) individuals' goals for themselves that are only their own personal goals, independent of others' (*independent* self-guides); (b) goals for themselves that their significant others also have for them (*shared* self-guides or identification); and (c) goals that their significant others have for them that they do *not* have for themselves (*introjected* self-guides or "the felt presence of others").[125]

In Western cultures at least, there is evidence that males' affective reactions to success and failure feedback are more influenced by their independent goals than by their parents' goals for them, whereas females' affective reactions are more influenced by the shared goals that they and their parents have for them. In addition, it is much more common for females than males to be emotionally influenced by introjected (i.e., *not* shared) goals that their mother holds for them—an emotional "felt presence" of the mother.[126] Even for people who might otherwise evaluate their success or failure in relation to their own goals for themselves, the activation of a significant other can cause them to evaluate themselves in relation to what that significant other would want them to attain. And how they actually feel about their success or failure will depend on whether that significant other's goal for them is associated with a promotion orientation (an ideal) or a prevention orientation (an ought).[127]

As an example of the impact that significant others can have on self-evaluation, participants in one study[128] were asked a variety of different questions about different people they knew. One question asked how much their father would ideally want them to do well on an anagram task (strength of *father ideal* for them), and another question asked how much their father felt they had a duty or obligation to do well on an anagram task (strength of *father ought* for them). Before performing the actual anagram task, they worked on some practice items, and while they worked they were subliminally (unconsciously) primed with father-related words (e.g., father; dad) or control non-words. After performing the anagram task, they received either success or failure feedback. Among the participants who had "father" subliminally primed, those whose fathers held a strong ideal for them felt cheerful after success feedback and dejected after failure feedback, whereas those whose fathers held a strong ought for them felt relaxed after success feedback and agitated after failure feedback.

SELF-ESTEEM FEELINGS AS FEEDBACK ABOUT SOCIAL ACCEPTANCE

The significance of feedback regarding others' viewpoint is not restricted to the effects of internally represented significant others. Individuals are highly sensitive to actual evaluative feedback from others as well. Consequential emotions like "shame" and "pride" can result from such feedback.[129] Indeed, Mark Leary, a leading figure in showing how interpersonal factors affect self-regulation, argues that self-esteem itself, which is often discussed as a strictly intrapersonal variable, is interpersonal at its core.[130] He proposes a "sociometer" mechanism motivated by the need to belong that controls a person's interpersonal behavior in the service of finding social acceptance and avoiding social rejection.

According to the "sociometer" theory, it is not people's need to feel good about themselves that underlies how self-esteem functions. Instead, feelings of high self-esteem provide feedback of belongingness success (i.e., having high relational value to others) and feelings of low self-esteem provide feedback of belongingness failure (i.e., having low relational value to others). If self-esteem is low, people take action to raise it—but this is not because they need to feel good about themselves, or even because low self-esteem feels unpleasant (although hedonic concerns do play a role). Rather, people take action to improve their belongingness, to raise their relational value to others.

Feedback from self-esteem feelings is different from the feedback described in most self-evaluation models because the self-esteem feelings are themselves the feedback signal about what is happening. In the other models, the affect is a product of what the feedback says about the condition of this relation (e.g., success or failure; congruency or discrepancy), together with the orientation that is associated with the goal (e.g., promotion or prevention). In Leary's "sociometer" theory, it is the self-esteem feelings themselves that directly provide the feedback.

"Feelings as Information" Feedback More Generally

A more general version of "feelings as information" feedback has been proposed by Norbert Schwarz, a pathbreaker in clarifying how feelings affect judgment and decision making. In his model, the focus is on affect itself and the feedback information it provides about a person's current condition.[131] The model proposes that our feelings inform us about the nature of our current psychological situation. Negative feelings inform us that our current condition is problematic, signaling either the lack of positive outcomes or the threat of negative outcomes. This feedback increases people's attempts to control what is or might be happening to them. Positive feelings, on the other hand, inform us that our current condition is non-problematic or benign, signaling either the presence of positive outcomes or the absence of the threat of negative outcomes. These positive feelings temporarily decrease control motivation. The information feedback from monitoring these good or bad feelings produces different processing strategies, such as individuals with positive feelings investing less cognitive effort than individuals with negative feelings.

If affect in general can provide information to people about their self-regulatory condition, is there anything special about self-esteem feelings *per se*? The "sociometer" model makes a distinction between feelings that signal what is happening right now and self-esteem feelings that signal something more stable that predicts the future. Rather than signaling something about people's current condition, self-esteem signals their eligibility for (or the likelihood of) having a stable condition of being accepted and having strong relational value. This is what gives self-esteem, as a self-regulatory signal, such power. Given this, I should note that it loses this power—and its validity—if it is falsely created. It needs to derive, in fact, from people's relational value to others. Interventions to boost self-esteem that do not increase actual relational value, such as a mother pretending that her son is popular with his peers when he is not, do more harm than good. It is equivalent to directly changing the fuel indicator in a car to signal full when no gasoline has been added to the empty tank.

The Rubicon Model Redux

I should mention another important kind of feedback that has received relatively little empirical attention—the postactional assessment phase of the

Rubicon Model. This phase includes feedback about whether the actual value of goal success (or failure) matches the expected value.[132] The monitoring and feedback require waiting some period after the goal pursuit has been completed to determine the actual consequences of goal success (or failure). The literature on affective forecasting suggests that it is quite common for the actual value of success (or failure) to be different than the expected value, with the actual value typically being less intense than expected.[133] In other words, one's affective forecasts of the value of a goal at the beginning of its pursuit are often mistaken. The function of the feedback about what actually happened after goal completion is *to improve future planning*, such as to improve affective forecasting. How well this function is generally served by the postactional assessment is not well known. It seems that people do not learn that well from their mistakes in affective forecasting. They also do not learn well from past mistakes in predicting how long they will take to complete a task (the planning fallacy).[134] But such slow learning may be more true for these kinds of forecasting than for other aspects of goal pursuit.

THE POWER OF WANTING EFFECTIVE CONTROL

I should note that people's motivation to experience themselves as having control, as managing what happens, is so strong that they will perceive themselves as having control over events that are actually outside of their control. They will even perceive themselves as having controlled events for which there are clear costs of taking personal responsibility. In brief, there are cases where wanting control trumps truth and trumps value.

Let me begin with an example of the first case—a phenomenon called *the illusion of control*.[135] As a stylus traveled down one of three possible paths, participants were asked to guess for which one of these paths a buzzer would sound as it traveled down it. The participants were told that the machine was preprogrammed so that on each trial which path would produce the buzzer sound was random. Thus, the participants had no control over whether the buzzer would sound as the stylus moved down a particular path on a particular trial.

Prior to the official task beginning, some participants were given "practice" doing the task, whereas others were given no practice. In addition, some participants moved the stylus themselves after selecting the path, whereas others only selected the path and the experimenter moved the stylus. Despite the randomness of success in turning on the buzzer, the participants who moved the stylus themselves and were given practice, compared to those who did not, were much more confident before the official task began that they would correctly select the path where the buzzer would sound.

This illusion of control from being responsible for some action, despite the outcome being independent of that action, is also found among some people playing craps in casinos, where they will throw the dice harder when they want high numbers to turn up and throw softer when they want low numbers to turn up. And people can have an illusion of control even when they are not themselves responsible for an action but simply anticipate what action will be taken by someone else. In one study, for example, an experimental assistant stood hidden from view behind the participants, and with extended hands forward on each side of the participant, made hand movements where the participant's hands would normally make the movements. When the participants could hear the instructions for what the assistant's hands should do next, and thus could anticipate what the hand movements would be, the participants felt like they themselves were controlling the hands of the person behind them.[136]

These cases demonstrate that people want to experience control, want to believe that they are managing to make things happen, even when they do not actually have control. They illustrate that *wanting control can trump wanting truth*. One would expect, however, that when it is *costly* to be responsible for making something happen people would no longer want to see themselves as being in control. In fact, people generally do take less responsibility for bad things that happen than for good things that happen.[137] Nonetheless, there are cases where *wanting control can trump wanting value*.

Take the example of a team competing with another team. One might expect that the team partners would remember that they were the more active partner on the team—they made more things happen than their partner—if their team won the competition, but *not* if their team lost the competition. But, win or lose, people remember that they were the more active partner on the team, attributing to themselves more than 50% of the team's actions.[138] Similarly, there are times when people are willing to take responsibility for having caused another person to suffer even though the other person's fate was simply chance or caused by someone else. In one study, for example, there were two participants at a time and one of them was told by the experimenter to draw a slip that would determine which of the two participants would receive an electric shock. Thus, the fact that one of the participants would receive a shock was determined by the experimenter, *not* by the participants, and which participant would receive the shock was *random*. Nonetheless, those participants who were told to draw the slip by the experimenter, and then happened to draw one that assigned the other participant to be shocked, were five times more likely to take responsibility for the other participant being shocked than other participants who were not given the task of drawing the shock-assignment slip.[139]

People are willing to take responsibility for causing something bad to happen not only when they are not responsible but even when they know they will be *punished* for taking responsibility. An extreme case of this is the phenomenon that criminal psychologists call "Confessing Sam." An infamous example was

Robert Hubert, who in 1666 confessed to having started the Great Fire of London, which destroyed most of the city, by throwing a type of fire grenade through the open window of a bakery. The problem with his confession was that Hubert, who was a sailor, had not even arrived in England until two days *after* the fire started. Moreover, the bakery itself had no windows. Despite all of this trial evidence against his confession, Hubert maintained that he was guilty, and he was executed by hanging.

In case you are thinking to yourself that perhaps Hubert was somehow guilty after all, I should note that when Charles Lindbergh's child was kidnapped, *over 100 different people* confessed to being the abductor. They could not have all been guilty. Such cases of "Confessing Sam," in fact, continue to be a major problem for police who end up wasting time checking out numerous false confessions after highly publicized crimes. What they illustrate is how strongly people can want to experience themselves as being effective at control, even if it requires distorting the truth to the point of fantasy and having undesired results to the point of execution—*control trumping both truth and value.*[140]

This chapter has reviewed control effectiveness—*managing what happens.* I have reviewed the two classic self-control issues of resisting temptation and controlling unwanted inner states. I have also described being effective at control beyond self-control *per se.* Specifically, I have described the selection, commitment, and feedback functions that must be managed more generally in order to control what happens in goal pursuit. This chapter has also begun to address the central theme of the book—the importance of *motivations working together.* For example, I described the significance of regulatory fit in goal pursuit—whether the strategic manner of goal pursuit sustains (fit) or disrupts (non-fit) the goal orientation of the actor. Regulatory fit represents a *relation* between goal orientations such as promotion versus prevention (two different value orientations) and strategic processes such as being eager versus vigilant (two different means of control)—a *value–control relation.* I should also note that feedback itself is information that establishes what's real regarding how we are doing in our self-regulation, and thus its use in control involves truth and control motivations working together—a *truth–control relation.* I will return to these particular relations in Chapters 8 and 9. But in the next chapter, I will consider more fully the value–truth relation.

PART THREE

Motivations Working Together

Value–Truth Relations

Creating Commitment

"Wheresoever you go, go with all your heart."

—Confucius

"The men who have succeeded are men who have chosen one line and stuck to it."

—Andrew Carnegie

"What this power is I cannot say; all I know is that it exists and it becomes available only when a man is in that state of mind in which he knows exactly what he wants and is fully determined not to quit until he finds it."

—Alexander Graham Bell

It is commonly believed that the most important single factor in the success of individuals or groups is their *commitment* to what they are doing. Alexander Graham Bell knew that commitment existed, but he wondered what was behind its power. What is it that motivates people to go with *all their heart* (Confucius) and *stick to their chosen path* (Andrew Carnegie)? Again, as I discussed briefly in Chapter 6, the usual answer is that the strength of people's commitment to something depends on its value to them and the likelihood that the value will, in fact, occur. To foreshadow my major take-away message in this chapter, what has received insufficient emphasis in the literature is the fact that "likelihood" is a motivational force in its own right; it is not simply a factor that qualifies or moderates value as *the* motivational force. To appreciate "likelihood" as a separate motivational force, it must be recognized that likelihood relates to its own motivation—the motivation to establish what's real (truth effectiveness). What is critical about commitment is that it derives from the two motivations of value and truth *working together*.

"Commitment" means *to pledge or bind oneself to some particular course of action*, and for such a pledge to occur the action must be seen as being worthwhile, as having what's desired. Thus, value is an important contributor to commitment. But value alone is not enough: the meaning of "commitment" also includes the concept of *putting your trust in something*.[1] And people must establish something as real in order to put their trust in it. Thus, commitment also requires truth, a belief in the likelihood that something will occur as a result of this commitment. Commitment, then, derives from a combination of value and truth—it involves value and truth working together. The purpose of this chapter is to review the different ways in which this combination operates.[2] When do people choose to commit to something? What conditions support such commitment? These are central issues in this chapter. I begin by discussing the *value–likelihood* relation—the best-known value–truth relation that creates commitment to something. I then discuss the different ways in which truth, represented as likelihood, is a motivational force in its own right that affects both commitment *and* value itself.

THE VALUE–LIKELIHOOD RELATION

In traditional models of motivation, commitment derives from the *value × likelihood function*, which is a multiplicative function of the subjective value of successful goal pursuit and the subjective likelihood of successful goal pursuit. However, as I previously discussed in Chapter 6, there is more to the story of commitment than just the value × likelihood function. For example, people will be strongly committed to a highly valued prevention goal even when the likelihood of its attainment is low. The purpose of this section, then, is to garner the lessons to be learned about commitment not only from what the "value × likelihood" function teaches us but also from other evidence regarding how value and likelihood work together. I have selected the "value × likelihood" model as the starting point for learning these lessons because of its historical and continuing status as the standard model of commitment. I begin by distinguishing between two versions of this model.

Subjective Expected Utility and Expectancy Value as Models of Commitment

People commit to taking action that they anticipate (likelihood) will result in their having what they desire in the future (value). This basic motivational effect of regulatory anticipation has been proposed in various forms for centuries[3] and by scholars across a broad range of areas.[4] What is being proposed is that the motivational force of a future desired outcome on current commitment to take action is quantified (i.e., made stronger or weaker) by the anticipation that the outcome will actually occur (i.e., will be real in the future).

The psychological nature of the anticipation that quantifies value is different in different models. It can be specific expectancies concerning each of the outcomes of performing some action or engaging in some activity.[5] It can be anticipation concerning the likelihood of effective performance from self-percepts of efficacy.[6] It can be general anticipations of success or failure from chronic achievement motives.[7] It can be perceptions of task difficulty or luck.[8] It can be anticipations that derive from simulations or predictions using pre-established norms (what would normally happen) or counterfactual thinking (what might happen instead).[9]

What interests me most here is how anticipation is treated by the two most influential models of commitment in psychology—the *subjective expected utility* model and the *expectancy value* model. What has received less attention than it deserves[10] is the fact that how *anticipation* quantifies value in these two models is quite different, despite these models having similar names. This is not to say that there are no similarities between the two models: there are significant similarities and, because they provide a useful general lesson about commitment, I will begin with a lesson from what these models have in common. But then I will discuss how these two models are more different than their names would suggest.

The subjective expected utility model and the expectancy value model both propose that commitment comes from the subjective value of the future outcomes that an action would produce, quantified by how strongly those outcomes are anticipated. And the quantification from anticipation produces a *multiplicative* function. The logic is that a high future value from taking action is not motivating if you know it will definitely not happen. The general lesson from both models, then, is that commitment is not just about contemplating the future value of taking action (value) because it matters to people whether that future value is real or imaginary (truth).

Despite these similarities, however, closer inspection of these models reveals major differences in the nature of the value–truth relation that they propose.

It is these differences that I will discuss in more detail because they have received insufficient attention in the literature.

THE SUBJECTIVE EXPECTED UTILITY (SEU) MODEL

This model assumes that the possible outcomes from taking some action are disjunctive; that is, the outcomes are *mutually exclusive* alternatives, joined by "or." For example, when deciding whether to commit to entering a race, a track star could think about the likelihood of coming in first (gold) *or* second (silver) *or* third (bronze) *or* worse than third (no medal). In addition, the outcomes are *exhaustive*, capturing all of the possible outcomes. Given these assumptions, the joint (subjective) probabilities of the possible outcomes sum to 100%.[11] In the simple case of succeeding or failing on a task, success and failure as outcomes are mutually exclusive and exhaustive. There is a subjective likelihood of success and a subjective likelihood of failure, and these sum to 100%.[12]

Consider another example. If I go to my boss to ask for a raise, one of three outcomes could happen: I could keep my job and get a raise, *or* I could keep my job but not get a raise, *or* I could lose my job and not get a raise. Each of these three possible outcomes has some likelihood of happening, and together their probabilities add to 100%. The remaining fourth possibility—my boss could fire me and give me a raise—is not logically possible (i.e., a likelihood of 0%), and thus it would not be included among the possible outcomes. Each of the three possible outcomes from going to my boss to ask for a raise has some subjective value to me. Keeping my job and getting a raise has high positive value to me. Keeping my job but not getting a raise would have moderately negative value to me. Losing my job and not getting a raise has very high negative value to me.

The subjective utility of my going to my boss to ask for a raise combines the three products of the three possible outcomes multiplied by each of their (subjective) probabilities of happening. I end with a resultant utility that is positive or negative of varying intensity. For instance, if I believe that it is extremely unlikely that my boss would fire me just for asking for a raise, and getting a raise is more likely than not getting a raise, then the resultant utility of asking for a raise would be positive. But if I believe that it is somewhat likely that my boss would fire me for asking for a raise, and getting versus not getting a raise is equally likely, then the resultant utility of my asking for a raise would be negative.

The utility of my going to my boss to ask for a raise is then compared to the utility of the alternative of my *not* going to my boss to ask for a raise. This alternative also has a resultant activity that combines the value × likelihood of the three different possible outcomes (i.e., keeping my job and getting a raise; keeping my job but not getting a raise; losing my job and not getting a raise). The (subjective) probabilities of these outcomes still sum to 100%, but the likelihood for each outcome would be different for this alternative of *not* going to my boss to ask for a raise. For example, getting a raise would be less likely, but keeping my job would be more likely. Finally, after comparing the resultant utilities for both alternatives—going to my boss and asking for a raise versus *not* going to my boss and asking for a raise—I then choose whichever alternative has the more positive utility.

A key feature of the SEU model is that it represents the outcomes from making a particular choice as the discrete, disjunctive, mutually exclusive *events that could happen from making that particular choice*, which together capture all the possible endings (i.e., exhaustive of all possibilities). But *only one of the possible events will actually happen*. It is like imagining a story with different endings, but only one of the endings actually happens in the story.

THE EXPECTANCY VALUE (EV) MODEL

Instead of the SEU model's mutually exclusive, disjunctive events joined together by "or," the EV model represents outcomes as *conjunctive*, inclusive alternatives joined together by "and." Multiple outcomes can *all* actually happen.[13] For example, Edward Tolman described the motivation of a rat to perform some action to attain food as being a joint function of the positive outcome of the expected food *and* the negative outcome of the expected work required to attain the food.[14] *Both* the positive food *and* the negative work are expected to actually happen.

To return to my earlier example, if I go to my boss to ask for a raise, I have some level of expectancy that I will keep my job and get a raise. I also have some level of expectancy that I will feel nervous and embarrassed when I ask for the raise; that my boss will be annoyed at me for having asked for a raise; that my fellow employees will disapprove of my asking for a raise; and that my spouse will be proud of me for asking for a raise. And more than one of these outcomes can happen; indeed, all of them can actually happen in the end.

Each outcome has a subjective value to me, some positive and some negative, and each has some (subjective) likelihood of happening. Because the likelihood that something positive will happen is quite high (combining the value × expectancy of all of the positive possibilities) and the likelihood that something negative will happen is also quite high (combining the value × expectancy of all of the negative possibilities), this model predicts *conflict and ambivalence* about taking action in a case like this where both positive and negative outcomes are likely to co-occur. Even if I combine all the outcomes and the overall result is positive, I will still experience some resistance to taking this action because I believe that it is highly likely that *something negative* will also occur. That is, I believe that overall there will be more positive outcomes than negative outcomes from taking some action, but I also believe that in the end I will experience something negative as well.

This is quite different from the SEU model. According to it, the resultant expected utility after summing the utilities of all the possible outcomes from taking some action must be either positive or negative (or perhaps neutral)—it cannot be both positive and negative. For the SEU model, when the possible outcomes of taking some action include a highly likely negative outcome in addition to other possible outcomes that are all highly likely to be positive, the presence of the highly likely negative outcome simply reduces the resultant positive utility of taking that action. In fact, the positive resultant could be more positive, and predict stronger commitment, than a case where there is no possible negative outcome and only moderately likely positive outcomes.

In contrast, for the EV model, when the possible outcomes of taking some action include a highly likely negative outcome in addition to other possible outcomes that are all highly likely to be positive, the presence of the highly likely negative outcome creates some conflict and ambivalence. This conflict and ambivalence could reduce commitment even though the result overall was more positive than the case where there is no possible negative outcome and only moderately likely positive outcomes. But what if the decision was made to take the action despite the conflict and ambivalence? This could function like overcoming resistance or opposing an interfering force that I discussed in Chapter 4, which would strengthen engagement in taking the action and increase its value.[15] The EV model raises these intriguing possibilities, whereas the SEU model does not.

Thus, the SEU model and the EV model, despite seeming like twins reared apart, have different implications for commitment when there are negative outcomes combined with positive outcomes. This difference has received little attention in the literature. And there is another difference between them that should be highlighted—*they emphasize different kinds of outcomes.* As illustrated in a murder mystery, two kinds of outcomes are important to the story: which character at the end of the story is arrested for the murder, and what effects the murder has on all of the characters. But these are different parts of the story. The EV model represents outcomes as all the possible ramifications of having made a particular choice, like all the twists and turns that can happen after the opening murder in the mystery story. The murder action has a multitude of effects on the different characters in the story. It is not about *the* final story ending—the one character who ends up being arrested for the murder—but about all of the effects on all of the characters. The outcome emphasized by the SEU model—which character is arrested at the end—is interesting, but it is *not* the whole story.

Imagine that I take the action of asking my boss for a raise. According to the SEU model, there will be only one ending to my story—either I keep my job and get the raise, or I keep my job but don't get the raise, or I get fired and don't get the raise. Any one of these mutually exclusive events will provide a simple end to the story. But is life so simple? Is it not more likely that, whatever my boss ends up doing, my outcomes will be mixed? Even the happy ending of keeping my job and getting the raise can include the negative outcomes of my boss liking me less and my colleagues being envious of me. This added complexity is nicely captured in the EV model.[16]

VALUE AS *THE* DRIVING FORCE OF COMMITMENT

Although the SEU and EV models differ in important ways, there is a major similarity in these models that needs to be highlighted as well. This is their assumption that value is *the* driving force of commitment. They propose that commitment to a choice alternative derives from the subjective value of the outcomes of that choice and the subjective likelihood that those outcomes will occur, with the relation between these two factors being multiplicative.[17] Even when the models do not formally describe the relation between value and likelihood as multiplicative, they include a discussion that suggests that it is multiplicative.[18]

What is notable about the proposed multiplicative relation is that it is *about value*. The contribution of subjective likelihood to this relation is to *moderate the strength of the value force*. Subjective likelihood is *not* treated as a motivational force in its own right. Once again, it is all about incentives for doing something; in this case, incentives for making a particular choice. It is all about wanting desired results. The more valued the desired results, the stronger the commitment to making the choice that will attain them. In the SEU and EV models, subjective likelihood makes no separate contribution to commitment as a motivational force in its own right. It simply qualifies the impact of subjective value on commitment by taking into account how likely it is that the desired results will actually happen. For example, I am not committed to winning an Olympic track medal, despite its being a highly valuable outcome, because I know it's impossible. Later in this section, I will question whether value is *the* driving force of commitment. But first I need to address several issues regarding the nature of value itself.

Different Kinds of Value in Value–Likelihood Models

The first issue is *which* "value" exactly is being referred to as the driving force of commitment. It turns out that different models refer to different kinds of "value" as the driving force. Is it the value from having been successful in attaining the goal, or is it the value associated with the positive outcomes that follow as a consequence of the success? Consider a second-year college woman who receives an "A" at the end of a course. Imagine that it was a difficult course and she naturally feels proud about her success at getting an "A." At the beginning of the course she had anticipated the pride of success in getting an "A" in this difficult course, and this motivated her to work hard in the course—the classic high need achiever.[19] This is one scenario, the kind of *achievement scenario* that McClelland and Atkinson describe in their standard model of achievement motivation. It is about success itself.

Consider now another scenario. The same student needs to receive an "A" in this course in order to be accepted into her preferred major. She understands her situation very well, and it is straightforward. She can work hard and end up getting the "A" needed for acceptance into the desired major, or she can *not* work hard and *not* end up getting the "A" needed for acceptance into the desired major. (She believes that not working hard and still ending up getting the "A," and working hard and not getting the "A," are both very low likelihood events.) She decides to work hard and, as predicted, she gets an "A" and is accepted into the major she wants. This is the kind of choice scenario that is described in standard decision-making models. It is about the anticipated consequences that follow from the success.

The events in these two scenarios are not mutually exclusive. Both the pride of succeeding and the positive consequences that follow from the success could happen to the same student. But the value that is treated as the driving force on commitment is different in these two scenarios. What is striking about the standard achievement scenario is that value ends with the student's success in getting an "A." Being effective in getting an "A" *is* value, *is* having desired results. The feedback signal of this success is the pride that is experienced (and, perhaps, joy or relief as well). It is anticipating this pride of success that motivates her hard work in the course. Remarkably, it is not *about* what follows after getting the "A"; it is not about the consequences or outcomes that result from getting the "A."

In the choice scenario, on the other hand, it *is* about the results that follow from something happening. It is *not* about the success *per se* in having made a choice between them. For our student in the choice scenario, what motivates her hard work in the course is getting the "A" needed for acceptance into the desired major. It is the outcome that follows from getting the "A," the outcome of acceptance into the desired major, that motivates her hard work in the course.[20]

So *which* value is the driving force on commitment? Is it simply the signal of successful goal pursuit, or is it the outcomes that follow from that success?

Are professionals motivated by "signs of success," such as receiving awards and prizes for their accomplishments, or are they motivated by the consequences of having received these awards and prizes, such as "fame and fortune" or the admiration and respect of friends and family? I think it is clear that both kinds of value can be motivating. What is not known as yet is which kind of value is more motivating and whether this varies across individuals and across situations. But what needs to be better recognized is that value is not just about the consequences that follow from success. Independent from and prior to whatever desired results follow from success, there is value in having been successful. Let me say a little more about this kind of value experience.

Value From Signals of Success

It is significant that for humans, and perhaps for other animals as well, simply the signals of success, signals of being effective, can themselves constitute having what's desired. Moreover, the signals can vary in intensity. People can feel mildly or extremely happy about their success, mildly or extremely proud of having been successful. Our student could feel proud after receiving an "A" or feel extremely proud after receiving an "A+." And these differences in signal intensity from different levels of success could be anticipated and could influence level of commitment. It is even possible that the anticipated outcomes when making choices could themselves function *in an achievement manner,* much like the effects of receiving an "A+" rather than an "A"—the difference between believing that we just made a great choice (an "A+" success) and we just made a good choice (an "A" success). Anticipation of the actual outcomes that will follow from goal success is still part of what commits people to a choice, but what is striking here is the potential contribution to commitment from simply succeeding at making an excellent choice—stronger commitment to one's choice because one feels so successful in having made such a good choice.

If this is so, it has interesting implications for the time course of value from signals of success as compared to value from the outcomes that follow from success. Value from such outcomes, such as the benefits of "fame and fortune" following high professional success, can last a long time. So too could the benefits to the student from being in her desired major, which was an outcome that followed from her receiving the "A" in the course. In contrast, the value of the signal of success, such as the award received by the professional or the value of the "A" in the course, decays relatively quickly. The student, for example, needs to turn her attention to a new goal pursuit in order to experience a new signal of success. Thus, there is a temporal difference in these two kinds of value. The value from the achievement success itself is relatively short-lived compared to the value from the post-success consequences. The phenomenon of people continually striving, moving from one success to another, never being satisfied with any single success, reflects the former kind of value (the signal of success) more than the latter (the post-success consequences).

Another implication is that being successful at something, especially a big something that took a long time to achieve, can produce a motivational letdown. The value from the achievement success signal decays quickly, and the goal pursuit itself is no longer motivating because it is completed. These factors could underlie the phenomenon of people becoming depressed a few months after receiving some major professional award—something they were striving after for years. And it is not just professional awards. People can pursue a relationship with another person as a sign of success, such as a "trophy wife." And again, once successful, there can be a motivational letdown. The benefits associated with that special wife are still present as post-success outcomes, but the motivation underlying the goal pursuit itself is over once the pursuit is successfully completed.

In sum, it is important to distinguish commitment from the value of succeeding in goal pursuit versus commitment from the outcomes that will follow from goal-pursuit success. Not surprisingly given the dominance of the hedonic principle, standard models of commitment have given more attention to the latter than the former, especially in decision-making models of choice. But it is clear that people want to make a "good choice" as an achievement success in addition to wanting the positive outcomes that follow from making a good choice. And they will remain committed to an earlier choice, and even forcefully defend it, despite the outcomes ending up negative. Independent of the value of the outcomes that actually followed their choice, people want to believe that they succeeded at the time they made their choice: "Yes, it turned out badly, but at the time that I made my choice, with the information available to me then, it was definitely the right choice. So I feel good about it."

Value as a Determinant of Subjective Likelihood Itself

The final issue regarding value as a driving force of commitment is a "bad news" story of its power as a driving force. Value can be so powerful as a force that likelihood no longer serves its function as an *independent* variable that moderates or qualifies the effect of value on commitment by providing information about whether the valued results will actually happen.

It has been recognized for a long time that the truth about the world—what reality is established—can be determined not only bottom-up by data but also top-down by which truth is desired, which reality is valued—"wishful thinking." This recognition took many forms during the 20th century, from the

Freudian perspectives on the effects of unconscious wishes on comprehending the world,[21] to the "New Look" studies of the effects of values and needs on perception,[22] to the motivated cognition work on self-enhancement and goal effects on judgment, reasoning, and decision making.[23]

Given that the subjective likelihood of something happening is an inference or judgment about the truth (i.e., what will be real in the future), it would not be surprising if people's subjective values (i.e., what desired results they *want* to have) can influence their subjective likelihoods. And, indeed, there is clear evidence that they can. Studies have found that the perceived likelihood of desired outcomes is higher than that of undesired outcomes.[24] In one study,[25] for example, it was found that people playing the lottery who had lower incomes (i.e., people for whom the subjective value of winning the lottery would be higher) believed that their likelihood of winning the lottery was higher than those playing the same lottery who had higher incomes. What this means is that a key assumption of value–likelihood models that value and likelihood are independent variables can be undermined by the fact that value can bias judgments of subjective likelihood.

LIKELIHOOD AS A DRIVING FORCE OF COMMITMENT

Clearly, value is a motivational force producing commitment, and I have just addressed several issues regarding the nature of that force. But is it *the* motivational force that value–likelihood models propose? As mentioned, what is remarkable about these models is that there is no discussion of the possibility that subjective likelihood could be a separate motivational factor that contributes to commitment in its own right. Even when value and likelihood are not formally described in terms of a multiplicative relation in which value is qualified by likelihood, there is no consideration of likelihood as a separate motivational force. If this notion of value being the only motivational force on commitment were correct, then studies of the impact of subjective value and subjective likelihood on choice commitment or goal commitment would find either just an effect of value alone (i.e., a main effect of value) or a multiplicative effect of value qualified or moderated by likelihood. But this is *not* what the literature finds. There is often a separate effect of subjective likelihood on commitment, such as a higher likelihood of a successful outcome increasing goal commitment separate from the value of a successful outcome.[26] Thus, there is empirical evidence that likelihood is a separate motivational force. Indeed, in some ways likelihood can be *the* driving force on commitment. What has received insufficient attention in value–likelihood models is that subjective likelihood is another way to *establish what's real*, and when something is real it is more engaging. Let us now consider the different ways that likelihood can motivate commitment.

James' "Ideo-motor Action" Notion

As with many things psychological, it was William James who first suggested that a critical force driving action is *beliefs about what is real*—that is, beliefs about what will or will not really happen.[27] James, however, was not explicitly contrasting value as a motivational force with likelihood as a motivational force; he was not even explicitly talking about likelihood *per se*. He was talking about the perception of reality, and how believing (vs. doubting) instigated action.

There are two steps in the Jamesian perspective. The first is to treat something as real: "Everyone knows the difference between imagining a thing and believing in its existence, between supposing a proposition and acquiescing in its truth. In the case of acquiescence or belief, the object is not only apprehended by the mind, but is held to have reality. Belief is thus the mental state or function of cognizing reality . . . 'Belief' will mean every degree of assurance, including the highest possible certainty and conviction."[28] For James, then, a belief reflects the highest possible likelihood that something is real, that something is the truth.

And for James a belief is not simply a cognition, not just stored information about something. It is a sense of reality, a sort of feeling that is more like an emotion than anything else. And this leads to the second step. James proposes that *a belief is a feeling of acquiescence* that relates to volition and then action: "It resembles more than anything what in the psychology of volition we know as consent. Consent is recognized by all to be a manifestation of our active nature. It would naturally be described by such terms as 'willingness' or the 'turning of our disposition.' What characterizes both consent and belief is the cessation of theoretic agitation, through the advent of an idea which is inwardly stable, and fills the mind solidly to the exclusion of contradictory ideas. When this is the case, motor effects are apt to follow."[29]

This proposal is James' famous "ideo-motor action" notion that a bare idea can be sufficient to prompt action: "We think the act, and it is done."[30] But what James makes clear is that the "ideo-motor action" notion is grounded in a sense of reality, in a feeling of acquiescence or consent in the truth of something. It reflects the notion that when something is treated as the highest possible likelihood of being real, there is a motivational force to take action that requires nothing else to make it happen. This proposal is the first and strongest version of when likelihood can be *the* driving force of commitment to take action. And, recently, it has inspired a substantial amount of research testing whether merely priming or activating a stored concept, even if done subliminally, can instigate action. Impressively, this research generally supports James' proposal, although it is not clear that the action taken is determined *solely* by the activated concept.[31]

Consider an example from a now-classic study by John Bargh and his colleagues.[32] This study tested whether simply priming people's stored knowledge of the "elderly"—their *idea* of the elderly—could instigate action. Part of people's idea of the elderly is that they walk slowly. Compared to a no priming condition, could priming the concept "elderly" subliminally (i.e., outside of awareness) make people afterwards walk *slowly* down a hallway, even in the absence of any elderly person? Amazingly, this is exactly what the study found.

This finding certainly supports James' "ideo-motor action" notion. But is it the case that the walking action was instigated *only* by activating the idea of the elderly? Joe Cesario, Jason Plaks, and I thought that value might also be contributing to the action that was taken.[33] We proposed that people's stored knowledge or ideas about things serve the function of preparing them to interact with such things, such as interacting with a member of the social category "elderly." The belief that elderly people walk slowly is used when preparing to interact with an elderly person and it will, indeed, be activated automatically when the concept "elderly" is primed. Moreover, the idea of an elderly person walking slowly can instigate motor action even in the absence of an elderly person—just as James suggested and Bargh found. However, we proposed that preparation for action, and the action actually taken, would also depend on the value of the category that was activated. In this case, it would depend on individuals' attitude toward the elderly.

Walking slowly would make strategic sense only for individuals who *like* the elderly and would want to walk slowly in order to interact with them better. Many of our participants liked the elderly, and when the concept "elderly" was subliminally primed, these participants afterwards walked slowly down the hallway (in the absence of any elderly person)—just as Bargh had found. But for those participants who *disliked* the elderly, they walked *quickly* down the hallway after being subliminally primed with the concept "elderly"—as if they were trying to avoid interaction with an elderly person (even though there was, again, no elderly person).

It seems, then, that activating a stored idea, even subliminally, can create a motivational force for action, but the nature of the particular action that is taken can also depend on additional motivational factors, such as the value associated with the idea.[34] This distinction has an interesting parallel in the development of Tolman's theory of learning and action. Tolman was a student of James. It is not surprising, then, that Tolman's original theory of learning and action emphasized the role of expectancies; specifically, contingency beliefs such as "when action X is taken, then Y event happens."[35] Like James' "ideo-motor action" notion, the contingency beliefs were considered to be sufficient to insti-gate action. Other psychologists did not agree; they did not consider beliefs to be sufficient by themselves. Among these was Edwin Guthrie, another pioneer in the study of animal learning.[36] As mentioned before, Guthrie famously said that Tolman's animals would be "buried deep in thought" and not take action.[37] At least partially in response to these criticisms, Tolman revised his theory and added, as intervening variables, drives and incentive-values within a drive-incentive–value system.[38] That is, he added value to expectancies such that, *working together*, they instigated action.

Commitment From Mental Contrasting Producing High Success Likelihoods

There is another recently proposed model of commitment that again gives homage to James but introduces a new underlying mechanism. Gabriele Oettingen, an expert in goal setting and goal commitment, has investigated how *mentally contrasting* a desired future with aspects of impeding reality can create binding goals.[39] Her research demonstrates that strong goal commitment can be induced by having people contrast the enjoyment of fantasizing a desired future self with imagining how to overcome the realistic obstacles that could hinder success. But this mental contrasting involving value has to result in a high subjective likelihood of success (truth) in order to strengthen commitment. If the subjective likelihood of success remains low, then mental contrasting is not effective.

In Oettingen's model, what is critical is *not* the subjective *value* of success alone, not just the value experienced from fantasizing the desired future self. Instead, the final subjective likelihood is the product of contrasting the fantasy with the obstacles that must be overcome. And it is the subjective likelihood that is the output of this contrasting that is critical to creating commitment. From this perspective, the key motivational force ultimately is the subjective likelihood of success (i.e., the truth about success from taking action). This emphasis on truth or reality is consistent with James' notion. Value is just part of the contrasting that is the source of this likelihood force.

Nonetheless, it should be noted that the final subjective likelihood product in Oettingen's model is not just a neutral belief. It is a belief that is associated with a desired end-state. It is a belief about a desired future self. Thus, once again, although likelihood is given a central role as a motivational force on commit-ment, it is not a mere idea—it is an idea that is related to value. Once again, it is value and truth working together, but this time truth is a star player rather than just a journeyman.

Commitment When Likelihood Is Certainty

Oettingen's work nicely illustrates one way in which the subjective likelihood of an outcome, in its own right, must be considered a motivational factor in commitment, a factor that influences the value of taking some action. And this is just one way in which subjective likelihood can play an important role in becoming committed to something. As I mentioned earlier, what has been overlooked in value–likelihood models is James' insight: the fact that subjective likelihood is another way to *establish what's real*, and when something is real it is more engaging. People take something more seriously, consider something more worthy of their sustained attention and their resources, when it is real rather than just imaginary.

One striking example of this is the effect on choosing between options when the outcome from choosing one option is certain whereas the outcome from choosing the other option is uncertain. In their highly influential paper on prospect theory,[40] Daniel Kahneman and Amos Tversky point out that people's preferences between positive prospects, such as choosing between Option A of a 50% chance to win $1,000 and a 50% chance to win nothing versus Option B of winning $500 for sure, are inconsistent with value–likelihood models because people are more attracted to the certain positive option (Option B) than the uncertain positive option (Option A) than would be predicted by these models, given that the subjective expected utility of the two options is the same (i.e., $500 for both options). People also give the certain option more weight than the uncertain option when choosing between negative prospects. For example, people are more repulsed by the certain negative Option C of losing $500 for sure than the uncertain negative Option D of 50% chance to lose $1,000 and 50% chance to lose nothing, and thus they choose the uncertain negative Option D (to avoid the certain negative Option C) more than would be predicted by value–likelihood models.

The power of certainty on commitment can also be appreciated intuitively by thinking about the prospect of winning something or losing something when the likelihood is 100% rather than 95% compared to when the likelihood is 95% rather than 90%. Although the increase in likelihood is 5% in each case, the increase in commitment to approach winning something or to avoid losing something is clearly greater for 100% (certainty) versus 95% compared to 95% versus 90%. Certainty is the strongest case of establishing something as real and thereby strengthening commitment.

Commitment to Taking Action From a Belief That the Action *Can* Be Taken

The fact that people take something more seriously when it is real influences their commitment in another way that I have not yet discussed—a way that is again independent of value, but not quite as James suggested. It is not simply that acquiescence or consent in the truth of something prompts action, that "We think the act, and it is done." The action is motivated by wanting to be effective. Examples of this motivation include White's effectance motivation, Deci and Ryan's self-determination, and Bandura's self-efficacy that I discussed in Chapter 2. People take action not just in order to attain desired end-states, not just to approach pleasure and avoid pain. They take action because it instantiates their competence, it reveals their efficacy. As when children jump into puddles, the outcomes can be unpleasant, including being punished. Despite these outcomes, the action *is* taken because it *can* be taken. It is *about* being competent, being efficacious. But a crucial underlying factor is that the actors *believe* that they can do it. They perceive that the subjective likelihood of their carrying out the action is high—*truth and control working together*. That is, their commitment to taking action derives from their belief that the likelihood that they can produce the act is high—independent of the consequences that accrue from having produced the act. It is not commitment to taking action from the high likelihood of attaining post-action outcomes, but commitment to taking action from a belief that the action *can* be taken.[41]

Commitment From Locomotion Concerns With High Likelihood

Another way in which commitment to taking an action can be created by high subjective likelihood, separate from the action's value, is when people are in a locomotion mode. In Chapter 5, I discussed how individuals with a strong locomotion orientation, in contrast to those with a strong assessment orientation, want to take action, to get started, to initiate and sustain movement. They are not concerned about the value outcomes their movement might produce; they are concerned with the movement itself, and they want it to be smooth and undisrupted. Recent studies have found that high locomotors across many different cultures are high in conscientiousness—that is, they are planful and well organized.[42] Being planful and well organized increases the likelihood that the action taken will be carried out smoothly and without disruption. Recall also the evidence mentioned in Chapter 6 that high locomotors are relatively sensitive to differences in likelihood of goal attainment that relate to potential obstacles in moving toward the goal that could disrupt smooth movement. In contrast, they are relatively insensitive to differences in the value of goal success that relate to outcomes.[43] Thus, when the subjective likelihood of completing an activity is high, individuals with a strong locomotion orientation will be committed to taking action *regardless* of the anticipated value outcomes from taking that action. For high locomotors, it is subjective likelihood rather than subjective value that is *the* driving force on commitment.

In sum, a strong argument can be made that in some cases subjective likelihood, rather than value, is the driving force of commitment. And this is not the end of the story regarding the role of likelihood as a separate motivational force. As it turns out, likelihood affects commitment, and value itself, in ways that are quite surprising and have only recently been recognized and researched.

HOW LIKELIHOOD AFFECTS VALUE

Thus far, I have discussed three general ways that likelihood can function to influence commitment. First, it can function as *a likelihood that qualifies or moderates value*. This is the function that is emphasized in standard value–likelihood models like SEU and EV. Second, likelihood can function as *a belief held with conviction* (acquiescence) that relates to volition and then action. This is the function emphasized in James' ideo-motor action proposal and Oettingen's notion of mental contrasting producing high likelihood beliefs. Third, likelihood can function as *a belief about what action can be initiated and sustained*. This function is emphasized in models of effectance, competence, and self-efficacy, and in the regulatory mode state of locomotion. The act *is* taken because a person believes it *can* be taken and sustained.

I will discuss in this section four additional ways that likelihood can function not only to influence commitment, but also to affect value itself: likelihood functioning as *perceived difficulty*; as *a norm*; as *psychological distance*; and as *reality preparation*.

Likelihood Functioning as Perceived Difficulty

We have already seen that subjective likelihood is a major motivational force in its own right. But likelihood not only contributes to commitment separate from value; likelihood functioning as perceived difficulty can also determine perceived value itself.

PERCEIVED DIFFICULTY FUNCTIONING AS MEANINGFULNESS

Some value–likelihood models, such as Lewin's and Atkinson's, explicitly recognize the effect of perceived difficulty on determining the value of success or failure.[44] In these models, as in most standard models, a multiplicative relation between value and likelihood is proposed in which likelihood qualifies value. But the new wrinkle is that value itself as a variable is operationalized in terms of likelihood. Specifically, the positive value of individuals succeeding in doing something or the negative value of their failing to do something is postulated to depend on their judgment of how likely it is that they will succeed or fail. For example, if a task is very easy, like landing a dart anywhere on a dartboard when standing 3 feet away, then the likelihood of success (i.e., landing a dart any-where on the board) is very high and the positive value of successfully doing so is low. As the task becomes more difficult, such as standing further and further away or landing a dart on the bull's eye, then the positive value of success increases. Conversely, if a task is very difficult, like landing a dart on the bull's eye from 20 feet away, then the likelihood of failure is very high and the nega-tive value of failure is low. As the task becomes easier, then the negative value of failure increases.

This analysis seems quite reasonable. What needs to be emphasized, how-ever, is that what is involved here is value and truth working together. It is *not* the hedonic properties of the desired end-state (landing a dart anywhere on the board) or the undesired end-state (missing the board completely) that are driv-ing value here. The desired end-state, for instance, could be landing the dart anywhere on the board, but what is critical is whether this end-state has a higher likelihood from standing 3 feet away or a lower likelihood from standing 20 feet away. And, notably, it is a *low* likelihood of success (i.e., a difficult task) that gives success *more* positive value rather than a high likelihood of success.

It is the likelihoods of success and failure that determine whether the end-state—success or failure—is personally meaningful. And an outcome is personally meaningful when it establishes something real about the person who has achieved the outcome.[45] Success in dart throwing at a farther distance and failure at a closer distance is more personally meaningful. The social psychological literature has described a couple of truth-seeking processes that can establish a personally meaningful outcome.

As I discussed in Chapter 5, one way to establish what's real is to find an explanation for *why* something happened. When individuals succeed on some task, for example, they can seek an explanation for why they succeeded. Imagine that they knew prior to engagement that the task was quite difficult. Given this, they cannot explain their success as due to the task being easy. It's possible that they were just lucky, and it's also possible that they worked especially hard, but people are more likely to explain their success as reflecting their high ability or competence.[46] With a high ability or competence explanation for the success, the success would have high value for them.

In contrast, if people knew that the task was easy, then they could attribute their success to low task difficulty rather than to high ability. In this case, suc-cess would not have high value for them. Because attributing success to ability rather than to task difficulty is more likely when a task is quite difficult rather than easy, success on a task has more positive value when the likelihood of suc-cess on the task is lower (i.e., higher in difficulty). The value derives from the success being personally meaningful—in this case, from attributing success to ability rather than to low task difficulty. Similarly, when likelihood of success on a task is high (i.e., the task is easy or low in difficulty), then failing on the task will have more negative value. The value derives from the failure being personally meaningful—in this case, from attributing failure to low ability rather than to high task difficulty.

An alternative truth-seeking route would be for people to use a hypothesis-testing process to decide whether or not their success or failure was *diagnostic* of their having high or low ability.[47] They would make the following comparison: if I had high ability, what is the likelihood that I would succeed on this difficult task; if I did not have high ability, what is the likelihood that I would succeed on this difficult task? For a difficult task, the likelihood of success is clearly greater when a person has versus does not have high ability. Therefore, success on a difficult task would be diagnostic of high ability, which would make success have high value. Success would have lower value for an easy task because success is likely even when a person does not have high ability; that is, success is non-diagnostic of high ability when success is likely (i.e., an easy task). And, once again, the value of success depends on the personal meaningfulness of the success—in this case, from concluding that success is diagnostic of high ability. Similarly, failure has more negative value for an easy task because failure is more diagnostic of low ability when the likelihood of success is high.

In sum, the likelihood of success can influence the value of succeeding or failing at something because it makes the valued outcome *more personally meaningful*. This is an important way that likelihood functioning as perceived difficulty can influence commitment and value. It is important because it shows how value is *not* independent of likelihood. And likelihood functioning as perceived difficulty has three other effects as well on value and commitment.

Perceived Difficulty Functioning as Anticipated Costs

An additional effect of perceived difficulty has to do with the amount of work or effort that is anticipated to be necessary in order to succeed. The more difficult the activity or task, the more work or effort will be required to succeed. This is *a cost of success* that should be weighed along with the benefits of success in a benefits/costs analysis. Although some value–likelihood models explicitly take this effect of task difficulty into account,[48] other models do not. The effect may not be a critical factor on an easy task where success requires minimal effort, such as successfully eating an ice-cream cone after deciding which flavor to buy, but it can become a significant factor when success requires substantial effort, such as successfully teaching a course after deciding which course to teach. The value of teaching a course (i.e., the benefits/costs ratio) would depend not only on the likelihood and outcomes of teaching it successfully, but also on the effort or work required (i.e., the costs) of teaching it successfully, which would increase with difficulty.

PERCEIVED DIFFICULTY FUNCTIONING AS RESISTANCE

Another effect of perceived difficulty is that it can create resistance. I discussed in Chapter 4 how opposing an interfering force can strengthen engagement, which would intensify the value reaction to the goal. Similarly, people naturally resist engaging in a difficult task that requires substantial work or effort, and they have to overcome this personal resistance to engage in the task nonetheless. Overcoming personal resistance also strengthens engagement, which intensifies the value reaction to the goal.[49]

The effect of perceived difficulty on strengthening engagement by opposing or overcoming resistance could contribute to the *scarcity effect* on value. When an item is scarce, such as a certain make and year of antique car, or a painting by a well-known (and deceased) artist, it tends to have higher value.[50] Even seeing a rare item, such as an owl in Manhattan, is highly valued. Scarce items are low in number, and thus the likelihood of even finding them is low. It is equivalent to high difficulty. Their scarcity functions like an obstacle to goal pursuit. If this obstacle is overcome, as when resistance to a difficult task is overcome, then engagement will be strengthened, and this will intensify the value reaction. For an item that is attractive to begin with, its attraction will intensify when it is scarce.[51]

PERCEIVED DIFFICULTY FUNCTIONING AS CERTAINTY

Another effect of perceived difficulty on value derives from its impact on perceived *certainty*. If a task is very difficult, then people can be quite certain of failure. If a task is very easy, then they can be quite certain of success. Thus, *both* very high and very low perceived difficulty can make people feel relatively certain about what the outcome will be. But if a task is moderate in difficulty— neither very easy nor very difficult—then people will be uncertain about whether they will succeed or fail. This difference in certainty of outcome produces another motivational effect. In Chapter 5, I discussed Sorrentino's distinction between *uncertainty-oriented* and *certainty-oriented* individuals. Uncertainty-oriented individuals should find the moderately difficult task more involving than the very easy or very difficult task because they can reduce uncertainty by performing the task. In contrast, certainty-oriented individuals should find a very easy or a very difficult task more involving than the moderately difficult task because they can maintain certainty by performing these tasks.

When a task is involving, high need achievers (those who anticipate pride from success) generally perform better than low need achievers (those who anticipate shame from failure). Given this, in those who are uncertainty oriented, high need achievers should outperform low need achievers more when the task is moderately difficult (i.e., uncertain) than when the task is very easy or very difficult (i.e., certain). But in those who are certainty oriented, the opposite should be true: high need achievers should outperform low need achievers more when the task is very easy or very difficult (i.e., certain) than when the task is moderately difficult (i.e., uncertain). This pattern is precisely what studies have found.[52]

What these various effects highlight is that even when likelihood is restricted to just being about the perceived difficulty of a goal pursuit, there are multiple ways that it can influence value and commitment.

Likelihood Functioning as a Norm

A significant effect of likelihood is to define what is normal or neutral.[53] For example, if most of the students in a class receive a grade of "B" on the mid-term exam, then that is the most likely grade and defines what is normal or neutral. Grades higher and lower than that are not normal and not neutral. Grades higher than "B" would be evaluated positively, and grades lower than "B" would be evaluated negatively. And this effect of likelihood or expectancy is not limited to the case of social comparison. Individual students, for example, could define what is normal or neutral for them in terms of the grade that they themselves have received most often on previous mid-term exams, rather than the grade most students received on this particular exam. For a particular student, the typical mid-term grade since starting college could be a "C," and this could define what is normal or neutral. Grades higher than "C" would be evaluated positively, and grades lower than "C" would be evaluated negatively. Note that the positive versus negative value of an outcome is being determined by whether that outcome is above or below some norm, where the norm is defined by the distribution of likely outcomes. Thus, once again, value is *not* independent of likelihood.

Using what has happened most often, what is most likely, to define what is normal or neutral is a kind of norm—a descriptive norm. As in the above examples, it can be used as a factual reference point to judge the value of something. Unexpected better events are evaluated positively, and unexpected worse events are evaluated negatively. In Chapter 5 I described both injunctive norms and descriptive norms. Whereas injunctive norms establish which behaviors are socially right or approved in which situations for which people, descriptive norms provide information about how people *are* behaving in some life domain (what is typical). Both injunctive and descriptive expectancies can influence value and commitment. They both involve value and truth working together. The nature of these relations is different, however.

LIKELIHOOD FUNCTIONING AS A DESCRIPTIVE NORM
Descriptive norms describe how people typically respond in particular situations. Thus, they provide information about what others are likely to do in the

future. For example, I could believe that it is common among my fellow workers to ask our boss for a raise or I could believe that it is rare, and thus it is something that, respectively, has high likelihood or low likelihood for people like us to do. When people are deciding what to do in a situation, they often consider what other people do in that situation. Robert Cialdini calls this "social proof" or "truths are us." Especially when individuals are uncertain what to do, they gain an understanding by considering what other people typically do, what is popular to do.[54] If most people on a picnic eat chicken with their fingers rather than with a fork, then I will choose to do so as well. This is yet another kind of value–truth relation that affects commitment to taking a particular action. If it is common for my fellow workers to ask my boss for a raise, then I will take this action as well.

What I am emphasizing here is the impact of the behaviors of others on *defining what is reasonable to do* in a particular situation, what it makes sense to do. And what is reasonable to do will have an impact on the value of my doing it and my commitment to doing it. I should note as well that what others do— descriptive norms—could also influence my perception of its difficulty: after all, if it was a difficult thing to do, then it would not be done by so many people. By influencing perceived difficulty, a descriptive norm could have the additional effects on value and commitment that I described earlier.[55]

LIKELIHOOD FUNCTIONING AS AN INJUNCTIVE NORM

Injunctive norms involve expectancies of other people's approval or disapproval for taking some action in a particular situation. Injunctive norms also define the situation, but they define *what is obligatory to do*, ought to be done, rather than what is reasonable to do, makes sense to do. This is yet another kind of value–likelihood relation that affects value and commitment. For example, it could be that my coworkers disapprove of anyone asking the boss for a raise; it is socially incorrect. This particular injunctive norm would decrease my commitment to asking my boss for a raise. Martin Fishbein and Icek Ajzen, pioneers in relating attitudinal and normative beliefs to behavior, have shown how beliefs about others' prescriptive expectations can have an impact on behavioral choices. Their work has shown that injunctive norms affect commitment to taking some action independent of the positive and negative outcomes of taking the action.[56]

Injunctive norms, as one's knowledge about what actions other people approve or disapprove of, could have another effect as well. Consider, for example, what could happen if you decide to take some action *despite* the fact that you know others would disapprove of it. People naturally resist doing something that is likely to produce others' disapproval or even punishment. But if they overcome their resistance and do it anyhow, this should strengthen engagement, which in turn should intensify their attraction and commitment to the chosen action.[57] Parents recognize the risk in disapproving of what their adolescent child is doing—that it could boomerang and make their child even more motivated to engage in the disapproved activity. This mechanism can be a factor in addictions, where the addicted behavior is typically counter to injunctive norms but is done despite the threat of disapproval and punishment. The stronger the injunctive norm against the addicted behavior, the more addicts will be committed and attracted to the behavior each time they choose to do it. But it is not only addictions: if I take seriously my coworkers' injunctive norm against asking our boss for a raise, but I decide to take that action nonetheless, then I will become even more committed to asking my boss for a raise.[58]

I should also note that the motivational force of injunctive norms should vary as a function of value orientation. I discussed in Chapter 6 how for prevention goals, like safety, the more valuable the goal is, the more people feel that they *must* attain it. They are strongly committed to pursuing a high value prevention goal because pursuing it is a *necessity*.[59] People with a prevention goal orientation represent their goals as something they ought to do, as their duty and responsibility. Injunctive norms concern the same imperative. Thus, there is a natural fit between injunctive norms and a prevention orientation. This means that the motivational force of injunctive norms should be greater for individuals with a stronger prevention orientation than for those with a stronger promotion orientation—yet another kind of value–truth relation. Consistent with this prediction, there is evidence that strong prevention managers are more likely than strong promotion managers to manage their subordinates in a style that copies how they themselves had been managed by their boss in the past—even when they disliked being managed in that way.[60]

Likelihood Functioning as Psychological Distance

One of the characteristics that define humans is their ability to transcend the "here and now" and to imagine what their lives will be like many years in the future. They can also imagine themselves being in different locations, such as imagining themselves instantly beamed—"Star Trek" fashion—to a sandy beach in Hawaii. We can imagine not only what is happening but what might be happening instead (i.e., counterfactual thinking). We are not stuck with how things actually are, right here, right now. How I actually am right here, right now, can be conceptualized as my starting point, my "0." Anything that moves me away from that—away from the present location and time, the present 100% reality—is increasing my *psychological distance* from "0." The ability to increase psychological distance—*to transcend the here and now*—is critical for humans to do the kind of complex and innovative planning that they do. But what is becoming clear from the recent landmark discoveries by Nira Liberman, Yaacov Trope, and their colleagues[61] is that psychological distance has other implications for judgment and decision making that had not previously been recognized.

My interest here is the recent work by this team on the effects of likelihood on determining the value of something. Objects and events have both central and peripheral characteristics. What is central to a theatrical event is the play itself, and the location of the theater building is peripheral. Imagine that a ticket to a play at a theater was a prize that could be won in a kind of lottery. Imagine that you had to choose between two versions of this theater ticket prize. One version of this prize had high value on the central characteristic but low value on the peripheral characteristic (e.g., a play with a famous cast at a theater in an inconvenient location) and the other version had the reverse (e.g., a play with a local cast at your local theater). Now imagine that before you made your choice between the two versions of the theater ticket prize, you were told that the like- lihood of winning the theater ticket prize was very high or the likelihood was very low. Would a high versus low likelihood of winning the prize influence which version of the prize you would choose?

Most people, I believe, would answer that the likelihood of winning the prize would not influence which version of the prize they would choose. Regardless of the likelihood of winning the prize, we would choose whichever version was more valuable to us overall. That is, for each version of the prize we would com- bine the value of its central characteristic and the value of its peripheral charac- teristic, and then we would compare the two versions and choose whichever version had the better combined value. And we would choose this version of the theater ticket prize—in case we won—regardless of whether the likelihood of winning the prize was high or low.

Generally speaking, we would expect that the preferred version of the prize would be that version that had the more valuable *central* characteristic; that is, the play with the famous cast. In fact, this was exactly what was found in a study that was very much like the imagined scenario I just described.[62] Overall, the participants selected the version of the prize with the more valuable central characteristic. But that study also found that the peripheral characteristic of each prize—the location of the theater—was given much *more weight* in the decision when the likelihood of winning the prize was *high* than when the like- lihood was low. Indeed, when the likelihood of winning the prize was high, the two versions of the prize were equally preferred by the participants, whereas the version with the more valuable central characteristic was much more preferred when the likelihood of winning the prize was low.

What's going on in this study? Why does the likelihood of winning some prize matter so much in choosing between the two versions of the prize? The answer is that the likelihood of something happening instantiates psychological distance in the same way that space and time do.[63] Something that has *high likelihood* functions like something that is here and now—it has *low psychological distance*. In contrast, something that has low likelihood functions like a distant time and distant place—it has high psychological distance. When something has high psychological distance, like an event taking place in the distant future or in a distant location, it is its essential or central characteristics that are emphasized.[64] This would also be true, then, for a low likelihood event. But when something has low psychological distance, like an event taking place in the here and now or a high likelihood event, its peripheral, less essential characteristics are also considered.

Likelihood Functioning as Reality Preparation

The likelihood functions that I have discussed thus far concern the likelihood that something "X" is true, or that something "X" will happen. Variations in likelihood influence commitment to "X," the value of "X," or the weight given to different characteristics of "X" (e.g., more central or peripheral). The final likelihood function that we will consider—*likelihood as the need to prepare for reality*—differs from these other functions because, according to this function, the likelihood that something "X" will happen can affect not only the value of "X" but also the value of something *else*: the value of "Y." This is because the likelihood that something "X" will happen can affect engagement strength. And strengthening engagement, as was discussed in Chapter 4, can intensify evaluative responses. If the high likelihood of a future event, by strengthening anticipatory engagement, could increase the value of something *else* in the present, this would be especially strong evidence for the independent contribution of likelihood to value and commitment.

Likelihood concerns perceptions or beliefs that something will or will not happen. As discussed already, the value–likelihood models of motivation assume that the subjective likelihood of a given outcome combines multiplicatively with the subjective value of *that* outcome to determine value intensity. For example, a high likelihood of attaining some positive outcome would produce a greater force of attraction toward *that* outcome than a low likelihood. In these models, a given likelihood belief has implications *only* for its associated outcome. Thus, as I start my day in the morning by reading the newspaper, a high likelihood that I will have cereal a little later would have no effect on my evaluative reaction to the newspaper story that I am reading now; it would only affect my commitment to having the cereal.

In these models, beliefs about the likelihood of a specific outcome are important because of the *information* they communicate about whether a particular future outcome is likely to occur, with the only motivating force (the pull) coming from the subjective value of that future outcome. In the SEU model, for example, when there are two possible future outcomes—"I will have cereal instead of eggs this morning" and "I will have eggs instead of cereal this morning"—a high likelihood of one outcome (e.g., 80% likelihood of having cereal) is *equivalent* to a low likelihood of the alternative outcome (e.g., 20% likelihood of having eggs). In this model, it is the future outcome that matters, and the likelihoods are providing the *same information* about what will happen in the future; that is, my having cereal is more likely to happen than my having eggs.

But what if subjective likelihood has a motivational force in its own right because it concerns another way of being effective (i.e., truth effectiveness)? What if, as James suggested, high subjective likelihood establishes something as real? If this were the case, then a subjective likelihood about a future event could contribute to value not only by providing information about whether *that* specific future outcome is likely to happen, but also by affecting strength of engagement now—preparatory engagement for a future reality. And this preparatory engagement could affect the value of something *else* in the *present* by intensifying current evaluative reactions.

When individuals experience high likelihood, future outcomes feel real. And because they need to prepare now for something that will really happen, their engagement in what they are doing in the present is strengthened. And stronger engagement will intensify evaluative reactions to what they are doing now. For example, thinking about the high likelihood of my having cereal a little later could strengthen my engagement now while reading the newspaper story, which would intensify my evaluative reaction to the story—more positive if I like the story and more negative if I dislike the story.

From this perspective, then, experiencing high likelihood of some future outcome, by strengthening engagement now, could affect the value of something else in the present. But if this is the case, then experiencing a high likelihood of my having cereal this morning is *not* equivalent to experiencing a low likelihood of my having eggs this morning because the high likelihood experience *strengthens* engagement by initiating preparation for having cereal, whereas the low likelihood does not do so because there is no need to prepare for having eggs. This has interesting implications for how the likelihood that one thing will happen (high or low) can affect the value of something *else*, such as how engaged I will be in reading the newspaper. A recent study has investigated these implications.[65]

Undergraduates believed that they were participating in a marketing study for a new dairy company that was trying to decide what would become their newest flavor of yogurt. The participants were told that in the first part of the study, they would taste two yogurt flavors that each represented a general flavor category (labeled A or B). Unbeknownst to participants, one yogurt was pre-tested to be good tasting (flavored with sugar and nutmeg) and the other yogurt was pre-tested to be bad tasting (flavored with clove). They were also told that in the second part of the study they would try more concentrations within just one of the two original general flavor categories. In the *expressed high likelihood* conditions, participants were told either that they had an 80% chance of later trying more yogurt concentrations from A or that they had an 80% chance of later trying more yogurt concentrations from B. In the *expressed low likelihood* conditions, participants were told either that they had a 20% chance of later trying more yogurt concentrations from A or that they had a 20% chance of later trying more yogurt concentrations from B.

In two experimental conditions, then, there was a high likelihood for later trying various concentrations of the *good* yogurt flavor—the 80% sugar and nutmeg condition and the 20% clove (and thus 80% sugar and nutmeg) condition. From a SEU perspective, these two conditions are equivalent. In the two other experimental conditions, there was a high likelihood for later trying various concentrations of the *bad* yogurt flavor—the 80% clove condition and the 20% sugar and nutmeg (and thus 80% clove) condition. From a SEU perspective, these two conditions are also equivalent. According to the SEU model, the high likelihood of later tasting sugar and nutmeg concentrations (and low likelihood of later tasting clove concentrations) would intensify positive anticipations of later trying more yogurt concentrations of the good yogurt, and the high likelihood of later tasting clove concentrations (and low likelihood of tasting sugar and nutmeg concentrations) would intensify negative anticipations of later trying more yogurt concentrations of the bad yogurt.

Strictly speaking, these anticipations of later tasting in the second part of the study either different concentrations of the good yogurt or different concentrations of the bad yogurt are irrelevant to evaluating now, in the first part of the study, one concentration of each of the two yogurts. But perhaps looking forward to tasting more of the good yogurt later would make people feel good now, and being upset about tasting more of the bad yogurt later would make people feel bad now, and these good or bad moods could affect evaluations of the two yogurts now. Possibly: but note that if there were such an effect of mood in the present from anticipating tasting future concentrations of either the good yogurt or the bad yogurt, this mood effect would be *opposite* for a high likelihood of the *good* yogurt versus a high likelihood of the *bad* yogurt. In addition, this mood effect, according to the SEU perspective, would be the same in the 80% sugar and nutmeg condition and the 20% clove condition because they are equivalent in anticipating the good yogurt, and it would be the same in the 80% clove condition and the 20% sugar and nutmeg condition because they are equivalent in anticipating the bad yogurt. But none of these predicted effects of mood were found in the study.

What was found in the study instead was an effect of describing the future activity of tasting different concentrations of a yogurt either in 80% likelihood terms or in 20% likelihood terms. Regardless of whether the likelihood was about tasting the good yogurt in the future or the bad yogurt in the future, describing the future activity as an 80% likelihood intensified evaluative reactions to both yogurts in the present more than describing the future activity as a 20% likelihood. Despite the 80% sugar and nutmeg condition and the 20% clove condition referring to the *same* future activity (a high likelihood of tasting different concentrations of the good sugar and nutmeg yogurt in the future), participants given the 80% sugar and nutmeg future description currently evaluated the good yogurt as better and the bad yogurt as worse than participants given the 20% clove future description. Similarly, despite the 80% clove condition and the 20% sugar and nutmeg condition referring to the *same* future activity (a high likelihood of tasting different concentrations of the bad clove yogurt in the future), participants given the 80% clove future description currently evaluated the good yogurt as better and the bad yogurt as worse than participants given the 20% sugar and nutmeg future description. In the future 80% likelihood conditions, the motivational system begins to prepare for something that is likely to happen, which strengthens engagement in the present, and this in turn intensifies positive reactions to the good yogurt and negative reactions to the bad yogurt.

The results of this study indicate that subjective likelihood is more than just a likelihood moderator or qualifier of the value of future outcomes. Because of its impact on *current* strength of engagement, it is a motivational force in its own right on the value of present things. This has important implications for the classic value–likelihood models of commitment because it clearly shows that subjective likelihood needs to be treated as an additional motivational force that affects not only commitment but also value. Consider what happened in this study. The likelihood of eating different concentrations of one type of yogurt in the future influenced the value of the yogurts being eaten now. If there was a high chance of eating a future yogurt, *whether that future yogurt was good or bad*, the value reactions to the current yogurts being eaten were intensified—with the good yogurt becoming better now and the bad yogurt becoming worse now. In sum, high likelihood can also affect value and commitment through a *reality preparation effect*.

Combining Reality Preparation and Perceived Difficulty Effects of Likelihood

Likelihood functioning as the need to prepare for reality raises a new question in relation to the perceived difficulty of a task. When something is difficult, it can function as a barrier or interference to goal attainment. This barrier or interference needs to be opposed for goal pursuit to continue, and this opposition strengthens engagement. For a positive value target, stronger engagement would intensify attraction toward it, thus increasing positive value. From this perceived difficulty perspective, then, *low* likelihood of attaining a goal leads to high perceived difficulty, which strengthens engagement and intensifies the value of a goal. In contrast, when likelihood functions as reality preparation, *high* likelihood of attaining a goal strengthens engagement and intensifies the goal's value. These two perspectives, then, predict *opposite* effects of likelihood on engagement strength and value intensification. How will this work out?

The essential difference between these two perspectives concerns the *role of control* in the overall value–truth relation. For likelihood as perceived difficulty, there is not only a value–truth relation but a critical *value–control* relation as well. When a goal pursuit has high perceived difficulty, making success happen will require high management skills (i.e., high control). The focus is on the control component of the value–truth–control relation—the control needed to oppose successfully the interference from difficulty. This mobilizes resources and strengthens engagement.

In contrast, the focus for likelihood as reality preparation is on the *truth* component of a *value–truth relation*. What is real? Will the event actually happen or not in the future? Do I need to prepare or not? There is no control issue *per se* because I cannot control what happens. In the yogurt study, for example, there was a *given likelihood* of tasting varieties of the good yogurt and a given likelihood of tasting varieties of the bad yogurt. There was no control over likelihoods, no control over what happens. The only control, given that an event was likely to happen, was to prepare for its future reality. In this study the likelihood of a particular event, such as getting the good yogurt, was 80% or 20%. The actual or perceived difficulty of making this happen was the *same* in both conditions—none at all. The participants did not have to make it happen; it was a given.

Although there is a natural correlation between outcome likelihood and perceived difficulty, these variables are, in fact, separate factors. In the yogurt study, actual or perceived difficulty was the *same* in both conditions—no personal control was necessary to make the event happen—but the likelihood of a particular event happening (i.e., getting the good yogurt) varied between 80% and 20%. As another example, in the "rat race" study I described earlier in the book, the rats in both the heavy obstacle and the light obstacle condition were successful in getting the food on every trial (i.e., 100% reinforcement). The perceived difficulty, and actual difficulty, was greater in the heavy than the light obstacle condition, but the likelihood of getting the food was the *same* in the heavy and the light obstacle conditions—100% in both conditions. In this study, then, likelihood as truth—likelihood as what would really happen—was the same in both the heavy and light obstacle conditions even though perceived difficulty (and actual difficulty) varied.

What this means is that both likelihood functioning as preparation for reality (truth) and likelihood functioning as perceived difficulty (control) can separately influence strength of engagement. Under some conditions, as in these two studies, one of these factors can vary across conditions while the other factor remains constant. But they are *both* contributing factors, and they *both* influence engagement strength and thus value and commitment. For example, if people believe that by working very hard at a difficult task (control) they are highly likely to succeed (truth)—like *The Little Engine That Could*—then they will engage very strongly and have strong value and commitment. And, if the task becomes too difficult and too costly, then disengagement will occur from ceasing to oppose the interfering force (control) and perceiving success as having very low likelihood (truth). In these cases, truth and control motivations are working together in the same direction to affect value and commitment. But there can be times when these motivations will not all work together, as when low likelihood of success can be engaging from opposing an interfering force (control) but disengaging from low reality preparation (truth).

This chapter has reviewed several different kinds of value–likelihood relations that create commitment. To begin with, the two standard value–likelihood models, the *subjective expected utility* model and the *expectancy value* model, have different assumptions about how value and likelihoods are combined to create commitment. The EV model allows for the possibility that people will experience ambivalence or conflict at the end of the decision process, whereas the SEU model is silent on this possibility. Where these models do agree is their assumption that value is the sole motivational force on commitment, and likelihood simply moderates or qualifies the motivational force of value. The remainder of the chapter provided evidence that the role of likelihood in commitment from likelihood's establishing what's real (truth effectiveness) is much greater than simply being a moderator or qualifier of value.

I first presented evidence of likelihood itself being a strong driving force on commitment, such as the effects on action of priming ideas or beliefs about what happens in the world, and high locomotors' concerns with likelihood as signaling whether there will be disruptions to maintaining smooth movement. I then presented evidence that likelihood can also contribute to creating value itself. Even the single case of likelihood functioning as perceived difficulty influences value and commitment in several different ways. But likelihood also functions as a norm, as psychological distance, and as reality preparation, and each of these additional functions affects value and commitment in different ways as well. Some of these ways are quite remarkable. Likelihood functioning as psychological distance influences which valued characteristics of something (i.e., its central or peripheral characteristics) are emphasized in preference choices. Likelihood functioning as reality preparation can intensify value reactions to things in the present from preparing for something *else* that will happen in the future, because preparing for a likely future event can strengthen engagement now.

What is clear is that not only is there more than one way that value and truth can combine in standard value–likelihood models, but there are also many other ways that value and truth combine to create commitment. And given that commitment itself is a central function that needs to be controlled in order to manage what happens in goal pursuit, as I discussed in Chapter 6, then value and truth can be managed in different ways to make goal pursuit more effective—a full-blown organization of value, truth, and control working together. I will discuss such full-blown organizations in more detail in Chapter 10, including how their effects on commitment could be controlled. Before that, however, I need next to consider more fully the two other pairs of relations (i.e., value–control and truth–control), beginning with value and control working together.

Value–Control Relations

It's the Fit that Counts

I've loved, I've laughed and cried
I've had my fill, my share of losing
And now, as tears subside, I find it all so amusing
To think I did all that
And may I say, not in a shy way,
"Oh, no, oh, no, not me, I did it my way"

—FRANK SINATRA

It's not whether you win or lose, it's how you play the game.

—GRANTLAND RICE

Whether about a game of sports or *the* game of living, the message in these epigraphs is that satisfaction from living is not about always winning. We can have our share of losing and still feel satisfied. We can have hedonic pain (crying; tears) and still feel satisfied. Rather than winning and seeking pleasure, satisfaction from living is about the *way* we live, *how* we pursue our goals. It is not about winning alone, having desired results alone (value). It is about the *relation* between value and control, the *relation* between desired results and how those results were attained . . . or not. This chapter is about the impact of value–control relations on how we feel about what we are doing and what we have done—whether we feel right or feel wrong in our journey.

To have desired results (*value*), people take action or undertake activities as means to make those desired results happen (*control*). These activities, such as working on a major term paper or a business project, are often carried out over an extended period of time before the final goal is reached and the desired results are attained. What motivates people to continue working on such activities, to persist for months at a time on their journey? There are two traditional answers.

The first and standard answer is *incentives*. People anticipate the rewards or positive outcomes that they will receive when they succeed at attaining the goal (e.g., getting a good grade on the term paper), and/or they anticipate the punishments or negative outcomes that they will receive if they fail to attain the goal (e.g., getting a bad grade on the term paper). From this incentives perspective, people engage in activities as an *instrumental* means to an end—*extrinsic* (or exogenous) motivation. The second answer is that an activity can have rewarding properties *in its own right*, such as reading interesting material for the term paper—*intrinsic* (or endogenous) motivation.

A hybrid version of these two answers is that extrinsic incentives initiate undertaking an activity but, once undertaken, valued intrinsic properties are discovered that motivate persisting with the activity—"Just get started, and you'll discover for yourself the pleasure of doing it." The hybrid answer suggests that undertaking an activity can be both extrinsically and intrinsically motivated—persisting with an activity to fulfill multiple extrinsic and intrinsic desired results. This is the concept of *multifinality* that I briefly discussed in Chapter 6. Multifinality is the condition where the same means serves to attain multiple goals. Reading a book for a course can be interesting while reading it, be the foundation for a fun discussion with a friend taking the same course, and provide the necessary background material for writing a report that receives a good grade. An activity that serves to attain multiple goals (including intrinsic motives) is an attractive activity, a valued activity. It can provide desired results in the immediate present (e.g., an interesting read), in the near future (e.g., a fun conversation with your classmate), in the not-too-distant future (e.g., a good grade on the report), and in the far future (e.g., graduating from college on time).

Although an activity means can be highly valued because of its multifinality, there are potential trade-offs. People, for example, could end up doing the activity for the sake of a motive other than the focal goal, such as beginning to do the means activity just for its own sake—*only* for intrinsic motivation. Rather than reading to attain the background material for the course report, the students begin to read simply because they find the material itself interesting. They can then decide to read other interesting material that has little to do with the topic of the course report, and end up not having enough time to complete the report by its due date. What began as an instrumental means to attain a goal has taken on *a life of its own* that is no longer tied to the original goal.

What happens in such cases is that the means activity has become, in Gordon Allport's terms, *functionally autonomous*.[1] As Robert Woodworth described it, activities and objects that earlier in the game were *means* to an end, now become *ends* in themselves:[2] "The fundamental drive towards a certain end may be hunger, sex, pugnacity or what not, but once the activity is started, the means to the end becomes an object of interest on its own account."[3] Even more strongly, Edward Tolman described the "strangle hold" that means activities acquire by "setting up in their own right."[4]

What is needed, then, for effective self-regulation is for people to be motivated to carry out the means activity without losing sight of the focal goal. It is not enough to have extrinsic and intrinsic motivation; there needs to be a motivation that supports the journey itself and sustains the original goal orientation. The purpose of this chapter is to discuss such a motivation. What I will argue is that, in a myriad of ways, *it's the fit that counts*.

WHEN GOALS AND THEIR MEANS OF ATTAINMENT HAVE A SPECIAL RELATIONSHIP

Let me begin with the nature of goal systems themselves, the concept of which has been developed most extensively by Arie Kruglanski and his colleagues.[5] A means activity can be valued because it fulfills multiple goals (i.e., *multifinality*), as in "many birds with one stone." A goal can also be fulfilled by multiple means (i.e., *equifinality*), as in "all roads lead to Rome." The association between a goal and its means of attainment is stronger when both multifinality and equifinality are low. There is evidence, for example, that the extent to which priming a means increases the accessibility of its goal (or vice versa), which is a measure of means–goal associative strength, is greater when the means fulfills only that goal and not other goals (low multifinality) and the goal is fulfilled by only that means and not other means (low equifinality). This reflects the goal systems property of *means–goal uniqueness*. An everyday example of means–goal uniqueness is using a Phillips screwdriver to take out a Phillips head screw. The advantage of uniqueness in the value–control relation is that simply thinking about or engaging in the means activity will automatically bring the goal to mind, which in turn will activate the intention to attain the goal (commitment). As the means–goal association becomes stronger, the transfer of goal commitment to the means activity is greater—the means activity will become tied to the goal.[6] Phenomenologically, it is possible that means–goal uniqueness strengthens commitment to the means activity by establishing the means as the *real* way, the *true* way, of attaining that goal (i.e., yet another case of value, truth, and control all working together).

Uniqueness of the means–goal association is one form of *value–control fit* because the means activity and the goal *uniquely go together*—as in the "right couple" that are "made for each other," whether it be love and marriage or horse and carriage. This particular form of fit concerns the worth of a means that derives from its special ability to fulfill some goal. There are other versions of this form of fit, which collectively can be called *compatibility*; again, like a couple being compatible. Compatibility refers to a specific action's instrumentality toward attaining some particular goal, and when there is means–goal uniqueness, that specific means is the most effective way to attain that particular goal (i.e., high instrumentality).

There is substantial evidence that specific actions or activities are valued to the extent that they support attaining a more general objective.[7] Research on *self-concordance* has found that the value of different actions increases for a person as its relevance to that person's broader aims increases.[8] People value more highly a process subgoal, such as "making conversation," that is compatible with the attainment of a broader purpose goal, such as "achieving interpersonal closeness."[9]

Another version of compatibility is the *message-matching effect* that has been found in the social-psychological literature on persuasion. There is considerable evidence that matching the specific content of a persuasive message to some particular characteristic of the message recipient's goals or needs can increase the persuasive power of the message.[10] The characteristics of the message recipient include the psychological needs served by the recipient's attitudes and the recipient's chronic promotion or prevention focus. An example of matching would be advocating using a particular brand of toothpaste to maintain healthy teeth (safety) when the message recipient has a prevention focus and advocating the same brand to have a brighter smile (advancement) when the message recipient has a promotion focus.[11] Importantly, there is evidence that a mediator of such message-matching effects is the degree to which participants expect that the action a message describes will be instrumental in affecting the outcome that is the focus of the message.[12]

What research studies on various forms of compatibility, including means–ends uniqueness, self-concordance, and message matching, have in common is that they all emphasize the special instrumental value of a specific means activity for attaining a particular goal or satisfying a particular need. They demonstrate how the special *relation* between a specific means activity and the attainment of a particular goal is an important source of the value of the means activity. These different versions of compatibility highlight the value of an activity that derives from its special contribution to attaining a particular goal or general purpose. But compatibility is not the only form of fit that increases the value of a means activity. The other form I call *regulatory fit*, which I discussed in Chapter 4. Regulatory fit concerns a different value–control relation: the relation between a particular *goal-pursuit orientation* (e.g., promotion; prevention) and the specific *manner* in which the goal is pursued (e.g., eager; vigilant).

Regulatory fit makes a critical contribution to value and control working together, which is why I highlight it in this chapter. I should emphasize, however, that regulatory fit is not restricted to value–control relations; it also applies to truth–control relations, to be discussed in Chapter 9. Thus, when I assert "It's the fit that counts," this is a claim not only about value–control relations but also about the organization of motives more generally. In fact, regulatory fit highlights the general theme of this book—how motivation goes beyond pleasure and pain. It is true that compatibility is not strictly about pleasure and pain either, but it does concern instrumentality, which involves the motive to attain goal outcomes. In contrast, regulatory fit is about the relation between a goal orientation and a manner of goal pursuit. Its effects can occur independent of goal outcomes, and thus these effects provide a compelling example of motivation beyond pleasure and pain. Indeed, there is evidence, which I will review later, that hedonic experience and regulatory fit can each have their own separate and independent effects on motivation.[13]

When two things fit with one another, they suit or agree with each other; they are in harmony.[14] This captures the general sense of "fit" as compatibility. In addition, when something is experienced as fitting, it feels correct, proper, or even just. This captures the sense of "fit" as feeling right about what is happening, which is a central element of *regulatory fit theory*.[15] According to regulatory fit theory,[16] people experience regulatory fit when the *manner* of their engagement in an activity *sustains* (vs. disrupts) their current regulatory orientation. Notably, the term "sustains" has two separate meanings in the dictionary.[17] One definition is to allow or admit as valid, to confirm, to support as true, legal, or just (as when a courtroom judge "sustains" a lawyer's objection). This definition relates to the sense of fit described as *feeling right* about something. The primary definition of "sustain," however, is to hold up or prolong, to give support, sustenance, or nourishment. This definition relates to the sense of fit as something that supplies what is needed to carry on. This captures the second central element of regulatory fit—*strong engagement in what one is doing*.

WAYS OF CREATING REGULATORY FIT

Regulatory fit can affect the value of things, the effectiveness of attempts at persuasion, and the quality of performance. In this section I will provide some examples of these effects while discussing the different ways that regulatory fit can be created. Regulatory fit effects are not restricted to the case of promotion or prevention orientations and the eager or vigilant strategies that do or do not fit these orientations. However, many regulatory fit studies have used these variables to create fit or non-fit, and so I will emphasize these variables in my review. Because of the centrality of regulatory focus variables in the regulatory fit literature, I need to review *regulatory focus theory* here.

According to regulatory focus theory,[18] when people have a promotion focus orientation they represent goals as hopes or aspirations (ideals) and are concerned with nurturance, accomplishment, and advancement. They are concerned with gains and non-gains. They are sensitive to the difference between the status quo or neutral state and a positive deviation from that state (the difference between "0" and "+1"). In contrast, when people have a prevention focus orientation, they represent goals as duties or obligations (oughts) and are concerned with security and safety. They are concerned with losses and non-losses. They are sensitive to the difference between "0" and "–1."[19]

Since both nurturance and security are necessary for survival, each regulatory focus orientation is available to all people (with varying accessibility) and all people will pursue goals in each focus at least some of the time. However, there are chronic individual differences in the strength of each orientation and in how often each orientation is emphasized. The distribution or percentage of individuals who are predominantly promotion focused versus predominantly prevention focused also varies across cultures. Moreover, and importantly, there are characteristics of situations that can momentarily induce either a promotion orientation or a prevention orientation in individuals within a given situation. This is because promotion and prevention orientations are *states.* Personality differences reflect chronic predispositions to be more often in a promotion state or a prevention state. Situations can be more likely to induce either a promotion state or a prevention state, including long-lasting situations found in organizations or in cultures (i.e., situations that have become institutionalized).

Regulatory focus theory also proposes that there are different *preferred strategies* of goal pursuit for each orientation. In other words, there is a strategic manner that *fits* a promotion orientation and a different strategic manner that *fits* a prevention orientation. The nature of this preference stems from the ability of a particular strategic manner to sustain (vs. disrupt) a given regulatory focus orientation. When individuals in a promotion focus pursue goals, they will prefer to use *eager strategies* of goal attainment. Eager strategies ensure gains (find ways to advance) and ensure against non-gains (do not close off possible advancements); they are sensitive to the difference between "0" and "+1." In contrast, when individuals in a prevention focus pursue goals, they will prefer to use *vigilant strategies* of goal attainment. Vigilant strategies ensure non-losses (be careful) and ensure against losses (avoid mistakes); they are sensitive to the difference between "0" and "–1."

Let me now consider the different ways that regulatory fit can be created. I begin with the prototypical case of individuals having a goal orientation that is sustained or disrupted by the manner in which they pursue the goal.

Regulatory Fit From Goal Orientation and Manner of Goal Pursuit

Regulatory fit can be created by experimentally manipulating both the goal-pursuit orientation and the manner in which the goal is pursued. In Chapter 6, for example, I described a study where the participants acted as scientists working with organic material in order to find as many four-sided objects as possible.[20] The participants' promotion or prevention orientation was manipulated at the beginning of the experimental session by asking them to describe either their hopes and aspirations in life (their ideals) or their beliefs about their duties and obligations in life (their oughts). Their manner of goal pursuit was manipulated by telling half of them that the way to do well on the task was to be *eager*, and telling the other half that the way to do well was to be *vigilant*. Participants in the *fit conditions* (promotion/eager; prevention/vigilant) enjoyed the task more than those in the *non-fit* conditions (promotion/vigilant; prevention/eager).

In this study the regulatory fit and non-fit conditions were created by *situationally* inducing participants' goal-pursuit orientation and goal-pursuit manner. It is also possible to create regulatory fit and non-fit by having different participants who vary *chronically* in their regulatory focus orientations and then having them pursue a goal in an eager or a vigilant manner. I described just such a regulatory fit study in Chapter 1—the *eager versus vigilant decision-making study* in which Columbia students chose between a coffee mug and a pen.[21]

In this study the students' chronic orientations were measured at the beginning of the experimental session to determine which students had a predominant promotion orientation and which had a predominant prevention orientation. Chronic regulatory focus orientations can be determined using the Self-Guide Strength measure. This idiographic measure asks respondents to list three attributes of their *ideal* self (where their *ideal* self is defined as the type of person they ideally would like to be, the type of person they hoped, wished, or aspired to be) and to list three attributes of their *ought self* (where their ought self is defined as the type of person they believed they ought to be, the type of person they believed it was their duty, obligation, or responsibility to be). The computer records the time each participant takes to produce each attribute. A total ideal strength assessment and a total ought strength assessment are calculated by summing attribute reaction times across the three ideal attributes and, separately, across the three ought attributes. Individuals with a stronger promotion orientation have faster reaction times when producing their ideal attributes. Individuals with a stronger prevention orientation have faster reaction times when producing their ought attributes.

As described before, when the participants arrived at the study they were asked to state their preference between a Columbia coffee mug and an inexpensive pen. Their manner of making the decision was manipulated by telling half of the participants to think about what they would gain by choosing the mug and what they would gain by choosing the pen (an eager manner of making a choice), and telling the other half to think about what they would lose by not choosing the mug or what they would lose by not choosing the pen (a vigilant manner of making a choice). After choosing the mug (the dominant option, as intended), the participants in the regulatory fit conditions (predominant promotion/eager decision manner; predominant prevention/vigilant decision manner) offered much more money to buy the *same* mug than did participants in the regulatory non-fit conditions (predominant promotion/vigilant decision manner; predominant prevention/eager decision manner).

Regulatory Fit From Shared Beliefs

In the studies just mentioned, the regulatory concern involved in the fit and non-fit relations was a desired end-state concern—a promotion or prevention desired end-state. But fit or non-fit is not restricted to desired end-state concerns. As described in Chapter 4, value concerns can also derive from *shared beliefs* about objectives and procedures. Social roles have prescriptions (i.e., shared beliefs) about how someone who takes on the role should carry out an activity and what should be emphasized. For example, the prescribed role of the seller and the prescribed role of the buyer in the classic two-person negotiation are quite different. When a negotiation activity is about price, which is common, it is the role of the seller to get as high a price as possible and it is the role of the buyer to get as low a price as possible.[22] Sellers want to maximize their gain of money and buyers want to minimize their loss of money.[23] This difference in the two roles can create regulatory fit and non-fit with negotiators' regulatory focus. For individuals with a promotion focus on gains, the seller role would be a fit but the buyer role would be a non-fit. In contrast, for individuals with a prevention focus on non-losses, the buyer role would be a fit but the seller role would be a non-fit.

The effects of regulatory fit and non-fit between negotiators' regulatory focus and negotiation role have been examined in a recent study.[24] At the beginning of the experimental session, undergraduate participants were given either $5 (the potential buyer) or a Columbia notebook (the potential seller). They were then told to engage in an actual negotiation for buying and selling the note-book. Because the negotiation was only about price, it was predicted that sellers with a promotion focus (wanting to gain as much money as possible when sell-ing the notebook) and buyers with a prevention focus (wanting to lose as little money as possible when buying the notebook) would experience regulatory fit and thus be more demanding in the negotiation. As predicted, the negotiators in the fit conditions (promotion/seller; prevention/buyer) reported feeling a better "fit with my assigned role," feeling more "engaged with my role," and feeling more that their "role is right" for them than participants in the non-fit conditions (promotion/buyer; prevention/seller). In addition, the negotiators in the fit conditions gave more demanding opening offers.[25]

The study also looked at how often the negotiation pairs could not come to an agreement (i.e., the rate of impasse). Given that negotiators in the fit condi-tions were more demanding, it is not surprising that dyads where both negoti-ating partners had regulatory fit (i.e., promotion-focused sellers paired with prevention-focused buyers) had a significantly higher rate of impasse than any other dyadic combination of regulatory focus. These results highlight the fact that regulatory fit has trade-offs. Regulatory fit strengthens engagement and makes people feel right about what they are doing. This can have benefits, such as making a negotiator more demanding in ways that often yield better out-comes, but this can also have costs, such as increasing the likelihood of impasse when both negotiators are *too* demanding.

In addition to shared beliefs about what should be emphasized when enact-ing a role, there are also shared beliefs about what should be emphasized when engaging in a particular activity. For example, there can be a shared belief that studying is an important activity rather than a fun activity, and there can be a shared belief that partying is a fun activity rather than an important activity. The manner in which people engage an activity can create a fit or non-fit with their shared beliefs about what kind of activity it is. For example, engaging in studying in a serious manner would be a fit, but engaging in a party in a serious manner would be a non-fit.

In a study that examined this kind of regulatory fit,[26] undergraduates' shared beliefs about different activities were determined in an initial pre-test. These participants rated different activities on the extent to which they agreed each was "fun" and each was "important." An activity was considered to have a shared or consensual orientation when a clear and significant majority of respondents rated it either as more "fun" than "important" (a consensual "fun" activity) or as more "important" than "fun" (a consensual "important" activity). The pre-test found that undergraduates had a shared belief that "Financial Duties" was among those activities that were "important," and that "Dating Game" was among those activities that were "fun." These two activities were selected for the experiment, which involved different participants than the pre-test.

The participants in the experiment were given a computer activity that was described as being either a Financial Duties task or a Dating Game task. The goal of the activity was the *same* for all participants: to determine how to use given cues to make predictions. However, the content of this activity was varied to transform it into either a Financial Duties task or a Dating Game task. For the Dating Game task, participants were asked to predict the eligibility ratings of fictitious bachelors on the basis of "Sense of Humor," "Good Looks," and "Intelligence," with the cues interpreted as "points" for a bachelor. For the "Financial Duties" task, participants predicted students' financial status on the basis of "Checking Accounts," "Savings Accounts," and "Credit Card Payments," with the cues interpreted as dollars.

For each of these two tasks, there were additional instructions that suggested that participants engage in the activity in either an *enjoyable manner* (i.e., "Experience doing the task as an enjoyable diversion from your 'real' academic work") or a *serious manner* (i.e., "Experience doing the task as an important part of your life"). The study found that participants' performance on the task depended on the regulatory fit between the participants' consensual shared belief about the concerns of each activity (important, fun) and the manner of engaging the task suggested by the instructions (serious, enjoyable). Performance was better when there was a fit (fun "Dating Game"/enjoyable engagement; important "Financial Duties"/serious engagement) than when there was a non-fit (fun "Dating Game"/serious engagement; important "Financial Duties"/ enjoyable engagement).

An important implication of this kind of regulatory fit is that teachers, managers, parents, and other supervisors who are in charge of instructing others how to do some activity need to know the shared beliefs of their pupils, subordinates, children, and so on regarding that activity. For example, many supervisors believe that they can increase the motivation of those they supervise by adding "fun" to an activity that they believe might be too serious otherwise. Following the "all-purpose energy" idea of motivation, they believe that adding "fun" is simply putting extra fuel in the tank—it can only help. But what if the supervisees have a shared belief that the concern of the activity is importance rather than fun? Might instructing the supervisees to engage in the activity in an enjoyable manner create a non-fit and decrease motivation and performance? Indeed, this is precisely what was found in the "make learning fun" study described in Chapter 1.[27] In that study, undergraduates worked on a task that they consensually considered to be one of "high importance and low fun," a paired-association task in which they had to learn the association between novel nonsense words and their definitions. The study found that participants who received "high importance and *low fun*" instructions for performing the task (i.e., a fit with the shared belief about the task) learned the paired associates *better* than those who received "high importance and *high fun*" instructions (a non-fit with the shared belief). That is, adding "high fun (enjoyable)" instructions *hurt* performance for this consensual "high importance and low fun" activity. And this was true despite the fact that participants reported having more fun in the "high fun (enjoyable)" than the "low fun" condition.

These findings suggest that when trying to motivate their supervisees on a task, supervisors' instructions need to match the supervisees' beliefs about the task in order to create regulatory fit and strengthen engagement. More generally, the results of these studies demonstrate how managing motives effectively requires going beyond the hedonic principle. Increasing pleasure by making an activity more enjoyable decreased rather than increased performance on the task. I discuss more fully the importance of regulatory fit in managing motives effectively in Chapter 12.

Regulatory Fit From an Incidental Activity

Thus far, I have described how regulatory fit can be created by having individuals with particular concerns regarding a goal activity engage in that activity in a manner that fits the concerns. Regulatory fit in this case is *integral* to the activity itself because the manner of engagement that fits the actor's concerns is part of the goal activity itself. But, importantly, regulatory fit (or non-fit) can be created independent of and prior to pursuing a goal—regulatory fit as *ambient* or *incidental* to a focal task.[28] Regulatory fit effects in such cases involve a transfer of engagement strength or "feeling right" from the fit that is created at one point in time to a subsequent goal-pursuit activity that occurs at a later period in time. The existence of such *incidental transfer effects* greatly broadens the significance of regulatory fit for motivation.

A study on object evaluation provides an illustration of such incidental transfer effects of regulatory fit. Undergraduate participants were asked first to think about their hopes and aspirations (promotion orientation goals) or their duties and obligations (prevention orientation goals), and then write down either five eager strategies or five vigilant strategies to attain the goals. This procedure experimentally created two regulatory fit conditions (i.e., eager action plans for promotion goals; vigilant action plans for prevention goals) and two regulatory non-fit conditions (i.e., vigilant action plans for promotion goals; eager action plans for prevention goals). After next filling out several other questionnaires, all participants were asked to rate the good-naturedness of some photographed dogs, supposedly as part of a general project to establish evaluative norms for different stimuli to be used in later studies. Participants in the fit conditions subsequently rated the dogs as more good-natured than did those in the non-fit conditions.[29] Thus, regulatory fit induced at one point in time from thinking of plans for attaining personal goals intensified participants' positive reactions to friendly-looking dogs at a later point in time.

Incidental transfer effects have also been found for the effectiveness of persuasive messages. In Chapter 4, for example, I described a study that tested the persuasiveness of an *identical* message as a function of regulatory fit or non-fit states induced *prior* to receiving the message. The same method of having participants think about eager or vigilant plans for attaining their personal promotion or prevention goals was used to experimentally create regulatory fit or non-fit conditions. After this, the participants received the same persuasive message on a proposed policy for a new after-school program for students.

For those participants who had a positive reaction to the message, the message was more persuasive if regulatory fit (vs. non-fit) had been induced prior to their receiving the message. But for those who had a *negative* reaction to the message, the message was *less* persuasive if regulatory fit (vs. non-fit) had been induced prior to their receiving the message.[30] This study not only demonstrates how an incidental transfer effect of regulatory fit can affect the effectiveness of a persuasive message, but it also shows how regulatory fit intensifies both positive reactions *and* negative reactions to a value target.

Regulatory Fit From Someone Else's Manner of Goal Pursuit

Thus far, all the ways of creating regulatory fit I have reviewed involve individuals' goal-pursuit concerns being sustained by those individuals' own manner of doing something. It is also possible, however, to have individuals with different goal-pursuit concerns interact with someone else, or receive a message from someone else, who displays a manner of goal pursuit that does or does not fit their concerns. There is substantial evidence, for example, that *the effectiveness of persuasive messages* can be enhanced when the source of the message uses a style of advocacy that fits the recipient's motivational orientation.[31]

In an early test of fit effects on persuasion,[32] the same goal of eating more fruits and vegetables—an advocated health behavior—was established in a persuasive message that either induced a promotion orientation by emphasizing concerns with accomplishment or induced a prevention orientation by emphasizing concerns with safety. The style of the message advocacy was either eager (describing the benefits that participants might obtain through complying with the message) or vigilant (describing the costs they might incur through not complying with the message). Thus, the style of advocacy was either a fit with the induced orientation (eager advocacy style for recipients with an induced promotion orientation; vigilant advocacy style for recipients with an induced prevention orientation) or a non-fit (vigilant for promotion; eager for prevention). For the next seven days after receiving the persuasive message, the participants recorded in a daily nutrition log how many servings of fruits and vegetables they ate. The participants in the regulatory fit conditions ate about 20% more fruits and vegetables over the following week than those in the non-fit conditions.

Similar results for health messages advocating eating fruits and vegetables were found in a large-scale study with recruits from the National Cancer Institute's Cancer Information Service. In this study, the fit or non-fit was between the respondents' chronic promotion or prevention orientation and messages that provided the same information but were framed in terms of either eagerly promoting health or vigilantly preventing disease.[33] Four months after receiving the persuasive message, more of the participants in the fit conditions than the non-fit conditions met the 5-A-Day guideline for the number of servings of fruits and vegetables that should be eaten per day.

There is also evidence of regulatory fit enhancing the effectiveness of health messages advocating more physical exercise.[34] In one study the participants were again either chronic promotion oriented or chronic prevention oriented. The promotion-fit "gain" message emphasized the potential benefits associated with being active (e.g., "Scientists say to accumulate physical activity throughout the day to stay healthy or improve your health"). The prevention-fit "stopping loss" message emphasized the potential costs associated with being physically inactive (e.g., "Scientists say failing to accumulate enough physical activity throughout the day can lead to poor health"). The study found that the level of physical activity two weeks after participants received the persuasive message was higher in the fit than the non-fit conditions.

A study on the persuasiveness of messages that are accompanied by *nonverbal cues* provides an especially powerful demonstration of the importance of the fit between a source's style of advocacy and the message recipient's motivational orientation.[35] All of the participants were exposed to a video message that again advocated implementing a new after-school program for grade schools. The speaker in the video was ostensibly a teacher who had worked on developing the program. The text of the persuasive messages was identical across all video conditions. What differed between the videos was the speaker's nonverbal cues while advocating for the new program; specifically, whether the speaker's body position, movements, nonverbal gestures, and speech rate constituted an eager style of advocacy or a vigilant style of advocacy.

In this study, the participants' chronic regulatory promotion or prevention orientation was determined using a questionnaire that measures individuals' general sense of being successful in promotion and in prevention.[36] The participants were either in regulatory fit conditions (predominant promotion participant/eager speaker style; predominant prevention participant/vigilant speaker style) or non-fit conditions (predominant promotion participant/ vigilant speaker style; predominant prevention participant/eager speaker style). The study found that participants more strongly "felt right" during the message presentation and were more persuaded by the message when they were in the fit than the non-fit conditions. In addition, the more strongly participants "felt right" during the message, the stronger was the effect of regulatory fit on persuasion. What this study suggests is that people's chronic goal orientation can be sustained or disrupted by the style in which *another person* advocates pursuing a goal.

These results have intriguing implications for those who are trying to influence another person. It means that sharing that person's goals may not be sufficient to make that person "feel right" about the influence attempt. It may also be necessary to display a *manner* of goal pursuit that fits that person's goal orientation, with the manner including *nonverbal* expressions. And this is not all that is necessary for effective persuasion. As we have seen, regulatory fit can intensify *negative* reactions as well as intensify positive reactions. Thus, when it comes to persuading others through regulatory fit, there is the additional complication that the recipient's initial reaction to whatever the message is advocating must be positive. Otherwise, creating regulatory fit by having a manner of message expression that fits the message recipient's goal orientation could backfire by intensifying the recipient's already negative reaction.

Indeed, there is evidence for just this effect on group reactions to an opinion deviate. Group members' reactions to opinion deviance is typically quite negative.[37] Might this negative reaction be intensified when there is a fit between a group's regulatory focus orientation (promotion vs. prevention) and the way a deviate delivers his or her deviant message (eager style vs. vigilant style)? This question was addressed in a study where groups of undergraduates discussed whether implementing a senior comprehensive examination was a good idea or a bad idea.[38] In some of the groups, a promotion state was experimentally induced in all of the members before they met for the discussion. In other groups, a prevention state was induced in all of the members. Each group then engaged in the discussion. As anticipated, all of the groups came to a unanimous group decision *against* implementing a senior comprehensive examination. They then watched a videotape of another student who ostensibly was also a psychology major at the university. This student read a message that *supported* the senior comprehensive exam requirement—a deviant position. The delivery style of the deviate's message presentation was experimentally manipulated to be either eager or vigilant.

The study found that the group members' subsequent evaluation of the deviate was *more negative* in the regulatory *fit* conditions (promotion group/eager advocacy; prevention group/vigilant advocacy) than in the non-fit conditions (promotion group/vigilant advocacy; prevention group/eager advocacy). That is, the usual negative response to a deviate was intensified in the fit conditions. What is quite remarkable about this effect is that, in a case like this, many psychologists might have predicted the opposite of what was found. After all, the deviate matched the group members more in the fit conditions by having a style that matched their current orientation (e.g., having an eager message style when addressing a promotion group). But rather than this producing the classic "similarity leads to liking" effect,[39] it intensified group members' initial negative reaction to the deviant position. What this highlights again is that regulatory fit does not necessarily make things better; rather, it intensifies whatever the evaluative reaction is.

Regulatory Fit From Different Kinds of Couplings

We have already seen how regulatory fit can increase the value of one's activity, such as finding four-sided objects on a sheet of paper. We have also seen how regulatory fit can increase the value of a chosen object, such as a Columbia coffee mug over a pen, as well as increase the effectiveness of persuasive messages and the intensity of reactions to them. In many of these studies, fit was created by coupling promotion with an eager manner of goal pursuit and coupling prevention with a vigilant manner. I will now review other kinds of couplings that can create regulatory fit.

REGULATORY FIT FROM GOAL ATTAINMENT VERSUS
GOAL MAINTENANCE

Pursuing goals in an eager manner versus a vigilant manner is one way in which the goal-pursuit process can vary. The goal pursuit process can vary in another way that is even more general—the difference between *goal attainment* and *goal maintenance*. People can try to attain a desired end-state they do not currently have or they can try to maintain a desired end-state that they do currently have. Because attaining a desired end-state involves advancing from a current status quo (i.e., changing from "0" to "+1"), it is a goal process that sustains a promotion orientation. In contrast, because maintaining a desired end-state involves stopping a loss from a current status quo (i.e., stopping change from "0" to "−1"), it is a goal process that sustains a prevention orientation. Can varying goal attainment versus goal maintenance also affect value by creating fit and non-fit with promotion and prevention orientations? There is evidence that, indeed, it can.[40]

Undergraduate participants earned tokens by solving anagrams, and they were all motivated to end up with enough tokens to win a coffee mug as a prize. However, half of the participants began with no tokens and needed to solve anagrams to add enough tokens to reach a criterion (the token *attainment* condition), whereas the other half began with tokens and needed to solve the anagrams to stop enough tokens from being subtracted to reach a criterion (the token *maintenance* condition). The strategic "addition" in the attainment condition fits promotion, whereas the strategic "stop subtraction" in the maintenance condition fits prevention. All participants reached the criterion and won the prize mug. They were then asked to assign a monetary price to it. Participants in the fit conditions (promotion/attainment; prevention/maintenance) assigned a higher monetary price to the mug than did participants in the non-fit conditions (promotion/maintenance; prevention/attainment).

REGULATORY FIT FROM RISKY OR CONSERVATIVE PLANNING
A study has also found a regulatory fit effect on value under conditions where either a promotion or a prevention orientation is activated by the kind of financial investment that individuals make—risky or conservative.[41] The same investment opportunity was described as either an individual *stock offered in a trading account* (a more risky promotion-related investment) or as a *mutual fund offered in an Individual Retirement Account* (a more conservative, prevention-related investment). The participants then chose between two brands of grape juice and between two brands of toothpaste.

For each decision, one of the two options represented a gain that fits promotion and the other option represented stopping a loss that fits prevention. Specifically, for the grape juice decision, Brand A was described as rich in vitamin C and iron, thus producing high energy (gain), whereas Brand B was described as rich in antioxidants, thus reducing the risk of cancer and heart diseases (stopping loss). For the toothpaste decision, Brand X's strength was in stopping cavities (stopping loss), whereas Brand Z's strength was in whitening teeth (gain). The study found that when the previous financial investment activated a promotion orientation (trading account stock) rather than a prevention orientation (IRA mutual fund), participants were more likely to choose the "gain" brands (Brand A; Brand Z) than the "stopping loss" brands (Brand B; Brand X).

Another study showed a regulatory fit effect on making financial investments.[42] Regulatory orientation was experimentally manipulated by having participants begin by performing two tasks, a proofreading task and an anagram task, with either promotion instructions for both tasks or prevention instructions for both tasks. The promotion instructions were to maximize the number of misspellings found on the proofreading task and to maximize the number of words found on the anagram task. The prevention instructions were to avoid missing any misspellings on the proofreading task and to avoid missing any words on the anagram task. After completing these two tasks, the participants then began the next (supposedly unrelated) part of the experimental session. They were asked to imagine that they had inherited $2,000 and had to decide how much of this money to invest in Stock A, a typical U.S. stock (risky gain emphasis) and how much to invest in Mutual Fund B, a typical U.S. mutual fund (conservative non-loss emphasis). The study found that the experimentally induced, promotion-oriented participants invested more money than the prevention-oriented participants in the risky Stock A versus the conservative Mutual Fund B.

REGULATORY FIT FROM USING FEELINGS VERSUS REASONS TO MAKE A DECISION

Yet another kind of fit involving regulatory focus occurs as a function of whether a decision is based on feelings or reasons—on the *heart* or the *head*. Earlier research had found that individuals with a promotion orientation prefer to rely more on their feelings, whereas those with a prevention orientation prefer to rely more on reasons.[43] Given this difference, if people are told to make a choice between two alternatives based either on how they feel about each alternative or on their reasons for choosing each alterative, this should produce regulatory fit or non-fit with promotion-oriented and prevention-oriented individuals, respectively. In a study testing this possibility,[44] chronic promotion-oriented and chronic prevention-oriented individuals chose between two brands of correction fluids in either an affect-based manner or a reason-based manner. The study found that chronic promotion-oriented participants were willing to pay much more for their chosen product if they had chosen it in an affect-based manner than in a reason-based manner. The reverse was true for chronic prevention-oriented participants.

As I discussed in Chapter 5, there is a centuries-old debate about whether decisions should be made with the heart or the head. The results of this study raise a separate question: Does a decision have greater *value* if it is made with the heart or the head? That is, independent of whether a decision *should* be made with the heart or the head, individuals could *value a decision more* when it is made with the heart or the head. For the participants in this study, there was an overall general effect of the choice being valued more when it was based on reasons than on feelings. But the strongest effect was the regulatory fit effect. A choice based on feelings was valued more by predominant promotion individuals, whereas a choice based on reasons was valued more by predominant prevention individuals.

In sum, there are several different ways in which regulatory fit can be created and then can have its effects on strengthening engagement, making people "feel right" about what they are doing, and intensifying their evaluative reactions. The goal-pursuit concerns can derive from a self-regulatory orientation (e.g., promotion; prevention) that is chronic for a person or is situationally induced, or it can derive from shared beliefs about a task activity (e.g., important; fun). The manner of goal pursuit that sustains or disrupts the goal orientation can be situationally induced strategies (e.g., eager; vigilant) or ways of doing an activity (e.g., enjoyable; serious) for oneself, or it can be reflected in someone else's way of doing something. The regulatory fit that has effects on a focal goal pursuit can derive from parts of the goal-pursuit activity itself (integral) or it can be independent of the focal activity and have transfer effects (incidental). Finally, there are many different kinds of couplings that create regulatory fit (e.g., eager vs. vigilant manner of goal pursuit; attainment vs. maintenance goal process; risky vs. conservative planning; using feelings vs. reasons in decision making).

MECHANISMS UNDERLYING REGULATORY FIT EFFECTS

We have now seen how regulatory fit created in many different ways can affect the value of things, the effectiveness of attempts at persuasion, and the quality of performance. In this section I will provide a fuller picture of such regulatory fit effects while discussing the different mechanisms that underlie them— fluency, strength of engagement, and "feeling right."

Fit and Fluency

Angela Lee and Jennifer Aaker, marketing scientists who have made major contributions to understanding how motivation affects consumer behavior, directly tested how fit effects on persuasion relate to fluency, where fluency was measured by the accessibility of keywords in the message or participants' self-reported ease of processing or ease of attending to the persuasive message.[45] The participants in one of their studies were presented with an advertisement for Welch's grape juice that emphasized either promotion concerns (e.g., energy creation; enjoyment of life) or prevention concerns (e.g., cancer and heart disease prevention) and either an eager strategy (seeking gains) or a vigilant strategy (stopping losses) to pursue these concerns.

The participants subsequently evaluated Welch's grape juice more positively in the fit conditions (promotion/eager; prevention/vigilant) than in the non-fit conditions (promotion/vigilant; prevention/eager). Processing fluency, as measured by participants' self-reported ease of processing and comprehensibility of the advertisement's message, was also higher in the fit than the non-fit conditions. Moreover, the study found that the effect of fit on positive evaluations depended on there being high processing fluency. In another study, participants first reviewed an appeal message that was framed in one of the same four fit or non-fit conditions. Then the participants had to identify target words from the message that were presented to them very briefly—an accessibility measure of processing fluency. The study found that more target words from the message were identified in the fit than the non-fit conditions.

There is also evidence that fluency as "ease of attention" relates to regulatory fit. Earlier I discussed a study where fit (or non-fit) was created in promotion or prevention message recipients by the eager or vigilant nonverbal behaviors of the person giving the message.[46] Processing fluency was measured by participants' subjective ease of attending to the persuasive message. The study found that processing fluency was higher in the regulatory fit conditions than in the non-fit conditions.

Processing fluency as indexed by ease of processing and comprehensibility and by accessibility is like a mild version of "being in the zone"—the psychological *flow* experience that psychologist Mihály Csikszentmihalyi has described.[47] If fluency were the mechanism underlying regulatory fit effects, how might it have its effect? There is evidence that the ease or difficulty of making preferential choices (i.e., preference fluency) can influence decision making because people use these experiences as information to make inferences about what their evaluations of the choices must be—the "feelings as information" mechanism that I discussed in Chapter 6.[48] One possibility, then, is that regulatory fit increases processing fluency, which makes people experience the choice process as being relatively easy, such as choosing between the pen and the Columbia coffee mug. They then use this information to infer that the chosen object, such as the mug, must have been of high value because it was easy to choose it over the alternative.

Although this "feelings as information" mechanism could contribute to past regulatory fit effects on value creation, it is unlikely to be a factor underlying all findings. For example, in the study where people evaluated the good-naturedness of photographed dogs, the manipulation of regulatory fit was incidental and prior to exposure to the photographs. In the regulatory fit manipulation in this study, the fluency from fit would be associated with the ease of processing eager (vs. vigilant) means for promotion goals or vigilant (vs. eager) means for prevention goals. If such fluency experiences functioned like "feelings as information," they would be relevant to evaluating the means of goal pursuit, such as evaluating the means more highly in the fit conditions, rather than to evaluating the photographed dogs that appear several minutes later.

Fit and Strength of Engagement

I presented evidence in Chapter 4 that engagement in a goal pursuit is strengthened when there is regulatory fit and is weakened when there is non-fit. In one
set of studies, for example, strength of engagement in an anagram task was
measured either in terms of persistence on the task (time spent working on
each anagram) or in terms of exertion on the task (arm pressure while working).[49] Engagement strength was measured both when the participants worked
on green-colored anagrams that added points to the total score (*eager anagram
strategy*) and when they worked on red-colored anagrams that stopped points
from being subtracted from the total score (*vigilant anagram strategy*).
Engagement strength generally increased from the first anagram to the final
anagram (the "goal looms larger" effect), but this increase differed for eager
versus vigilant responses. As described earlier, for both the persistence and the
exertion measures of engagement strength, engagement strength increased
over time more for the eager responses than the vigilant responses when the
participants had a strong promotion focus, whereas the reverse was true when
the participants had a strong prevention focus. Moreover, the participants
solved more anagrams when there was fit (vs. non-fit) between their promotion
or prevention orientation and their eager or vigilant anagram strategy.

As I have discussed earlier in the book, strengthening engagement from regulatory fit intensifies evaluative reactions. When people choose between attractive options, for example, those who make their decision in a manner that fits
their motivational orientation will find their final choice to be more attractive
than those who made their decision in a non-fit manner. I described a study in
Chapter 5 that illustrates this fit effect. The participants in this study chose one
book-light from a set of book-lights.[50] At the beginning of the study, either a
locomotion orientation or an assessment orientation was experimentally
induced. Half of the locomotion participants and half of the assessment participants were given the decision strategy of eliminating the worst alternative
at each phase until only one alternative remains (a progressive elimination
strategy)—a manner of decision making that fits a locomotion orientation more
than an assessment orientation. The other participants were given the decision
strategy of making comparisons among all of the alternatives for all of the attributes and then choosing the best option overall (a full evaluation strategy)—a
manner of decision making that fits an assessment orientation more than a
locomotion orientation. All of the participants chose the same book-light that
had been pre-selected to be the best. The measure of interest was how much
they valued their choice as revealed in how much money they offered to buy it.
The participants offered much more money in the fit conditions (assessment/"full
evaluation"; locomotion/"progressive elimination") than in the non-fit conditions (assessment/"progressive elimination"; locomotion/"full evaluation").

The results of this study are consistent with the conclusion that fit strength-ened engagement, which in turn intensified attraction toward the chosen book-light. It is also possible, however, that the fluency of the decision-making process was higher in the fit than the non-fit conditions, and higher fluency created stronger feelings of attraction toward the chosen book-light. In fact, both higher fluency and stronger engagement could occur under conditions of regulatory fit, and both could have separate effects on value creation. It is also possible that in some cases the stronger engagement from fit produces the higher fluency, and it is the stronger engagement rather than the higher fluency that is the major contributor to the fit effect. There is some evidence from recent research that supports this second possibility.[51]

The regulatory fit examined in this research was between promotion and pre-vention orientations that were experimentally induced and the manner in which an advertised product (e.g., elliptical trainer; MP3 player) was construed—at either a high construal level (e.g., using abstract language to describe the product; discussing *why* to use the product) or a low construal level (e.g., using concrete language to describe the product; discussing *how* to use the product). Prior research had found that a high-level construal fits promotion, while a low-level construal fits prevention.[52] One study tested whether fit does strengthen engagement by creating fit and non-fit advertising conditions and then measuring the effect of regulatory fit on a subsequent incidental anagram task. If fit strengthens engagement, then those participants in the advertising fit conditions (promotion/high-level construal; prevention/low-level construal) should perform better on the subsequent anagram task than those in the non-fit conditions (promotion/low-level construal; prevention/high-level construal). This is what was found.

Another study examined the effect of regulatory fit on attitudes toward the advertised product and took measures of both engagement strength (how moti-vated participants felt while reviewing the message information) and fluency (their perceived ease of processing the message information). The study found that attitudes toward the product were more positive for participants in the advertising fit conditions than those in the non-fit conditions. When just fluency was examined, there was evidence that fit resulted in higher fluency than non-fit, and higher fluency predicted more positive attitudes toward the product. Similarly, when just engagement strength was examined, there was evidence that fit resulted in stronger engagement than non-fit, and stronger engagement predicted more positive attitudes toward the product. Importantly, however, there was also evidence that stronger engagement was associated with higher fluency, and when both fluency and engagement strength were exam-ined together, the engagement strength effect on attitudes remained but the fluency effect was eliminated. These results indicate that engagement strength as a mechanism can underlie fit effects separate from fluency as a mechanism.

Fit and "Feeling Right"

The underlying mechanism that was emphasized when regulatory fit theory was being initially developed was the experience of "feeling right" about what you were doing when there was a fit between your goal-pursuit orientation and the manner of goal pursuit.[53] Because "feeling right" from fit is itself a positive experience, and "feeling wrong" from non-fit is a negative experience, it is important to distinguish these fit and non-fit feelings from general pleasure–pain feelings.

Having a pleasant hedonic experience is *not* the same as the experience of "feeling right" that regulatory fit creates. The experience of "feeling right" is its own special kind of feeling, and it can be another mechanism that underlies regulatory fit effects on value—a mechanism that is potentially different from both fluency and engagement strength. "Feeling right" is different from pleasant hedonic experience because it has an additional "correctness" property. It is not just value; it is also truth. Fit "sustains" someone's current concern, in the sense of "sustain" as meaning "to allow or admit as valid, to confirm, to support as true, legal, or just." The "feeling right" experience thus adds the elements of being *true* and *just*, which adds something beyond hedonic pleasure.

Consider first the element of being *true* as it relates to feeling confident in one's judgments. In a study that incidentally manipulated regulatory fit prior to participants receiving the identical persuasive message (using the manipulation described earlier of listing promotion or prevention goals and eager or vigilant ways to attain them), those participants in the regulatory fit conditions were more *confident* in their attitude toward the advocated issue than those in the non-fit conditions.[54] There is also evidence that regulatory fit increases people's confidence in how well they performed a task, independent of their actual performance.[55]

Consider next the element of being *just* as it relates to moral rightness. There is evidence that people in regulatory fit are more likely than those in non-fit to believe that their judgments are *morally right*—an unconscious transfer from a regulatory fit "feel right" to a moral "*is* right." As one example of this phenomenon,[56] participants in one study were asked to think back to a time in their lives when they had a conflict with an authority figure, and it was the authority figure who determined how to resolve the conflict. Different participants were asked to recall different kinds of resolution. For example, some participants recalled a pleasant resolution in which the authority figure encouraged them or set up opportunities for them to succeed (the pleasant/eager condition), and other participants remembered a pleasant resolution in which the authority figure safeguarded them against anything that might cause trouble or made them alert to potential dangers (the pleasant/vigilant condition). The participants judged the resolution to be *more morally "right"* if they were predominantly promotion focused and the conflict was resolved in an eager manner or they were predominantly prevention focused and the conflict was resolved in a vigilant manner. And, importantly, this fit effect was independent of the participants' pleasant or painful mood while making their judgments.

What studies like this show is that the *true* and *just* elements of the regulatory fit "feeling right" experience can contribute in their own unique ways to creating value. In addition, the experience can have an even more general effect by making people feel right about both their positive and their negative evaluative reactions to something. This more general effect functions like engagement strength to intensify the value of things. Although this effect could occur together with engagement strength, there is evidence that it can make its own independent contribution.

For example, there are studies where, after regulatory fit has been induced, people are made aware that something has produced their "feeling right" experience prior to their being asked to evaluate a separate value object. Under these circumstances, people should recognize that this experience could potentially bias their evaluation and should try to control for this potential bias.[57] Indeed, when people's attention is drawn to their regulatory fit-induced "feeling right" experience, the regulatory fit effects on subsequent evaluations are reduced or eliminated.[58]

These results suggest that the "feeling right" experience under normal conditions (i.e., when people's attention is *not* drawn to it) contributes to regulatory fit effects on value. More direct evidence for the role of this experience in evaluations was obtained in another nonverbal persuasion study like the one I described earlier.[59] The measure of "feeling right" in this study was taken after the measure of message effectiveness. As before, the study found that regulatory fit from having messages delivered with eager versus vigilant nonverbal styles to recipients who were chronically promotion oriented or prevention oriented increased the persuasive effectiveness of the message. Significantly, the study also found that the effect of fit on persuasion was greater for participants who "felt right" from regulatory fit (i.e., "feeling right" mediated the effect).

In sum, there are three different mechanisms that can underlie regulatory fit effects—fluency, strength of engagement, and "feeling right." These mechanisms can function independently to underlie fit effects or they can function together. Future research needs to identify the conditions when one or another mechanism is more likely to underlie regulatory fit effects, and whether a specific mechanism relates to a particular kind of regulatory fit effect.

REGULATORY FIT MECHANISMS AS DISTINCT FROM
HEDONIC MECHANISMS

I have just reviewed evidence that regulatory fit effects from the "feeling right" mechanism are distinct from hedonic effects from pleasure and pain. In this section I address the broader question of whether regulatory fit effects can be explained in terms of the hedonic mechanism of approaching pleasure and avoiding pain.

Fit Effects Are Not Approach–Avoidance Effects

Regulatory focus theory distinguishes between the focus of a goal pursuit (promotion vs. prevention) and the direction of a goal pursuit (approaching a desired end-state vs. avoiding an undesired end-state).[60] A promotion system approaches gains and avoids non-gains, and a prevention system approaches non-losses and avoids losses. In most cases people are approaching desired end-states, and do so with a promotion or prevention orientation. Thus, fit effects involving regulatory focus are distinct from a simple approach–avoidance system; that is, they are distinct from the hedonic principle of approaching pleasure and avoiding pain.

A recent study directly tested whether the fit effect on persuasion conforms more to the hedonic principles of approach and avoidance or to the regulatory orientations of promotion and prevention.[61] Participants first saw an advertisement of a foot deodorizer that functioned as the prime. They then saw an advertisement of an antiperspirant that functioned as the target. Each advertisement had pictures of the product as well as captions supposedly capturing the purpose of the product. The *prime* advertisement that appeared first had either gain-framed captions (e.g., "Feeling confident") or loss-framed captions (e.g., "Feeling humiliated"). The *target* advertisement that appeared second had either negative, non-gain-framed captions (e.g., "Not feeling great") or positive, non-loss-framed captions ("Freedom from embarrassment"). The participants evaluated the brand of antiperspirant shown in the target advertisement.

If the fit effect relies on a hedonic *valence match* of approach versus avoidance, then gain-primed participants (positive valence prime) should evaluate the positive, non-loss target (a valence match between the positive valence prime and a positive valence target) more favorably than the negative, non-gain target (a valence mismatch between the positive valence prime and a negative valence target). Similarly, the loss-primed participants (negative valence prime) should evaluate the negative, non-gain target (a valence match between the negative valence prime and a negative valence target) more favorably than the positive, non-loss target (a valence mismatch between the negative valence prime and a positive valence target). However, if the fit effect instead relies on a *regulatory focus match* of promotion versus prevention, then gain-primed participants (a promotion prime) should evaluate the non-gain target (a focus match between the promotion prime and a promotion target) more favorably than the non-loss target (a focus mismatch between the promotion prime and a prevention target), and the loss-primed participants (a prevention prime) should evaluate the non-loss target (a focus match between the prevention prime and a prevention target) more favorably than the non-gain target (a focus mismatch between the prevention prime and a promotion target).

The results clearly supported the regulatory focus account rather than the hedonic valence account. In addition, the study found that the effect of regulatory fit on enhancing evaluations of the target product depended on fluency of processing (i.e., fluency mediation) and *not* on hedonic mood. This study provides clear evidence that the regulatory fit effect on persuasion does *not* derive from an underlying hedonic mechanism. Let me discuss this issue in more detail next.

Fit Effects Are Not Hedonic Mood Effects

There is an alternative *feeling* mechanism associated with fluency that could also contribute to regulatory fit effects on value: *positive mood transfer*. There is evidence that processing fluency can elicit positive affect.[62] It is possible, then, that when regulatory fit increases processing fluency, positive affect is generated and transfers to objects and activities, thereby increasing their value. Moreover, positive affect from fit could be an ambient or incidental factor that transfers positivity when later evaluating something, such as the photographed dogs. Can positive mood, then, account for the effects of regulatory fit?

This possibility was addressed in another "mug versus pen" study.[63] The procedure for this study was basically the same as I described earlier. After participants had made their choice between the mug and the pen, they were given a questionnaire that asked them how good, positive, happy, relaxed, and content they felt. The study found that the chosen mug was assigned a higher price in the fit conditions, replicating previous results. The study also found that this effect was *independent* of the participants' positive mood.

The independence of regulatory fit effects from positive mood was also tested in a study (discussed earlier) that involved a different kind of evaluation: evaluating the "rightness" of a conflict resolution. The study found not only that participants' evaluations of "rightness" were stronger when the manner of the conflict resolution fit their regulatory focus (i.e., an eager manner of resolution for promotion participants; a vigilant manner of resolution for prevention participants) but also that this regulatory fit effect was independent of the positivity of participants' mood.[64] Rather than the fit effect on value deriving from positive mood transfer, the results of this study support "feeling right" as being the underlying mechanism.

More direct support for the independence of regulatory fit effects on value from hedonic mood is provided in studies where participants made prospective evaluations of how good or bad they would feel if they were to make a choice that produced a positive or negative outcome.[65] The participants imagined buying a book and choosing to pay for it with cash or a credit card, with the price of the book being higher if they paid with a credit card. In one study, the scenario was written either to induce a promotion focus by framing the difference in price as a "discount" for using cash instead of a credit card (using cash as a gain) or to induce a prevention focus by framing the difference in price as a "penalty" for using a credit card instead of cash (using cash as a non-loss). The outcomes were framed either in gain-related or loss-related terms.

This study examined the implications for fit effects on value of an important *asymmetry* between the promotion and prevention orientations. In a promotion focus, a positive outcome (a gain) is a fit because it maintains the eagerness that is needed to sustain promotion, whereas a negative outcome (a non-gain) is a non-fit because it reduces eagerness. In a prevention focus, however, a negative outcome (a loss) is a fit because it maintains the vigilance that is needed to sustain prevention, whereas a positive outcome (a non-loss) is a non-fit because it reduces vigilance. The study found that both feeling good and feeling bad were intensified in the regulatory fit conditions: feeling good when imagining a positive outcome was greater for promotion/gain than prevention/non-loss; and feeling bad when imagining a negative outcome was greater for prevention/loss than promotion/non-gain.

The specific intensification mechanism examined in such studies as this one was fit increasing motivational intensity, where motivational intensity is engagement strength. It was predicted that the fit effect on motivational force would have an effect on "feeling good" and "feeling bad" that was separate from the effect of hedonic experience. In addition to measuring how good or bad participants felt about the imagined decision outcome, separate measures of pleasure/pain intensity and strength of motivational force were taken. In one study, for example, *pleasure–pain intensity* was measured by asking the participants how pleasant the positive outcome would be or how painful the negative outcome would be; and *strength of motivational force* was measured by asking them how motivated they would be to make the positive outcome happen and the negative outcome not happen. The studies found that pleasure/pain intensity and strength of motivational force *each* made significant and *independent* contributions to the goodness and badness evaluations of the positive and negative outcomes.[66] What is clear from this study and the other studies is that regulatory fit effects on intensifying positive and negative reactions to things do *not* derive from a pleasant mood effect.

These studies also address another issue about regulatory fit effects. Because regulatory fit concerns a manner of goal pursuit that "feels right," it could be conceptualized as involving success in attaining a separate process goal. According to *the theory of goal systems* proposed by Arie Kruglanski and his colleagues,[67] pursuing goals in a particular way is itself a goal—*a process goal*. Thus, goal pursuit can be considered to involve two separate goals, one associated with the outcomes being pursued and the other associated with *how* the goal is pursued. From this perspective, the added value from successfully pursuing goals in a suitable manner need not derive from something different than hedonic experiences. Instead, there would simply be *two separate hedonic experiences adding together*—one deriving from the outcomes of the goal pursuit and another deriving from the process of goal pursuit. However, this viewpoint would not expect regulatory fit to contribute to "feeling good" by creating a strong motivational force that was *separate* from hedonic intensity. More importantly, this viewpoint would not expect regulatory fit, if it were just a positive success experience regarding the goal pursuit process, to intensify *negative* reactions to things. Yet, as we have seen, there is evidence for both of these regulatory fit effects.

REGULATORY FIT EFFECTS ON PERFORMANCE

In the above review of the different ways that regulatory fit can be created and the different mechanisms that underlie regulatory fit effects, the studies that have received the most emphasis are those showing regulatory fit intensifying people's positive and negative reactions to things and its affecting the effectiveness of persuasive messages. (This was the emphasis in Chapter 4 as well.) I have reviewed some evidence of regulatory fit effects on performance, but such effects are broader than I have discussed thus far. In this section, I will provide a fuller account of regulatory fit effects on performance.

Fit Effects on Performance From Framing Incentives

I have already described an anagram study where arm pressure was used as a measure of engagement strength, and fit both strengthened engagement and increased performance.[68] Another study in this research program, which also used arm pressure as a measure of engagement strength, created regulatory fit in a different way than this earlier study. Instead of promotion and prevention participants solving anagrams in an eager or vigilant way, the anagram task instructions were framed in different ways: either in terms of promotion success ("If you find 90% or more of all possible words, you will get an extra dollar"), promotion failure ("If you don't find 90% or more of all possible words, you will not get an extra dollar"), prevention success ("If you don't miss 10% or more of all possible words, you will not lose a dollar"), or prevention failure ("If you miss 10% or more of all possible words, you will lose a dollar").[69] Again, promotion success (a gain that increases eagerness) and prevention failure (a loss that increases vigilance) are a fit, whereas promotion failure (a non-gain that reduces eagerness) and prevention success (a non-loss that reduces vigilance) are a non-fit.

This study found that participants in the promotion framing condition pressed harder overall—an overall measure of engagement strength—when the framing was a potential success (a fit) than when the framing was a potential failure (a non-fit), whereas participants in the prevention framing condition pressed harder overall when the framing was a potential failure (a fit) than when the framing was a potential success (a non-fit). Moreover, performance in solving anagrams was especially high for participants in the promotion condition when the framing was a potential success (a fit) *and* they were pressing upward on the plate (a fit), and was especially high for participants in the prevention condition when the framing was a potential failure (a fit) *and* they were pressing downward on the plate (a fit).

Other studies have also found that performance is higher for promotion-focused participants when a task is framed in terms of gaining payment by doing well (a gain) rather than in terms of avoiding losing payment by doing well (a non-loss), whereas the reverse is true for prevention-focused participants. This is especially true when the means for doing well are eager means for the promotion-focused participants (e.g., getting a good score by adding points) and vigilant means for the prevention-focused participants (e.g., getting a good score by stopping points from being subtracted).[70] What these findings again highlight is that it is not only incentives that increase motivation and improve performance. All of the participants in these studies were told that they would end up with more money if they performed better. But it is not about the incentives; it is about the fit. I return to this important point in Chapter 12.

It should also be noted that it is not the case that describing payments in a "pleasant" or "reward" manner is more effective than describing them in a "painful" or "punishment" manner. For individuals with a prevention orientation, whether from chronic predisposition or from situational induction, motivation is increased and performance is improved when the payments are described in terms of not losing money (i.e., avoiding "punishment") rather than gaining money (i.e., approaching "reward"). For these individuals, motivation and performance are enhanced when the means of success is stopping something bad from happening rather than making something good happen.

Fit Effects on Performance From Framing the Task

Regulatory fit effects from framing tasks in ways to fit a promotion or preven-tion orientation are not restricted to monetary incentives; the nature of the task itself can be framed in different ways. One study, for instance, framed a math test as being either diagnostic of strong math ability but nondiagnostic of weak ability (potential for gain) or diagnostic of weak math ability but nondiagnostic of strong ability (potential for loss).[71] The study found that performance on the math test was better in the fit conditions (predominant promotion/potential for gain; predominant prevention/potential for loss) than in the non-fit conditions (predominant promotion/potential for loss; predominant prevention/potential for gain).

This effect on performance has also been demonstrated recently for the interesting case of shooting penalty shots in soccer.[72] The participants in the study were active soccer players in a regional league of the German Football Association. The study was conducted in the middle of the season during one of the official training sessions. Each player participant took five penalty shots. The participants varied in their chronic promotion and prevention orientations. The task framing of how to succeed in the penalty shootout was experimentally manipulated. In the "success as gain (eager shooting)" condition, the partici-pants were told: "You are going to shoot five penalties. Your aspiration is to score at least three times." In the "success as avoiding loss (vigilant shooting)" condition, the participants were told: "You are going to shoot five penalties. Your obligation is not to miss more than two times." Even for these seasoned soccer players, who are always highly motivated to do their best, the shootout performance was about 30% better in the fit conditions (predominant promo-tion/gain; predominant prevention/avoid loss) than in the non-fit conditions (predominant promotion/avoid loss; predominant prevention/gain).

Another study in this research program found evidence of another kind of regulatory fit: selection of what sport to play. It is reasonable to assume that sports vary in whether their demands fit more of a promotion focus or more of a prevention focus. Given this, people should end up selecting those sports that fit their regulatory focus orientation. This would produce differences among sports in how promotion or prevention oriented the players are in those sports. Not surprisingly, there was evidence that people who play sports are generally more promotion oriented than prevention oriented. But controlling for this, there were sports differences, with basketball being relatively more promotion oriented ("get baskets") and gymnastics being relatively more prevention ori-ented ("stop deductions"). Within a sport, such as soccer, those who played as attackers were more promotion oriented and those who played as defenders were more prevention oriented.

The use of different task instructions to create regulatory fit and affect performance was also demonstrated in the research I discussed earlier on introducing an activity, such as paired-associate learning, as something to treat as *fun* or as *important*. This program of research found fit effects of instructions not only for tasks involving making predictions and paired-associate learning but also for a task involving remembering what one saw in a documentary film.[73] Watching a documentary film is an activity that some people believe is "fun" and others believe is "important." Participants who had one or the other of these prior orientations to watching documentary films were selected for the study.

When the participants arrived, the task instructions were experimentally manipulated, with half of the participants being told that the film was selected because previous viewers had found it enjoyable to watch and the other half being told it was selected because previous viewers had considered watching it to be a serious activity. Some events in the film were central to the story whereas others were not. The study found no fit effect on the non-central events, but the central events were better remembered by participants in the fit conditions (fun orientation/introduced as enjoyable; important orientation/introduced as serious) than in the non-fit conditions (fun orientation/introduced as serious; important orientation/introduced as enjoyable).

This study again demonstrates the importance for performance of using task instructions that fit someone's prior orientation toward the task. This is also true for the effectiveness of introducing implementation strategies, which, as I discussed in Chapter 6, can be framed as either eager ways or vigilant ways for carrying out the *when*, *where*, and *how* steps. And the effectiveness of these different framings depends on the actors' goal orientation. In the study I discussed, participants in the fit conditions (predominant promotion/eager steps; predominant prevention/vigilant steps) were much more likely to turn in a report about how they would spend the upcoming Saturday (in order to receive a cash payment) than participants in the non-fit conditions (predominant promotion/vigilant steps; predominant prevention/eager steps).[74]

Fit Effects on Leadership Performance

In these various performance studies, the motivational force associated with engagement strength is the likely mechanism underlying the better performance when there is regulatory fit than non-fit. Engagement strength relates to being absorbed in what one is doing or giving it one's full attention. What is clear from these studies is that fit effects on performance are wide-ranging, from intellectual to athletic tests to tests of self-control. There is recent evidence, for example, that regulatory fit can help people not only control their food intake better (i.e., choose a healthy apple over a chocolate bar for a snack), but even squeeze a handgrip longer as a measure of self-control.[75]

Regulatory fit also applies to the area of leadership performance. For example, fit effects on leader effectiveness have been demonstrated for regulatory mode orientations. One study, for instance, examined leadership effectiveness in diverse organizational contexts.[76] The study compared the effectiveness of two leadership styles: (1) a "forceful" leadership style, represented by coercive, legitimate, and directive kinds of strategic influence and (2) an "advisory" leadership style, represented by expert, referent, and participative kinds of strategic influence. A forceful leadership style fits individuals high in locomotion more than an advisory leadership style because forceful leaders push for moving a task along (a fit with locomotion) whereas advisory leaders wait to allow reflection before moving ahead (a non-fit with locomotion). In contrast, an advisory leadership style fits individuals high in assessment more than a forceful leadership style because advisory leaders allow for critical comparison of alternatives (a fit with assessment) whereas forceful leaders dictate the one course of action that they prefer (a non-fit with assessment). The study found that subordinates who were high in locomotion preferred forceful leadership over advisory leadership, and they also reported greater job satisfaction with forceful than advisory leadership. The opposite pattern was found for subordinates who were high in assessment.

Another research program examined the fit effects between regulatory mode and transformational, or change-oriented, leadership.[77] This research program used experimental laboratory tests as well as data collected from a survey of executives. Leadership effectiveness was measured in terms of an executive's increasing the motivation of followers and being evaluated positively by the followers. Transformational leadership fits followers who have a locomotion orientation more than followers who have an assessment orientation because such leaders emphasize movement and change through their strong sense of purpose, perseverance, and direction. Indeed, the studies found that transformational leaders were more effective with locomotion-oriented followers than assessment-oriented followers.

A Caveat on Regulatory Fit Improving Performance

It is not always the case that regulatory fit improves performance. Whether it does or does not depends on whether the strategy that fits the actor's goal orientation is the strategy needed to be effective on a particular task. For example, consider what is needed to work on a difficult task while being distracted by something in the environment, such as working on a math assignment while fun videos are playing in the background. To perform well, people need to be vigilant in ignoring the distraction. Such vigilance would be a fit for individuals with a prevention focus, but it would be a non-fit for promotion-focused individuals whose eager strategy, though usually a fit for them, is not what is needed to be effective for this kind of task.

Indeed, one study found that participants who received promotion-focused instructions for a math task performed worse in the presence of an attractive distractor than when the distractor was absent, but participants who received prevention-focused instructions actually performed *better* when the distractor was present than absent.[78] What this study demonstrates is that a task or an activity can have inherent demands or opportunities for how to engage it. These demands or opportunities create a natural fit or non-fit with different self-regulatory orientations. Given this, we cannot assume that all tasks are totally malleable with respect to allowing a fit with any orientation that thereby enhances performance. Tasks themselves have properties that allow fit more easily with some orientations than others. For instance, bookkeeping fits a prevention orientation better than a promotion orientation, and the reverse is true for creative problem solving. These differences in turn can have other self-regulatory effects, such as whether positive or negative feedback on a task is more motivating and yields higher performance. A recent study, for example, found that participants who received negative (vigilant-related) feedback subsequently improved their task performance more than those who received positive (eager-related) feedback when the task was error detection in arithmetic calculations (a task that fits prevention), but the opposite was true when the task was generating different uses for an object (a task that fits promotion).[79]

The fact that tasks themselves have properties that naturally fit better with some orientations than others adds some complexity regarding how best to manipulate value–control relations. But understanding the demands and opportunities inherent to a task or activity can facilitate selecting the self-regulatory orientation that best fits it, as well as selecting the self-regulatory features that suit that orientation (e.g., positive vs. negative feedback). This issue, too, will be discussed more fully in Chapter 12. But the more general caveat needs to be highlighted. Regulatory fit strengthens regulatory orientations and the strategic preferences associated with them. If the strategy that is strengthened by fit is not what is needed on a current task, then fit will impair rather than facilitate performance on the task.

REGULATORY FIT AS BEING ABOUT BOTH STRATEGIES *AND* TACTICS

I close this chapter with an even more important caveat. It is natural to think of control in terms of general strategies. But regulatory fit is not only about strategies: it is also about specific *tactics*. As in war, sports, and romance, strategies have to be translated into effective tactics to be successful. For example, should the strategic vigilance preferred by prevention-focused individuals be translated into a risky tactic or a conservative tactic when making a choice between different options? Psychologists have paid relatively little attention to the relation between strategies and tactics.[80] This is surprising given that psychologists, and others as well, want to predict the actions of others (what people actually do), and tactics are one step closer to actions than are strategies. Tactics are one step closer because they are embedded in specific contexts and situations that compel action, whereas strategies are relatively context and situation independent.[81] Given a particular goal orientation and the strategy that serves it, different situations or contexts will determine which tactics are appropriate for that orientation and strategy.

A recent program of research on stock investment decisions provides a compelling example of the importance of making this distinction.[82] In an initial study that had participants invest their own money, participants arrived at the lab and completed a battery of questionnaires that included a measure of their chronic promotion and prevention orientation. After completing the questionnaires, they were paid for their participation. They were then given a choice to leave the study or to invest their payment in a second, stock-investment study. They were told that past participants generally made additional money in the second study but that there was a chance that they could lose money. Most participants chose to participate in the second study. After making their initial investment decision, participants tracked the performance of their stock over time. At the end of the opening round of the second study, all participants learned that they had lost not only their original investment but also their payment from the first study.

At this point, when all the participants were in *a condition of loss*, they were given a choice for the next round of investing between two stocks: a risky one and a conservative one. The two stocks had the same expected value (i.e., the same product of the monetary value of the outcome × the probability of the outcome), but the risky stock was riskier in the sense that it was less certain (i.e., had greater variance) than the conservative stock and was experienced by the participants as being the riskier option. Previous studies have found that individuals with a promotion focus are generally riskier than individuals with a prevention focus; they are more willing to commit an error in order not to miss the opportunity for a "hit."[83] But this difference had been found in situations where individuals' current condition was satisfactory (i.e., "0") or even good (i.e., "+1"). Would this same difference be found when the current condition was poor (i.e., "−1"), as was the case for the participants in this study? Does riskiness as a tactic for promotion-oriented and prevention-oriented individuals vary as a function of whether the current state is "0 or +1" versus "–1"?

This is where the distinction between strategy and tactic becomes important. There is substantial evidence to support regulatory focus theory's proposal that promotion-focused individuals are strategically eager and prevention-focused individuals are strategically vigilant. This strategic difference should be found across different contexts and situations. In addition, one might expect that willingness to be risky would serve well someone who was strategically eager, and that being more conservative (i.e., less risky) would serve well someone who was strategically vigilant. And, generally speaking, this is the case. But tactics are contextualized. Given this, it might not always be the case that being conservative would serve strategic vigilance. Indeed, when people's current condition is poor (i.e., "–1"), being risky might serve strategic vigilance better than being conservative. Why would this be?

Consider what it means to be vigilant for prevention-focused individuals when the current situation is negative. What matters to these individuals is the difference between a satisfactory status quo (i.e., "0") and an unsatisfactory state (i.e., "–1"). They do whatever is necessary to maintain a satisfactory state. They don't take unnecessary risks that might create a maintenance failure that puts them in an unsatisfactory state. But once they find themselves in an unsatisfactory state, they must do everything necessary to return to the satisfactory state. And "everything necessary" includes taking risks if that is the only way to return to the satisfactory state.

Thus, under the circumstances of a current unsatisfactory state (i.e., "–1"), being risky *is* in the service of being vigilant for prevention-focused individuals. If so, then such individuals in a current state of loss in the investment study should prefer the riskier stock. In fact, the study found that as the strength of chronic prevention focus increased, the probability of selecting the risky option also increased substantially, and prevention-focused individuals were, if anything, *more risky* than promotion-focused individuals.

In this study, *only* the risky option had the potential of returning participants to their breakeven point, the satisfactory status quo. The conservative option could improve participants' condition but it could not restore the status quo. What would happen if a new set of participants again found themselves down after an investment (i.e., again in a loss "–1" condition), but this time were given a risky and a conservative option that *both* could return them to their breakeven point? If prevention-focused individuals can be vigilant by choosing a conservative tactic that could return them to the status quo, then it would no longer be necessary to choose the risky option. Indeed, given that its outcome is more certain than the outcome of the risky option, the conservative option would better serve the vigilance of the prevention-focused individuals. With this new context, the new study found that as the strength of chronic prevention focus increased, now the probability of selecting the conservative option increased substantially. Now the prevention-focused individuals were *more conservative* than promotion-focused individuals.

What these studies show is that when prevention-focused individuals find themselves in a negative condition, their vigilance motivates them to do whatever is necessary to restore a satisfactory state. But what tactics serve this vigilance vary as a function of their situational circumstances—*the tactical preference is contextualized.* When a risky tactic is the only way to restore the status quo, they will choose the risky tactic to serve their vigilance. When a conservative tactic could restore the status quo without it being necessary to be risky, then they will choose the conservative tactic to serve their vigilance. Thus, regulatory fit occurs at the level of tactics as well as the level of strategies, and what counts as a fit depends on people's current condition (i.e., a poor, satisfactory, or good state) and their situational circumstances (i.e., what is afforded by different tactical options). In trying to maximize performance through regulatory fit, this fuller picture of regulatory fit must be considered.

This chapter has presented evidence for the importance of regulatory fit as a value–control relation. I have reviewed the many different ways it can be created, which accounts for its pervasiveness. I have also reviewed its broad-ranging impact on value, persuasion, and performance. Finally, I have considered the mechanisms that underlie regulatory fit effects. These mechanisms include fluency, the experience of "feeling right", and strength of engagement. In the final chapters of this book, I will discuss how the principle of regulatory fit can be applied to better understand the nature of personality and culture (Chapter 11), to manage motives effectively (Chapter 12), and to enhance well-being and have "the good life" (Chapter 13). I turn now to the third and final two-element relation—the *truth–control* relation.

Truth–Control Relations

Going in the Right Direction

The great thing in the world is not so much where we stand, as in what direction we are moving.

—OLIVER WENDELL HOLMES

The good life is a process, not a state of being. It is a direction, not a destination.

—CARL ROGERS

Leaders establish the vision for the future and set the strategy for getting there; they cause change. They motivate and inspire others to go in the right direction . . .

—JOHN KOTTER

When Adam and Eve chose to eat from the "tree of the knowledge of good and evil" despite being explicitly forbidden to do so by God's command, they were expelled from the Garden of Eden, where they could have enjoyed a life of all pleasure and no pain *forever*. From a hedonic perspective, their choice makes no sense. Nor, from a hedonic perspective, does it make sense that Neo in *Matrix* and Truman in *The Truman Show* would choose to give up a guaranteed life of hedonic pleasure for a life-threatening alternative. However, as the above epigraphs illustrate, people do understand that people are motivated not only by desired results but also by truth and control. We intuitively know what motivates the choices of Adam and Eve and Neo and Truman. We are like Neo who, when asked if he believed in fate, said he did not, "because I don't like the idea that I'm not in control of my life." Like Neo, Truman, and Adam and Eve, our lives are not all about maximizing pleasure and minimizing pain. As we see from these examples, truth and control are very important to us. We want to be effective in establishing what's real and in managing what happens. And *going in the right direction* constitutes having both truth and control.

The motivations of truth and control work together as a very powerful partnership. They can trump the motivation to maximize pleasure and minimize pain. How might this partnership be characterized? I believe that the epigraphs at the start of this chapter provide a good answer. Their combined message is that we have to manage to move in some direction, which is *control*. But to have a good life we cannot move just anywhere; we need to move in the *right* direction. And to know which direction is right, we need to have *truth* as well. Indeed, according to the *Oxford English Dictionary*, "direction" is defined as *putting or keeping in the right way or course*.[1] That is, "direction" is defined in terms of both control (*putting or keeping* the way or course) and truth (the *right* way or course).

What needs to be distinguished here is that going in the right direction does *not* necessarily mean that we will end with having desired results. For Adam and Eve, one consequence of eating the fruit from the "tree of the knowledge of good and evil" was that they had direction for the first time. When they were in a state of paradise, they had neither truth nor control. Now they had direction, but this led, at least initially, to the undesired result of being banished by God. Neo and Truman also had direction for the first time when they chose truth and control over hedonic pleasure, but again this led initially to a dangerous situation for them. As Carl Rogers said, the good life is a direction and not a destination.

Historically, the psychological relations that have received the most attention in the literature are those where value plays the central role. This traditional emphasis on value is consistent with the predominance of pleasure and pain in theories of motivation. In contrast, this chapter considers truth–control relations where value does not play the central role. This is not to say that these relations have nothing to do with value. As I discuss in the next chapter, Chapter 10, motivation is typically a story of how *all three* ways of being effective work together. Normally, truth–control relations function to facilitate having desired results, to facilitate success at value. But the story is not always about value as the lead player, with truth and control having only supporting roles. Sometimes the emphasis can be on truth or control rather than on value, and when truth and control work together as partners they can trump value motivationally.

TRUTH AND CONTROL AS PARTNERS IN CONTROL SYSTEMS

Truth and control as partners in self-regulation have received the most attention in theories of *"control systems"*—devices or mechanisms that manage,
direct, or regulate how things behave. Norbert Wiener, an applied mathematician and the founder of cybernetics,[2] was a pioneer in formulating the role of
feedback in control systems. They can include feedback systems that regulate in
relation to some set point or reference value, as when air conditioning systems
vary their output as the temperature changes in order to maintain a temperature that was set as the reference value. Such systems are often assumed to
contain two functional elements: a *testing* component designed to evaluate a
system's current state (truth), and an *action* component designed to move it
toward the desired state (control). A thermostat, for instance, has sensors to
detect whether the desired temperature has been reached (truth), and a switching mechanism to activate or deactivate the heating or the cooling process
(control). Together, these two functional elements ensure that the temperature
is *going in the right direction*. Similarly, bodily mechanisms detect low hydra-
tion levels, which indicate that the activity of drinking is called for, or low blood
glucose levels, which produce hunger that motivates eating.

In Chapter 2 I discussed a control system model proposed by Miller, Galanter,
and Pribram—the TOTE model (for Test-Operate-Test-Exit).[3] TOTE units
function at strategic and behavioral levels. At the strategic planning level of
hammering a nail, for example, there are the phases of lifting the hammer and
striking the nail. But what tells us when to stop hammering? There needs to be
feedback comparing where the head of the nail currently is in relation to the
reference value of being flush with the surface of the work. We stop our hammering (i.e., exit) when the operation of hammering is followed by a test of
the current state of the nail head in relation to the reference value of the work
surface, and the test informs us that the nail head is flush with the surface.

According to the TOTE model, then, being effective at hammering a nail
requires a truth–control partnership. Effective truth involves establishing the
current reality of the relation between the nail head and the work surface.
Effective control involves managing to carry out the strategic plan at the behavioral level, such as lifting the hammer and striking the nail. Working together,
truth and control arrive at the stopping or exit point where the nail head is flush
with the surface—thereby having the desired result (value).

The partnership described in the TOTE model is the type of truth–control
relation that has received the most attention in the motivational literature.
Truth and control are working together in order to have desired results; that is,
it is *a truth–control relation in the service of value*. A similar model is the
influential *self-regulation model of Carver and Scheier*[4] that I also previously

discussed. In their theory, there are two self-regulatory systems. One system involves a desired end-state as the reference value and an operational control function that is concerned with reducing any existing discrepancy between the current state and the desired reference value. A second self-regulatory system involves an undesired end-state as the reference value and an operational control function that is concerned with amplifying the distance between the current state and the undesired reference value. In each case there is a monitoring and feedback *truth* function that compares the current state with the reference value and provides progress information regarding the amount and rate of distance reduction or amplification—*the truth regarding "how am I doing?"* Once again, truth and control are partners in the service of value, where value is either the desired result of eliminating the discrepancy between the current state and the desired end-state, or the desired result of establishing sufficient distance between the current state and the undesired end-state.

The type of truth–control relation emphasized in Miller, Galanter, and Pribram's TOTE model and Carver and Scheier's control-process model is one in which the self-regulatory functions of truth (i.e., monitoring and providing feedback about current reality) and control (i.e., managing operations) are intertwined in relation to a reference value that defines their purpose. Certainly, value, truth, and control *do* work together in this way. But, again, I need to emphasize that a desired result is not a necessary outcome of a powerful truth–control relation. My favorite example is Walt Disney's Mickey Mouse in his role as the sorcerer's apprentice in the movie *Fantasia*. Mickey used his apprentice-level of knowledge of magic (truth) to manage a broom (control) to do his chore of carrying buckets of water. Unfortunately for him, going in what he thought was the right direction—and clearly enjoying it—did not have desired results because he did not know how to stop the process, and the castle became flooded.

In addition, truth and control are not always equal partners when they work together. There are times when the motivation for truth is primary and control operates in its service, and this can occur even when the behaviors required to establish truth have unpleasant consequences. There are other times when the motivation for control is primary and truth operates in its service, and once again this can occur even when the behaviors required for successful control have unpleasant consequences. Perhaps most significant, rather than being conceptualized as interdependent functions in the service of value, truth and control can be conceptualized as *separate functions* that can motivationally receive *differential emphasis* in different situations and from different individuals. It is these less traditional, non-standard types of truth–control partnerships that I wish to highlight in this chapter.

ASSESSMENT AND LOCOMOTION AS TRUTH
AND CONTROL CONCERNS

The assessment and locomotion modes of self-regulation, introduced briefly in Chapters 5 and 6, are one such truth-control partnership. To appreciate more fully how truth and control work together as partners, it is important to understand how assessment and locomotion work together. And to understand how they work together, it is important to learn more about the distinct motivational nature of each of them. Just as truth and control can be conceptualized as separate functions that can receive differential emphasis, so too can assessment and locomotion. Indeed, this is precisely how regulatory mode theory treats them. Within this partnership, either assessment or locomotion can receive differential emphasis in different situations and from different individuals. Let us now consider these distinct functions more fully.

Assessment and Locomotion as Distinct Self-Regulatory Functions

Distinguishing between assessment and locomotion modes of self-regulation began when Arie Kruglanski and I were discussing the fundamental nature of control systems. Before long, we became convinced that the test and operate functions, or the monitoring and reducing/amplifying functions, could be conceptualized more broadly as distinct and general self-regulatory functions. More important, we felt that these functions need not be conceived as inseparable parts of a self-regulation whole, as always being functionally integrated and interdependent. Instead, we decided that there were two separate and independent functions of self-regulation—assessment and locomotion—that had wide ranges of applicability and could work together (or not) with varying degrees of emphasis on one or the other function (high emphasis on just one; high emphasis on both; high emphasis on neither).[5]

Rather than just testing or monitoring the current state of affairs relative to some reference value end-state, we conceptualized the assessment mode as being concerned more generally with making comparisons between some target and some standard. This includes assessing the relation between the current state and the reference value end-state. But it also includes assessing the end-state itself by comparing it to alternative end-states that could be pursued, as well as assessing alternative means for attaining whichever end-state had been selected to pursue. Indeed, assessment would apply beyond personal self-regulation to include critical evaluation of other people's self-regulation as well (i.e., their goals, their means, their progress). The concept of assessment motivation is captured in the maxim, "Get it right!" Most broadly, the assessment mode is concerned with *the process of making comparisons*. And what matters is engaging in this truth-finding comparison process rather than the desired results that might follow from doing so—"I would rather be right than happy."

Similarly, the locomotion mode was not restricted to operations or procedures for reducing discrepancies to desired end-states or amplifying distance from undesired end-states. The central feature of the locomotion mode is its concern simply with movement; that is, movement for its own sake. In contrast to control system models, locomotion movement is not restricted to the case of moving toward a desired end-state or moving away from an undesired end-state. Taking our cue from Lewin's field theory,[6] we conceptualized locomotion as concerned with any change of position that occurred in any region within the life space. It was about movement in an experiential or psychological sense, in physical space or mental space. And the reference point that matters is only the current state because locomotion is just about movement itself. Movement away from the current state is locomotion regardless of where the movement is going. The concept of locomotion motivation is captured in the maxim, "Just do it!" Locomotion is concerned with initiating movement and then sustaining it smoothly, without interruptions—no matter what the destination. Most broadly, the locomotion mode or function is concerned with *movement from state to state*. Note that, once again, it is the movement and change that matters rather than the desired results that might follow from doing so—"Doing anything is better than doing nothing."

Conceptualizing assessment and locomotion as independent functions has a significant implication. Specifically, on any one task there could be a strong emphasis on assessment but a weak emphasis on locomotion, or a strong emphasis on locomotion but a weak emphasis on assessment, or a strong emphasis on both, or a weak emphasis on both. This is in contrast to control system models that implicitly assume that on any one task both the testing (or monitoring) function and the operating (or discrepancy reduction) functions will receive equal and strong emphasis overall (albeit at different phases of the task).

Moreover, assessment and locomotion modes are conceptualized as motivational states and, as such, their emphasis can vary across situations and across individuals. When assessment and locomotion modes vary chronically across individuals, they become personality differences. Some individuals can be chronically high in locomotion and low in assessment, others can be chronically high in assessment and low in locomotion, others can be chronically high in both, and still others can be chronically low in both. This perspective on how assessment and locomotion function across situations and individuals predicts motivational phenomena that are not predicted by control system models. In particular, it predicts that *how* people go about pursuing goals and making decisions in their lives—their *activity selections* and *preferred strategies*—will vary depending on the relative strength of their locomotion concerns and assessment concerns.

It occurred to me while writing this book that assessment and locomotion have different relations to truth and control concerns. The assessment function relates more to truth concerns than to control concerns, given its emphasis on making comparisons and critical evaluations in order to establish what is correct, what is right. Assessment refers to determining the rate, amount, size, value, or importance of something. It concerns critical appraisal or evaluation for the purpose of understanding or interpreting.[7] Thus, assessment is a fundamental part of establishing what's real. In contrast, the locomotion function relates more to control concerns than to truth concerns, given its emphasis on initiating and sustaining movement in order to manage what happens. Thus, when assessment and locomotion work together as partners, they constitute a truth–control relation. When assessment is emphasized more than locomotion, truth is being emphasized more than control; and when locomotion is emphasized more than assessment, control is being emphasized more than truth. Given this, the research on regulatory mode provides valuable new insights into truth–control relations and what it means to place relatively more emphasis on assessment–truth or on locomotion–control during goal pursuits and decision making. Moreover, research has shown that people's performance is often at its best when *both* locomotion and assessment are emphasized—the condition for *going in the right direction*.[8]

How Emphasis on Assessment Versus Locomotion Affects What We Do

What does it mean, then, to emphasize assessment versus locomotion in our lives? To begin with, it influences which activities people decide to invest their efforts in.

ACTIVITY SELECTION AND INVESTMENT AS A FUNCTION OF ASSESSMENT VERSUS LOCOMOTION

In one study, participants were asked a couple of questions to determine their motives for engaging in different activities.[9] To determine how much their assessment concerns motivated their engagement, they were asked the extent to which they engaged in each activity "because it involves evaluating, measuring, or interpreting information. It satisfies my need for critically appraising and evaluating something in order to be sure I am doing it correctly." To determine how much locomotion concerns motivated engagement, they were asked the extent to which they engaged in each activity "because it involves action or movement away from the current situation. It satisfies my need for change, to do something, anything different, regardless of what I am currently doing."

Some activities were engaged in for both assessment and locomotion reasons, such as "going places" ("traveling, exploring, or going places in general"). But there were other activities that people did primarily for assessment reasons or primarily for locomotion reasons. The activities that were motivated primarily by assessment included attending cultural events, participating in academic activities ("required learning and course work"), dealing with financial duties (e.g., paying bills), and obtaining news. In contrast, the activities that were motivated primarily by locomotion included playing sports, exercising, dancing, and partying.

One implication of this difference is that people are likely to *select* those activities that satisfy their self-regulatory concerns. Individuals with assessment–truth concerns, for instance, are more likely to seek out cultural events and news more than individuals with locomotion–control concerns. In contrast, individuals with locomotion–control concerns are more likely to seek out opportunities to play sports and exercise than individuals with assessment–truth concerns. And, of course, those individuals who have both high assessment and high locomotion concerns will seek out both kinds of activities.

Another implication is that when we are engaged in a particular kind of activity—and almost all of us spend some time exercising and some time reading or watching the news—the *amount of effort we are willing to expend* on the activity is likely to be greater if there is a fit between how much that activity satisfies assessment or locomotion concerns and how much we personally emphasize assessment–truth or locomotion–control. Indeed, there is evidence that the amount of energy that individuals report they would put into an assessment activity, like carrying out financial duties, is positively related to the level of their general assessment concerns, but it has no relation to the level of their general locomotion concerns. In contrast, the amount of energy that individuals say they would put into a locomotion activity, like exercising, is positively related to the level of their general locomotion concerns, but it has no relation to their general assessment concerns.

Overall, then, our concerns with assessment–truth versus locomotion–control can influence which activities we select to do and how much effort we expend on them.[10] If individuals are high in *both* assessment and locomotion, their preference for an activity and the effort they are willing to put into it will be especially high for activities like traveling that satisfy both assessment and locomotion concerns. But beyond this fit, traveling is enjoyed by many people because, by combining truth with control as partners, it gives people the experience of "going in the right direction."

THINKING AS AN ASSESSMENT VERSUS LOCOMOTION ACTIVITY

Thinking can also be considered to be a type of activity. Is this also something that those with assessment–truth concerns are more motivated to do than those with locomotion–control concerns? Generally speaking, there is evidence that this is the case. Participants in the study just described did report that the activity of "thinking" ("problem solving, idea generation") satisfied their need for assessment (i.e., "for critically appraising and evaluating something in order to be sure I am doing it correctly") more than their need for locomotion (i.e., "for change, to do something, anything different, regardless of what I am currently doing").

An especially interesting case of thinking occurs when something bad happens and people think about what they might have done differently ("If only I had . . ."; "If only I hadn't . . ."). Such *counterfactual* thinking can have the benefit of finding solutions for past problems that can be applied in future situations to ensure that the problem doesn't happen again. It can also have the cost of people dwelling on the past—*ruminative* thinking—and experiencing painful *regret* for past decisions.[11] Because counterfactual thinking involves critically evaluating why something went wrong and searching for some alternative to what happened that would make it right instead of wrong, it is the kind of activity that people with a proclivity toward assessment–truth concerns should be more likely to do. And if they do engage in this activity, they should experience regret about their past decisions. In fact, there is evidence that individuals with stronger assessment concerns (whether as a chronic personality disposition or situationally induced) do engage more in counterfactual thinking and experience more regret about past decisions.[12]

What about individuals with locomotion–control concerns? Counterfactual thinking involves spending time in the present thinking about past events. Individuals with locomotion–control concerns want to make things happen going forward, *to get on with it*. For them, thinking about the past is like getting stuck in the past; it is interfering with moving ahead now. Thus, counterfactual thinking is the kind of activity that people with locomotion–control concerns should *not* want to do. And by not doing it, they should experience less regret from past decisions. In fact, there is evidence that individuals with stronger locomotion concerns do engage less in counterfactual thinking and experience less regret about past decisions.[13]

I am not suggesting that, compared to people with locomotion–control concerns, people with assessment–truth concerns engage more in all forms of thinking. After all, there are many different kinds of thinking, and some are more like locomoting in the mind, as Lewin suggested.[14] One clear example is *planning for the future*. This involves thinking about how to move from one's current state to the future state that is one's goal, like planning a trip from here to there. Good planning involves thinking about how to get started and about how to carry on smoothly, with minimal interruptions along the way. This kind of thinking should be a fit for people with locomotion–control concerns.

There is evidence, in fact, that strength of locomotion concerns positively relates to this kind of thinking. The evidence has to do with the personality trait of *conscientiousness*. Being conscientious relates to being planful, responsible, organized, thorough, and efficient.[15] Across various countries, from the United States, Italy, and Israel to India and Japan, a consistent finding is that individuals who have stronger locomotion concerns are more conscientious.[16] In contrast, no relation has been found between individuals' strength of assessment concerns and their conscientiousness.

Personality Styles as Strategies Serving Assessment or Locomotion

Conscientiousness, more generally, is *a way of getting along in the world* and is considered to be one of the major ways in which individuals differ from one another—one of the so-called "Big Five" personality trait dimensions that also include extraversion, openness to experience, and agreeableness.[17] How do these various dimensions relate to the strength of individuals' locomotion or assessment concerns?

Clearly, for individuals with strong locomotion concerns, taking time for planning, or being conscientious more generally, can be considered as a way to satisfy their locomotion concerns. From this perspective, the personality trait of conscientiousness can be considered *a strategic style* that is *in the service of* locomotion concerns. This is a different way to conceptualize personality traits. From this "in the service of" perspective, rather than personality traits being chronic needs or inner forces that drive one to behave in particular ways, they are instead strategic styles that are in the service of more general motivational concerns. For the case of conscientiousness, rather than individuals being driven, perhaps genetically, to behave conscientiously, they would instead behave conscientiously in the service of their locomotion concerns.[18]

From this new "in the service of" perspective, a strategic style like conscientiousness could even serve locomotion concerns that are momentarily created by a situation rather than only being associated with someone's chronic personality. Moreover, and importantly, a strategic style like conscientiousness could serve *more than one* motivational concern. Indeed, there is consistent evidence from several cultures that individuals who have stronger prevention concerns also behave more conscientiously.[19] In this case, behaving conscientiously would be a strategy in the service of satisfying prevention concerns with fulfilling duties and obligations, with behaving as one ought to behave.

This suggests that some aspects of conscientiousness could be more in the service of locomotion, while other aspects could be more in the service of prevention. Evidence indicates that being conscientious in the sense of *being careful and non-negligent* relates more to prevention concerns with maintaining a satisfactory status quo (i.e., maintaining "0" rather than "–1"), whereas being conscientious in the sense of *being steady, thorough, and systematic* relates more to locomotion concerns with maintaining smooth and uninterrupted movement.[20]This highlights how the same general trait style can play out with somewhat different emphases in the service of different motivational concerns.

With this new perspective on personality in mind, which I develop more fully in Chapter 11, let us look at other personality traits to see how differential emphasis on locomotion–control versus assessment–truth could yield different ways of getting along in the world.

LOCOMOTION AND EXTRAVERSION

Since the early work of Carl Jung and Hans Eysenck, two pioneering figures in the area of personality, the distinction between *extraverts* and *introverts* has become probably the best-known personality distinction. In comparison to introverts, extraverts are relatively more active, sociable, adventurous, assertive, and forceful.[21] If we consider extraversion as a strategic style, which concerns would this style serve more? If your answer was "locomotion–control concerns," then the research supports your answer. In every nation studied, individuals with stronger locomotion concerns were more extraverted. In contrast, extraversion was not related to the strength of individuals' assessment concerns.[22]

Evidence from many different cultures also indicates that extraversion in the sense of being active and energetic relates to both locomotion and promotion concerns. But once again, there are also distinct ways that extraversion serves locomotion and promotion.[23] Extraversion in the sense of being *unreserved (not shy)* relates more to promotion concerns with eagerly (unreservedly) trying to maximize desired results. In contrast, extraversion in the sense of being *bold and daring* relates more to locomotion concerns with initiating movement and wanting change for its own sake.

LOCOMOTION, ASSESSMENT, AND OPENNESS TO EXPERIENCE

Now consider a more difficult case: the trait of openness to experience (sometimes called intellect). In comparison to those who are low in openness, individuals high in openness are relatively more imaginative, reflective, and complex, as well as being bright and inquisitive.[24] Which concerns would openness to experience as a strategic style serve? If your answer was "locomotion–control concerns," then, once again, the research supports your answer. In every nation studied, individuals with stronger locomotion concerns were higher in openness. And yet, if your answer was "assessment–control concerns," then the research also supports your answer. In most (but not all) nations studied, individuals with stronger assessment concerns were also higher in openness.[25]

Both locomotion and assessment concerns are served by people being bright and inquisitive. But, once again, there are also distinct relations between ways of being open to experience and locomotion versus assessment concerns.[26] Openness in the sense of being *innovative and imaginative* has been found to relate more to locomotion concerns, which is consistent with locomotion-oriented individuals being open to change. Indeed, such individuals want change and movement to new states—in this case, new states of mind. In contrast, openness in the sense of being *complex and introspective* has been found to relate more to assessment concerns, which is consistent with assessment-oriented individuals wanting to make critical evaluations in relation to multiple standards.

Altogether, what this suggests is that individuals who have strong locomotion–control concerns *and* strong assessment–truth concerns would be especially high in openness to experience. It is interesting in this regard that a study of 11 nations from Europe, North America, Asia, and the Middle East found that Israel had the strongest assessment concerns and the second-strongest locomotion concerns (only Italy was stronger in locomotion). To the extent that Israelis are unusually curious, reflective, complex, and imaginative, one explanation would be that they are motivated to be this way in order to serve their unusual combination of strong locomotion–control and strong assessment–truth concerns.

LOCOMOTION, ASSESSMENT, AND AGREEABLENESS

Let us consider one more case: the trait of agreeableness. In comparison to those who are low in agreeableness, individuals high in agreeableness are relatively more warm and trusting, less fault-finding, more forgiving and cooperative. Which concerns would agreeableness as a strategic style serve? If your answer was "locomotion–control concerns," then, once again, the research supports your answer. In almost every nation studied, individuals with stronger locomotion concerns were higher in agreeableness. This makes sense because being forgiving of the past, trusting others in the future, helping others, and cooperating with others all satisfy locomotion–control concerns with moving on to the next project, with making things happen.

But what about assessment–truth concerns? In most of the nations studied the relation was *negative*: individuals with stronger assessment concerns score high on being harsh, uncooperative, and distrustful.[27] Why is it that, generally speaking, individuals with stronger assessment concerns behave less agreeably? My guess is that such individuals would not consider themselves as being disagreeable people but rather as being honest and accurate in searching for what is "right" or correct through critical evaluation. To serve their assessment–truth concerns, they could appear to be cold and "fault-finding" when they are only being evaluatively critical in the search for truth. The problem, of course, is that when the target of their strategic style is another person, that person can find the *truth-giving* behavior disagreeable.

Thus, the relation of agreeableness as a personality trait to locomotion–control concerns and assessment–truth concerns is in *opposite* directions. This is interesting precisely because it is possible for someone to have *both* strong locomotion–control concerns and strong assessment–truth concerns. What happens in this case? To take a concrete example, what might happen to Israelis who, generally speaking, are strong in both kinds of concerns? I believe that they would behave in a manner that can satisfy both kinds of concerns. They would be warm and trusting (high agreeableness) under conditions where this provided an opportunity to make things happen, and they would be fault-finding (low agreeableness) when this provided an opportunity to be critically evaluative and determine what was "right." In direct contrast to traditional ways of thinking about personality traits where a person cannot be both high and low on a personality trait (e.g., both high and low in agreeableness), this perspective permits different aspects of a strategic style to appear under different conditions as a function of which regulatory function—locomotion–control or assessment–truth—can be served.[28]

Decision Styles Better Serving Assessment Versus Locomotion Concerns

Earlier in this book I have described research that examined the fit between locomotion and assessment concerns and two different styles of decision making—the "full evaluation" decision style and the "progressive elimination" style. The actual instructions given to the participants were as follows:[29]

For the "full evaluation" decision style:

Look at brand number 1. Compare it to the rest of the brands based on each of the attributes. Now look at brand number 2. Compare it to the rest of the brands based on each of the attributes. Now look at brand number 3. Compare it to the rest of the brands based on each of the attributes. Do so until you have looked at all the brands and at all the attributes. After you are done comparing between the brands, decide which brand you prefer most. Mark this brand as your chosen brand.

For the "progressive elimination" style:

Look at the first attribute, Amount of light provided, brand by brand. Exclude the brand that has the worst value on this attribute. Now you are left with 4 brands. Go to the second attribute, Light adjustability, and again look at it

for all the remaining brands. Exclude the brand that has the worst value on
this attribute. Follow this procedure until you are left with only one brand.
Mark this brand as your chosen brand.

Which of these two ways of making a decision would you prefer to use?
When I give an audience in the United States the basic scenario of this study
and then ask them which decision style they would prefer, most prefer the "progressive elimination" style. They are surprised when others raise their hands in
support of the "full evaluation" style, and they say things like, "Why would you
choose that one? It's so boring to wait until the end to actually do anything." In
contrast, in Japan or South Korea most prefer the "full evaluation" style and are
surprised when others show support for the "progressive elimination" style.
They say things like, "But you can't make the right choice that way! You're missing too much information." It is notable that cross-cultural studies have found
that locomotion concerns are generally stronger than assessment concerns in
the United States, whereas just the opposite is true in Japan and Korea. Indeed,
among many nations studied, Japan and Korea have the weakest locomotion
concerns and among the strongest assessment concerns.

Might there be other, even more general aspects of decision making that also
better fit or satisfy either locomotion or assessment concerns? Is it even possible
that the two major factors in commitment discussed in Chapter 7—the *value* of
an outcome and the *likelihood* of an outcome—vary in whether they satisfy
locomotion or assessment? In fact, there is evidence that they do. To understand
why outcome value and outcome likelihood might vary in the extent to which
they satisfy locomotion–control concerns versus assessment–truth concerns,
we need to consider more fully how each of them relate to each of these
concerns.

LOCOMOTION AND OUTCOME VALUE AND LIKELIHOOD

Individuals with locomotion concerns are motivated to initiate movement and
then have it continue in a smooth and steady manner. The end-state or destination of the movement is less important than the movement itself. It is change
from state to state that matters, and the new state need not be better than the
old one. It is about *wanting change*, wanting something different—"I don't care
what it is as long as it is different." There is recent evidence, for example, that
when individuals are deciding whether or not to initiate change, such as whether
or not to quit smoking or to begin exercising regularly, they are more likely to
commit to change when they have stronger locomotion concerns—whether
those stronger concerns are a chronic personality variable or are situationally
induced. Moreover, and importantly, this greater *commitment to change* is
independent of the perceived benefits and costs of the change; that is, it is

independent of the value of the change.[30] What this means is that the value of possible outcomes should *not* be a critical factor for commitment when individuals have strong locomotion concerns.

In contrast, the likelihood of possible outcomes *should* matter to individuals with strong locomotion concerns. Why would this be? Recall that the likelihood of possible outcomes can be experienced as the difficulty of the goal pursuit—the higher the likelihood, the lower the perceived difficulty. When we perceive a goal pursuit as being easy (i.e., as a high outcome likelihood), we predict that the process of goal attainment will *flow smoothly and steadily*. It should matter, then, to individuals with strong locomotion concerns whether the likelihood of possible outcomes is high or low because high outcome likelihood would satisfy their concerns for a smooth and steady goal-pursuit process. And because high outcome likelihood would satisfy their concerns, they would even have a motivational bias to perceive future success as being likely. If this were so, then we would expect, more generally, that individuals with stronger locomotion concerns would be more optimistic about their future. In fact, there is separate evidence that such individuals have more positive expectations about future goal attainment[31] and are generally more optimistic.[32]

In a test of the predictions relating locomotion concerns to goal attainment value and likelihood, participants in one study[33] listed five personal goals that they wanted to attain. They then rated the value to them of attaining each goal and the likelihood of its attainment. If it were outcome value that satisfied locomotion concerns, then the goals should have higher attainment value for individuals with stronger locomotion concerns. If, on the other hand, it were outcome likelihood that satisfied locomotion concerns, as hypothesized, then the goals should have higher attainment likelihood for individuals with stronger locomotion concerns. The study found, as predicted, that participants with stronger locomotion concerns did have goals with *higher attainment likelihoods*, but they did *not* have goals with higher attainment value.

Assessment and Outcome Value and Likelihood

Assessment concerns *are* about value. Individuals with strong assessment concerns want to make the *right* choice, which would be the choice that maximizes value. After all, effective critical *evaluation* is all about comparing the value of different alternatives in order to choose the best alternative—the best means and the best ends. Individuals with strong assessment concerns should care about whether a goal is *really* worth it, *truly* worthwhile. This predicts that higher outcome value would satisfy assessment concerns. Individuals with stronger assessment concerns should have goals with higher attainment value. This is exactly what was found in the above study where participants rated the attainment value and attainment likelihood of their personal goals.

What about the relation between strong assessment concerns and attainment likelihood in this study? Individuals with strong assessment concerns should want to know what the likelihood of attainment *really* is. They should want to know whether the *true* likelihood is high or low. Because likelihood information relates to truth, individuals with strong assessment concerns should be strongly motivated to find out whether the *true* likelihood is high or low. But note that it does not matter whether the likelihood is high or is low. All that matters for the truth is whether the *perceived* likelihood—*whether high or low*—is accurate. Individuals with strong assessment concerns do not want a high likelihood *per se*; rather, they want to know what's real regarding the likelihood. Evidence from other studies indicates that individuals with stronger assessment concerns want *predictability*, want to be able to know what will or will not happen in the future.[34] It is about wanting to have accurate predictions about attainment likelihood rather than about wanting the high attainment likelihoods themselves. This then predicts *no relation* between stronger assessment concerns and attainment likelihood. And in the same study on goal attainment, stronger assessment concerns did *not* predict having goals with higher attainment likelihood—in contrast to what was found for stronger locomotion concerns.

However, this is not the full story of what was found in this study. Rather than finding no relation between stronger assessment concerns and attainment likelihood, the study found a *negative* relation. Why would individuals with stronger assessment concerns perceive attaining their goals as *less* likely? It turns out that this question needs to be answered more generally because there is evidence from other research that assessors are generally more pessimistic, anxious, and depressed about the future.[35] What can account for this negative relation? It is possible that such negativity about the future is an unintended consequence of the critical evaluations associated with strong assessment concerns. Perhaps this is a downside of being *too* effective in establishing what's real. It has been suggested, after all, that having a dose of positive illusions can be healthy in some ways, and the flipside is that being *too* realistic might be unhealthy in some ways.[36] However, there may be something else going on with assessors as well, which I consider next.

THE DEVELOPMENT OF LOCOMOTION AND ASSESSMENT CONCERNS

To my knowledge, it was Erik Erikson, a psychoanalyst and pioneer in the area of social development, who first discussed the development of locomotion and assessment concerns during early childhood[37] (albeit not quite in the same way as regulatory mode theory). Erikson regarded development from 3 to 6 years of age to be especially significant, with two key periods. First is a period of *initiative* when the child is "on the make," "attacking" a task for the sake of being active and on the move. Erikson explicitly relates this to *locomotion*, to being curious and exploring the unknown. Second is a period of *critical self-evaluation*, of conscience and a sense of moral responsibility. He discusses the danger that the child will have a sense of *guilt* over what is being initiated, guilt over the pleasure in attack and conquest.

Erikson refers to what is happening during this period as "Initiative *Versus* Guilt" (italics are mine). This highlights the idea that for different children there could be more initiative–locomotion or more guilt–assessment. Children during this period create a shared reality with their significant others about how much locomotion should be emphasized in self-regulation, with motivational viewpoints such as "Just do it!" and "Doing anything is better than doing nothing," versus how much assessment should be emphasized, with motivational viewpoints such as "Get it right!" and "It is better to be right than happy." And, despite the *Versus* in Erikson's label for the period, it is possible to develop strong concerns for *both* locomotion and assessment.[38]

From an Eriksonian perspective, therefore, assessment concerns are not neutral. Assessment is negatively tinged with guilt and harsh self-criticism. I am not suggesting that all individuals with strong assessment concerns have an Eriksonian guilt or anxiety associated with these concerns. But some might, and others may experience an internal pressure or demand to abstain from initiating action until they are certain it is the right thing to do. Indeed, there is evidence that individuals with strong assessment concerns have high fear of invalidity, fear of failure, and introjection (i.e., the "felt presence of others"),[39] which is consistent with their experiencing an internal pressure or demand to be right. This would bias attention toward potential negatives to be avoided.

It is possible, then, that individuals with strong assessment concerns have a more negative than positive tone to their critical evaluations—both when evaluating themselves and when evaluating others. When evaluating themselves, this would make them vulnerable to anxiety, depression, and pessimism. When evaluating others, this could make them appear disagreeable. This negativity and pessimism could account for why there is a negative relation between stronger assessment concerns and perceived likelihood of goal attainment.

Assessment and Locomotion as Non-hedonic Motives

The positive association between stronger assessment concerns and greater anxiety, depression, pessimism, and disagreeableness is interesting because it illustrates once again the need for the science of motivation to go beyond pleasure and pain. If people simply wanted to avoid pain, then individuals with strong assessment concerns would not be so critical in their evaluations given that such criticism is painful. Their decision-making emphasis has a different motivational source—to make critical comparisons in the service of knowing what is right, knowing the truth. They are motivated to seek the truth *even* if they—and others—might suffer for it. The pain of anxiety, depression, and being disagreeable are the *unintended consequences of this truth motivation*. It is not about pleasant and painful outcomes *per se*; it is not about value *per se*. It is about engaging in the process of making critical comparisons because that is what is needed to establish what's real. The motivation to make comparisons is so strong for individuals with strong assessment concerns that they are even willing to sacrifice hedonic outcomes for its sake.

A recent study provides a striking illustration of this point.[40] Participants made a choice between an option that offered a better expected return versus an option that offered more alternatives for making comparisons and evaluations.[41] The participants were asked to decide which of two business firms they would like to represent. Each firm provided the opportunity to form different business alliances with different expected rates of return for each alliance. Choosing to represent one of the two firms would mean having more opportunities to form more different alliances, but the overall outcome (i.e., the expected utility) was less positive for this firm. If having desired results was what mattered, a participant should not choose this firm. However, those participants who had strong assessment concerns did choose this firm, thereby sacrificing a better outcome for the sake of being able to make more comparisons and evaluations. In contrast, participants who didn't have strong assessment concerns chose the *other* firm with the better expected return.

Individuals with strong assessment concerns make comparisons and evaluations in order to seek the truth. Their desire to know what *is* right is not the same as the experience of "feeling right" from regulatory fit. But if feeling positive were the critical motivation, then individuals should be content with "feeling right." Would individuals with strong assessment concerns sacrifice the positive experience of *feeling* right for the sake of knowing what *is* right? Another recent experiment addressed this question.[42] The study used the same basic paradigm that I discussed in Chapter 8 where participants in an actual negotiation received either $5 (the potential buyer) or a Columbia notebook (the potential seller) at the beginning of the experimental session. The participants varied in the strength of their promotion and prevention focus, which created two regulatory fit conditions (promotion/seller; prevention/buyer) and two regulatory non-fit conditions (promotion/buyer; prevention/seller).

In the fit conditions, the participants "feel right" about their role in the negotiation, and this experience normally translates into feeling confident about the upcoming negotiation (e.g., anticipate performing better). Indeed, this was what happened for those participants who had weaker assessment concerns. But for those participants who had strong assessment concerns, the regulatory fit conditions had the *opposite* effect: they felt *less* confident about the upcoming negotiation. Because individuals with strong assessment concerns want to do what *is* right and not just *feel* right, these participants corrected for "feeling right" about the upcoming negotiation (i.e., reversed the normal implications of what it means to "feel right"), which reduced their confidence. For the *sake of the truth*, they ended up *losing* confidence.

What the results of these two studies demonstrate is that the motivation of individuals with strong assessment–truth concerns to know what is right by making comparisons and critical evaluations can be so strong that they will sacrifice positive outcomes and positive feelings for its sake. It is not that they are insensitive to outcome value; we have seen that they care about the attainment value of their goals. But the motivation is still to do what is right, to be effective in having made the comparisons and critical evaluations that led to the best goals. In addition, we have seen that individuals with strong locomotion–control concerns, for different reasons, are also not motivated simply by outcome value. For them, it is about change, about movement from state to state, and this matters independent of whether or not the new state happens to be more valuable than the old one.

I should note that people who have strong locomotion concerns or strong assessment concerns would select high- over low-value options if given a direct choice. But their assessment and locomotion concerns are not themselves about value *per se*, and if those concerns conflict with value, they can trump value. What this highlights is the importance of separating the independent functions of locomotion and assessment from the overall system of pursuing desired end-states. In control system models, the functions of operating and monitoring are in the service of having desired results, are in the service of value. According to regulatory mode theory, however, the locomotion–control and assessment–truth functions are *motivating in themselves*. They are separate and independent motivational forces with broad ranges of applicability.

Only by treating locomotion and assessment as separate and independent motivational forces can we appreciate fully their motivational significance and recognize the extent to which they influence decisions and behavior beyond pleasure and pain. In addition, only by treating them as separate and independent can we appreciate how they work together as partners to help us go in the right direction. And they do work together: they do combine as partners to attain and maintain desired end-states, including in the manner proposed by control system models. But when locomotion and assessment work together, they need not be equal partners, as suggested in control system models. In addition, even while they serve value in having desired results, they still work together serving the broader concerns of locomotion–control and assessment–truth. This is a deeper and richer motivational picture of self-regulation than is provided by control system models. It is a picture of value, truth, and control working together as an organization of motives that I will develop more fully in Chapter 10. Here I will give just one example of how locomotion–control and assessment–truth can work together to serve value in having desired results— the important case of achievement.

ASSESSMENT AND LOCOMOTION AS PARTNERS IN ACHIEVEMENT

From the perspective of traditional control system models, it is not reasonable to ask whether the operating function or the monitoring function is more important for successful achievement because both functions are equally critical in these models. In contrast, by separating the independent functions of locomotion and assessment, it *is* possible for regulatory mode theory to address the question of whether strong locomotion concerns or strong assessment concerns are more important for successful achievement. Two studies have addressed this question—one predicting the grade point averages (GPAs) of undergraduates and one predicting the completion of training in an elite military unit of the U.S. Army.[43]

Locomotion and Assessment as Predictors of General Achievement

The first study with college undergraduates restricted participation to those who had completed at least three semesters of courses. The participants' chronic locomotion and assessment concerns were measured. In the analysis predicting the students' cumulative GPA achievement, the participants' gender and score on the Scholastic Aptitude Test (SAT) were controlled for. The study found that the strongest regulatory mode predictor of the students' academic achievement was the strength of their locomotion concerns, with their achievement increasing as their strength of locomotion concerns increased.

Strength of assessment concerns by itself did *not* significantly predict academic achievement. However, the study also found that strength of assessment concerns did matter *as a partner with locomotion concerns*. Specifically, the better academic achievement for students with stronger locomotion concerns was more pronounced for those who also had stronger assessment concerns. Indeed, if students' assessment concerns were less strong than those of the median or typical student, then having stronger locomotion concerns did not yield stronger academic achievement. It is as if a certain level of assessment concerns is necessary, and, then, once that level is reached, it is the strength of locomotion concerns that predicts academic achievement and not the strength of assessment concerns. Before discussing this further, let me turn now to the second study.

All of the participants in this study were already in military service. The military training program they entered was highly selective and extremely demanding—so demanding that approximately 60% of the participants never completed the program. The measure of achievement in this study was whether a participant did or did not complete the training program. In the analysis predicting the soldiers' achievement of completing the program, the participants' military status (i.e., commissioned officer; enlisted soldier), technical and other abilities, and prior training as an Army Ranger were controlled for. The study found that the strongest regulatory mode predictor of soldiers' completing the program was the strength of their locomotion concerns, with program completion increasing as strength of locomotion concerns increased.

Again, strength of assessment concerns by itself did not significantly predict completion of the program. But again, paralleling the academic achievement study, assessment concerns *did* matter when they were partnered with locomotion concerns. As before, the better achievement for participants with stronger locomotion concerns was more pronounced for those participants who also had stronger assessment concerns: when the soldiers' assessment concerns were less strong than those of the median or typical soldier in the program, then having stronger locomotion concerns did not yield stronger achievement. Once more, it was as if a certain level of assessment concerns was necessary, and, then, once that level was reached, it was the strength of locomotion concerns that predicted achievement in the program and not the strength of assessment concerns.

The results of these two studies were the same even though the participants and the type of achievement were very different. What the studies found was that variability in locomotion concerns was a stronger predictor of achievement than variability in assessment concerns. Stronger locomotion, by itself, predicted higher achievement. Stronger assessment, by itself, did not. But a certain level of assessment concerns had to be reached before stronger locomotion concerns translated into higher achievement. This represents an interesting kind of truth–control relation—in this case, assessment–truth in the service of locomotion–control but still a partner.

The fact that stronger locomotion–control concerns do not translate into more effective achievement until a certain level of assessment–truth concerns is reached makes a lot of sense. After all, effective achievement requires having some idea of which goals are good and which means are good. Without this truth, individuals with strong locomotion–control concerns could be effective in moving from state to state without the movement being in the *right* direction toward a desired destination. Something has to establish a basic reality about where the movement should be headed. This is the job of assessment. Thus, there could be a limit on how strong the locomotion motivation can be if when locomotion becomes too strong it overwhelms the contribution of assessment. If this were to happen, then extremely strong locomotors might not move in the *right* direction. Once assessment has done its job, however, then the strength of motivation to initiate and maintain smooth and steady movement becomes the essential factor. This provides a new insight into how the partnership of truth and control provides the motivational underpinnings of effective achievement.

There is also an irony here that you might have noticed. Individuals with strong locomotion concerns select goals to pursue that have high (vs. low) likelihood of attainment, whereas individuals with strong assessment concerns select goals that have high (vs. low) value. But it is locomotion rather than assessment that is the dominant player in effective achievement in these studies. Once again, as I discussed in Chapter 7, this demonstrates how likelihood can play a central role in commitment.

Locomotion and Assessment as Complementary Partners

The contributions of locomotion–control and assessment–truth concerns to achievement in these studies were examined at a general level of overall performance. It is also possible to consider them with respect to a particular task. On a specific task, there can be more of an equal partnership from locomotion concerns and assessment concerns emphasizing different aspects of a task—a complementary partnership. This is especially true when there is more than one criterion defining effective performance, such as in tasks for which both speed and accuracy are important.

Speed and accuracy should be differentially emphasized by individuals with strong locomotion concerns versus strong assessment concerns. Individuals with strong locomotion concerns would want to initiate action quickly and move quickly from state to state. They would emphasize speed in the task. As part of the same study that I described earlier where the participants listed personal goals to pursue,[44] after they had reported the attainment value and attainment likelihood for their different goals, they were asked to type in as quickly as possible the best means for attaining each of the attributes. The stronger the participants' locomotion concerns, the faster they were in choosing the best means. In contrast, the speed of choosing the best means was not related to participants' strength of assessment concerns. In another study,[45] participants were given the opportunity to wait for background information about nine different tasks, one of which they would choose to do, or if they preferred they could just randomly choose a task and get started immediately. Participants with stronger locomotion concerns were more likely to choose to begin immediately, whereas there was no relation between choosing to begin immediately and strength of assessment concerns.

While an emphasis on speed relates to strong locomotion concerns, an emphasis on accuracy should relate to strong assessment concerns given its association with wanting to do what is right or correct. In a follow-up to the nine-tasks study,[46] the quality of the background information about the different tasks in the choice set was also manipulated. This study found not only that participants with stronger assessment concerns spent more time investigating the background information about the different tasks, but also that this effort was more true for the high-quality (i.e., more accurate) information than for the low-quality information.

A third study on proofreading[47] tested for both speed and accuracy emphases. The participants were told that the study was about ease of reading and detection of errors as a function of the different types of print font used in a passage. Participants were asked to check for any differences between a Sample Copy and a Master Copy (e.g., spelling errors). The study found that stronger locomotion concerns (but not stronger assessment concerns) predicted quicker completion time, whereas stronger assessment concerns (but not stronger locomotion concerns) predicted finding more errors. I should also note that, consistent with their assessment negativity bias, participants with stronger assessment concerns more often identified errors that were *not* errors.

These studies were not designed to examine truth–control relations directly, and thus we do not know whether those individuals who had *both* strong locomotion concerns and strong assessment concerns managed to be *both* relatively fast and relatively accurate—although this seems likely given the overall findings. Fortunately, there is a study of group performance that did directly test this question.[48] The composition of four-member groups was experimentally manipulated by inducing either strong locomotion concerns or strong assessment concerns in the individual members prior to their becoming a group.[49] Groups were then created that contained all high locomotors, all high assessors, or half high locomotors and half high assessors.

The group task was a "homicide investigation" where different bits of evidence concerning three suspects were distributed among the group members. After the group members read, reviewed, and discussed the evidence, each group's mission was to reach a consensus on the likely culprit.[50] The study found that the strong locomotion groups were *faster* in reaching a consensus than the strong assessment groups, whereas the strong assessment groups were more *accurate* in their final judgment than the strong locomotion groups. So far this sounds like a trade-off between speed and accuracy: you can either be fast by having strong locomotion or be accurate by having strong assessment. However, the groups with an even mix of high locomotors and high assessors were *as fast* as the strong locomotion groups and *as accurate* as the strong assessment groups!

This study provides a nice illustration of how locomotion–control and assessment–truth can work together effectively as partners. With strong locomotion–control and strong assessment–truth, individuals can be effective at *going in the right direction*. In this case the partnership was between members of a group whose locomotion or assessment concerns emphasized one or the other aspect of task achievement (i.e., speed or accuracy, respectively). But the same partnership could occur within a person who has both strong locomotion and strong assessment concerns.

We have now seen how assessment–truth can serve locomotion–control for the sake of general achievement, and how assessment–truth and locomotion–control can function to complement each other on a particular task that emphasizes different achievement criteria (speed vs. accuracy). I turn now to other kinds of truth–control relations, including cases where truth serves control and control serves truth.

WHEN TRUTH SERVES CONTROL: THE CASE
OF RESISTING TEMPTATION

The function of *self-regulatory feedback* in goal pursuit involves both evaluating our goal pursuits while they are still ongoing ("How am I doing?") and evaluating their success or failure after they are completed ("How did I do?"). These questions, as I discussed in Chapter 6, are trying to establish what's real in the present and in the past. By knowing the truth about how we are doing in the present, we can better manage what happens in our current goal pursuit. We can stick with our current strategies and tactics if the feedback is that things are going fine, or we can switch them or modify them if the feedback is that this is not the case. Similarly, by knowing the truth about how we did in our completed goal pursuit, we can better manage future goal pursuits by retaining strategies or tactics that were effective and efficient or searching for new strategies or tactics that could be more effective or efficient.

Self-regulatory feedback, then, is an important case where truth is in the service of control. Another important case where truth is in the service of control is the classic self-control problem of resisting temptation that I discussed in Chapter 6. This is the case that I will discuss in more detail in this section. The problem of resisting temptation has been traditionally treated as just a control issue. I believe, however, that it can be re-conceptualized as a truth–control relation where truth can serve control as a partner in helping to resist temptation. Unfortunately, as we will see, truth as a partner can also make things worse.

Delay of Gratification as a Truth–Control Relation

Let me begin by reconsidering the influential studies of Walter Mischel on *delay of gratification*—the willingness and ability to wait for something we want that is at the core of *willpower*. To review his basic "marshmallow test"[51] paradigm, preschoolers sat at a table and were shown a pretzel, which they liked, and a marshmallow, which they liked better. To get the marshmallow, each child must wait alone with the two objects on the table until the experimenter returns. The child could ring a bell at any time to signal the experimenter to return, but at the cost of getting the pretzel to eat rather than the preferred marshmallow. To eat the marshmallow, the child must delay gratification *and* resist the impulse to ring the bell.

Which strategies for resisting temptation worked and which did not work? Mischel and his colleagues found that having the children think about the marshmallow's yummy properties and how delicious it would be to eat it did *not* work. Indeed, this strategy of paying attention to wanting to eat something delicious made it *more* difficult to wait.[52] What did work for children was to mentally transform the marshmallow into a non-consummatory object, such as a white fluffy cloud. The explanation given for why this transformation strategy worked was that the concrete "hot" marshmallow object had been mentally transformed into an abstract "cool" object.[53] There is another possibility, however, that introduces truth as a partner serving control.

It is possible that control succeeded in this case by *reducing the object's truth*— a strategy that takes advantage of a truth–control relation. The marshmallow, after all, was not really a white fluffy cloud. Thus, this mental transformation made the tempting object *less real*. By being less real, its motivational force, its pull, was reduced. This should make it easier to wait, easier to delay gratification. This is an interesting kind of truth–control relation because, unlike the other cases considered in this chapter, *truth is being reduced in the service of control*. In contrast, making the desire to eat something *more real* by directing children's attention to the delicious properties of the marshmallow made it more difficult to wait.

Let me reconsider as well other studies by Mischel and his colleagues that also demonstrated the power of the mental transformation strategy.[54] While the children waited, they were shown color pictures of the objects rather than the actual objects, or they faced the actual objects but were asked to think of them as color pictures. Delay of gratification (i.e., how long the children were willing to wait) also increased in these "treat as a picture" conditions. In contrast, delay of gratification decreased when the children were shown pictures of the objects but were instructed to think of them as the actual objects (i.e., a "treat as real" condition).

I believe that these conditions might also be manipulating truth in ways that enhance or impair control effectiveness. When the children in these studies were shown color pictures of the objects or were told to think of the actual objects as color pictures, they were explicitly instructed to think of them as *not real* ("The ____ aren't real; they're just a picture"). It is notable that the representations in these conditions were not like the "white fluffy cloud" representation of the marshmallow. The properties of the actual objects were depicted, but the objects were being experienced as *not real*; they were either just pictures or thought of as being just pictures. Being experienced as "not real" made the tempting objects easier to resist.

And the reverse is true for the condition where the children were shown pictures of the objects but were instructed to think of them as the actual objects. Here, the children were told to think of them not as pictures but as being "real" objects, which made the depicted tempting objects harder to resist. This is a case where the truth, where making a tempting object *more real*, made it *more* difficult to resist temptation.

In sum, resisting the tempting objects (i.e., control effectiveness) increased or decreased as a function of whether the tempting objects were experienced as real or not. When the tempting objects had *less* reality, *less* truth, the children were more successful at delaying, more successful at resisting temptation, because the motivational force of the tempting object was reduced. When the tempting objects had *more* reality, *more* truth, the children were less successful at resisting temptation because the motivational force of the tempting object was increased.

Truth as a Factor in Other Strategies to Resist Temptation

Another common strategy that children used successfully to resist temptation was *distraction*. For example, in the marshmallow test, they avoided looking at the objects by covering their eyes or trying to sleep or they distracted themselves by engaging in pleasant activities, such as singing to themselves. Actually removing the tempting objects from the children's sight was also effective.[55] The success of such conditions in increasing resistance to temptation can also be thought of in truth–control terms because they involved *decreasing or removing attention* from the tempting objects, which would also make them feel less real and thereby reduce their motivational force.

A final strategy that children used successfully to delay gratification was to explicitly remind themselves—by *verbalizing*—about the outcome contingencies involved in the control situation, such as "If I wait, I get the marshmallow. If I hit the bell, I get the pretzel." This strategy was successful both when children used it spontaneously and when they were instructed to use it.[56] I suggested previously that verbalizing the contingencies can be considered a value–control strategy because the contingencies involve propositions about which actions will result in having desired results. But it is not only that: laying out the causal relations for waiting established by the experimenter in the role of epistemic authority should make the consequences of waiting versus not waiting *more real*. This in turn should increase the motivational force of what is gained by waiting and lost by not waiting. This then would be a powerful strategy indeed, because value, truth, and control motivations would all be working together as a full-blown organization.

What about the evidence that sometimes an effective way to resist temptation is *prior exposure to the temptation itself*? Remember, for example, the study that found that participants with a diet goal who were exposed in a waiting room to stimuli related to tempting fattening foods, compared to other participants who were not exposed to tempting food stimuli, were later more likely to choose a healthy apple over a chocolate bar. This study also found that plans to resist specific tempting fattening foods in the near future were stronger for those participants who had been exposed to tempting stimuli. The participants in this study were selected specifically to have had previous experience in restricting their dietary intake. Thus, specific plans for abstaining from tempting fattening foods were associated with their goal of dieting. Such previous experience and specific plans would make the *idea of resisting* tempting foods *more realistic* for them than it would be for other types of people. Once again, this additional truth component would facilitate control.

Recall as well *counteractive control* strategies for resisting temptation. People can anticipate that when faced with a future choice between a tempting alternative and the alternative that they actually prefer, they will fail to resist temptation, such as failing to resist the temptation of not showing up for a medical appointment that makes them anxious but is good for their long-term health. Counteractive control mechanisms can be instituted to deal with the influence of the short-term costs that produce failure,[57] such as promising another person that we will make a checkup appointment by the end of the month. In addition to creating future social penalties for failure to keep our promises, such tactics could also enlist truth by increasing the future reality of our promises (e.g., to make the appointment) through creating a *shared reality* with the other person regarding this action.

Back to Freud for Truth Serving Control

I began my Chapter 6 discussion of resisting temptation with Freud's description of how civilization demands that individuals curb their personal pleasures, how the development of civilization imposes restrictions on freedom. His description of toilet training illustrates such conflict, where the anal eroticism of young children must be controlled through their learning the rules of civilized defecation. Children's resisting the temptation to defecate whenever and wherever they wish is Freud's prime example of how the conflict between the Id and the Superego can produce guilt and frustration. It is his prime example of self-control—being effective or not in managing when and where defecation happens and doesn't happen.

How is the conflict between the Id and the Superego managed? One might argue that it is enough that the Superego works to control the selfish impulses of the Id in the service of society. But it is well known, especially to psychoanalysts, that the Superego can be, and typically is, overly harsh in its demands. It is as if nothing that is wanted by the Id is acceptable. Given this, there is a need to manage the conflict between the Id and the Superego because neither motivational force is realistic about the balance between the legitimate wants of both the individual and society. Enter the *Ego* and the *reality principle* that it represents! According to Freud, it is the role of the Ego with its reality principle to find the balance, to resolve the conflict between the Id and the Superego *according to what is real.*[58]

What has been underappreciated by psychologists is the fact that when Freud proposes that the Id–Superego conflict should be controlled by the Ego's reality principle, he is proposing a truth–control relation where *truth is serving control.* As we have seen, truth serving control could play a major role more generally in successful resistance to temptation. And the effective strategies include not only increasing reality, which was emphasized by Freud, but also decreasing reality, such as making tempting objects *less* real. By recognizing that resistance to temptation can be enhanced through strategies that manipulate truth, new strategies could be developed that take advantage of what we know about establishing what's real and what's not real.

WHEN CONTROL SERVES TRUTH: THE CASE OF TAKING ACTION FROM AN IDEA

When it comes to truth–control relations, there are also cases where control serves truth. Indeed, I have already described such cases in this book, but without highlighting their significance in this regard. For example, the phenomena associated with Festinger's cognitive dissonance theory and Heider's balance theory that I discussed in Chapter 5 provide striking examples of control being in the service of truth. The truth in this case concerns individuals' need for consistency among their beliefs, their need to establish an organized, coherent truth about the world. It is the motivation to maintain or establish this truth that is emphasized in these theories. And what the evidence shows is that beliefs will be managed, through addition, deletion, and distortion, in order to make this truth happen. That is, the control of beliefs is in the service of truth.

How Control Serves Truth in the Form of Ideas

In this section I return to William James' intriguing notion of "ideo-motor action," discussed in Chapter 7, where *a bare idea can be sufficient to prompt action*. James' notion has been traditionally treated as just a truth issue (i.e., as being about the activation of a stored idea or belief). However, I believe that the action consequences of activating a stored idea or belief can be re-conceptualized as a truth–control relation where control serves truth as a partner in guiding action.

For James, to believe in something was to acquiesce in its truth, to experience it as real. And according to him, when an idea or belief is activated, it "fills the mind solidly to the exclusion of contradictory ideas,"[59] then action follows: "We think the act, and it is done." What James is proposing is the direct effect of truth on action. However, it is more likely that, rather than functioning alone, truth guides action by working together with other motivations to be effective.

I previously discussed how truth can work together with value to determine what action is taken. I gave the example of a study in which the concept "elderly" was activated (outside of awareness) for all participants in the "elderly priming" condition, but the value of elderly people (liking or disliking them) was different for different participants in this priming condition.[60] Compared to a "no priming" condition, activating the belief that the elderly walk slowly, which is part of people's idea of the elderly, did affect participants' actions. This is generally consistent both with James' proposal that ideas instigate action and with a study by John Bargh and his colleagues that tested James' proposal.[61] But it was not the case that activating the belief that elderly people walk slowly led all primed participants to walk slowly afterwards. The action taken by participants depended on the value of elderly people to them—whether they liked or disliked them. If they liked the elderly, they walked slowly down the hallway (in the absence of any elderly person), but if they disliked the elderly, they walked *quickly* down the hallway.

Truth alone, then, did not determine action. The action taken also depended on control, i.e., controlling walking speed, in the service of value (liking vs. disliking). This illustrates how truth, control, and value can all work together to determine what action is taken following belief activation from priming.[62] Are there other ways that truth and control can work together to determine what action is taken following belief activation from priming? There is evidence that there are.

How Control Serves Truth By Taking the Current Situation Into Account

It is common in everyday life—at home, at work, and at play—for individuals to team up with a partner to work on a task. The social-psychological literature has found that the effort individuals expend on team tasks depends on situational factors. One such factor is individuals' ideas or beliefs about how effective their partner will be on the task. When individuals believe that their team partner (or partners) will be effective on the task, they often take it easy—the well-known *social loafing* phenomenon.[63] On the other hand, when individuals believe that their team partner will be ineffective, they actually work harder in order to make up for it—*social compensation*.[64]

Our ideas regarding whether a future team partner will be effective or ineffective on an upcoming task can be based on more general beliefs about the social group to which the partner belongs. For example, part of our idea about males might be that they have high math skills but low verbal skills, and part of our idea about females might be that they have high verbal skills but low math skills. Would simply learning that our team partner was a male or a female, and thus activating our ideas about males or females, be enough to make us take action according to those ideas about those social categories? Would our actions occur *before the actual teamwork even began* (in the absence of our partner)? And, if so, what would our actions be? James' ideo-motor notion would predict a direct effect of idea activation that would result in our performing better on a solo practice math test, which did not count toward the team score, when the idea of "male" was primed than when the idea of "female" was primed, and performing better on a solo practice verbal test when the idea of "female" was primed than when the idea of "male" was primed—a mimicking or *similarity* pattern of responses.

A different prediction would be made if there was a truth–control relation in which the truth contained in the idea instigated action with *control* then serving to regulate the effort involved. This predicts that we would automatically (without awareness) reduce effort or loaf—*even on the practice test*—when the primed category idea meant the partner had high skill on the upcoming task. However, we would increase effort or compensate when the primed category idea meant the partner had *low* skill on the upcoming task—a *complementarity* pattern of responses rather than a similarity pattern. For this latter compensation case, we should perform better on the solo practice math test when the idea of "female" was primed than when the idea of "male" was primed, and perform better on the solo practice verbal test when the idea of "male" was primed than when the idea of "female" was primed. This pattern of complementarity responses rather than similarity responses for the compensation case was precisely what Jason Plaks and I found in a study on how activating social category beliefs about a male or female team partner affected performance on the practice test prior to the team performance.[65]

How Control Can Serve a Combination of Truths

Control serving a truth idea is not restricted to the case of a single idea. There can be more than one idea involved, and control has to serve the combination of truths. A recent study on the *role of ecology* in automatic priming effects on motivation has tested this more complex situation.[66] Some participants were primed subliminally (i.e., *outside conscious awareness*) with pictures of young black males (the "Black" condition) and others were primed subliminally with pictures of young white males. The participants also varied in the extent to which their idea about the social category "Black" was associated with danger; that is, the extent to which they believed that members of the "Black" social category are a threat. For half of the participants the experiment took place in a laboratory booth. For the other half it took place in an open field.

Following the subliminal priming of black or white faces, the accessibility of "fight" or "flight" concepts was measured. The participants were asked to judge whether a target letter string was a fight-related or escape-related word. Participants registered their responses on a box with buttons labeled "fight" and "escape." The box was positioned so that the "fight" response required participants to move their arm forward ("as if you are moving forward to attack") and the "escape" response required participants to move their arm back ("as if you are moving away to avoid").

The simple ideo-motor notion predicts that subliminal priming of the "black" social category will produce fast "fight" responses because, stereotypically, young black men are associated with aggressive behavior. But the truth–control perspective makes a different prediction as a function of control serving other truths as well. First, there is the additional truth associated with participants' belief about whether young black men are a threat or not. Second, there is the additional truth associated with the ecology of being in a booth versus being in an open field, where the open field affords escape from threat but the booth does not, making a fight response to threat necessary in the booth but not in the open field. Combining all of these truths, for participants primed with "black" faces (compared to those primed with "white" faces), control would mean faster "escape" responses in the open field but faster "fight" responses in the booth for participants who believe young black men are a threat (compared to participants who do not believe young black men are a threat). This pattern of control responses that suits the combination of truths was the pattern observed in the study.

What these studies demonstrate is that stored ideas that are associated with social categories need not be translated directly into behaviors. The ideo-motor notion of direct expression is too simple. Instead, activation of ideas—the "truth"—about a social category simply establishes the initial conditions for preparing to interact with a social category member.[67] The actual response could be to imitate or mimic some attribute associated with the category, such as walking slowly when "elderly" is activated (if we like the elderly), but it could also be a complementary response such as walking quickly when "elderly" is activated (if we dislike the elderly) or compensating with higher performance on a task when a team partner's social category is associated with low performance on that kind of task. Our response could be whatever response allows us to handle the upcoming interaction with a social category member given our current circumstances (e.g., open vs. confined space) and whatever control we have over the resources that are necessary to deal with the situation. It is not just about ideas or truth: it is also about control. It is a truth–control relation.

IMPLICATIONS OF TRUTH–CONTROL RELATIONS FOR INTERPRETING IMPLICIT ATTITUDES

The above conclusion has important implications for a social-psychological issue that has received increasing attention, including in the popular media. Various experimental techniques have been invented to measure people's evaluative response to the members of different social categories. These new *implicit* measures of attitudes—often referred to as implicit attitudes—are taken outside of people's conscious awareness and explicit control.[68] The ability of these techniques to measure stored associations between a social category and evaluations of that category has been demonstrated in many studies.[69] The controversy concerns how to interpret the findings from such measures. In both scientific papers and the popular media, the most common interpretation is that what is being measured are individuals' personal biases—either in favor of or against some social group. For example, if individuals show a stronger positive association to the category label "White" and a stronger negative association to the category label "Black," then it is concluded that they have a favorable bias toward whites and a hidden, unconscious bias against blacks. There is often the implication as well that the unconscious bias against blacks supposedly revealed in these measures could also produce discriminatory behavior toward blacks.[70]

In most of these studies the response to the social category that is measured is an evaluative response such as "good" versus "bad" or "positive" versus "negative." Given that the stored social category has associated with it a positive or negative stereotypical attribute, such as "good" being associated with "White" and "bad" being associated with "Black," then the participants' responses could be characterized as imitating or mimicking these attributes in their responses. If so, then these responses could be seen as a kind of ideo-motor action: the positive or negative idea is activated, and we respond in kind. From this perspective, it is not clear whether the evaluative responses should, strictly speaking, be called prejudice because this term is typically used for people who endorse or *approve* responding negatively to the members of some social category.[71] However, it would be reasonable to conclude that discriminatory behavior could occur because responding positively or negatively to group members (i.e., carrying out the associated ideas) need not be restricted to evaluative judgments: discriminatory behaviors would be another way to carry out the associated ideas.

If we take the truth–control perspective, on the other hand, a different picture emerges. It *is* true that the associations of "bad" with "Black" and "good" with "White" reflect stereotypes. But as such they are like other cases of stored categorical information, such as the ideas we have that are commonly associated with dogs ("loyal") or cats ("independent"). And people can have these stored associations independent of whether they like or dislike the members of a social category. For example, they can associate "walk slowly" with the elderly independent of whether they like or dislike the elderly. Indeed, there is evidence that people commonly associate the same attributes with the social category "Black" (e.g., "aggressive"; "poor") regardless of whether they are high or low in prejudice toward them; that is, *knowledge* of the cultural stereotype can be independent of prejudice.[72]

From the truth–control perspective, stereotypical ideas about members of social categories function as a situation—in this case a culturally defined situation. That still permits individuals to control how they behaviorally respond to the activated ideas. It is not just, as James suggested, that "We think the act, and it is done." For low-prejudice individuals, knowledge of the cultural stereotype that associates "Black" with "bad" is a social and interpersonal situation that they try to deal with by responding in *non*-discriminatory ways. They don't simply act out the associated attribute but, instead, try to control their response given this situation. This is not to say that they are always successful, especially when control or managing processes are undermined in some ways, such as being under stress. But the point is that evidence of their possessing the stereotypical association from implicit measures does not permit either a conclusion regarding unconscious prejudice or a conclusion that discriminatory behaviors are likely to occur. And, once again, this is because their actions are not best understood in terms of the ideo-motor perspective but rather in terms of the truth–control perspective, where "truth" in this case is the cultural stereotype rather than their own personal attitudes or feelings.

If the truth–control perspective on motivated action is correct, shouldn't a current situation be capable of changing even the evaluative response to the stereotyped category? For example, shouldn't control within a current situation be capable of changing the negative response bias to the category "Black"? The answer is yes. One study, for example, found that the automatic negative response bias to the category "Black" was greatly reduced among white participants who anticipated interacting with a black person under circumstances where their situational power in the interaction would be less than the black person's power, as compared to circumstances where white participants were assigned a superior role.[73] In another related study involving actual interethnic contact, the automatic negative response bias to the category "Black" was eliminated among white participants who interacted with a black experimenter, while it remained for white participants who interacted with a white experimenter.[74] This latter finding is notable because, if anything, an ideo-motor perspective would predict that the negative idea associated with "black," and thus the negative response bias, would be even greater when interacting with a black rather than a white experimenter.

If the truth–control perspective is correct, then people's responses should go beyond simply expressing directly the ideas associated with a stored category. They should depend on their personal feelings, needs, and goals regarding the category, just as walking speeds following the priming of "elderly" varied as a function of individuals' feelings about the elderly. A study on gender stereotypes, for example, found that male participants who held chronic *egalitarian* goals, compared to males without a goal of gender fairness, *preconsciously* controlled automatic activation of stereotypical responses to the "female" category.[75] Other studies concerning responses to other categories such as food items and cigarette smoking have also found that automatic positive and negative responses will vary depending on individuals' current need states, such as their current food or nicotine deprivation.[76]

If the truth–control perspective is valid, shouldn't there be ways in which people can learn to exert control over their automatic behavioral responses to categories? Fortunately, there are, and I gave an example when discussing resistance to temptation. When a preferred goal is clearly a priority, such as eating healthy foods, then exposure to a temptation will activate the goal with its higher priority, and activating the preferred goal will override the temptation.[77] For this to work associations must be established not only between the temptation and the preferred goal, but between the temptation and the resolve to oppose it for the sake of the preferred goal. For example, if individuals have the goal of dieting, direct activation of this goal is less effective than if they are presented with tempting foods that automatically activate not only the goal of dieting but also the resolve to abstain from the tempting foods. This is precisely what effective self-regulators do.[78]

Returning to the issue of prejudicial or discriminatory responses, another control technique is to monitor our failures to control our responses. If we represent non-prejudicial responding as our obligation toward members of other groups, as how we ought to behave toward them, then a failure to meet this *ought self-guide* will automatically produce feelings of agitation and guilt. There is evidence that these feelings can function as cues that help people to exert more control over their automatic prejudiced responses.[79] This control technique uses a prevention focus to provide helpful control cues (i.e., guilt from an ought discrepancy). The downside of this technique is that the anxiety-related feelings that serve as cues can also deplete self-regulatory control resources. An alternative technique would be to monitor success and failure within a system where the feedback cues are not anxiety-related. This can be accomplished by having the monitoring done within the promotion system.

In a recent study that took this approach to improving control over prejudicial responses,[80] white participants were told prior to an interracial interaction either to approach the interaction as an opportunity to have an enjoyable intercultural dialogue (a promotion focus induction) or to avoid appearing prejudiced during the interaction (a prevention focus induction). After the promotion or prevention induction, the participants were taken to a different room where they interacted with a Black experimenter who asked them questions on various topics, including topics related to race (e.g., campus diversity). Following this interaction, a measure of self-regulatory control was taken. The study found that, after interacting with the Black experimenter, self-regulatory control was more depleted for the prevention-focused participants than the promotion-focused participants. This suggests that there may be advantages to controlling our possible negative responses to a stereotyped category by monitoring our behaviors with a promotion rather than a prevention focus.

TRUST AS A TRUTH–CONTROL RELATION

The motivational significance of truth and control working together is also well captured in the concept of *trust*. We all recognize the importance of trust to humans: it is fundamental to our close relationships with other individuals and to intergroup relationships as well.[81] Erikson proposed that "Basic Trust Versus Basic Mistrust" is the first and critical stage of motivational development: "The infant's first social achievement, then, is his willingness to let the mother out of sight without undue anxiety or rage, because she has become an inner certainty as well as an outer predictability. Such consistency, continuity, and sameness of experience provide a rudimentary sense of ego identity."[82] Note how Erikson's trust has the elements of certainty, predictability, consistency, and continuity— elements that are all related to *reliability*. If people lose trust in themselves, in others, or in the world around them, they feel helpless and hopeless. It is a devastating condition and is a major cause of suicide.[83] Independent of value *per se*, people lose the motivation to live when trust is gone, when they can no longer rely on truth and control.

When you trust others, you believe that you can count on them to care about and be responsive to your present and future needs and interests.[84] Generally speaking, I believe that, together as partners, truth and control *build this trust*. Truth is essential for trust, which is reflected in "truth" and "trust" having the common meaning of being "true." For trust there must be *reliability*, and something that is not real, not the truth, is not reliable. But something is also not reliable if it is uncontrollable. Control is also essential for trust. Consistent with this, "trust" has been defined as *assured reliance on the strength or truth of someone or something*.[85] My only quibble with this definition is that it should say "strength *and* truth" to capture the full essence of what trust is: control (i.e., strength) and truth.

Trusting someone to be responsive to our needs and interests adds the element of having desired results, which would make trust a full-blown value–truth–control organization of motives. But while trust is important motivationally when it does exist, I do not believe that the additional element of value, of having desired results, is necessary in order to establish trust. Trust is not restricted to wanting someone to create desired results for us. We can trust people who tell us that if we do X, then they will reward us, but if we do Y, then they will *punish* us. If we believe that they are telling the truth (i.e., not joking or lying to us) *and* that they have control over making the reward and punishment happen, then we will trust them. We don't have to like them, or believe that they like us, in order to trust them. It can be enough to believe that they will keep their word. This is the case in many negotiations or social conflict situations where the parties are not friends or family and can even be enemies. Building trust requires that each party believes that the other party is telling the *truth* about what he or she promises and that he or she has the *strength* to keep those promises. And promises can be about rewards *or* punishments.[86]

Trust, then, illustrates the motivational significance of truth and control working together as partners even without value as a third partner. In this chapter, I've described other ways that truth and control work together as partners, beyond pleasure and pain, to have a myriad of motivational effects: activity selection, personality styles, decision-making styles, emphasis on outcome value versus outcome likelihood, resistance to temptation, and taking action from an idea. What should be clear from these examples is that this partnership of truth–control relations has a broad impact on the choices that we make, the way we deal with problems, and the way we carry out our lives. And this happens independent of whether we end up having desired results. Much of what matters to us is about having truth and control for their own sake. This is because truth and control, working together as partners, help us *go in the right direction*. And to paraphrase Carl Rogers, going in the right direction is a central part of living "the good life." But this is not to say that truth and control do not work together with value: they *do* work together with value in multiple ways that have been described in earlier chapters. It is time to consider more fully how value, truth, and control work together as *an organization of motives*. In the next chapter we will see that understanding how they do so provides a more complete picture of how motivation works.

10

Value–Truth–Control Relations

Organization of Motives

I have described in this book a myriad of ways in which motivation goes beyond pleasure and pain. Even when it comes to having desired results, there is more to value than just maximizing pleasure and minimizing pain. There is an experience of effectiveness, an experience of success at having desired results, that is not simply feeling pleasure. And there are ways of being effective beyond value. There is the truth effectiveness of establishing what's real and the control effectiveness of managing what happens. But the most significant way that motivation goes beyond pleasure and pain lies in its multidimensional nature. Yes, motivation is not just about the hedonic dimension of pleasure and pain. But motivation is also not just about adding the dimension of truth or the dimension of control either. What motivation is fundamentally about is the relations between and among motivational dimensions—*the organization of motives*. It is about value, truth, and control working together to create commitment, fit, and going in the right direction. Motivations organized and working together is why motivation is *Beyond Pleasure and Pain*.

In Chapters 7, 8, and 9, I have discussed how value, truth, and control work together as pairs of motivations. The commitment, fit, and direction created by such partnerships are central to the story of motivation. But the story would not be complete without considering how all three motivations work together as an *organization* of motives. Indeed, this part of the story is so important that my original title for the book was *Organization of Motives: Value, Truth & Control Working Together*. There were two inspirations for this original title: Donald Hebb's book *The Organization of Behavior*[1] and Kurt Lewin's book *Field Theory in Social Science*.[2] Part of the inspiration was personal. Hebb was my first psychology teacher when I was an undergraduate student at McGill University. Lewin was the mentor of my first psychology teacher, Stanley Schachter, when I was a graduate student at Columbia University. Not surprisingly, I learned about Hebb's theories and research in that first undergraduate class, and I learned a lot about Lewin's theories and research (as well as Schachter's) in that first graduate class.

Hebb and Lewin had a profound influence on me at the time and their influence has lasted. Only much later, however, did I fully appreciate a basic commonality between them. Simply put, they both believed that the elements that determined behavior did not work independently, each with its own separate effect, but, instead, they worked together as interrelated, organized elements where the whole was not only greater than, but also different from, the sum of its parts. It is the purpose of this chapter to describe the motivationally significant properties of the organization formed by value, truth, and control working together. But before describing these properties, I need to provide some examples of different organizations and to describe the relation between their whole and their parts.

MOTIVATIONS WORKING TOGETHER IN PROMOTION AND PREVENTION

I will begin by revisiting the distinct motivational systems of promotion and prevention. The self-regulatory orientations of promotion and prevention both concern *value*. Promotion is concerned with the value of accomplishment and advancement in goal pursuit, the value of moving from "0" to "+1." Prevention is concerned with the value of safety and security in goal pursuit, the value of maintaining "0" and stopping "–1." Each focus orientation has a preferred *control* strategy for goal pursuit, a preferred way to make things happen that *fits* the orientation. For promotion it is using eager means that ensure advancement, and for prevention it is using vigilant means that ensure against making mistakes. So far, the differences between these two sets of value–control elements are simply differences in content (i.e., promotion + eager; prevention + vigilant)—not really wholes different from the sum of their parts. But what happens when the third truth element is added?

Adding the truth element to the promotion and prevention value–control relations forms the full-blown organization of value, truth, and control working together. The actual or anticipated outcome of a goal pursuit is success or failure.

As outcomes, success is success and failure is failure. Success and failure are the same *truth* elements (i.e., what *really* happened) in both the promotion and the prevention systems. But when they are organized together with the value and control elements, something *different* is created. Success (actual or anticipated) *strengthens* promotion eagerness, but it *weakens* prevention vigilance. Failure (actual or anticipated) *strengthens* prevention vigilance, but it *weakens* promotion eagerness. Why is this? Because wholes are different from their parts.

Wholes Different From Their Parts

The organization of value–truth–control elements in promotion and prevention, when working together, creates wholes that differ from the sum of their parts. How does this happen? I stated previously that success is a fit for promotion but a non-fit for prevention, whereas failure is a fit for prevention but a non-fit for promotion. This is true whether success or failure has already occurred or is simply anticipated. When people have a promotion focus, success (fit) increases the eagerness that sustains promotion and it strengthens engagement, which is reflected in feeling happy and encouraged; failure (non-fit) reduces the eagerness that sustains promotion and it weakens engagement, which is reflected in feeling sad and discouraged. In contrast, when people have a prevention focus, success (non-fit) reduces the vigilance that sustains prevention and it weakens engagement, which is reflected in feeling calm and relaxed; failure (fit) increases the vigilance that sustains prevention and strengthens engagement, which is reflected in feeling tense and worried.

These differences between the promotion and prevention systems highlight how the entire organization of motives—the way in which value, truth, and control work together—must be taken into account to understand motivation. Yes, generally speaking, success brings pleasure and failure brings pain. But that alone does not tell us the motivational effects of success and failure. The motivational effects of success and failure, as truth elements, on promotion and prevention also depend on how these truth elements work together with the value and control elements within promotion and within prevention.

Defensive Pessimists

The motivational significance of the organization of motives beyond pleasure and pain is well illustrated in the behavior of defensive pessimists. These are individuals who are effective in the prevention system. Studies have found that defensive pessimists actually have better outcomes when they adopt a *negative* outlook, rather than a positive outlook, for future anticipated events.[3] From a hedonic perspective, this is surprising: after all, adopting a negative outlook for future anticipated events makes people feel tense and worried, which is unpleasant. Thus, we would expect that people would not adopt this outlook unless they had to, such as their having a history of failure and needing to be realistic about the future in light of this history. But defensive pessimists take a negative outlook even when they have had *a history of success*. They "expect the worst" when entering a new situation, despite the fact that they generally have the same history of success as others who have an optimistic outlook.[4] I mentioned previously, for example, that prior to an exam, successful students who are defensive pessimists will avoid interacting with others who might try to encourage them by reminding them of their past successes.[5]

Why ultimately do defensive pessimists adopt a negative outlook that makes them feel unpleasant even when they have had a history of success? In brief, because they want to be vigilant. For defensive pessimists, having a negative outlook keeps them vigilant, which fits their prevention focus, strengthens their engagement in what they are doing, and works motivationally by strengthening their system overall. Although their past successes would justify more pleasant feelings of optimism and enthusiasm, they need to maintain their vigilance by adopting a negative outlook in order to perform effectively—even if it means feeling unpleasant. Indeed, if the inconsistency between their present negative expectations and their past positive performance is pointed out to defensive pessimists, it disrupts their vigilance and their performance suffers.[6]

The advantage to defensive pessimists of having a negative outlook is evident not only for task performance but also for interpersonal performance. In one experiment, for example, participants arrived for a study and were told that they would be having a "get acquainted" conversation with another participant— a social situation that could go well or badly. Prior to the conversation, some participants filled out a questionnaire that highlighted the possibilities for positive outcomes in the upcoming discussion, whereas other participants filled out a questionnaire that highlighted the negative possibilities.[7] The study found that defensive pessimists who had considered *negative* possibilities prior to the conversation (compared to those who had considered positive possibilities) exhibited more positive behaviors during the social interaction—they talked more and exerted more effort, and the conversations were rated more positively by their interaction partners. For defensive pessimists, considering the possibility of failure increases vigilance that strengthens engagement, which enhances their performance. It is not about pleasure and pain—it is about an organization of motives that works.

Expectancies Following Success and Failure

So far we've seen that the difference in the organization of motives for the promotion and prevention systems derives from a difference in how success and failure—as truth elements— relates to value (promotion vs. prevention) and control (being eager vs. vigilant). This difference affects motivation and performance by strengthening or weakening engagement. It can also affect how beliefs about future truth (i.e., beliefs about what will happen in the future) are updated from the reality of a recent success or failure.

According to classic motivational models, such as Lewin's "level of aspiration" model,[8] success on a present task increases expectancy of succeeding again on the task in the future, while failure on a present task decreases expectancy of future task success. These effects of a present reality on establishing beliefs about a future reality seem obvious and are treated as a law of behavior for human and non-human animals alike.[9] There is evidence, however, that this "obvious" law of motivation works differently in the promotion and prevention systems. One study, for example, found that after success, promotion-focused participants did raise their expectations for future success, but prevention-focused participants did *not*. After failure, prevention-focused participants did lower their expectations for future success, but promotion-focused participants did *not*.[10]

Thus, inconsistent with the "obvious" law of motivation, people's expectation of future success does not necessarily increase as a result of success at a present task, nor does people's expectation of future failure necessarily decrease as a result of failure at a present task. Because the prevention organization needs to maintain vigilance, beliefs about success in the future are *not* raised after having just succeeded like they are in promotion. And because the promotion organization needs to maintain eagerness, beliefs about success in the future are *not* lowered after having just failed like they are in prevention.

What this study highlights is that truth (i.e., the meaning of success or failure in this case) can serve the organization of motives as a whole. That is, effectiveness in establishing what is real is not just about accuracy, not just about "the whole truth and nothing but the truth." Nor is it about feeling good. It is about *the truth that works*. And what works depends on the other elements in the organization of motives. The truth that works with promotion value and eager control is different from the truth that works with prevention value and vigilance control. For truth to work together effectively with value and control, those in a promotion focus need to establish expectations about the future beyond what past outcomes alone would justify, such as what a recent failure would justify, in order to support the eagerness that sustains promotion. And those in a prevention focus also need to establish expectations about the future beyond what past outcomes alone would justify, such as what a recent success would justify, in order to support the vigilance that sustains prevention. Moreover, as the case of prevention illustrates, this shaping of truth is *not* in the service of making people *happy*. Rather, it is in the service of an effective organization of motivations as a whole.

MOTIVATIONS WORKING TOGETHER TO
ESTABLISH CONSISTENCY

Earlier in the book (Chapter 5), I described another case of one motivational element being in the service of another within an organization of motivations. This was the case of value being altered for the sake of establishing what's real—*shaping value in the service of truth*. The classic example of this are the studies testing Festinger's cognitive dissonance theory, especially the "effort justification" studies. In these studies, the value of working on some task or joining some group increases when people freely choose to engage with the task or group despite there being substantial costs of engagement. Under these conditions, cognitive dissonance theory suggests that people experience an inconsistency between their choice to engage and the costly outcomes of engagement. To make sense of their choice—to succeed at establishing a sensible reality—people increase the benefits of the value of their engagement as a way to justify their choice. Thus, value is shaped in the service of truth.

When the value of something is increased to resolve dissonance, then the pleasantness of life is increased, and it could be argued that this fulfills the general hedonic principle of preferring pleasure over pain. But this hedonic principle would not predict that people would make a positive thing *less* positive simply to resolve an inconsistency. Yet studies testing cognitive dissonance theory, and balance theory, indicate that this can happen as well. As one example, if children freely choose not to play with a very attractive toy after receiving only a mild threat that makes this toy "forbidden," their choice not to play with the toy is inconsistent with the normal behavior of playing with such an attractive toy. This choice, then, must be justified, and this process is a control process. Children under these circumstances will subsequently *derogate* the attractive toy—a kind of "sour grapes" phenomenon that establishes consistency by diminishing something's positivity.[11]

A balance theory example of shaping value in the service of truth even when it reduces positivity in the world would be experiencing imbalance because an acquaintance you like (a "+" sentiment relation) becomes a close friend (a "+" unit relation) with someone else you dislike intensely (a "–" sentiment relation). To resolve this imbalance, you decide after reflection that you don't really like this acquaintance after all (changing the "+" sentiment relation with the acquaintance to a "–" sentiment relation). This phenomenon of people increasing negativity in the world to achieve balance among inconsistent cognitions is quite common. There is evidence that children as young as 8 years of age have the ability and motivation to infer negativity in the world in order to achieve balance.[12] In such cases, the value of something in the world has become more *negative* in the service of truth.

What is clear in these examples is that people are motivated to make sense of what they or others do, to establish a reality that works for them. It is not accuracy for each of the specific elements that matters but, rather, establishing a structural pattern of beliefs that is consistent or coherent. Given this, a single element will be altered if that is necessary to make the entire structure work— the *structural whole* being more important than any one part. And this is the case even if it requires making a part of the world less positive than it would otherwise be. It is *overall truth*, then, and not accuracy of any particular thing that matters, and people are motivated to make this overall truth happen. To this extent, control processes, such as the justification process of dissonance, are used to establish what's real. The value of things, such as the value of the acquaintance, can be altered by control processes in the service of truth, and this new truth can then be used to make things happen in the future, such as avoiding the now-disliked acquaintance. The change in value creates a new organization of motives that directs future choices.

ORGANIZATIONAL PROPERTIES

Changing truth for the sake of value and control, and changing value for the sake of truth and control, illustrate different ways in which value, truth, and control can work together— how one form of being effective can function in the service of other forms of being effective. This represents the general organizational property of *supportiveness*, where the different ways of being effective support one another. It is the first of the organizational properties of motivations working together.

Supportiveness

Traditional models of motivation emphasize just one version of supportiveness: truth and control both being used to support value. In traditional models, truth and control are instrumental means that are in service of having desired results (value). This is one kind of supportiveness—*instrumental means* supportiveness. As we have seen, however, the principle of supportiveness is more general than just instrumental means supportiveness. For example, truth can be *altered* to support value and control, and value can be *altered* to support truth. These other cases of supportiveness illustrate that one way of being effective is not just a tool, used as given, for achieving the success of some other way of being effective. Rather, one way of being effective can be changed or altered to suit what is needed. Indeed, the support can involve one effectiveness element being *sacrificed* for other ways of being effective. For example, the accuracy of a truth element, or the pleasantness of a value element, can be reduced in order that another effectiveness element succeed, as when defensive pessimists adopt a less pleasant outlook about future desired results for the sake of control effectiveness (i.e., strengthening the vigilance they need).

This is a different kind of structural supportiveness—*sacrificing* supportiveness—and it has generally been overlooked in traditional models of motivation. Subjective expected utility and expectancy value models, for example, treat individuals' beliefs about the likelihood of a future outcome as being subjectively accurate predictions that are used as a tool in current decision making. Certainly, this can be the case—but it is not always the case. For example, the accuracy or truth of outcome likelihood beliefs or expectancies can be sacrificed in the service of managing what happens; that is, *truth serving control.* I described in Chapter 6 the phenomena called "the illusion of control" where wanting control trumps truth (i.e., truth is sacrificed for the experience of control success). And earlier in this chapter I described how individuals with a strong promotion focus will enhance the likelihood of their future success because such optimism supports the eagerness that underlies their effectively managing what happens. In such cases, accuracy in expectancies or perceived likelihoods is sacrificed for the sake of control. Such sacrificing of one way of being effective for another way of being effective is an intriguing property of the organization of motives, and it highlights its dynamic nature. It reminds me of the organization called a *family.*

The simple *instrumental means* supportiveness that has been emphasized in traditional models and the *sacrificing* supportiveness are two kinds of supportiveness. A third kind, which is also dynamic, is where one way of being effective *makes up for* the limitations of another way of being effective. This is *compensation* supportiveness. Research testing locomotion and assessment as regulatory modes provides a good example of how this compensation dynamic works.

The locomotion aspect of self-regulation, given its concern with initiating and sustaining movement, is associated with managing what happens. In contrast, the assessment aspect of self-regulation, given its concern with identifying the right course of action, is more associated with establishing what is real. As discussed in Chapter 9, studies have consistently found that performance is generally better when strong locomotion concerns are combined with strong assessment concerns.[13]

Strong assessment alone has the potential performance cost of becoming "lost in thought" and not taking action. In contrast, strong locomotion concerns push for taking action, for getting on with it, which helps to *bridge the gap* between thought and action. But a major limitation of strong locomotion derives from its lack of concern with moving in the *right* direction. This means that decisions can be made that initiate or sustain movement, but in a direction that will not produce desired results. Strong assessment will set constraints on the impatience of strong locomotion to just get going, and it will delay movement until the right direction has been determined. Strong assessment concerns can work together with strong locomotion concerns by each *compensating* for the limitation of the other.

Research has consistently found that individuals with strong locomotion benefit from their also having strong assessment.[14] Moreover, the advantage of having strong assessment compensate for the downside of strong locomotion operating alone has been found to apply to groups as well, with the personal performance of an individual high locomotor improving from working with team members who are high assessors. In this case, the strong assessment of others compensates for an individual's strong locomotion to improve that individual's performance.[15]

The above research findings illustrate the *dynamic* functioning of the organizational property of *supportiveness*. This property plays out in different ways: with one way of being effective functioning as an *instrumental means* in the service of another way of being effective; with one way of being effective being *sacrificed* for another way of being effective; and with one way of being effective *compensating* for the limitations of another way of being effective. The property of supportiveness in the organization of motivations is very important for understanding how they work together. It is not the only important organizational property, however; two other important properties of organization relate to its *structural nature*—the overall *significance* of the structure and *spreading* among the elements of the structure.

Significance

When something is *significant* it has both *meaning and importance*. When the motivational elements of value, truth, and control are organized together, they can create many possible structural patterns. But not all of the possible structural patterns are equally meaningful or important motivationally, nor are they equally stable.[16] There are different possible structural patterns because the value, truth, and control can each receive different degrees of emphasis as ways to be effective. Although emphasis is a continuous variable, I will illustrate the notion of significance by treating emphasis as a binary variable where the emphasis on each of the dimensions of value, truth, and control is either high or low. Given that the emphasis on value, truth, and control can each be high or low, this means that there are, potentially, eight different kinds of motivational structures or patterns that can be formed from these motivational elements. These structures can occur at the individual level and at levels higher than the individual (e.g., at the level of culture) and lower than the individual (e.g., at the level of an attitude).

Structural Forms at the Individual Level

The *Protestant Work Ethic* is a classic motivational structure where value, truth, and control all receive high emphasis.[17] Specifically, hard work (high control) is seen as necessary for worldly success (high value) and is also a duty—that is, the right thing to do (high truth). An alternative motivational structure would be high emphasis on value and low emphasis on both truth and control. In this motivational structure, what matters is the desired results, and how they are achieved is secondary. If outright lies yield desired results, that's fine. If desired results are obtained independent of one's contribution to making it happen, that's fine too. This is the motivational structure represented in the *Divine Right of Kings*, where the king's high status (high value) is ascribed rather than achieved (low control) and the king can do no wrong (low truth). A third motivational structure is value and control both being high but truth being low, as is stereotypically found with "crooked salesmen" or "political strategists" who want desired results (high value), are motivated to work hard to personally manage what happens (high control), but care little about the veracity of what they are saying (low truth).

These three motivational structures have received the most attention in the academic literature. Note that value is high in all three, consistent with the hedonic principle. More explicit consideration of other possibilities is needed, especially those that include *value* as being *low*. The *Cynics* in ancient Greece, for example, were philosophers who rejected the conventional desired results of having wealth, health, power, or fame (low value) and emphasized instead the importance of establishing the truth about reality (high truth) and rigorously managing one's everyday life free from all possessions (high control). Religious ascetics and religious hermits might also be characterized as having this kind of motivational structure. All those who have this motivational structure do have some desired end-states or goals that they want, but compared to other people, they place relatively greater emphasis on truth and control than on value, and certainly material value.

Perhaps individuals currently suffering from depression provide an even clearer case of a motivational structure that contains a low emphasis on value. A central symptom of depression is having "no interest in anything." The force of attraction toward objects and activities can become so reduced that these individuals are no longer motivated to engage with them, which results in inactivity and immobility. This is clearly a low value motivational state. Depression also typically includes an element of *low control*, where individuals believe that changing their condition is not something they can manage, which creates a feeling of helplessness. They also believe that the present reality will continue into the future, which creates a feeling of hopelessness (i.e., it will never change). Notably, because their negative view of their present and future reality is experienced as *the truth*, they have high confidence in their negative outlook. Thus, their motivational structure includes a *high truth* element along with low value and low control.

In the case of depressed individuals, the high truth element combined with the low control and low value elements makes matters worse than if they had a low truth element (i.e., low confidence in the reality of their negative view). This illustrates, once again, how the significance of the structure as a whole—how the elements work together—is different from a simple combination of the separate elements. That is, adding high (vs. low) truth to the structure *hurts* rather than helps the depressed person. Indeed, the motivational structure of low value, low control, and high truth could be a reason why attempted suicide is a particular risk among depressed individuals because it can seem like the only *real* solution when they feel both helpless and hopeless.

CULTURAL STRUCTURAL FORMS

At a higher level than the individual, we could consider the significance of structures involving a culture's emphases on institutions that are concerned with value, truth, and control. In Chapter 3, I suggested that the institutions of Monarchy, Government, and Business have concerns with value; the institutions of Church, Media, and Academia (or Education) have concerns with truth; and the institutions of Military, Courts, and Police have concerns with control. Cultures vary in the power that is assigned to these different institutions, where power would be a proxy for emphasis.

As speculation, it is possible that a culture—through its leadership—could place high or low emphasis on the institutions associated with each of the three effectiveness elements and thereby create a structure that has motivational significance for that culture. For example, David McClelland's description of the "Achieving Society"[18] is a culture where the institutions associated with *all three* effectiveness elements—the value, the truth, and the control institutions—all receive high emphasis. The "American Culture," with its emphasis on value-related Business and Government, on truth-related Media and Academia (i.e., Education), and on control-related Courts and Police, is the prototype of such an "Achieving Society." In fact, the U.S. system of government was itself originally designed to place high emphasis on all three elements—the Executive Branch's high emphasis on getting desired results (value), the Judicial Branch's high emphasis on establishing what's right and correct (truth), and the Legislative Branch's high emphasis on writing bills and laws that manage what happens (control).

It is also possible for a nation to place high emphasis on the value institutions (Monarchy, Government, and/or Business) and high emphasis on the control institutions (Military, Courts, and/or Police) but place low emphasis on the truth institutions (Church, Media, and/or Academia)—as some mid-20th-century Fascist nations could be characterized as having done. Might such Fascist nations be analogous to some combination of "crooked salesmen" and "political strategists"?

To continue speculating for a moment, the significance of the motivational structures created by value, truth, and control could also be considered at the level of artistic forms. For example, the motivational emphasis in mystery or detective stories (found in plays, movies, or novels) is on establishing what's real (e.g., "whodunit" stories). Although control and value are also elements, the emphasis is on truth. In contrast, the motivational emphasis in action or adventure stories (e.g., "action hero" stories) is on making things happen. Although truth and value are also elements, the emphasis is on control. The emphasis in comedies is also on control, on trying to make things happen, and they are funny because the lead characters have difficulties making things happen (unlike action heroes, who are extremely competent in making things happen). What about value? I believe that value takes center stage in romantic stories where the motivational emphasis is on desired results—continually hoping for, but not always getting, a "happy ending" (e.g., the Cinderella story). Such differences among stories in their motivational emphases could make them more or less engaging to different people. There is evidence, for example, that individuals with strong locomotion concerns, where control is emphasized, especially like action/adventure movies and comedies.[19]

STRUCTURAL FORMS AT THE LEVEL OF ATTITUDE

What about motivational structures at a lower level than an individual's different ways of being effective? As an illustration of a lower-level structure, let us consider the elements that, together, make up *an attitude* toward an object. According to the traditional "tripartite model of attitudes," attitudes are composed of three elements: affect (feelings toward the attitude object), cognition (beliefs about the attitude object), and behavior (action or behavioral intentions associated with the attitude object).[20] Although the match is not perfect, the affect element of attitudes functions like value given that it has to do with people's feelings of attraction toward or repulsion from an attitude object; the cognition element functions like truth given that it has to do with people's beliefs about what an attitude object is really like (James' "idea"); and the behavior element functions like control given that it has to do with managing what actions will be taken regarding the attitude object.

Thus, the tripartite model of an attitude could be treated as a motivational structure with value, truth, and control elements. Doing so raises the question of what would be the motivational significance of different tripartite structures that vary in the quality of their affect–value, cognition–truth, and behavior–control.

This question for the most part has not been considered in the traditional literature on attitudes. Instead, the attitude literature has mostly considered the antecedents and consequences of each attitude element independent of the others, with the affective or evaluative like/dislike element receiving the most emphasis.[21]

A rare example of research that has considered the motivational significance of different tripartite structures *as a whole* (i.e., as holistic patterns) was carried out by Orit Tykocinski in her doctoral dissertation.[22] A key insight in her work is that, contrary to the standard assumption in the psychological literature, inconsistency among elements can be a stable and significant condition rather than a transient or spurious condition destined to move toward consistency.[23] Consider the following example:

A woman believes that smoking is bad for her health. This cognition-truth element has the directional force of avoiding smoking. But the woman smokes regularly, which is a behavior-control element with the directional force of approaching smoking. These two elements are inconsistent and, according to standard consistency models, there should be a change toward consistency, such as quitting smoking or deciding that smoking is not so bad for one's health after all. But this inconsistency between cognition-truth and behavior-control can be highly stable. What is its motivational significance?

To answer this question, it would be useful to now add the third, affect-value element to the picture and examine the entire structure or pattern. Let us first imagine that the affect-value element is positive for this woman because she enjoys smoking. The motivational significance of the entire structure would then be that this woman loves smoking—so much so that she is willing to risk the health costs in order to keep smoking. Now imagine instead that the affect-value element is not positive for this woman because she no longer enjoys smoking. The motivational significance of the entire structure would then be that this woman is physically (or psychologically) addicted to smoking and can't give it up despite no longer enjoying it and knowing that her health is at risk—smoking as an activity she *wants* to do rather than something she hedonically *likes* to do.[24] What this demonstrates is that the same so-called inconsistency between the cognition-truth and behavior-control elements can have an entirely different significance—liking versus wanting—as a function of the nature of the third affect-value element and its contribution to the overall structure. *It is the organization of motives that matters.*

Tykocinski's studies investigated undergraduates' attitudes toward studying. Not surprisingly, the students uniformly believed that studying was a good idea, and thus their attitude structure contained a positive cognition–truth element. What varied among students was whether this positive cognition–truth element was consistent or inconsistent with the affect–value element and whether it was consistent or inconsistent with the behavior–control element. Logically, this can create four different types of patterns, but I want to highlight just two of them here (where C is cognition–truth, A is affect–value, and B is behavior-control): (1) a "C = A = B" structure where students believe studying is important, they like studying, and they have managed to study in the past and (2) a "C = B > A" structure where students believe studying is important and they have managed to study often in the past, but they dislike studying.

The most common structure found in the study was the "C = A = B" structure. Because it involves all positive elements and all consistent relations, this structure was called *intrinsic* by Tykocinski to capture the idea that students with this attitude structure are more likely to experience studying as being an end in itself. In contrast, because the "C = B > A" structure involves a negative affect element that is inconsistent with both the positive cognition and positive behavior elements, it was called *extrinsic* to capture the idea that students with this attitude structure are likely to experience studying as just a means to an end, something unpleasant that has to be done because of its known importance. Supporting these characterizations of these two structures, those students with the extrinsic "C = B > A" attitude structure were especially likely to describe their studying as being in order to get good grades rather than a goal in itself, whereas students with the intrinsic "C = A = B" structure were especially likely to report that they did not have inner conflicts about studying.

How did these two different structures relate to performance? The students with the *extrinsic* structure spent *more* hours studying in the course than those with the intrinsic structure, and they also tended, if anything, to perform better. Moreover, the affect element, *when considered alone*, did *not* predict hours spent studying or performance. It was the structural difference that predicted hours spent studying for the course. What is happening here?

Again, the motivational significance of each structure *as a whole* must be considered. What is striking about the extrinsic pattern is its especially strong association with the following measures of studying style: "I exercise a lot of self-discipline in relation to my studies" and "Studying is a major part of my life." These students know studying is important to attain their goals, but their dislike of studying functions like an interfering force or barrier in carrying out their goal to study. This interfering force must be opposed to continue their goal pursuit, and these students have opposed it successfully in the past, as evident in the positive behavior–control element of their attitude structure. Their experience of successfully opposing the interfering force is nicely captured in their report that they exercise a lot of self-discipline in relation to their studies.

This successful opposition to the interfering force would *strengthen their engagement* in the important activity of studying, which in turn would make them *want* to study more—even more than the students with the intrinsic attitude structure—because its perceived importance would increase. And this would happen despite the fact they *liked* studying less than the students with the intrinsic attitude structure. This phenomenon is analogous to the smoking example; it is as if the students with the extrinsic attitude structure became "addicted" to studying!

HOW TO TEST WHETHER ELEMENTS ARE STRUCTURALLY INTERCONNECTED

How do we know that these attitude elements really do form a structure? If there is a structural interconnection among the elements, then activation of one element should automatically spread across the connections and activate other elements in the structure.[25] But is there any evidence for this attitude structure? Indeed, another study by Tykocinski provides such evidence.

If the students' intrinsic or extrinsic attitudes were actual structures, then activating or priming the cognition element—which was the same positive element in both structures—should spread to the affect–value element, which should make the students with the intrinsic attitude structure feel better than they did before the priming but make the students with the extrinsic attitude structure feel worse. A mood measure was taken before the priming of the cognition element and then again 10 minutes after the priming, with the 10-minute delay being filled by the students performing a shape-copying task. The priming of the cognition element was accomplished by having the students listen to a taped conversation of other students who talked about a variety of topics, one of which concerned the importance of studying. As predicted, this priming—which was exactly the same for everyone—made the students with the intrinsic attitude structure feel *better* over time, but it made the students with the extrinsic attitude structure feel *worse*. No such mood changes were found in a control condition where no priming occurred. These results support the idea that the students' intrinsic and extrinsic attitudes were, indeed, structures.

IMPLICATIONS FOR REGULATORY FOCUS AND REGULATORY MODE STRUCTURES

Together, these studies on the tripartite notion of attitudes illustrate that the cognition–truth, affect–value, and behavior–control elements are organized as structures that have motivational significance. Despite the fact that students with an extrinsic attitude structure had negative feelings while studying whereas students with an intrinsic attitude structure had positive feelings while studying, the former students studied more than the latter. Once again this demonstrates the need to go beyond the logic of the hedonic principle, beyond pleasure and pain, in order to understand how motivation works.

More research is needed on the motivational significance of other structures that contain the value, truth, and control elements. Some research has distinguished among structures or patterns that combined individuals' promotion goals (value) with their "Future self" beliefs about their future reality (truth) and their "Can self" beliefs about what they were capable of managing (control). This research found that when their current self was discrepant from their promotion–value element, individuals suffered from different kinds of emotional problems depending on the rest of the structure. They suffered from *hopelessness* when the structure also contained a Future-self (truth) element that was discrepant from their promotion–value element, whereas they suffered from *helplessness* when the structure also contained a Can-self (control) element that was discrepant from their promotion–value element.[26]

Given the association between control and locomotion concerns, and the association between truth and assessment concerns, one direction for future research would be to examine how promotion value and prevention value work together with locomotion and assessment. High or low promotion can combine with high or low locomotion and high or low assessment, which yields eight possible structural combinations. There would be another eight possible structural combinations with high or low prevention combining with high or low locomotion and high or low assessment. It is not clear at present whether all 16 of these possible structures have clear motivational significance or what their motivational significance would be.

An additional general question is what motivation states would be produced when people with each of these 16 possible structures succeed or fail in what they are doing. What is notable, however, is that a relatively few motivational principles—regulatory focus (promotion; prevention), regulatory mode (locomotion; assessment), and success/failure—have the potential when combined of describing 32 different kinds of motivational states (16 × the two possible outcomes, success or failure). The question for the future is whether such a framework could capture a substantial portion of the significant motivational states that vary across persons, situations, organizations, and cultures.

I have discussed the significance of different structural forms at the individual level, the cultural level, and the attitude level. Before leaving this section, I should mention that motivational theories themselves can have different structural forms. For many scientists, motivation in general is captured by subjective expected utility or expectancy value models (see Chapter 7). For many other scientists, motivation in general is captured by cybernetic or control system models (see Chapter 9). The former motivational perspective places high emphasis on value and truth and little emphasis on control. Its significance is having commitment to something, with little attention to how to make it happen. The latter motivational perspective places high emphasis on truth and control and little emphasis on value. Its significance is going in the right direction, with little attention to why reaching the destination would be a desired result. A truly general theory of motivation needs to emphasize all three ways of being effective and examine how they work together.[27]

Spreading

I have already introduced this third property of motivational organization in my discussion of spreading activation from one element in a structure to another element in the same structure. The Tykocinski study, where priming the cognition–truth element spread within the tripartite attitude structure to the affect–value element, illustrates such spreading activation. There is also evidence of spreading among the elements involved in promotion and prevention self-regulation. To understand how and why this occurs, I need to discuss an especially important feature in human self-regulation: the *monitored self*.[28]

Between 3 and 6 years of age a motivational revolution occurs in children. They begin to make inferences about the thoughts, expectations, motives, and intentions of others.[29] Children now understand that other people have different attitudes about different types of behaviors, that they prefer some types of behaviors over others. They understand that performing the types of behavior preferred by others relates to how these others respond to them. Thus, they are motivated to learn which types of behavior are preferred by their significant others. Children learn about these preferences both from how significant others react to what they do and from observing how significant others react to other people (i.e., observational learning). For example, children can observe how their mother reacts to what their brother or sister does and thereby infer which types of behavior their mother prefers.[30] The critical development during this period is that children learn that how another person responds to what they do depends on an *inner state* of that person—that person's *standpoint* on their behavior.[31] They can now represent the fact that it is the relation (match or mismatch) between their behavior and a significant other's standpoint on that behavior that underlies the significant other's response to them.

This is a discovery of shattering importance. Children at this age are still totally dependent on older adults for survival. It is clear to them that these older people are different from them, especially in their possession of essential resources. Their highest priority is to figure out what determines how these resource-rich persons allocate such resources. Children want to tame these powerful animals called Mommy and Daddy by learning what motivates them. By taking others' standpoint on them into account—a new and critical kind of shared reality—children can plan their actions to increase the likelihood that others will use their resources for them and not against them. This increasing ability to take others' inner motives into account is also demonstrated in children's increasing ability to cooperate and collaborate with one another in a way that is not found in other animals, including other primates.[32]

By taking into account others' standpoints on them, children develop a new kind of social consciousness and a new kind of actual-self function. These standpoints become standards of self-evaluation—*self-guides*.[33] Children now use self-guides as a basis for self-evaluation by assessing or monitoring the amount of congruency or discrepancy between their current self-state and the end-state that a significant other desires or demands of them (e.g., "How am I doing in relation to what Father wants or demands of me?"). They can then respond to any perceived discrepancy by taking action to reduce it.

SELF-DISCREPANCY STRUCTURES OF THE MONITORED SELF

The possibility of a self-related motivational structure, where activating one self element would spread activation to another self element, has been considered most fully for the monitored self.[34] In particular, *self-discrepancy theory* postulated that "a self-discrepancy is a cognitive structure interrelating distinct self-beliefs."[35] Given that a self-discrepancy is postulated to be a structure within the self-regulatory system, it would be a structure that has motivational significance. And its motivational significance should vary depending on which elements constitute the structure. Indeed, there is evidence that activating a self-discrepancy structure with a promotion–value element has different emotional and motivational effects than activating a self-discrepancy structure with a prevention–value element. This is illustrated in an early study by Tim Stauman and I that used a covert and idiographic (i.e., individually tailored) priming technique to activate the elements in each participants' belief system.[36]

The study was supposedly investigating the "physiological effects of thinking about other people." The participants were given phrases of the form, "An X person . . . " (where X would be a positive trait adjective such as "friendly" or "intelligent"), and they were asked to complete each sentence as quickly as possible. Although they were completing phrases about *other people*, the X trait adjective in each phrase primed a promotion-related ideal trait or a prevention-related ought trait possessed by a participant. For each phrase completion, rate of speech was measured and skin conductance amplitude was recorded as a measure of physiological arousal. The participants also reported their mood on scales that measured dejection-related emotions (e.g., "feeling sad") and agitation-related emotions (e.g., "feeling nervous"). On the basis of their responses to a questionnaire obtained weeks before the experiment, participants were selected whose actual-self beliefs were discrepant predominantly to either their ideal self-guides (promotion-related) or their ought self-guides (prevention-related). Thus, the participants' monitored-self structures contained either an actual-self belief element (truth) combined with a promotion element (value) in a discrepancy relation or an actual-self element combined with a prevention element, also in a discrepancy relation.

The study found that, despite the fact that the trait primed in the phrase was always *positive*, the participants' mood became *more negative* after the priming. This could have happened only if there was a monitored-self structure where activating the value element in the structure (ideal self guides for promotion or ought self-guides for prevention) spread activation to the truth element in the structure (the actual self) that had a discrepancy relation to the value element—thereby producing a negative emotion from the discrepancy. Moreover, the study also found that the motivational significance of the structure was clearly different depending on whether it contained a promotion value element or a prevention value element.

Independent of the content of the prime—that is, the *same* X trait could be either an ideal self-guide for one participant or an ought self-guide for another participant—the priming produced different motivational-emotional syndromes when it was a promotion value element or a prevention value element. When the prime was a promotion value element in participants' self-belief structure, the priming made them feel dejected and talk more slowly, and it lowered their physiological arousal—a *depression-related* syndrome. In contrast, when the prime was a prevention value element, the priming made them feel agitated and talk more quickly, and it raised their physiological arousal—an *anxiety-related* syndrome. And the participants reported having no idea why the task was creating these experiences. This was because, naturally, they would have no notion that their experiences were produced by the unconscious activation of structural relations that had specific motivational significance for them.

The results of this study, and others like it,[37] suggest that different self-belief structures can have different motivational significance. Activation of one element in the structure can spread to another element and produce a motivational state that is associated with the psychological situation represented by the elements *as a whole*. As a whole, a discrepancy relation between a promotion element (value) and an actual-self element (truth) represents the psychological situation of "absence of positive outcomes," which is a dejection–depression condition. As a whole, a discrepancy relation between a prevention element and an actual-self element represents the psychological situation of "presence of negative outcomes," which is an agitation–anxiety condition.[38]

A More Stringent Test for Self-Discrepancy
Structures of the Monitored Self

Although the results of such studies are consistent with there being structural spreading, they were not specifically designed to test directly for spreading activation effects. Indeed, it is possible to interpret them as activating standards of self-evaluation that are used *during the study itself* for appraising the current condition of the actual self—an online self-monitoring process of checking "how am I doing?" There is other research, however, that tested for structural effects in a more stringent manner. Let me now discuss the logic behind, and the findings of, this research program.

Within cognitive psychology, one standard method for testing whether object categories are organized together (i.e., interconnected) in memory[39] involves the use of the Stroop task, in which people have to name as quickly as possible the color of target words, with each word appearing in a different-colored ink. Before each target word appears, participants are given a memory-load word, which functions as the prime and which they have to repeat after they name the color of the target word. The critical experimental manipulation involves the relation between the priming word and the target word.

When there is a structural relation between the priming word's concept and the target word's concept in long-term memory, then activating the priming word's concept in memory will spread and activate the target word's concept. This will make the target's concept more accessible to the participants and thus harder to ignore when the target word appears. And when this happens it will take longer to name just the *ink color* of the target word because the target word's *concept* cannot be ignored. For example, if the target word is "oak" in blue ink, then it will take longer to name the ink color as blue when the priming word is "maple," because priming with one type of tree will spread and make other tree concepts (e.g., oak) more accessible and thus interfere with just naming "blue" as the color of the ink. Simply put, the stronger the organization in long-term memory between the priming word's concept and the target word's concept, the worse participants will perform on the Stroop task at just naming the color of the ink.

What is nice about this paradigm is that the predicted effect from organization is *opposite* to what the participants are *trying* to do, which is to name the ink color of the target word as quickly as possible. That is, the effect of structural organization is predicted to occur *despite* the task goal of the participants. This paradigm has been successful in demonstrating the organization that exists among object categories, such as showing that the concepts associated with the words "maple" (as a priming word) and "oak" (as a target word) are organized together in long-term memory (i.e., semantically related as trees), whereas the concepts associated with the words "story" (as a priming word) and "potato" (as a target word) are not.

This paradigm was also selected to examine how self-beliefs are organized together.[40] Participants' actual-self attributes, or self-descriptive traits, were obtained by finding those traits that participants perceived as being both highly applicable to themselves and highly relevant to themselves (important). Their non–self-descriptive traits were obtained by finding those traits that participants perceived as not relevant to themselves and as neither high nor low in applicability.[41] The initial studies consistently found that pairs where both the prime and the target were self-descriptive did *not* slow response times in the Stroop task more that mixed pairs (i.e., where only one trait was self-descriptive). The same studies also included object categories and *did* find evidence that identifying pairs where both the prime and the target were members of the same object category (e.g., both prime and target were types of trees) was slower than with mixed pairs (only one object from any specific object category). Thus, the paradigm was effective at detecting structural organization for object categories, but there was *no* evidence of structure for self-descriptive traits.

This finding was initially surprising to social-personality psychologists because each self-descriptive trait is, by definition, connected to the "self." But the fact that both are connected to the "self" does *not* mean that they are connected to *each other*. What, then, might produce an organization of self beliefs where they *are* connected to each other? In the previous research that I described, there was evidence suggesting that an actual-self belief (a truth element) can be organized in a discrepancy relation with a promotion or a prevention self-guide (a value element). If these are structurally organized together, then the discrepant actual-self attributes themselves could become organized together in the category of *problematic self traits*. Thus, when a prime and a target are both *problematic* traits, there could be evidence of organization. And this is precisely what was found in a subsequent study that included actual-self traits that were or were not discrepant from participants' personal ideal or ought self-guides. For the prime–target pairs containing discrepant (i.e., problematic) actual-self traits, the response times on the Stroop task *were* slower than for prime–target pairs that did not contain discrepant actual-self traits. Evidence for structure among actual-self traits was finally found!

Why would discrepant or problematic actual-self traits be more likely to become interconnected or organized? In the social cognition literature more generally, it has been suggested that the attributes that are most likely to form the basis for interconnectedness are those that fail to meet expectations for what a target is like.[42] If this notion is broadened to failure to meet expectations for what a target ought to be like or ideally should be like, and the target is the self, then discrepant or problematic actual-self traits would be likely candidates for organization. In addition, discrepant or problematic actual-self traits are more likely to receive an individual's attention, which in turn would mean that they are more likely to be repeatedly and concurrently stimulated, and this would lead to structural interconnectedness.[43]

What this suggests, then, is that an organization of the actual-self–truth element and the promotion value or prevention value elements is especially likely when the elements involve a discrepancy relation. This conclusion is consistent with the unfortunate phenomena of depressed individuals (with their actual–ideal discrepancies) having *global* negative views of themselves and anxious individuals (with their actual–ought discrepancies) feeling *generally* threatened in the world—both of which would be resistant to change because of the strength provided by interconnectedness, by structure. The experience of global or general negativity would occur each time the activation of one negative self belief spread activation to other negative self beliefs within the self belief structure.

Spreading as Stopping

It should be noted that interconnectedness among structural elements does not always mean that the activation of one element strengthens another element (excitation): activation of one element can also weaken another element (inhibition). When discussing resistance to temptation in Chapter 6, for example, I described the case of there being already-established associations not only between the temptation and the preferred goal, but also between the temptation and the resolve to oppose it for the sake of the preferred goal. When the preferred goal is clearly a priority, then exposure to the temptation will activate this goal with its higher priority, and this activated goal will then override (i.e., inhibit) the temptation.[44]

More generally, when motivations are organized together and are functioning dynamically, one motivational dimension can set constraints on another motivational dimension whose preferences are receiving too much emphasis. Consider a previous example: when strong assessment's preference for making exhaustive comparisons is creating a state of becoming "lost in thought," then strong locomotion can stop the comparison process in order to initiate action. And the reverse is also true: strong assessment can stop locomotion from initiating just any action and insist on first determining which direction is the *right* direction. Spreading as strengthening (excitation) has received more research attention than spreading as weakening (inhibition), but the organizational dynamics of constraints and stop rules are an important part of motivation that need to be examined more closely.

Spreading as Transfer

In my discussion thus far, I have focused on the case of *spreading activation* among interconnected elements. This is the most straightforward meaning of spreading as it relates to psychological organization, but there is another kind of spreading that also has important motivational effects. This kind has been called *transfer* in the social-psychological literature. For example, Dolf Zillman, who was inspired by Stanley Schachter's pioneering research on misattribution of arousal,[45] conducted a classic study on "excitation transfer." His research demonstrated that arousal from one's simply working out on an exercise bicycle was later transferred to anger intensity that increased aggressive behavior toward another person.[46] This kind of spreading as transfer was not originally conceptualized in structural terms, but it is useful to consider whether the organization of motives could produce transfer.

What might such spreading as transfer look like? In Chapter 4, I described a model of value experience as the force of attraction toward or repulsion from a target. According to this model, sources of motivational force direction and motivational force intensity, together, create the holistic experience of the target's value. Importantly, there are sources, such as a value target's hedonic properties, that contribute to both motivational force direction and intensity, but there are other sources that contribute to just motivational force intensity. In particular, there are sources of *engagement strength* that contribute to the intensity of a target's attractiveness or repulsiveness independent of whether the sources themselves are associated with pleasant or painful experiences.

When I discussed this model in Chapter 4, I did not describe it as an organization of motives—a motivationally significant structure—that involves transfer. But it can, and should be, conceptualized this way. The output of this structure is the value experience of a force of attraction toward or repulsion from the value target. These experiences constitute the motivational significance of the structure. The motivational significance of the structure has direction and intensity, and it is determined by the nature of its structural elements and their interconnectedness.

What, then, are the structural elements in the experience of something that has value? I propose that the elements are value, truth, and control effectiveness. It is not surprising to claim that the motive to have desired results (i.e., value effectiveness) contributes to the value experience of something. The more that something has the desired result of providing pleasure or satisfying a need, the stronger should be the force of attraction toward it. As I discussed in Chapter 7, the classic value–likelihood models of commitment would include truth as well as value in the structure given that the force of attraction toward something with a desired result would vary as a function of the belief that the desired result is likely to happen.

What has not been included in classic models of value is the *control* element. Although I did not explicitly discuss control in Chapter 4, it is involved in the engagement strength contribution to the overall value experience. When people are strongly engaged in something, they have sustained attention; they are fully absorbed or engrossed in what they are doing. To sustain attention without being distracted, to continue with a goal despite interference and resistance, is to manage what happens. Thus, strong engagement itself involves effective control. As I said at the beginning of this book, value effectiveness relates to outcomes (benefits vs. costs) and truth effectiveness relates to reality (real vs. illusion), but control effectiveness relates to *strength*.

I believe that it is useful to conceptualize the resultant value experience as a holistic experience that derives from a dynamic structure of interconnected value, truth, and control elements that affect one another. In this dynamic structural model, strengthening the *engagement–control* element would spread to strengthen the entire value experience as a whole. Similarly, strengthening the likelihood–truth element would spread to strengthen the entire value experience as a whole.

There is an intriguing question raised by this dynamic structural model. Is it possible that the engagement–control element could spread to the truth element itself and strengthen it as an element? For instance, if engagement in a goal pursuit was strengthened by creating a condition of regulatory fit, such as having promotion-oriented individuals pursue the goal eagerly or prevention-oriented individuals pursue the goal vigilantly, would the actors perceive a greater likelihood that goal attainment would produce those outcomes (truth)?[47]

There is some evidence that engagement–control can spread to the truth element. I discussed one of these studies in Chapter 8. Participants who had either a predominant promotion orientation or a predominant prevention orientation thought back to a time in their lives when they had a conflict with an authority figure who determined how to resolve the conflict.[48] Some participants recalled an eager resolution of the conflict, whereas others recalled a vigilant resolution. Thus, some participants were in a regulatory fit condition when they thought about the resolution (predominant promotion/eager resolution; predominant prevention/vigilant resolution), whereas other participants were in a non-fit condition (predominant promotion/vigilant resolution; predominant prevention/eager resolution). Those in the fit conditions judged the resolution to be more morally right. That is, they judged the resolution to have truth effectiveness—the resolution *is* right. But the manipulation was only a regulatory fit manipulation where engagement–control and "*feeling* right" were strengthened in the fit conditions. Nonetheless, strengthening the control element transferred to the truth element—what *is* right.

Once again, William James was early in appreciating how strengthening our experience of control can have an impact on establishing what's real—believing that we have the power to make something happen transfers to establishing that thing as real. In his chapter on *Will* in Volume II of *The Principles of Psychology*, he writes the following:

> We desire to feel, to have, to do, all sorts of things which at the moment are not felt, had, or done. If with the desire there goes a sense that attainment is not possible, we simply *wish*; but if we believe that the end is in our power, we *will* that the desired feeling, having, or doing shall be real; and real it presently becomes, either immediately upon the willing or after certain preliminaries have been fulfilled.[49]

Transfer of strength from the control element to the truth element underlies a very old idea, at least as old as the writings of the ancient Greeks: *might makes right*. Apart from its usual bellicose connotation, one interpretation of this statement is that strength in managing what happens (control as might) can transfer to strength in establishing what's real (truth as right). But in 1860, as part of his speech at Cooper Union in New York City, Abraham Lincoln reversed this statement and declared instead: "Let us have faith that right makes might." What he was proposing expresses a message similar to the famous maxim, "The truth shall set you free." This means that a strong *truth* element in the organization of motives can also transfer to strengthen the *control* element. If you know you are right, you feel strong and in control and therefore act with increased vigor and determination.

SUMMARY

This chapter has considered the relations among all three ways of being effective—value, truth, and control—as an organization of motivations working together. To date, there is much less research addressing the implications of the full organization of these three motivations than the separate dyadic relations among them that I reviewed in earlier chapters. The purpose of this chapter was to provide some ways of thinking about the structural organization of motivations working together and to review what evidence exists for there being such a structure.

I proposed three properties of the organization of motives as a holistic structure—*supportiveness, significance,* and *spreading*. Regarding structural *supportiveness*, I discussed how the organization of motivations goes beyond the classic case of truth (e.g., likelihood) and control (e.g., means) being just tools in the instrumental service of attaining desired results (value). For example, I reviewed evidence that value itself can be *sacrificed* in the service of truth, such as reducing the positivity of some value target in order to achieve cognitive consistency. I also discussed the *compensation* version of supportiveness, as when high assessment concerns can compensate for the "just do it" costs of high locomotion and thereby improve performance.

Regarding the holistic structural *significance* of motivations working together, I discussed how the motivational significance of the whole structure can be different from the sum of its parts. I presented evidence, for example, that having a negative value element (disliking studying) can increase motivation to study *more* than having a positive value element (liking studying) when these value elements are components in a tripartite attitude structure that also includes cognition–truth and behavior–control. Whereas studying is something you "like" to do for individuals with the latter structure, it is something you "want" to do, "need" to do, for individuals with the former structure.

Regarding structural *spreading* within holistic organizations, I presented evidence for *spreading activation*, as when priming an actual-self belief that has a discrepant relation with an ideal-value element or an ought-value element will spread and activate other actual-self beliefs with discrepant relations, thereby creating global and generalized affective problems. I then discussed the notion of *spreading as transfer*. For example, I described how strengthening engagement as a control element can spread to value and intensify the holistic experience of attraction toward or repulsion from a value target. I also described how strengthening control as an element can strengthen the experience of truth ("might makes right"), and how establishing what's real can strengthen the experience of control ("right makes might").

In this chapter, I also discussed the possibility that there are various ways that the motivations of promotion, prevention, locomotion, and assessment can work together as structural organizations—different patterns from each of these motivations receiving differential emphasis in the structure. Promotion and prevention are distinct *value* orientations. Locomotion is concerned with *control*, and assessment is concerned with *truth*. There are specific ways of dealing with or perceiving the world that fit each of these particular orientations. When these various orientations receive different emphasis, different ways of dealing with or perceiving the world are emphasized. Because of these differences in emphasis, it is possible that distinct personalities and distinct cultures can emerge. This possibility is considered in the next chapter.

PART FOUR

Implications of Motivations Working Together

Personality and Culture

Ways of Seeing and Coping With the World

We are all fascinated with how different people can be, whether in terms of their personality or their cultural attributes. We are surprised, for example, by how different extraverts are from introverts or by how different Americans are from the Japanese. We can be fascinated with such personality and cultural differences without thinking much about where they come from. What causes them? The answers typically are the classic nature-or-nurture explanations for behavior. That is, some people prefer to explain both cultural and personality differences in terms of genetic differences, whereas others prefer to explain them both in terms of differences in socialization. Of course, there are other possible answers as well, such as thinking that culture is more nurture than nature (i.e., has more to do with socialization) whereas personality is more nature than nurture (i.e., has more to do with genetics).

What such answers don't do is provide a general framework for how to think about personality and cultural differences in the first place. Not surprisingly given the theme of this book, my position on this issue will highlight the role of motivational mechanisms in personality and cultural differences. A motivational emphasis is not unusual for thinking about personality differences, although it is somewhat unusual for cultural differences, where differences in belief systems have received more emphasis than differences in motivation. But beyond its emphasis on motivation, what is new about my position is the proposal that *both* personality and cultural differences derive from the *same* set of *universal* mechanisms and principles.[1]

Because this assertion—*differences from universals*—might sound like a contradiction, let me clarify what I mean by using regulatory focus as an example. Briefly, I believe that there are universal principles of motivational functioning that underlie both personality and culture, such as eager strategies of advancement being a fit with a promotion orientation and vigilant strategies of maintaining a satisfactory state being a fit with a prevention orientation. And this is true whether the promotion and prevention states are chronic (e.g., stable in a person or institutionalized in a society) or are momentary (e.g., situationally induced). Importantly, these *functional relations* between the tendency to use eager strategies increasing with promotion strength, and the tendency to use vigilant strategies increasing with prevention strength, are found within every person and within every culture: *they are universal.*

However, within each person and within each culture, the promotion and the prevention orientations themselves can receive different emphasis—promotion could receive high emphasis while prevention receives low emphasis; prevention could receive high emphasis while promotion receives low emphasis; both promotion and prevention could receive low emphasis; and both could receive high emphasis. These personality or cultural differences in emphasis play through the universal functions to produce personality or cultural differences in people's tendency to use eager strategies, or vigilant strategies, or neither strategy, or both strategies during their decision making, problem solving, and task performance. In this way, significant differences can derive from universals.

I believe that most personality and cultural differences derive from a relatively small number of universal self-regulatory principles working together. It is not possible in this chapter to develop fully what I have in mind, but I will try to illustrate my perspective using the motivational principles of regulatory focus, regulatory mode, and regulatory fit. I begin with a discussion of personality differences and then extend that discussion to cultural differences.

WHAT IS PERSONALITY AND WHEN IS IT REVEALED?

Most of us have an intuitive sense of when others' behaviors or attributes reveal their personality. Typically, it is not when they are walking down the street or drinking a glass of water. It is also not the color of their eyes or how tall they are. Instead, it is how they respond to failure or rejection, or how they interpret some ambiguous remark of another person—the way one person versus another reacts to the world.

Individual differences alone do not reveal personality because differences in eye color or height are individual differences and yet they typically are not considered to reveal personality. Still, the issue of personality would not even arise if individual differences were not somehow a factor. If all earthworms behave in the same way, then we are unlikely to think that they have different personalities. But now imagine that you observe some earthworms consistently burrow through soil quickly and smoothly, whereas others consistently tunnel at a slow and jerky pace. Would you now think that earthworms have different personalities— the "quick and smooth" earthworm type and the "slow and jerky" earthworm type? Or would you still think that this type of individual difference by itself is not enough to be considered a personality difference?

The earthworm example suggests that not all individual differences are created equal. And this is true for humans as well. For most of us, individual differences in walking speed—"fast" walkers and "slow" walkers—would not, by itself, constitute a personality difference.[2] Which individual differences, then, reveal personality? I believe that the individual differences that reveal *personality* are those that reflect *motivated* preferences and biases. Specifically, personality is revealed through *motivated preferences and biases in the ways that someone sees the world and copes in the world.*[3] Notably, the "someone" does not refer only to humans, as pet owners would quickly point out; indeed, there is a growing interest in personality in non-human animals.[4]

From this perspective on personality, "fast" versus "slow" human walkers, and "quick and smooth" versus "slow and jerky" earthworms, would be personality differences to the extent that we believed they reflected differences in motivated preferences and biases. For the human case of walking speed, for example, we would ask ourselves if this might be a behavioral choice reflecting a motivated preference. Might "fast" walkers be eager promotion individuals or high locomotors? For individual differences in walking speed, then, it seems possible that it might be a personality difference, whereas individual differences in eye color would not.

The notion that motivation is central to personality is not new. Many theories of personality have given a primary role to the motives of an individual, from early psychodynamic theories of personality[5] to more recent social-cognitive approaches to personality.[6] In his classic book on personality, Gordon Allport defined personality traits not in terms of a tendency to behave the same way across situations but, rather, as an individual characteristic that "renders many stimuli functionally equivalent"[7] and, given this rendering, initiates and guides equivalent responses to these stimuli. The "rendering stimuli equivalent" feature relates to biases and preferences in the ways an individual *sees the world*. The "guides equivalent responses" feature relates to preferences and biases in the ways an individual *copes in the world*. For example, a person can have a chronically accessible construct, such as "conceited," that creates functional equivalence by categorizing the different behaviors of different people as all being "conceited," even when there is little evidence to support this categorization.[8] And this categorization in turn can produce equivalent responses in how that person copes with these "conceited" people.

Low-Demand and High-Demand Situations as Revealing Personality

Individuals' "ways of seeing" the world and "ways of coping" in the world are two different kinds of *sensitivities* that can define personality. Significantly, different kinds of situations reveal these different kinds of sensitivities. Sensitivity in "ways of seeing" (e.g., a person's chronically accessible constructs) is revealed in *low-demand* situations where input is minimal or unclear, where reality constraints or demands are low. Low-demand situations provide opportunities to observe how individuals' perceptions, judgments, and evaluations are shaped by their "ways of seeing." In contrast, sensitivity in "ways of coping" is revealed in *high-demand* situations where an individual's self-regulatory system is taxed or stressed. High-demand situations provide opportunities to observe how the way an individual handles personal problems and pressures is shaped by his or her "ways of coping."[9]

In psychology, two classic instruments that have been used to reveal personality have been Mischel's "marshmallow test" of resisting temptation that I described earlier in this book[10] and projective tests, such as the Rorschach or the Thematic Apperception Test (TAT), which ask individuals to describe vague or ambiguous pictures they are shown.[11] What is it about these tests that reveal personality? The "marshmallow test" is a high-demand situation, and the actors' responses in this situation can reveal differences in their *ways of coping* in the world. The TAT or Rorschach is a low-demand situation, and the actors' responses in this situation reveal differences in their *ways of seeing* the world.

My proposal that personality is revealed through motivated preferences and biases in the ways that someone sees and copes in the world is consistent with my first starting position in this book that what it means to be motivated is to have preferences that direct choices. If personality is revealed through motivation, then it must be revealed through *preferences that direct choices*. To count as personality, there must be some stability in the preferences underlying someone's choices, and there must be some difference between these stable preferences and those of someone else.

Stability in someone's preferences should not be confused with someone making the same behavioral choice across all situations (i.e., cross-situational consistency). An underlying preference could be revealed in a stable *pattern* of choices that involves someone consistently making choice X in situation A, but consistently making choice Y in situation B. This involves stable consistency *within* each situation but not across situations—what Walter Mischel and Yuichi Shoda refer to as the stable "if–then" profile that is someone's *personality signature*.[12] The underlying status bias that motivates the choices of an authoritarian personality, for example, is a stable "if–then" profile of consistently choosing *submissive* behaviors when interacting with a higher-status person, but consistently choosing *dominant* behaviors when interacting with a lower-status person.[13]

The Importance of Control and Truth Processes for Revealing Personality

My second starting position in this book is that what people really want is to be effective in life pursuits. This position also underlies my proposal that personality is revealed through the ways that someone sees and copes in the world as revealed, respectively, in low-demand and high-demand situations. People want to be effective in establishing what's real (truth) and in managing what happens (control), both for their own sake and in order to have desired results (value). Truth-effectiveness and control-effectiveness concern the goal-pursuit process, whereas value-effectiveness concerns the goal-pursuit outcome.

Personality is more likely to be revealed in the processes of goal pursuit than in the outcomes of goal pursuit. This is because individuals' outcomes, what desired results they do or do not end up having, may have little to do with their personality. Their desired results, for example, could be determined by what others do rather than what they do. And when individuals end up with the same desired result, such as getting high grades in school or having a high-paying job or having a long-lasting marriage, their personalities may be revealed less by these outcomes than by how they went about pursuing them.

It is the goal-pursuit system as a whole that matters, and differences between systems are often revealed by differences in goal-pursuit processes rather than outcomes. For example, the difference between people with a strong promotion orientation versus a strong prevention orientation, which is a value difference, has been revealed less in the type of desired results they want—which can often be the same (e.g., getting an "A" in a course)—than in how they see those results (i.e., an accomplishment vs. a fulfilled duty) and how they try to attain them (i.e., using eager means vs. vigilant means). Indeed, research on regulatory focus differences has typically controlled for the outcomes, such as what money or reward would be received from successful performance, and examined the effects of regulatory focus on people's strategic ways of managing the goal pursuit (control) and ways of representing goal success or failure (truth).

My emphasis on truth (ways of seeing) and control (ways of coping) is different from some of the traditional personality perspectives that emphasized the different needs that people have (i.e., value). For example, some models distinguish between individuals who are motivated to approach desired results versus those who are motivated to avoid undesired results. For instance, they propose that there is the personality difference between those with high need achievement who approach opportunities for success versus those with low need achievement who avoid possible failure, and that there is the personality difference between those with high need for affiliation, who approach opportunities for acceptance, versus those with low need for affiliation, who avoid possible rejection.[14] This traditional perspective retains a close connection with the hedonic principle in its emphasis on distinguishing between individuals who approach pleasure versus those who avoid pain.

What this perspective leaves out are the *different ways* in which people approach pleasure and avoid pain. I believe that it is the different ways of seeing and different ways of coping with pleasure and pain that are more revealing of personality.[15] For example, there is more than one way in which people are high need achievers. There is the way that people are high need achievers when they have a promotion focus, and there is the way they are high need achievers when they have a prevention focus.[16]

According to McClelland and Atkinson's classic theory of achievement motivation,[17] over time a new achievement task elicits the feelings associated with past achievement engagements. For individuals with a history of success, a new achievement task elicits a feeling of *pride*, which produces anticipatory goal reactions that energize and direct behavior to approach the new task. In contrast, for individuals with a history of failure, a new achievement task elicits a feeling of shame, which produces anticipatory goal reactions that energize and direct behavior to avoid the new task. But is this the whole story, or even the most informative story? If we were to consider, for example, just those individuals with a subjective history of success, is it best to characterize them as high need achievers whose anticipatory goal reactions *energize* and *direct* them to approach achievement tasks?

Individuals, in fact, can have a subjective history of either successful promotion or successful prevention. The former have promotion pride and the latter have prevention pride.[18] How they represent their past success and anticipate their potential success in the future is *different*. For example, those with promotion pride are optimists, whereas those with prevention pride are defensive pessimists. That is, they both *value* success, but their *truth* about success is different.

Importantly, their *control* of success is also different. Promotion pride individuals approach achievement tasks with strategic eagerness, whereas prevention pride individuals approach achievement tasks with strategic vigilance. That is, although they both approach an achievement task to have a desired result, promotion pride individuals use *strategic approach* means to advance (eager means), whereas prevention pride individual use *strategic avoidance* means to be careful (vigilant means)—two very different ways of achieving. To treat promotion pride and prevention pride individuals as if they were the same because they both value success and have pride in success overlooks the fact that they are completely different regarding the truth and control of success. Once again, it is necessary to go beyond pleasure and pain to understand more deeply the essential nature of the underlying motivational system. *And* it is necessary to go beyond the notion that motivation is about directing some general, all-purpose energy.

Let me make a quick comment about need for affiliation as well. In this case, it is individuals with a history of affiliation failure who have received the most attention in the literature. According to the traditional model, they can be characterized as being motivated to avoid possible rejection (i.e., avoid pain). This suggests that such individuals would simply avoid affiliating with other people in order to avoid rejection. But, once again, this is too simple. Among people who have a history of affiliation failure, there are different ways that they mentally represent such failures (i.e., truth) and cope with such failures (i.e., control). And there is substantial evidence that it is these different "ways of seeing" and "ways of coping" that create different personalities.[19]

For example, both children who are "avoidant" and children who are "anxious/ambivalent" experience affiliation failure when their caregivers thwart their attempts to attain security. But the coping strategy of "avoidant" children is to stay away from the caretaker (i.e., deactivate the attachment system), whereas the coping strategy of "anxious/ambivalent" children is to cling to the caregiver one moment and angrily push the caregiver away the next (i.e., hyperactivate the attachment system).[20] Moreover, as I discuss later, individuals who are high in rejection sensitivity use both approach and avoidance coping strategies, and the preferred strategies or tactics that they use depend on their relations to other motivational elements, such as the strength of their prevention orientation.[21]

How Are Individual Differences in Truth and Control Revealed?

As both the achievement motivation and affiliation motivation literatures illustrate, personality differences are not captured adequately by simply distinguishing between individuals who approach desired results and individuals who avoid undesired results in some motivational domain. It is not just about hedonic value differences. It is also about differences in truth and in control—in the *how* of goal pursuit and not just the outcome of goal pursuit. The question, then, becomes: How are individual differences in truth and control processes revealed?

For *truth*, differences are less likely to be revealed when everything is straightforward and simple for everyone—that is, when the truth about something is unambiguous, totally obvious. However, when the truth about something is not clear, then differences in people's choices emerge. This is what Solomon Asch found in his research on people's decisions to agree or disagree with the unanimous majority's incorrect answer about which line matched the target line. Individual differences in choosing to agree or disagree with the majority were most evident when the correct answer was unclear. This illustrates how personality differences in "ways of seeing" are revealed when the truth about the world is unclear (i.e., reality constraints or demands are low).

How are individual differences in *control* processes revealed? When a goal-pursuit process goes smoothly and routinely, few conflicts between different managing options need to be dealt with; minimal choices between managing trade-offs have to be made. Differences between managing preferences, between strategic biases, are more likely to be observed when difficulties in goal pursuit require choosing between alternatives that each have trade-offs. For example, a difficult task may have a "speed/accuracy" trade-off where greater speed and greater accuracy are in conflict with one another. Individuals with a strong promotion orientation have a preference for strategic eagerness, which is revealed in their choosing speed over accuracy in this high-demand situation. In contrast, individuals with a strong prevention orientation have a preference for strategic vigilance, which is revealed in their choosing accuracy over speed.[22] This illustrates how in high-demand situations personality differences in control, in "ways of coping," are revealed that might not be observed in less-taxing situations. Let us now consider in more detail how individual differences in "ways of seeing" and in "ways of coping" function as windows into understanding personality.

WAYS OF SEEING: PERSONALITY DIFFERENCES IN TRUTH

The notion that differences in "ways of seeing" could reveal personality took hold in the mid-20th century with the emergence of the "New Look" in perception. What was new was the idea—and research supporting the idea—that the perception of objects, events, and other individuals in the world was influenced by a perceiver's expectancies, needs, and beliefs.[23] As envisioned in George Kelly's personal constructs theory, for example, individuals scan the perceptual field to "pick up blips of meaning" (p. 145) that relate to their chronically accessible constructs, like scanning others' behaviors and picking up signs of conceitedness.[24] Indeed, inspired by the work of the pioneering psychoanalyst Carl Jung, some of the earliest research in personality used differences in "ways of seeing" to explore differences in personality.[25] Although the terminology differed, early work by David McClelland and John Atkinson emphasized that differences in perception were driven by differences in an individual's highly accessible constructs, including motives.

Projective tests of personality such as the TAT or the Rorschach inkblot test rely on the assumption that the meaning an individual imposes on ambiguous or vague stimuli reveals highly accessible motives.[26] While much of the initial work was focused on chronically accessible motives, even early work demonstrated that motives could become temporarily accessible through the priming of a motivational construct, such as achievement or affiliation.[27] And subsequent research demonstrated that situationally induced accessibility can combine with individuals' chronic accessibility and, together, influence how others' behaviors are evaluated.[28] It is not surprising, then, that individual differences in construct accessibility now play an important role in many social-cognitive theories of personality.[29]

The idea that differences in ways of seeing the world reflect differences in personality was also the core assumption in the *cognitive styles* approach to personality, which is a precursor to many social-cognitive theories of personality.[30] Perhaps the best-known cognitive style difference is the distinction between field-dependent and field-independent individuals. With respect to object perception, this difference concerns the ability to discriminate visual, auditory, or tactile cues from their surrounding environments (e.g., to separate figures from their backgrounds), with field-independent individuals being better able to do so than field-dependent individuals. Field-dependent individuals, on the other hand, are more responsive to environmental cues (i.e., the surrounding background) than field-independent individuals.[31] Significantly, this cognitive style difference was believed to reflect a global perceptual difference that would affect *social* perception as well as object perception. And there was evidence for such effects, such as field-dependent individuals being more responsive to the social cues contained in their surrounding social environment than field-independent individuals.[32]

Of particular relevance to the current discussion, there was also evidence that this difference in sensitivity to social information emerged primarily when situations were *ambiguous*. For instance, field-dependent individuals were not generally more likely to seek information from others when making decisions, but were more likely to do so when there was ambiguity about the best decision.[33] This illustrates my previous point: personality as sensitivity in "ways of seeing" is more likely to be revealed in low-demand situations. While personality as sensitivity in "ways of seeing" can be revealed in almost any context, the evidence suggests that ambiguous or vague situations (i.e., low-demand situations) afford particularly clear opportunities to observe biased motives.

As Walter Mischel aptly described it: "To the degree that the situation is 'unstructured,' the subject will expect that virtually *any* response from him is equally likely to be equally appropriate . . . and variance from individual differences will be the greatest."[34] It is in this way that projective tests of personality take advantage of the supposition not only that an individual's motives will be reflected in what he or she sees, but also that these motives will be more clearly revealed when the stimuli being perceived or interpreted are vague or ambiguous. There is greater potential for chronically accessible motives to influence behavior in such low-demand situations, given that the expression of people's motives, particularly for preferred outcomes, would otherwise be bounded by reality constraints.[35] To understand how low-demand situations reveal personality differences in "ways of seeing," I believe that it is useful to apply the general principles of knowledge activation to individual differences in judgment.[36]

Implications of Knowledge Activation Principles for "Ways of Seeing"

Low-demand or unstructured situations can be either vague or ambiguous. Vague situations are those in which no particular response or behavior is clearly *applicable* to the situation (i.e., there is no stored response category whose features or characteristics match those of the situation). When the situation is vague, there is a low demand for *any* response to the situation. Ambiguous situations, on the other hand, are those in which there are at least two alternative responses that are clearly and equally applicable to the situation; that is, there are at least two stored response categories whose features or characteristics match those of the situation. When the situation is ambiguous, there is a low demand for any *one* particular response.[37] Under such ambiguous low-demand conditions, motivational biases or preferences associated with a personality difference can determine which response is given because the situation itself does not have the reality constraints that clearly demand one particular response.

In previous publications, I have proposed a "general principles" perspective on personality, arguing that the same general underlying principles, such as the general principles of knowledge activation, underlie both "person" and "situation" variables.[38] Rather than distinguishing between "person" explanatory principles and "situation" explanatory principles, I have argued that the same psychological principles underlie both explanations. This approach provides not only a common language for personality and social psychologists, but also a richer understanding of how a given principle plays out in a number of conditions. For example, it clarifies how chronic individual differences in construct accessibility interact with situationally induced differences in construct accessibility.[39]

Importantly, none of us knows the extent to which a construct we use to judge some person comes to mind because the features of the construct match the observed features of the person (the construct is applicable) or because our long-term concerns have made that construct chronically accessible (the construct reflects our personal way of seeing the world). That is, we don't know what our judgment is actually "about."[40]

To understand how sensitivity in "ways of seeing" works, it is important to distinguish among accessibility, applicability, and judged usability of a knowledge construct.[41] Two critical factors influence the probability that a stored construct will be activated and become ready for use in making a judgment of some target. The first factor is the accessibility of the knowledge prior to the appearance of the target. The second factor is the applicability of the construct to the target (i.e., the overlap of features between the stored construct and the target).

As accessibility and applicability increase, the probability that the construct will be activated and ready for use also increases. Accessibility and applicability work together in knowledge activation. Thus, when applicability is greater—when the situational input is clear and unambiguous—there is less need for high accessibility in order for stored knowledge to be activated. In the case of high applicability, then, individual differences in chronic accessibility become a less important factor in knowledge activation. This is why personality as a sensitivity in truth seeking or "ways of seeing" is less likely to be revealed when reality is clear—different "ways of seeing" matter less for knowledge activation when applicability is high.

But as applicability decreases, as when the input is vague, accessibility must be greater in order for the construct to be activated. In this case, individual differences in chronic accessibility become a more important contributor to knowledge activation and thus reveal personality. Indeed, if an individual's sensitivity for seeing the world in a certain way is great enough, then a construct will be activated even when the applicability is very low. In one study, for example, the construct "conceited" was made accessible by priming it as part of another task, and this accessibility combined with the chronic accessibility for "conceited" that the different participants possessed (i.e., the personality sensitivity factor). The study found that when participants' chronic accessibility for "conceited" was very high, they formed an impression of a female target as being a conceited person even though her behavior was so vague that it provided no evidence at all of conceitedness; in fact, no one else in the study described her as conceited.[42] In contrast to vague input, when target information is ambiguous (i.e., when applicability is high for two or more constructs), then even low levels of chronic accessibility of a construct are sufficient to tip the balance in favor of that construct. Thus, low-demand vague input, like the

TAT or Rorschach, is an even better measure of sensitivities in "ways of seeing" than is low-demand ambiguous input.

A given individual's past experiences, such as socialization, can make different types of knowledge more chronically accessible and thus influence how likely it is that a construct like "conceited" will be used by that individual to characterize a vague or ambiguous social world. A recent study, for example, found a relationship between the speed with which participants classify words as negative or neutral and the intensity of their daily negative affect.[43] In other words, the more that evaluatively negative constructs have become chronically accessible for some individuals, the easier it becomes for them to "see" negativity in the world.

The third key factor in sensitivity to "ways of seeing" is *judged usability*. Even when there is both accessibility and applicability, the activated knowledge may not be used to make a judgment of a target. For instance, when individuals are aware that an activated construct is inappropriate to the task at hand, they will try to minimize or correct its impact on their behavior. Judged usability is the judged appropriateness of applying an activated construct to a particular target. If people decide that an activated construct should not be used, as when they believe that it relates to a stereotype associated with a target person's social group, they may try to suppress its use in their judgment of the target. This can lead to contrast rather than assimilation effects, such as deciding that a Hollywood star is "confident" rather than the Hollywood stereotype of being "conceited."[44]

Importantly, the judged usability of knowledge may itself be influenced by motivational factors that reflect a personality difference. What information is deemed appropriate to use depends on a person's prior beliefs (mental models or implicit theories) about the appropriateness of using some information under different conditions. And individuals can differ in their prior beliefs. Some senior professionals, for example, might suppress using the activated construct "mousy" when interviewing a female job candidate because they believe that it is an inappropriate, stereotypical label, whereas others might believe it is appropriate to use this label.

Sources of Individual Differences in "Ways of Seeing"

There are various sources of individual differences in sensitivity to "ways of seeing." It is not possible for me here to review all of these sources in detail. However, some illustrations will provide a richer picture of the underpinnings of this personality factor.[45]

EFFECTS OF CHRONIC ACCESSIBILITY ON WAYS OF SEEING
Individual differences in chronic accessibility are an essential part of understanding personality because they affect how the behaviors of others are judged

and remembered, which in turn can shape the social relationships that play a primary role in human functioning.[46] The study I just mentioned where individuals with a chronically accessible "conceited" construct formed an impression of a female target as being a conceited person illustrates this point.

In another early study on chronic accessibility,[47] participants' chronically accessible constructs were measured by asking them to list the traits of the type of person they liked, disliked, sought out, avoided, and frequently encountered, thereby identifying which traits came to mind first for each participant. A week later, participants read about the behaviors of a target person where some of the behaviors related to a participant's own chronically accessible constructs whereas other target behaviors did not. The study found that what participants remembered about the target person, and what impressions they formed of the target, depended on those behaviors of the target that related to their chronically accessible constructs rather than the other behaviors that did not relate to their accessible constructs.

The importance for interpersonal relations of individual differences in what social knowledge is chronically accessible is strikingly illustrated in the work of Susan Andersen, who has made major contributions to the interface of social and clinical psychology. Andersen and her colleagues propose that all of us have multiple selves that are experienced in relationships with our significant others, and that our representations of our significant others include not only their characteristics and motives but also our habitual ways of being with them. A stored representation of a particular significant other can be situationally activated, such as meeting someone who happens to resemble a significant other in some way, which can result in our remembering, feeling about, and behaving toward this new person as if he or she *were* our significant other—the process called *transference* in the clinical literature.[48] Indeed, participants in Andersen's studies reported *high* confidence that they saw some characteristic in a target person who superficially resembled a significant other, despite no information about the characteristic actually being presented, when the significant other possessed that characteristic.[49]

The process of transference investigated by Andersen is part of the general attachment process. Psychiatrist John Bowlby highlighted the importance of "working models" in his pioneering work on the attachment process, whereby children develop mental representations of their attachment figures' responses to them and their responses to the attachment figures.[50] These working models are chronically accessible constructs that can be activated not only by the attachment figures themselves but also by other individuals whose attributes or responses are similar to those of the attachment figures (i.e., have sufficient applicability). This results in individuals, not only when they are children but also later when they are adults, relating to new people they meet as if they were their own parents or some other early attachment figure.[51] As Bowlby described this process: a person "tends to assimilate any new person with whom he may form a bond, such as a spouse, or child, or employer, or therapist, to an existing model (either of one or other parent or of self), and often continues to do so despite repeated evidence that the model is inappropriate. Similarly, he expects to be perceived and treated by them in ways that would be appropriate to his self-model, and to continue with such expectations despite contrary evidence."[52]

An example of "different ways of seeing" that are associated with personality differences in attachment styles is the two-dimensional space created by beliefs about the self and beliefs about others.[53] Securely attached individuals have positive beliefs about both the self and others: they perceive themselves as being worthy and lovable and they have positive expectations about how others behave. "Anxious/ambivalent" individuals have negative beliefs about the self combined with positive beliefs about others: they perceive themselves as unworthy and unlovable while evaluating others positively. Because this pattern of beliefs creates the motive to find ways to gain acceptance from valued others, it has also been called "preoccupied." "Avoidant" individuals have negative beliefs about both self and others: they perceive themselves as unworthy and unlovable and have negative expectations about how others behave. Finally, "dismissive" individuals have positive beliefs about the self and negative beliefs about others. These individuals dismiss intimacy and maintain a sense of independence and invulnerability.

Each of these patterns of beliefs is a chronically accessible mental model that, typically, developed during childhood and continues to shape adults' current relationships when applicable.[54] They illustrate complex truth–control relations beyond just approaching acceptance and avoiding rejection (i.e., value) because they represent stable preferences for how to approach acceptance and avoid rejection. The personality differences reside in these stable strategic preferences.

THE INFLUENCE OF PREFERRED CONCLUSIONS ON WAYS OF SEEING

There are both directional and non-directional conclusions that people want to believe are the truth about the world.[55] Directional conclusions reflect desires to reach particular conclusions about reality, such as "I am an intelligent and kind person" or "My spouse is generous and attractive." An especially interesting individual difference in directional conclusion preference is that between *optimists* and *pessimists*. The popular description of these different personalities is that when confronted with a glass half filled with water, optimists see it as a "glass half full" whereas pessimists see it as a "glass half empty." Notice both of these ways of seeing are reasonable because the state of a glass half filled with water is ambiguous; that is, it is a low-demand situation with respect to what's the truth.

Despite its popularity, the glass metaphor does not, strictly speaking, capture the nature of this personality difference because optimists and pessimists differ in their beliefs about what *will* happen in the future rather than in their positive or negative judgments of a current state or condition. Optimists believe that their future reality will be having desired results, whereas pessimists believe that their future reality will not be having desired results (or will be having undesired results). The popular song "High Hopes" *is* an optimistic statement. Murphy's Law ("Anything that can go wrong, will go wrong") *is* a pessimistic statement. The "glass half full" and the "glass half empty" *would* be optimistic and pessimistic statements, respectively, if they meant the glass was at the halfway point to becoming full in the future versus halfway to becoming empty in the future. I raise this distinction because I believe that optimism and pessimism readily reveal themselves as a personality difference precisely because they concern "ways of seeing" a potential reality in the future. By being about the *future*, the directional conclusion is less constrained by present realities. It is a low-demand situation.

Individual differences in preferred directional conclusions constitute a value difference (i.e., a difference in what conclusion is preferred), and it affects what truth is established. In contrast, *non-directional* outcomes are about general concerns rather than specific outcomes, such as the desire of individuals high in need for closure for an answer that is definite.[56] A high need for closure biases judgments and decisions towards attaining an answer, *any answer*, quickly and permanently—"seizing" and "freezing."

Individuals with a high need for closure are often contrasted with individuals with a high need for accuracy, and the differences between them affect "ways of seeing." Individuals with a high need for accuracy consider detailed information about a target that individuates that target from other people. In contrast, those with a high need for closure rely instead on more categorical information during impression formation that treats individuals as being just like other members of the category to which they belong. This contributes to sterotyping.[57] In addition, a construct whose accessibility has been increased from priming is more likely to be used by individuals with a high need for closure and less likely to be used by individuals with a high need for accuracy.[58] There is also evidence that individuals are more likely to infer that another person's behavior is evidence of possessing a certain trait or attitude if they have a high need for closure than if they have a high need for accuracy.[59]

The Influence of Preferred Strategies on Ways of Seeing

Individuals differ not only in the conclusions they prefer to draw (i.e., in what truth they are seeking and how soon and permanently they want the truth) but also in which specific strategies they prefer to use to process information and draw conclusions (i.e., in what strategic ways they prefer to seek the truth). These individual differences in preferred strategies can have a major impact on memory and judgment of what is seen. There is evidence, for example, that when asked to identify vague stimulus objects depicted in photos, individuals who have a strong promotion orientation and therefore a preference for eager strategies generate more alternatives for the identity of the objects than do individuals who have a strong prevention orientation and therefore a preference for vigilant strategies.[60] More generally, the eagerness of individuals with a strong promotion orientation also underlies their openness to change and to new ideas, which contributes to their seeing things more creatively than prevention-oriented individuals.[61]

The difference between optimists and pessimists in their ways of seeing future reality has also been found to be related to individual differences in regulatory focus. It is individuals with a strong promotion orientation and preference for eager strategies who are optimists.[62] Optimism about the future supports the eagerness that sustains a strong promotion orientation. Optimism is in the service of promotion–eagerness. In contrast, optimism about the future could reduce the vigilance that sustains a strong prevention orientation. Thus, something other than optimism is needed to serve prevention–vigilance. But pessimism *per se* can cause people to give up and avoid pursuing goals. This would not support effective goal pursuit in the service of prevention–vigilance. What would work is *defensive* pessimism, which involves predicting future failure *unless* vigilant strategies are carried out in the present. This representation of the truth does sustain prevention–vigilance and, indeed, it is an effective "way of seeing" for strong prevention individuals, as I discussed in Chapter 6.

A recent study on strategic differences between men and women in romantic-sexual relationships also relates to regulatory focus.[63] People can have regrets about what was not done but should have been done (i.e., regrets of omission or inaction), or they can have regrets about what was done but should not have been done (i.e., regrets of commission or action).[64] For the sexual aspect of romantic relationships particularly, men were found to have stronger regrets of inaction than regrets of action, whereas there was no difference for women. Moreover, this sex difference in what was regretted was *not* found for non-romantic relationships, such as friendship relationships.

Previous research has found that regrets of inaction correspond to promotion failure (errors of omission), whereas regrets of action correspond to prevention failure (errors of commission).[65] What this suggests, then, is that men more than women regret not being eager enough in their sexual relationships—they should have tried to advance more. Indeed, another study found that men, more than women, emphasized promotion–eagerness over prevention–vigilance in their romantic-sexual relationships; once again, this difference was *not* found for friendship relationships.[66]

This difference between males and females in the emotional significance they assign to past action or inaction in their sexual relationships (i.e., a sex difference in "ways of seeing" sexual relationships) is especially interesting given its relation to evolutionary theories of mate preference and selection.[67] From this viewpoint, differences between men and women in mate choice relate to reproductive biological differences between them. Women would naturally be more cautious (i.e., strategically vigilant) when pursuing romantic-sexual possibilities because of the higher costs of producing offspring and of making a mistake in mate selection.[68] Men, on the other hand, can increase their chances of producing viable offspring by mating with more partners, which means that they should be more eager for sexual relationships and thus regret more when they fail to do so.

WAYS OF COPING: PERSONALITY DIFFERENCES IN CONTROL

We have seen how individual differences in "ways of seeing" shed light on the nature of personality—on personality differences in truth-seeking processes and the impact of those differences on what truth is found. Let us now consider how individual differences in "ways of coping" also teach us about personality—about personality differences in control processes that affect how goal pursuits are managed. While low-demand situations provide the clearest opportunities for revealing motivated preferences or biases in "ways of seeing," high-demand situations that tax or stress individuals provide the clearest opportunities for revealing the motivations and strategies underlying an individual's "ways of coping."[69] The coping literature suggests that it is differences in the ways people cope with stressful situations, rather than the nature of the stress itself, that is the best predictor of psychological and physical outcomes.[70]

Early psychoanalytic approaches emphasized the importance of exploring differences in "ways of coping" in order to understand personality, giving special attention to the defenses that individuals use to deal with conflict and frustration.[71] When unwanted or disturbing thoughts become conscious, an individual has to find some way to cope because such thoughts or impulses cannot be gratified in an acceptable manner. Following on her father's pioneering work,[72] Anna Freud, a pioneer in psychoanalysis in her own right, developed psychoanalytic ideas about the core *defense mechanisms*.[73] Importantly, she not only identified several new defense mechanisms but she also noted that individuals differ in their preferences for using some defense mechanisms more than others. Moreover, she argued that some coping defenses are more adaptive than others, and that particular defense "styles" are associated with specific pathologies.

In recent years, self-control and coping in human functioning has received increasing attention.[74] This attention is because, for a variety of reasons, self-control and coping are so difficult,[75] especially in demanding or stressful situations. For example, when attending to information about their personal liabilities, *repressors* prefer avoidant strategies such as denial and *sensitizers* prefer approach strategies such as rumination, but these different behaviors are greater following a recent failure than following a recent success.[76] As another example, although individuals with Type A personalities are not more hostile than individuals with Type B personalities in general, they are more hostile following frustration.[77]

In the following review, I have identified just a few high-demand situations to illustrate how "ways of coping" reveal personality: (1) failure or anticipated failure; (2) interpersonal rejection; and (3) conditions that tax self-regulatory capacity, such as delay of gratification or resisting temptation.[78] Before beginning this review, there are two general points I want to emphasize. First, when I refer to high-demand situations, I mean taxing or stressful situations, as well as situations involving trade-offs that produce conflicts in people. I am *not* referring to situations with strong motivational forces that are likely to induce the *same* motivational system in almost everyone, such as promotion–eagerness when your child smiles at you and gives you a hug. These *strong force* situations are less likely to reveal personality differences because they produce a similar control response in most people.

Second, personality differences *do* occur when the situation is not taxing, stressful, or conflictual, but any differences in "ways of coping" are less likely to be observed in less-demanding situations. For example, I described earlier in this book differences between strong promotion versus strong prevention individuals that occurred after success in task performance. Strong promotion individuals felt happier and were optimistic about future task success, whereas strong prevention individuals felt more relaxed but remained guarded about their future success (i.e., defensively pessimistic). These differences in responses to success reflect a control difference between managing the eagerness that sustains promotion versus the vigilance that sustains prevention. There is, then, a difference in managing what happens in these situations, but the psychological literature would not call it a difference in coping. Coping differences occur after failures, and the personality differences associated with them are typically more observable—hence my focus in this review on failures and other high-demand situations.

Ways of Coping With Failure or Potential Failure

When I discussed judged usability in my earlier description of knowledge activation principles, I mentioned that individuals have mental models or implicit theories about how the world works (e.g., what behavior is appropriate in a particular situation) that can create biases and preferences. These implicit theories can be conceptualized as meaning systems about the self and the world, and thus they contribute to establishing what's real (truth). With her colleagues, Carol Dweck, a major contributor to discovering the role of mental models in motivation, has studied two different implicit theories that individuals hold about the nature of intelligence—the *incremental* view that intelligence is malleable and can change through effort over time, and the *entity* view that intelligence is fixed and stable. These different implicit theories of intelligence are associated with differences in managing goal pursuits, with incremental theorists setting *learning* goals about developing their intelligence and entity theorists setting *performance* goals about validating or proving their intelligence.

There is evidence that the effects of these different implicit theories are especially likely to emerge in challenging situations that increase the threat of failure. When facing failure, incremental theorists typically have "mastery-oriented" strategies whereas entity theorists typically have "helpless-oriented" strategies.[79] In the research by Dweck and her colleagues, students were followed across the transition to junior high school, a transition where students generally encounter greater challenges and potential failures in their courses than they had experienced in elementary school. When the entity and incremental theorists began junior high school, there was no difference in their math grades. Subsequently, however, the math grades of incremental theorists steadily increased, while those of entity theorists decreased. This difference was due to the incremental theorists adopting more positive beliefs about effort and more mastery-oriented strategies than entity theorists when facing challenges and failure.[80]

Another example of personality emerging when coping with failure involves the difference in managing challenges that is associated with individuals' sense of personal efficacy—their belief that they can (or cannot) produce desired results by their actions. Self-efficacy beliefs can develop from our own experiences of overcoming obstacles, from observing others overcome obstacles, from social support situations that increase the likelihood of our succeeding, and from inner signals of self-efficacy such as feeling energetic.[81] Self-efficacy beliefs are typically context or task specific, with individuals having high self-efficacy in some domains but not others.[82] For example, there are life phase differences in self-efficacy that relate to daily challenges, such as older adults having higher self-efficacy than younger adults in dealing with excessive demands by family members to baby-sit their children.[83]

Once again, differences between individuals with high and low self-efficacy often emerge in high-demand situations. When challenges arise, individuals with higher self-efficacy will invest more time and effort to meet the challenge.[84] Whereas individuals with low self-efficacy tend to see more risks and ruminate about dangers and their own inadequacies when facing stressful situations, those with high self-efficacy are able to transform stressful situations to make them more controllable.[85] The high demands that adolescents face provide a good example of the role of self-efficacy in effective control. Adolescence is a period of heightened demands and increased potential for failure, both academically and interpersonally. Research has shown that those adolescents who have high efficacy beliefs about their ability to resist peer pressure achieve higher grades, have fewer behavior problems, and are more popular among their peers.[86]

Defensive pessimists exemplify yet another kind of managing style. They have a belief in a future reality of failure *if* they do not carry out specific activities in the present, such as failing an upcoming exam *unless* they study hard now. For them, the issue is not coping with an actual failure but coping with a potential future failure. Defensive pessimists are different from individuals with high or low self-efficacy. Those with high self-efficacy believe they are capable of performing actions that will produce a desired result. This belief can produce optimism about success in the relevant domain. Those with low self-efficacy believe they are not capable of performing actions that will produce a desired result. This belief can produce pessimism about success in the relevant domain. Defensive pessimists, on the other hand, believe that they will not succeed in a particular domain *unless* they carry out some specific activities now. They have better outcomes when they anticipate future failure, "expect the worse," rather than anticipating future success because they manage the potential future failure by vigilantly doing what's necessary now to avoid it.

Ways of Coping With Rejection

Rejection could be considered a kind of personal failure, but it can happen even when people do not experience it as a failure on their part. In cases of discrimination, for example, people have to cope with rejection that they believe is caused by the prejudice toward their group that others have. But rejection needs to be coped with whether it is experienced as a personal failure or not because it has special psychological significance for us given the importance of belonging.[87] Classic psychodynamic models of personality, such as those of Adler and Sullivan, highlight how problems in early relationships with significant others create the strategic biases and preferences that play out later in adult relationships.[88] More recent social-cognitive models of personality also address how people cope with interpersonal rejection and the threat of rejection. A prime example is the rejection sensitivity model of Geraldine Downey and her colleagues.[89]

This model posits that individuals who are high in rejection sensitivity anxiously expect, readily perceive, and tend to overreact with hostility to rejection, often producing the very rejection they most want to avoid—an unfortunate version of the self-fulfilling prophecy. Such individuals exhibit strategic biases in the ways they interpret and cope with social situations where rejection might occur. There is evidence, for example, that women high in rejection sensitivity show an automatic association between rejection and hostility,[90] having a readiness to identify hostility-related words that women low in rejection sensitivity do not have. Moreover, other evidence shows that this readiness is not simply due to hostility-related words being more chronically accessible for women who are high (vs. low) in rejection sensitivity, because the difference is revealed only after a rejection has occurred recently.[91]

When in a state of threat, individuals with high rejection sensitivity are highly motivated to detect threat-congruent cues, showing a higher startle response than individuals with low rejection sensitivity to rejection-themed art, but not to other images.[92] This startle response reflects the activation of the defensive motivational system.[93] There is also evidence that people high in rejection sensitivity may respond differently depending on whether they think that ultimate rejection is preventable or not. When future rejection is perceived as possible but not irrevocable, those high in rejection sensitivity can take extreme measures to adapt the self to the relationship in an attempt to prevent rejection. In one study, for example, males high in rejection sensitivity were willing to engage in ingratiating behaviors, such as doing menial tasks for group members and agreeing more with them, if earlier they had received from them e-mail messages that were only moderately cold rather than clearly rejecting.[94]

The coping strategies or tactics of persons high in rejection sensitivity also depend on their motivational orientation. A couple of studies examined how strong (vs. weak) prevention-oriented individuals who were high in rejection sensitivity coped with the anxiety of anticipated rejection and with the negative feelings produced by perceived rejection.[95] The studies found that those high in rejection sensitivity with a strong prevention orientation were more likely to use covert and passive forms of negative coping (vs. more overt and active forms) with perceived rejection. They expressed their hostility passively, such as by withdrawing their love and support from their partner, while at the same time suppressing direct acts of hostility such as yelling, presumably to prevent things from getting worse.

Ways of Coping With Temptation

There are also individual differences in how well people resist temptation and in the strategies they use to do so. And, once again, these differences are most clearly revealed when people are placed in a highly tempting situation and try to resist it. This is precisely the high-demand situation that Mischel created for his young participants in the "marshmallow test," where the children were presented with a treat available immediately plus the option of receiving an even better treat if they waited until the experimenter returned to the room after some delay.[96]

As I discussed earlier, different children used different strategies to resist the temptation to eat the treat available now to get the better treat later, and some strategies were more effective than others. Those children who used effective strategies, such as cognitive and attentional strategies, were also found to have effective school-related competencies years later as adolescents.[97] Recent research has found that some of the children who delay gratification best are able to flexibly shift their attention between the hot, consummatory features of the temptation and a more abstract, cool representation of it, which maintains the motivation to delay while reducing the frustration from delay.[98]

Another type of resisting temptation occurs when we are working on some task and a tempting diversion, such as overhearing that there is interesting "breaking news" on television, threatens to distract us from what we are supposed to be doing. In such circumstances, the temptation is functioning like an obstacle or interference on our path to the goal. We must oppose the interference by maintaining our attention on the task and being careful not to be distracted. This sounds like "a job for super-vigilance!," which means that a prevention orientation would be most effective. This is exactly what was found in a study that provided evidence that for coping with temptation, as for coping with rejection, there is a value–control relation involving strength of prevention orientation. Whether deciphering encrypted messages or solving math problems, participants with a stronger prevention orientation reported *better* performance and *greater* enjoyment when the task required (vs. did not require) vigilantly ignoring attractive, distracting video clips. The opposite was true for participants with a stronger promotion orientation.[99]

This last study demonstrates how there can be outcome benefits from using control strategies or tactics that are in the service of a particular orientation, in this case performance and enjoyment benefits from vigilant resistance to temptation that serves a strong prevention orientation—a *regulatory fit*. The implications of such regulatory fit can be extended to cultural differences in personality. Indeed, it provides a new perspective on where cultural differences in personality come from. Once again, it's the fit that counts.

CULTURE AND PERSONALITY

People have been interested in the relation between culture and personality for well over a century. The original question about culture and personality that interested them was, "What is the personality character of different nationalities?"

Unfortunately, this question led not just to relatively harmless answers like Germans are "scientific-minded," Italians are "passionate," and Canadians are "polite," but also to insulting answers like Germans are "heartless," Italians are "chaotic," and Canadians are "compliant"—answers that function like national stereotypes.[100] Answers like this go back at least to the middle of the 19th century, when renowned scholars such as Francis Galton, a pioneer in eugenics, felt confident to describe a nation's character. According to Galton, for example, the American character was "enterprising, defiant, and touchy; impatient of authority; . . . very tolerant of fraud and violence; possessing much high and generous spirit, and some true religious feeling, but strongly addicted to cant."[101]

The "national character" question had its heyday in the first half of the 20th century. The dominant answers to where "national character" comes from were psychodynamic, proposing that a culture's members would have a personality that was different from other cultures as a result of a distinct type of socialization.[102] As a "culture and personality" question, "What is the personality character of different nationalities?" came under increasing criticism in the 1950s for stereotyping the members of different cultures, and it continues to be a question treated with suspicion for this reason. Since the mid-1990s, however, there has been a renewed interest in "culture and personality" by a new generation of psychologists who are being guided by new questions, such as, "What are the basic psychological principles that underlie the interplay of personality and cultural processes?"[103]

As I stated in the beginning of this chapter, I believe that cultural differences derive from a relatively small number of universal principles that play out at different levels of analysis. Among them are motivational principles such as regulatory focus, regulatory mode, and regulatory fit. I believe that these universal principles of human functioning underlie both culture and personality, such as eager strategies being a fit with promotion and vigilant strategies being a fit with prevention, and this is true whether the promotion and prevention states are chronic (e.g., stable in a person or institutionalized in a society) or momentary (e.g., situationally induced). What varies across individuals and across cultures is the relative emphasis that each principle receives. The differences in emphasis play through the universal functions to produce personality and cultural differences. It is in this way that differences derive from universals. Let me now develop this proposal more fully.[104]

Difficulties in Relating Culture and Personality

To address any "culture and personality" question, the terms themselves need to be defined. How they are defined is critical to determining not only how culture and personality are related, but even *whether* they can be related conceptually.

Personality can be conceptualized in a way that is so intertwined with culture that the two become basically inseparable.[105] Alternatively, "culture" and "personality" can be defined in a way that makes them too separate to be related, as when personality is conceptualized as "nature" (i.e., biological heredity) and culture as "nurture."[106] An example of this kind of choice is the approach taken by Robert McCrae, a father of the influential five-factor theory (FFT) of personality, who argues that "One distinctive feature of FFT is the postulate that the basis of traits is solely biological: there are no arrows connecting culture to personality traits" (p. 5).[107]

Another difficulty in relating culture and personality has been the tendency to treat these concepts differently with respect to the area of psychology that is emphasized. When considering personality, most psychologists have emphasized stable individual differences in motivational variables (whether biologically based or not), such as needs, concerns, impulses, goals, trait dispositions, and so on, along with preferred ways of dealing with these motivational states. In contrast, when considering culture, most psychologists have emphasized cognitive variables, such as shared meaning systems or "knowledge traditions" involving a network of knowledge that is produced, distributed, and reproduced by a collection of interconnected individuals.[108] It is difficult conceptually to relate culture conceived mostly in cognitive terms to personality conceived mostly in motivational terms. It would be simpler to relate culture and personality if they were conceived in common terms, still maintaining their different levels of analysis. I believe that there are advantages in conceiving both personality and culture in terms of motivational principles, although I certainly recognize that a fuller picture of these concepts must also include common cognitive principles, such as those of knowledge activation (e.g., chronic accessibility) that have been fruitfully applied to understanding both personality and culture.[109]

Before I present my motivational proposal for relating culture and personality, however, I need first to address another difficulty with the tendency to conceive of culture as cognition but personality as motivation—a difficulty in how human evolution has been conceptualized.[110] Darwin's seminal work in the second half of the 19th century had a revolutionary effect on scientists' understanding of what it meant to be human.[111] Given that humans evolved from other animals, why not discover what it meant to be human by using the characteristics of non-human animals as a reference point? Darwinian logic, however, permitted two different kinds of conclusions—each associated with a different meaning of *evolve.*

One meaning of *evolve* is "to derive," which means to be formed by or made up of. Thus, one implication of Darwinian evolution is that if humans evolved from—*derived from*—non-human animals, they must share characteristics with non-human animals. But another meaning of *evolve* is "to develop," which means growth and elaboration of possibilities. Thus, a different implication of Darwinian evolution is that if humans evolved from—*developed from*—non-human animals in a direction of increasing complexity, then humans must have some special or distinct capacities that make them advanced in some way compared to other animals. The "derived from" implication suggests that psychologists should look for evidence of humans having *similar* characteristics to other animals that cause them to function in similar ways. In contrast, the "developed from" conclusion suggests that psychologists should look for evidence of humans having *new* characteristics that allow them to function in different and often more elaborate ways (i.e., less "primitive" ways).

What largely happened in psychology was that the "developed from" implication was chosen for the domain of cognition whereas the "derived from" implication was chosen for the domain of motivation. When it came to cognition, researchers in psychology, and other disciplines as well, were impressed by how humans' use of symbol systems and cultural artifacts, such as language and the arts, was so unusual and advanced compared to the cognitive expressions of non-human animals. When it came to motivation, however, what impressed people was how humans' needs, desires, and underlying self-regulation, such as the hedonic principle, were so much like those of other animals. This combination created an image of humans as having *the mind of a god and the motives of a brute.*

This image creates a difficulty for relating culture and personality because it requires relating the higher human functioning emphasized in cultural cognition, such as language, to the lower human functioning emphasized in personality motivation, such as the hedonic principle. The solution I prefer is to emphasize higher human functioning in *both* culture and personality. This requires considering how unique *human* motives developed.

Relating Culture and Personality Through Universal *Human* Motives[112]

To relate culture and personality, I believe the following criteria must be met: (1) to identify universal principles of human functioning that underlie both culture and personality; (2) to treat those common principles at different levels of analysis for culture and personality; (3) to define culture and personality in terms of those common principles in a manner that maintains the integrity of these distinct concepts; (4) to select specific psychological factors that, because of their survival value, are present in every culture and individual, although to varying degrees; and (5) to postulate how different cultures and personalities emerge from variability in the predominance of those specific psychological factors. I believe that all of these criteria can be met by relating culture and personality through universal motivational states that receive differential emphasis by different individuals and cultures. Let me now consider each of these criteria in turn.

IDENTIFYING UNIVERSAL PRINCIPLES THAT UNDERLIE CULTURE AND PERSONALITY AND TREATING THEM AT DIFFERENT LEVELS OF ANALYSIS

The culture and personality issue is a version of the following classic question in social psychology and personality: How do the variables of concern to personality psychologists relate to the variables of concern to social psychologists? The classic answer was that there were *separate* personality variables and social psychological variables that independently contributed to behavior, such that behavior was the product of both the person variables and the situation variables, often by co-constructing an event's psychological significance.[113] An alternative way is to identify *one set of general principles* for which *both* persons and situations are sources of variability.[114] In this way, "person" and "situation" variables can be understood in terms of the *same* general principles. Personality is re-conceptualized as just one source of variability in the functioning of psychological principles that also vary across momentary situations—as well as varying across age, groups, and culture.

Let me say a little more about what I mean by "source of variability." Imagine measuring the psychological states of a representative sample of individuals from various cultures who engage in different types of activities across time. When studying these states, personality psychologists would be interested in finding differences *across individuals* regarding which psychological states displayed stability over time. When studying the *same* states, social psychologists would be interested in finding differences *across situations* regarding which psychological states were induced by which type of situation. And, again, when studying the *same* states, cross-cultural psychologists would be interested in the differences *across cultures* regarding which psychological states were modal or typical among the members of a culture.

Note that in each case the same sample of psychological states of the same persons are being compared; the data are the same. What differs among the studies by personality psychologists, social psychologists, and cross-cultural psychologists is which kind of variability they are interested in examining. Because the same psychological states are involved, the same general principles can be used to describe and understand what is happening from a personality perspective, a social psychological perspective, and a cross-cultural perspective. Importantly, the fact that the same general principles can be applied across these different areas does *not* mean that these areas can be reduced to one level of analysis. The levels of analysis remain separate because what is being compared remains separate; that is, the data as units for comparison are being aggregated in different ways. Thus, both Criterion 1 and Criterion 2 for relating culture and personality can be met: universal principles that underlie both culture and personality can be identified (Criterion 1), and those principles can be treated at different levels of analysis for culture and personality (Criterion 2).

DEFINING CULTURE AND PERSONALITY

The next step is to define the concepts of culture and personality in terms of psychological states related to general principles, while at the same time maintaining the integrity of the concepts. In addition, higher human functioning should be emphasized for both culture and personality. In a recent paper I wrote with Thane Pittman,[115] we proposed that there were four fundamental developments of the human animal that together produced distinct *human* motives: (1) social consciousness or awareness that the significance of individuals' actions depends upon how others react to them; (2) recognizing inner states (e.g., beliefs, feelings, goals) as causal mechanisms that underlie outward behaviors (i.e., inner states as mediators); (3) mental time travel or relating present states to both past and future states; and (4) sharing reality with other people.

The development of the motives to comprehend, manage, and share inner states is basic to the development of both human culture and human personality. Indeed, culture is typically defined in terms that presuppose that the members of a culture comprehend, manage, and share inner states. The word "culture" derives from "cultura," which means cultivation, tillage. This etymology is reflected in the primary meaning of culture as representing the act of developing the intellectual and moral faculties, especially through education and training,[116] which presupposes the motives to comprehend, manage, and share inner states. Culture, then, can be defined as follows: *the members of a network of interconnected actors comprehending, managing, and sharing their inner states—their knowledge, feelings, moral standards, goals, and so on.*

In contrast to culture, personality has generally not been explicitly defined in a way that presupposes the motives to comprehend, manage, and share inner states. Most classic approaches to human personality, however, do assume that people take others' inner states into account, which is a requisite for the development of a Superego and the guilt or harsh self-criticism that its development can produce. For humans, more than for any other animal, taking others into account is necessary for personal survival. Children need adults to provide them with nurturance and security for many years, and this dependency requires getting along with others. To survive, people need to predict and influence (i.e., comprehend and manage) what others do, and what others do depends on their inner states—their thoughts, feelings, attitudes, goals, and so on. The social world of self and others that is perceived by people comprise inner states of thoughts, feelings, desires, and so on, and not simply observable behaviors.

And what people try to control or manage are not just the actions of self and others but the inner states of self and others—their thoughts, feelings, desires, and so on. For this reason, then, I define human personality as follows: *personality is the set of stable preferences and biases in the ways a person sees and copes with the outer world and the inner states of self and others.*

From this perspective, then, human culture and personality have in common the fact that people are motivated to comprehend, manage, and share the inner states of self and others. Within this commonality, however, there is a difference in emphasis for culture and personality. For culture, the emphasis is more on the processes and products of sharing among the actors of an interconnected network, especially sharing information and knowledge. For personality, the emphasis is more on the processes and products of comprehending ("ways of seeing") and managing ("ways of coping") self and significant others. Criterion 3 has now been met: to define culture and personality in terms of common principles in a manner that maintains the integrity of these distinct concepts. It is time to turn to Criterion 4: to select specific psychological factors that, because of their survival value, are present in every culture and individual, although to a varying extent.

REGULATORY FOCUS AND REGULATORY MODE AS UNIVERSAL SURVIVAL FACTORS

As I said earlier, a full picture of culture and personality would need to include cognitive factors like knowledge activation principles that are universal and contribute to survival. Especially given the nature of this book, I will emphasize motivational factors, and particularly those that I have already discussed—the regulatory focus principles of promotion and prevention, and the regulatory mode principles of locomotion and assessment. There are good reasons for emphasizing these principles.[117] First, there is substantial research both on how these self-regulatory principles function, strategically and tactically, and on the cognitive, affective, and behavioral consequences of their functioning. Second, promotion, prevention, locomotion, and assessment refer to motivational states that vary not only across individuals but across situations and across groups. To link personality to culture and culture to geographical/ecological factors, it is necessary to have motivational states that vary across different levels. Third, regulatory focus and regulatory mode are basic to all self-regulation. Let me expand on this third reason.

As I have discussed before, regulatory focus theory proposes that nurturance-related regulation involves a promotion focus whereas security-related regulation involves a prevention focus. Given that nurturance and security needs must both be met for survival, all persons have both the promotion and prevention systems available to them. For individuals to survive, each individual must be in a promotion state on occasion and in a prevention state on occasion, but how often an individual is in either state could vary greatly. Similarly, for cultures to survive, each culture must have at least some members in a promotion state on occasion and at least some individuals in a prevention state on occasion. How often or how many cultural members are in either state could vary markedly.

The regulatory mode orientations of locomotion and assessment present a similar case. When people self-regulate, they decide what they want that they don't currently have; they figure out what they need to do to get what they want; and then they do it. Two essential functions of self-regulation are captured here: *assessing* both the different goals to pursue and the different means to pursue them, and *locomoting* or "moving" from a current state to some alternative state. All major models of self-regulation contain some version of these two functions.[118] Because the functions of locomotion and assessment are both vital to all goal pursuits that are necessary for survival, all persons have both locomotion and assessment systems available to them. For both cultures and individuals to survive, locomotion states and assessment states must be present at least some of the time, but cultures can vary in how many of their members are in either state and individuals can vary in how often they are in either state.

I described in Chapters 9 and 10 the special significance of the period from 3 to 6 years of age for developing human motivation. This period is critical in the development of the human forms of regulatory mode and regulatory focus. Regarding what happens in regulatory mode during this period, I drew on the insights of Erik Erikson, who identifies it as a period of *initiative*—with children being "on the make," "attacking" a task for the sake of being active and on the move—which he explicitly related to *locomotion*.[119] He uses the example of walking, but he clearly means something broader because he describes children's curiosity and intrusion into the unknown during this period. Erikson also says that this is a period in which there is the danger that children will have a sense of *guilt* over what they are initiating, over the pleasure in attack and conquest. This is the period of critical self-evaluation, of conscience. Notably, such critical self-evaluation is a defining characteristic of the assessment mode for humans. Because Erikson describes this period as "Initiative *Versus* Guilt" [my italics], it highlights that for different children there could be more initiative or more guilt (i.e., more locomotion or more assessment). From a personality or a cultural perspective, this period could be the beginning of differences in the strength of, and relative emphasis on, the different regulatory mode orientations of locomotion and assessment.

This period between 3 and 6 years of age is also important to the development of the human form of regulatory focus. Given that a promotion focus is concerned with nurturance and growth and a prevention focus is concerned with safety and security, children before 3 years of age, as well as other animals, can have a promotion or prevention focus in their self-regulation. However, there is a unique development that occurs in children from 3 to 6 years of age that transforms the regulatory focus systems of promotion and prevention such that self-regulation is never the same again for children, and it differs from any other animal.

Children develop a new kind of social consciousness during this period by taking into account others' wishes and expectations for them. As I have described before, these standpoints become self-guides that function both as standards of self-evaluation and as desired end-states to be attained or maintained. For young children, the desired-end state is a shared reality with a significant other about what the child will ideally accomplish in the future (promotion ideals) or what the child's duties and responsibilities are (prevention oughts).

From socialization episodes involving different kinds of parent–child interactions, children learn to share what their significant others wish, expect, and demand of them (i.e., share others' inner states regarding them). These interactions can emphasize fulfilling promotion-focus ideals or fulfilling prevention-focus oughts.[120] By comprehending what significant others emphasize for them, by managing to fulfill those emphases, and by sharing the reality of those emphases, children during this period begin the process of creating what will become personality differences and cultural differences.

Criterion 4 has now been met. I have selected locomotion, assessment, promotion, and prevention as specific psychological factors that, because of their survival value, are present in every culture and individual, although to varying degrees. I have discussed the distinctive human form of these universal orientations for personality and culture in terms of their involving the comprehending, managing, and sharing of inner states. I propose that it is variability across individuals and across cultures in these motivational states that provides an important link between culture and personality. I turn now to Criterion 5, the final criterion that must be met in order to relate human culture and personality: to postulate how cultural variability and personality variability in these motivational factors can influence one another.[121]

Culture and Personality's Bidirectional Influence From Motivation

I first need to consider the background context in which this influence occurs. Undoubtedly biological differences among people are part of the story, but I prefer to begin at a higher level of analysis. Specifically, I prefer to begin with ecological or geographical factors within a region whose influence on broad economic and social forces places demands, sets constraints, and provides opportunities for people who live in the region. An excellent illustration of this general approach is provided in Richard Nisbett's book *The Geography of Thought: How Asians and Westerners Think Differently . . . and Why.*[122] Nisbett proposes a schematic model of influences that move from ecology to economy to social structure to attention and so on. Significantly, his model posits bidirectional influences, as do I, and we both consider social processes to be critical. Where Nisbett's model and my proposal differ is his emphasis on cognitive processes and my emphasis on motivational processes.

I propose five steps in the bidirectional influence between culture and personality. The first three steps concern how cultures influence which personalities emerge among the cultural members to become the modal personalities. The last two steps concern how those modal personalities that emerged within a culture then influence the culture.

In Step 1 of my proposal, I hypothesize that the humans living in a particular region have specific demands, constraints, and opportunities. In response to these environmental forces, they cooperate with one another to survive, and this cooperation involves comprehending, managing, and sharing their inner states. Importantly, these inner states include the orientations of promotion, prevention, locomotion, and assessment. Step 2 of my proposal concerns the fit between the environmental forces and the different motivational orientations with their preferred strategies of goal pursuit. I hypothesize that the extent to which promotion, prevention, locomotion, or assessment states contribute to surviving environmental forces depends on the nature of the specific forces in a particular region. For example, promotion eagerness would be more effective than prevention vigilance in an environment that is generally safe and provides opportunities for growth and improvement. However, the opposite would be true for an environment where it is difficult to maintain safety and failures to be careful are highly costly; now prevention vigilance would be more effective.

Step 3 of my proposal concerns truth and control working together—cultures going in the right direction to suit their environmental forces. I hypothesize that, based upon their experiences, the network of interconnected actors in a particular region comprehend and share an understanding (a *truth* that is not necessarily conscious) that some motivational states need to be emphasized more than others in order to best manage (i.e., *control*) their environmental forces. Together over time, they construct social structures and institutions—a culture—that increase the likelihood that the cultural members will be in some motivational states more often than other states. I propose that it is this cultural solution to the environmental forces that determines which personalities will become modal within a culture. Again, all motivational states will occur within each culture and within each person at least some of the time, but within this dynamic of variability, cultural forces will press for the culturally preferred motivational states. As a function of their roles and positions within the culture's social structures and institutions, some individuals will be exposed more often than others to these cultural forces, and thus their self-regulation will more often involve an emphasis on the culturally preferred motivational states. Within this dynamic flow of culturally preferred motivational states, an order of modal personalities will emerge.[123]

The next two steps describe how the personalities that emerge within a culture influence the culture. Regulatory fit plays a major role in the influence of emergent personalities on culture. In Step 4 of my proposal, I hypothesize that individuals will naturally prefer to pursue goals in the manner that fits their dominant motivational orientations (i.e., their personality). These goal-pursuit strategies will become chronically preferred procedures for getting along in the world (i.e., control preferences). Given that some motivational orientations have emerged as modal personalities in a particular culture, the goal-pursuit strategies preferred by those orientations will become *descriptively normative* because they will be the strategies that most members of the culture use most of the time.[124]

In Step 5, the final step in my proposal, I hypothesize that those members of a culture who most possess the modal personalities within the culture are likely to become more influential within that culture. This would occur because those members of the culture who most possess the modal personalities will be more prototypical within their culture, and research has shown that group members who are perceived to be highly prototypical of the group are more influential.[125] As they become leaders within the group, they will have influence on which goal-pursuit strategies are used by the other group members. They will prefer the goal-pursuit strategies that fit their personal motivational orientations (i.e., their personalities) not only because those strategies will "feel right" but also because they will experience them as morally "right," given the tendency for people to transfer regulatory fit experiences to moral experiences.[126]

In this way, those goal-pursuit strategies will become *prescriptively normative* in addition to being descriptively normative. Similarly, leaders could influence the identity of a group, including influencing which group-defining strategies are adopted by its members. This in turn would affect how the group members behave. There is evidence, for example, that promotion and prevention strategies, as reflected in group mottos (e.g., "An ounce of prevention is worth a pound of cure"), can become part of the identity of a group—a *collective* regulatory focus—and then influence the behavior of individual group members.[127]

Steps 4 and 5 describe how the modal personalities that emerge within a culture can influence which descriptive and prescriptive norms develop within that culture. These norms will become part of the customs and practices of that culture, which will then have their own influence on cultural members through culturally defined situations that press for using the goal-pursuit strategies associated with these norms. Given such bidirectional influences, the impact within a culture from using particular goal-pursuit strategies will be considerably greater than one would expect from just the presence of the modal personalities *per se*.

Criterion 5 has now been met: describing how cultural variability and personality variability in motivational factors can influence one another. First, the network of interconnected actors in a particular region share an understanding that some motivational states need to be emphasized more than others in order to best manage their environmental forces, and thus they construct social structures and institutions—a culture—that increase the likelihood that the cultural members will be in some motivational states more often than other states. It is this cultural solution to the environmental forces that determines which personalities will become modal within a culture, which is how cultural variability affects personality variability. Second, the modal personalities that emerge within a culture influence which descriptive and prescriptive norms develop within that culture—norms that underlie the customs and practices of that culture—which is how personality variability affects cultural variability.

Cultural Differences in Big Five Traits and Self-Esteem From Regulatory Fit Universals

It is time to return to the proposal with which I began this section of the chapter: *Cultural differences derive from universals.* Is there evidence to support this proposal? Indeed there is. Antonio Pierro, Arie Kruglanski, and I,[128] with the assistance of many other researchers, examined the relations between promotion, prevention, locomotion, and assessment orientations and the following widely studied personality dimensions: *self-esteem*[129] and the Big Five trait dimensions of *agreeableness, extraversion, conscientiousness,* and *openness.*[130] We conceptualized these personality dimensions as ways of getting along in the world, as different *manners of goal pursuit.*[131] As such, we predicted that they would function as strategic conduits or channels, which would have regulatory fit or non-fit with each of the four motivational orientations. The purpose of our research was as follows: (1) to demonstrate that there are cross-cultural *differences* in the predominance of promotion, prevention, locomotion, and assessment orientations; (2) to show that there are cross-cultural *universals* in how these motivational orientations relate to self-esteem, agreeableness, extraversion, conscientiousness, and openness; and (3) to examine whether combining the cross-cultural *differences* from (1) with the cross-cultural *universals* from (2) could yield previously identified cross-cultural differences, such as self-esteem generally being higher in the United States than in Japan.

To measure promotion, prevention, locomotion, and assessment, the studies used the Regulatory Focus Questionnaire[132] and the Regulatory Mode Questionnaire,[133] each of which has been shown to possess good reliability, validity, and psychometric properties. The nations for which we obtained measures of promotion and prevention and all of the personality dimensions were Australia, India, Israel, Italy, Japan, and the United States. The nations for which we obtained measures of locomotion and assessment and all of the personality dimensions were India, Israel, Italy, Japan, and the United States.[134] All of the participants were college students.[135]

As hypothesized, we did find clear cross-cultural *differences* in the predominance of promotion, prevention, locomotion, and assessment orientations. Across all the nations for which promotion and prevention scores were obtained, Japan was significantly different from all other nations (except India) in its higher percentage of *predominant prevention individuals* (i.e., individuals with prevention being higher than promotion). In contrast, the United States and Italy were significantly different from all other nations in their higher percentage of *predominant promotion individuals* (i.e., individuals with promotion being higher than prevention). Across all the nations for which locomotion and assessment scores were obtained, Japan was significantly different from all other nations in its higher percentage of *predominant assessment individuals* (i.e., individuals with assessment being higher than locomotion). In contrast, Italy was significantly different from all other nations in its higher percentage of *predominant locomotion individuals* (i.e., individuals with locomotion being higher than assessment).

As hypothesized, there were also clear cross-cultural *universals* in how promotion, prevention, locomotion, and assessment relate to the strategic conduits of self-esteem, agreeableness, extraversion, conscientiousness, and openness.[136] For regulatory focus, we found in every nation that stronger *promotion* was positively related to higher *self-esteem, extraversion,* and *openness.*[137] In contrast, in every nation stronger prevention was either unrelated or negatively related to these personality characteristics. Both stronger promotion and stronger prevention were related to higher *conscientiousness* in every nation.[138] Generally speaking, but less universal, both stronger promotion and stronger prevention tended to be positively related to higher *agreeableness.* For regulatory mode, we found in every nation that stronger locomotion was positively related to higher *self-esteem, extraversion, conscientiousness,* and *agreeableness.*[139] In contrast, stronger assessment in every nation was either unrelated or negatively related to these personality characteristics. Both stronger locomotion and stronger assessment were positively related to higher *openness* in every nation.[140]

I believe that the universal relations we found between particular motivational orientations (e.g., promotion and locomotion) and specific personality characteristics (e.g., self-esteem and extraversion) derive from specific personality characteristics sustaining particular orientations; that is, they derive from regulatory fit.[141] Let us consider how this would work, with *extraversion* as an initial example. In every nation we found that stronger promotion, but not stronger prevention, positively related to higher extraversion. We also found that stronger locomotion, but not stronger assessment, positively related to higher extraversion. Individuals who are high in extraversion are enthusiastic, carefree, sociable, and eager to meet new people. This strategic way of getting along in the world would clearly sustain a strong promotion orientation that prefers an eager manner of goal pursuit. Because extraverted responses to social situations also support entering and engaging in situations, enthusiastically moving ahead without hesitation or care, this manner of goal pursuit would also sustain a strong locomotion orientation.

Let us now consider the personality characteristic of *self-esteem*. Cross-cultural differences in levels of self-esteem, or positive views of the self, have received considerable attention in the literature. Studies have found, for example, that people in the United States and Eastern Asian nations like Japan differ in their level of self-esteem—differ in their self-evaluative "ways of seeing."[142] Generally speaking, level of self-esteem is higher in the United States than Japan. One explanation for this difference is that self-esteem itself is emphasized more in an independent (or individualistic) culture like the United States than in an interdependent (or collectivistic) culture like Japan.[143] I believe there is an alternative explanation, however: I believe that this difference derives instead from a cross-cultural *difference* between the United States and Japan in modal promotion, prevention, locomotion, and assessment personalities, combined with cross-cultural *universals* in how these motivational orientations relate to self-esteem as a "way of seeing" that fits promotion and locomotion but not prevention and assessment.

As I have discussed in earlier chapters, studies testing regulatory fit have found that for strong promotion-oriented individuals, anticipating goal-pursuit success is a fit (by increasing eagerness) whereas anticipating failure is a non-fit (by decreasing eagerness). In contrast, for strong prevention-oriented individuals, anticipating goal-pursuit success is a non-fit (by decreasing vigilance) whereas anticipating failure is a fit (by increasing vigilance). Given this, strong promotion-oriented individuals should tactically boost their optimism and confidence to remain eager, whereas predominant prevention individuals should tactically dampen their optimism and confidence to remain vigilant. These differences in adaptive, tactical self-regulation would result in self-esteem being higher for strong promotion-oriented individuals than strong prevention-oriented individuals.

Similarly, it makes sense that strong locomotion-oriented individuals would tactically use high confidence about the future to get themselves moving forward, whereas strong assessment-oriented individuals would tactically engage in critical, post-action assessments to do what's right the next time. These differences in tactical self-regulation would result in self-esteem being higher for strong locomotion-oriented individuals than strong assessment-oriented individuals.

What are the implications of these regulatory fit relations for the self-esteem levels of different nations, such as the United States and Japan? Our research found that both countries have some individuals who are predominant promotion, some who are predominant prevention, some who are predominant locomotion, and some who are predominant assessment. However, the relative distributions of predominant orientations (i.e., the modal personalities) in the United States and Japan are different. The United States has more predominant promotion and predominant locomotion individuals than Japan; Japan has more predominant prevention and predominant assessment individuals than the United States. Given the universal relations between these different orientations and self-esteem, with self-esteem being higher for predominant promotion and locomotion than predominant prevention and assessment, self-esteem should be higher overall in the United States than Japan. This is what we found in our research and what others have found as well. But what is novel from our findings is the possibility that, rather than arising from self-esteem working differently in "independent" United States versus "interdependent" Japan, this difference arises from a cross-cultural difference between United States and Japan in modal personalities *combined with* cross-cultural *universals* in how self-esteem fits the motivational orientations of these personalities.

What I am proposing is that regulatory fits (vs. non-fits) between specific ways of getting along in the world—"ways of seeing" and "ways of coping"— and particular motivational characteristics function as universals that, when combined with differences among cultures in their predominant or modal motivational orientations, yield cultural differences in personality. Regulatory fit could contribute to cultural differences in another way as well that I should also mention. Not only is there fit and non-fit between individuals' chronic motivational orientations and the ways in which they see and cope with the world, there is also fit and non-fit between individuals' chronic orientations and the ways of dealing with the world that are demanded by the *modal situations* in which they find themselves in a particular culture, including the normative demands of other people about how to behave.[144]

Predominant promotion individuals in Japan, for example, might prefer to sustain their eagerness by boosting their self-esteem, but they are likely to find themselves, at least some of the time, in situations where humility and self-effacement are demanded. These situations could create a situational non-fit that would make them "feel wrong" about their eagerness and weaken their engagement, thereby diminishing their quality of life. Regulatory fit and non-fit relations between individuals' chronic orientations and the behavioral demands of the surrounding culture, as embodied in traditional situations, need to be taken into account when predicting individual and cross-cultural differences in life experiences. Indeed, there is recent evidence for such a personality–culture fit.[145] In a study of 28 different societies, the well-being of individuals with predominant promotion or predominant locomotion was found to be higher when there was a fit between their particular personality and the cultural situation, or "cultural norm," created by the aggregate societal personality.

The interactions between chronic individual orientations with their preferred ways of seeing and coping and the ways of seeing and coping that are induced by institutionalized situations are also important to consider at levels of analysis lower than a nation's culture. A management team in a company can have its own lower-level "culture," as can a family or school classroom. Even at these lower levels, there are interactions between different chronic situations and the "ways of seeing" and "ways of coping" that are associated with different individuals' chronic predispositions. Indeed, personnel could be selected or chronic situations created that would create a fit for individuals in a company team or classroom. This could be done as an effective approach to managing others' motives. I consider this precise possibility in the next chapter.

Managing Motives Effectively

Working Backwards From What You Want

I mentioned earlier in this book that I taught a class in motivation years ago for the Columbia Business School's Senior Executive Program. At the beginning of the class, I asked the executives to answer the following two questions:

1. "As a manager, what are the most effective ways to motivate others?"
2. "If you could influence the motives of those you manage, which motives would you want *them* to have?"

Not surprisingly, their answers to the first question were mostly about using incentives; that is, telling others that they would receive future benefits from performing well. Among the incentives that were mentioned, the most common were material rewards like salary or bonus incentives, but social rewards like praising accomplishments or public recognition were also frequently mentioned.

My guess is that the use of incentives would be the most common answer for other business managers, as well as for teachers, coaches, parents, and other "managers" more generally. After all, the classic psychological research on motivation was all about the effects of different kinds of incentives. And the advice available today in the media is still all about incentives, as in the message I came across on the Internet, "Incentives are everywhere." This message came with the advice to managers to find *that* particular incentive that motivates each specific subordinate they are working with. And the advice includes using the threat of punishment, such as the threat of firing subordinates, as well as the promise of reward.

Given that incentives involve anticipated rewards and punishments, their logic is *working forward*. The first step is to find the particular incentive that motivates a specific subordinate. This incentive will then create motivation in the present that can later be directed toward whatever future desired outcome is wanted. These managers first think about what a subordinate wants—"What should I offer now that would be motivating?" Then they offer that incentive to their subordinate contingent on that subordinate behaving a certain way now. The concept of motivation that typically underlies this managerial approach is that motivation is "energy (to be directed)." Once the energy has been created in the present from offering the incentive, it can be directed toward some future destination later: working forward from the present incentive-induced energy to whatever future destination is wanted. Indeed, all of these business executives who said incentives are the most effective way to motivate others also gave some version of "energy (to be directed)" to describe motivation itself. As I mentioned in Chapter 2, they believed that what they needed to do was use the appropriate incentive to get a subordinate "energized," "fired up," and then the subordinate could be directed to whatever destination was wanted.

According to this approach to managing others, all that really matters is that the anticipation of the future desired result "energize" or "fire up" the subordinate in the present. The energy itself is "all-purpose" and can be directed to any destination. The source of the energy does not matter—it could be a monetary bonus, social recognition, or job security. And once the incentive—whatever it is—has done its job of energizing the subordinate, the subordinate can be directed to whatever destination the manager wants.

There is a serious problem with the "working forward, energy (to be directed)" approach that underlies the popularity of using incentives as motivators. To illustrate the problem, let me give you an example of a management failure that a colleague of mine at Columbia Business School told me about.[1] A student in his Executive MBA course was the CEO of a company that employs drivers. The drivers had been told that they would receive a monetary bonus at the end of the year if they had a safe driving record. This bonus plan did not work—the safety record did not improve. Why not?

Perhaps the bonus plan did not work because the monetary bonus was not valued by the drivers (i.e., a low-value incentive) or they did not believe that they could finish the year with a safe driving record (i.e., a low-expectancy incentive). Perhaps the reward was too temporally distant; that is, the drivers would have to wait a year before receiving the bonus for having a safe driving record. Possibly, the bonus would have worked if it had a shorter time delay. According to standard reward or reinforcement principles, a shorter delay should be a more powerful motivator. But I don't think the problem was reward delay or low-value incentive or low-expectancy incentive. What, then, was the problem for the CEO's bonus plan? I believe the problem was that the CEO used a working forward model rather than a working backwards model.

WORKING BACKWARDS FROM WHAT YOU WANT

Instead of "working forward" with some incentive, I propose that managers work in the opposite direction. When managing someone, begin by asking yourself *what you want*. Begin with *your* preferred final destination, *your* desired result, for that person. Then work backwards to identify a *fit* between that person's goal orientation and manner of goal pursuit that would naturally produce the kinds of behaviors needed to reach the destination. Using this "working backwards" approach, let's reconsider the CEO's "safe driving record" problem.

According to the "working backwards" approach, the CEO (who was male) should begin with what he wants—that by the end of the year the company drivers will have a good safety record. Now, *working backwards*, he should ask himself which motivational state the drivers could have that would naturally lead to driving safely. One obvious answer is "vigilance." If the drivers were motivated to be careful when driving, making an effort to avoid mistakes (i.e., behavioral tactics that serve vigilance), then it is likely that they would drive more safely. What can the CEO do in order to ensure that the drivers will be in a vigilant motivational state? *Working backwards* again, the CEO should ask himself what motivational orientation would make it more likely that the drivers would naturally prefer to be vigilant. Recall that people prefer to be vigilant in their goal pursuits when they have a prevention orientation; vigilance *fits* prevention. *Working backwards* again, the CEO should ask himself, "What could be done, then, to induce a prevention focus in the drivers?"

There are different ways that a prevention focus could be induced in the drivers. Which method the CEO chooses to use should depend on his other goals. Imagine, for example, that the CEO believed that it would be fair if drivers with a good safety record finished the year financially better off than drivers without a good safety record. This fairness goal would have been met by the original bonus plan, but it was a *gain/non-gain* contingency plan that would induce a *promotion* focus rather than a prevention focus, and it is prevention vigilance that is needed for safe driving rather than promotion eagerness. What the CEO could have done instead is announce that money has been set aside for each driver in an account that will become active at the end of the year. The money will be maintained in the account (i.e., a non-loss) if at the end of the year the driver has a good enough safety record, but will be removed from the account (i.e., a loss) if at the end of the year the driver does not have a good enough safety record. This is a *non-loss/loss* contingency plan. It would induce a prevention focus, increase vigilance, and support safe driving behaviors.

In the actual story, the CEO did change the bonus plan after it had failed to improve the safety record. Instead of rewarding a good safety record with a bonus, the CEO switched to fining drivers who had an accident (despite the cost of an accident being recovered from the insurance company). This is another form of *non-loss/loss* contingency and should also induce a prevention focus, increase vigilance, and support safe driving behaviors. And, in fact, it did work better than the original bonus plan. The drivers' safety record improved. It should be noted, however, that this negative version of a non-loss/loss contingency, which is about stopping a future negative state (i.e., being fined), could be perceived as being unfair and lower morale. For this reason, an alternative positive version of *non-loss/loss* contingency (i.e., not losing the money set aside for safe driving), would be preferable because drivers would perceive it as a fairer policy.

The "working backwards" approach to managing does not assume that there is some "all-purpose energy" that can simply be directed toward a desired destination. Instead, it makes the following three assumptions: (1) There are different strategic motives that support attaining different valued outcomes (e.g., being eager supports creative outcomes; being vigilant supports safety outcomes); (2) Different strategic motives are a fit or a non-fit with different goal orientations (e.g., promotion–eager fit and prevention–vigilant fit vs. promotion–vigilant non-fit and prevention–eager non-fit); and (3) Different conditions induce different goal orientations (e.g., gain/non-gain conditions induce promotion; loss/non-loss conditions induce prevention). And, importantly, the "working backwards" approach is not restricted to the variables associated with promotion versus prevention orientations. It can also be applied to locomotion versus assessment orientations, fun versus important orientations, need for closure orientations, and so on, with different strategic motives being a fit or a non-fit with these different orientations. For example, when making a choice among different options, a strategy of critically comparing all of the features of all of the different options is a fit for an assessment orientation but a non-fit for a locomotion orientation. Or, for an activity that is considered important, engaging in a serious manner is a fit whereas engaging in an enjoyable manner is a non-fit.

It is critical to work backwards rather than forwards because, otherwise, a plan could be instituted that does, indeed, create a strong motivational state (i.e., high "energy") but a state that naturally prefers behaving in ways that work *opposite* to what is needed. This was clearly illustrated in the example of a bonus plan that can create "high energy" from stronger eagerness but works opposite to the vigilance that is needed to improve safety.

What About the Folly of Rewarding A, While Hoping for B?

I believe that the failure of the CEO's bonus plan was a failure from his working forwards with incentives rather than working backwards from what he wanted. I do not believe the failure was because the reward was delayed too long or the reward had low incentive value or low expectancy value. However, there is another possible way that the incentive might have failed that I have not yet discussed: perhaps the bonus plan was really rewarding something other than having a safe driving record. Let me consider this possibility in more detail because it is often used as an explanation, or an excuse, for when the use of incentives fails.

In the area of business management, there is an "Academy Classic" paper by Steven Kerr called "On the folly of rewarding A, while hoping for B."[2] The paper describes cases in which people use an incentive system that is faulty and they end up rewarding and increasing a behavior A rather than the behavior B they wanted to reward and increase. Is this why the CEO's bonus plan failed? Was the failure of the bonus plan just another example of "the folly of rewarding A, while hoping for B"? I don't think so. Driving safely was clearly the behavior that the plan rewarded with a bonus. The drivers *were* given a clear contingent reward for the "hoped-for" behavior of driving safely. Thus, the problem with the CEO's bonus plan was *not* the problem raised by Kerr. But let's consider one of Kerr's own examples—rewarding professors.

According to Kerr, society wants university professors to give substantial time and attention to their teaching but instead creates an incentive system that rewards professors for doing research and publishing scholarly papers. Given the incentive system, it is rational for professors to concentrate on their research at the expense of their teaching. In this example, the incentive system in universities is not working as society hoped it would. Is this because there is a problem with the "working forward, energy (to be directed)" approach that underlies the use of incentives as motivators? Not according to Kerr. He proposes instead that the problem is that the right incentive has not been used. He describes the problem as follows:

> "Rewards for good teaching are usually limited to outstanding teacher awards, which are given to only a small percentage of good teachers and usually bestow little money and fleeting prestige. Punishments for poor teaching are also rare."[3]

According to this framing of the problem, what universities need to do is give more professors more awards that bestow more money for good teaching, sustain longer the public recognition associated with these awards, and introduce punishments for poor teaching. Would this work?

It is probably true that new teaching award incentives would increase teaching motivation, thereby increasing the "energy" associated with teaching. But what type of motives would be induced? The new monetary and recognition gains from teaching are likely to induce a promotion focus. Professors would eagerly pursue the new awards. To receive the awards, they would have to meet some standard set for "good teaching." This standard would have criteria, such as student course ratings. The professors would work hard to fulfill the criteria. For example, they would be responsive to the expressed concerns and interests of the students. They would do what is needed to receive high ratings from the students. Responsiveness to students would become a means to the end of receiving high ratings rather than being an end in itself. The teaching would be about fulfilling the criteria, about getting high student ratings, rather than being about what the students learn. Is this what is meant by "responsible teaching"? Would these motives create the kind of teaching that society wants?

What about the effects of introducing punishments for poor teaching? Doing so would introduce a prevention focus. A prevention focus could reduce creative thinking in the classroom, thereby shifting the teaching even further from what society really wants. Moreover, the prevention focus motivation induced by punishing poor teaching could conflict with the promotion focus motivation induced by the good teaching awards. The "energy" notion includes the idea that adding new incentives will further increase motivation; in this case, the energy already created by the good teaching awards would be increased even further by punishing poor teaching. And, supposedly, all this energy could be directed toward the valued destination. But motivation doesn't work like that. Instead, what would be created is conflict between different motivational systems that have different concerns and different strategic preferences.[4]

Rather than introducing stronger incentives for teaching, what is needed first is to determine what exactly society wants with respect to professors' teaching. This first step is critical. Only when we know what society wants can we begin the process of working backwards to determine which strategic motives would naturally support that valued desired outcome. Then the backward process would continue from determining which strategic motive is needed, then identifying which goal orientation that strategy fits, and finally to the conditions that induce that goal orientation.

Imagine that society wants professors both to teach students to be critical thinkers and to provide a model of critical thinking in their lectures through their discussions of alternative viewpoints and their presentation of evidence for and against these viewpoints.[5] Working backwards, the motivation to make critical comparisons would support both modeling and teaching critical thinking, and making critical comparisons fits an assessment goal orientation. Thus, conditions that induce an assessment orientation are needed, such as conditions that emphasize the importance of truth, of establishing what's real. Providing lucrative awards for good teaching and punishing bad teaching place an emphasis on *value*, rather than an emphasis on *truth*. It could bring about effects that are *opposite* to what is wanted.

The Importance of Answering Question 2 First

You'll recall that the second question I asked the business students in my course was, "If you could influence the motives of those you manage, which motives would you want *them* to have?" The most common answers were that, as managers, they wanted their subordinates to be motivated to be creative and open to change ("think out of the box"); to be optimistic and enthusiastic; to build team spirit, have respect for others, be loyal to the team ("perform for the public good"); to have personal initiative and pride in personal achievement; and to keep learning and improving. Like parents regarding their children, these managers wanted their subordinates to have all of these "good" motives.

I have done this exercise several times and have found consistently that most managers do not consider *the relation between* their answer to Question 1 ("As a manager, what are the most effective ways to motivate others?") and their answer to Question 2. If you are a manager and your answer to Question 1 is that a bonus plan for personal achievement is an excellent way to motivate subordinates because it provides a strong incentive, how does this relate to your answer to Question 2 about what motives you want your subordinate to have? If among your answers to Question 2 your priority was that your subordinates be motivated to build team spirit and loyalty, then is your answer to Question 1—the use of a bonus plan for individual achievement—a good idea?

Once again, it is critical to work backwards; in this case, to work backwards from your answer to Question 2 *before* selecting an answer to Question 1. Working backwards and asking what the best way is to motivate your subordinates so that their motive will be to build team spirit and loyalty, it is evident that your bonus plan would need to reward the entire *team* performance rather than individual achievement. But working backwards could also make it clear that there are even better ways to build team spirit and loyalty than bonus incentives of any kind. Bonus incentives, after all, relate to having desired results (even when they are team results), which emphasizes value. But team spirit and loyalty may be more about managing what happens (control) or establishing a shared reality (truth) than about having desired results (value). Emphasizing truth and control variables, like improving information flow and feedback among team members, might be the better way to create a preference for building team spirit and loyalty.

What if your answer to Question 2 was that you wanted your subordinates to be motivated to keep learning and improving (i.e., mastery and intrinsic motives)? Once again, bonus incentives relating reward to performance would *not* be a good idea: such *contingent rewards* have been shown to *undermine* mastery and intrinsic motives. Working backwards, conditions that induce an orientation toward self-determination or autonomy might be the better way to create a preference for learning and improving.[6]

Consider the case of managing the success of a product. An initial decision might be whether product quantity or product quality should be emphasized. If the decision were to emphasize product quality, then the next decision might be whether to emphasize reliability or innovation. As a class exercise, I ask my students to imagine they are the CEO of an aircraft manufacturer (e.g., Boeing) who wants to improve product reliability. What would they do to motivate their subordinates to emphasize product reliability more? Once again, the students' most common solution is to introduce bonus incentives contingent on improving product reliability. We know that bonus incentives induce promotion eagerness. Does promotion eagerness support product reliability? No! Research shows that it supports product quantity, *not* quality, and product innovation, *not* product reliability.[7] Thus, this incentive plan would be a mistake because it would produce motives that work in the *opposite* direction to what is wanted. Working backwards from the product reliability the CEO wants, reliability is naturally preferred when someone is motivationally vigilant, and vigilance fits a prevention orientation. What is needed, then, are conditions that induce a prevention orientation.

Earlier I suggested that trying to *maintain* (not lose) money already set aside to reach some goal (e.g., driving safely; emphasizing reliability) is one way to induce a prevention orientation. But it is certainly *not* the only way. It is not necessary to use any form of incentive at all. What is needed is a condition that induces prevention, and there are non-incentive ways to do this. For example, a manager could emphasize each worker's obligation and responsibility to have a product that customers can rely on, which would induce prevention by priming *oughts*. Pride from fulfilling a duty will induce prevention and produce a natural preference for vigilance that would be served by increasing reliability. But note that it would not always be beneficial to emphasize pride from fulfilling a duty. This would be counterproductive if a CEO wanted to emphasize innovation rather than reliability because a preference for innovation is associated with promotion eagerness rather than prevention vigilance.

I am not suggesting that a bonus incentive is a bad thing. My point is that, in itself, a bonus incentive is neither inherently good nor bad. Depending on how it is framed (e.g., gain framing vs. non-loss framing), it will induce a particular orientation, such as the usual gain-framed bonus incentive inducing a promotion orientation. A promotion orientation, in itself, is also neither inherently good nor bad. It all depends on what end-state you as a manager want. If you want those you manage to emphasize quantity output or to emphasize an innovative, creative product, then inducing a promotion orientation with a gain-framed bonus incentive would be a good idea. If you also want your subordinates to be enthusiastic and optimistic, which many of my student managers said they did, then a gain-framed bonus incentive is a *very* good idea because enthusiasm and optimism fit promotion-related eagerness. But if you want your subordinates to emphasize reliability and defensive pessimism (e.g., believe that "only the paranoid survive," like Andy Groves, Intel's early CEO),[8] or if you want them to have strong analytic thinking rather than creative thinking,[9] then a gain-framed bonus incentive is *not* a good idea and a non-loss-framed incentive *is* a good idea.

The Need to Consider Motivations as a Whole, Working Together

The "working backwards" approach does not assume that an incentive is inherently good or bad. Rather, it assumes that its effectiveness or ineffectiveness depends on its motivational relation to what a manager wants. More generally, this approach assumes that it is important to consider motivations as a whole, working together. This means considering the conditions that induce a goal orientation and the strategy that fits that orientation. It means going beyond the kind of "pleasure and pain," "carrot and stick" thinking that underlies the use of incentives—that attaining pleasure and avoiding pain is energizing, and energizing others is all we need to do to get them to move to our desired destination. As previously described, this kind of thinking can result in managers using incentives that lead to the opposite of what they wanted.

It is true that the "working forward, energy (to be directed)" approach has the apparent advantage of being simple and straightforward compared to my "working backwards from what you want" approach. After all, the energy is considered to be "all-purpose" energy that is effective for everything. In contrast, the concept of motivational states working together as an organization that will be effective for some ends but not others is more complex. To make use of this concept, managers must know first precisely what they want and, by working backwards, find that specific organization of motivations that works for that particular desired result. This takes planning and motivational expertise regarding which conditions induce which orientation, which strategic motive fits which orientation, and which tactics serving which strategies will sustain the behaviors needed to yield the end-state that is wanted.

Yes, this definitely sounds more complicated than putting a battery in the Energizer bunny. But becoming a proficient golfer also takes more than just learning to swing hard. A proficient golfer knows that his or her swing might have to be changed when unusual circumstances prevail, such as gusty winds. This is true for effective management as well. Imagine that you are the CEO of a financial investment firm. Things have gotten out of hand lately, with your subordinates taking great risks that could spell disaster for the company. You want your subordinates to be more prudent, to be more conservative in their decisions. This sounds straightforward. Working backwards, you know that strategic vigilance, generally speaking, supports making conservative decisions. Thus, working backwards, what you need to do is set conditions to induce a prevention orientation for which vigilance is a fit.

But what if the current circumstances are unusual? What if you know that your subordinates feel that they and the company are *currently in trouble*? They experience their current state as a negative or "–1" rather than as a "0" or a "+1." Given this circumstance, it would be a mistake to induce a prevention orientation. As I discussed in Chapter 8, when the current state is "–1," prevention-related vigilance can produce *very risky* decisions rather than conservative decisions because prevention-focused people in a "–1" condition will do whatever is necessary, no matter how risky, to return to a satisfactory status quo ("0").

This example illustrates that, like a proficient golfer, effective managers need to take the current circumstances into account. They need to look at the full picture and then appreciate how motivations work together. The CEO mentioned above who wanted his drivers to improve their safety record and, after the bonus plan failed, began fining the drivers when they had an accident set the conditions to induce prevention and vigilance, which *was* effective in improving driving safety. But the policy of fining accidents could also have been seen as unfair, which would have unintended negative consequences. It might have been better to set conditions that induced prevention and vigilance without this potential downside.

There are usually alternative conditions that could be set in order to induce the orientation system needed to get what a manager wants. At the final step of working backwards to set the conditions to induce the preferred orientation system, the additional effects of each condition option should be considered as well. Fairness, for example, relates to doing what is right or correct and thus relates to truth (as well as value). As I discussed in Chapter 10, the organization of motivations is a structure that, as a whole, has its own motivational significance. The holistic significance of setting each condition option should be considered at this final step.

Admittedly, managing motives by "working backwards from what you want" may be more complex than using incentives to create some "all-purpose" energy that can then be directed. But, as we have seen, there is actually no neutral "all-purpose" energy from incentives to begin with. Instead, different incentives produce different motivational orientations, each having their own specific strategic preferences and their own directional forces. Simply ignoring this complexity isn't going to make the problem go away. The apparent simplicity of incentives and their to-be-directed "all-purpose" energy is an illusion.

Appreciating that motivations work together is a major advantage of the "working backwards" approach. When compared to using incentives, it has an additional benefit that I haven't highlighted yet. When managers use incentives, they are trying to motivate their subordinates to perform in some way because, by so doing, they will receive a future reward or avoid a future punishment. This is, in fact, more complex than it seems because those being managed have to continue to want the incentive over time, to believe that they can continue over time to do what is necessary to receive the incentive, and to trust that whoever is offering the incentive can and will follow through on the promised contingency. Any break in this contingency chain will doom the effectiveness of the incentive. Compare this to the case where those who are managed want, *by themselves*, to do exactly what is needed to reach the destination that their managers want for them. Like magic, they would carry out exactly those behaviors that end up at the destination. There would be no need for extrinsic incentives to perform in some particular way.

This *is* the magic of the "working backwards" approach because it takes advantage of the regulatory fit principle that inducing a specific goal orientation creates a *natural preference* for a particular strategic way of doing things. Once managers have worked backwards and found the right conditions to induce the orientation that creates the needed strategic preference, then all they have to do is set those conditions for their subordinates and let the motivational system play out. With the right conditions, the subordinates will have an orientation that prefers precisely the strategy (i.e., the strategy that fits) that yields the tactical behaviors that support reaching the destination managers want.

APPLYING REGULATORY FIT TO MANAGE MOTIVES EFFECTIVELY

In this section, I review evidence of how managing motivation effectively by setting regulatory fit conditions can enhance the task performance and satisfaction of company workers or students. I then discuss how regulatory fit can be used to increase openness to change and improve the consequences of change. I focus on change because how people deal with change has become a major issue in several life domains.

Regulatory Fit and Students' Task Performance and Satisfaction

There is an unfortunate tendency among some social scientists and laypeople to think of laboratory studies with college students as having little external validity, as being somehow not generalizable to everyday life. But this is not the case for many laboratory studies involving task performance. College students who participate in such studies are, after all, still students and the task performance that is under investigation is taking place at the college along with those tasks they regularly perform as students. Their researched performance does not count toward their course grades, but they take the tasks seriously and want to perform well—just as they do when they perform in their courses. The manager in these cases is the experimenter who is setting the conditions, but the manager role could be a college teacher. Thus, the results of such studies are directly relevant to learning about the conditions that can enhance task performance for college students.[10]

Some of the studies I discussed in previous chapters involved students, and so they warrant a second review here because they provide strong evidence of the utility of applying regulatory fit to managing motives effectively in students. One study (in Chapter 8) framed the instructions for performing an anagram task in four different ways: either in terms of promotion success ("If you find 90% or more of all possible words, you will get an extra dollar"), promotion failure ("If you don't find 90% or more of all possible words, you will not get an extra dollar"), prevention success ("If you don't miss 10% or more of all possible words, you will not lose a dollar"), or prevention failure ("If you miss 10% or more of all possible words, you will lose a dollar").[11] Note that these four different conditions distinguish not only between reward incentives (gain or not gain a dollar) and punishment incentives (lose or not lose a dollar), but also between whether a *promotion fit* or a *prevention fit* is created. Promotion success (a gain that increases eagerness) and prevention failure (a loss that increases vigilance) are a fit, whereas promotion failure (a non-gain that reduces eagerness) and prevention success (a non-loss that reduces vigilance) are a non-fit.

The study found that a reward incentive of gaining a dollar versus a punishment incentive of losing a dollar was *not* the distinction that affected performance. What mattered was the distinction between fit and non-fit. As compared to the two non-fit conditions, performance in solving the anagrams was higher for the students in the promotion framing condition when the framing was a potential gain–success (a fit) and for the students in the prevention framing condition when the framing was a potential loss–failure (a fit). Other studies have also found that performance is enhanced when promotion is combined with a potential gain–success and prevention is combined with a potential loss–failure. And this is especially true when the means for doing well are eager means for promotion (e.g., getting a good score by adding points) and vigilant means for prevention (e.g., getting a good score by stopping points from being subtracted).[12]

Studies like these use different framing of incentives as a method for creating regulatory fit. It is not the incentives themselves that matter but, rather, the way they are framed to create fit (or non-fit). But it is not necessary to use incentives at all in order to create regulatory fit. Regulatory fit can be created by framing the task itself in different ways that either fit promotion or fit prevention. Recall, for example, the study in which a math test was framed as being either diagnostic of strong math ability but non-diagnostic of weak ability (potential for gain) or diagnostic of weak math ability but non-diagnostic of strong ability (potential for loss). The participants varied in whether they dispositionally had a chronic promotion focus or a chronic prevention focus. Performance on the math test was better in the fit conditions (promotion/potential for gain; prevention/potential for loss) than in the non-fit conditions (promotion/potential for loss; prevention/potential for gain).[13]

I described in Chapter 6 how implementation strategies can themselves be framed as either eager ways or vigilant ways for carrying out the *when*, *where*, and *how* steps. Again, this framing has nothing to do with incentives. It takes advantage of the control element that implementation strategies represent and it frames them to create fit (and non-fit) with the promotion and prevention value orientations. The study found that college students were much more likely to turn in papers for extra credit when they were in the fit conditions (promotion/eager steps; prevention/vigilant steps) than when they were in the non-fit conditions (promotion/vigilant steps; prevention/eager steps).[14]

I also described in Chapter 8 how creating regulatory fit can enhance the performance of college students when fit is created by combining participants' "fun" or "important" orientation toward a task with "enjoyable" or "serious" task instructions about how to engage the task (i.e., how to treat it). Prior to the "documentary film" study,[15] for example, some students were given a "fun" orientation toward watching a documentary film whereas others had an "important" orientation. When they arrived at the study, half of the students were told that previous viewers had found the film enjoyable to watch and the other half were told that previous viewers had considered watching the film to be a serious thing to do. The central events of the film were better remembered by the students in the fit conditions (fun orientation/introduced as enjoyable; important orientation/introduced as serious) than those in the non-fit conditions (fun orientation/introduced as serious; important orientation/introduced as enjoyable).

These various studies demonstrate how creating conditions of regulatory fit can enhance students' task performance. There is also evidence that it can enhance students' task satisfaction. The "four-sided objects" study that I described previously is an example.[16] It showed that students who had been induced to have a promotion orientation had a more enjoyable time doing the task when they were instructed to eagerly rather than vigilantly look for four-sided objects on a sheet of paper with dozens of multiply shaped objects. Similarly, students induced with a prevention orientation had a more enjoyable time doing this task when they were instructed to perform it in a vigilant rather than an eager manner.

Using regulatory mode orientations rather than regulatory focus orientations, a recent study created regulatory fit for high school students in Italy.[17] The study examined students' satisfaction with their classroom as a function of how autonomy-supportive versus controlling their teacher was. The degree to which the students perceived their teacher as supporting their autonomy during class was measured with questionnaire items such as, "My teacher tries to understand how I see things before suggesting a new way to do things." The degree to which the students perceived their teacher as being controlling was measured with items such as, "My teacher constantly checks our preparation and knowledge of course materials." The study found that, overall, the students' satisfaction with their classroom was higher when the teachers' classroom style was more autonomy-supportive than controlling. This general effect of managing an environment is consistent with previous findings in work organizations in which employees' job satisfaction is positively related to their managers' autonomy-supportive style,[18] and it suggests that this may be generally true for school classroom settings as well.

This classroom study, however, also examined the fit between autonomy-supportive versus controlling classroom climates and the students' mode orientations. Students with a strong locomotion orientation want to maintain smooth action that reduces disruption and obstacles in their goal pursuits. Engaging in classroom activities with greater flow would be a fit for them. In contrast, students with a strong assessment orientation want opportunities for critical evaluation. Having teachers disrupt task flow for the sake of providing critical feedback would be a non-fit for locomotors by disrupting the flow, but it would be a fit for assessors by providing an opportunity for critical self-evaluation. Consistent with this prediction, the generally higher satisfaction for the autonomy-supportive than the controlling classroom was especially pronounced among students who were predominant locomotors (i.e., higher locomotion than assessment). And the *opposite* pattern was found for predominant assessors (i.e., higher assessment than locomotion). They were more satisfied with a *controlling* classroom climate than an autonomy-supportive climate.

Regulatory Fit and Employees' Task Performance and Satisfaction

The leadership style of business managers can also create either a fit or a non-fit that affects the task performance and satisfaction of their subordinates.

In Chapter 8, I briefly discussed research that examined such fit effects between regulatory mode and transformational leadership.[19] Transformational leadership is a style characterized by perseverance, a strong sense of purpose, a compelling vision, and the ability to motivate subordinates to persist in and maintain their goal pursuit.[20] Full-time employees working in a range of diverse industries rated their boss on transformational leadership.[21] They also reported how much they felt their boss motivated them to exert effort beyond the ordinary.

Generally speaking, the subordinates reported being more highly motivated when their boss had a strong transformational style of leadership. But this effect was stronger when the transformational style created a regulatory fit with the subordinates. Specifically, the motivational impact of bosses being transformational leaders was stronger when the subordinates were high (vs. low) locomotors because the compelling vision and strong sense of purpose of such leaders initiate action, and their perseverance is a driving force for maintaining steady movement—in short, a leadership style that sustains (i.e., fits) the orientation of strong locomotion subordinates. This fit effect of transformational leadership on strengthening the motivation of strong locomotion subordinates is important because other research has found that strongly motivated locomotors are more involved with their job, invest more effort in it, and perform better.[22]

Regulatory Fit and Openness to Change

Change is something that we make happen or that happens to us. An example of the former is when we commit ourselves to changing our lifestyle by exercising more, eating a healthier diet, stopping smoking, and so on. An example of the latter is when our job changes at work, which is becoming increasingly common in business settings. Being open to change, willing to change, is an important motive to manage. Which motivational orientations might prefer change over no change?

There is evidence across many cultures that openness, as a general personality trait, increases as certain orientations increase.[23] Specifically, openness increases as promotion, locomotion, and assessment orientations increase. This is because openness as a strategic way of getting along in the world serves (i.e., fits) each of these orientations *for different reasons*. Openness relates to being imaginative and curious, as well as having wide interests. Having wide interests and high curiosity would motivate engagement in a broad range of activities and provide new opportunities for advancement and for movement, which serves both a promotion orientation and a locomotion orientation. Imagination and curiosity also provide opportunities for making multiple comparisons and evaluations, which serves an assessment orientation.

These relations suggest that it might be possible to heighten people's openness to change by setting conditions that appropriately strengthen these particular orientations. In an early set of studies addressing this issue,[24] undergraduates' promotion strength was increased in a couple of ways prior to testing their openness to change. One study had the participants describe their hopes and aspirations (i.e., priming their ideals) before testing their willingness to exchange a new object for an old object they had received earlier. Another study gave participants the opportunity to gain points for good performance on a task before testing their openness to replace this task with a new one. Compared to conditions that strengthened a prevention orientation instead (i.e., priming oughts or losing points for poor performance), the students whose promotion orientation was strengthened were more open to change.

The impact of regulatory fit on employees' response to change in their business organization was recently investigated by Jill Paine in her doctoral dissertation.[25] The participants in the study were employees in a multinational energy company, an online marketing firm, a healthcare organization, and a law firm—all of which were undergoing or had recently undergone large-scale change. The employees' perceptions of their supervisors' messages about the organizational change were measured with respect to the messages' strength of "vision," such as how well they had articulated the compelling benefits of the change or had emphasized optimism about potential positive outcomes of the change.[26]

The study found that supervisors' messages with a stronger vision created a regulatory fit for subordinates with a strong (vs. weak) promotion orientation. For these subordinates, a stronger vision message was related to their being more strongly absorbed or engaged in their work (e.g., "I am immersed in my work"; "I get carried away when I am working"[27]) and their being more favorable to the change (e.g., "As a result of this change, people in this group/team find their work more interesting"; "As a result of this change, people's quality of life at work has improved"[28]). There was no such effect of a strong vision message for subordinates with a strong (vs. weak) prevention orientation.

There has also been research on the relation between employees' strength of locomotion orientation and their ability to cope with organizational change at work.[29] In separate studies with hospital nurses and with postal workers, the measure of coping with organizational change captured both coping with change (e.g., "The changes in this organization cause me stress," scoring *reversed*), and ability to adapt to change (e.g., "When dramatic changes happen in this organization, I feel I handle them with ease").[30] Both studies found that employees with stronger locomotion were much better able to cope with the changes that were happening at work. Given that change means movement and movement from state to state is something that high locomotors want, it is not surprising that they are especially able to cope with change—*they naturally prefer it.*

Another study with postal workers examined not only the relation between employees' strength of locomotion orientation and their ability to cope with changes at work but also the consequences of being better at coping with change.[31] This study used a longitudinal design to measure differences in the employees' strength of locomotion a month before measuring their ability to cope with work changes, and the consequences of their coping on job satisfaction and organizational commitment (e.g., "I would be very happy to spend the rest of my career with this organization"). Consistent with earlier findings, this study found that employees with a stronger locomotion orientation coped better with the organizational changes. And, importantly, their better coping predicted higher job satisfaction and higher organizational commitment afterwards. Thus, not only do high locomotors cope better with change because change fits their orientation, but this better coping also has benefits for them and their employer.

Thus far, I have cited studies demonstrating that individuals with a stronger promotion orientation or a stronger locomotion orientation are more open or willing to change and cope better with change. These results suggest that setting conditions that induce a promotion or locomotion orientation would benefit individuals who are undergoing change or are being asked to change. These studies, however, were not designed to create conditions of regulatory fit experimentally. Can such conditions be created that would increase willingness to change and commitment to change? Recent research suggests that they can, and that by so doing individuals with a strong locomotion orientation can become more willing and committed to change.

As part of her doctoral dissertation research,[32] Abigail Scholer investigated whether increased commitment to change can result from strengthening individuals' locomotion orientation during the deliberation phase of planning future actions. College students each chose a domain in their lives where they were considering making a change, such as stopping smoking or exercising more, but were currently ambivalent about whether to change or not. They were all asked to consider the pros and the cons of changing versus not changing from their current state to the new state. They also received one of two messages that differentially framed *what this deliberation process was about.* In the "movement" framing condition, the deliberation was about initiating movement and making progress, about adopting a "just do it" attitude to move out of their ambivalence toward change. In the "critical comparison" framing condition, the deliberation was about thoughtfully making comparisons and weighing options, about adopting a "do it right" attitude to solve their ambivalent state.

The students' continuing commitment to the goal to change in their chosen domain was measured three weeks after the deliberation process.[33] The study found a regulatory fit effect. For those students who had engaged in the deliberation process with the "movement" framing, those with a stronger locomotion orientation were more committed to the goal to change (a fit effect). In contrast, those with a stronger locomotion orientation were *less* committed to the goal to change if they had engaged in the deliberation process with the "critical comparison" framing (a non-fit effect). In fact, high locomotors in the "movement" framing condition had much stronger commitment to the goal to change—by 50%—than high locomotors in the "critical comparison" framing condition.

Importantly, this study also examined the role of two other possible factors that could increase commitment to change: the subjective value of the new state and self-efficacy beliefs. For the subjective value of the new state, participants had been asked, after their deliberation in the first session, how positive making a particular change would be for them, and how negative making a particular change would be for them. For self-efficacy, they reported how difficult they felt making the change would be and how certain they were that they'd be able to make the change. The study found that the beneficial effect of regulatory fit on commitment to the goal to change was independent of both subjective value of the new state and self-efficacy beliefs about the ability to carry out the change. Thus, regulatory fit can have a substantial motivational effect separate from the classic factors of value and expectancy.

Additional studies by Scholer were inspired by the insight that perhaps change need not be experienced as just a means to an end, but, rather, could be experienced as an end in itself—*change itself being what someone wants*. Scholer reasoned that this experience of change as an end in itself should come naturally to individuals with a strong locomotion orientation. She first tested this possibility by developing a measure that assessed the value of change in general. Respondents indicated on different scales how they would complete the sentence "Change *in general* is . . ." (e.g., bad/good, harmful/beneficial, worrying/reassuring, unpleasant/pleasant, punishing/rewarding, foolish/wise).[34] As predicted, Scholer found that as locomotion strength increased, the value of change in general increased.

Scholer also developed a laboratory measure of people's decision to make a change under conditions of ambivalence that would, as closely as possible, mimic some of the qualities of real-life change decisions that people confront. The participants began the session by working on a set of activities that had both positive and negative aspects. They were then given the choice to continue with this initial set of activities or to change to a new set of activities that were described as also having both positive and negative aspects. This mimics many real-life decisions where the current state has both positive and negative aspects—for example, the current state of not exercising permits more sleep in the morning, but lack of exercise contributes to feeling out of shape—and the potential new state of exercising also has both positive and negative aspects— looking fit and trim but spending less time relaxing with friends. The study found that higher locomotors were more likely to choose to change from the old set to the new set of activities. Moreover, the positive relation between stronger locomotion and stronger value of change in general accounted for this effect.

Raising the Bar on Creating Regulatory Fit Conditions

In the studies I have discussed so far, regulatory fit has been created either by emphasizing different strategies for individuals carrying out a task or by having managers with different leadership styles for their students or subordinates. These methods play out at the individual and dyadic levels of analysis. There are other situations, however, where it could be useful to raise the level of analysis from individuals and dyads to social networks and groups and even to entire institutions and cultures. Recent research conducted by Canny Zou as part of her dissertation nicely illustrates how regulatory fit and non-fit can play out at such higher levels.[35]

Zou's starting point was the evidence, beginning with the pioneering work of Emile Durkheim, the great French sociologist,[36] that social ties play an important role in emotional well-being. There is general agreement that social networks can affect many aspects of social life that are central to well-being, including conversation partners, friendship development, social integration, and so on.[37] What is less clear is which type of social network most benefits well-being.

Social capital is created through wide-ranging participation in social life and from social ties.[38] But social capital could be created either by establishing diverse social ties (i.e., high network range) or by establishing interconnections among existing contacts (i.e., high network density). Some researchers argue that "closure" networks, which have a large number of strong ties and high network density, are beneficial because they enhance trust and social support that contribute to well-being.[39] However, other researchers argue that "brokerage" networks, which have lower network density, are beneficial because they enrich social roles that enhance well-being.[40] It is a confusing picture.[41]

To resolve this confusion, Zou proposed that different social networks create a regulatory fit for individuals with different motivational orientations. For example, a closure network, with its large proportion of strong ties and high network density, provides a sense of personal belonging, builds a coherent set of normative expectations within the network, and establishes trust from structural embeddedness.[42] This kind of network uniquely fits individuals with a strong prevention orientation because it allows them to establish a coherent set of normative expectations within a group (i.e., establish obligations and responsibilities to others) and maintains stability and cohesion, while also supporting information checks and quality control.[43] In contrast, a person in a brokerage or open network has a large proportion of connections to others who are themselves unconnected, which has competitive advantages from having exclusive exchange partners and gaining exclusive information from others.[44] This kind of network uniquely fits individuals with a strong promotion orientation because it allows them to exploit their unique position in the structure to create value and gain information.

In one of Zou's studies, the participants were students in Columbia's Executive MBA program, who mostly held managerial positions in large companies or prominent consulting firms. They completed a network survey that allowed each participant to list up to 24 contacts whom they deemed as important in their professional network. They then indicated who knew whom within their network. A general life satisfaction measure was taken.[45] A measure of interpersonal distance asked participants how close they felt to each of their contacts. From this measure, the *number of strong ties* was calculated (the number of contacts that each participant felt close to or very close to) and the *number of weak ties* was calculated (the total number of ties minus the number of strong ties). Network density (the extent to which the contacts were connected to each other) was also measured.[46] Weak ties, which are indicative of a brokerage or open network, had a positive effect on general life satisfaction for managers with a stronger promotion focus but a negative effect on managers with a stronger prevention focus. Higher network density, which is associated with a closure network, had a positive effect on general life satisfaction for managers with a stronger prevention focus but a negative effect on managers with a stronger promotion focus. This demonstrates how regulatory fit at the social network level of analysis can affect the general life satisfaction of individuals.

Zou's research illustrates the importance of considering different levels of analysis when "working backwards" to manage motives effectively. Her findings suggest that interventions in the social networks of employees or students that influence regulatory fit could have an impact on their subjective well-being. Other research covered in this chapter suggests that regulatory fit interventions could be used to enhance performance as well. For example, when students in an elementary school classroom have a dominant prevention orientation, which is likely to be the case if they have an East Asian background, then setting conditions for them to establish strong interconnecting ties within the classroom should enhance their performance and their subjective well-being.

In this chapter, I have discussed the benefits of managing others by working backwards from the end-state that you want. The working backwards approach assumes that there are different strategic motives that support attaining different desired end-states, that these different strategic motives are a fit or a non-fit with different goal orientations, and that different conditions induce different goal orientations. Thus, once the right conditions are set, there will be a natural flow from conditions to goal orientation to strategic motive to the behaviors needed to attain the desired end-state. The working backwards approach can be used with incentives, but incentives are not necessary to use this approach. The emphasis of this chapter has been on managing others' motives effectively in order to enhance task performance and work satisfaction. Only with Zou's research did I consider how motivational orientations and regulatory fit relate to subjective well-being. But the motivational determinants of well-being is a major issue in its own right. I have touched on well-being issues briefly throughout this book, but it is now time to consider them in more detail.

What is The Good Life?

Well-Being From Being Effective

For centuries, people have wanted the answer to the question, "What is the good life?" The scholar who coined the phrase "the good life" was also the one who provided the Western world with its most influential answer to this question. To Aristotle, the secret to having "the good life" was to avoid extremes of all sorts—"seek moderation in all things." From my perspective, Aristotle's thinking was insightful because he went beyond pleasure and pain in his account of the good life, taking seriously the importance of the goal-pursuit *process* rather than just goal-pursuit outcomes. He believed that pleasure was not the good life in itself; rather, activities that are worthwhile often have their own distinctive pleasures. Indeed, for Aristotle, contemplation and other intellectual activities, which involve truth effectiveness, were the highest form of genuine "happiness." Like Aristotle, I believe that well-being not only involves being effective in having desired results (value) in ways that go beyond approaching pleasure and avoiding pain, but also involves being effective in managing what happens (control) and establishing what's real (truth). Control and truth are vital to "the good life" and well-being.

But this is not all. A good life and well-being are not just about combining separate motivational elements, such as combining the Aristotelian virtues of contemplation and ethical behavior. Rather, they are about the *relations* among motivations, such as the relations involved in regulatory fit. More generally, they are about motivations, such as promotion, prevention, assessment, and locomotion, working together effectively. The major take-away message of this chapter is that a good life and well-being are about *motivations working together effectively*.

DIFFERENT PERSPECTIVES ON THE ROLE OF VALUE, TRUTH, AND CONTROL IN WELL-BEING

A modern version of the Aristotelian perspective can be found in the *positive psychology* movement that was founded by Martin Seligman in the 1990s.[1] A basic tenet of this movement is that the field of psychology has historically emphasized mental illness and "the bad life," rather than mental wellness and "the good life." With Christopher Peterson, Seligman has identified six classes of "core virtues," made up of 24 character strengths,[2] that have been highly valued by people across history and across cultures, both Eastern and Western. Together, these virtues and strengths lead to increased "happiness" or well-being. Let's consider these virtues and strengths from the perspective of motivations working together effectively.

The six core virtues that Peterson and Seligman identify are *Wisdom and Knowledge* (strengths that involve the acquisition and use of knowledge, such as open-mindedness and love of learning); *Courage* (strengths that allow one to accomplish goals in the face of opposition, such as persistence and integrity); *Humanity* (strengths of tending and befriending others, such as love and social intelligence); *Justice* (strengths that build healthy community, such as fairness and teamwork); *Temperance* (strengths that protect against excess, such as prudence and self-control); and *Transcendence* (strengths that forge connections to the larger universe and provide meaning, such as appreciation of beauty and spirituality).

Well-Being From Truth and Control Effectiveness

What I find striking about these core virtues and character strengths is their close relation to *truth* effectiveness and *control* effectiveness. Indeed, they can be conceptualized as *ways of being* that support or fit establishing what's real (truth) and managing what happens (control). The relation between establishing what's real (truth) and *Wisdom and Knowledge* as a core virtue, with its various character strengths, is straightforward. But character strengths associated with the other core virtues also relate to truth effectiveness. For example, *Integrity* refers to consistency among actions, feelings, and beliefs and relates to both honesty and truthfulness, and *Fairness* refers to being free of bias or dishonesty and doing what is right. Other character strengths, such as *Persistence*,

Teamwork, and *Self-Control,* clearly involve being effective in managing what happens (control), while *Social Intelligence* involves both truth and control effectiveness in referring to knowledge of social situations and managing social relations wisely and effectively.

I should note that the emphasis on truth and control effectiveness found in "the good life" of Aristotle and in Peterson and Seligman's "happiness" is found elsewhere as well. Consider, for example, the following rules or precepts from ancient Delphi:

> *As a child, learn good manners.*
> *As a young man, learn to control your passions.*
> *In middle age be just.*
> *In old age give good advice.*
> *Then die without regret.*

That is, having had "the good life" through being effective in both truth ("be just"; "give good advice") and control ("learn good manners"; "control your passions"), *and* in a manner that *fits* each stage of life, a person can die fulfilled.

The emphasis on truth and control effectiveness is notable for another reason as well. I discussed in Chapter 11 how personality concerns "ways of seeing" the world, which relates to ways of being effective in establishing what's real (truth effectiveness), and "ways of coping" in the world, which relates to being effective in managing what happens (control effectiveness). Thus, the emphasis on truth and control effectiveness in Aristotle's "good life" and Peterson and Seligman's "happiness" connects well-being to personality. And, indeed, this is consistent with their emphasis on *character strengths,* which can be thought of as personality. This perspective highlights once again the importance of distinguishing truth and control effectiveness from value effectiveness—the need to go beyond pleasure and pain to understand both personality and well-being.

What About Well-Being From Value Effectiveness?

It is reasonable to argue that having desired results (i.e., value effectiveness) would come with having many of the character strengths associated with the core virtues, such as those associated with *Humanity* and *Justice,* because these character strengths would support having the desired results of love and belongingness. But if having desired results makes a separate contribution to having "the good life" or well-being, why restrict character strengths to those that support love and belongingness? What about Machiavellianism or ambition? Why are they not considered character strengths that support having other kinds of desired results?

Let's consider Machiavellianism. The term refers to the character traits needed to be an effective Prince in Niccolo Machiavelli's *The Prince*. They include those interpersonal skills needed to make *and break* alliances, promises, and rules—practices that lead to political success.[3] Richard Christie and Florence Geis developed a personality measure of *Machiavellianism* that assessed the extent to which an individual deceives and manipulates others for personal gain. They found that those who scored high on the measure were exceptionally effective in making and breaking alliances and promises in the service of ending up with the greatest share of the pie.[4]

In one of their studies, three participants were given 10 one-dollar bills, and whichever two participants could agree on how to divide it between them—the "winning coalition"—could then divide it according to their agreement, with the third participant ending up with nothing. Each set of three participants had one person who was high in Machiavellianism (High Mach), one who was medium (Medium Mach), and one who was low (Low Mach). If what happened during the negotiations were random, we would expect that across the different negotiation triads the High Mach member of the triad would on average finish with $3.33 (1/3 of $10). In fact, the High Mach members of the triad finished with $5.57 on average—in comparison to Low Machs, who ended up with $1.28 on average. The High Machs used their techniques to always end up on the winning coalition pair, and then they usually negotiated a larger share of the pie. High Machs, then, are effective in having desired results (value).

Now let's consider ambition. The prototypic individuals who are ambitious are high need achievers who not only have the motive to succeed but also do succeed more than low need achievers. Thus, ambitious individuals are also effective in having desired results (value). If the selection of character strengths depended on value effectiveness rather than on truth and control effectiveness, then characteristics like Machiavellianism or ambition would be included. Why are they not included?

One of Peterson and Seligman's criteria for selection stipulates that a character trait cannot be included that conflicts with (i.e., rivals) another character trait. Character traits associated with *Humanity* and *Justice*, which contain a *cooperation* element, could conflict with Machiavellianism or ambition, which contain a *competitive* element. Given this rule, it makes sense that Machiavellianism or ambition would not appear in Peterson and Seligman's list of character strengths.

But, beyond this rule, I believe that their exclusion of character traits like Machiavellianism or ambition reflects an unstated (but important) assumption about how ways of being effective contribute to well-being. For them, "happiness" or well-being is not simply about having desired results or being prosperous. Instead, well-being concerns *ways of being* that have *truth* and *control* effectiveness. Consistent with this perspective is the fact that well-being means *being well*, and "well" refers to behaving "in a good or proper manner (justly, rightly)," "in a kindly or friendly manner," "with skill or aptitude," "with careful or close attention," "without doubt or question (clearly)," and "in a way appropriate to the circumstances (fittingly; rightly)."[5] These definitions of being "well" concern ways of being that have truth or control effectiveness.

This emphasis on truth and control processes rather than just outcomes is captured in the maxims: "It is not enough to do good; one must do it in the right way," "What counts is not whether you win or lose, but how you play the game," "The ends don't justify the means," and "Never good through evil." This emphasis would rule out high Machiavellianism as a character strength. And, as I mentioned in Chapter 4, this emphasis on truth and control processes rather than just outcomes is not just about behaving morally or ethically. As reflected in the meanings of "well," it concerns what is fitting and appropriate as much as what is just or moral. What matters is not being moral or ethical *per se*, but, more generally, *being well* with respect to process. It is this emphasis on process for "the good life" or "well-being" that is of critical importance.

Peterson and Seligman's viewpoint on "the good life" is consistent with Aristotle's. He too emphasized establishing what's real (truth) and managing what happens (control) more than having desired results (value). For Aristotle, an important part of managing what happens is maintaining "moderation in all things." Interestingly, Machiavelli also believed that virtuous behavior (at least for a prince) lies in moderation, in the mean or middle of things, such as being neither overly violent nor overly civil, and in acting appropriately given the situation, such as having the ability to be powerful like a lion, when necessary, and to be cunning like a fox, when necessary.[6] But for Machiavelli results *did* matter. Truth itself was managed, as were social relationships, *in the service of having desired results*. The techniques of political manipulation were not carried out for their own sake, but were a means to attain desired results. The ends *did* justify the means. "The good life" was about the prince having his desired results, and truth and control were just means to an end.

Whereas truth and control for Aristotle and for Peterson and Seligman are *intrinsically* motivating, they are *extrinsically* motivating for Machiavelli. For Freud as well, control factors like the defense mechanisms, as well as resolving the conflicts among the Id, Ego, and Superego, are not carried out for their own sake but are in the service of approaching pleasure and avoiding pain.[7] This is different from the virtues of Peterson and Seligman or Aristotle, which are carried out for their own sake—they have intrinsic value. Indeed, for Peterson and Seligman, being "intrinsically valuable" is one of the explicit criteria for inclusion as a character strength. This highlights a critical difference in viewpoint on what is "the good life" between Machiavelli (and Freud) on the one hand, and Aristotle (and Peterson and Seligman) on the other.[8]

According to the Machiavellian viewpoint, "the good life" is about having desired results, about *value* effectiveness. This also seems to be the predominant viewpoint in the popular media today, where "the good life" of the "rich and famous" is depicted and viewers try to emulate it as closely as they can—looking beautiful and healthy and enjoying the best that the world has to offer. This viewpoint is about maximizing desired outcomes. But according to the alternative Aristotelian viewpoint, "the good life" is mostly about the character strengths that involve being effective at *truth* and *control*—being wise and knowledgeable, courageous, humane, and temperate. So what is "the good life"?

Well-Being From All Three Ways of Being Effective

I believe that both of these viewpoints tell an important part of the story, and thus each viewpoint alone is only part of the story. I believe "the good life" or well-being is *being effective in all three ways*—establishing what's real, managing what happens, *and* having desired results. I have already mentioned that the different meanings of being "well" refer to both truth and control effectiveness. Notably, other meanings of being "well" also include value effectiveness: "with good effect," "as one could wish," "with material success," "in a prosperous or affluent manner."[9] Thus, all three ways of being effective are included among the dictionary meanings of being "well."[10]

I should also note that the three ways of being effective can function in simpler and more ordinary forms than how the "good life" is often described—whether by the popular media or by scholars. Having desired results can be drinking a hot cup of tea. Rather than requiring challenging character strengths such as creativity, bravery, or leadership, which are three other truth and control traits on the Peterson and Seligman list, managing what happens can be boiling the water for the tea (control), and establishing what's real can be knowing that your favorite tea is Formosa Oolong (truth). And well-being from regulatory fit occurs when a promotion-focused individual makes tea in an enthusiastic manner and a prevention-focused individual makes tea in a careful manner. Sound trivial? Think about how we spend a good part of our day—not searching for the Big Truth or dealing with a Big Control issue or raking in the Big Value. A large part of our day is spent in the common and ordinary details of daily living in which the three ways of being effective work together without our even knowing it.

The life story of Buddha illustrates the importance of all three ways of being effective for "the good life" or well-being. Prince Siddhartha, who later came to be known as Buddha Gautama, was born around 560 B.C. His father the king tried to protect him from anything unpleasant. He grew up in beautiful palaces filled with comforts and luxuries. Because of his father's orders to protect him from unpleasant thoughts or sights, Prince Siddhartha grew up not knowing about the pain and misery in life. His was a life of fun and joy. Even into his late 20s, he continued to live in splendor protected from painful thoughts or sights. But he became progressively dissatisfied with his life. On one eventful day, while traveling outside the palace, he saw old age, suffering, and death for the first time. Now his protected and joyful life in the palace was no longer enough. A subsequent meeting with a religious ascetic on another trip inspired him to give up his protected and joyful life of pleasure in the palace. He gave up his family and royal lifestyle and began to live as an ascetic in the clothes of a beggar, renouncing pleasure, joy, and protection to search for the highest truth.

If the story ended there—and some storytellers choose to end it there—then this would be Aristotle's idea of "the good life." A life of wisdom and seeking truth trumps a life of pleasure, trumps a life of promotion–value (joy) and prevention–value (protection). As an ascetic beggar seeking the truth, Buddha has a life of control and truth effectiveness, and he willingly gives up value effectiveness. His story is reminiscent of Adam and Eve leaving the Garden of Eden after choosing to eat from "the tree of the knowledge of good and evil."

However, and significantly, Buddha's life story does *not* end there. After becoming an ascetic, Siddhartha practiced physical discipline that included enduring pain and fasting nearly to starvation. *But he was still dissatisfied.* And *then* he had a major insight: he realized that in trying to renounce all pleasure he had simply chosen to live the opposite of pleasure—a life of pain. He now realized that life should be neither of these extremes, neither a life of pleasure nor a life of pain. There needed to be a Middle Way. Truth and control, yes; but also value. Also enjoying good food and enjoying life—a smiling Buddha with a noticeably full belly.

Buddha's life story illustrates the first lesson of this chapter: well-being and "the good life" involve being effective in all three ways—value, truth, and control. But again, this is not the only message of this chapter. Well-being and the "good life" are also about the relations among these three ways of being effective. They involve promotion and prevention as value, locomotion as control, and assessment as truth, *all working together effectively.*

The next question, then, is how can value, truth, and control work together effectively? To answer this question, it is necessary to recognize that motivations have *trade-offs.* Strong promotion, prevention, locomotion, and assessment all contribute to "the good life" in important ways, but they also have potential costs to our well-being. The next two sections discuss these trade-offs—the costs and benefits associated with having predominance in any one of these orientations—and the implications of these trade-offs for defining well-being and "the good life." I then present different solutions to the trade-off problem that are considered accepted wisdom today—Aristotle's "moderation in all things" and the notion of "a perfect balance"—and I reconsider whether such solutions are really what is needed for well-being and "the good life." Finally, I propose an alternative solution to the problem of these trade-offs—how strong motivations working together can reduce the downside of trade-offs.

WELL-BEING BENEFITS AND COSTS FROM PROMOTION AND PREVENTION

How can promotion–value and prevention–value work together effectively? The answer may seem obvious. First identify the positive tendencies that are associated with promotion (e.g., joyful; fast) and those with prevention (e.g., peaceful; accurate). Next find the negative tendencies that are associated with promotion (e.g., sad; inaccurate) and those with prevention (e.g., anxious; slow). Now set the conditions to ensure that the positive feelings and motives occur and the negative feelings and motives do not. There are some psychologists who advocate this kind of solution. They believe that there are psychological factors underlying positive well-being that are distinct from the factors that underlie negative suffering. They believe that researchers and practitioners should pay more attention to the factors underlying positive motivation and less attention to the factors underlying negative motivation that have dominated the field of psychology for so long.

The solution is not that easy, however. As I have noted elsewhere in this book, the same set of psychological factors functions across individuals, situations, cultures, and so on. And these factors underlie both positive well-being and negative suffering. In other words, good life experiences and bad life experiences derive from the *same* basic factors. Moreover, all psychological factors have *trade-offs*, have both benefits and costs. There is not one set of factors for the benefits and a separate set for the costs.[11] It is not possible, for example, to strengthen promotion in order to benefit from joy without risking the downside of sadness. And if you try to reduce sadness by weakening promotion, such as giving someone a drug to weaken promotion, then you reduce the potential benefits of joy.

It would be nice to believe there is one set of beneficial factors and another set of costly factors because then we could strengthen the beneficial factors and weaken or eliminate the costly factors. But we can't do that. If we rid ourselves of anxiety, for example, through some surgical procedure or shock therapy as was done in the past, we impair psychological factors that also have benefits for us.

This is *not* the solution to well-being. We need instead to fully appreciate the trade-offs of each factor, and then consider how the relations between motivations can affect these trade-offs. I will begin by discussing the trade-offs associated with promotion and prevention orientations.

Distinguishing Absolute From Relative Levels of Motivational Strength

The trade-offs associated with a motivational factor do not derive simply from that factor being strong. It is not the absolute level of a factor that is critical but rather its level relative to other competing factors. It is the *difference in strength* that matters. For example, if an individual performs a signal detection task (for evaluatively neutral stimuli) where either a conservative bias or a risky (lenient) bias can underlie a judgment, the likelihood that a clear bias will occur depends on the difference between the individual's promotion strength and prevention strength. For individuals who have a much stronger promotion than prevention orientation, a risky bias will occur. For individuals who have a much stronger prevention than promotion orientation, a conservative bias will occur. But no clear bias will occur for individuals who have *both* a strong promotion and a strong prevention orientation.

What this means is that the trade-offs of having a strong promotion orientation that involves the benefits of being risky and the costs of not being conservative enough will be revealed when it is combined with a *weak* prevention orientation. And the trade-offs of having a strong prevention orientation that involves the benefits of being conservative and the costs of not being risky enough will be revealed when it is combined with a *weak* promotion orientation. It is when a particular value orientation—either promotion or prevention—dominates in strength that the trade-offs from a bias will occur. It is not only about strength; it is also about predominance. Thus, the trade-offs of motivational factors are observed when one orientation is both strong and stronger than its alternative.

So it is the relations that matter—not just the strength of promotion or prevention but their *relative* strength. Thus, it is a mistake to treat motives as being separate and independent and then simply combine them additively. The relations between them are critical. Second, there are times when having *two strong motives working together* can produce the *most* beneficial outcome. In the above example, having strong promotion and strong prevention working together reduces both the risky bias and the conservative bias in signal detection, thereby enhancing the accuracy of the overall detection performance. It is having *both* motives *strong* that yields the best results. Contrary to what Aristotle said, "moderation in all things" is *not* always the best advice. Instead, competing strong motives can be best at certain times. At other times one strong motive dominating a weaker motive can be best. Note that neither of these cases involves "moderation in all things."

Emotional Trade-Offs of Orientation Predominance

The difference in strength between two motivational orientations can be a chronic personality condition, such as someone's promotion ideals being more chronically accessible than prevention oughts, or it can be situationally induced, such as priming someone's promotion ideals, which makes them temporarily more accessible than prevention oughts. Research on promotion and prevention orientations has revealed several emotional trade-offs from one or the other being predominant.

Research testing self-discrepancy theory was the first to examine the well-being implications of self-regulation in the promotion–ideal and prevention–ought systems.[12] It investigated the emotional and motivational suffering that occurs when individuals have self-discrepancies. The self-discrepancies can be either between who these individuals believe they actually are (i.e., their *actual* selves) and the type of person they hope or aspire to be (i.e., their *ideal* selves [or self-guides]), or between their actual selves and the type of person they believe it is their duty or obligation to be (i.e., their *ought* selves [or self-guides]).

As discussed earlier in the book, when people have actual–ideal discrepancies they experience dejection-related states like feeling sad for mild discrepancies and feeling depressed for severe discrepancies. In contrast, when people have actual–ought discrepancies they experience agitation-related states like feeling nervous for mild discrepancies and feeling generalized anxiety for severe discrepancies. There are also distinct motivational vulnerabilities associated with these different discrepancies. Actual–ideal discrepancies produce discouragement (or *hypo*-eagerness) and actual–ought discrepancies produce guardedness (or *hyper*-vigilance). In severe cases, the former can lead to "loss of interest in everything" and extreme motor retardation, and the latter can lead to "general fear of everything" and extreme motor agitation.

There was one trade-off that received special emphasis in self-discrepancy theory. The theory postulated that children would develop stronger or weaker self-guides depending on different kinds of caretaker–child interactions, and that there was a trade-off from the strength of self-guides.[13] The trade-off derives from the fact that self-guides function both as goals to be attained and as standards of self-evaluation. It was predicted that strong self-guides would strongly motivate goal attainment, and thus would result in individuals having fewer actual–self discrepancies in relation to their ideal and ought self-guides. That is the *benefits* side of the story. However, individuals would suffer more from any discrepancy that remained because their strong self-guides would function as strong standards of self-evaluation. That is the *costs* side of the story.

Evidence consistent with these predicted trade-offs has been found for females, who generally have stronger self-guides than males, and for first-borns (including one-child families), who generally have stronger self-guides than later-borns.[14] Adult females have fewer conduct and substance abuse disorders than males (strong behavioral control), but they suffer more from depression and anxiety (strong negative self-evaluation). First-borns have smaller self-discrepancies than later-borns, but they suffer more emotionally from whatever discrepancies they do have.[15]

The positive side of having strong ideals or strong oughts was emphasized more in regulatory focus theory than it had been in self-discrepancy theory.[16] The more positive viewpoint was captured in the names of the two kinds of regulatory focus—promotion and prevention. Promotion and prevention, after all, are two ways of being effective. Moreover, they produce the positive feeling states of "feeling happy and cheerful" for promotion effectiveness and "feeling calm and relaxed" for prevention effectiveness.[17] In addition to emphasizing more the positive side of the story, what regulatory focus theory did was to consider other trade-offs from strong promotion or prevention self-regulation beyond just the emotional trade-offs emphasized in self-discrepancy theory.[18]

Motivational Trade-Offs From Promotion and Prevention

To return to what it means to be motivated, the preferences that direct choices for individuals in a promotion focus derive from emphasizing the difference between "0" and "+1," on wanting to use eager means to advance and make progress. In contrast, the preferences that direct choices for individuals in a prevention focus derive from emphasizing the difference between "0" and "–1," on wanting to use vigilant means to maintain a satisfactory state and to stop or undo any unsatisfactory state. This difference produces choice trade-offs for both value orientations. For example, when the current state is satisfactory and there is a choice between being relatively risky and accepting something as being true or right, such as "Yes, that statement is correct" or "Yes, that stock is worth buying," or instead being relatively conservative and rejecting something as being true or right, such as "No, that statement is not correct" or "No, that stock is not worth buying," then predominant promotion individuals will have a risky bias whereas predominant prevention individuals will have a conservative bias.

Note that both promotion preferences and prevention preferences direct *biased* choices. The trade-off for "acceptance" promotion is the benefit of ending up with something that is true or right that otherwise would have been missed, but the cost is ending up with something that is false or wrong. The trade-off for "rejection" prevention is the benefit of rejecting something that is false or wrong and thereby avoid making a mistake, but the cost is rejecting something that is true or right. Which bias is better, being risky or being conservative? To have "the good life," is predominant promotion or predominant prevention better? Before addressing these questions, let us consider two more examples of predominant promotion and predominant prevention trade-offs—the trade-off between speed versus accuracy and the trade-off between creative versus analytical thinking.

Often when people perform a task, performing more quickly increases the likelihood that errors will be made—the common "speed/accuracy" trade-off (or "quantity/quality" conflict). For over a century, psychologists have studied the personality and situational factors that relate to when people are fast, when they are accurate, and what the relation is between speed and accuracy.[19] What had not been considered was the possibility that speed and accuracy might support different *strategic preferences*—that is, different ways of managing what happens that were in the service of different value orientations. By working quickly, progress is made faster, gains are made sooner. This serves promotion concerns with moving from "0" to "+1." In contrast, by working to ensure accuracy, mistakes are avoided, which serves prevention concerns with stopping a "−1."

In one set of studies,[20] participants were asked to complete a series of four "connect-the-dot" pictures, where each picture when correctly completed depicted a cartoon animal, such as a hippopotamus. The measure of speed of goal completion for each picture was the number of dots participants connected for each picture within the allotted time frame. The measure of accuracy of goal completion was the number of dots participants missed when connecting the dots (up to the highest dot they reached for each picture). The studies found that predominant promotion participants were faster (i.e., got through a greater percentage of the pictures in the allotted time), whereas predominant prevention participants were more accurate (i.e., made fewer errors in the portions of the pictures that they had completed).

Because there was a series of pictures, these studies could also investigate what happens as the participants get closer and closer to completing the task (i.e., as they move from the first to the fourth picture). According to the classic "goal looms larger" effect, motivation increases as people get closer to completing their goal pursuit.[21] If this increased motivation applies to *strategic* motivation as well, then the greater speed of predominant promotion than predominant prevention participants and the greater accuracy of predominant prevention than predominant promotion participants should become more pronounced as the participants get closer and closer to completing the task. Indeed, this effect was also found. Thus, the difference in speed performance versus accuracy performance between participants with predominant promotion and those with predominant prevention became greater and greater as the participants became more and more motivated.

Trade-offs between predominant promotion and predominant prevention also occur in creative thinking versus logical analytical reasoning. To be creative or innovative, individuals need to free themselves from the restrictions or constraints of the status quo or what is normative. They need to move beyond what is given. To be good at logical analytical reasoning, however, the opposite is the case. To correctly relate the different components of a system to identify its true inner relationships, individuals must methodically follow the rules and stick with what is given. Individuals with a predominant promotion orientation want to move beyond the status quo, move beyond "0." They want to accomplish "new" things, gain new knowledge. These preferences support creative thinking but, if anything, they impair analytical reasoning that requires sticking to what is given and methodically following the rules of logic. In contrast, individuals with a predominant prevention orientation want to maintain the status quo and carefully follow prescribed logical rules. This should support analytical reasoning but impair creative thinking.

In fact, there is evidence that individuals with a predominant promotion orientation are more creative than individuals with a predominant prevention orientation, such as thinking of more different ways that a brick could be used or trying different approaches to solve a problem. And there is also evidence that individuals with a predominant prevention orientation are better at analytical reasoning than individuals with a predominant promotion orientation, such as scoring higher on the Graduate Record Examination (GRE) Analytical Writing test, whose problems involve evaluating the truth value of propositions given an initial set of basic facts.[22]

In sum, having a predominant promotion orientation produces more risky decision making, faster performance, and better creative thinking, while it also produces less conservative decision making, less accurate performance, and poorer analytical reasoning. Having a predominant prevention orientation produces the opposite pattern of trade-offs. What these trade-offs highlight is that *there is no one best system of self-regulation*. It cannot reasonably be argued that generally being risky is better than being conservative, that speed is better than accuracy, or that creative thinking is better than analytical thinking. Nor can the reverse be argued. Instead, what should be concluded is that predominant promotion and predominant prevention both have trade-offs that produce benefits under some conditions and costs under other conditions. Not only is it the case that one cannot assert that either predominant promotion or predominant prevention is better than the other, but it is also the case that one cannot even assert that either predominant promotion alone or predominant prevention alone is necessarily good. Each has costs as well as benefits. One of the major implications from this conclusion is that the search for well-being or "the good life" must find a solution other than choosing one or the other of these value orientations to *anoint* as the "good" motive. But that is precisely what psychology has done.

The Problem With Anointing "Happiness" and Promotion for Well-Being

Some might argue that there is one difference between effective promotion and effective prevention that does prove that predominant promotion *is* clearly preferable to predominant prevention: the fact that "happiness" is higher after promotion success than after prevention success. However, this difference simply highlights a fundamental problem with treating "happiness" as if it were the same as well-being.

As I discussed earlier in the book, feeling happy is a feedback signal of successful promotion, just as feeling calm (or relieved) is a feedback signal of successful prevention. These differences in feelings reflect differences in which value orientation—promotion or prevention—was involved in the goal pursuit that was successful. They do *not* reflect differences in which goal was successfully pursued. Indeed, it can be precisely the *same* goal that was successful, such as getting an "A" in a course or arriving on time at a destination during a car trip. In both cases, a person was effective in achieving a desired result and in managing to make it happen. What differed was whether the goal of getting an "A" or arriving on time was represented as an accomplishment to attain or as a responsibility to fulfill. To argue that these different representations of the goal reflect a difference in well-being is unreasonable. And, if that is unreasonable, then so is measuring well-being in terms of how much "happiness" is felt.

In addition, "happiness" can be considered to be either a desired end-state (value) or a feedback signal about how we are doing in our goal pursuit (control). As a feedback signal, feeling happy functions *like any other feedback signal* to help manage what happens next—it has *no special status* in this regard. Feeling "sadness," for example, is also a feedback signal. As a feedback signal, it also contributes to control effectiveness and thus contributes to well-being.[23] Given this, why not use greater "sadness" as an indicator of greater well-being? Why anoint only the feedback signal of "happiness" for this role?

The failure in the well-being literature to recognize that "happiness" is just a feedback signal that happens to be associated with success in a specific self-regulatory system (the promotion system), and that success in prevention has its own positive feedback signal, is part of a larger problem. The well-being literature generally fails to distinguish between what it means to be effective in promotion self-regulation and what it means to be effective in prevention self-regulation. It acts as if feeling "joy" has more status than feeling the calm of "peace"—despite the fact that several religions describe the equivalent of Heaven as a condition where the deceased feel both "peace" and "joy." There is a general tendency to assume that whatever is associated with effective promotion self-regulation represents higher well-being than whatever is associated with effective prevention self-regulation.

The problem begins with measures of well-being. It is common for such measures to ask people how often or how much they feel happy (greater happiness being scored as higher well-being) and how often or how much they feel nervous or tense (greater nervousness being scored as lower well-being).[24] It has even become common to define *the basic positive emotions* as being promotion-success emotions like feeling "happy," "joyful," or "cheerful," and to *exclude* prevention-success emotions like feeling "calm," "relaxed," or "at ease." At the same time, it has become common when defining *general negative affect* to use prevention-failure emotions like feeling "afraid," "nervous," "jittery," and so on rather than promotion-failure emotions like "sad."[25] Controlling for actual effectiveness in life (i.e., frequency of successes and failures), these measurement biases make promotion-oriented people more likely to score higher in well-being than prevention-oriented people because promotion success (vs. prevention success) will score positively and prevention failure (vs. promotion failure) will score negatively.

The measurement bias in favor of promotion includes anticipatory feelings as well. Effective promotion-oriented people anticipate success in order to support the eagerness that sustains or fits their orientation, and by anticipating success they feel not only the "basic positive emotions" like "happy," "joyful," or "cheerful," but they also feel "confident" and "bold," which themselves are also included as "basic positive emotions" and raise the well-being score. In contrast, effective prevention-related people anticipate the possibility of failure—defensive pessimism—in order to support the vigilance that sustains or fits their orientation. Anticipating the possibility of failure can make them feel tense and nervous, which would count as "general negative affect" and lower their well-being score. Thus, when promotion and prevention individuals are *both being effective* and feeling right from regulatory fit, the promotion individuals score higher on well-being and the prevention individuals score lower.

Because the measures of well-being are themselves problematic, it is not surprising that conclusions about which motivational factors, or types of personality, contribute to high well-being are also problematic. For example, in an influential paper on personality traits associated with well-being, Warner Wilson concluded that the happy person is "extraverted, optimistic, worry-free," as well as having high self-esteem.[26] The person being described here is an effective promotion-oriented person. Promotion effectiveness is positively related to higher extraversion, higher optimism (thus less worrying about the future), and higher self-esteem. These positive relations occur because higher extraversion, optimism, and self-esteem are all in the service of supporting the eagerness that fits promotion. They do *not* support the vigilance that fits prevention. This doesn't mean that promotion effectiveness is better than prevention effectiveness. *It is just different.* Nonetheless, the literature has concluded that what fits predominant promotion counts as high well-being whereas what fits predominant prevention does not.

WELL-BEING BENEFITS AND COSTS FROM LOCOMOTION AND ASSESSMENT

Promotion and prevention are motivational states that can vary chronically across individuals as a personality variable or can be situationally induced. This is also true for locomotion and assessment. In a predominant locomotion state, individuals want to initiate action and then keep it running smoothly over time. Initiating and maintaining smooth movement is in the service of managing what happens—*control effectiveness.* In a predominant assessment state, individuals want to critically evaluate alternative options by thoroughly comparing them. Critical evaluation and thorough comparison is in the service of establishing what's real—*truth effectiveness.*

The functions of locomotion and assessment in self-regulation have been treated, historically, as being *means* for attaining desired end-states. For example, in the standard control system models that I discussed in Chapter 9, assessment and locomotion are worthwhile to the extent that they contribute to achieving the desired state. But *well-being from locomotion or assessment is not about hedonic outcomes or achieving desired results.* Locomotion and assessment are separate from value effectiveness. Assessment and locomotion are worthwhile independent of whether they are effective in achieving desired results. This is a major feature of these regulatory mode states that has received insufficient attention. The process of critically evaluating alternative options by thoroughly comparing them is *intrinsically* worthwhile as a way to be effective by establishing what's real (truth effectiveness). The process of initiating and maintaining smooth movement is *intrinsically* worthwhile as a way to be effective by managing what happens (control effectiveness).

I am not suggesting that having desired results at the end does not matter for well-being. As I said earlier, being "well" also means being effective in having valued outcomes. But effective locomotion and effective assessment independently contribute to "the good life" and well-being. For example, famous

American businessmen have told others that the secret to "success" in life is to take action, to change, to keep moving (i.e., to locomote), as the following quotations illustrate:

> "Success seems to be connected with action. Successful people keep moving. They make mistakes, but they don't quit." *Conrad Hilton*
> "The way to get started is to quit talking and begin doing." *Walt Disney*
> "You have to pretend you're 100 percent sure. You have to take action; you can't hesitate or hedge your bets. Anything less will condemn your efforts to failure." *Andrew Grove*
> "Willingness to change is a strength, even if it means plunging part of the company into total confusion for a while." *Jack Welch*
> "Punishing honest mistakes stifles creativity. I want people moving and shaking the earth and they're going to make mistakes." *Ross Perot*

Certainly, these businessmen also want to end up with desired outcomes, and, to some extent at least, strong locomotion is a means to this end. Nonetheless, they believed that strong locomotion itself is worthwhile, and I believe that they also felt that a life of strong locomotion is "the good life" and contributes to well-being. The independence of the worth of locomotion from the worth of desired outcomes is more explicit in the following two quotes:

> "One should not think about the result; one does not travel to reach a destination, but to travel." *Johann Wolfgang von Goethe*
> "Move. Go forward or backward, whatever it takes. Just move!" *Anonymous*

At the same time, Western literature more generally has also emphasized the importance of truth for well-being, including the willingness of humans to give up hedonic pleasure for the sake of the truth. From Adam and Eve risking the loss of paradise to eat from the "tree of the knowledge of good and evil," to Neo in "Matrix" giving up the blue pill that offers a life of hedonic pleasure for the red pill that offers only the truth, the message is that "the good life" is more than just having hedonic outcomes. It is about being effective in establishing what's real in addition to being effective in managing what happens. Indeed, pleasure will be forgone and pain taken on in the service of truth and control effectiveness.

In sum, locomotion–control and assessment–truth contribute to well-being independent of value effectiveness. This is important to recognize explicitly. But this is not to say that they are the saviors of well-being; they too have their own trade-offs.

The Downsides of Predominant Locomotion and Assessment

Individuals in a predominant locomotion state want to *initiate action*. They would rather do *anything* than nothing at all. And, as reflected in the quote from *Anonymous*, this means going backwards as well as forwards—as long as they move. But this can result in their moving to a state that is *worse* than where they began. Yes, they would have locomotion–control effectiveness from moving, but they would have wasted resources only to end up in a less desirable state. If they had planned more (i.e., had assessed more), they could have had control effectiveness from moving *and* have used resources efficiently to end up in a more desirable state: an example of well-being resulting from truth and control working together to create value.

There is also a potential downside from strong locomotion wanting to *maintain smooth, uninterrupted movement*. This could result in movement continuing even though it is no longer productive (i.e., when it would be better to stop and do something else). Strong locomotion in this sense can be like a train without a driver moving smoothly but blindly down the track without stopping at any stations. A train driver who assesses when to move, when to stop, and how long to stop is necessary for the train to fulfill its purpose. Again, managing to make things happen by maintaining smooth movement would have control effectiveness, but resources would be used to keep on moving when stopping is needed to yield the desired results. By assessing when it is time to stop, when smooth movement should be interrupted, as well as when movement should be maintained, truth can contribute to using resources efficiently to attain desired results. Thus, achievement performance is increased when strong locomotion works together with assessment.

It is not only predominant locomotion that has potential downsides: predominant assessment does as well. It can yield the prototypical case of individuals becoming "lost in thought" and doing nothing. Whether selecting goals, strategies, or tactics, the process of goal pursuit for such individuals involves many options to be considered. There are also many different standards or reference points that can be used when critically evaluating and comparing the attributes of the different options. An exhaustive and thorough assessment process could continue for a very long time only to yield no dominating option at the end of the process. The more that all possible reference points are used in an exhaustive and thorough process, the more choice *conflict* will be generated that reduces commitment to any one option. This is also very inefficient because substantial resources are expended only to produce *choice paralysis*. In the end, nothing happens. High assessors would rather do nothing than the wrong thing, and this can sound reasonable. However, strong assessment can make no choice look like the right decision even when each of the options is actually superior to doing nothing at all.

There are other downsides to predominant assessment. The use of different standards or reference points in making evaluations can produce changes in evaluation over time, as when people feel good when they compare themselves to those doing worse than they are (downward comparison) but feel bad when they compare themselves to those doing better than they are (upward comparison).[27] The downside of such shifting evaluations is reflected in individuals with strong assessment being more emotionally unstable and neurotic.[28] Another downside is that strong assessors would be more even-handed than most people (in order to make all possible comparisons) and would weigh negative evaluations heavily in overall evaluations. This tendency would produce more overall "failure" evaluations for high assessors than other people, which is reflected in predominant assessors being both more anxious and more depressed.[29]

It is clear, then, that predominant locomotion and predominant assessment can each have their own costs for desired results. When they function alone without the input of the other, goal pursuit is inefficient and can not only decrease desired results but even produce undesired results. But there is more than just these value costs. Additionally, when each mode functions without the constraint or countervailing force of the other, effective control and effective truth are actually reduced. Without assessment to counterbalance the move-at-any-cost nature of individuals with predominant locomotion, their failure to stop movement or to stop long enough when necessary would be a failure to manage what happens and would reduce this hallmark of control effectiveness. Thus, predominant locomotion alone can impair control effectiveness.

And when predominant assessors fail to understand that in many cases there is not one *a priori* correct standard or reference point,[30] when they keep changing the point of comparison in order to be exhaustive and thorough, or when they are critical to the extent of becoming depressed or anxious, they are not being effective in finding *the* truth. Individuals who are emotionally unstable, depressed, or anxious have their own biases and distortions of reality. It is not realistic to choose comparison points that generate debilitating self-views. Indeed, individuals suffering from depression or anxiety disorders have irrational or *unrealistic* views of themselves, of others, and of the world around them.[31] In addition, they can ruminate and obsess about these views in a manner that further reduces the ability to establish what's real.[32] What can help is a push from locomotion to end the assessment and move on. Without such locomotion, there can be a failure to establish what's real. Thus, ironically, predominant assessment alone can impair truth effectiveness.

SOLVING THE PROBLEM OF TRADE-OFFS

What, then, is the solution to this problem of downsides and costs from predominant motivations, whether they are predominant promotion, prevention, locomotion, or assessment? Given that predominance involves one motivation being at a high or strong level and its competing motivation (or motivations) being at a low or weak level, the solution seems obvious. And Aristotle has already given it: "Moderation in all things." Thus, his solution would be to eliminate the costs of predominance by reducing the strong motivation to a more moderate level and raising the weak motivation to a more moderate level. Now we have what we want! We have eliminated the predominance by making the motivations equally moderate. And by eliminating the predominance, we have eliminated its costs. Thus, the answer to how to achieve well-being would seem to be "moderation in all things." Or is it?

Why "Moderation in All Things" Is *Not* the Solution

As a solution to the problem of costs from predominant motivations, "moderation in all things" has three effects. First, it reduces a motivation from being strong to being moderate. Second, it eliminates a motivation's predominance. Third, it creates "a perfect balance" of moderate motivations. I believe that each of these effects is problematic for well-being and "the good life" and therefore that "moderation in all things" is not the best solution. Indeed, it is a bad idea. Let me explore each of its effects to demonstrate why it is a bad idea and what solutions would be better.

THE PROBLEM WITH REDUCING A MOTIVATION FROM
BEING STRONG TO MODERATE

It is true that predominant promotion, prevention, locomotion, and assessment have potential costs for value, truth, and control effectiveness. Why, then, not solve these problems by reducing their strength to moderate levels? There are both emotional and motivational reasons why this is not a good idea.

Regarding emotion, reducing promotion and prevention to moderate levels would mean giving up the benefits of experiencing a strong promotion success or a strong prevention success: feeling less joy from a promotion success and feeling less peace from a prevention success. Reducing their strength to moderate levels would reduce the strength of these positive emotional experiences.

Regarding motivation, reducing promotion and prevention to moderate levels would also reduce the strength of motivation to attain promotion and prevention goals, which in turn would make success itself less likely. Reducing locomotion and assessment to moderate levels would also hurt performance for a somewhat different reason. As I described in Chapter 9, research has consistently shown that the combination of moderate locomotion and moderate assessment produces significantly *worse* performance than the combination of strong locomotion and strong assessment. Moderate levels, generally speaking, simply don't work as well for performance.

When locomotion and assessment, or promotion and prevention, have costs from being predominant, rather than reducing them to moderate levels, a better solution is to *ensure that both motivations are strong*. When both locomotion and assessment are strong, they set *constraints* or *limits* on one another that, as just discussed, reduce the potential costs from one or the other being too predominant. When both promotion and prevention are strong, they can work together to improve performance. Strong promotion insists that errors of omission be avoided, while strong prevention insists that errors of commission be avoided. By working to ensure against both of these errors, decision bias is minimized.

Thus, the solution to the trade-offs of predominant motivations is *not* to reduce the strength of the predominant motivation in order that both motivations end up at a moderate level. Rather, the solution is to increase the strength of the weaker motivation so that it has the strength to set constraints and limits on the now-less-predominant motivation. The good life and well-being are not created by combining independent, moderate-strength motivations. Instead, they are created by having motivations strong enough that they can work together to maximize the benefits and minimize the costs of each.

There is an implicit mechanism underlying my proposed solution of having *strong motivations working together* that I need to make explicit. The "moderation in all things" solution to well-being and the more general notion of well-being as combining core virtues and character strengths treat these motivations as independent motives that can be added together to produce a high level of well-being. My proposed solution does not suggest an additive model. Instead, it involves a *dynamic, relational system*. It proposes that combining strong motivations works because the strong motivations set constraints and limits on one another. Such constraints and limits should not be understood as conflict, like Freud's conflicts among the Ego, Id, and Superego. They should be understood as dynamic cooperation. Motivations have a relation to one another; they cooperate—work together—in a way that enhances overall effectiveness. And they often work best together when they are both strong.

I believe that Aristotle and others have overlooked the significance of dynamically cooperating motivations to "the good life" and well-being. I believe that they have failed to distinguish between the behavioral expressions of motivations they observe and the actual motivations that underlie these behavioral expressions. Like the classic correspondence bias described in the person perception literature, where an "X" (aggressive; friendly) behavior is assumed to derive from an "X" (aggressive; friendly) trait or disposition,[33] it is as if the moderate behaviors that are preferred over extreme behavior are assumed to derive from underlying moderate motivations. But moderate behaviors can result from underlying strong motivations that work together in a mutually constraining and limiting manner. In fact, this may be the only way that the preferred "moderate" behaviors will be produced.

The Problem With Eliminating a Motivation's Predominance

The solutions of "moderation in all things" and "a perfect balance" also involve eliminating the predominance of the predominant motivation. By reducing the predominant motivation from a strong to a moderate level, and raising the weak motivation to a moderate level, the predominance itself is eliminated. Again, I believe it is a mistake to reduce the predominant motivation from strong to moderate, and have suggested instead to raise the weak motivation all the way to being strong. But doesn't this mean that the previously predominant motivation will no longer be predominant? Because the two motivations will both be strong, won't the predominance be eliminated? Is this a good thing for well-being?

I have argued that it can be beneficial when two motivations working together are *both strong*. By this, I was *not* suggesting that the motivations had to be *equally* strong. For example, it might be that promotion and prevention *do* need to be equally strong to minimize decision biases, but when assessment is strong it is possible that achievement is maximized when locomotion is *even stronger*. Motivation science needs to learn more about when it is better for motivations working together to be equally strong and when it is better for one motivation to be stronger than the other. But here I simply want to emphasize that the benefits to well-being from strong motivations working together do not mean that they should always be equally strong.

The Problem With Creating a "Perfect Balance"
of Moderate Motivations

The more general problem is the notion that the best solution to the costs of extremity is to create a perfect balance of moderate motivations. This solution overlooks the principle of trade-offs. A perfect balance of moderate motivations will eliminate the costs of a predominant motivation, but there is always the risk that it will *eliminate its benefits as well*. For example, if predominant prevention hurts creative thinking, then eliminating its predominance would reduce this cost. However, by eliminating it, especially by reducing it from strong to moderate as proposed in the "moderation in all things" solution, the benefits to analytical thinking from predominant prevention would be lost. There are times when analytical thinking is needed and we would want individuals to have a strong and predominant prevention orientation. There are other times when creative thinking is needed and we would want individuals to have a strong and predominant promotion orientation. And this is also true for strong and predominant locomotion and for strong and predominant assessment. At these times, the predominant motivation *must be both strong and stronger than the other motivation*—it will not be effective if it is equally moderate.

There is an additional problem from eliminating predominance if this is done by creating "a perfect balance" of moderate motivations. The problem is that this could result in a *stalemate*—no choice being made, no action being taken. Many times in life we choose between a set of positive alternatives, such as choosing between different menu options or vacation trips. Any choice would be better than no choice at all. If we have moderate motivations that prefer different options, and if the moderate motivations are perfectly balanced in strength—like Aristotle's famous perfect balance of bodily humors—then we could end up with no clearly preferred choice (no "dominating alternative"). This could result in no choice being made, despite the fact that *any* choice is better than *no* choice, which is clearly not good for well-being. The solution in such cases is to have one of the alternative solutions being both strong and stronger than its rival alternatives—neither moderation nor a perfect balance.

The Problem With Aristotle's Idea of *The* Good Life

Not only are there several problems with Aristotle's proposal that "the good life" can be attained through "moderation in all things" and "a perfect balance," there is also a problem with "the good life" idea to begin with. I discussed in Chapter 10 how promotion, prevention, locomotion, and assessment can receive different emphases and that different structural patterns are created when these different emphases combine, with each pattern having a distinct motivational significance. I believe that a full appreciation of well-being and what it means to have "the good life" must take into account how motivations work together and the fact that there can be different structural patterns that function effectively. Rather than there being *the* "good life," this means that there would be different kinds of "good life."

As I said earlier, I disagree with the additive model of well-being that proposes that there is a set of independent character strengths and it is best to have as many of them as possible. I believe that the *relations* among a person's "strengths" must be taken into account because the whole is different than the sum of its parts. For example, adding together the strong sense of responsibility that is associated with a prevention orientation (a *Justice* character strength) and eager-related hope and optimism (a *Transcendence* character strength) creates a regulatory *non-fit*. Indeed, because this combination is a non-fit, it would reduce strength of engagement or vitality. The *Courage* character strength would be low when engagement strength and vitality are low. Thus, combining *Justice* and *Transcendence* does not result in a simple additive product; they interact as a regulatory non-fit that can have negative consequences for *Courage*. Fit and non-fit relations between character strengths need to be taken into account to predict well-being. How motivations work together dynamically matters.

The importance of fit and non-fit to well-being was investigated in a field study on the emotional effects of dealing with life's everyday hassles and challenges.[34] As part of a daily diary study, participants at the end of each day reported the "most upsetting or bothersome incident" that happened to them that day and their current level of emotional distress. They also completed a coping measure that assessed their use of eager and vigilant strategies to cope with the upsetting incident. Notably, it was possible for participants to cope with the incident by using several eager and several vigilant strategies, using several eager but few (or no) vigilant strategies, using several vigilant but few (or no) eager strategies, or using few of either strategy. It was also possible for participants to be strong in both promotion and prevention, be strong in promotion but not prevention, be strong in prevention but not promotion, or be strong in neither.

The study found both a regulatory fit effect and a regulatory non-fit effect. First, distress from the upsetting incident was *less* at the end of the day the more that strong promotion participants used eager strategies to cope with the incident (e.g., "I looked for additional means to advance my goals") and the more that strong prevention participants used vigilant strategies (e.g., "I was very cautious—I didn't want any other bad incidents to happen"). That is, there was a well-being *benefit* from a value–control *fit* relation. Second, distress from the upsetting incident was *more* at the end of the day the more that strong promotion participants used vigilant strategies to cope with the incident and the more that strong prevention participants used eager strategies. Thus, there was also a well-being *cost* from a value–control *non-fit* relation. What mattered for well-being was whether the individuals used coping control strategies that fit or did not fit their value orientations. What mattered for well-being was whether the value and control motivations were or were not working together effectively.

As I have noted throughout this book, *regulatory fit* is a major motivational mechanism underlying effective self-regulation. For example, it is central to managing motives by working backwards from what we want (Chapter 12). It can tip the balance between two strong motivations with opposing preferences by sustaining one motivation more than the other. It can increase or decrease suffering when coping with life's everyday hassles and challenges. It is time to consider more fully the implications of regulatory fit's contribution to well-being because it provides an especially clear case of the need to go beyond just valued outcomes, beyond pleasure and pain, when thinking about how well-being and a "good life" can be established.

REGULATORY FIT AND WELL-BEING

In considering how regulatory fit can contribute to well-being, I begin with its potential contribution to allowing strong promotion and strong prevention to work together effectively. I should note from the beginning that the question of how strong promotion and strong prevention can work together to enhance well-being refers to their working together on the same goal pursuit or task activity, such as working together "to plan a fun vacation" or "to cook a delicious dinner." This is the challenge of coordination.

It is a different case than when there are separate goals or task activities that will be pursued at different times. For the case of temporally separated activities, the potential advantage in having both strong promotion and strong prevention available as orientation options is more obvious. It would be an advantage, for example, to have a strong prevention orientation when preparing your home for an oncoming thunderstorm and a strong promotion orientation when you are decorating your home for an upcoming birthday party. It can also be advantageous during a task to be in a promotion orientation at one point in time and in a prevention orientation at some other point in the task, such as having strong promotion when generating ideas during the initial planning stage of a project (e.g., to promote creativity) but having strong prevention in the post-planning stage when the decisions have to be carried out (e.g., to prevent execution errors).[35] These cases do not involve the challenge of coordination. Having strong prevention during one activity or phase of a task and strong promotion during a different activity or phase does not involve promotion and prevention working *together*. Integration or coordination of promotion and prevention is not necessary in these cases. There is also no potential conflict between promotion and prevention orientations when they are functioning in separate activities or temporal phases.

The case I wish to consider is how promotion and prevention can be effectively coordinated to enhance well-being when they are functioning at the same time for the same task activity. And this case applies both to *inter*personal coordination and to *intra*personal coordination. I will begin by considering interpersonal coordination between individuals because the conditions underlying effective coordination have been identified most clearly for this case. I will then consider how the identified conditions for this case could be applied to effective coordination of promotion and prevention within one individual to enhance a person's well-being.

Interpersonal Coordination of Promotion and Prevention in Couples

Having satisfying close relationships enhances personal well-being.[36] Thus, the question for well-being is whether partners in a close relationship who have opposite regulatory focus orientations—one strong promotion and the other strong prevention—can coordinate effectively to form a satisfying relationship. If they can, they would illustrate how complementarity in relationships can be beneficial. This issue relates more generally to a classic question in the area of social attraction and close relationships: Is partner similarity or partner complementarity more important for forming a strong and satisfying relationship? Both alternatives are supported in folk wisdom, as reflected in there being both a maxim that similarity matters ("Birds of a feather flock together") and a maxim that complementarity matters ("Opposites attract"). So which is better for creating the satisfying relationships that enhance well-being—similarity or complementarity?

For a close relationship with both a strong promotion partner and a strong prevention partner (i.e., *opposite* value orientations), it is easy to see why complementarity could harm rather than help relationship satisfaction and why similarity would be better. This is because, as noted earlier, there is the potential for *goal conflict* when the partners have opposite value orientations. When planning what to do during a vacation, for example, the promotion partner would want an exciting vacation with novel activities that provided opportunities to accomplish new things, whereas the prevention partner would want a peaceful vacation with familiar activities where past enjoyments could be experienced again. Such differences are likely to result in different vacation preferences, which, in turn, could produce conflict and dissatisfaction in the relationship.

It is critical for relationship satisfaction that the partners agree on common goals, that they have a shared reality on what they want to do. When they do not have such a shared reality, opposite value orientations can be a problem. In this case, the possibility of goal conflict can make the partners' dissimilarity a disadvantage because the conflict would reduce relationship satisfaction. Indeed, generally speaking, the psychological literature has found, for friendships as well as romantic relationships, that similarity between relationship partners predicts stronger and more satisfying relationships than dissimilarity.[37]

But what happens when relationship partners have established common goals, when they have a shared reality on what they want to do? Now there would be a need for a different kind of coordination between the partners. Now the partners have to coordinate on the means for reaching their common goal. Which partner is going to carry out which of the different aspects of the goal-pursuit process that need to be done to reach the goal? For example, consider a romantic couple who have the common goal of cooking a delicious dinner together. There are many different things that need to be done to reach this goal, from preparing special sauces to ensuring that each ingredient is cooked just the right amount of time. Being creative could support preparing special sauces, and being careful could support cooking each ingredient for the right amount of time.

Now there should be an advantage if the relationship partners have opposite value orientations because the promotion partner can eagerly work on the special sauces while the prevention partner vigilantly keeps track of the cooking time (and the cooking temperature) for each ingredient. Not only would each aspect of the meal preparation have an appropriate person working on it, which could enhance the desired results, but each partner would be acting in a *strategic manner* that fit his or her value orientation. By both partners experiencing regulatory fit, they would be more strongly engaged in, and "feel right" about, what they were doing. Moreover, these fit effects could intensify the partners' attraction toward both the meal and each other—*a recipe for romance*. What this predicts is that when relationship partners share common goals, having opposite value orientations can increase relationship satisfaction. If so, then this could be a way for strong promotion and strong prevention to work together to enhance well-being.

This prediction about the benefits of *strategic compatibility* in close relationships was proposed and investigated by Vanessa Bohns as part of her doctoral dissertation.[38] Additional research was also conducted in collaboration with experts in the area of close relationships.[39] A necessary initial condition to test this proposal is that the relationship partners have shared common goals. The likelihood of having shared common goals is greater for married than unmarried couples, and among married couples the likelihood of having shared common goals is greater for couples who have been married longer. Thus, length of marriage was used as a proxy in one study for having established shared common goals. Having shared common goals is also more likely when married partners experience themselves as more of a "we" rather than separate experiences of "I." In another study, a measure of closeness that captures this sense of "we" was used as a proxy for having shared common goals.[40]

The measure of relationship well-being was a composite of four different measures that are commonly used in the close-relationships literature: *satisfaction, commitment, trust,* and *dyadic adjustment,* where dyadic adjustment assesses qualities of a couple's well-being such as affection and intimacy. The studies found that the more that couples were likely to have established shared common goals (i.e., couples married longer; couples experiencing themselves as more of a "we" than separate "I's"[41]), the more benefit there was for relationship well-being from the partners being complementary (vs. similar) in their value orientations. These studies demonstrate the potential advantage from coordinating strong promotion and strong prevention.[42] For a couple, the advantage derives from each partner performing those aspects of the joint activity that fit his or her predominant regulatory focus. The partners work together such that the promotion partner takes on those aspects of the activity that benefit from eagerness and the prevention partner takes on those aspects that benefit from vigilance. Each partner is strongly engaged and "feels right" from working in a manner that fits his or her predominant value orientation. Positive reactions to the joint activity and to each other are intensified.

It should be noted, however, that for these well-being benefits from complementarity to work, it is necessary that the activity have both eager and vigilant aspects that can be divided. As Bohns points out in her dissertation, it is important to distinguish between task activities that have divisible roles (*divisible* tasks) and those that do not (*unitary* tasks) when predicting benefits from complementarity.[43] She found in another study that when participants were given a choice between working together with someone they thought had a strong promotion focus or someone they thought had a strong prevention focus, they chose as their partner that person whose value orientation was *opposite* to their own *when* their joint task had *divisible* roles, such as "cooking together." When the joint task did not have divisible roles, such as "watching a movie together," then the participants were more likely to choose as their partner that person whose value orientation was similar to their own.[44]

Intrapersonal Coordination of Promotion and Prevention in an Individual

The research program just described has identified conditions for interpersonal coordination on a joint activity where well-being can be enhanced from having both strong promotion and strong prevention working together. Can these conditions be generalized in some way to *intra*personal coordination to enhance the well-being of an individual from having strong promotion and strong prevention working together on the same task activity? I believe that it can, and "cooking a meal" provides a good example of how it can be done.

Cooking a meal is an activity with multiple aspects that permits different roles to be assigned to different individuals. But one individual can take on all the roles. One individual can do both the eager parts and the vigilant parts. Indeed, there is an advantage of one individual having both strong promotion and strong prevention orientations because the different aspects can intermingle and overlap in the task. For example, once the sauce is made and is then added to the cooking pan with the other main ingredients, tasting and re-tasting, adding this and that, raising and lowering the heat, are all going on during the same short period. Some new spice is eagerly added while the heat is vigilantly lowered. A cook who has strong promotion and strong prevention, working together, is just what is needed. And such cooks experience fit between their strong promotion and their eagerly adding a new spice and their strong prevention and their carefully lowering the heat. Their engagement in what they are doing is very strong, their "feel right" experience is intense, and their attraction toward their cooking activity and their finished dish is very strong.

As with interpersonal coordination between team partners or couples, intrapersonal individual coordination of opposite value orientations will enhance well-being *when* the activity is divisible into different aspects that permit a fit with each value orientation. Then the opposite value orientations can work together harmoniously and productively, and the fit with both value orientations will create exceptionally high engagement strength, "feel right" experiences, and positive value experiences. These are the conditions where well-being will clearly be enhanced from strong promotion and strong prevention working together. Thus, it is not necessary to have "moderation in all things." For both interpersonal and intrapersonal coordination, having strong promotion and strong prevention working together can be good for well-being. The secret is to know the conditions where they work together effectively and to appreciate the importance of regulatory fit in enhancing well-being.

I should also note that these conditions are not always met. When the activity is *not* divisible into different aspects that permit a fit with each value orientation, an individual can experience a conflict between his or her strong promotion and prevention orientations regarding which strategy to use in the task activity—whether it would be better to be eager or vigilant. Moreover, going back a step, the strong promotion and prevention orientations could create a conflict over which goal or task activity to pursue in the first place—the one that satisfies accomplishment or the one that satisfies security. Thus, to benefit from strong promotion and prevention working together, a person needs to select a goal or task activity that can satisfy both promotion and prevention concerns, such as "cooking a tasty and nutritious meal," and that can be divided into eager and vigilant aspects. Fortunately, the ability to frame or represent events in multiple ways makes this possible.

There is an additional caveat. Even when the activity *is* divisible and regulatory fit is created for both value orientations, something could go wrong during the activity, such as burning the sauce from too high a heat or leaving the stove too long to do something else, such as talking on the phone. When this happens, the exceptionally high engagement strength produced by the regulatory fit with both value orientations can intensify the negative reactions to the "disaster." What this highlights is that there is no failsafe plan for enhancing well-being. But nobody said it would be easy.

Implications for Well-Being of Engagement Strength From Regulatory Fit

It is not always best for well-being to be strongly engaged in what we are doing, as the case of addiction makes clear. In order to "feel alive" we must engage in life's activities, but it is important for all of us to know when to disengage from some activity. With that proviso, the maxim "Get engaged in life!" is generally good advice for enhancing well-being.

Among all of the clinical disorders, it is depression that is associated with the weakest engagement in life activities. Depression is associated with a failure of the promotion system; a promotion failure reduces eagerness, which creates a regulatory non-fit, which in turn will weaken engagement. If this condition is stable over time, as it is with depression, then the continuous weak engagement will generally de-intensify or reduce attraction to the positive things in the world that normally motivate the promotion system (i.e., reduce the potential gains in life). The result is "no interest in things," which is a central symptom of depression. It is no accident, I believe, that suicidal thoughts (and suicide) are relatively frequent among those who are depressed compared to those with other mental health problems. Choosing to end one's life is more likely when one doesn't "feel alive" to begin with.

It should be emphasized, however, that being strongly engaged in life's activities does not necessarily mean having more pleasant outcomes. It is not greater *pleasure* that underlies the contribution of stronger engagement to well-being. After all, as I discussed in Chapter 4, stronger engagement intensifies both negative and positive reactions to things. What stronger engagement does, especially, is contribute to control effectiveness, contribute to managing what happens. As the following maxim suggests, what counts is to get engaged: "You can't win if you don't play." Moreover, there is more than one way to play the game with strong engagement. You can play in an eager way or you can play in a vigilant manner—as long as you play in a way that fits your orientation. This does not necessarily yield an overall advantage for having desired emotional results, because winning will feel more positive but losing will feel more negative. But the experience of managing what happens while playing (i.e., control effectiveness) will be more intense, and this will contribute to well-being independent of whether you end up winning or losing: "What counts is not whether you win or lose, but how you play the game"[45].

The story of regulatory fit and engagement strength has even broader well-being implications that must also be considered. Weaker engagement from failure in the promotion system has costs—the loss of interest in things that is associated with depression. But too-strong engagement can also have costs under some conditions. There are two versions of such potential costs—one in the promotion system and the other in the prevention system. In the promotion system, individuals can be overeager (i.e., hyper-eager), which would create an even stronger fit with promotion and strengthen engagement even more. If the hyper-eagerness is stable, then the continuous super-high engagement strength will make positive things generally super-attractive, such as making potential accomplishments and advancements extremely attractive. An extreme version of this is the unreasonable enthusiasm that is associated with *manic* states. Indeed, excessive involvement in activities is a central symptom of mania.

Overly strong engagement can also come from the prevention system. When people fail in the prevention system they become more vigilant, which fits the prevention system and strengthens engagement. If the failure or anticipated failure is stable and severe, the continuous hyper-vigilance and super-high engagement strength will generally intensify anticipated negative things in life (i.e., all the "–1" things that must be prevented). An extreme version of this is the excessive or unreasonable guardedness or hyper-vigilance that is associated with *generalized anxiety disorder*.

Fortunately, these cases of hyper-eagerness and hyper-vigilance from continuous super-high engagement strength in the promotion and prevention systems are rare, and thus they do not contradict the argument that well-being generally benefits from strong rather than moderate motivations. But they can occur. Well-being and "the good life" *are* reduced when people are continuously hyper-eager or hyper-vigilant. This does not mean that Aristotle is correct in saying "all things in moderation" because the problem here is having extremely strong motivations rather than having strong or even very strong motivations. Moreover, it is not only the fact that the eagerness or vigilance is "hyper" (i.e., extreme), but also the fact that it is continuous and insensitive to circumstances. There are circumstances, such as getting engaged to be married, where very high enthusiasm and very high engagement strength is appropriate, and there are other circumstances, such as getting your family out of a burning building, where very high vigilance and very high engagement strength is appropriate. Being "moderate" in such circumstances does not contribute to "the good life" or well-being. Rather, what is necessary is to be flexible and responsive to what is appropriate and needed in different circumstances.

Regulatory Fit and Well-Being in Non-human Animals

It is clear that regulatory fit is an important factor in human motivation. Is the motivation of non-human animals also affected by regulatory fit? If it is, then this would demonstrate the significance of regulatory fit as a motivational variable with broad applicability. Moreover, it would mean that regulatory fit should be taken into account by caretakers of non-human animals.

Indeed, there is recent evidence that non-human animals are affected by regulatory fit. A master's thesis study by Becca Franks provides a compelling illustration of regulatory fit functioning in monkeys.[46] The inspiration for the research was the increasing interest among scientists in stable animal personalities,[47] such as the difference found in many species between "bold" versus "shy" animals. The standard animal personality perspective predicts cross-situational consistency in behavior, such as "bold" animals being consistently faster than "shy" animals to explore or check out new objects in their environment. From the perspective of regulatory fit, however, engagement strength as measured by speed of exploration or checking behavior would depend on whether this manner of behaving does or does not serve an animal's regulatory orientation.

Franks studied cotton-top tamarin monkeys. The monkeys were repeatedly observed in their cages to distinguish between promotion-oriented monkeys, who ate in the open more than the other monkeys (i.e., risking safety to gain food), and prevention-oriented monkeys, who hid more often than the other monkeys. Then the behavior of both sets of monkeys was examined when familiar and unfamiliar objects were introduced into their cage. Prior to the experimental test, the monkeys had learned that objects with one color had food hidden inside them, whereas objects with a different color did not. In addition, some objects were unfamiliar to the monkeys (three or fewer prior exposures to the object), whereas other objects were familiar to them (more than three prior exposures).

For the unfamiliar objects, the "promotion" monkeys moved toward them and explored them more quickly than did "prevention" monkeys, who cautiously checked them. This finding is consistent with "promotion" monkeys being more eager and "prevention" monkeys being more vigilant or cautious when approaching a goal. However, the same differential behavior would be predicted if "promotion" monkeys were actually "bold" monkeys and "prevention" monkeys were actually "shy" monkeys. What about the familiar objects? When the familiar object was a "food"-colored object, the "promotion" monkeys again approached it faster than the "prevention" monkeys. But when the familiar object was a "no food"-colored object, suddenly the "prevention" monkey looked more "bold" than the "promotion" monkeys. The "promotion" monkeys were slow to approach the familiar "no food"-colored object. After all, there was no food to be gained in this condition. But the "prevention" monkeys still approached this object to check that it was safe. This meant that they approached the familiar "no food"-colored object *faster* than the "promotion" monkeys. This is precisely the pattern that would be predicted for "promotion" versus "prevention" animals behaving in a regulatory fit manner, but it would not be predicted for "bold" versus "shy" animals.

These findings support the conclusion that non-human animals are affected by regulatory fit and non-fit. They also demonstrate that within a species there can be some individual animals who are more promotion oriented and others who are more prevention oriented. It is also possible that some animal species generally have a higher proportion of promotion-oriented individuals and other animal species generally have a higher proportion of prevention-oriented individuals. If so, this has implications for how animals in zoos, and personal pets, should be taken care of.[48]

Generally speaking, zookeepers create promotion-related conditions for the animals they care for—an environment in which animals can reliably gain positive outcomes like food, and in which punishment and danger are removed. This environment is more strongly promotion than is the natural environment in the wild. Zookeepers want their animals to be happy and free of pain, and creating promotion environments would seem to support this goal. However, a promotion environment may not be best for the well-being of those animals that are prevention oriented. To have the regulatory fit that strengthens engagement in their activities, prevention-oriented animals need to be vigilant, and vigilance is increased by the anticipation of future negative outcomes.

For prevention-oriented animals, well-being would be greater if they were treated as defensive pessimists rather than as optimists. The typical zoo environment, with its provision of reliably obtainable positive outcomes like receiving food and its rare negative outcomes, creates conditions that support optimism rather than defensive pessimism. For prevention-oriented animals, it would be better if defensive pessimism conditions were created (i.e., conditions with "if I do not do X, then negative Y will happen" contingencies). Otherwise, prevention-oriented animals will not experience regulatory fit and will not engage strongly in their activities. It could even be argued that defensive pessimism conditions are needed for these animals to "feel alive." And this would be true for prevention-oriented home pets as well. More generally, caretakers of prevention-oriented animals need to create environments where the animal needs to be vigilant in order to succeed. "One size fits all" is not a good plan for supervising or taking care of human or non-human animals.

WELL-BEING DURING THE BOOKENDS OF LIFE

In this chapter I have discussed how well-being can be enhanced when strong motivations work together to set constraints on one another that reduce each of their potential costs while maintaining their unique benefits. I have described how regulatory fit can strengthen engagement, make people "feel alive" and "feel right" about what they are doing. It is clear that "the good life" is not just having desired results, not just having "moderation in all things," and not just having independent motivations that combine additively. The importance for well-being of having strong motivations that go beyond pleasure and pain and work together is highlighted by the nature of well-being in early childhood and in old age. This section discusses how folk wisdoms regarding these bookends of life are generally consistent with the proposals in this chapter, but the take-away messages from these folk wisdoms are implicit and need to be made more explicit.

Folk Wisdom on Parenting for the Sake of Children's Well-Being

Parents naturally want the best for their children. They want to do everything they can to make their children happy and content. This would suggest that parents want to maximize their children's desired results. If this were the case, then value effectiveness would be all that parents wanted for their children and they would do whatever they could to make that happen. They would try to ensure that their children experience both promotion success and prevention success all the time. But is this, in fact, what most parents do? The folk wisdom expressions that capture people's understanding that such parenting is not good for children's well-being include the following derogatory labels: "spoiling" and "overprotective." What do these labels mean and why is such parenting bad for children's well-being?

Several years ago I wrote a paper on the different ways that parents, or care-takers more generally, interact with children that influence whether and how these children develop effective self-regulation. As self-discrepancy theory and regulatory focus theory developed over the years, I continued to elaborate on this socialization model of self-regulation, but its basic gist remained the same.[49] I distinguished between caretaker–child modes of interaction that support chil-dren developing a promotion orientation and modes that support their devel-oping a prevention orientation. Because a single caretaker can interact with a child in either mode at different times, and a child can interact with different caretakers who use different modes, a child can develop both strong promotion and strong prevention orientations. Often, however, one mode dominates and either promotion or prevention is emphasized (as I discussed in Chapter 11 regarding culture and personality).

Importantly, modes of caretaker–child interaction vary not only in whether promotion or prevention is emphasized but also in whether they set conditions for children to learn about self-regulatory contingencies—that is, to learn con-tingency rules like "When I do A, then X happens; but when I do B, then Y happens." Children are more likely to learn about self-regulatory contingencies when caretakers use *managing* modes. A promotion-oriented managing mode is the *bolstering* mode, as when a parent encourages a child to overcome difficulties and continue advancing toward the goal. A prevention-oriented managing mode is the *prudent* mode, as when a parent trains a child how to do something safely. These managing modes involve engineering and planning a child's environment so that he or she will learn how to overcome difficulties, meet challenges, and maintain satisfactory states in the face of potential dangers. In brief, managing modes set conditions for strong learning of self-regulatory contingencies.

In contrast to managing modes, *doting* modes (which I originally called "smothering") do *not* set conditions for strong learning of self-regulatory contingencies. According to my model, *spoiling* is a promotion-oriented doting mode, as when a parent praises and rewards a child no matter what the child does. *Overprotective* is a prevention-oriented doting mode, as when a parent child-proofs the house and restricts the child's activities to ensure that he or she cannot get hurt. These doting modes do not allow a child to learn self-regulatory contingencies because the outcomes are totally controlled by the parent and are independent of whatever the child does—that is, the outcomes are non-contingent.

It is important to emphasize that children do have desired results when the caretaking mode is doting. Indeed, it could be argued that, overall, the children have *more* desired results when the caretaking is doting rather than managing. This is because children receiving the managing mode can make mistakes and can fail, whereas only successful desired results are permitted in the doting mode. What, then, is the problem with the doting mode? Why does folk wisdom about parenting use the terms "spoiling" and "overprotective"—as well as "overpermissive"—in a derogatory manner? I believe it is because people understand, at least tacitly, that the doting modes undermine children's opportunity to learn those realistic self-regulatory contingencies that will support their well-being now and in the future.

And exactly what do these self-regulatory contingencies do that support children's well-being? First, these contingencies establish realities about the world regarding what happens or does not happen as a function of how children behave or do not behave. That is, these contingencies involve *truth* effectiveness. Second, these contingencies are used by children when they plan and manage what happens in their world. That is, these contingencies involve *control* effectiveness. What this means, then, is that the doting modes of "spoiling" and "overprotective" can have an advantage for children having desired results (value effectiveness), but they have a major disadvantage for children learning how the world really works (truth effectiveness) and for them managing what happens (control effectiveness). What the folk wisdom is expressing—consistent with the overall theme of this book—is that value effectiveness is *not* enough. For well-being, truth effectiveness and control effectiveness are necessary. And that is why "spoiling" and "overprotective" parenting is bad for children.

The prototype of the child whose well-being suffers from such parenting is "the poor little rich kid."[50]

Earlier I discussed the role of regulatory fit in taking care of zoo animals and pets. I discussed how zookeepers, and pet owners as well, want their animals to be happy and free of pain. Given the above discussion, one might even argue that when a "spoiling" or "overprotective" environment is created for some zoo animals and pets, the animals become equivalent to "the poor little rich kid." I also discussed the need for caretakers of zoo animals and pets to create an environment that motivationally fits the animals in their care. This take-away message applies to taking care of children as well. For example, a promotion environment may not be best for the well-being of children who are more prevention oriented. For prevention-oriented children, well-being might be greater if they were treated as vigilant defensive pessimists rather than as eager optimists. More generally, there needs to be a fit between the promotion, prevention, locomotion, and assessment orientations of children and the environment that is created for them by their caretakers. A fit might occur more naturally with a parent because the child's orientation would *itself* be influenced by the environment that the parent creates. But rather than having a single parent as the only caretaker, most children have multiple caretakers—a mother, a father, grandparents, older siblings, teachers, coaches, and so on—and thus there is the potential for a non-fit between the child's orientation and the environment that is created by a particular caretaker. Children also need a fit to "feel alive," and future research needs to examine how a caretaker's interactions with a child can be *tailored* to fit that child's motivational orientation for the sake of the child's well-being.

Old Age and Well-Being

For many people, it was a surprise when lifespan development researchers reported that there was, if anything, an *increase* in well-being in old age rather than the expected decline.[51] Why would most people expect a decline? I believe that it is because most people, myself included, would think about the physical discomforts, the "aches and pains," that are associated with old age. If well-being is about having pleasant rather than unpleasant experiences, and old age is a period of "aches and pains," then well-being should decline during old age.

But what if well-being is about being effective? Consider first value effectiveness, having desired results. On the downside of old age there would be the undesired results of having "aches and pains." Yet having desired results is more than just having positive hedonic experiences: it is also looking back to desired results that have been achieved, like having a spouse and family, taking care of children as they grew up, having a job and a home, and so on. Precisely because older people have had a long life, they have a long history of past successes that they can remember as having desired results. They can look back to a "life fulfilled" in a way that younger people cannot because they are still striving and do not yet feel fulfilled. This is an upside of old age regarding value effectiveness that could compensate for a decline in current hedonic pleasures.

However, the secret of old age may not concern value effectiveness to begin with. Instead, it could be about control and truth effectiveness. The literature on aging describes how older people manage effectively in ways that younger people do not. Older people are more selective in choosing when and with whom to have social interactions. They are also more selective in choosing which goals to pursue, and concentrate their resources more on selected priorities rather than exploring many different pathways of life.[52]

Thus, one secret of old age is that there are increases in effectively managing what happens, such as effective selection of what to do and whom to see (i.e., control effectiveness). This effective management can contribute to well-being—benefits that most of us had not recognized. But it is, perhaps, truth effectiveness that is most overlooked when people are surprised at hearing that well-being increases in old age. This way of being effective receives insufficient attention in lay theories of what contributes to well-being and the "good life." I believe that it receives insufficient attention by scientists as well when they consider the well-being of older people. It would receive more attention if people remembered Aristotle's emphasis on contemplation and intellectual activities.

For Aristotle's vision of the "good life," and for Peterson and Seligman's positive psychology vision of "happiness," *Wisdom and Knowledge* as a core virtue is a major contributor to well-being. And, notably, old age is associated not only with "aches and pains" but also with "older and wiser." Thus, perhaps, greater wisdom in old age—greater truth effectiveness—could be one of the secrets of well-being in old age. According to Erik Erikson, true wisdom develops in the eighth and final stage of life.[53]

The "success story" of old age, then, highlights once again the importance for well-being of truth and control effectiveness rather than just hedonic pleasure. And the contribution of truth and control motivations to well-being could be especially great when they work together effectively—a life of going in the right direction. More generally, regulatory fit and motivations working together effectively may be a significant part of the "success story" of old age, although this has not yet been studied to my knowledge. For example, one important consequence of being successful in truth and control could be learning which strategic manner fits which situation or circumstance. Such learning could increase with age, and could be part of what is meant by "older but wiser." Well-being is about learning the truth—about when to be promotion–eager, when to be prevention–vigilant, and when to be both; when to locomote, when to assess, and when to do both; when to be strongly engaged and when to disengage—and then acting on this knowledge and managing to make it happen. Effectiveness is about finding the right motivation (or motivation partnership) in the right circumstance, and this can come with experience and maturity.

Precisely because there are *trade-offs* of promotion, prevention, locomotion, assessment, and engagement strength, learning how to change motivational states in changing circumstances contributes greatly to having a good life and well-being. Well-being is *not* about "moderation in all things." It is about being effective in *tailoring* motives *to fit* the situation. It's the fit that counts. And for there to be fit, value effectiveness cannot stand alone: it must work together with truth and control. Well-being is beyond pleasure and pain. It is about value, truth, and control *working together* effectively.

CONCLUDING THOUGHTS

Despite the popular media's emphasis on pleasure, what is clear is that a good life and well-being are not all about maximizing pleasure and minimizing pain. In extending the analysis of the non-hedonic factors, I have emphasized the importance of establishing what's real (truth effectiveness) and managing what happens (control effectiveness) for having a good life and well-being, rather than just having desired results (value effectiveness). I have also emphasized the role of regulatory fit in the overall story. Regulatory fit highlights the importance for well-being of motivations working together effectively. I believe that this part of the story is critically important and needs to receive more research attention in the future.

Consider, for example, coordinating the motivations of the members of a team. If you were the manager of the team, would you want every team member to be moderately strong on his or her predominant motivation, or would you want him or her to be very strong on his or her predominant motivation? President Abraham Lincoln wanted his team to be composed of individuals who would each strongly advocate his personal viewpoint—a "Team of Rivals."[54] President Barack Obama also said that this was the kind of Cabinet that he wanted. Justice in court trials is also supposed to be produced by the prosecuting lawyers and defense lawyers *strongly* advocating their different positions. What makes such a group composition effective is that the members challenge and constrain one another such that a product emerges that is different from and better than just the sum of the parts. For this dynamic to work effectively, the different motivations need to be strong, but not necessarily equally strong, and, most important, they need to work together and not just combine as independent motivations.

Whether coordinating team members' different motivations or coordinating our own personal motivations, future research needs to consider more fully how promotion, prevention, locomotion, and assessment can work together to create well-being. It will not always be the case that the best combinations will involve all the motivations being strong. But I do believe that Aristotle was wrong when he proposed "moderation in all things" and "a perfect balance." I have illustrated this with examples of how strong promotion working together with strong prevention can be an advantage, as can strong locomotion working together with strong assessment. I am also confident that we will find that the significance of motivations functioning dynamically as integrative structures is different from, and sometimes greater than, the sum of independent motivational parts. In this sense, we have only begun to understand where a good life and well-being come from. Research on the effects of regulatory fit and motivations like assessment and locomotion *working together* is a beginning to this new story of how motivation works.

NOTES

Chapter 1

1. See Comer & Laird (1975).
2. See Lewis (1965).
3. See Bianco, Higgins, & Klem (2003).
4. A "sniglet" is a neologism, which is defined as a word that doesn't appear in the dictionary, but should. It is intended to be funny. The term was created by comedian Rich Hall when he performed on the comedy series "Not Necessarily the News" for HBO in the 1980s. An example of a sniglet is: "Elbonics—*n*. The actions of two people maneuvering for one armrest in a movie theater."
5. See Higgins, Idson, Freitas, Spiegel, & Molden (2003).
6. Readers who are familiar with Kahneman & Tversky's (1979) prospect theory might find it surprising that there was no effect on value from the "gain" of eager framing versus the "loss" of vigilant framing. But both framing conditions referred to the positive qualities of the mug and the pen, to be gained or not lost, and thus it was not the case that some participants were in an area of gains whereas others were in an area of losses. This study is described in more detail in Chapter 4.
7. I should note that when people decide to carry out a goal pursuit despite its having unpleasant properties, there could also be an inferential process that could create value. For example, people could infer that they must value the goal a lot if they are willing to suffer to attain it. Such evaluative inferences will be considered in Chapter 4. But, notably, it is unlikely that the rats in this study are making such inferences. And for those readers familiar with cognitive dissonance theory, I will also be discussing how dissonance might account for such findings, while also being skeptical that a dissonance-like justification process is the mechanism underlying such findings with rats.
8. In Chapter 7, I will discuss in more detail the role of likelihood in each of these two theories, and will describe the different ways in which likelihood functions as a separate motivational force, including being itself a source of value rather than just a moderator of value.
9. See *Webster's Ninth New Collegiate Dictionary* (1989).

CHAPTER 2

1. For Freud's instinctual energy concept, see Freud (1957/1915).

2. For Hull's general drive concept, see Hull (1943; 1952). Performance was determined by this general drive interacting with habit strength, with habit strength increasing when a behavior had been previously rewarded frequently.

3. See Kimble (1961), p. 396.

4. See Kimble (1961), p. 434.

5. See Hebb (1955), p. 249.

6. Lewin's field theory: see Lewin (1951).

7. Lewin's version of the "energy (to be directed)" viewpoint varies somewhat from the more common version described earlier where one first creates the energy in a person (or a car or a toy) and then guides or directs the person toward the goal. In Lewin's model, by introducing a goal for a person, one creates an energy force within that person for movement toward it. In this sense, Lewin's version of "energy (to be directed)" is less "all-purpose" than some other versions because each directional goal itself creates the energy for locomotion to reach it. The sense in which it remains "all-purpose" is that distinctions are not made between different types of tension systems for different types of directional forces—the tension system and forces are all-purpose across different directional goals.

8. This "flow" or "in the zone" phenomenon is a fascinating one (see Csikszentmihalyi, 1975, 1990), and I will return to it later in the book. For now, let me simply suggest that it is an experience of efficiency, where experts in an activity domain (e.g., long-distance running, mountain climbing, math problem solving) can become so *efficient* that they can direct full attention to the task and be highly productive with relatively little effort expenditure.

9. The car was a rental in France with no indication that it had a diesel engine, but most important, the fuel nozzle restrictor that usually comes with such cars was missing. But the silver lining was that once the car broke down in a small town, I got to practice my French.

10. See Higgins (2009).

11. See Bianco, Higgins, & Klem (2003).

12. Animal learning/biological models: see Gray (1982); Konorski (1967); Lang (1995); Miller, (1944); Mowrer (1960).

13. Cybernetic-control models: see Carver & Scheier (1990); Miller, Pribram, & Galanter (1960); Powers (1973).

14. Dynamic models: see Atkinson (1964); McClelland, Atkinson, Clark, & Lowell (1953).

15. For Wiener's cybernetic model about feedback loops, see Wiener (1948).

16. For Miller, Galanter, & Pribram's Test-Operate-Test-Exit model of feedback loops, see Miller et al. (1960).

17. For a fuller discussion of the distinction between regulatory anticipation and regulatory reference, see Higgins (1997).

18. Carver and Scheier's control theory: see Carver & Scheier (1981; 1990; 1998).

19. Powers' control theory: see Powers (1973).

20. Even this asymmetry is exaggerated because actual movement need not occur. Actions that are "close" or "distant" from a reference value need not require actual

movement and need not be conceptualized in such terms. Much of human problem solving, for example, involves mental processes without any actual movement, what Lewin referred to as locomotion at the level of irreality (Lewin, 1951).

21. See Carver & Scheier (1981; 1990).

22. See Bandura's social cognitive theory (Bandura, 1986) and my self-discrepancy theory (Higgins, 1987).

23. See Higgins (1997) for a fuller discussion of matches and mismatches to end-states as an alternative conception to the "movement" metaphor.

24. For a discussion of "decision utility," see Kahneman (1999).

25. For example, for research and discussion on the distinction between distributive justice versus procedural justice, see Tyler & Smith (1998).

26. For fuller discussions of regulatory focus theory's distinction between promotion and prevention orientations, see Higgins (1997, 1998b) and Scholer & Higgins (in press, d).

27. For a discussion of the strategic preferences associated with promotion and prevention, see Higgins (2000a); Higgins & Spiegel (2004).

28. See Scholer & Higgins (in press, a).

29. See Scholer & Higgins (2008).

30. Darwin's theory of evolution: see Darwin (1859).

31. The faulty inference that "survival" must be the answer is an example of a very pervasive inferential error called the "aboutness principle." This refers to the inference that whatever something is "about," in this case that "survival" is what the phrase "survival of the fittest" is all "about," must also be the source of what it is you are trying to explain—that a basic motivation to survive is the source of the phenomenon called "survival of the fittest." For a fuller discussion of this inferential error, see Higgins (1998).

32. For a classic description of this viewpoint, see Woodworth (1918).

33. See Woodworth & Schlosberg (1954).

34. For a fuller discussion of terror management theory, see Becker (1973); Pyszczynski, Greenberg, & Solomon (1997).

35. See Damasio (1994) for a discussion of the importance of affective experience in motivating decisions.

36. See *Webster's Ninth New Collegiate Dictionary* (1989), p. 561.

37. See Jeremy Bentham (1781/1988).

38. See Jeremy Bentham (1781/1988), p. 2.

39. See Freud's *Beyond the Pleasure Principle*, Freud (1920/1950).

40. See Lewin (1935).

41. See Mowrer (1960).

42. See Atkinson (1964).

43. See Kahneman & Tversky (1979).

44. See Kahneman, Diener, & Schwarz (1999).

45. For a review of this evidence, see Eisenberger (1972).

46. For a review of these early studies, see Woodsworth & Schlosberg (1954).

47. See Olds & Milner (1954).

48. Berridge & Robinson (2003).

49. For a fuller discussion of this point, see Higgins (1997).

50. See McMahon (2002).
51. See Dodes (2002), p. 206.
52. For fuller discussions of the "liking" versus "wanting" distinction, and its relation to addiction, see Berridge & Robinson (2003); Robinson & Berridge (2003).
53. For this quote and a fuller description of extreme sports, see Wikipedia "Extreme sport."
54. See Brymer (2005).
55. See Keynes (1936/1951), Chapter 12, Part VII, pp. 161–162.
56. See Heidbreder (1933) for a fuller discussion of the Dynamic Psychology movement (also known, proudly in my department, as the Columbia School of Psychology), as well as the six other major movements in the early development of psychology as a discipline.
57. See Woodworth (1940), p. 374.
58. See Thorndike (1911).
59. See Hebb (1955). NOW ADD
60. See Hebb (1930).
61. See Hebb (1955).
62. See Hebb (1955).
63. See Bexton, Heron, & Scott (1954).
64. For earlier evidence of a similar bell-shaped curve relating strength of stimulus to rate of learning, see Yerkes & Dodson (1908).
65. See White (1959).
66. See White (1959), p. 297.
67. Note that White does accept the notion, like the drive theorists Freud and Hull, that what it means to be motivated is "directed energy," as reflected in his constant use of the term "energies."
68. See Groos (1901). Note that according to Groos, children's play was preparation or practice for the later demands of life.
69. See Piaget (1952).
70. See Piaget (1951), p. 90. Notably, the notion of play being in the service of affecting the environment rather than serving organic needs is extended by Woodworth (1958) to the case of social play, where he says that the playmates afford the opportunity to do something interesting in the environment rather than satisfying organic needs or even needs for affection.
71. See Piaget (1952). For another discussion of children's motivation to be effective, see Hunt (1961).
72. See White (1959), p. 317.
73. See White (1959), p. 317.
74. See White (1959), p. 322.
75. See Bandura (1982), p. 122.
76. See Neufeld & Thomas (1977). See also Goldberg, Weisenberg, Drobkin, Blittner, & Gunnar Gotestam (1997).
77. See Bandura (1986).
78. See Deci (1975; 1980); Deci & Ryan (1985; 2000).
79. See Deci & Ryan (2000), p. 229.

80. See Webster (1989). For a fuller discussion of the role of volition in human motivation, see deCharms (1968).
81. For a similar distinction among motives influencing choices, see Kelman (1958).
82. See *Oxford English Dictionary* (1971).
83. See Higgins (2000a), Higgins & Spiegel (2004), and Molden & Higgins (2008).
84. See Higgins (1996a; 1996c).
85. See Higgins (2001).
86. See Higgins (2000a) and Higgins (2010).
87. See Higgins (2006) and Higgins (2008).
88. See Higgins (1996a; 1996c).
89. See Frijda (1986), Mandler (1984), and Simon (1967). For a more recent account of how positive and negative feelings provide information about whether current conditions are, respectively, non-problematic or problematic, see Schwarz (1990).
90. This argument is consistent with a position taken many decades ago by Gordon Allport (1937a) in an important paper called "The functional autonomy of motives."
91. See Brehm & Self (1989) and Wright (2008).

CHAPTER 3

1. For thorough and thoughtful discussions of how self-esteem relates to experiencing acceptance or rejection from others, see Leary & Baumeister (2000) and Leary, Tambor, Terdal, & Downs (1995).
2. See Tulving (2005) and Higgins & Pittman (2008).
3. For a discussion of how overcoming obstacles and opposing interfering forces can increase strength of engagement, see Higgins (2006).
4. For discussions of this difference, see Dweck (1999) and Nicholls (1984).
5. See *Oxford English Dictionary* (1971).
6. It is interesting that the definitions in the *Oxford English Dictionary* (1971) allow non-living things like machinery to "fail" more than they allow them to "succeed." You can test this in your own knowledge of discourse. For me at least, I could talk about a machine failing, the ground beneath me failing (when walking on a beach, for example), the winds failing while sailing, and so on, but I would not talk about a machine succeeding, the ground beneath me succeeding, or the winds succeeding while sailing. This is intriguing and suggests to me that humans are not willing to give human-like credit to non-living things for success—which we will take credit for, thank you very much—but we *are* willing to blame them.
7. For discussions of motivation as goal pursuit, see Elliot & Fryer (2008), Elliott & Dweck (1988), Kruglanski et al. (2002), McDougall (1914), and Pervin (1989).
8. For a review, see Elliot & Fryer (2008).
9. See Woodworth (1921), p. 70.
10. See Lewin (1935) and Lewin (1951) for discussions of goal pursuit and valence in a field of forces. In Chapter 4, I will return to the important question "Where does value come from?" and will reconsider the forces of attraction and repulsion in terms of the contributions of value effectiveness, truth effectiveness, and control effectiveness to the experience of these forces.

11. See *Oxford English Dictionary* (1971) and *Webster's Ninth New Collegiate Dictionary* (1989).

12. See *Oxford English Dictionary* (1971) and *Webster's Ninth New Collegiate Dictionary* (1989).

13. James (1948/1890), p. 462.

14. See *Oxford English Dictionary* (1971) and *Webster's Ninth New Collegiate Dictionary* (1989). I should note that there is another meaning of control that relates to checking or verifying the accuracy of something, such as a statement or story or conclusion. Although such checking or verifying typically involves procedures, competencies, and resources, and thus would involve control effectiveness in that regard, it is in the service of determining what is accurate, valid, or real, and thus will be considered here to reflect truth effectiveness.

15. See Carder & Berkowitz (1970).

16. See Ross & Sicoly (1979). I should note that Ross & Sicoly's (1979) explanation for this phenomenon has more to do with cognitive accessibility biases regarding our own actions versus someone else's actions. They suggest that motivational biases like self-enhancement could not account for what happened because credit was being taken for a bad outcome. But this argument applies to value effectiveness more than control effectiveness. I believe that control effectiveness motivation is also a factor in the general phenomenon of people taking responsibility for joint projects, even when they fail. I should note as well that there is also evidence that people mainly take credit for good joint outcomes.

17. See Nozick (1974).

18. See Osgood, Suci, & Tannenbaum (1957).

19. It is interesting that both value effectiveness and truth effectiveness were part of the evaluation dimension because when people evaluate whether to take a particular action or engage in an activity, they need to take into account both the value effectiveness and truth effectiveness associated with that action or activity. As I discuss later, it is this value–truth relation that underlies commitment to a particular action or activity.

20. For the full report of this study, see Iyengar & Lepper (1999).

21. For a review of children's perceptions of motivation as a function of child vs. significant other choosing an activity, see Costanzo & Dix (1983).

22. For a similar argument with respect to cultural differences in the experience of choice, see Hernandez & Iyengar (2001).

23. See Iyengar & Lepper (1999).

24. See Bandura (1982), p. 142.

25. For the full report of this study, see Lepper, Greene, & Nisbett (1973). For other classic studies demonstrating the same basic phenomenon, see Deci (1971), Kruglanski, Friedman, & Zeevi (1971), and Ross (1975).

26. In Chapter 4 I will discuss in more detail how making an effort, choosing to engage in an activity that has some undesired properties associated with it (i.e., overcoming personal resistance), can increase strength of engagement in an activity and thereby increase value (see also Higgins, 2006). I will also present evidence in Chapter 8 of how an instrumental reward for doing an activity can *enhance* interest in doing that activity again if the reward matches or fits the orientation toward the activity.

27. See Horner (1968).
28. See Shaver (1976).
29. See Feather (1989).
30. See Tesser (1988).
31. See Swann (1987).
32. For discussions of the distinction between promotion and prevention concerns and their relation to emotional experiences, see Higgins (1997; 2001). These emotional experiences and the mechanisms underlying them are discussed in more detail in Chapter 4.
33. See Ortony, Clore, & Collins (1988).
34. See, for example, Gellner (1988) and Spruyt (1994).
35. See *Oxford English Dictionary* (1971) and *Webster's Ninth New Collegiate Dictionary* (1989).
36. See Eagly & Chaiken (1993).
37. I should note that the Declaration's choice of "Liberty" for control effectiveness and the Declaration's choice of "the pursuit of Happiness" for value effectiveness are, in fact, not the only possible choices. As we will see later in Chapter 4 and Chapter 6, these are the choices that fit specific motivational orientations—locomotion and promotion, respectively. And, as will be discussed in Chapter 11, locomotion and promotion are still the predominant orientations in America. But they are not predominant in all nations, nor are they predominant among all Americans. They would be a good choice for the Declaration, however, because they would have been a fit for most of the audience, and, as discussed in Chapter 8, this would have strengthened the message for those in the audience and made them "feel right" about it.
38. See Epstein (1992), Deci & Ryan (2000), Maslow (1943), Murray (1938), and Pittman & Zeigler (2007).
39. See Baumeister & Leary (1995), Bowlby (1969), Fiske (2004), and Hazan & Shaver (1987).
40. It is notable that my examples of ways of being effective not being the whole story of what people really want are all cases of hedonic pleasure. This deserves further comment. People are motivated to have pleasant sensual experiences. Generally speaking, they are not motivated to have painful sensual experiences and, when they do choose to have them, it is usually because they are instrumental, as when people apply painful cold treatments followed by painful hot treatments to reduce swelling after an injury. Typically, people avoid painful sensual experiences, and what they do to make this happen involves control effectiveness. And successful pain avoidance means that the pain is not actually experienced. Thus, there is an asymmetry here between pleasure and pain. The evidence for the importance of hedonic experience as a motivator beyond just effectiveness is stronger for the case of pleasure than pain.

CHAPTER 4

1. See Thorndike (1911).
2. See Deci (1971) and Lepper, Greene, & Nisbett (1973).

3. For the full report of this study, see Lepper, Greene, & Nisbett (1973). For other classic studies demonstrating the same basic phenomenon, see Deci (1971), Kruglanski, Friedman, & Zeevi (1971), and Ross (1975).

4. See Allport (1961), p. 543.

5. See Eagly & Chaiken (1993).

6. See *Oxford English Dictionary* (1971); *Webster's Ninth New Collegiate Dictionary* (1989).

7. For a discussion of the concept of "affordance," see Gibson (1979).

8. See Smith (1776/1994).

9. See Weiner (1972).

10. See Woodworth (1918).

11. See Eagly & Chaiken (1993).

12. See Eagly & Chaiken (1993).

13. See Fang, Singh, & AhluWalia (2007), Freitas, Azizian, Travers, & Berry (2005), Titchener (1910), and Zajonc (1968).

14. See Hovland, Janis, & Kelley (1953) and Rogers (1975).

15. See Clary, Snyder, Ridge, Miene, & Haugen (1994), Katz (1960), and Smith, Bruner, & White (1956).

16. See Deci (1975; 1980) and Deci & Ryan (1985; 2000).

17. See Rokeach (1980), p. 262. See also Williams (1979).

18. See Merton (1957) p. 133. See also Rokeach (1979) and Schwartz (1992).

19. See Thibaut & Walker (1975) and Tyler & Lind (1992).

20. See Rokeach (1973), Schwartz & Bilsky (1987), and Seligman, Olson, & Zanna (1996).

21. See Lewin (1952).

22. See Carver & Scheier (1981; 1990), Miller, Galanter, & Pribram (1960), Powers (1973), and Wiener (1948).

23. For discussions of self-discrepancy theory, see Higgins (1987; 1991; 1998b) and Moretti & Higgins (1999). For related ideas, see also James (1890/1948) and Rogers (1961).

24. See Bandura (1986), Boldero & Francis (2002), Carver & Scheier (1990), Duval & Wicklund (1972), and Higgins (1987; 1996d).

25. See Higgins (1987; 1989a).

26. See Tesser (1988).

27. See Hyman (1942) and Merton & Kitt (1952).

28. See Wicklund & Gollwitzer (1982).

29. See Cialdini, Borden, Thorne, Walker, Freeman, & Sloan (1976) and Tesser (1988).

30. See Tajfel & Turner (1979).

31. See Bem (1965; 1967).

32. See Heider (1958), Jones & Davis (1965), and Schachter & Singer (1962).

33. See Skinner (1953; 1957).

34. See Kruglanski (1975), Lepper, Greene, & Nisbett (1973), and Salancik & Conway (1975).

35. See Andersen (1984) and Schwarz & Clore (1988).

36. See Schwarz & Clore (1983).
37. See Gilovich (1981), Holyoak & Thagard (1997), and Tversky & Kahneman (1974).
38. Examples include Bayesian logic (e.g., Trope, 1986a) or the information gain logic that is proposed in Higgins and Trope's activity engagement theory (e.g., Higgins, Trope, & Kwon, 1999).
39. See Kohlberg (1969; 1976) and Piaget (1932/1965).
40. For a critical discussion of this viewpoint, see Haidt (2001).
41. See Tyler & Smith (1998).
42. See Helson (1964), Higgins & Stangor (1988), Higgins, Strauman, & Klein (1986), and Sherif & Hovland (1961).
43. See Thaler (1999).
44. See Kahneman & Miller (1986), Kahneman & Tversky (1982), and Roese (1997).
45. See Haidt (2001) and Williams (1985).
46. See Freud (1923/1961).
47. See Haidt (2001).
48. See Bentham (1781/1988), Hume (1777/1975), and Smith (1759/1997).
49. See Eisenberger (1972) and Woodsworth & Schlosberg (1954).
50. See Jeremy Bentham (1781/1988, p. 1).
51. See Kahneman, Diener, & Schwarz (1999) and Kahneman & Tversky (1979).
52. See Kahneman (2000a).
53. See Redelmeier and Kahneman (1996).
54. See Miller (1963), Mowrer (1960), and Spence (1958).
55. See Spinoza (1677/1986).
56. See Frijda (1986a), Mandler (1984), and Simon (1967).
57. See Diener & Emmons (1984), Frijda, Kuipers, & ter Schure (1989), Feldman Barrett & Russell (1998), Green, Goldman, & Salovey (1993), Larsen & Diener (1985), Ortony, Clore, & Collins (1988), Roseman (1984), Russell (1980), Scherer (1988), Schlosberg (1952), Smith & Ellsworth (1985), Watson & Tellegen (1985), and Wundt (1896/1999).
58. See Eagly & Chaiken (1993).
59. See Kahneman & Tversky (1979) and Lopes (1987).
60. See Higgins (1987).
61. See Ortony et al. (1988), Roseman (1984), and Russell (1980).
62. See Rozin (2000), p. 9.
63. For a fuller discussion of regulatory engagement theory, see Higgins (2006) and Higgins & Scholer (2009a).
64. See Lewin (1951).
65. See Higgins (2006).
66. See Berlyne (1960), Berlyne (1973), and Mandler (1984).
67. See Higgins (2006) and Higgins & Scholer (2009a).
68. See Förster, Grant, Idson, & Higgins (2001) and Förster, Higgins, & Idson (1998).
69. See Cacioppo, Priester, & Berntson (1993).
70. See Higgins, Idson, Freitas, Spiegel, & Molden (2003).

71. For a fuller discussion of how strength of engagement influences the intensity of the value experiences of attraction and repulsion, see Higgins (2006). It should also be noted that stronger engagement from regulatory fit can be associated with an experience of "feeling right" about what one is doing, and that weaker engagement from regulatory non-fit can be associated with an experience of "feeling wrong" about what one is doing. Again, these experiences of "feeling right" or "feeling wrong" from regulatory fit and non-fit differ from hedonic and ethical experiences. For a fuller discussion of this, see Higgins (2007).

72. See Cesario, Grant, & Higgins (2004).

73. See Tyler & Blader (2000; 2003).

74. See Higgins, Camacho, Idson, Spiegel, & Scholer (2008).

75. There was some additional evidence in this research program supporting both the idea that the participants in the "Right Way" condition were more strongly engaged in the decision-making activity than participants in the "Best Choice" condition, and the idea that the greater attraction of the mug for participants in the "Right Way" condition was independent of their perception of future hedonic outcomes.

76. See March (1994).

77. Woodworth (1940), p. 396.

78. See Lewin (1935).

79. See Brehm (1966), Brehm & Brehm (1981), and Wicklund (1974).

80. See Brehm, Stires, Sensenig, & Shaban (1966).

81. See Lewin (1935).

82. See Bushman & Stack (1996).

83. See by Fitzsimons & Lehmans (2004).

84. I should note that there is considerable variability across individuals in the extent to which perceived threats to freedom will produce reactance. See Bushman & Stack (1996), Fitzsimons & Lehmans (2004), and Friestad & Wright (1994).

85. See Lewis (1965).

86. See Lewin (1935) and Zeigarnik (1938).

87. See Cartwright (1942).

88. See Mischel & Masters (1966).

89. See Mischel & Patterson (1978).

90. See Freitas, Liberman, & Higgins (2002).

91. See Higgins, Marguc, & Scholer (2010).

92. See Higgins, Marguc, & Scholer (2010).

93. See Lewin (1935; 1951).

94. See Higgins & Scholer (2009a).

95. See Brehm & Self (1989) and Wright (1996; 2008).

96. See Brehm & Self (1989).

97. See Brickman (1987).

98. See Brehm & Cohen (1962), Festinger (1957), and Wicklund & Brehm (1976). I will also be discussing cognitive dissonance theory in Chapter 5 as it relates to truth effectiveness.

99. Wanting to make sense of the world and resolve inconsistent cognitions is part of the motivation to have an understanding of the world that is real. Thus, cognitive

dissonance theory will be reconsidered in Chapter 5 when the motivation for truth is considered. What this highlights is that the same phenomena, such as those examined in cognitive dissonance studies, can involve more than one kind of motivation to be effective, in this case both value motivation (wanting to have what's desired) and truth motivation (wanting to establish what's real).

100. See Aronson & Mills (1959).

101. See also Brickman (1987) and Deci (1980).

102. See Lawrence & Festinger (1962).

103. To be honest, I am not a fan of this explanation of the results because not only am I, frankly, skeptical that rats engage in such justifications, but also it is not clear to me why there would be dissonance at all in this situation. According to Festinger (1957), there is no dissonance if a decision can be explained or rationalized. If the only way to get to the food is to go up the inclined runway, regardless of whether it is 50 degrees or 25 degrees, then there is no choice but to go up the incline. The fact that there is no choice is a sufficient explanation or rationalization for the choice. Thus, there should be no dissonance to begin with.

104. Although these rat studies were inspired by cognitive dissonance theory, they do not seem easily explained in terms of truth motivation (i.e., the rats trying to make sense of the world by cognitively justifying the costs of their high effort). This is a case where the value explanation relating stronger engagement to intensifying attraction seems to be clearly superior. As will be seen in Chapter 5, however, there are other studies inspired by cognitive dissonance theory where an explanation in terms of truth motivation is highly reasonable.

105. See Cairns (1967).

106. See Hess (1959).

107. See Lawrence & Festinger (1962).

CHAPTER 5

1. This was the question that Philip Brickman (1978) asked decades ago in a provocative chapter from the book series on "New Directions in Attribution Research."

2. See Johnson, Foley, & Leach (1988).

3. Loftus & Palmer (1974).

4. Higgins & Rholes (1978).

5. See Perky (1910). For additional research on this phenomenon, see Segal (1970).

6. See Johnson & Sherman (1990) and Johnson & Raye (1981). For a psychoanalytic perspective on distinguishing what is real from what is imaginary, see Lacan (1991).

7. See Johnson & Sherman (1990) and Johnson & Raye (1981).

8. See Segal (1970), p. 111.

9. See James (1948/1890).

10. See James (1948/1890).

11. See Case (1985), Piaget (1965/1932), and Werner (1957).

12. See Gopnik (1996).

13. See Asch (1952), p. 131.

14. See Griffin & Ross (1991) and Ross & Ward (1995).
15. Indeed, this is one way of characterizing the classic "actor–observer" difference in person perception (see Jones & Nisbett, 1972; Storms, 1973).
16. Admittedly, it is not always easy to distinguish between motivational and cognitive mechanisms. For discussions of cognitive mechanisms, see Johnson (2006), Johnson & Sherman (1990), Johnson & Raye (1981), and Schooler, Gerhard, & Loftus (1986).
17. See Hardin & Higgins (1996).
18. See Johnson & Raye (1981).
19. See Brickman (1978).
20. See Higgins & Pittman (2008).
21. See Brickman (1978).
22. See Hilton, Fein, & Miller (1993).
23. See Heider (1958), Jones & Davis (1965), and Malle (2004). Malle (2004) makes the important point that people seek *causes* for behaviors they believe were unintentionally produced (e.g., unconscious impulses) and seek *reasons* for behaviors they believe were intentionally produced, with reasons referring to inner states of the actor such as the actor's beliefs, desires, or attitudes.
24. For a well-known example of this, see Jones & Davis (1965).
25. See Brewer (1988), Gilbert (1990), Higgins, Strauman, & Klein (1986), Ross & Olson (1981), and Trope (1986a).
26. See Trope (1986a). It should also be noted, as mentioned by Higgins, Strauman, & Klein (1986), that situational context can influence the first step representation as well, such as whether turned-up corners of a mouth are represented as a smile or a grimace.
27. See Higgins (1996b).
28. See Higgins (1998a).
29. See, for example, Higgins, Rholes, & Jones (1977).
30. See Brown (1958b).
31. The level of abstraction selected can itself have important subsequent effects because level of abstraction relates to psychological distance, and psychological distance has been shown to have major motivational effects (see Liberman, Trope, & Stephan, 2007).
32. See Macrae & Bodenhausen (2000).
33. See Bandura & Walters (1963).
34. See Tolman (1948).
35. See Tolman & Honzik (1930). See also Blodgett (1929).
36. See Hull (1952).
37. For recent reviews of this extensive literature, see Hilton (2008), Kruglanski & Sleeth-Keppler (2007), Malle (2004), and Uleman, Saribay, & Gonzalez (2008).
38. See Heider (1958), Jones & Davis (1965), Trope & Higgins (1993), and Weiner, Frieze, Kukla, Reed, Rest, & Rosenbaum (1971).
39. See Tulving (2005).
40. See Jones & Davis (1965) and Kelley (1973) for discussions of trait attributions and the principle that when situational forces would make most people behave a certain

way, then observers are less likely to attribute a trait to an actor who behaved that way in that situation (the discounting principle).

41. See Higgins & Winter (1993).
42. See Higgins & Winter (1993).
43. See Chen (2003), Idson & Mischel (2001), and Uleman, Saribay, & Gonzalez (2008). For a general discussion of personality "if–then" profiles, see Mischel & Shoda (1995).
44. See Anderson, Krull, & Weiner (1996) and Uleman, Saribay, & Gonzalez (2008).
45. See Fiske, Kitayama, Markus, & Nisbett (1998), Miller (1984), and Uleman, Saribay, & Gonzalez (2008).
46. See Comer & Laird (1975).
47. See Newcomb (1968), p. xv.
48. For overviews of and commentaries on cognitive consistency theories, see Abelson (1983), Abelson, Aronson, McGuire, Newcomb, Rosenberg, & Tannenbaum (Eds.) (1968), Kruglanski (1989), and Zajonc (1968b).
49. See Heider (1958).
50. See Abelson (1983), p. 40.
51. I should note that Abelson (1983) had a different motivational account that was more about signaling a real-world problem to be solved (value) than about truth *per se*. His example was Heider trying to solve the problem of having two of his friends together as guests in his home, at the same time, knowing that these two guests hated each other. The cognitive imbalance was a functional signal of potential future disaster. What could he do to prevent them from fighting? In this case, there is no attempt to establish a new understanding, a new reality, about the different parts in the pattern. In Abelson's discussion, the pattern is accepted as the reality; it has to be dealt with as an interpersonal reality. What I am suggesting is quite different. I am suggesting that the cognitive imbalance could lead Heider to rethink the parts in the pattern in order to establish a new reality. "Perhaps because I like both of them, and both of them will be doing fun things together with me, they will learn to like each other and become friends. Now that makes sense; they will become friends in the future while visiting me."
52. Heider (1958), p. 180.
53. See Spiro (1977).
54. See Festinger (1957), p. 260.
55. See Festinger (1957), p. 3.
56. See Festinger, Riecken, & Schachter (1956).
57. See Festinger (1957), p. 5. See also Festinger (1964).
58. See Lewin (1951).
59. I should note that Festinger (1957, p. 2) distinguishes this dissonance-resolving process from the common process of rationalization. If a man, for example, rationalized that the only car he could afford to buy was the foreign option, then there would no longer be any inconsistency, and the dissonance process would not begin.
60. For a discussion of the difference between the availability and the accessibility of cognitions, see Higgins (1996b).
61. See Aronson & Carlsmith (1963).

62. See Zanna, Lepper, & Abelson (1973). See also McGregor, Newby-Clark, & Zanna (1999).

63. In the classic paradigm neither the forbidden toy nor the mild threat is made accessible, and thus it is possible that the effect of reduced attractiveness of the forbidden toy is not due to re-establishing reality in the service of truth. It is possible that the effect occurs from value, as discussed in Chapter 4. Specifically, when there is only a mild threat it is difficult for the children to resist the temptation of the forbidden toy. To cope with this adversity, the children could disengage from the forbidden toy by taking attention away from it. This decrease in engagement strength would reduce the intensity of the attractiveness toward the forbidden toy, which is the standard effect.

64. See Jost, Banaji, & Nosek (2004), Jost & Hunyady (2005), and Jost, Pietrzak, Liviatan, Mandisodza, & Napier (2008).

65. See Jost, Pelham, Sheldon, & Sullivan (2003).

66. See Zajonc (1968b).

67. See Kruglanski (1980), Kruglanski (1989), and Kruglanski (1990).

68. See Kruglanski (1989) and Kruglanski & Webster (1996).

69. See Kruglanski & Webster (1996). See also Snyder & Wicklund (1981). I should note that individuals with a need to avoid nonspecific closure do not necessarily have the goal of creating ambiguity. They could have the goal of being as accurate as possible, wanting a truth-seeking process that can be fully justified to others, and these motives could produce a hypothesis-testing strategy that ends up creating ambiguity.

70. See Asch (1946).

71. See Kruglanski & Webster (1996).

72. See Higgins, Rholes, & Jones (1977).

73. See Ford & Kruglanski (1995) and Thompson, Roman, Moskowitz, Chaiken, & Bargh (1994).

74. Because different desired end-states are associated with the different epistemic motivations (Kruglanski, 1989), what is happening motivationally is best characterized as a value–truth relation. Indeed, the different epistemic motivations are associated with differences in commitment, which is a product of value–truth relations. Given this, I will be discussing Kruglanski's theory of epistemic motives again in Chapter 7.

75. See Sorrentino & Short (1986) and Sorrentino & Roney (2000).

76. See Sorrentino & Roney (2000), p. 157.

77. See Driscoll, Hamilton, & Sorrentino (1991).

78. See Mayseless & Kruglanski (1987).

79. See Liberman, Molden, Idson, & Higgins (2001). See also Crowe & Higgins (1997).

80. See Higgins, Kruglanski, & Pierro (2003) and Kruglanski, Thompson, Higgins, Atash, Pierro, Shah, & Spiegel (2000).

81. See Avnet & Higgins (2003).

82. I will discuss in Chapter 8 how regulatory fit basically involves a value–control relation between a value orientation toward goal pursuit and a manner or strategy of goal pursuit. In this study the preferred strategy concerned how to establish

what was the right choice, and thus truth was also involved in partnership with control (see Chapter 9). Overall, then, this study provides a good example of how all three effectiveness motivations—value, control, and truth—can work together during goal pursuit.

83. See Chaiken & Trope (1999) for a broad variety of such models. See also Epstein (1991), Smith & DeCoster (2000), Strack (1992), and Strack & Deutsch (2004).

84. This binary distinction is probably too simple, however. The properties of presence vs. absence of consciousness (or awareness), presence vs. absence of intentionality, presence vs. absence of controllability, and presence vs. absence of effort can be independent of one another and occur in various combinations. In addition, each of these properties is itself not binary; rather it is multilevel or continuous. For thoughtful general discussions of these issues, see Bargh (1989), Kruglanski, Erbs, Pierro, Mannetti, & Chun (2006), and Kruglanski & Thompson (1999).

85. See, for example, Gawronski & Bodenhausen (2006) and Strack & Deutsch (2004).

86. See Dijksterhuis & Nordgren (2006), Wilson, Lisle, Schooler, Hodges, Klaaren, & LaFleur (1993), and Wilson & Schooler (1991).

87. See Wilson, Lisle, Schooler, Hodges, Klaaren, & LaFleur (1993).

88. See Gawronski & Strack (2004), Strack (1992), and Strack & Deutsch (2004).

89. See Strack (1992).

90. See Gawronski & Strack (2004).

91. See Higgins & Bargh (1987), Kruglanski (1989), Swann (1984), Trope (1986b), and Wood (1989).

92. See Trope (1986a). For other discussions on this and related issues on biased hypothesis testing, see Higgins & Bargh (1987), Kruglanski (1989), Kunda (1990), Miller & Ross (1975), Nisbett & Ross (1980), and Tetlock & Levi (1982).

93. See Higgins & Bargh (1987).

94. You might be wondering why there tends to be an overall positive bias given that people could begin with a negative hypothesis or question, such as "Am I an unfriendly person?," and draw an "unfriendly" conclusion. It is true that this is logically possible, but there is an inherent bias toward the positive version of the hypothesis or question. For many adjectives, the name of the dimension as a whole (i.e., the "unmarked" form of the adjective) is the same name as the positive end of the dimension, such as "friendliness," "intelligence," "kindness," "honesty," and so on (see Huttenlocher & Higgins, 1971). This characteristic of language biases the form of the hypothesis or question in the direction of the positive end of the dimension. The question seems neutral because it uses the unmarked form of the adjective, but it primes stored information matching the positive end of the dimension and, if anything, inhibits stored information matching the negative end of the dimension.

95. See Trope (1980).

96. See Swann (1984; 1987; 1990). For other research and discussions on the motivation for self-consistency, see Aronson (1969) and Lecky (1945).

97. For a recent review, see Kwang & Swann (2010).

98. See Swann, Hixon, Stein-Seroussi, & Gilbert (1990).

 99. See Hardin & Higgins (1996) for evidence of self-verification being stronger when self-views are shared with significant others.

100. See Swann (1984).

101. See Festinger (1950; 1954).

102. See Asch (1952).

103. See Asch (1952), p. 456–457.

104. See Asch (1952), p. 459.

105. See Levine (1999).

106. Participants in Asch's study could be motivated by wanting to establish what's real, or wanting to be in agreement with the group, or both. It should be noted, however, that if wanting to be in agreement were the only motivation, then it would not matter how incorrect the group's judgment was on the incorrect trials. But it did matter: the naïve participants were much more likely to go along with the group's incorrect judgment on incorrect trials where the discrimination was relatively difficult. On trials where the discrimination was easy, it was rare for the naïve participants to go along with the group's incorrect judgment. This pattern is more consistent with wanting to establish what's real than simply wanting agreement with the group.

107. See Sherif (1935; 1936).

108. See Jacobs & Campbell (1961).

109. See Durkheim (1951/1897) and Weber (1971).

110. Deutsch & Gerard (1955), Homans (1950), Kelley (1952), Merton (1957), and Parsons (1964).

111. See Cialdini (2003).

112. See Fu, Morris, Lee, Chao, Chiu, & Hong (2007).

113. See Cialdini (1993) and Cialdini & Goldstein (2004).

114. See Cialdini (2003).

115. See Cialdini, Reno, & Kallgren (1990).

116. See Thomas & Thomas (1928). For a thorough and thoughtful discussion of symbolic interactionism, see Stryker & Statham (1985).

117. See Kruglanski (1989).

118. See Cialdini (1993), Hovland, Janis, & Kelley (1953), and Kruglanski, Raviv, Bar-Tal, Raviv, Sharvit, Ellis, Bar, Pierro, & Mannetti (2005).

119. See Milgram (1974). I discuss Milgram's study in some detail because it is so well known and is, indeed, a powerful example of epistemic authority. More importantly, it is widely misunderstood and mischaracterized, and I want to do what I can to correct this.

120. Milgram (1974), p. 123.

121. See Cialdini (1993).

122. Milgram (1974), p. 18.

123. Milgram (1974), p. 176.

124. See Arendt (1963).

125. Whenever I teach my Social Psychology course, I spend one class discussing both what I believe actually happened in Milgram's study and the ethical implications of Milgram conducting this research program. Let me make a brief comment here on the latter issue. It is likely that Milgram did not know beforehand how much the

participant teachers would suffer in this study. Once he did know, however, he should have ended the research program. There is no excuse for his continuing with this research. Indeed, he later introduced conditions that made the participant teachers suffer even more (e.g., by making the teacher shock the learner in closer and closer physical proximity). In subsequent studies, the one person who had full responsibility for making individuals actually suffer, and did so knowingly, was Milgram. His excuse for all this was that it had scientific benefits. There are still those who excuse what he did for this reason. It is as if they are saying, as Milgram did, that "scientific truth" required him to carry on with the research—he *had no choice but to do what he did.* In contrast to Milgram making an analogy between the participant teachers and SS guards, some might say that a better analogy is between Milgram's excuse and those defending themselves at Nuremberg. But such an analogy also goes too far. We all need to see beyond simple analogies to the psychological conditions that are created in specific situations.

126. See Higgins (1996d).
127. See Bowlby (1988).
128. See Collins & Read (1990), Mikulincer (1998), and Mikulincer & Shaver (2003).
129. For a discussion of such "phonetic symbolism," see Brown (1958a).
130. See Higgins (1981; 1992), Echterhoff, Higgins, & Groll (2005), and Echterhoff, Higgins, Kopietz, & Groll (2008).
131. See Higgins & Rholes (1978). For an even earlier demonstration of audience tuning in communication, see Zimmerman & Bauer (1956).
132. For reviews, see Higgins (1992), Echterhoff, Higgins, Kopietz, & Groll (2008), and Echterhoff, Higgins, & Levine (2008).
133. See Echterhoff, Higgins, Kopietz, & Groll (2008).
134. See Festinger (1950), Kruglanski, Pierro, Mannetti, & De Grada (2006), and Suls, Martin, & Wheeler (2002).
135. See Echterhoff, Higgins, & Groll (2005), Echterhoff, Higgins, Kopietz, & Groll (2008), and Echterhoff, Higgins, & Levine (2008).
136. See Echterhoff, Higgins, & Levine (2008), Hausmann, Levine, & Higgins (2008), Jost, Ledgerwood, & Hardin (2008), and Lau, Chiu, & Lee (2001).
137. See Hausmann, Levine, & Higgins (2008) and Lyons & Kashima (2003).
138. See Hardin & Higgins (1996).
139. See *Oxford English Dictionary* (1971).
140. See Ross, Greene, & House (1977).
141. See Fields & Schuman (1976), Marks & Miller (1987), and Ross, Greene, & House (1977).
142. See Asch (1952). See also Allen (1975).
143. For a fuller discussion of these unique human motives, see Higgins & Pittman (2008).
144. See Call (2005).
145. See Nelson (2005) and Terrace (2005).
146. See Kruglanski & Mayseless (1987).
147. See Dunn, Brown, Slomkowski, Tesla, & Youngblade (1991), Gopnik (1996), and Perner, Ruffman, & Leekam (1994).
148. See Doise & Mugny (1984).

149. See Perner, Ruffman, & Leekam (1994).
150. I should also note that there are important similarities among these different routes to the truth regarding the "if–then" logic of deriving truth from evidence. For a thoughtful and clear discussion of such similarities, see Kruglanski (1989) and Kruglanski, Dechesne, Orehek,& Pierro (in press).

CHAPTER 6

1. See Freud (1961b).
2. See Freud (1961a) and Freud (1961b).
3. See Mischel (1974) and Mischel & Ebbesen (1970).
4. As this test has been dubbed in the media; e.g., Goleman (1995).
5. See Mischel (1999), Mischel, Shoda, & Rodriguez (1989), and Shoda, Mischel, & Peake (1990).
6. See Mischel & Ebbesen (1970) and Mischel, Shoda, & Rodriguez (1989).
7. See Metcalfe & Mischel (1999) and Mischel (1999). In Chapter 9 I discuss another possibility for why this strategy works—using truth in the service of control.
8. Mischel & Moore (1973) and Mischel (1974).
9. See Mischel & Ebbesen (1970).
10. See Mischel (1999). In a similar fashion, Mischel & Patterson (1978) describe the self-control effectiveness of providing children with an elaborated plan about how to resist the tempting distractions of an attractive toy clown and to continue working on the focal task. For additional evidence of the self-control advantages of specific instructions, including self-instructions, see Hartig & Kanfer (1973) and Miller, Weinstein, & Karniol (1978).
11. See Hoffman (1970).
12. See Fishbach, Friedman, & Kruglanski (2003), Fishbach & Shah (2006), and Shah, Friedman, & Kruglanski (2002).
13. See Freitas, Liberman, & Higgins (2002) Shah, Friedman & Krulganski (2002), and Shah & Higgins (1997).
14. See Freitas, Liberman, & Higgins (2002).
15. See Fishbach, Friedman, & Kruglanski (2003), Fishbach & Shah (2006), and Shah, Friedman, & Kruglanski (2002).
16. See Fishbach, Friedman, & Kruglanski (2003).
17. See Fishbach, Friedman, & Kruglanski (2003).
18. See Trope & Fishbach (2000).
19. See Kuhl (1985) for a discussion of the self-regulatory effectiveness more generally of creating a social commitment by making one's intentions public.
20. See Trope & Fishbach (2000).
21. See Fujita (2008) and Fujita, Trope, Liberman, & Levin-Sagi (2006).
22. See Trope & Liberman (2003).
23. See Fujita, Trope, Liberman, & Levin-Sagi (2006).
24. See Baumeister, Bratslavsky, Muraven, & Tice (1998), Baumeister & Heatherton (1996), Baumeister, Heatherton, & Tice (1994), and Baumeister, Schmeichel, & Vohs (2007). See also Mischel (1996).
25. See Vohs, Baumeister, Schmeichel, Twenge, Nelson, & Tice (2008).
26. See also Baumeister, Bratslavsky, Muraven, & Tice (1998).

27. See Masicampo & Baumeister (2008).
28. See Freud (1961a) and Freud (1965).
29. See Freud (1961a, p. 24).
30. See Larsen & Prizmic (2004).
31. See Pennebaker, Colder, & Sharp (1990) and Weinberger, Schwartz, & Davidson (1979).
32. See Tangney, Baumeister, & Boone (2004). It is notable in this regard that Tangney et al. (2004) also report that feelings of *shame* are *negatively* related to effective self-control. Repressing shame, then, might be an effective tactic, although even shame might be useful as a signal of interpersonal problems that need to be dealt with.
33. See Kross, Ayduk, & Mischel (2005) and Pennebaker, Mayne, & Francis (1997).
34. See Pennebaker & Francis (1996).
35. See Pennebaker, Mayne, & Francis (1997).
36. It is notable that each of these proposed benefits would also contribute to truth effectiveness through the "What?," "Why?," and cognitive consistency mechanisms.
37. See Nolen-Hoeksema (2000) and Teasdale (1988).
38. See Pennebaker, Mayne, & Francis (1997).
39. See Kross, Ayduk, & Mischel (2005).
40. See Kross, Ayduk, & Mischel (2005).
41. These examples suggest that self-control techniques are especially effective when they are combined with establishing what's real (truth). I will return to this issue in Chapter 9 when I discuss how control motivation and truth motivation work together as partners. I should also note that the tactics of verbalization and of self-distancing plus "Why?" questioning could reveal alternative truths rather than increasing truth *per se*. George Kelly (1955, 1969), a pioneer of cognitive approaches to clinical treatment, described how constructive alternativism could be a strategy for improving control effectiveness. His core idea was that events could always be construed differently, and thus people could change their views about past events and themselves in ways that worked better for them.
42. For reviews of these mechanisms, see Gross (1999), Larsen & Prizmic (2004), and Morris & Reilly (1987).
43. See Koole & Kuhl (2007).
44. See also Wegner (1996) for a discussion of the factors that determine the mental states that people prefer.
45. See Erber, Wegner, & Therriault (1996).
46. See Lazurus (1966) and Lazurus & Folkman (1984).
47. See Penley, Tomaka, & Wiebe (2002).
48. See Tice, Bratslavsky, & Baumeister (2001).
49. See Cheng (2003) and Compas, Malcarne, & Fondacro (1988). Similarly, Miller (1979) has found that people are more likely to use *monitoring* strategies (attending to and scanning for threatening cues) when a stress is controllable and more likely to use *blunting* strategies (e.g., self-distraction) when a stress is uncontrollable.
50. See Cheng (2003) and Chiu, Hong, Mischel, & Shoda (1995).
51. See Larsen & Prizmic (2004).
52. See Larsen & Prizmic (2004), Parkinson, & Totterdell (1999), and Parkinson, Totterdell, Briner, & Reynolds (1996).

53. See Gross (2001).
54. See Gross (1998), Ochsner & Gross (2004), and Richards & Gross (2000). See also Wegner (1989) and Wegner (1994) for a discussion of how suppression of thoughts can also backfire and make the thoughts *more* rather than less accessible.
55. See Bandura (1973) and Geen & Quanty (1977).
56. See Larsen & Prizmic (2004).
57. See Higgins (2006).
58. See Diener & Seligman (2002).
59. See Cutrona & Russell (1990).
60. See Bolger & Amarel (2007).
61. See also Coyne, Wortman, & Lehman (1988).
62. For the interested reader, there are some excellent recent reviews of goal pursuit functions in Moskowitz & Grant (2009) and Vohs & Baumeister (2011).
63. See Gollwitzer (1990) and Heckhausen & Gollwitzer (1987).
64. See Lewin, Dembo, Festinger, & Sears (1944).
65. See McClelland (1980) and Murray (1938).
66. See Carver & Scheier (1981).
67. See Higgins (1997).
68. See Elliot & McGregor (2001), Elliot & Sheldon (1997), Elliot & Sheldon (1998), and Elliot, Sheldon, & Church (1997).
69. See Higgins (1997) and Scholer & Higgins (in press). For clinical implications of patients distinguishing between the reference points and orientations they select in their goal pursuits, see Strauman, Vieth, Merrill, Kolden, Woods, Klein, Papadakis, Schneider, & Kwapil (2006).
70. See Shah & Kruglanski (2002).
71. See Förster, Higgins, & Bianco (2003).
72. For a review of these levels and the conflicts that can occur within and between levels, see Scholer & Higgins (in press).
73. Gollwitzer (1990).
74. For a review of how different levels of self-regulation do and do not work together effectively, see Scholer & Higgins (in press).
75. See Gollwitzer (1996), Gollwitzer & Brandstatter (1997), and Gollwitzer, Fujita, & Oettingen (2004).
76. See Spiegel, Grant-Pillow, & Higgins (2004).
77. See Cantor (1994), Norem & Cantor (1986a), and Showers (1992).
78. See Cantor, Norem, Niedenthal, Langston, & Brower (1987).
79. See Norem & Cantor (1986a; 1986b) and Showers (1992)
80. See Norem & Illingworth (1993) and Showers (1992).
81. See Norem & Cantor (1986a; 1986b).
82. See Cantor (1994).
83. For a fuller discussion of this issue, see Higgins (2005b).
84. See Anderson (1983), Bargh (1990), and Kruglanski, Shah, Fishbach, Friedman, Chun, & Sleeth-Keppler (2002).
85. See Bargh (1990), Bargh (1996), and Bargh (2005).
86. See Bargh, Gollwitzer, Lee-Chai, Barndollar, & Trotschel (2001).
87. See Hassin, Bargh, & Zimerman (2009).

88. See Scholer & Higgins (in press).

89. See Bandura (1982) and Bandura (1986).

90. See Atkinson (1957), Atkinson (1964), and Kruglanski, Shah, Fishbach, Friedman, Chun, & Sleeth-Keppler (2002).

91. See Shah & Higgins (1997).

92. See Brendl & Higgins (1996).

93. See Study 1 in Shah & Higgins (1997).

94. See Study 2 in Shah & Higgins (1997).

95. See also Higgins, Kruglanski, & Pierro (2003) and Kruglanski, Thompson, Higgins, Atash, Pierro, Shah, & Spiegel (2000).

96. For evidence of high locomotors being motivated to change for the sake of change itself, see Scholer & Higgins (2009).

97. See Kruglanski, Thompson, Higgins, Atash, Pierro, Shah, & Spiegel (2000).

98. For early discussions of these phenomena, see Lewin (1935) and Lewin (1951). See also Miller (1944) and Miller (1959) for a discussion of the "goal looms larger" effect, and Henle (1944) for a discussion of "resumption of an interrupted task."

99. See Förster, Grant, Idson, & Higgins (2001).

100. See Förster, Higgins, & Idson (1998).

101. See Förster, Grant, Idson, & Higgins (2001) and Förster, Higgins, & Idson (1998).

102. See Liberman, Idson, Camacho, & Higgins (1999).

103. See Liberman, Idson, Camacho, & Higgins (1999).

104. See Kruglanski, Thompson, Higgins, Atash, Pierro, Shah, & Spiegel (2000).

105. See Shah, Friedman, & Kruglanski (2002).

106. See Kuhl (1986).

107. See Shah, Friedman, & Kruglanski (2002).

108. See Locke & Kristof (1996), Locke & Latham (1990), and Locke & Latham (2002).

109. See Kuhl (1978).

110. See Kruglanski, Thompson, Higgins, Atash, Pierro, Shah, & Spiegel (2000).

111. See Kruglanski, Thompson, Higgins, Atash, Pierro, Shah, & Spiegel (2000).

112. See Sansone, Weir, Harpster, & Morgan (1992).

113. See Arkes & Blumer (1985).

114. See Mischel, Cantor, & Feldman (1996).

115. For an exception, see Gollwitzer, Parks-Stamm, Jaudas, & Sheeran (2008).

116. See Carver (2004), Carver & Scheier (1998), and Carver & Scheier (2008).

117. See also Miller, Galanter, & Pribram (1960), Powers (1973), and Wiener (1948).

118. I should also note that when a difficult goal is set, feedback about progress in meeting that goal has been found to benefit performance (see Locke & Kristof, 1996; Locke & Latham, 1990; Locke & Latham, 2002). This could be because the feedback makes clear when a difficult goal has still not been met and thus requires additional effort.

119. See Higgins (1996c) and Higgins (2001).

120. I should note an important difference, however, in how affect is conceptualized in Carver and Scheier's model versus in self-discrepancy theory. In Carver and Scheier's model, affect is produced during the goal-pursuit process as a function of the rate of progress being above or below some criterion. In self-discrepancy

theory, emotions are produced at the completion of the goal pursuit as a function of whether the goal pursuit succeeded or failed to attain the desired end-state. This is a difference between feeling good or bad, respectively, as a function of being effective or ineffective in managing what happens (control effectiveness feelings) versus feeling specific emotions as a function of being effective or ineffective in having what's desired (value effectiveness feelings). Future research should examine the functional significance of this difference for subsequent motivation.

121. See Brodscholl (2005) and Koo & Fishbach (in press).

122. See Carver (2004) and Carver & Scheier (2008).

123. For a discussion of self-discrepancy theory and the motivational consequences of self-evaluative processes, see Higgins (1987, 1989b, 1991). For an additional discussion of how self-evaluative processes affect motivation, see Bandura (1986) and Bandura (1989).

124. See A. Freud (1937), S. Freud (1961a), Horney (1939), Kohut (1971), Sandler (1960), Schafer (1968), and Sullivan (1953).

125. See Higgins (1987), Moretti & Higgins (1999a), and Moretti & Higgins (1999b).

126. See Moretti & Higgins (1999a), and Moretti & Higgins (1999b).

127. See Andersen & Chen (2002), Higgins (1987), Higgins (1991), and Shah (2003). For additional evidence of the impact that significant others can have on self-evaluation, see also Baldwin, Carrell, & Lopez (1990) and Baldwin & Holmes (1987).

128. See Shah (2003).

129. See Leary (2007).

130. See Leary (2004), Leary & Baumeister (2000), and Leary, Tambor, Terdal, & Downs (1995); see also Higgins (1996d) for a related point on self-evaluation being embedded in social relationships and their success/failure feedback.

131. See Schwarz (1990). For other discussions of how affect can provide informative feedback that influences judgments and actions, see Carver (2004), Schwarz & Clore (1988), and Simon (1967).

132. See Gollwitzer (1990).

133. See Gilbert, Lieberman, Morewedge, & Wilson (2004), Mellers & McGraw (2001), Schkade & Kahneman (1998), Wilson & Gilbert (2003), and Wilson, Wheatley, Meyers, Gilbert, & Axsom (2000).

134. See Buehler, Griffin, & Ross (1994).

135. See Langer (1975). See also Langer & Roth (1975).

136. See Wegner, Sparrow, & Winerman (2004).

137. See Miller & Ross (1975).

138. See Ross & Sicoly (1979) and Lerner (1970).

139. Lerner (1970).

140. In this section on people's motivation to experience themselves as having control, I have described how people want so strongly to manage what happens that they will perceive themselves as having control over events that are actually outside of their control and as having controlled events for which there are clear costs of taking personal responsibility. Additional evidence for the power of wanting effective control can be found from studies of what happens when people perceive themselves as failing to have control. For example, the literatures on learned

helplessness (e.g., Abramson, Seligman, & Teasdale,1978; Seligman, 1975), control deprivation (e.g., Pittman & D'Agostino, 1989; Pittman & Pittman, 1980), and perceived lack of control (e.g., Weary, Elbin, & Hill, 1987) provide substantial evidence of the motivational impact of control failure on emotions and cognitive processing.

CHAPTER 7

1. See *Oxford English Dictionary* (1971) and *Webster's Ninth New Collegiate Dictionary* (1989).
2. This is not a chapter about *how* commitment works. I discussed the *how* of commitment in Chapter 6 on control effectiveness, with commitment being one of the three central functions of goal pursuit that needs to be managed to be effective. As I mentioned there, controlling or managing commitment involves a full-blown *value–truth–control relation* because it entails managing both value and truth.
3. See, for example, Bernoulli (1738/1954).
4. See, for example, Atkinson (1957), Edwards (1955), Freud (1920/1950), Lewin (1935), Mowrer (1960), Rotter (1954), and Tolman (1932).
5. See Ajzen & Fishbein (1970 and Rotter (1954).
6. See Bandura & Cervone (1983).
7. See Atkinson (1957; 1964) and Feather (1961).
8. See Weiner et al. (1971).
9. See Kahneman & Miller (1986) and Kahneman & Tversky (1982).
10. For an important exception, see Ajzen (1996).
11. As psychological examples of a subjective expected utility model, see Atkinson (1957), Edwards (1955), Coombs (1958), Lewin, Dembo, Festinger, & Sears (1944), Luce (1959), and Thurstone (1927).
12. See Atkinson (1957).
13. As psychological examples of an expectancy value model, see Fishbein (1963), Fishbein & Ajzen (1975), Rosenberg (1956), Rotter (1954), and Tolman (1955).
14. See Tolman (1955).
15. See Brickman (1987) and Higgins (2006).
16. See Ajzen (1996).
17. See, for example, Atkinson (1957), Edwards (1955), Lewin, Dembo, Festinger, & Sears (1944), and Vroom (1964).
18. See, for example, Tolman (1955) and Rotter (1954). For a discussion of these issues, see Feather (1959).
19. See McClelland, Atkinson, Clark, & Lowell (1953).
20. This difference between the EV and SEU models in what is the value driving commitment should not be confused with intrinsic vs. extrinsic motivation—as if it were success for its own sake vs. success as just a means to an end. In both cases the activity of studying hard can be extrinsic, can be just a means to an end. For EV achievement, studying hard is a means to feeling pride in having done well in a difficult course. For SEU, studying hard is a means of getting acceptance into the desired major. In neither case is the activity of studying hard being done just for its own sake.
21. See A. Freud (1937) and S. Freud (1923/1961a; 1930/1961b; 1933/1965).

22. See Bruner (1957a), Bruner & Goodman (1947), Bruner & Postman (1948), and Erdyli (1974).
23. See Dunning (1999), Gollwitzer & Bargh (1996), Kruglanski (1989; 1996), Kunda (1990), and Sorrentino & Higgins (1986).
24. See Biner, Angle, Park, Mellinger, & Barber (1995), Irwin (1953), and Marks (1951),
25. See Biner, Angle, Park, Mellinger, & Barber (1995).
26. See Feather (1990), Kuhl (1986), and Shah & Higgins (1997). Kuhl (1986) makes the excellent point that to test the multiplicative model you cannot just aggregate across individuals; you need to look at what each individual does under different parameters of value and expectancy. Little evidence exists for the multiplicative function of value × expectancy. Some use value and ignore expectancy; others use expectancy and ignore value.
27. See James (1890/2007).
28. See James (1890/2007), p. 283.
29. See James (1890/2007), p. 283.
30. See James (1890/2007), p. 522.
31. I will return to this issue in Chapter 9 on truth–control relations, where I will discuss research suggesting that the action taken depends not only on the stored idea or belief (i.e., truth), but also on situational factors that relate to control.
32. See Bargh, Chen, & Burrows (1996).
33. See Cesario, Plaks, & Higgins, (2006). Lashley (1951) was, perhaps, the first psychologist to use the term *priming* to describe the preparatory function of thought as part of his historical discourse on the sequential organization of behavior.
34. See also the discussion of additional situational or ecological factors in Chapter 9.
35. See Tolman (1932; 1948).
36. See Guthrie (1935; 1952).
37. See Guthrie (1952).
38. See Tolman (1955).
39. See Oettingen (1996), Oettingen, & Mayer (2002), and Oettingen, Pak, & Schnetter (2001).
40. See Kahneman & Tversky (1979).
41. Bandura (1977) makes this distinction when discussing why perceived self-efficacy is a different mechanism in human agency than outcome expectancy. The emphasis in previous models of commitment was on people's outcome expectancies, and the control issue was individuals' belief that whether they attained a desired result or not was under their personal control or was under the control of others (i.e., locus of control; see, for example, Rotter, 1966). In contrast, perceived self-efficacy concerned people's belief that were or were not capable of producing a particular action, independent of whether or not their action would lead to desired results.
42. See Higgins, Pierro, & Kruglanski (2008).
43. See Kruglanski, Thompson, Higgins, Atash, Pierro, Shah, & Spiegel (2000).
44. See, for example, Atkinson (1957) and Lewin, Dembo, Festinger, & Sears (1944).
45. Success or failure in doing something could also be informative about the difficulty of the task or activity (see Heider, 1958; Weiner et al., 1971), but in the models that I am discussing the difficulty of the task or activity is established prior to performance (i.e., it is a given).

46. See Weiner et al. (1971).

47. See Trope (1986b) and Trope & Liberman (1996).

48. See, for example, Tolman (1955) and Hull (1943).

49. See Brickman (1987) and Higgins (2006).

50. See Cialdini (1993).

51. Sometimes people talk about scarcity as if it always increases the attractiveness of things, as if it adds positivity by itself. But if scarcity as a situation functions like an obstacle that strengthens engagement, then it should intensify negative reactions to things as well as intensify positive reactions. Indeed, there is recent evidence that this also occurs (Sehnert, Franks, & Higgins, 2009).

52. See Sorrentino & Roney (2000) and Sorrentino, Short, & Raynor (1984).

53. See Brendl & Higgins (1996). See also Kahneman & Miller (1986).

54. Cialdini (1993; 2001; 2003).

55. And these effects could work in opposite directions. As one example, believing that an action is easy to do because everyone does it could increase my commitment to taking the action because I anticipate that the costs of taking that action will be low. I could infer that the costs of asking my boss for a raise must be low if so many of my coworkers do it. On the other hand, believing that an action is easy to do could decrease my commitment to taking the action because I infer that the personal meaningfulness of the action, the value of the action, is low. I infer that it doesn't take much courage to ask my boss for a raise because it a common thing to do among my coworkers, and thus neither I nor my wife will feel much pride if I were to do it too.

56. See Ajzen (1985), Ajzen & Fishbein (1980), and Fishbein & Ajen (1975).

57. See Higgins (2006). See also Brehm's discussion of *reactance* (e.g., Brehm, 1966).

58. This kind of effect is not discussed in Fishbein and Ajzen's model. In their model, the injunctive norms are a separate component whose product is combined with the product of the anticipated outcomes of taking the action, yielding an overall resultant behavioral intention. In the overall result, no special status is given to the case of choosing to take the action despite the injunctive norms against it. The additional effect on commitment when individuals oppose or overcome resistance from injunctive norms is not included in their model.

59. See Liberman & Forster (2008), Liberman, Molden, Idson, & Higgins (2001), and Shah & Higgins (1997).

60. See Zhang, Higgins, & Chen (2011).

61. See Liberman & Trope (2008), Liberman, Trope, & Stephan (2007), and Trope & Liberman (2003).

62. See Todorov, Goren, & Trope (2007).

63. See Todorov, Goren, & Trope (2007) and Wakslak, Trope, Liberman, & Alony (2006).

64. See Liberman, Trope, & Stephan (2007) and Trope & Liberman (2003).

65. See Higgins, Franks, & Pavarini (2008).

CHAPTER 8

1. See Allport (1937a).

2. See Woodworth (1918), p. 145.

3. See Woodworth (1918), p. 201.
4. See Tolman (1935), p. 370.
5. See Kruglanski et al. (2002)
6. See Kruglanski et al. (2002). For a related consequence of structural uniqueness in connections, see Andersons (1974; 1983).
7. See Carver & Scheier (1981) and Shah & Kruglanski (2000). For a general review of goal supportiveness, see Brendl & Higgins (1996).
8. See Sheldon & Elliot (1999).
9. See Harackiewicz & Sansone (1991), Sansone & Harackiewicz (1996), and Tauer & Harackiewicz (1999).
10. See Millar & Tesser (1986) and Petty & Wegener (1998).
11. See Clary, Snyder, Ridge, Miene, & Haugen (1994) and Evans & Petty (2003).
12. See DeSteno, Petty, Rucker, Wegener, & Braverman (2004).
13. For examples of the separate, independent effects of regulatory fit and hedonic pleasure, see Cesario, Grant, & Higgins (2004) and Higgins, Idson, Freitas, Spiegel, & Molden (2003).
14. See *Webster's* (1989).
15. See Higgins (2000a; 2005c).
16. See Higgins (2000a).
17. See *Webster's* (1989).
18. See Higgins (1997; 1998b).
19. See Brendl & Higgins (1996).
20. See Freitas & Higgins (2002).
21. See Higgins, Idson, Freitas, Spiegel, & Molden (2003).
22. See Barry & Friedman (1998), Neale & Bazerman (1992), and Van Poucke & Buelens (2002).
23. See Monga & Zhu (2005) and Neale, Huber, & Northcraft (1987).
24. See Appelt, Zou, Arora, & Higgins (2009).
25. See Galinsky & Mussweiler (2001).
26. See Bianco, Higgins, & Klem (2003).
27. See Bianco, Higgins, & Klem (2003).
28. See Cesario, Higgins, & Scholer (2008) and Lee & Higgins (2009).
29. See Higgins, Idson, Freitas, Spiegel, & Molden (2003).
30. See Higgins, Idson, Freitas, Spiegel, & Molden (2003).
31. See Cesario, Higgins, & Scholer (2008) and Lee & Higgins (2009).
32. See Spiegel, Grant-Pillow, & Higgins (2004).
33. See Latimer, Williams-Piehota, Katulak, Cox, Mowad, Higgins, & Salovey (2008).
34. See Latimer, Rivers, Rench, Katulak, Hicks, Hodorowski, Higgins, & Salovey (2008).
35. See Cesario & Higgins (2008).
36. See Grant & Higgins (2003) and Higgins, Friedman, Harlow, Idson, Ayduk, & Taylor (2001) for information about the reliability and validity of this Regulatory Focus Questionnaire.
37. See Levine (1989) and Levine & Kerr (2007).
38. See Alexander, Levine, & Higgins (2010).
39. See Byrne (1971) and Griffitt & Veitch (1974).

40. See Brodscholl, Kober, & Higgins (2007).
41. See Zhou & Pham (2004).
42. See Zhou & Pham (2004).
43. See Pham & Avnet (2004).
44. See Avnet & Higgins (2006).
45. See Lee & Aaker (2004).
46. See Cesario & Higgins (2008).
47. See Csikszentmihalyi (1975; 1990).
48. See Novemsky, Dhar, Schwarz, & Simonson (in press).
49. See Cacioppo, Priester, & Berntson (1993).
50. See Avnet & Higgins (2003).
51. See Lee, Keller, & Sternthal (2010).
52. See Lee, Keller, & Sternthal (2010).
53. See Camacho & Higgins (2003), Cesario, Grant, & Higgins (2004), and Lee & Aaker (2004).
54. See Cesario, Grant, & Higgins (2004).
55. See Freitas & Higgins (2002).
56. See Camacho, Higgins, & Luger (2003).
57. For discussions of such correction processes, see Martin & Achee (1992). Schwarz & Clore (1983), and Wegener & Petty (1995).
58. See Cesario, Grant, & Higgins (2004) and Higgins, Idson, Freitas, Spiegel, & Molden (2003).
59. See Cesario & Higgins (2008).
60. See Higgins (1997).
61. See Labroo & Lee (2006).
62. See Winkielman & Cacioppo (2001).
63. See Higgins, Idson, Freitas, Spiegel, & Molden (2003).
64. See Camacho, Higgins, & Luger (2003).
65. See Idson, Liberman, & Higgins (2004). These studies used a modified version of a scenario from Thaler (1980).
66. It was these findings from this research program that ultimately led to the model of value that I described in Chapter 4 where value intensity derives not only from hedonic sources (and other sources of value direction) but also, and separately, from engagement strength (Higgins, 2006).
67. See Kruglanski et al. (2002).
68. See Förster, Higgins, & Idson (1998). For replications of the fit effect for both the arm pressure and persistence measures of engagement strength, see Förster, Grant, Idson, & Higgins (2001).
69. See Förster, Higgins, & Idson (1998).
70. See Shah, Higgins, & Friedman (1998).
71. See Keller & Bless (2006).
72. See Plessner, Unkelbach, Memmert, Baltes, & Kolb (2009).
73. See See Bianco, Higgins, & Klem (2003).
74. See Spiegel, Grant-Pillow, & Higgins (2004).
75. See Hong & Lee (2008).
76. See Kruglanski, Pierro, & Higgins (2007).

77. See Benjamin & Flynn (2006).
78. See Freitas, Liberman, & Higgins (2002).
79. See Van Dijk & Kluger (2010).
80. But see Cantor & Kihlstrom (1987).
81. See Cantor & Kihlstrom (1987) and Scholer & Higgins (in press, b).
82. See Scholer, Zou, Fujita, Stroessner, & Higgins (2010).
83. See Crowe & Higgins (1997) and Friedman & Förster (2001).

CHAPTER 9

1. See *Oxford English Dictionary, The Compact Edition*, Volumes I & II (1971).
2. See Wiener (1948).
3. See Miller, Galanter, & Pribram (1960).
4. See Carver & Scheier (1981; 1990; 1998). See also Powers (1973).
5. See Higgins, Kruglanski, & Pierro (2003) and Kruglanski, Thompson, Higgins, Atash, Pierro, Shah, & Spiegel (2000).
6. See Deutsch (1968) and Lewin (1951).
7. See *Webster's Ninth New Collegiate Dictionary* (1989).
8. See Higgins, Kruglanski, & Pierro (2003).
9. See Taylor & Higgins (2002).
10. See Taylor & Higgins (2002).
11. See Nolen-Hoeksema (2000), Roese (1997), Roese & Olson (1993), and Sanna (1996).
12. See Pierro, Leder, Mannetti, Higgins, Kruglanski, & Aiello (2008).
13. See Pierro, Leder, Mannetti, Higgins, Kruglanski, & Aiello (2008).
14. See Lewin (1951).
15. See John (1990) and John & Srivastava (1999).
16. See Higgins (2008) and Higgins, Pierro, & Kruglanski (2008).
17. See Goldberg (1990), John (1990), John & Srivastava (1999), and McCrae & Costa (1987). The fifth trait dimension is neuroticism. It differs from the other four trait dimensions in referring more to a type of outcome (emotional instability) than a way of dealing with the world. For this reason, it will not be discussed here.
18. See Higgins (2008) and Higgins, Pierro, & Kruglanski (2008).
19. This unpublished study includes United States, Canada, Italy, Israel, India, and Japan and the relations of locomotion, assessment, promotion, and prevention—entered simultaneously in the analysis in order to test for their unique, independent relations—to each of the Big Five trait dimensions as well as self-esteem.
20. See Higgins & Scholer (2009b).
21. See John (1990).
22. See Higgins, Pierro, & Kruglanski (2008).
23. See Higgins & Scholer (2009b).
24. See John (1990).
25. See Higgins, Pierro, & Kruglanski (2008).
26. See Higgins & Scholer (2009b).
27. See Higgins, Pierro, & Kruglanski (2008).
28. For a complementary perspective on how individuals' personalities can play out differently in different situations, thereby producing distinctive person–situation "signatures," see Mischel & Shoda (1995) and Shoda, Mischel, & Wright (1994).

29. This strategy is a variation of the equal-weight strategy (Bettman, Luce, & Payne, 1998). In the equal-weight strategy, a choice is made according to the highest value achieved. This value is obtained for each alternative by summing all of the attribute values for that option, and the alternative with the highest value is selected.

30. See Scholer & Higgins (2009).

31. See Kruglanski, Pierro, Higgins, & Capozza (2007).

32. See Kruglanski, Thompson, Higgins, Atash, Pierro, Shah, & Spiegel (2000).

33. See Kruglanski, Thompson, Higgins, Atash, Pierro, Shah, & Spiegel (2000).

34. See Kruglanski, Thompson, Higgins, Atash, Pierro, Shah, & Spiegel (2000).

35. See Kruglanski, Thompson, Higgins, Atash, Pierro, Shah, & Spiegel (2000).

36. For discussions of the possible upsides of being unrealistically positive about the future and the possible downsides of being realistically negative about the future, see Alloy & Abramson (1979), Taylor (1991), and Taylor & Brown (1988).

37. See Erikson (1950/1963).

38. See Higgins (2008).

39. See Kruglanski, Thompson, Higgins, Atash, Pierro, Shah, & Spiegel (2000).

40. See Appelt, Zou, & Higgins (2009).

41. This scenario study was a modification of a widely used negotiation case called "Federated Science Fund" (see Mannix, 1997).

42. See Appelt, Zou, & Higgins (2010).

43. See Kruglanski, Thompson, Higgins, Atash, Pierro, Shah, & Spiegel (2000).

44. See Kruglanski, Thompson, Higgins, Atash, Pierro, Shah, & Spiegel (2000).

45. See Klem, Higgins, & Kruglanski (1996). For a discussion of this study, see Higgins, Kruglanski, & Pierro (2003).

46. See Klem, Higgins, & Kruglanski (1996). For a discussion of this study, see Higgins, Kruglanski, & Pierro (2003).

47. See Kruglanski, Thompson, Higgins, Atash, Pierro, Shah, & Spiegel (2000).

48. See Mauro, Pierro, Mannetti, Higgins, & Kruglanski (in press).

49. The induction used the procedure devised by Avnet & Higgins (2003) where participants either recalled three behavioral instances when they acted like high locomotors or recalled three behavioral instances when they acted like high assessors and described those instances in a short written paragraph.

50. This task was devised by Stasser and Stewart (1992).

51. As this test has been dubbed in the media; e.g., Goleman (1995).

52. See Mischel & Ebbesen (1970) and Mischel, Shoda, & Rodriguez (1989).

53. See Metcalfe & Mischel (1999) and Mischel (1999).

54. Mischel & Moore (1973) and Mischel (1974).

55. See Mischel & Ebbesen (1970).

56. See Mischel (1999). In a similar fashion, Mischel & Patterson (1978) describe the self-control effectiveness of providing children with an elaborated plan about how to resist the tempting distractions of an attractive toy clown and continue working on the focal task. For additional evidence of the self-control advantages of specific instructions, including self-instructions, see Hartig & Kanfer (1973) and Miller, Weinstein, & Karniol (1978).

57. See Trope & Fishbach (2000).

58. See Freud (1961a). The importance of Ego control of impulsive behavior was further developed by Jack Block and his collaborators (e.g., Block, 2002; Block & Block, 1980). For Block, ego control was central to personality functioning. He distinguished between people along a dimension from "ego undercontrol" at one end to "ego overcontrol" at the other end, with undercontrollers being impulsive and immediate gratifiers and overcontrollers being constrained and overdelaying gratification.

59. See James (1890/2007), p. 283.

60. See Cesario, Plaks, & Higgins, (2006).

61. See Bargh, Chen, & Burrows (1996).

62. For a fuller discussion of how motivational relevance from value, truth, and control underlies priming effects on judgment and action, see Eitam & Higgins (2010).

63. See Karau & Williams (1993) and Latane, Williams, & Harkins (1979).

64. See Williams & Karau (1991) and Williams, Karau, & Bourgeois (1993).

65. See Plaks & Higgins (2000).

66. See Cesario, Plaks, Hagiwara, Navarrete,& Higgins (2010).

67. For a fuller discussion of the theory of *motivated preparation*, see Cesario, Plaks, & Higgins, (2006) and Cesario, Plaks, Hagiwara, Navarrete, & Higgins (2010).

68. See Fazio, Jackson, Dunton, & Williams (1995), Fazio & Olson (2003), Fazio, Sanbonmatsu, Powell, & Kardes (1986), Greenwald, Banaji, Rudman, Farnham, & Nosek (2002), Greenwald, McGhee, & Schwartz (1998), and Olson & Fazio (2004).

69. See Schwarz & Bohner (2001), however, for a discussion of whether what is being measured is previously stored associative structures or relations constructed in the moment.

70. See Gladwell (2005) and Kristof (2008), for example, for discussions of how unconscious prejudice can produce racial discrimination.

71. See also Brendl, Markman, & Messner (2001) and Karpinski & Hilton (2001) for other reasons to question whether implicit measures of prejudice actually measure prejudice.

72. See Devine (1989).

73. See Richeson & Ambady (2003).

74. See Lowery, Hardin, & Sinclair (2001).

75. See Moskowitz, Gollwitzer, Wasel, & Schaal (1999).

76. See Ferguson (2008) and Sherman, Presson, Chassin, Rose, & Koch (2003).

77. See Fishbach, Friedman, & Kruglanski (2003), Fishbach & Shah (2006), and Shah, Friedman, & Kruglanski (2002).

78. See Fishbach, Friedman, & Kruglanski (2003).

79. See Monteith, Ashburn-Nardo, Voils, & Czopp (2002).

80. See Trawalter & Richeson (2006).

81. See Brewer (2007), Erikson (1950/1963), and Simpson (2007).

82. See Erikson (1950/1963), p. 247.

83. See Abramson, Metalsky, & Alloy (1989), Abramson, Seligman, & Teasdale (1978), Beck, Rush, Shaw, & Emery (1979), and Seligman (1975).

84. See Holmes & Rempel (1989) and Miller & Rempel (2004).

85. See *Webster's Ninth New Collegiate Dictionary* (1989).

86. Value influences trust in another way as well. If we believe that people will use their control and truth effectiveness to benefit us (for us), then we see them as worthy of our trust (i.e., trustworthy). Alternatively, if we believe that they will use their control and truth effectiveness to hurt us (against us), then we see them as not worthy of our trust (i.e., untrustworthy). Thus, the concept of *trustworthiness* combines the truth and control partnership in trust with value or worth—a full-blown organization of motives.

CHAPTER 10

1. See Hebb (1949).
2. See Lewin (1951).
3. See Norem & Cantor (1986a, 1986b) and Showers (1992).
4. See Cantor et al. (1987).
5. See Cantor (1994).
6. See Norem & Cantor (1986b).
7. See Showers (1992).
8. See Lewin, Dembo, Festinger, & Sears (1944).
9. See Rescorla & Solomon (1967) and Rescorla & Wagner (1972).
10. See Förster, Grant, Idson, & Higgins (2001).
11. See Aronson & Carlsmith (1963), Lepper, Zanna, & Abelson (1970), and Pepitone, McCauley, & Hammond (1967).
12. See Wells & Higgins (1989).
13. See Higgins, Kruglanski, & Pierro (2003) and Kruglanski, Thompson, Higgins, Atash, Pierro, Shah, & Spiegel (2000).
14. See Higgins, Kruglanski, & Pierro (2003) and Kruglanski, Thompson, Higgins, Atash, Pierro, Shah, & Spiegel (2000).
15. See Pierro, Kruglanski, & Higgins (2011).
16. For readers familiar with chaos theory, we can think of some forms as functioning like attractors in chaos theory that other unstable forms ultimately settle into after a dynamic period of instability.
17. See McClelland (1961).
18. See McClelland (1961).
19. See Higgins, Kruglanski, & Pierro (2003).
20. See Eagly & Chaiken (1993), Krech, Crutchfield, & Ballachey (1962), Ostrom (1969), Rosenberg & Hovland (1960), Smith (1947), and Zanna & Rempel (1988).
21. See Eagly & Chaiken (1993) and Ostrom (1969).
22. See Tykocinski (1992).
23. For discussions of inconsistency suggesting its transient or spurious nature, see Festinger (1957), Heider (1958), McGuire (1966), Osgood & Tannenbaum (1955), and Rosenberg & Abelson (1960).
24. Especially in the area of addiction, but also more generally, it is important to distinguish wanting from liking. For a thoughtful discussion of this distinction, see Berridge & Robinson (2003) and Robinson & Berridge (2003).
25. For discussions of this property of structures, see Collins & Loftus (1975) and Higgins (1989).

26. See Higgins, Tykocinski, & Vookles (1990) and Higgins, Vookles, & Tykocinski (1992).
27. It is notable that the one motivational element that is shared by both kinds of models is truth effectiveness. This suggests that truth makes a critical contribution to motivation. But the irony is that scientists who prefer the former kind of model emphasize the value contribution to motivation, and scientists who prefer the latter kind of model emphasize the control contribution to motivation. The critical contribution of truth to motivation has been overlooked. Indeed, the importance of truth to motivation is one of the most important lessons I learned while writing this book. In retrospect, this should have been obvious to all of us. If nothing is real, what is there to be motivated about?
28. The "monitored self" is one of three forms of self-regulation that, together, form the *self digest*. The other two are the "instrumental self" and the "expectant self." The self digest is self-knowledge that summarizes information about ourselves *as a unique object in the world*, especially interpersonal contingency rules how about we need to relate to our significant others to be effective (see Higgins, 1996d; Higgins, 2010; Higgins & May, 2001).
29. See Nelson (2005), Shantz (1983), and Wellman (1990).
30. See Bandura (1977; 1986) and Bandura & Walters (1963).
31. See Turner (1956).
32. See Povinelli (2000) and Tomasello (1999).
33. See Higgins (1989c; 1991).
34. See Higgins (1987; 1989b).
35. See Higgins (1989b), p. 97.
36. See Strauman & Higgins (1987).
37. See Strauman (1989) for a replication of this research with clinical populations.
38. See Higgins (1987; 1989b) for a fuller discussion of the psychological situations associated with different self-discrepancies.
39. See Warren (1972).
40. See Higgins, Van Hook, & Dorfman (1988).
41. This was basically the same procedure used by Markus (1977) to identify self-schematic and self-aschematic traits.
42. See Wyer & Gordon (1984).
43. See Hebb (1949) and Wyer & Gordon (1984).
44. See Fishbach, Friedman, & Kruglanski (2003), Fishbach & Shah (2006), and Shah, Friedman, & Kruglanski (2002).
45. See Schachter & Singer (1962).
46. See Zillmann, Johnson, & Day (1974).
47. Although previous studies have not generally found that regulatory fit increases perceived efficiency or perceived effectiveness, the goals pursued were quite simple to attain, such as choosing between a Columbia coffee mug and an inexpensive pen. But more important, these measures of perceived efficiency and perceived effectiveness were judgments about the efficiency or effectiveness of the goal-pursuit process itself. They were not about outcome value or outcome likelihood for the post-goal attainment outcomes. Stronger control–engagement from regulatory fit might not affect perceptions of whether a goal will be attained but could still

affect perceptions of the value and likelihood of the outcomes that goal attainment would produce. This possibility has not been examined in previous studies.
48. See Camacho, Higgins, & Luger (2003).
49. See James (1890/2007), p. 486.

Chapter 11

1. See Higgins (2000b) and Higgins (2008).
2. Of course, it might constitute a personality difference if it were combined with other characteristics, like "small and neat handwriting" when combined with repetitive actions and constant checking can be seen as evidence for a "compulsive" personality.
3. See Higgins & Scholer (2008) and Scholer & Higgins (2010).
4. See Weinstein, Capitanio, & Gosling (2008).
5. See Freud (1914/1955).
6. See Bandura (1986), Cantor & Kihlstrom (1987), Dweck & Leggett (1988), Grant & Dweck (1999), Higgins (1997), and Mischel & Shoda (1995).
7. See Allport (1937b), p. 295.
8. See Higgins & Brendl (1995).
9. See also Caspi & Moffit (1993) and Wright & Mischel (1987).
10. See Mischel & Ebbesen (1970)
11. See Rorschach (1921/1951) and Murray (1938).
12. See Mischel & Shoda (1995; 1999). For a similar perspective on personality stability despite cross-situational changes, see also Cantor & Kihlstrom (1987), Murray (1938), McClelland (1951), and Pervin (2001).
13. See Adorno, Frenkel-Brunswick, Levinson, & Sanford (1950), Dustin & Davis (1967), and Wells, Weinert, & Rubel (1956).
14. See McClelland (1951) and Murray (1938).
15. See Higgins (1997).
16. See Higgins, Friedman, Harlow, Idson, Ayduk, & Taylor (2001).
17. See Atkinson (1964), McClelland (1951; 1961) and McClelland, Atkinson, Clark, & Lowell (1953).
18. Some individuals have both high promotion pride and high prevention pride.
19. See Ainsworth (1967), Ainsworth, Blehar, Waters, & Wall (1978), Bartholomew & Horowitz (1991), Bowlby (1969; 1973); Hazan & Shaver (1987), Main, Kaplan, & Cassidy (1985), and Mikulincer & Shaver (2003).
20. See Ainsworth (1967), Ainsworth, Blehar, Waters, & Wall (1978), and Main, Kaplan, & Cassidy (1985).
21. See Ayduk, May, Downey, & Higgins (2003), Downey & Feldman (1996), and Downey, Freitas, Michaelis, & Khouri (1998).
22. See Förster, Higgins, & Bianco (2003).
23. See Bartlett (1932), Bruner (1957a, b), Hebb (1949), Kelly (1955), and Wertheimer (1923).
24. See Kelly (1955), p. 145. See also Higgins, King, & Mavin (1982) and Robinson (2004).
25. See McClelland & Atkinson (1948), McClelland, Atkinson, Clark, & Lowell (1953), and Murray (1938).

26. For the TAT, see Murray (1938). For the Rorschach, see Rorschach (1921/1951) and Exner (1993). For further discussion of how these methods measure individual differences in chronically accessible constructs (i.e., "ways of seeing"), see Sorrentino & Higgins (1986).

27. See Atkinson, Heyns, & Veroff (1954) and McClelland, Atkinson, Clark, & Lowell (1953).

28. See Bargh, Bond, Lombardi, & Tota (1986) and Higgins & Brendl (1995).

29. See, for example, Andersen & Chen (2002), Cervone (2004), Higgins (1990), Higgins, King, & Mavin (1982), Kruglanski (1989), and Mischel & Shoda (1995).

30. For reviews, see Cantor & Kihlstrom (1987) and Kagan & Kogan (1970).

31. See Witkin, Dyk, Faterson, Goodenough, & Karp (1962).

32. See Witkin & Goodenough (1977).

33. See Witkin & Goodenough (1977).

34. See Mischel (1973), p. 276.

35. For further discussion of this issue, see Dunning, Meyerowitz, & Holtzberg (1989), Kunda (1990), and Kruglanski (1996b).

36. For a fuller discussion of the general principles of knowledge activation, see Higgins (1996).

37. See Higgins (1996).

38. See Higgins (1990; 1999; 2000b).

39. See Bargh, Bond, Lombardi, & Tota (1986), Bargh, Lombardi, & Higgins (1988), Higgins, Bargh, & Lombardi (1985), and Higgins & Brendl (1995). For an overview, see Higgins (1996).

40. See Higgins (1998a) for a fuller discussion of the problem of "aboutness."

41. For a fuller discussion of these distinctions, see Higgins (1996).

42. See Higgins & Brendl (1995).

43. See Robinson, Vargas, Tamir, & Solberg (2004).

44. See Lombardi, Higgins, & Bargh (1987) and Martin (1986). For a fuller discussion of judged usability and contrast effects, see Higgins (1996).

45. For a fuller discussion of these consequences, see Higgins & Scholer (2008) and Scholer & Higgins (2010).

46. See Baumeister & Leary (1995) and Fiske (2003).

47. See Higgins, King, & Mavin (1982).

48. See Andersen & Baum (1994), Andersen & Chen (2002), Andersen, Reznick, & Chen (1997), Andersen, Reznik, & Glassman (2005), Andersen & Saribay (2005), Berk & Andersen (2000), Chen & Andersen (1999), and Hinkley & Andersen (1996). For related findings, see Baldwin & Holmes (1987) and Shah (2003).

49. See Andersen, Glassman, Chen, & Cole (1995), Andersen & Cole (1990), and Glassman & Andersen (1999).

50. See Bowlby (1969; 1973). See also Bretherton (1991) and Main, Caplan, & Cassidy (1985).

51. See Bretherton (1991) and Mikulincer & Shaver (2003). See also Sullivan (1953).

52. See Bowlby (1979), pp. 141–142.

53. See Bartholomew & Horowitz (1991).

54. See Bartholomew & Horowitz (1991). See also Mikulincer & Shaver (2003).

55. See Kruglanski (1996b) and Kunda (1990).

56. See Kruglanski & Webster (1996).
57. See Dijksterhuis, van Knippenberg, Kruglanski, & Schaper (1996), Fiske & Neuberg (1990), Kruglanski & Freund (1983), Moskowitz (1993), and Neuberg & Fiske (1987).
58. See Ford & Kruglanski (1995) and Thompson, Roman, Moskowitz, Chaiken, & Bargh (1994).
59. See Tetlock (1985) and Webster (1993).
60. See Liberman, Molden, Idson, & Higgins (2001).
61. See Crowe & Higgins (1997) and Friedman & Förster (2001).
62. See Grant & Higgins (2003).
63. See Roese, Pennington, Coleman, Janicki, & Kenrick (2006).
64. See Roese & Olson (1993).
65. See Pennington & Roese (2003) and Roese, Hur, & Pennington (1999).
66. See Roese, Pennington, Coleman, Janicki, & Kenrick (2006).
67. See Buss & Schmitt (1993), Kenrick, Trost, & Sundie (2004), and Li, Bailey, Kenrick, & Linsenmeier (2002).
68. See Trivers (1972).
69. See Cox & Ferguson (1991) and Wright & Mischel (1987).
70. See Folkman & Moskowitz (2004) and Zeidner & Endler (1996).
71. See Breuer & Freud (1956/1893).
72. See Freud (1914/1955).
73. See A. Freud (1937).
74. For a review, see Baumeister, Schmeichel, & Vohs (2007).
75. See Mischel & Mischel (1983), Salovey, Hsee, & Mayer (1993), and Martijn, Tenbult, Merckelbach, Dreezens, & de Vries (2002).
76. See Mischel, Ebbesen, & Zeiss (1973).
77. See Strube, Turner, Cerro, Stephens, & Hinchey (1984).
78. For a fuller review of how people cope in a demanding world, see Higgins & Scholer (2008) and Scholer & Higgins (in press).
79. See Dweck (1999), Dweck, Chiu, & Hong (1995), and Molden & Dweck (2006).
80. See Dweck & Sorich (1999), Henderson & Dweck (1990), and Molden & Dweck (2006).
81. See Bandura (1977; 1997; 1999), Cervone (2000), and Cervone & Scott (1995).
82. See Bandura (1977), Cervone (1997), and Cervone, Shadel & Jencius (2001).
83. See Artistico, Cervone, & Pezzuti (2003).
84. See Bandura (1977), Bandura & Cervone (1983), Cervone & Peake (1986), and Schunk (1981).
85. See Sanderson, Rapee, & Barlow (1989) and Williams (1992).
86. See Caprara, Barbaranelli, Pastorelli, & Cervone (2004).
87. See Baumeister & Leary (1995) and Fiske (2003).
88. See Adler (1954) and Sullivan (1953).
89. See Downey & Feldman (1996) and Downey, Freitas, Michaelis, & Khouri (1998).
90. See Ayduk, Downey, Testa, Yen, & Shoda (1999).
91. See Ayduk, Downey, Testa, Yen, & Shoda (1999) and Downey, Frietas, Michaelis, & Khouri (1998).
92. See Downey, Mougios, Ayduk, London, & Shoda (2004).
93. See Lang, Bradley, & Cuthbert (1990).

94. See Romero-Canyas & Downey (2005).
95. See Ayduk, May, Downey, & Higgins (2003).
96. See Mischel (1974) and Mischel & Ebbesen (1970).
97. See Mischel (1999), Mischel, Shoda, & Rodriguez (1989), and Shoda, Mischel, & Peake (1990).
98. See Peake, Hebl, & Michel (2002).
99. See Freitas, Liberman, & Higgins (2002).
100. See Inkeles & Levinson (1969), Katz & Braly (1933), McCrae & Terracciano (2006), Peabody (1985), and Terracciano et al. (2005).
101. See Galton (1865).
102. For reviews, see Church & Ortiz (2005) and LeVine (2001).
103. See Benet-Martinez & Oishi (2008) and Chiu, Kim, & Wan (2008).
104. For a fuller discussion of these issues, see Higgins (2008) and Higgins, Pierro, & Kruglanski (2008).
105. See Markus & Kitayama (1998) and Shweder (1991).
106. For a review, see Chiu, Kim, & Wan (2008).
107. See McCrae (2004), p. 5.
108. See Chiu & Hong (2006), Chiu, Kim, & Wan 2008 Shweder & Sullivan (1993), and Triandis (1996).
109. See Cervone (2004), Higgins (1990), Hong, Morris, Chiu, & Benet-Martinez (2000), Hong, Wan, No, & Chiu (2007), Mendoza-Denton & Hansen (2007), Mischel & Shoda (1995), and Morris, Menon, & Ames (2001).
110. For a fuller discussion of this issue, see Higgins & Pittman (2008).
111. See Darwin (1859).
112. The following discussion was originally developed in Higgins (2008).
113. See Endler (1982), Lewin (1935), Marlowe & Gergen (1969), Mischel (1968), Murray (1938), and Rotter (1954).
114. See Higgins (1990, 1999, 2000b).
115. See Higgins & Pittman (2008).
116. See *Webster's Ninth New Collegiate Dictionary* (1989).
117. I am *not* suggesting that these are the only motivational factors that could be included. A motivational principle that is considered to be only a personality variable, or only a social psychological variable, or only a cultural variable, would not be included, nor would a motive that did not capture what it means to be human. But there are other motivational factors that would meet my criteria for inclusion. A clear example of a motivational principle that *does* meet my criteria is need for closure, which I have discussed earlier in this book (see Fu, Morris, Lee, Chao, Chiu, & Hong, 2007; Kruglanski & Webster, 1996).
118. See Carver & Scheier (1990), Heckhausen & Gollwitzer (1987), Kuhl (1984), Miller, Galanter, & Pribram (1960), and Wiener (1948).
119. See Erikson (1950/1963).
120. See Higgins (1991; 1996d).
121. The following discussion was originally developed in Higgins (2008).
122. See Nisbett (2003). See also Triandis & Suh (2002).
123. For a fuller discussion of how order emerges from dynamic flow, see Vallacher & Nowak (2007).

124. For a discussion of the difference between descriptive norms and injunctive or prescriptive norms, see Cialdini (2003).
125. See Hogg (2007) and Hogg & van Knippenberg (2003).
126. See Camacho, Higgins, & Luger (2003).
127. See Faddegon, Scheepers, & Ellemers (2007).
128. See Higgins, Pierro, & Kruglanski (in press).
129. See Rosenberg (1979).
130. See John (1990) and John & Srivastava (1999).
131. It is unclear how to conceptualize the fifth Big Five dimension of *neuroticism*, because it might be conceptualized either as a manner of goal pursuit or as an emotional outcome of maladaptive goal pursuit. Given this ambiguity, I will not describe here the results for this dimension. They are described in Higgins, Pierro, & Kruglanski (2008).
132. See Higgins, Friedman, Harlow, Idson, Ayduk, & Taylor (2001).
133. See Kruglanski, Thompson, Higgins, Atash, Pierro, Shah, & Spiegel (2000).
134. In every nation where English was not the first language of the participants, all the measures were translated and back-translated for accuracy.
135. By having the samples in every nation be college students, we created a conservative test of our hypothesis because this would make it *less* likely to find cross-cultural differences in our four motivational orientations.
136. We computed the *partial* correlations between promotion (statistically controlling for prevention) and each of the personality characteristics (self-esteem and Big Five), and the *partial* correlations between prevention (statistically controlling for promotion) and each of the personality characteristics. We also computed the partial correlations between locomotion (statistically controlling for assessment) and each of the personality characteristics (self-esteem and Big Five), and the partial correlations between assessment (statistically controlling for locomotion) and each of the personality characteristics.
137. Except Israel for openness.
138. Except Australia for promotion.
139. Except Israel for agreeableness.
140. Except Israel for both and Italy for assessment.
141. For a fuller discussion of how regulatory fit could underlie the obtained findings, see Higgins, Pierro, & Kruglanski (2008. See Chapter 9 for a regulatory fit account of the positive relation between strong locomotion and high conscientiousness.
142. Heine & Hamamura (2007) and Heine, Kitayama, Lehman, Takata, Ide, Leung, & Matsumoto (2001).
143. See, for example, Markus & Kitayama (1991).
144. See Kitayama & Park (2007).
145. See Fulmer, Gelfand, Kruglanski, Kim-Prieto, Diener, Pierro, & Higgins (2010).

CHAPTER 12
1. I am grateful to Paul Ingram for this case example.
2. See Kerr (1975).
3. See Kerr (1975), p. 773.

Notes

4. I am not suggesting that having both the promotion and prevention systems active together necessarily leads to conflict. As I discuss in Chapter 13, there can be benefits from having both systems working together, as when promotion concerns with errors of omission and prevention concerns with errors of commission can work together to enhance accuracy in decision making. However, there can be times when they are in conflict, and it cannot be assumed that motivational energy from one system can simply be added to the motivational energy from the other system to produce a higher sum total of motivational energy.

5. I must confess that I have been a member of a committee at Columbia that selects the Presidential Award for Outstanding Teaching—just the kind of rare and financially small award described by Kerr. From my experience on this committee, I believe that this is the kind of teaching that the "society" of Columbia wants.

6. See, for example, Deci, Connell, & Ryan (1989).

7. See Crowe & Higgins (1997) and Liberman, Molden, Idson, & Higgins (2001).

8. See Grove (1996).

9. See Förster & Werth (2009) and Seibt & Förster (2004).

10. I have observed this attitude among college teachers and have myself been guilty in the past of unthinkingly sharing this attitude. What made me realize the folly of overlooking such research was a question I received when I became a member of the Board of Advisors of the Teagle Collegium for Neuroscience, Cognition, and Student Learning (Columbia University). Another member of the Board (Professor Lois Putnam) asked me how I applied my research findings on motivation to my classroom teaching. I realized that I had not done so. Upon reflection, I recognized that this was because I had not appreciated its direct relevance. Since then I have tried to apply the research findings to improving student learning and performance.

11. See Förster, Higgins, & Idson (1998).

12. See Shah, Higgins, & Friedman (1998).

13. See Keller & Bless (2006).

14. See Spiegel, Grant-Pillow, & Higgins (2004).

15. See See Bianco, Higgins, & Klem (2003).

16. See Freitas & Higgins (2002).

17. See Pierro, Presaghi, Higgins, & Kruglanski (2009).

18. See Deci, Connell, & Ryan (1989).

19. See Benjamin & Flynn (2006).

20. See Bass (1998; 1999).

21. For more details about this study, see Benjamin & Flynn (2006).

22. See Pierro, Kruglanski, & Higgins (2006).

23. See Higgins (2008) and Higgins, Pierro, & Kruglanski (2008).

24. See Liberman, Idson, Camacho, & Higgins (1999).

25. See Paine (2009).

26. To increase the objectivity of the measure of perceived "vision" of a supervisor's message, an aggregate (mean score) across employees in each team was used (see Ostroff, 2007).

27. For more details on this work engagement measure, see Schaufeli, Bakker, & Salanova (2006).

28. For more details on this measure of favorability toward change, see Fedor, Caldwell, & Herold (2006).
29. See Kruglanski, Pierro, Higgins, & Capozza (2007).
30. See Judge, Thoresen, Pucik, & Welbourne (1999).
31. See Kruglanski, Pierro, Higgins, & Capozza (2007).
32. See Scholer (2009).
33. Commitment to the goal to change was assessed using the goal commitment scale developed by Klein, Wesson, Hollenbeck, Wright, & DeShon (2001).
34. This measure was based on previous research by Sheeran, Conner, & Norman (2001).
35. See Zou (2009).
36. See Durkheim (1897/1951).
37. See, for example, Berkman, Glass, Brissette, & Seeman (2001), Campbell, Converse, & Rodgers (1976), Cohen (2004), Fowler & Christakis (2008), House, Umberson, & Landis (1988), Marsden (1987), McPherson, Smith-Lovin, & Brashears (2006), and Seeman (1996).
38. See Putnam (2000).
39. See, for example, Stokes (1985)and Wellman, Carrington, & Hall (1988).
40. See, for example, Berkman (1995) and Berkman & Syme (1979); Cohen, Doyle, Skoner, Rabin, & Gwaltney (1997).
41. See Zou (2009) for a fuller discussion of this issue.
42. See Coleman (1990) and Granovetter (1985).
43. See Baker (1984) and Baker & Iyer (1992).
44. See Burt (1992), Cook & Emerson (1978), Freeman (1977), and Granovetter (1973).
45. See Diener, Emmons, Larsen, & Griffin (1985).
46. The network density measure was calculated by dividing the total number of identified relationships between the contacts by the total possible number of ties.

CHAPTER 13

1. See Seligman (1990; 2002).
2. See Peterson & Seligman (2004).
3. See Machiavelli (1513/2004).
4. See Christie & Geis (1970).
5. See *Webster's Ninth New Collegiate Dictionary* (1989).
6. I am grateful to Kayla Higgins for these insights about the relation between the viewpoints on virtue of Machiavelli and Aristotle (see K. A. Higgins, 2008).
7. See Freud (1920/1950).
8. I should also note, thanks to other insights in Kayla Higgins' paper (see K. A. Higgins, 2008), that the Aristotelian and Machiavellian viewpoints differ not only in whether truth and control are treated as intrinsically worthwhile (Aristotle) versus just as extrinsic means for having desired results (Machiavelli), but also in their general orientation toward the goal of having "the good life." For Aristotle, the aim of mankind was to fulfil human's highest potential—a promotion value orientation. For Machiavelli, the aim of mankind (or at least a Princely man) was to maintain his state and keep it stable and enduring—a prevention value orientation.

If Aristotle was a promotion optimist, then Machiavelli was a prevention *defensive pessimist*. And Freud's viewpoint was even darker than Machiavelli's. Freud was a true *pessimist* who described a constant conflict between the Id and the Superego. Like Machiavelli, Freud had a prevention orientation. But for Freud it was a story of reducing prevention failure, reducing anxiety as a constant, whereas for Machiavelli it was a story of prevention success as long as one did what was necessary. I believe that it was Freud's pessimism that, ultimately, inspired the development of the positive psychology movement. There was a positive story to tell, and the positive psychology movement wanted it told. And the preferred positive story was even more positive than Machiavelli's prevention success with its defensive pessimism. The preferred positive story was promotion success with its hopes and optimism—more like Aristotle's story.

9. See *Webster's Ninth New Collegiate Dictionary* (1989).
10. For monetary wealth or material success, there is evidence that well-being or "happiness" is improved by having some basic level of material resources, but beyond that level, having more material resources does not enhance well-being or "happiness" (see Diener & Diener, 1995; Ryan & Deci, 2001). Moreover, there is evidence that having monetary wealth or material success as your highest goal priority is, if anything, negatively related to well-being (e.g., Kasser & Ryan, 1993).
11. For a further discussion of the trade-offs of basic psychological principles, see Higgins (1991; 2000c).
12. See, for example, Higgins (1987; 1989b; 1998b), Higgins, Bond, Klein, & Strauman (1986), Strauman (1989), and Strauman & Higgins (1987, 1988).
13. See Higgins (1989c; 1991).
14. See Higgins (1991).
15. See Newman, Higgins, & Vookles (1992).
16. See Higgins (1997; 1998b).
17. See Higgins (2001).
18. For a fuller discussion and description of the trade-offs in the promotion and prevention systems, see Scholer & Higgins (2011).
19. See Dickman & Meyer (1988), Meyer, Smith, & Wright (1982), and Woodworth (1899).
20. See Förster, Higgins, & Bianco (2003).
21. See Lewin (1935) and Miller (1944; 1959).
22. See Crowe & Higgins (1997), Förster & Werth (2009), and Friedman & Förster (2001).
23. See Lucas & Diener (2008).
24. See Lucas & Diener (2008) and Roysamb, Harris, Magnus, Vitterso, & Tambs (2002).
25. See Watson, Clark, & Tellegen (1988) and Watson & Tellegen (1985).
26. See Wilson (1967), p. 294.
27. See Suls, Martin, & Wheeler (2002), Tesser (1988), and Wood (1989).
28. See Kruglanski, Thompson, Higgins, Atash, Pierro, Shah, & Spiegel (2000).
29. See Kruglanski, Thompson, Higgins, Atash, Pierro, Shah, & Spiegel (2000).
30. For a discussion of all the different possible—and legitimate—standards for self-evaluation, see Higgins, Strauman, & Klein (1986).

31. See Beck (1967) and Ellis (1973).
32. See Nolen-Hoeksema (2000).
33. See Jones (1979) and Ross (1977).
34. See Scholer, Grant, Baer, Bolger, & Higgins (2009).
35. For discussions of the advantages of having strong promotion versus strong prevention for different tasks or for different temporal phases of the same task, see Brockner, Higgins, & Low (2004) and Lam & Chiu (2002).
36. See Berscheid & Reis (1998).
37. See Berscheid (1985), Byrne (1971), Byrne & Blaylock (1963), Byrne, Clore & Smeaton (1986), Carli, Ganley, & Pierce-Otay (1991), Coombs (1966), Deutsch, Sullivan, Sage, & Basile (1991), and Newcomb (1961).
38. See Bohns Lake (2008).
39. These experts were Michael K. Coolsen, Eli J. Finkel, Madoka Kumashiro, Gale Lucas, Daniel C. Molden, and Caryl E. Rusbult.
40. See Aron, Aron, & Smollan (1992) for a description of the "Inclusion of Other in the Self" scale.
41. In this study, the relationship well-being composite measure included the same variables as in the first study except for the variable of commitment.
42. There are also potential advantages in business organizations from having the top managers include both a strong promotion individual and a strong prevention individual (Brockner, Higgins, & Low, 2004). This kind of business relationship needs to be directly examined in future research.
43. For a broader discussion of the difference between divisible and unitary tasks, see Steiner (1972).
44. See Bohns & Higgins (in press).
45. The full quote shows that this maxim, from Grantland Rice, an American sportswriter, also had a moral "rightness" intent related to truth effectiveness: "For when the One Great Scorer comes,/To write against your name,/He marks—not that you won or lost—/But how you played the Game."
46. See Franks (2009).
47. See Weinstein, Capitanio, & Gosling (2008).
48. The following discussion of the well-being of animals is based on unpublished papers (e.g., Franks & Higgins, 2005), and many conversations with Becca Franks, who is an expert in this area. And our conversations were not restricted to just the well-being of animals but concerned well-being in general. I am indebted to Becca for her insights and wisdom regarding the nature of well-being.
49. See Higgins (1989c; 1991) and Higgins & Silberman (1998).
50. This argument can be extended from caretakers of children to caretakers of the elderly or the infirm and caretakers of non-human animals. Regarding non-human animals, there is no question that zoo caretakers and pet-owners not only care *for* their animals but also care *about* them. Like loving parents, they want the best for their animals. Indeed, they try to ensure that the animals have a life of desired results—for food, water, shelter, and so on. The animals, then, have desired results (value effectiveness). My concern is that, at least in some cases, zoo animals or pets may be "spoiled" and "overprotected." There may be too much "doting" and not enough "managing." Animals need to be allowed to make mistakes and experience

failure in order to learn the self-regulatory contingencies that support their well-being. Only in this way can they have the truth effectiveness and control effectiveness that they need for well-being.

51. See Neugarten, Havighurst, & Tobin (1961) and Ryff (2008).
52. See Brandtstadter, Wentura, & Rothermund (1999), Carstensen (1995), and Freund & Baltes (2002).
53. See Erikson (1950/1963).
54. See Goodwin (2005).

REFERENCES

Aaker, J. L., & Lee, A. Y. (2001). I seek pleasures and we avoid pains: The role of self regulatory goals in information processing and persuasion. *Journal of Consumer Research, 28*, 33–49.

Abelson, R. P. (1983). Whatever became of consistency theory? *Personality and Social Psychology Bulletin, 9*, 37–54.

Abelson, R. P., Aronson, E., McGuire, W. J., Newcomb, T. M., Rosenberg, M. J., & Tannenbaum, P. H. (Eds.) (1968). *Theories of cognitive consistency: A sourcebook.* Chicago: Rand McNally.

Abramson, L. Y., Metalsky, F. I., & Allo'y, L. B. (1989). Hopelessness depression: A theory based subtype of depression. *Psychological Review, 96*(2), 358–372.

Abramson, L. Y., Seligman, M. E. P., & Teasdale, J. D. (1978). Learned helplessness in humans: Critique and reformulation. *Journal of Abnormal Psychology, 87*, 49–74.

Adler, A. (1954). *Understanding human nature.* New York: Fawcett.

Adorno, T. W., Frenkel-Brunswick, E., Levinson, D. J., & Sanford, R. N. (1950). *The authoritarian personality.* New York: Harper.

Ainsworth, M. D. S. (1967). *Infancy in Uganda: Infant care and the growth of love.* Baltimore: Johns Hopkins University Press.

Ainsworth, M. D. S., Blehar, M. C., Waters, E., & Wall, S. (1978). *Patterns of attachment.* Hillsdale, NJ: Erlbaum.

Ajzen, I. (1985). From intentions to actions: A theory of planned behavior. In J. Kuhl & J. Beckmann (Eds.), *Action-control: From cognition to behavior* (pp. 11–39). Heidelberg: Springer.

Ajzen, I. (1996). The social psychology of decision making. In E. T. Higgins & A. W. Kruglanski (Eds.), *Social psychology: Handbook of basic principles* (pp. 297–325). New York: Guilford.

Ajzen, I., & Fishbein, M. (1970). The prediction of behavior from attitudinal and normative variables. *Journal of Experimental Social Psychology, 6*, 466–487.

Ajzen, I., & Fishbein, M. (1980). *Understanding attitudes and predicting social behavior.* Englewood Cliffs, NJ: Prentice-Hall.

Alexander, K. M., Levine, J. M., & Higgins, E. T. (2010). *Regulatory fit and reaction to deviance in small groups.* Unpublished manuscript, University of Pittsburgh

Allen, V. L. (1975). Social support for nonconformity. In L. Berkowitz (Ed.), *Advances in experimental social psychology* (Vol. 8, pp. 1–43). New York: Academic Press.

Alloy, L. B., & Abramson, L. Y. (1979). Judgment of contingency in depressed and non-depressed students: Sadder but wiser? *Journal of Experimental Psychology: General, 108,* 441–485.

Allport, G. W. (1937a). The functional autonomy of motives. *American Journal of Psychology, 50,* 141–156.

Allport, G. W. (1937b). *Personality: A psychological interpretation.* New York: Holt.

Allport, G. W. (1961). *Pattern and growth in personality.* New York: Holt, Rinehart & Winston.

Alvarez, J. M., Ruble, D. N., & Bolger, N. (2001). Trait understanding or evaluative reasoning? An analysis of children's behavioral predictions. *Child Development, 72,* 1409–1425.

Andersen, S. M. (1984). Self-knowledge and social inference: II. The diagnosticity of cognitive/affective and behavioral data. *Journal of Personality and Social Psychology, 46,* 294–307.

Andersen, S. M., & Baum, A. (1994). Transference in interpersonal relations: Inferences and affect based on significant-other representations. *Journal of Personality.* (Special Issue: Psychodynamics and social cognition: Perspectives on the representation and processing of emotionally significant information), *62,* 459–497.

Andersen, S. M., & Chen, S. (2002). The relational self: An interpersonal social-cognitive theory. *Psychological Review, 109,* 619–645.

Andersen, S. M., & Cole, S. W. (1990). "Do I know you?": The role of significant others in general social perception. *Journal of Personality and Social Psychology, 59,* 384–399.

Andersen, S. M., Glassman, N. S., Chen, S., & Cole, S. W. (1995). Transference in social perception: The role of chronic accessibility in significant-other representations. *Journal of Personality and Social Psychology, 69,* 41–57.

Andersen, S. M., Reznik, I., & Chen, S. (1997). The self in relation to others: Motivational and cognitive underpinnings. In J. G. Snodgrass & R. L. Thompson (Eds.), *The self across psychology: Self-recognition, self-awareness, and the self concept.* Annals of the New York Academy of Sciences (Vol. 818, pp. 233–275). New York: New York Academy of Sciences.

Andersen, S. M., Reznik, I., & Glassman, N. S. (2005). The unconscious relational self. In R. R. Hassin, J. S. Uleman, & J. A. Bargh (Eds.), *The new unconscious.* Oxford Series in Social Cognition and Social Neuroscience (pp. 421–481). New York: Oxford University Press.

Andersen, S. M., & Saribay, S. A. (2005). The relational self and transference: Evoking motives, self-regulation, and emotions through activation of mental representations of significant others. In M. W. Baldwin (Ed.), *Interpersonal cognition* (pp. 1–32). New York: Guilford Press.

Anderson, C. A., Krull, D. S., & Weiner, B. (1996). Explanations: Processes and consequences. In E. T. Higgins & A. W. Kruglanski (Eds.), *Social psychology: Handbook of basic principles* (pp. 271–296). New York: Guilford.

Anderson, J. R. (1974). Retrieval of propositional information from long-term memory. *Cognitive Psychology, 6,* 451–474.

Anderson, J. R. (1983). *The architecture of cognition*. Cambridge, MA: Harvard University Press.

Appelt, K. C., Zou, X., Arora, P., & Higgins, E. T. (2009). Regulatory fit in negotiation: Effects of "prevention-buyer" and "promotion-seller" fit. *Social Cognition, 27*, 365–384.

Appelt, K. C., Zou, X., & Higgins, E. T. (2009). *Choosing truth over value: How strong assessment changes negotiation decisions*. Unpublished manuscript, Columbia University.

Appelt, K. C., Zou, X., & Higgins, E. T. (2010). Feeling right or being right: When strong assessment yields strong correction. *Motivation and Emotion, 34*, 316–324.

Arendt, H. (1963). *Eichmann in Jerusalem: A report on the banality of evil*. London: Faber & Faber.

Arkes, H. R., & Blumer, C. (1985). The psychology of sunk cost. *Organizational Behavior and Human Decision Processes, 35*, 124–140.

Armitage, C. J. (2005) Can the theory of planned behavior predict the maintenance of physical activity? *Health Psychology, 24*, 235–245.

Aron, A., Aron E. N., & Smollan, D. (1992). Inclusion of other in the self scale and the structure of interpersonal closeness. *Journal of Personality and Social Psychology, 63*, 596–612.

Aronson, E. (1969). The theory of cognitive dissonance: A current perspective. In L. Berkowitz (Ed.), *Advances in Experimental Social Psychology* (Vol. 4, pp. 1–34). New York: Academic Press.

Aronson, E., & Carlsmith, J. M. (1963). The effect of the severity of threat on the devaluation of forbidden behavior. *Journal of Abnormal and Social Psychology, 66*, 584–588.

Aronson, E., & Mills, J. (1959). The effect of severity of initiation on liking for a group. *Journal of Abnormal and Social Psychology, 59*, 177–181.

Artistico, D., Cervone, D., & Pezzuti, L. (2003). Perceived self-efficacy and everyday problem solving among young and older adults. *Psychology and Aging, 18*, 68–79.

Asch, S. E. (1946). Forming impressions of personality. *Journal of Abnormal and Social Psychology, 41*, 258–290.

Asch, S. E. (1952). *Social psychology*. Englewood Cliffs, NJ: Prentice-Hall.

Atkinson, J. W. (1957). Motivational determinants of risk-taking behavior. *Psychological Review, 64*, 359–372.

Atkinson, J. W. (1964). *An introduction to motivation*. Princeton, NJ: D. Van Nostrand.

Atkinson, J. W., Heyns, R. W., & Veroff, J. (1954). The effect of experimental arousal of the affiliation motive on thematic apperception. *Journal of Abnormal & Social Psychology, 49*, 405–410.

Aviles, A. I. (2009). *The effects of regulatory focus on learning and value of information*. Unpublished honors thesis, Columbia University.

Avnet, T., & Higgins, E. T. (2003). Locomotion, assessment, and regulatory fit: Value transfer from "how" to "what." *Journal of Experimental Social Psychology, 39*, 525–530.

Avnet, T., & Higgins, E. T. (2006). How regulatory fit impacts value in consumer choices and opinions. *Journal of Marketing Research, 43*, 1–10.

Ayduk, O., Downey, G., Testa, A., Yen, Y., & Shoda, Y. (1999). Does rejection elicit hostility in rejection sensitive women? *Social Cognition. Special Issue: Social Cognition and Relationships, 17*, 245–271.

Ayduk, O., May, D., Downey, G., & Higgins, E. T. (2003). Tactical differences in coping with rejection sensitivity: The role of prevention pride. *Personality and Social Psychology Bulletin, 29*, 435–448.

Baker, W. E. (1984). The social structure of a national securities market. *American Journal of Sociology, 89*, 775–811.

Baker, W. E., & Iyer, A. V. (1992). Information networks and market behavior. *Journal of Mathematical Sociology, 16*, 305–332.

Baldwin, M. W., Carrell, S. E., & Lopez, D. F. (1990). Priming relationship schemas: My advisor and the Pope are watching me from the back of my mind. *Journal of Personality and Social Psychology, 26*, 435–454.

Baldwin, M. W., & Holmes, J. G. (1987). Salient private audiences and awareness of the self. *Journal of Personality and Social Psychology, 52*, 1087–1098.

Banaji, M. R., & Greenwald, A. G. (1994). Implicit stereotyping and prejudice. In M. P. Zanna & J. M. Olson (Eds.), *The psychology of prejudice: The Ontario symposium* (Vol. 7, pp. 55–76). Hillsdale, NJ: Erlbaum.

Banaji, M. R., Hardin, C., & Rothman, A. J. (1993). Implicit stereotyping in person judgment. *Journal of Personality and Social Psychology, 65*, 272–281.

Bandura, A. (1973). *Aggression: A social learning theory analysis*. Englewood Cliffs, NJ: Prentice-Hall.

Bandura, A. (1977). Self-efficacy: Toward a unifying theory of behavioral change. *Psychological Review, 84*, 191–215.

Bandura, A. (1982). Self-efficacy mechanism in human agency. *American Psychologist, 37*, 122–147.

Bandura, A. (1986). *Social foundations of thought and action: A social cognitive theory*. Englewood Cliffs, NJ: Prentice-Hall.

Bandura, A. (1989). Self-regulation of motivation and action through internal standards and goal systems. In L. A. Pervin (Ed.), *Goal concepts in personality and social psychology* (pp. 19–85). Hillsdale, NJ: Erlbaum.

Bandura, A. (1997). *Self-efficacy: The exercise of control*. New York: Freeman.

Bandura, A. (1999). Social cognitive theory of personality. In D. Cervone & Y. Shoda (Eds.), *The coherence of personality: Social-cognitive bases of consistency, variability, and organization* (pp. 185–241). New York: Guilford Press.

Bandura, A., & Cervone, D. (1983). Self-evaluative and self-efficacy mechanisms governing the motivational effects of goal systems. *Journal of Personality and Social Psychology, 45*, 1017–1028.

Bandura, A. L., & Walters, R. H. (1963). *Social learning and personality development*. New York: Holt, Rinehart and Winston.

Bargh, J. A. (1989). Conditional automaticity: Varieties of automatic influence in social perception and cognition. In J. S. Uleman & J. A. Bargh (Eds.), *Unintended thought* (pp. 3–51). New York: Guilford.

Bargh, J. A. (1990). Auto-motives: Preconscious determinants of social interaction. In E. T. Higgins & R. M. Sorrentino (Eds.), *Handbook of motivation and cognition: Foundations of social behavior,* (Vol. 2, pp. 93–130). New York: Guilford.

Bargh, J. A. (1996). Automaticity in social psychology. In E. T. Higgins & A. W. Kruglanski (Eds.), *Social psychology: Handbook of basic principles* (pp. 169–183). New York: Guilford.

Bargh, J. A. (2005). Bypassing the will: Toward demystifying the nonconscious control of social behavior. In R. R. Hassin, J. S. Uleman, & J. A. Bargh (Eds.), *The new unconscious* (pp. 37–58). New York: Oxford University Press.

Bargh, J. A., Bond, R. N., Lombardi, W. J., & Tota, M. E. (1986). The additive nature of chronic and temporary sources of construct accessibility. *Journal of Personality and Social Psychology, 50,* 869–878.

Bargh, J. A., Chen, M., & Burrows, L. (1996). Automaticity of social behavior: Direct effects of trait construct and stereotype activation on action. *Journal of Personality and Social Psychology, 71,* 230–244.

Bargh, J.A., Gollwitzer, P.M., Lee-Chai, A., Barndollar, K., & Trotschel, R. (2001). The automated will: Nonconscious activation and pursuit of behavioral goals. *Journal of Personality and Social Psychology, 81,* 1014–1027.

Bargh, J. A., Lombardi, W. J., & Higgins, E. T. (1988). Automaticity of chronically accessible constructs in person × situation effects on person perception: It's just a matter of time. *Journal of Personality and Social Psychology, 55,* 599–605.

Baron, R. A., & Lawton, S. F. (1972). Environmental influences on aggression: The facilitation of modeling effects by high ambient temperatures. *Psychonomic Science, 26,* 80–82.

Barry, B., & Friedman, R.A. (1998). Bargainer characteristics in distributive and integrative negotiation. *Journal of Personality and Social Psychology, 74,* 345–359.

Bartholomew, K., & Horowitz, L. M. (1991). Attachment styles among young adults: A test of a four-category model. *Journal of Personality and Social Psychology, 61,* 226–244.

Bartlett, F. C. (1932). *Remembering.* Oxford, England: Oxford University Press.

Bass, B. M. (1998). *Transformational leadership: Industry, military, and educational impact.* Mahwah, NJ: Erlbaum.

Bass, B. M. (1999). Two decades of research and development in transformational leadership. *European Journal of Work and Organizational Psychology, 8,* 9–32.

Batson, C. D. (1975). Rational processing or rationalization? The effect of disconfirming information on a stated religious belief. *Journal of Personality and Social Psychology, 32,* 176–184.

Baumeister, R. F., Bratslavsky, E., Muraven, M., & Tice, D. M. (1998). Ego depletion: Is the active self a limited resource? *Journal of Personality and Social Psychology, 74,* 1252–1265.

Baumeister, R. F., & Heatherton, T. F. (1996). Self-regulation failure: An overview. *Psychological Inquiry, 7,* 1–15.

Baumeister, R. F., Heatherton, T. F., & Tice, D. M. (1994). *Losing control: How and why people fail at self-regulation.* San Diego, CA: Academic Press, Inc.

Baumeister, R. F., & Leary, M. R. (1995). The need to belong: Desire for interpersonal attachments as a fundamental human motivation. *Psychological Bulletin, 117,* 497–529.

Baumeister, R. F., Schmeichel, B. J., & Vohs, K. D. (2007). Self-regulation and the executive function: The self as controlling agent. In A. W. Kruglanski & E.T. Higgins (Eds.), *Social psychology: Handbook of basic principles* (pp. 516–539). New York: Guilford.

Beck, A. T. (1967). *Depression: Causes and treatment.* Philadelphia: University of Pennsylvania Press.

Beck, A. T., Rush, A. J., Shaw, B. F., & Emery, G. (1979). *Cognitive therapy of depression.* New York: Guilford Press.

Becker, E. (1973). *The denial of death.* New York: Free Press.

Bem, D. J. (1965). An experimental analysis of self-persuasion. *Journal of Experimental Social Psychology, 1,* 199–218.

Bem, D. J. (1967). Self-perception: An alternative interpretation of cognitive dissonance phenomena. *Psychological Review, 74,* 183–200.

Bem, S. L. (1974). The measurement of psychological androgyny. *Journal of Consulting and Clinical Psychology, 42,* 155–162.

Benet-Martinez, V., & Oishi, S. (2008). Culture and personality. In O. P. John, R. W. Robins, & L. A. Pervin (Eds.), *Handbook of personality: Theory and research* (3rd ed., pp. 542–567). New York: Guilford Press.

Benjamin, L., & Flynn, F. J. (2006). Leadership style and regulatory mode: Value from fit? *Organizational Behavior and Human Decision Processes, 100,* 216–230.

Bentham, J. (1988). *The principles of morals and legislation.* Amherst, NY: Prometheus Books. (Originally published 1781)

Berk, M. S., & Andersen, S. M. (2000). The impact of past relationships on interpersonal behavior: Behavioral confirmation in the social-cognitive process of transference. *Journal of Personality and Social Psychology, 79,* 546–562.

Berkman, L. F. (1995). Role of social-relations in health promotion. *Psychosomatic Medicine, 57,* 245–254.

Berkman, L. F., Glass, T., Brissette, I., & Seeman, T. E. (2001) From social integration to health: Durkheim in the new millennium. *Social Science & Medicine, 51,* 843–857.

Berkman, L. F., & Syme, S. L. (1979). Social networks, host resistance, and mortality: A 9-year follow-up study of Alameda County residents. *American Journal of Epidemiology, 109,* 186–204.

Berlyne, D. E. (1960). *Conflict, arousal and curiosity.* New York: McGraw-Hill.

Berlyne, D. E. (1973). The vicissitudes of aplopathematic and thelematoscopic pneumatology (or The hydrography of hedonism.) In D. E. Berlyne & K. B. Madsen (Eds.), *Pleasure, reward, preference.* New York: Academic Press.

Berne, E. (1964). *Games people play.* New York: Ballantine Books.

Bernoulli, D. (1954). Specimen theoriae novae de mensura sortis. St. Petersburg, 1738. Translated in *Econometrica, 22,* 23–36.

Berridge, K. C., & Robinson, T. E. (2003). Parsing reward. *Trends in Neurosciences, 26,* 507–513.

Berscheid, E. (1983). Emotion. In H. H. Kelley, E. Berscheid, A. Christensen, J. Harvey, T. Huston, G. Levinger, E. McClintock, A. Peplau, & D. R. Peterson (Eds.), *Close relationships.* San Francisco: Freeman.

Berscheid, E. (1985). Interpersonal attraction. In G. Lindzey & E. Aronson (Eds.), *Handbook of social psychology* (3rd ed., pp. 413–484). New York: Random House.

Berscheid, E., & Reis, H. T. (1998). Attraction and close relationships. In D. T. Gilbert, S. T. Fiske, & G. Lindzey (Eds.), *The handbook of social psychology* (4th ed., pp. 193–281). New York: McGraw Hill.

Bettman, J. R., Luce, M. F., & Payne, J. W. (1998). Constructive consumer choice processes. *Journal of Consumer Research, 25,* 187–217.

Bexton, W. H., Heron, W., & Scott, T. H. (1954). Effects of decreased variation in the sensory environment. *Canadian Journal of Psychology, 8*, 70–76.

Bianco, A. T., Higgins, E. T., & Klem, A. (2003). How "fun/importance" fit impacts performance: Relating implicit theories to instructions. *Personality and Social Psychology Bulletin, 29*, 1091–1103.

Biner, P. M., Angle, S. T., Park, J. H., Mellinger, A. E., & Barber, B. C. (1995). Need and the illusion of control. *Personality and Social Psychology Bulletin, 21*, 899–907.

Biner, P. M., Huffman, M. L., Curran, M. A., & Long, K. R. (1998). Illusory control as a function of motivation for a specific outcome in a chance-based situation. *Motivation and Emotion, 22*, 277–291.

Blanchard, D. C., Hynd, A. L., Minke, K. A., Minemoto, T., & Blanchard, R. J. (2001). Human defensive behaviors to threat scenarios show parallels to fear- and anxiety-related defense patterns of non-human animals. *Neuroscience and Biobehavioral Reviews, 25*, 761–770.

Block, J. H. (2002). *Personality as an affect-processing system: Toward an integrative theory*. Mahwah, NJ: Erlbaum.

Block, J. H., & Block, J. (1980). The role of ego-control and ego-resiliency in the organization of behavior. In W. A. Collins (Ed.), *Minnesota symposium on child psychology* (Vol. 13, pp. 39–101). Hillsdale, NJ: Erlbaum.

Blodgett, H. C. (1929). The effect of the introduction of reward upon the maze performance of rats. *University of California Publications in Psychology, 4*, 113–134.

Boldero, J., & Francis, J. (2002). Goals, standards, and the self: Reference values serving different functions. *Personality and Social Psychology Review, 6*, 232–241.

Bolger, N., & Amarel, D. (2007). Effects of social support visibility on adjustment to stress: Experimental evidence. *Journal of Personality and Social Psychology, 92*, 458–475.

Bohns Lake, V. K. (2008). *Strategic compatibility in social relationships: The case of regulatory focus complementarity*. Unpublished doctoral dissertation, Columbia University.

Bohns, V. K., & Higgins, E. T. (in press). Liking the same things, but doing things differently: Outcome versus strategic compatibility in partner preferences for joint tasks. *Social Cognition*.

Bowlby, J. (1969). *Attachment* (Attachment and Loss, Vol. 1). New York: Basic Books.

Bowlby, J. (1973). *Separation: Anxiety and anger* (Attachment and Loss, Vol. 2). New York: Basic Books.

Bowlby, J. (1979). *The making and breaking of affectional bonds*. London: Tavistock.

Bowlby, J. (1988). *A secure base: Clinical applications of attachment theory*. London: Routledge.

Brandtstadter, J., Wentura, D., & Rothermund, K. (1999). Intentional self-development through adulthood and later life: Tenacious pursuit and flexible adjustment of goals. In J. Brandtstadter & R. M. Lerner (Eds.), *Action and self-development: Theory and research through the life span* (pp. 373–400). Thousand Oaks, CA: Sage.

Brehm, J. W. (1956). Post-decision changes in desirability of alternatives. *Journal of Abnormal and Social Psychology, 52*, 384–389.

Brehm, J. W. (1959). Increasing cognitive dissonance by fait accompli. *Journal of Abnormal and Social Psychology, 58*, 379–382.

Brehm, J. W. (1966). *A theory of psychological reactance.* New York: Academic Press.

Brehm, J. W., & Cohen, A. R. (1962). *Explorations in cognitive dissonance.* New York: Wiley.

Brehm, J. W., & Self, E. A. (1989). The intensity of motivation. *Annual Review of Psychology, 40,* 109–131. Palo Alto, CA: Annual Reviews Inc.

Brehm, J. W., Stires, L. K., Sensenig, J., & Shaban, J. (1966). The attractiveness of an eliminated choice alternative. *Journal of Experimental Social Psychology, 2,* 301–313.

Brehm, S. S., & Brehm, J. W. (1981). *Psychological reactance: A theory of freedom and control.* New York: Academic Press.

Brendl, C. M., & Higgins, E. T. (1996). Principles of judging valence: What makes events positive or negative? In M. P. Zanna (Ed.), *Advances in experimental social psychology* (Vol. 28, pp. 95–160). New York: Academic Press.

Brendl, C. M., Markman, A. B., & Messner, C. (2001). How do indirect measures of evaluation work? Evaluating the inference of prejudice in the Implicit Association Test. *Journal of Personality and Social Psychology, 81,* 760–773.

Bretherton, I. (1991). Pouring new wine into old bottles: The social self as internal working model. In M. R. Gunnar & L. A. Sroufe (Eds.), *Self processes and development: The Minnesota symposia on child psychology* (Vol. 23, pp. 1–41). Hillsdale, NJ: Erlbaum.

Breuer, J., & Freud, S. (1956). On the psychical mechanism of hysterical phenomena (1893). *International Journal of Psycho-Analysis, 37,* 8–13.

Brewer, M. B. (1988). A dual-process model of impression formation. In T. K. Srull & R. S. Wyer, Jr. (Eds.), *Advances in social cognition* (Vol. 1, pp. 1–36). Hillsdale, NJ: Erlbaum.

Brewer, M. B. (2007). The social psychology of intergroup relations: Social categorization, ingroup bias, and outgroup prejudice. In A. W. Kruglanski & E. T. Higgins (Eds.), *Social psychology: Handbook of basic principles* (2nd ed., pp. 695–715). New York: Guilford.

Brickman, P. (1978). Is it real? In J. H. Harvey, W. Ickes, & R. F. Kidd (Eds.), *New directions in attribution research* (Vol. 2, pp. 5–34). Hillsdale, NJ: Lawrence Erlbaum Associates.

Brickman, P. (1987). *Commitment, conflict, and caring.* Englewood Cliffs, NJ: Prentice-Hall.

Brockner, J., Higgins, E. T., & Low, M.B. (2004). Regulatory focus theory and the entrepreneurial process. *Journal of Business Venturing, 19,* 203–220.

Brodscholl, J. C. (2005). *Regulatory focus and utility in goal pursuit.* Unpublished doctoral dissertation, Columbia University.

Brodscholl, J. C., Kober, H., & Higgins, E. T. (2007). Strategies of self-regulation in goal attainment versus goal maintenance. *European Journal of Social Psychology, 37,* 628–648.

Brody, N. (1983). *Human motivation: Commentary on goal-directed action.* New York: Academic Press.

Broverman, I., Broverman, D. M., Clarkson, F. E., Rosenkrantz, P. S., & Vogel, S. R. (1970). Sex-role stereotypes and clinical judgments of mental health. *Journal of Consulting and Clinical Psychology, 34,* 1–7.

Brown, R. W. (1958a). *Words and things.* New York: Free Press.

Brown, R. W. (1958b). How shall a thing be called? *Psychological Review, 65,* 14–21.

Brook, A. T., Garcia, J., & Fleming, M. (2008). The effects of multiple identities on psychological well-being. *Personality and Social Psychology Bulletin, 34,* 1601–1612.

Bruner, J. S. (1957a). On perceptual readiness. *Psychological Review, 64,* 123–152.

Bruner, J. S. (1957b). Going beyond the information given. In H. Gruber et al. (Eds.), *Contemporary approaches to cognition.* Cambridge, MA: Harvard University Press.

Bruner, J. S., & Goodman, C. C. (1947). Value and need as organizing factors in perception. *Journal of Abnormal and Social Psychology, 42,* 33–44.

Bruner, J. S., & Postman, L. (1948). Symbolic value as an organizing factor in perception. *Journal of Social Psychology, 27,* 203–208.

Brymer, E. (2005). *Extreme dude: A phenomenological perspective on the extreme sports experience.* University of Wollongong, Australia.

Buehler, R., Griffin, D., & Ross, M. (1994). Exploring the "planning fallacy": Why people underestimate their task completion times. *Journal of Personality and Social Psychology, 67,* 366–381.

Burt, R. S. (1992). *Structural holes.* Cambridge, MA: Harvard University Press.

Bushman, B. J., & Stack, A. D. (1996). Forbidden fruit versus tainted fruit: Effects of warning labels on attraction to television violence. *Journal of Experimental Psychology: Applied, 2,* 207–226.

Buss, D. M., & Schmitt, D. P. (1993). Sexual Strategies Theory: A contextual evolutionary analysis of human mating. *Psychological Review, 100,* 204–232.

Byrne, D. (1971). *The attraction paradigm.* New York: Academic Press.

Byrne, D., & Blaylock, B. (1963). Similarity and assumed similarity of attitudes between husbands and wives. *Journal of Abnormal and Social Psychology, 67,* 636–640.

Byrne, D., Clore, G., & Smeaton, G. (1986). The attraction hypothesis: Do similar attitudes affect anything? *Journal of Personality and Social Psychology, 51,* 1167–1170.

Cacioppo, J. T., Priester, J. R., & Berntson, G. G. (1993). Rudimentary determinants of attitudes II: Arm flexion and extension have differential effects on attitudes. *Journal of Personality and Social Psychology, 65,* 5–17.

Cairns, R. B. (1967). The attachment behavior of animals. *Psychological Review, 73,* 409–426.

Call, J. (2005). The self and other: A missing link in comparative social cognition. In H. S. Terrace & J. Metcalfe (Eds.), *The missing link in cognition: Origins of self-reflective consciousness* (pp. 321–341). Oxford: Oxford University Press.

Camacho, C. J., Higgins, E. T., & Luger, L. (2003). Moral value transfer from regulatory fit: "What feels right *is* right" and "what feels wrong *is* wrong." *Journal of Personality and Social Psychology, 84,* 498–510.

Campbell, A., Converse, P. E., & Rodgers, W. L. (1976). *The quality of American life.* New York: Russell Sage Foundation.

Cantor, N. (1994). Life task problem-solving: Situational affordances and personal needs. *Personality and Social Psychology Bulletin, 20,* 235–243.

Cantor, N., & Kihlstrom, J. F. (1987). *Personality and social intelligence.* Englewood Cliffs, NJ: Prentice Hall.

Cantor, N., Norem, J. K., Niedenthal, P. M., Langston, C. A., & Brower, A. M. (1987). Life tasks, self-concept ideals, and cognitive strategies in a life transition. *Journal of Personality and Social Psychology, 53,* 1178–1191.

Caprara, G. V., Barbaranelli, C., Pastorelli, C., & Cervone, D. (2004). The contribution of self-efficacy beliefs to psychosocial outcomes in adolescence: predicting beyond global dispositional tendencies. *Personality and Individual Differences, 37,* 751–763.

Carder, B., & Berkowitz, K. (1970). Rats' preference for earned in comparison with free food. *Science, 167,* 1273–1274.

Carli, L., Ganley, R., & Pierce-Otay, A. (1991). Similarity and satisfaction in roommate relationships. *Personality and Social Psychology Bulletin, 17,* 419–426.

Carstensen, L. L. (1995). Evidence for a life-span theory socioemotional selectivity. *Current Directions in Psychological Science, 4,* 151–156.

Cartwright, D. (1942). The effect of interruption, completion and failure upon the attractiveness of activity. *Journal of Experimental Psychology, 31,* 1–16.

Carver, C. S. (2004). Self-regulation of action and affect. In R. F. Baumeister & K. D. Vohs (Eds.), *Handbook of self-regulation: Research, theory, and applications* (pp. 13–39). New York: Guilford Press.

Carver, C. S., & Scheier, M. F. (1981). *Attention and self-regulation: A control-theory approach to human behavior.* New York: Springer-Verlag.

Carver, C. S., & Scheier, M. F. (1990). Origins and functions of positive and negative affect: A control-process view. *Psychological Review, 97,* 19–35.

Carver, C. S., & Scheier, M. F. (1998). *On the self-regulation of behavior.* New York: Cambridge University Press.

Carver, C. S., & Scheier, M. F. (2008). Feedback processes in the simultaneous regulation of action and affect. In J. Y. Shah & W. L. Gardner (Eds.). *Handbook of motivation science* (pp. 308–324). New York: Guilford Press.

Case, R. (1985). *Intellectual development: Birth to adulthood.* New York: Academic Press.

Caspi, A., & Moffitt, T. E. (1993). When do individual differences matter? A paradoxical theory of personality coherence. *Psychological Inquiry, 4,* 247–271.

Cervone, D. (1997). Social-cognitive mechanisms and personality coherence: Self-knowledge, situational beliefs, and cross-situational coherence in perceived self-efficacy. *Psychological Science, 8,* 43–50.

Cervone, D. (2000). Thinking about self-efficacy. *Behavior Modification, 24,* 30–56

Cervone, D. (2004) The architecture of personality. *Psychological Review, 111,* 183–204.

Cervone, D., & Peake, P. K. (1986). Anchoring, efficacy, and action: The influence of judgmental heuristics on self-efficacy judgments and behavior. *Journal of Personality and Social Psychology, 50,* 492–501.

Cervone, D., & Scott, W. D. (1995). Self-efficacy theory of behavioral change: Foundations, conceptual issues, and therapeutic implications. In W. T. O'Donohue & L. Krasner (Eds.), *Theories of behavior therapy: Exploring behavior change.* (pp. 349–383). Washington, D. C.: American Psychological Association.

Cervone, D., Shadel, W. G., & Jencius, S. (2001). Social-cognitive theory of personality assessment. *Personality and Social Psychology Review, 5,* 33–51.

Cesario, J., Grant, H., & Higgins, E. T. (2004). Regulatory fit and persuasion: Transfer from "feeling right." *Journal of Personality and Social Psychology, 86,* 388–404.

Cesario, J., & Higgins, E. T. (2008). Making message recipients "feel right": How nonverbal cues can increase persuasion. *Psychological Science, 19,* 415–420.

Cesario, J., Higgins, E. T., & Scholer, A. A. (2008). Regulatory fit and persuasion: Basic principles and remaining questions. *Social and Personality Psychology Compass, 2,* 444–463.

Cesario, J., Plaks, J. E., Hagiwara, N., Navarrete, C. D., & Higgins, E. T. (2010). The ecology of automaticity: How situational contingencies shape action semantics and social behavior. *Psychological Science, 21,* 1311-1317.

Cesario, J., Plaks, J. E., & Higgins, E. T. (2006). Automatic social behavior as motivated preparation to interact. *Journal of Personality and Social Psychology, 90,* 893–910.

Chaiken, S., & Trope, Y. (1999). *Dual-process theories in social psychology.* New York: Guilford Press.

Chen, S. (2003). Psychological-state theories about significant others: Implications for the content and structure of significant-other representations. *Personality and Social Psychology Bulletin, 29,* 1285–1302.

Chen, S., & Andersen, S. M. (1999). Relationships from the past in the present: Significant-other representations and transference in interpersonal life. In M. P. Zanna (Ed.), *Advances in experimental social psychology* (Vol. 31, pp. 123–190). New York: Academic Press.

Cheng, C. (2003). Cognitive and motivational processes underlying coping flexibility: A dual process model. *Journal of Personality and Social Psychology, 84,* 425–238.

Chiu, C-Y., & Hong, Y-Y. (2006). *Social psychology of culture.* New York: Psychology Press.

Chui, C-Y., Hong, Y-Y., Mischel, W., & Shoda, Y. (1995). Discriminative facility in social competence: Conditional versus dispositional encoding and monitoring-blunting of information. *Social Cognition, 13,* 49–70.

Chiu, C-Y., Kim, Y-H., & Wan, W. (2008). Personality: Cross-cultural perspectives. In G. J. Boyle, G. Matthews, & D. H. Salofske (Eds.), *Sage handbook of personality theory and testing. Vol. 1: Personality theory and testing.* London: Sage.

Christie, R., & Geis, F. L. (1970). *Studies in Machiavellianism.* New York: Academic Press.

Church, A. T. & Ortiz, F. A. (2005). Culture and personality. In V. J. Derlaga, B. A. Winstead, & W. H. Jones (Eds.), *Personality: Contemporary theory and research* (3rd ed., pp. 420–456). Belmont, CA: Wadsworth.

Cialdini, R. B. (1993). *Influence: The psychology of persuasion* (rev. ed.). New York: Quill.

Cialdini, R. B. (2001). *Influence: Science and practice* (4th ed.). Boston, MA: Allyn & Bacon.

Cialdini, R. B. (2003). Crafting normative messages to protect the environment. *Current Directions in Psychological Science, 12,* 105–109.

Cialdini, R. B., Borden, R. J., Thorne, A., Walker, M. R., Freeman, S., & Sloan, L. R. (1976). Basking in reflected glory: Three (football) field studies. *Journal of Personality and Social Psychology, 34,* 366–375.

Cialdini, R. B., & Goldstein, N. J. (2004). Social influence: Compliance and conformity. *Annual Review of Psychology, 55,* 591–621.

Cialdini, R. B, Reno, R. R., & Kallgren, C. A. (1990). A focus theory of normative conduct: Recycling the concept of norms to reduce littering in public places. *Journal of Personality and Social Psychology, 58,* 1015–1026.

Clary, E. G., Snyder, M., Ridge, R. D., Miene, P. K., & Haugen, J. A. (1994). Matching messages to motives in persuasion: A functional approach to promoting volunteerism. *Journal of Applied Social Psychology, 24,* 1129–1149.

Cohen, S. (2004). Social relationships and health. *American Psychologist, 89,* 676–684.

Cohen, S., Doyle, W. J., Skoner, D. P., Rabin, B. S., & Gwaltney, J. M., Jr. (1997). Social ties and susceptibility to the common cold. *Journal of the American Medical Association, 277,* 1940–1944.

Coleman, J. S. (1990). *Foundations of social theory.* New York: Free Press.

Collins, A. M., & Loftus, E. F. (1975). A spreading-activation theory of semantic processing. *Psychological Review, 82,* 407–428.

Collins, N. L., & Read, S. J. (1990). Adult attachment, working models, and relationship quality in dating couples. *Journal of Personality and Social Psychology, 58,* 644–663.

Comer, R., & Laird, J. D. (1975). Choosing to suffer as a consequence of expecting to suffer: Why do people do it? *Journal of Personality and Social Psychology, 32,* 92–101.

Compas, B. E., Malcarne, V. L., & Fondacaro, K. M. (1988). Coping with stressful events in older children and young adolescents. *Journal of Consulting and Clinical Psychology, 56,* 405–411.

Cook, K. S., & Emerson, R. M. (1978). Power, equity and commitment in exchange networks. *American Sociological Review, 43,* 721–739.

Cooley, C. H. (1964). *Human nature and the social order.* New York: Schocken Books. (Original work published 1902)

Coombs, C. H. (1958). On the use of inconsistency of preferences in psychological measurement. *Journal of Experimental Psychology, 55,* 1–7.

Coombs, R. H. (1966). Value consensus and partner satisfaction among dating couples. *Journal of Marriage and the Family, 28,* 165–173.

Costanzo, P. R., & Dix, T. H. (1983). Beyond the information processed: Socialization in the development of attributional processes. In E. T. Higgins, D. N. Ruble, & W. W. Hartup (Eds.), *Social cognition and social development: A sociocultual perspective* (pp. 63–81). New York: Cambridge University Press.

Cox, T., & Ferguson, E. (1991). Individual differences, stress and coping. In C. L. Cooper & R. Payne (Eds.), *Personality and stress: Individual differences in the stress process* (pp. 7–30). *Wiley Series on Studies in Occupational Stress.* Oxford: John Wiley & Sons.

Coyne, J. C., Wortman, C. B., & Lehman, D. R. (1988). The other side of support: Emotional overinvolvement and miscarried helping. In B. H. Gottlieb (Ed.), *Marshaling social support: Formats, processes, and effects* (pp. 305–330). Newbury Park, CA: Sage.

Crowe, E., & Higgins, E. T. (1997). Regulatory focus and strategic inclinations: Promotion and prevention in decision-making. *Organizational Behavior and Human Decision Processes, 69,* 117–132.

Csikszentmihalyi, M. (1975). *Beyond boredom and anxiety.* San Francisco: Jossey-Bass.

Csikszentmihalyi, M. (1990). *Flow: The psychology of optimal experience.* New York: Harper & Row.

Cutrona, C. E., & Russell, D. W. (1990). Type of support and specific stress: Toward a theory of optimal matching. In B. R. Saronson, I. G. Sarason, & G. R. Pierce (Eds.), *Social support: An interactional view* (pp. 319–366). New York: Wiley.

Damasio, A. R. (1994). *Descartes' error: Emotion, reason, and the human brain.* New York: G. P. Putnam's Sons.

Darwin, C. (1859). *Origin of species.* London: John Murray.

deCharms, R. (1968). *Personal causation: The internal affective determinants of behavior.* New York: Academic Press.

Deci, E. L. (1971). Effects of externally mediated rewards on intrinsic motivation. *Journal of Personality and Social Psychology, 18,* 105–115.

Deci, E. L. (1975). *Intrinsic motivation.* New York: Plenum Press.

Deci, E. L. (1980). *The psychology of self-determination.* Lexington, MA: D. C. Heath.

Deci, E. L., Connell, J. P., & Ryan, R. M. (1989). Self-determination in a work organization. *Journal of Applied Psychology, 74,* 580–590.

Deci, E. L., & Ryan, R. M. (1985). *Intrinsic motivation and self-determination in human behavior.* New York: Plenum Press.

Deci, E. L., & Ryan, R. M. (2000). The "what" and the "why" of goal pursuits: Human needs and the self-determination of behavior. *Psychological Inquiry, 11,* 227–268.

DeSteno, D., Petty, R. E., Rucker, D., Wegener, D. T., & Braverman, J. (2004). Discrete emotions and persuasion: The role of emotion-induced expectancies. *Journal of Personality and Social Psychology, 86,* 43–56.

Deutsch, F., Sullivan, L., Sage, C., & Basile, N. (1991). The relations among talking, liking, and similarity between friends. *Personality and Social Psychology Bulletin, 17,* 406–411.

Deutsch, M. (1968). Field theory in social psychology. In G. Lindzey & E. Aronson (Eds.), *The handbook of social psychology* (Vol. 1, pp. 412–487). Reading, MA: Addison-Wesley.

Deutsch, M., & Gerard, H. B. (1955). A study of normative and informational social influences upon individual judgment. *Journal of Abnormal and Social Psychology, 51,* 629–636.

Devine, P. G. (1989). Stereotypes and prejudice: Their automatic and controlled components. *Journal of Personality and Social Psychology, 56,* 5–18.

Dickman, S. J., & Meyer, D. E. (1988). Impulsivity and speed-accuracy tradeoffs in information processing. *Journal of Personality and Social Psychology, 54,* 274–290.

Diener, E., & Diener, M. (1995). Cross-cultural correlates of life satisfaction and self-esteem. *Journal of Personality and Social Psychology, 68,* 653–63.

Diener, E., & Emmons, R. A. (1984). The independence of positive and negative affect. *Journal of Personality and Social Psychology, 47,* 1105–1117.

Diener, E., Emmons, R. A., Larsen, R. J., & Griffin, S. (1985). The Satisfaction with Life Scale. *Journal of Personality Assessment, 49,* 71–75.

Diener, E., Sandvik, E., Pavot, W., & Fujita, F. (1992). Extraversion and subjective well-being in a U.S. national probability sample. *Journal of Research in Personality, 26,* 205–215.

Diener, E., & Seligman, M. E. P. (2002). Very happy people. *Psychological Science, 13,* 81–84.

Dijksterhuis, A., & Nordgren, L. F. (2006). A theory of unconscious thought. *Perspectives on Psychological Science, 1,* 95–109.

Dijksterhuis, A., van Knippenberg, A., Kruglanski, A. W., & Schaper, C. (1996). Motivated social cognition: Need for closure effects on memory and judgment. *Journal of Experimental Social Psychology, 32,* 254–270.

Dodes, L. M. (2002). *The heart of addiction*. New York: HarperCollins.

Doise, W., & Mugny, G. (1984). *The social development of the intellect*. Oxford: Pergamon Press.

Downey, G., & Feldman, S. I. (1996). Implications of rejection sensitivity for intimate relationships. *Journal of Personality and Social Psychology, 70*, 1327–1343.

Downey, G., Freitas, A. L., Michaelis, B., & Khouri, H. (1998). The self-fulfilling prophecy in close relationships: Rejection sensitivity and rejection by romantic partners. *Journal of Personality and Social Psychology, 75*, 545–560.

Downey, G., Mougios, V., Ayduk, O., London, B. E., & Shoda, Y. (2004). Rejection sensitivity and the defensive motivational system: Insights from the startle response to rejection cues. *Psychological Science, 15*, 668–673.

Driscoll, D. M., Hamilton, D. L., & Sorrentino, R. M. (1991). Uncertainty orientation and recall of person-descriptive information. *Personality and Social Psychology Bulletin, 17*, 494–500.

Dunn, J., Brown, J., Slomkowski, C., Tesla, C., & Youngblade, L. (1991). Young children's understanding of other people's feelings and beliefs: Individual differences and their antecedents. *Child Development, 62*, 1352–1366.

Dunning, D. (1999). A newer look: Motivated social cognition and the schematic representation of social concepts. *Psychological Inquiry, 10*, 1–11.

Dunning, D., Leuenberger, A., & Sherman, D. A. (1995). A new look at motivated inference: Are self-serving theories of success a product of motivational forces? *Journal of Personality and Social Psychology, 69*, 58–68.

Dunning, D., Meyerowitz, J. A., & Holzberg, A. D. (1989). Ambiguity and self-evaluation: The role of idiosyncratic trait definitions in self-serving assessments of ability. *Journal of Personality and Social Psychology, 57*, 1082–1090.

Durkheim, E. (1951). *Suicide: A study in sociology*. New York: The Free Press. (Original work published 1897)

Dustin, D. S., & Davis, H. P. (1967). Authoritarianism and sanctioning behavior. *Journal of Personality and Social Psychology, 6*, 222–224.

Duval, S., & Wicklund, R. A. (1972). *A theory of objective self-awareness*. New York: Academic Press.

Dweck, C. S. (1975). The role of expectations and attributions in the alleviation of learned helplessness. *Journal of Personality and Social Psychology, 31*, 674–685.

Dweck, C. S. (1999). *Self-theories: Their role in motivation, personality, and development*. Philadelphia: Psychology Press.

Dweck, C. S., Chiu, C., & Hong, Y. (1995). Implicit theories and their role in judgments and reactions: A world from two perspectives. *Psychological Inquiry, 6*, 267–285.

Dweck, C. S., & Leggett, E. L. (1988). A social-cognitive approach to motivation and personality. *Psychological Review, 95*, 256–273.

Dweck, C. S., & Sorich, L. (1999). Mastery-oriented thinking. In C. R. Snyder (Ed.), *Coping* (pp. 232–251). New York: Oxford University Press.

Eagly, A. H., & Chaiken, S. (1993). *The psychology of attitudes*. New York: Harcourt Brace Jovanovich.

Echterhoff, G., Higgins, E. T., & Groll, S. (2005). Audience-tuning effects on memory: The role of shared reality. *Journal of Personality and Social Psychology, 89*, 257–276.

Echterhoff, G., Higgins, E. T., Kopietz, R., & Groll, S. (2008). How communication goals determine when audience tuning biases memory. *Journal of Experimental Psychology: General, 137*, 3–21.

Echterhoff, G., Higgins, E. T., & Levine, J. M. (in press). Shared reality: Experiencing commonality with others' inner states about the world. *Perspectives on Psychological Science.*

Edwards, W. (1955). The prediction of decisions among bets. *Journal of Experimental Psychology, 51*, 201–214.

Eisenberger, R. (1972). Explanation of rewards that do not reduce tissue needs. *Psychological Bulletin, 77*, 319–339.

Eitam, B., & Higgins, E. T. (2010). Motivation in mental accessibility: Relevance Of A Representation (ROAR) as a new framework. *Social and Personality Psychology Compass, 4*, 951–967.

Elliot, A.J. (2006). The hierarchical model of approach-avoidance motivation. *Motivation and Emotion, 30*, 111–116.

Elliot, A. J., & Fryer, J. W. (2008). The goal construct in psychology. In J. Y. Shah & W. L. Gardner (Eds.). *Handbook of motivation science* (pp. 235–250). New York: Guilford Press.

Elliot, A.J., & McGregor, H. (2001). A 2×2 achievement goal framework. *Journal of Personality and Social Psychology, 80*, 501–519.

Elliot, A.J., & Sheldon, K.M. (1997). Avoidance achievement motivation: A personal goals analysis. *Journal of Personality and Social Psychology, 73*, 171–175.

Elliot, A. J., & Sheldon, K. M. (1998). Avoidance personal goals and the personality-illness relationship. *Journal of Personality and Social Psychology, 75*, 1282–1299.

Elliot, A. J., Sheldon, K. M., & Church, M. A. (1997). Avoidance personal goals and subjective well-being. *Personality and Social Psychology Bulletin, 23*, 915–927.

Elliott, E. S., & Dweck, C. S. (1988). Goals: An approach to motivation and achievement. *Journal of Personality and Social Psychology, 54*, 5–12.

Ellis, A. (1973). *Humanistic psychotherapy: The rational-emotive approach.* New York: McGraw-Hill.

Endler, N. S. (1982). Interactionism comes of age. In M. P. Zanna, E. T. Higgins, & C. P. Herman (Eds.), *Consistency in social behavior: The Ontario Symposium* (Vol. 2, pp. 209–249). Hillsdale, NJ: Erlbaum.

Epstein, S. (1973). The self-concept revisited: Or a theory of a theory. *American Psychologist, 28*, 404–416.

Epstein, S. (1991). Cognitive-experiential self theory: Implications for developmental psychology. In M. R. Gunnar & L. A. Sroufe (Eds.), *Self processes and development: The Minnesota symposia on child psychology* (Vol. 23, pp. 79–123). Hillsdale, NJ: Erlbaum.

Epstein, S. (1992). Coping ability, negative self-evaluation, and overgeneralization: Experiment and theory. *Journal of Personality and Social Psychology, 62*, 826–836.

Erber, R., Wegner, D. M., & Therriault, N. (1996). On being cool and collected: Mood regulation in anticipation of social interaction. *Journal of Personality and Social Psychology, 70*, 757–766.

Erdelyi, M. H. (1974). A new look at the new look: Perceptual defense and vigilance. *Psychological Review, 81*, 1–25.

Erikson, E. H. (1963). *Childhood and society* (rev. ed.; original edition, 1950). New York: W. W. Norton & Co.

Evans, L. M., & Petty, R. E. (2003). Self-guide framing and persuasion: Responsibly increasing message processing to ideal levels. *Personality and Social Psychology Bulletin*, 29, 313–324.

Exner, J. E., Jr. (1993). *The Rorschach: A comprehensive system, vol. 1: Basic foundations* (3rd ed.). Wiley Series in Personality Processes. Oxford, England: John Wiley & Sons.

Eysenck, H. J. (1971). *Readings in extraversion-introversion*. New York: Wiley.

Faddegon, K., Scheepers, D., & Ellemers, N. (2007). If *we* have the will, there will be a way. Regulatory focus as a group identity. *European Journal of Social Psychology*, 37, 1–16.

Fang, X., Singh, S., & AhluWalia, R. (2007). An examination of different explanations for the mere exposure effect. *Journal of Consumer Research*, 34, 97–103.

Fazio, R. H., Jackson, J. R., Dunton, B. C., & Williams, C. J. (1995). Variability in automatic activation as an unobtrusive measure of racial attitudes: A bona fide pipeline? *Journal of Personality and Social Psychology*, 69, 1013–1027.

Fazio, R. H., & Olson, M. A. (2003). Implicit measures in social cognition: Their meaning and use. *Annual Review of Psychology*, 54, 297–327.

Fazio, R. H., Sanbonmatsu, D. M., Powell, M. C., & Kardes, F. R. (1986). On the automatic activation of attitudes. *Journal of Personality and Social Psychology*, 50, 229–238.

Feather, N. T. (1959). Subjective probability and decision under uncertainty. *Psychological Review*, 66, 150–164.

Feather, N. T. (1961). The relationship of persistence at a task to expectation of success and achievement-related motives. *Journal of Abnormal and Social Psychology*, 63, 552–561.

Feather, N. T. (1989) Attitudes towards the high achiever: The fall of the tall poppy. *Australian Journal of Psychology*, 41, 239–267.

Feather, N. T. (1990). Bridging the gap between values and action: Recent applications of the expectancy-value model. In E. T. Higgins & R. M. Sorrentino (Eds.), *Handbook of motivation and cognition: Foundations of social behavior* (Vol. 2, pp. 151–192). New York: Guilford.

Fedor, D. B., Caldwell, S., & Herold, D. M. (2006). The effects of organizational changes on employee commitment: A multilevel investigation. *Personnel Psychology*, 59, 1–29.

Feldman Barrett, L., & Russell, J. A. (1998). Independence and bipolarity in the structure of current affect. *Journal of Personality and Social Psychology*, 74, 967–984.

Ferguson, M. J. (2008). On becoming ready to pursue a goal you don't know you have: Effects of nonconscious goals on evaluative readiness. *Journal of Personality and Social Psychology*, 95, 1268–1294.

Festinger, L. (1950). Informal social communication. *Psychological Review*, 57, 271–282.

Festinger, L. (1954) A theory of social comparison processes. *Human Relations*, 1, 117–140.

Festinger, L. (1957). *A theory of cognitive dissonance*. Evanston, IL: Row, Peterson.

Festinger, L. (1964). *Conflict, decision, and dissonance*. Stanford, CA: Stanford University Press.

Festinger, L., Riecken, H. W., & Schachter, S. (1956). *When prophecy fails: A social and psychological study of a modern group that predicted the destruction of the world.* New York: Harper & Row.

Fields, J. M., & Schuman, H. (1976). Public beliefs about the beliefs of the public. *Public Opinion Quarterly, 40,* 427–448.

Fischer, K. W. (1980). A theory of cognitive development: The control and construction of hierarchies of skills. *Psychological Review, 87,* 477–531.

Fishbach, A., Friedman, R. S., & Kruglanski, A. W. (2003). Leading us not unto temptation: Momentary allurements elicit overriding goal activation. *Journal of Personality and Social Psychology, 84,* 296–309.

Fishbach, A., & Shah, J. Y. (2006). Self-control in action: Implicit dispositions toward goals and away from temptations. *Journal of Personality and Social Psychology, 90,* 820–832.

Fishbach, A., & Trope, Y. (2005). The substitutability of external control and internal control in overcoming temptation. *Journal of Experimental Social Psychology, 41,* 256–270.

Fishbein, M. (1963). An investigation of the relationships between beliefs about an object and the attitude toward that object. *Human Relations, 16,* 233–240.

Fishbein, M., & Ajzen, I. (1975). *Belief, attitude, intention, and behavior: An introduction to theory and research.* Reading, MA: Addison-Wesley.

Fiske, A. P., Kitayama, S., Markus, H. R., & Nisbet, R. E. (1998). The cultural matrix of social psychology. In D. T. Gilbert, S. T. Fiske, & G. Lindzey (Eds.), *Handbook of social psychology* (4th ed., pp. 915–981). New York: McGraw-Hill.

Fiske, S. T. (2003). Five core social motives, plus or minus five. In S. J. Spencer, S. Fein, M. P. Zanna, & J. M. Olson (Eds.), *Motivated social perception. Ontario symposium on personality and social psychology* (Vol. 9, pp. 233–246). Mahwah, NJ: Lawrence Erlbaum Associates.

Fiske, S. T. (2004). *Social beings: A core motives approach to social psychology.* New York: Wiley.

Fiske, S. T., & Berdahl, J. (2007). Social power. In A. W. Kruglanski & E. T. Higgins (Eds.), *Social psychology: Handbook of basic principles* (2nd ed., pp. 678–692). New York: Guilford.

Fiske, S. T., & Neuberg, S. L. (1990). A continuum of impression formation, from category-based to individuating processes: Influences of information and motivation on attention and interpretation. In M. P. Zanna (Ed.), *Advances in experimental social psychology* (Vol. 23. pp. 1–74). New York: Academic Press.

Fitzsimons, G. M., & Bargh, J. A. (2003). Thinking of you: Nonconscious pursuit of interpersonal goals associated with relationship partners. *Journal of Personality and Social Psychology, 84,* 148–163.

Fitzsimons, G. J., & Lehman, D. R. (2004). Reactance to recommendations: When unsolicited advice yields contrary responses. *Marketing Science, 23,* 82–94.

Folkman, S., & Moskowitz, J. T. (2004). Coping: Pitfalls and promise. *Annual Review of Psychology, 55,* 745–774.

Ford, T. E., & Kruglanski, A. W. (1995). Effects of epistemic motivations on the use of accessible constructs in social judgment. *Personality and Social Psychology Bulletin, 21,* 950–962.

Förster, J., Grant, H., Idson, L. C., & Higgins, E. T. (2001). Success/failure feedback, expectancies, and approach/avoidance motivation: How regulatory focus moderates classic relations. *Journal of Experimental Social Psychology, 37,* 253–260.

Förster, J., Higgins, E. T., & Bianco, A. T. (2003). Speed/accuracy decisions in task performance: Built-in trade-off or separate strategic concerns? *Organizational Behavior and Human Decision Processes, 90,* 148–164.

Förster, J., Higgins, E. T., & Idson, L. C. (1998). Approach and avoidance strength during goal attainment: Regulatory focus and the "goal looms larger" effect. *Journal of Personality and Social Psychology, 75,* 1115–1131.

Förster, J., & Werth, L. (2009). Regulatory focus: Classic findings and new directions. In G. B. Moskowitz & H. Grant (Eds.), *The psychology of goals* (pp. 392–420). New York: Guilford Press.

Fowler, J. H., & Christakis, N. A. (2008). Dynamic spread of happiness in a large social network: longitudinal analysis over 20 years in the Framingham Heart Study. *British Medical Journal, 337,* a2338.

Franks, B. (2009). *Regulatory focus and fit in monkeys: Relating individual differences in behavior to differences in motivational orientations.* Unpublished master's thesis, Columbia University.

Franks, B., & Higgins, E. T. (2005). How motivational studies in humans could provide new insights to animal enrichment science. In *Proceedings of the Seventh International Conference on Environmental Enrichment,* July 31, 2005–August 5, 2005, 33–38. New York: Wildlife Conservation Society.

Freedman, J. L. (1975). *Crowding and behavior.* San Francisco: W. H. Freeman & Company.

Freeman, L. C. (1977). Set of measures of centrality based on betweenness. *Sociometry, 40,* 35–41.

Freitas, A. L., Azizian, A., Travers, S., & Berry, S. A. (2005). The evaluative connotation of processing fluency: Inherently positive or moderated by motivational context? *Journal of Experimental Social Psychology, 41,* 636–644.

Freitas, A. L., & Higgins, E. T. (2002). Enjoying goal-directed action: The role of regulatory fit. *Psychological Science, 13,* 1–6.

Freitas, A. L., Liberman, N., & Higgins, E. T. (2002). Regulatory fit and resisting temptation during goal pursuit. *Journal of Experimental Social Psychology, 38,* 291–298.

Freud, A. (1937). *The ego and the mechanisms of defense.* New York: International Universities Press.

Freud, S. (1950). *Beyond the pleasure principle* (Original work published 1920). New York: Liveright.

Freud, S. (1955). History of the psychoanalytic movement. In J. Strachey (Ed. & Trans.), *The standard edition of the complete psychological works of Sigmund Freud* (Vol. 14). London: Hogarth Press. (Original work published 1914)

Freud, S. (1957). Instincts and their vicissitudes. In J. Strachey (Ed. & Trans.), *The standard edition of the complete psychological works of Sigmund Freud* (Vol. 14). London: Hogarth Press. (Original work published 1915)

Freud, S. (1961a). The ego and the id. In J. Strachey (Ed. & Trans.), *The standard edition of the complete psychological works of Sigmund Freud* (Vol. 19, pp. 3–66). London: Hogarth Press. (Original work published 1923)

Freud, S. (1961b). *Civilization and its discontents* (J. Strachey, Ed. & Trans). New York: W. W. Norton. (Original work published 1930)

Freud, S. (1965). *New introductory lectures on psychoanalysis* (J. Strachey, Ed. & Trans). New York: W. W. Norton. (Original work published 1933)

Freund, A. M., & Baltes, P. B. (2002). Life-management strategies of selection, optimization, and compensation: Measurement by self-report and construct validity. *Journal of Personality and Social Psychology, 82,* 642–662.

Friedland, N., Keinan, G., & Regev, Y. (1992). Controlling the uncontrollable: Effects of stress on Illusory perceptions of controllability. *Journal of Personality and Social Psychology, 63,* 923–931.

Friedman, R. S., & Förster, J. (2001). The effects of promotion and prevention cues on creativity. *Journal of Personality and Social Psychology, 81,* 1001–1013.

Friestad, M., & Wright, P. (1994). The persuasion knowledge model: How people cope with persuasion attempts. *Journal of Consumer Research, 21,* 1–31.

Frijda, N. H. (1986). *The emotions.* New York: Cambridge University Press.

Frijda, N. H., Kuipers, P., & ter Schure, E. (1989). Relations among emotion, appraisal, and emotional action readiness. *Journal of Personality and Social Psychology, 57,* 212–228.

Fu, J. H., Morris, M. W., Lee, S., Chao, A., Chiu, C., & Hong, Y. (2007). Epistemic motives and cultural conformity: Need for closure, culture, and context as determinants of conflict judgments. *Journal of Personality and Social Psychology, 92,* 191–207.

Fujita, K. (2008). Seeing the forest beyond the trees: A construal-level approach to self-control. *Social and Personality Psychology Compass, 2/3,* 1475–1496.

Fujita, K., Trope, Y., Liberman, N., & Levin-Sagi, M. (2006). Construal levels and self-control. *Journal of Personality and Social Psychology, 90,* 351–367.

Fulmer, C. A., Gelfand, M. J., Kruglanski, A. W., Kim-Prieto, C., Diener, E., Pierro, A., & Higgins, E. T. (2010). On "feeling right" in cultural contexts: How person-culture match affects self-esteem and subjective well-being. *Psychological Science, 21,* 1563-1569.

Galinsky, A. D., & Mussweiler, T. (2001). First offers as anchors: The role of perspective-taking and negotiator focus. *Journal of Personality and Social Psychology, 81,* 657–779.

Galton, F. (1865). Hereditary talent and character. *MacMillan's Magazine.*

Gawronski, B., & Bodenhausen, G. V. (2006). Associative and propositional processes in evaluation: An integrative review of implicit and explicit attitude change. *Psychological Bulletin, 132,* 692–731.

Gawronski, B., & Strack, F. (2004). On the propositional nature of cognitive consistency: Dissonance changes explicit, but not implicit attitudes. *Journal of Experimental Social Psychology, 40,* 535–542.

Geen, R. G., & O'Neal, E. (1969). Activation of cue elicited aggression by general arousal. *Journal of Personality and Social Psychology, 11,* 289–292.

Geen, R. G., & Quanty, M. B. (1977). The catharsis of aggression: An evaluation of an hypothesis. In L. Berkowitz (Ed.), *Advances in experimental social psychology* (Vol. 10, pp. 1–37). New York: Academic Press.

Gellner, E. (1988). *Plough, sword and book: The structure of human history.* Chicago: University of Chicago Press.

Gibson, J. J. (1979). *The ecological approach to visual perception.* Boston: Houghton-Mifflin.

Gilbert, D. T. (1990). How mental systems believe. *American Psychologist, 46,* 107–119.

Gilbert, D. T., Morewedge, C. K., Risen, J. L., & Wilson, T. D. (2004). Looking forward to looking backward: The misprediction of regret. *Psychological Science, 15,* 346–350

Gilovich, T. (1981). Seeing the past in the present: The effect of associations to familiar events on judgments and decisions. *Journal of Personality and Social Psychology, 40,* 797–808.

Gladwell, M. (2005). *Blink: The power of thinking without thinking.* New York: Little, Brown & Company.

Glassman, N. S., & Andersen, S. M. (1999). Activating transference without consciousness: Using significant-other representations to go beyond what is subliminally given. *Journal of Personality and Social Psychology, 77,* 1146–1162.

Goldberg, J., Weisenberg, M., Drobkin, S., Blittner, M., & Gunnar Gotestam, K. (1997). Effects of manipulated cognitive and attributional set on pain tolerance. *Cognitive Therapy and Research, 21,* 525–534.

Goldberg, L. R. (1990). An alternative "Description of personality": The Big-Five factor structure. *Journal of Personality and Social Psychology, 59,* 1216–1229.

Goleman, D. (1995). *Emotional intelligence.* New York: Bantam Books.

Gollwitzer, P. M. (1990). Action phases and mind-sets. In E. T. Higgins & R. M. Sorrentino (Eds.), *Handbook of motivation and cognition: Foundations of social behavior* (Vol. 2, pp. 53–92). New York: Guilford.

Gollwitzer, P. M. (1996). The volitional benefits of planning. In P. M. Gollwitzer & J. A. Bargh (Eds.), *The psychology of action: Linking cognition and motivation to behavior* (pp. 287–312). New York: Guilford.

Gollwitzer, P. M., & Bargh, J. A. (Eds.). (1996). *The psychology of action: Linking cognition and motivation to behavior.* New York: Guilford.

Gollwitzer, P. M., & Brandstatter, V. (1997). Implementation intentions and effective goal pursuit. *Journal of Personality and Social Psychology, 73,* 186–199.

Gollwitzer, P. M., Earle, W. B., & Stephan, W. G. (1982). Affect as a determinant of egotism: Residual excitation and performance attributions. *Journal of Personality and Social Psychology, 43,* 702–709.

Gollwitzer, P. M., Fujita, K., & Oettingen, G. (2004). Planning and the implementation of goals. In R. F. Baumeister & K. D. Vohs (Eds.), *Handbook of self-regulation: Research, theory, and applications* (pp. 211–228). New York: Guilford Press.

Gollwitzer, P. M., & Kinney, R. F. (1989). Effects of deliberative and implemental mind-sets on illusion of control. *Journal of Personality and Social Psychology, 56,* 531–542.

Gollwitzer, P. M., Parks-Stamm, E. J., Jaudas, A., & Sheeran, P. (2008). Flexible tenacity in goal pursuit. In J. Y. Shah & W. L. Gardner (Eds.). *Handbook of motivation science* (pp. 325–341). New York: Guilford Press.

Goodwin, D. K. (2005). *Team of rivals: The political genius of Abraham Lincoln.* New York: Simon & Schuster.

Gopnik, A. (1996). The scientist as child. *Philosophy of Science, 63,* 485–514.

Granovetter, M. (1973). The strength of weak ties. *American Journal of Sociology, 78,* 1360–1380.

Granovetter, M. (1985). Economic action and social structure: The problem of embeddedness. *American Journal of Sociology, 91*, 481–510.

Grant, H., & Dweck, C. S. (1999). A goal analysis of personality and personality coherence. In D. Cervone & Y. Shoda (Eds.), *The coherence of personality: Social-cognitive bases of consistency, variability, and organization.* (pp. 345–371). New York: Guilford Press.

Grant, H., & Higgins, E. T. (2003). Optimism, promotion pride, and prevention pride as predictors of quality of life. *Personality and Social Psychology Bulletin, 29*, 1521–1532.

Gray, J. A. (1982). *The neuropsychology of anxiety: An enquiry into the functions of the septo-hippocampal system.* New York: Oxford University Press.

Green, D. P., Goldman, S. L., & Salovey, P. (1993). Measurement error masks bipolarity in affect ratings. *Journal of Personality and Social Psychology, 64*, 1029–1041.

Greenwald, A. G., Banaji, M. R., Rudman, L. A., Farnham, S. D., & Nosek, B. A. (2002). A unified theory of implicit attitudes, stereotypes, self-esteem, and self-concept. *Psychological Review, 109*, 3–25.

Greenwald, A. G., McGhee, D. E., & Schwartz, J. L. K. (1998). Measuring individual differences in implicit cognition: The Implicit Association Test. *Journal of Personality and Social Psychology, 74*, 1464–1480.

Griffin, D., & Ross, L. (1991). Subjective construal, social inference, and human misunderstanding. In M. P. Zanna (Ed.), *Advances in experimental social psychology* (Vol. 24, pp. 319–359). San Diego, CA: Academic Press.

Griffitt, W., & Veitch, R. (1974). Preacquaintance attitude similarity and attraction revisited: Ten days in a fallout shelter. *Sociometry, 37*, 163–173.

Groos, K. (1940). *The play of man* (E. L. Baldwin, Trans.) Cambridge, MA: Harvard University Press. (Original published in 1901 in New York by Appleton.)

Gross, J. J. (1998). The emerging field of emotion regulation: An integrative review. *Review of General Psychology, 2*, 271–299.

Gross, J. J. (1999). Emotion regulation: Past, present, future. *Cognition and Emotion, 13*, 551–573.

Gross, J. J. (2001). Emotion regulation in adulthood: Timing is everything. *Current Directions in Psychological Science, 10*, 214–219.

Grove, A. S. (1996). *Only the paranoid survive.* New York: Doubleday Business.

Guthrie, E. R. (1935). *The psychology of learning.* New York: Harper.

Guthrie, E. R. (1952). *The psychology of learning* (rev. ed.). New York: Harper.

Haidt, J. (2001). The emotional dog and its rational tail: A social intuitionist approach to moral judgment. *Psychological Review, 108*, 814–834.

Harackiewicz, J. M., & Sansone, C. (1991). Goals and intrinsic motivation: You can get there from here. In M. L. Maehr & P. R. Pintrich (Eds.), *Advances in motivation and achievement* (Vol. 7, pp. 21–49). Greenwich, CT: JAI Press.

Hardin, C., & Higgins, E. T. (1996). "Shared reality": How social verification makes the subjective objective. In R. M. Sorrentino & E. T. Higgins (Eds.), *Handbook of motivation and cognition: The interpersonal context* (pp. 28–84). New York: Guilford.

Harmon-Jones, C., Schmeichel, B. J., & Harmon-Jones, E. (2009). Symbolic self-completion in academia: Evidence from department web pages and email signature files. *European Journal of Social Psychology, 39*, 311–316.

Hartig, M., & Kanfer, F. H. (1973). The role of verbal self-instructions in children's resistance to temptation. *Journal of Personality and Social Psychology, 25,* 259–267.

Hassin, R. R., Bargh, J. A., & Zimerman, S. (2009). Automatic and flexible: The case of non-conscious goal pursuit. *Social Cognition, 27,* 20–36.

Hausmann, L. R. M., Levine, J. M., & Higgins, E. T. (2008). Communication and group perception: Extending the "saying is believing" effect. *Group Processes & Intergroup Relations, 11,* 539–554.

Hazan, C., & Shaver, P. R. (1987). Romantic love conceptualized as an attachment process. *Journal of Personality and Social Psychology, 52,* 511–524.

Hebb, D. O. (1930). Elementary school methods. *Teach Magazine* (Montreal), *12,* 23–26.

Hebb, D. O. (1949). *The organization of behavior.* New York: John Wiley & Sons.

Hebb, D. O. (1955). Drives and the C. N. S. (Conceptual Nervous System). *Psychological Review, 62,* 243–254.

Heckhausen, H., & Gollwitzer, P. M. (1987). Thought contents and cognitive functioning in motivational versus volitional states of mind. *Motivation and Emotion, 11,* 101–120.

Heidbreder, E. (1933). *Seven psychologies.* New York: Appleton-Century-Crofts.

Heider, F. (1958). *The psychology of interpersonal relations.* New York: Wiley.

Heine, S. J., & Hamamura, T. (2007). In search of East Asian self-enhancement. *Personality and Social Psychology Review, 11,* 4–27.

Heine, S. J., Kitayama, S., Lehman, D. R., Takata, T., Ide, E., Leung, C., & Matsumoto, S. (2001). Divergent consequences of success and failure in Japan and North America: An investigation of self-improving motivations and malleable selves. *Journal of Personality and Social Psychology, 81,* 599–615.

Helson, H. (1964). *Adaptation-level theory: An experimental and systematic approach to behavior.* New York: Harper & Row.

Henderson, V., & Dweck, C. S. (1990). Achievement and motivation in adolescence: A new model and data. In S. Feldman & G. Elliot (Eds.), *At the threshold: The developing adolescent* (pp. 308–329). Cambridge, MA: Harvard University Press.

Henle, M. (1944). The influence of valence on substitution. *Journal of Psychology, 17,* 11–19.

Hernandez, M., & Iyengar, S. S. (2001). What drives whom? A cultural perspective on human agency? *Social Cognition, 19,* 269–294.

Hess, E. H. (1959). Imprinting. *Science, 130,* 130–141.

Higgins, E. T. (1981). The "communication game": Implications for social cognition and persuasion. In E. T. Higgins, C. P. Herman, & M. P. Zanna (Eds.), *Social cognition: The Ontario Symposium* (pp. 343–392). Hillsdale, NJ: Erlbaum.

Higgins, E. T. (1987). Self-discrepancy: A theory relating self and affect. *Psychological Review, 94,* 319–340.

Higgins, E. T. (1989a). Knowledge accessibility and activation: Subjectivity and suffering from unconscious sources. In J. S. Uleman & J. A. Bargh (Eds.), *Unintended thought: The limits of awareness, intention and control* (pp. 75–123). New York: Guilford Press.

Higgins, E. T. (1989b). Self-discrepancy theory: What patterns of self-beliefs cause people to suffer? In L. Berkowitz (Ed.), *Advances in experimental social psychology* (Vol. 22, pp. 93–136). New York: Academic Press.

Higgins, E. T. (1989c). Continuities and discontinuities in self-regulatory and self-evaluative processes: A developmental theory relating self and affect. *Journal of Personality*, 57, 407–444.

Higgins, E. T. (1990). Personality, social psychology, and person-situation relations: Standards and knowledge activation as a common language. In L. A. Pervin (Ed.), *Handbook of personality: Theory and research* (pp. 301–338). New York: Guilford Press.

Higgins, E. T. (1991). Development of self-regulatory and self-evaluative processes: Costs, benefits, and tradeoffs. In M. R. Gunnar & L. A. Sroufe (Eds.), *Self processes and development: The Minnesota symposia on child psychology* (Vol. 23, pp. 125–165). Hillsdale, NJ: Erlbaum.

Higgins, E. T. (1992). Achieving "shared reality" in the communication game: A social action that creates meaning. *Journal of Language and Social Psychology*, 11, 107–131.

Higgins, E. T. (1996a). Shared reality in the self-system: The social nature of self-regulation. *European Review of Social Psychology* (Vol. 7, pp. 1–29). New York: John Wiley & Sons.

Higgins, E. T. (1996b). Knowledge activation: Accessibility, applicability, and salience. In E. T. Higgins & A. W. Kruglanski (Eds.), *Social psychology: Handbook of basic principles* (pp. 133–168). New York: Guilford.

Higgins, E. T. (1996c). Emotional experiences: The pains and pleasures of distinct regulatory systems. In R. D. Kavanaugh, B. Zimmerberg, & S. Fein (Eds.), *Emotion: Interdisciplinary perspectives* (pp. 203–241). Mahwah, NJ: Erlbaum.

Higgins, E. T. (1996d). The "self digest": Self-knowledge serving self-regulatory functions. *Journal of Personality and Social Psychology*, 71, 1062–1083.

Higgins, E. T. (1997). Beyond pleasure and pain. *American Psychologist*, 52, 1280–1300.

Higgins, E. T. (1998a). The aboutness principle: A pervasive influence on human inference. *Social Cognition*, 16, 173–198.

Higgins, E. T. (1998b). Promotion and prevention: Regulatory focus as a motivational principle. In M. P. Zanna (Ed.), *Advances in experimental social psychology* (Vol. 30, pp. 1–46). New York: Academic Press.

Higgins, E. T. (1999). Persons or situations: Unique explanatory principles or variability in general principles? In D. Cervone & Y. Shoda (Eds.), *The coherence of personality: Social-cognitive bases of consistency, variability, and organization* (pp. 61–93). New York: Guilford Press.

Higgins, E. T. (2000a). Making a good decision: Value from fit. *American Psychologist*, 55, 1217–1230.

Higgins, E. T. (2000b). Does personality provide unique explanations for behavior? Personality as cross-person variability in general principles. *European Journal of Personality*, 14, 391–406.

Higgins, E. T. (2000c). Social cognition: Learning about what matters in the social world. *European Journal of Social Psychology*, 30, 3–39.

Higgins, E. T. (2001). Promotion and prevention experiences: Relating emotions to nonemotional motivational states. In J. P. Forgas (Ed.), *Handbook of affect and social cognition* (pp. 186–211). Mahwah, NJ: Lawrence Erlbaum Associates.

Higgins, E. T. (2005a). Humans as applied motivation scientists: Self-consciousness from "shared reality" and "becoming." In H. S. Terrace & J. Metcalfe (Eds.), *The missing link in cognition: Origins of self-reflective consciousness* (pp. 157–173). Oxford: Oxford University Press.

Higgins, E. T. (2005b). Motivational sources of unintended thought: Irrational intrusions or side effects of rational strategies? In R. R. Hassin, J. S. Uleman, & J. A. Bargh (Eds.), *The new unconscious* (pp.516–536). New York: Oxford University Press.

Higgins, E. T. (2005c). Value from regulatory fit. *Current Directions in Psychological Science, 14,* 208–213.

Higgins, E. T. (2006). Value from hedonic experience *and* engagement. *Psychological Review, 113,* 439–460.

Higgins, E. T. (2007). Value. In A. W. Kruglanski & E. T. Higgins (Eds.), *Social psychology: Handbook of basic principles* (2nd ed., pp. 454–472). New York: Guilford.

Higgins, E. T. (2008). Culture and personality: Variability across universal motives as the missing link. *Social and Personality Psychology Compass, 2,* 608–634.

Higgins, E. T. (2009). Regulatory fit in the goal-pursuit process. In G. B. Moskowitz & H. Grant (Eds.), *The psychology of goals* (pp. 505–533). New York: Guilford Press.

Higgins, E. T. (2010). Sharing inner states: A defining feature of *human* motivation. In G. R. Semin & G. Echterhoff (Eds.), *Grounding sociality: Neurons, minds, and culture* (pp. 149–174). New York: Psychology Press.

Higgins, E. T., & Bargh, J. A. (1987). Social cognition and social perception. *Annual Review of Psychology, 38,* 369–425.

Higgins, E. T., Bargh, J. A., & Lombardi, W. J. (1985). Nature of priming effects on categorization. *Journal of Experimental Psychology: Learning, Memory, and Cognition, 11,* 59–69.

Higgins, E. T., Bond, R. N., Klein, R., & Strauman, T. (1986). Self-discrepancies and emotional vulnerability: How magnitude, accessibility, and type of discrepancy influence affect. *Journal of Personality and Social Psychology, 51,* 5–15.

Higgins, E. T., & Brendl, M. (1995). Accessibility and applicability: Some "activation rules" influencing judgment. *Journal of Experimental Social Psychology, 31,* 218–243.

Higgins, E. T., & Bryant, S. (1982). Consensus information and the "fundamental attribution error": The role of development and in-group versus out-group knowledge. *Journal of Personality and Social Psychology, 43,* 889–900.

Higgins, E. T., Camacho, C. J., Idson, L. C., Spiegel, S., & Scholer, A. A. (2008). How making the same decision in a "proper way" creates value. *Social Cognition, 26,* 496–514.

Higgins, E. T., Cesario, J., Hagiwara, N., Spiegel, S., & Pittman, T. (in press). Increasing or decreasing interest in activities: The role of regulatory fit. *Journal of Personality and Social Psychology.*

Higgins, E. T., & Eccles-Parsons, J. (1983). Social cognition and the social life of the child: Stages as subcultures. In E. T. Higgins, D. N. Ruble, & W. W. Hartup (Eds.), *Social cognition and social development: A socio-cultural perspective* (pp. 15–62). New York: Cambridge University Press.

Higgins, E. T., Franks, K. R., & Pavarini, D. (2008). *Value intensity from likelihood as a source of engagement strength.* Unpublished manuscript, Columbia University.

Higgins, E. T., Friedman, R. S., Harlow, R. E., Idson, L. C., Ayduk, O. N., & Taylor, A. (2001). Achievement orientations from subjective histories of success: Promotion pride versus prevention pride. *European Journal of Social Psychology, 31*, 3–23.

Higgins, E. T., Idson, L. C., Freitas, A. L., Spiegel, S., & Molden, D. C. (2003). Transfer of value from fit. *Journal of Personality and Social Psychology, 84*, 1140–1153.

Higgins, E. T., King, G. A., & Mavin, G. H. (1982). Individual construct accessibility and subjective impressions and recall. *Journal of Personality and Social Psychology, 43*, 35–47.

Higgins, E. T., Kruglanski, A. W., & Pierro, A. (2003). Regulatory mode: Locomotion and assessment as distinct orientations. In M. P. Zanna (Ed.), *Advances in experimental social psychology* (Vol. 35, pp. 293–344). New York: Academic Press.

Higgins, E. T., Lee, J., Kwon, J., & Trope, Y. (1995). When combining intrinsic motivations undermines interest: A test of activity engagement theory. *Journal of Personality and Social Psychology, 68*, 749–767.

Higgins, E. T., Loeb, I., & Ruble, D. N. (1995). The four A's of life transition effects: Attention, accessibility, adaptation, and adjustment. *Social Cognition, 13*, 215–242.

Higgins, E. T., Marguc, J., & Scholer, A. A. (2008). *Working under adversity: How opposing versus coping affects value.* Unpublished manuscript, Columbia University.

Higgins, E. T., & May, D. (2001). Individual self-regulatory functions: It's not "we" regulation, but it's still social. In C. Sedikides & M. B. Brewer (Eds.), *Individual self, relational self, collective self* (pp. 47–67). Philadelphia, PA: Psychology Press.

Higgins, E. T., Pierro, A., & Kruglanski, A. W. (2008). Re-thinking culture and personality: How self-regulatory universals create cross-cultural differences. In R. M. Sorrentino & S. Yamaguchi (Eds.), *Handbook of motivation and cognition across cultures* (pp. 161-190). New York: Academic Press.

Higgins, E. T., & Pittman, T. (2008). Motives of the *human* animal: Comprehending, managing, and sharing inner states. *Annual Review of Psychology, 59*, 361–385.

Higgins, E. T., & Rholes, W. S. (1978). "Saying is believing": Effects of message modification on memory and liking for the person described. *Journal of Experimental Social Psychology, 14*, 363–378.

Higgins, E. T., Rholes, W. S. & Jones, C. R. (1977). Category accessibility and impression formation. *Journal of Experimental Social Psychology, 13*, 141–154.

Higgins, E. T., & Scholer, A. A. (2008). When is personality revealed? A motivated cognition approach. In O. P. John, R. W. Robins, & L. A. Pervin (Eds.), *Handbook of personality: Theory and research* (3rd ed., pp. 182–207). New York: Guilford Press.

Higgins, E. T., & Scholer, A. A. (2009a). Engaging the consumer: The science and art of the value creation process. *Journal of Consumer Psychology, 19*, 100–114.

Higgins, E. T., & Scholer, A. A. (2009b). *How the same personality trait can serve different motivational concerns in distinct ways.* Unpublished manuscript, Columbia University.

Higgins, E. T., Shah, J., & Friedman, R. (1997). Emotional responses to goal attainment: Strength of regulatory focus as moderator. *Journal of Personality and Social Psychology, 72*, 515–525.

Higgins, E. T., & Silberman, I. (1998) Development of regulatory focus: Promotion and prevention as ways of living. In J. Heckhausen & C. S. Dweck (Eds.), *Motivation and self-regulation across the life span* (pp. 78–113). New York: Cambridge University Press.

Higgins, E. T., & Spiegel, S. (2004). Promotion and prevention strategies for self-regulation: A motivated cognition perspective. In R. F. Baumeister & K. D. Vohs (Eds.), *Handbook of self-regulation: Research, theory, and applications* (pp. 171–187). New York: Guilford Press.

Higgins, E. T., & Stangor, C. (1988). A "change-of-standard" perspective on the relations among context, judgment, and memory. *Journal of Personality and Social Psychology, 54,* 181–192.

Higgins, E. T., Strauman, T., & Klein, R. (1986). Standards and the process of self-evaluation: Multiple affects from multiple stages. In R. M. Sorrentino & E. T. Higgins (Eds.), *Handbook of motivation and cognition: Foundations of social behavior* (pp. 23–63). New York: Guilford Press.

Higgins, E. T., & Trope, Y. (1990). Activity engagement theory: Implications of multiple identifications for intrinsic motivation. In E. T. Higgins & R. M. Sorrentino (Eds.), *Handbook of motivation and cognition: Foundations of social behavior* (Vol. 2, pp. 229–264). New York: Guilford.

Higgins, E. T., Trope, Y., & Kwon, J. (1999). Augmentation and undermining from combining activities: The role of choice in activity engagement theory. *Journal of Experimental Social Psychology, 35,* 285–307.

Higgins, E. T., Tykocinski, O., & Vookles, J. (1990). Patterns of self-beliefs: The psychological significance of relations among the actual, ideal, ought, can, and future selves. In J. M. Olson & M. P. Zanna (Eds.), *Self-inference processes: The Ontario Symposium* (Vol. 6, pp. 153–190). Hillsdale, NJ: Erlbaum.

Higgins, E. T., Van Hook, E., & Dorfman, D. (1988). Do self attributes form a cognitive structure? *Social Cognition, 6,* 177–207.

Higgins, E. T., Vookles, J., & Tykocinski, O. (1992). Self and health: How "patterns" of self-beliefs predict types of emotional and physical problems. *Social Cognition, 10,* 125–150.

Higgins, E. T., & Winter, L. (1993). The "acquisition principle": How beliefs about a behavior's prolonged circumstances influence correspondent inference. *Personality and Social Psychology Bulletin, 19,* 605–619.

Higgins, K. A. (2008). *Aristotle and Machiavelli: A clash not on virtue, but on human nature.* Unpublished paper for "Classics of social and political thought," University of Chicago.

Hilton, D. (2007). Causal explanation: From social perception to knowledge-based attribution. In A. W. Kruglanski & E. T. Higgins (Eds.), *Social psychology: Handbook of basic principles* (2nd ed., pp. 232–253). New York: Guilford.

Hilton, J. L., Fein, S., & Miller, D. T. (1993). Suspicion and dispositional inference. *Personality and Social Psychology Bulletin, 19,* 501–512.

Hinkley, K., & Andersen, S. M. (1996). The working self-concept in transference: Significant-other activation and self change. *Journal of Personality and Social Psychology, 71,* 1279–1295.

Hoffman, M. L. (1970). Moral development. In P. H. Mussen (Ed.), *Carmichael's manual of child psychology* (Vol. 2, pp. 261–359). New York: Wiley.

Hogg, M. A. (2007). Social psychology of leadership. In A. W. Kruglanski & E. T. Higgins (Eds.), *Social psychology: Handbook of basic principles* (2nd ed., pp. 716–733). New York: Guilford.

Hogg, M. A., & van Knippenberg, D. (2003). Social identity and leadership processes in groups. In M. P. Zanna (Ed.), *Advances in experimental social psychology* (Vol. 35, pp. 1–52). San Diego, CA: Academic Press.

Holmes, J. G., & Rempel, J. K. (1989). Trust in close relationships. In C. Hendrick (Ed.), *Close relationships: Review of personality and social psychology* (Vol. 10, pp. 187–220). London: Sage.

Holyoak, K. J., & Thagard, P. (1997). The analogical mind. *American Psychologist, 52,* 35–44.

Homans, G. C. (1950). *The human group.* New York: Harcourt, Brace & World.

Hong, J., & Lee, A. Y. (2008). Be fit and be strong: Mastering self-regulation through regulatory fit. *Journal of Consumer Research, 34,* 682–695.

Hong, Y-Y., Morris, M., Chiu, C., & Benet-Martinez, V. (2000). Multicultural minds: A dynamic constructivistic approach. *American Psychologist, 55,* 709–721.

Hong, Y-Y., Wan, C., No, S., & Chiu, C-Y. (2007). Multicultural identities. In S. Kitayama & D. Cohen (Eds.), *Handbook of cultural psychology* (pp. 323–345). New York: Guilford Press.

Horner, M. S. (1968). *Sex differences in achievement motivation and performance in competitive and non-competitive situations.* Unpublished doctoral dissertation, University of Michigan.

Horney, K. (1939). *New ways in psychoanalysis.* New York: Norton.

House, J. S., Umberson, D., & Landis, K. R. (1988). Structures and processes of social support. *Annual Review of Sociology, 14,* 293–318.

Hovland, C. I., Janis, I. L., & Kelley, H. H. (1953). *Communication and persuasion: Psychological studies of opinion change.* New Haven, CT: Yale University Press.

Hull, C. L. (1943). *Principles of behavior.* New York: Appleton-Century-Crofts.

Hull, C. L. (1952). *A behavior system: An introduction to behavior theory concerning the individual organism.* New Haven, CT: Yale University Press.

Hume, D. (1975). *An equiry concerning the principles of morals* (J. B. Schneewind, Ed.). Cambridge, England: Hackett. (Originally published 1777)

Hunt, J. M. (1961). *Intelligence and experience.* New York: The Ronald Press.

Huttenlocher, J., & Higgins, E. T. (1971). Adjectives, comparatives, and syllogisms. *Psychological Review, 78,* 487–504.

Hyman, H. H. (1942). The psychology of status. *Archives of Psychology, 269.*

Idson, L. C., Liberman, N., & Higgins, E. T. (2004). Imagining how you'd feel: The role of motivational experiences from regulatory fit. *Personality and Social Psychology Bulletin, 30,* 926–937.

Idson, L. C., & Mischel, W. (2001). The personality of familiar and significant people: The lay perceiver as a social-cognitive theorist. *Journal of Personality and Social Psychology, 80,* 585–596.

Inkeles, A., & Levinson, D. J. (1969). National character: The study of modal personality and sociocultural systems. In G. Lindzey & E. Aronson (Eds.), *The handbook of social psychology* (pp. 418–506). Reading, MA: Addison-Wesley.

Irwin, F. W. (1953). Stated expectations as functions of probability and desirability of outcomes. *Journal of Personality, 21,* 329–335.

Iyengar, S. S., & Lepper, M. R. (1999). Rethinking the value of choice: A cultural perspective on intrinsic motivation. *Journal of Personality and Social Psychology, 76,* 349–366.

Jacobs, R. C., & Campbell, D. T. (1961). The perpetuation of an arbitrary tradition through several generations of a laboratory microculture. *Journal of Abnormal and Social Psychology, 62,* 649–658.

James, W. (1948). *Psychology.* New York: The World Publishing Company. (Original publication, 1890)

James, W. (2007). *The principles of psychology* (Vol. 2). New York: Cosimo. (Original publication, 1890)

Jensen, G. D. (1963). Preference for bar pressing over "freeloading" as a function of number of rewarded presses. *Journal of Experimental Psychology, 65,* 451–454.

John, O. P. (1990). The "big five" factor taxonomy: Dimensions of personality in the natural language and in questionnaires. In L. A. Pervin (Ed.), *Handbook of personality: Theory and research* (pp. 66–100). New York: Guilford Press.

John, O. P., & Srivastava, S. (1999). The big-five taxonomy: History, measurement, and theoretical perspectives. In L. A. Pervin & O. P. John (Eds.), *Handbook of personality: Theory and research* (2nd ed., pp. 102–138). New York: Guilford Press.

Johnson, M. K. (2006). Memory and reality. *American Psychologist, 61,* 760–771.

Johnson, M. K., Foley, M. A., & Leach, K. (1988). The consequences for memory of imagining in another person's voice. *Memory and Cognition, 16,* 337–342.

Johnson, M. K., & Raye, C. L. (1981). Reality monitoring. *Psychological Review, 88,* 67–85.

Johnson, M. K., & Sherman, S. J. (1990). Constructing and reconstructing the past and the future in the present. In E. T. Higgins & R. M. Sorrentino (Eds.), *Handbook of motivation and cognition* (Vol. 2, pp. 482–526). New York: Guilford.

Jones, E. E. (1979). The rocky road from acts to dispositions. *American Psychologist, 34,* 107–117.

Jones, E. E., & Davis, K. E. (1965). From acts to dispositions: The attribution process in person perception. In L. Berkowitz (Ed.), *Advances in experimental social psychology* (Vol. 2, pp. 219–266). New York: Academic Press.

Jones, E. E., & Nisbett, R. E. (1972). The actor and the observer: Divergent perceptions of the causes of behavior. In E. E. Jones, D. Kanouse, H. H. Kelley, R. E. Nisbett, S. Valins, & B. Weiner (Eds.), *Attribution: Perceiving the causes of behavior* (pp. 79–94). New York: General Learning Press.

Jost, J. T., Banaji, M. R., & Nosek, B. A. (2004). A decade of system justification theory: Accumulated evidence of conscious and unconscious bolstering of the status quo. *Political Psychology, 25,* 881–919.

Jost, J. T., & Hunyady, O. (2005). Antecedents and consequences of system-justifying ideologies. *Current Directions in Psychological Science, 14,* 260–265.

Jost, J. T., Ledgerwood, A., & Hardin, C. D. (2008). Shared reality, system justification, and the relational basis of ideological beliefs. *Social and Personality Psychology Compass, 2,* 171–186.

Jost, J. T., Pelham, B. W., Sheldon, O., & Sullivan, B. N. (2003). Social inequality and the reduction of ideological dissonance on behalf of the system: Evidence of enhanced system justification among the disadvantaged. *European Journal of Social Psychology*, *33*, 13–36.

Jost, J. T., Pietrzak, J., Liviatan, I., Mandisodza, A. N., & Napier, J. L. (2008). System justification as conscious and nonconscious goal pursuit. In J. Y. Shah & W. L. Gardner (Eds.). *Handbook of motivation science* (pp. 591–605). New York: Guilford Press.

Judge, T. A., Thoresen, C. J., Pucik, V., & Welbourne, T. M. (1999). Managerial coping with organizational change: A dispositional perspective. *Journal of Applied Psychology*, *84*, 107–122.

Jung, C. G. (1971). *Psychological types*. Princeton, NJ: Princeton University. (Original publication, 1921)

Kagan, J., & Kogan, N. (1970). Individual variation in cognitive processes. In P. Mussen (Ed.), *Carmichael's manual of child psychology* (Vol. 1, pp. 1273–1365). New York: Wiley.

Kahneman, D. (1999). Objective happiness. In D. Kahnemen, E. Diener, & N. Schwarz (Eds.), *Well-being: The foundations of hedonic psychology* (pp. 3–25). New York: Russell Sage Foundation.

Kahneman, D. (2000a). Experienced utility and objective happiness: A moment-based approach. In D. Kahneman & A. Tversky (Eds.), *Choices, values, and frames* (pp. 673–692). New York: Cambridge University Press.

Kahneman, D. (2000b) New challenges to the rationality assumption. In D. Kahneman & A. Tversky (Eds.), *Choices, values, and frames* (pp. 758–774). New York: Cambridge University Press.

Kahneman, D., Diener, E., & Schwarz, N. (1999). *Well-being: The foundations of hedonic psychology*. New York: Russell Sage.

Kahneman, D., & Miller, D. T. (1986). Norm theory: Comparing reality to its alternatives. *Psychological Review*, *93*, 136–153.

Kahneman, D., & Tversky, A. (1979). Prospect theory: An analysis of decision under risk. *Econometrica*, *47*, 263–291.

Kahneman, D., & Tversky, A. (1982). The simulation heuristic. In D. Kahneman, P. Slovic, & A. Tversky (Eds.), *Judgment under uncertainty: Heuristics and biases* (pp. 201–208). New York: Cambridge University Press.

Karau, S. J., & Williams, K. D. (1993). Social loafing: A meta-analytic review and theoretical integration. *Journal of Personality and Social Psychology, 65*, 681–706.

Karpinski, A., & Hilton, J. L. (2001). Attitudes and the implicit association test. *Journal of Personality and Social Psychology, 81*, 774–788.

Kasser, T., & Ryan, R. M. (1993). A dark side of the American dream: correlates of financial success as a central life aspiration. *Journal of Personality and Social Psychology, 65*, 410–422.

Katz, D. (1960). The functional approach to the study of attitudes. *Public Opinion Quarterly, 24*, 163–204.

Katz, D., & Braly, K. W. (1933). Racial stereotypes of 100 college students. *Journal of Abnormal and Social Psychology, 28*, 280–290.

Keller, J., & Bless, H. (2006). Regulatory fit and cognitive performance: The interactive effect of chronic and situationally induced self-regulatory mechanisms on test performance. *European Journal of Social Psychology, 36*, 393–405.

Kelley, H. H. (1952). Two functions of reference groups. In G. E. Swanson, T. M. Newcomb, & E. L. Hartley (Eds.), *Readings in social psychology* (2nd ed., pp. 410–420). New York: Holt, Rinehart & Winston.

Kelley, H. H. (1973). The process of causal attribution. *American Psychologist, 28,* 107–128.

Kelly, G. A. (1955). *The psychology of personal constructs.* New York: W. W. Norton.

Kelly, G. A. (1969). *Clinical psychology and personality. The selected papers of George Kelly* (B. Maher, Ed.). New York: Wiley.

Kelman, H. C. (1958). Compliance, identification, and internalization: Three processes of attitude change. *Journal of Conflict Resolution, 2,* 51–60.

Kenrick, D. T., Trost, M. R., & Sundie, J. M. (2004). Sex-roles as adaptations: An evolutionary perspective on gender differences and similarities. In A. H. Eagly, A. Beall, & R. Sternberg (Eds.), *Psychology of gender* (pp. 65–91). New York: Guilford.

Kerr, S. (1975). On the folly of rewarding A, while hoping for B. *Academy of Management Journal, 18,* 769–783.

Keynes, J. M. (1951). *The general theory of employment, interest, and money.* London: MacMillan & Co. (Original publication, 1936)

Kimble, G. A. (1961). *Hilgard and Marquis' conditioning and learning.* New York: Appleton-Century-Crofts.

Kitayama, S., & Park, H. (2007). Cultural shaping of self, emotion, and well-being: How does it work? *Social and Personality Psychology Compass, 1,* 202–222.

Klein, H. J., Wesson, M. J., Hollenbeck, J. R., Wright, P. M., & DeShon, R. P. (2001). The assessment of goal commitment: A measurement model meta-analysis. *Organizational Behavior and Human Decision Processes, 85,* 32–55.

Klem, A., Higgins, E. T., & Kruglanski, A. W. (1996). *Getting started on something versus waiting to do the "right" thing: Locomotion and assessment as distinct regulatory modes.* Unpublished manuscript, Columbia University.

Kohlberg, L. (1969). Stage and sequence: The cognitive-developmental approach to socialization. In D.A. Goslin (Ed.), *Handbook of socialization theory and research.* Chicago: Rand McNally.

Kohlberg, L. (1976). Moral stages and moralization. In T. Lickona (Ed.), *Moral development and behavior.* New York: Holt, Rinehart, & Winston.

Kohut, H. (1971). *The analysis of the self: A systematic approach to the treatment of narcissistic personality disorders.* Madison, CT: International Universities Press.

Konorski, J. (1967). *Integrative activity of the brain: An interdisciplinary approach.* Chicago: University of Chicago Press.

Koo, M., & Fishbach, A. (in press). Dynamics of self-regulation: How (un)accomplished goal actions affect motivation. *Journal of Personality and Social Psychology.*

Koole, S. L., & Kuhl, J. (2007). Dealing with unwanted feelings: The role of affect regulation in volitional action control. In J. Y. Shah & W. L. Gardner (Eds.). *Handbook of motivation science* (pp. 295–307). New York: Guilford Press.

Krantz, D. H., & Kunreuther, H. C. (2007). Goals and plans in decision making. *Judgment and Decision Making, 2,* 137–168.

Krech, D., Crutchfield, R. S., & Ballachey, E. L. (1962). *Individual in society: A textbook of social psychology.* New York: McGraw-Hill.

Kristof, N. D. (2008, Oct. 4). Racism without racists. Opinion column, *New York Times.*

Kross, E., Ayduk, O., & Mischel, W. (2005). When asking "why" does not hurt: Distinguishing rumination from reflective processing of negative emotions. *Psychological Science, 16,* 709–715.

Kruglanski, A. W. (1975). The endogenous-exogeneous partition in attribution theory. *Psychological Review, 82,* 387–406.

Kruglanski, A.W. (1980). Lay epistemo-logic—process and contents: Another look at attribution theory. *Psychological Review, 87,* 70–87.

Kruglanski, A. W. (1989). *Lay epistemics and human knowledge: Cognitive and motivational bases.* New York: Plenum.

Kruglanski, A. W. (1990). Motivations for judging and knowing: Implications for causal attribution. In E. T. Higgins & R. M. Sorrentino (Eds.), *Handbook of motivation and cognition: Foundations of social behavior* (Vol. 2, pp. 333-368). New York: Guilford.

Kruglanski, A. W. (1996a). Goals as knowledge structure. In P. M. Gollwitzer & J. A. Bargh (Eds.), *The psychology of action: Linking cognition and motivation to behavior* (pp. 599–618). New York: Guilford Press.

Kruglanski, A. W. (1996b). Motivated social cognition: Principles of the interface. In E. T. Higgins & A. W. Kruglanski (Eds.), *Social psychology: Handbook of basic principles* (pp. 493–520). New York: Guilford Press.

Kruglanski, A. W. (2006). The nature of fit and the origins of "feeling right": A goal-systemic perspective. *Journal of Marketing Research, 43,* 11–14.

Kruglanski, A. W., Dechesne, M., Orehek, E., & Pierro, A. (in press). Three decades of lay epistemics: The why, how and who of knowledge formation. *European Review of Social Psychology.*

Kruglanski, A. W., Erbs, H-P., Pierro, A., Mannetti, L., & Chun, W. Y. (2006). On parametric continuities in the world of binary either ors. *Psychological Inquiry, 17,* 153–165.

Kruglanski, A. W., & Freund, T. (1983). The freezing and unfreezing of lay-inferences: Effects on impressional primacy, ethnic stereotyping, and numerical anchoring. *Journal of Experimental Social Psychology, 19,* 448–468.

Kruglanski, A. W., Friedman, I., & Zeevi, G. (1971). The effects of extrinsic incentive on some qualitative aspects of task performance. *Journal of Personality, 39,* 606–617.

Kruglanski, A. W., & Mayseless, O. (1987). Motivational effects in the social comparison of opinions. *Journal of Personality and Social Psychology, 53,* 834–853.

Kruglansk, A. W., Pierro, A., & Higgins, E. T. (2007). Regulatory mode and preferred leadership styles: How fit increases job satisfaction. *Basic and Applied Social Psychology, 29,* 137–149.

Kruglanski, A. W., Pierro, A., Higgins, E. T., & Capozza, D (2007). "On the move," or "staying put": Locomotion, need for closure and reactions to organizational change. *Journal of Applied Social Psychology, 37,* 1305-1340.

Kruglanski, A. W., Pierro, A., Mannetti, L., & De Grada, E. (2006). Groups as epistemic providers: Need for closure and the unfolding of group-centrism. *Psychological Review, 113,* 84–100.

Kruglanski, A. W., Raviv, A., Bar-Tal, D., Raviv, A., Sharvit, K., Ellis, S., Bar, R., Pierro, A., & Mannetti, L. (2005). Says who? Epistemic authority effects in social judgment. In M. P. Zanna (Ed.), *Advances in experimental social psychology* (Vol. 37, pp. 345–392). New York: Academic Press.

Kruglanski, A. W., Shah, J. Y., Fishbach, A., Friedman, R., Chun, W. Y., & Sleeth-Keppler, D. (2002). A theory of goal systems. In M. P. Zanna (Ed.), *Advances in experimental social psychology* (Vol. 34, pp. 331–378). San Diego, CA: Academic Press.

Kruglanski, A. W., & Sleeth-Keppler, D. (2007). The principle of social judgment. In A. W. Kruglanski & E. T. Higgins (Eds.), *Social psychology: Handbook of basic principles* (2nd ed., pp. 116–137). New York: Guilford.

Kruglanski, A. W., & Thompson, E. P. (1999). Persuasion by a single route: A view from the unimodel. *Psychological Inquiry, 10*, 83–109.

Kruglanski, A. W., Thompson, E. P., Higgins, E. T., Atash, M. N., Pierro, A., Shah, J. Y., & Spiegel, S. (2000). To "do the right thing" or to "just do it": Locomotion and assessment as distinct self-regulatory imperatives. *Journal of Personality & Social Psychology, 79*, 793–815.

Kruglanski, A. W., & Webster, D. M. (1996). Motivated closing of the mind: "Seizing" and "freezing." *Psychological Review, 103*, 263–283.

Kuhl, J. (1978). Standard setting and risk preference: An elaboration of the theory of achievement motivation and an empirical test. *Psychological Review, 85*, 239–248.

Kuhl, J. (1984). Volitional aspects of achievement motivation and learned helplessness: Toward a comprehensive theory of action control. In B. A. Maher (Ed.), *Progress in experimental personality research* (Vol. 12, pp. 99–170). New York: Academic Press.

Kuhl, J. (1985). Volitional mediation of cognition-behavior consistency: Self-regulatory processes and action versus state orientation. In J. Kuhl & J. Beckman (Eds.), *Action control: From cognition to behavior* (pp. 101–128). Berlin, Germany: Springer-Verlag.

Kuhl, J. (1986). Motivation and information processing: A new look at decision making, dynamic change, and action control. In R. M. Sorrentino & E. T. Higgins (Eds.), *Handbook of motivation and cognition: Foundations of social behavior* (pp. 404–434). New York: Guilford.

Kunda, Z. (1990). The case for motivated reasoning. *Psychological Bulletin, 108*, 480–498.

Kwang, T., & Swann, Jr., W. B. (2010). Do people embrace praise even when they feel unworthy? A review of critical tests of self-enhancement versus self-verification. *Personality and Social Psychology Review, 14*, 263–280.

Labroo, A., & Lee, A. Y. (2006). Between two brands: A goal fluency account of brand evaluation. *Journal of Marketing Research, 43*, 374–385.

Lacan, J. (1991). *The seminar of Jacques Lacan: Book II: The ego in Freud's theory and in the technique of psychoanalysis 1954–1955.* New York: W. W. Norton.

Lam, T. W., & Chiu, C-Y (2002). The motivational function of regulatory focus in creativity. *Journal of Creative Behavior, 36*, 138–150.

Lang, P. J. (1995). The emotion probe: Studies of motivation and attention. *American Psychologist, 50*, 372–385.

Lang, P. J., Bradley, M. M., & Cuthbert, B. N. (1990). Emotion, attention, and the startle reflex. *Psychological Review, 97*, 377–395.

Langer, E. J. (1975). The illusion of control. *Journal of Personality and Social Psychology, 32*, 311–328.

Langer, E. J., & Roth, J. (1975). Heads I win, tails it's chance: The illusion of control as a function of the sequence of outcomes in a purely chance task. *Journal of Personality and Social Psychology, 32*, 951–955.

Larsen, R. J. (2000). Toward a science of mood regulation. *Psychological Inquiry, 11,* 218–225.

Larsen, R. J., & Diener, E. (1985). A multitrait, multimethod examination of affect structure: Hedonic level and emotional intensity. *Personality and Individual Differences, 6,* 631–636.

Larsen, R. J., & Prizmic, Z. (2004). Affect regulation. In R. F. Baumeister & K. D. Vohs (Eds.), *Handbook of self-regulation: Research, theory, and applications* (pp. 40–61). New York: Guilford Press.

Lashley, K. S. (1951). The problem of serial order in behavior. In L. A. Jeffress (Ed.), *Cerebral mechanisms in behavior: The Hixon symposium* (pp. 112–136). New York: Wiley.

Latane, B., Williams, K., & Harkins, S. (1979). Many hands make light the work: The causes and consequences of social loafing. *Journal of Personality and Social Psychology, 37,* 822–832.

Latimer, A. E., Rivers, S. E., Rench, T. A., Katulak, N. A., Hicks, A., Hodorowski, J. K., Higgins, E. T., & Salovey, P. (2008). A field experiment testing the utility of regulatory fit messages for promoting physical activity. *Journal of Experimental Social Psychology, 44,* 826–832.

Latimer, A. E., Williams-Piehota, P., Katulak, N. A., Cox, A., Mowad, L. Z., Higgins, E. T., & Salovey, P. (2008). Promoting fruit and vegetable intake through messages tailored to individual differences in regulatory focus. *Annals of Behavioral Medicine, 35,* 363–369.

Lau, I. Y-M., Chiu, C-Y., & Lee, S-L. (2001). Communication and shared reality: Implications for the psychological foundations of culture. *Social Cognition, 19,* 350–371.

Lawrence, D. H., & Festinger, L. (1962). *Deterrents and reinforcement.* Stanford, CA: Stanford University Press.

Lazarus, R. S. (1966). *Psychological stress and the coping process.* New York: McGraw-Hill.

Lazarus, R. S., & Folkman, S. (1984). *Stress, appraisal, and coping.* New York: Springer.

Leary, M. R. (2004). The sociometer, self-esteem, and the regulation of interpersonal behavior. In R. F. Baumeister & K. D. Vohs (Eds.), *Handbook of self-regulation: Research, theory, and applications* (pp. 373–391). New York: Guilford Press.

Leary, M. R. (2007). Motivational and emotional aspects of the self. *Annual Review of Psychology, 58,* 317–344.

Leary, M. R., & Baumeister, R. F. (2000). The nature and function of self-esteem: Sociometer theory. In M. Zanna (Ed.), *Advances in experimental social psychology* (Vol. 32, pp. 1–62). San Diego, CA: Academic Press.

Leary, M. R., Tambor, E. S., Terdal, S. K., & Downs, D. L. (1995). Self-esteem as an interpersonal monitor: The sociometer hypothesis. *Journal of Personality and Social Psychology, 68,* 518–530.

Lecky, P. (1945). *Self-consistency: A theory of personality.* New York: Island Press.

Lee, A. Y., & Aaker, J. L. (2004). Bringing the frame into focus: The influence of regulatory fit on processing fluency and persuasion. *Journal of Personality and Social Psychology, 86,* 205–218.

Lee, A. Y., Aaker, J. L., & Gardner, W. L. (2000). The pleasures and pains of distinct self-construals: The role of interdependence in regulatory focus. *Journal of Personality and Social Psychology, 78,* 1122–1134.

Lee, A. Y., & Higgins, E. T. (2009). The persuasive power of regulatory fit. In M. Wänke (Ed.), *The social psychology of consumer behavior* (pp. 319-333). New York: Psychology Press.

Lee, A. Y., Keller, P. A., & Sternthal, B. (2010). Value from regulatory construal fit: The persuasive impact of fit between consumer goals and message concreteness. *Journal of Consumer Research, 36,* 735–747.

Lefcourt, H. M. (1976). *Locus of control: Current trends in theory and research.* Hillsdale, NJ: Erlbaum.

Lepper, M. R., Greene, D., & Nisbett, R. E. (1973). Undermining children's intrinsic interest with extrinsic reward: a test of the overjustification hypothesis. *Journal of Personality and Social Psychology, 28,* 129–137.

Lepper, M. R., Zanna, M. P., & Abelson, R. P. (1970). Cognitive irreversibility in a dissonance-reduction situation. *Journal of Personality and Social Psychology, 16,* 191–198.

Lerner, M. J. (1970). The desire for justice and reactions to victims. In J. Macaulay & L. Berkowitz (Eds.), *Altruism and helping behavior.* New York: Academic Press.

Levine, J. M. (1989). Reaction to opinion deviance in small groups. In P. B. Paulus (Ed.), *Psychology of group influence* (2nd ed., pp. 187–231). Hillsdale, NJ: Erlbaum.

Levine, J. M. (1999). Solomon Asch's legacy for group research. *Personality and Social Psychology Review, 3,* 358–364.

Levine, J. M., & Thompson, L. (1996). Conflict in groups. In E. T. Higgins & A. W. Kruglanski (Eds.), *Social psychology: Handbook of basic principles* (pp. 745–776). New York: Guilford Press.

LeVine, R. A. (2001). Culture and personality studies, 1918–1960: Myth and history. *Journal of Personality, 69,* 803–818.

Lewin, K. (1935). *A dynamic theory of personality.* New York: McGraw-Hill.

Lewin, K. (1951). *Field theory in social science.* New York: Harper.

Lewin, K. (1952). Constructs in field theory [1944]. In D. Cartwright (Ed.), *Field theory in social science: Selected theoretical papers by Kurt Lewin* (pp. 30–42). London: Tavistock.

Lewin, K., Dembo, T., Festinger, L., & Sears, P. S. (1944). Level of aspiration. In J. McHunt (Ed.), *Personality and the behavior disorders* (Vol. 1, pp. 333–378). New York: Ronald Press.

Lewis, M. (1965). Psychological effect of effort. *Psychological Bulletin, 64,* 183–190.

Li, N. P., Bailey, J. M., Kenrick, D. T., & Linsenmeier, J. A. W. (2002). The necessities and luxuries of mate preferences: Testing the tradeoffs. *Journal of Personality and Social Psychology, 82,* 947–955.

Liberman, N., & Forster, J. (2008). Expectancy, value and psychological distance: A new look at goal gradients. *Social Cognition, 26,* 629–647.

Liberman, N., Idson, L. C., Camacho, C. J., & Higgins, E. T. (1999). Promotion and prevention choices between stability and change. *Journal of Personality and Social Psychology, 77,* 1135–1145.

Liberman, N., Molden, D. C., Idson, L. C., & Higgins, E. T. (2001). Promotion and prevention focus on alternative hypotheses: Implications for attributional functions. *Journal of Personality and Social Psychology, 80,* 5–18.

Liberman, N., & Trope, Y. (2008). The psychology of transcending the here and now. *Science, 322,* 1201-1205.

Liberman, N., Trope, Y., & Stephan, E. (2007). Psychological distance. In A. W. Kruglanski & E. T. Higgins (Eds.), *Social psychology: Handbook of basic principles* (2nd ed., pp. 353-381). New York: Guilford.

Lindskold, S. (1978). Trust development, the GRIT proposal, and the effects of conciliatory acts on conflict and cooperation. *Psychological Bulletin, 85,* 772-793.

Locke, E. A., & Kristof, A. L. (1996). Volitional choices in the goal achievement process. In P. M. Gollwitzer & J. A. Bargh (Eds.), *The psychology of action: Linking cognition and motivation to behavior* (pp. 365-384). New York: Guilford Press.

Locke, E. A., & Latham, G. P. (1990). *A theory of goal setting and task performance.* Englewood Cliffs, NJ: Prentice-Hall.

Locke, E. A., & Latham, G. P. (2002). Building a practically useful theory of goal setting and task motivation: A 35-year odyssey. *American Psychologist, 57,* 705-717.

Loftus, E. F., & Palmer, J. C. (1974). Reconstruction of automobile destruction: An example of the interaction between language and memory. *Journal of Verbal Learning and Verbal Behavior, 13,* 585-589.

Lombardi, W. J., Higgins, E. T., & Bargh, J. A. (1987). The role of consciousness in priming effects on categorization. *Personality and Social Psychology Bulletin, 13,* 411-429.

Lopes, L. L. (1987). Between hope and fear: The psychology of risk. In L. Berkowitz (Ed.), *Advances in experimental social psychology* (Vol. 20, p. 255-295). New York: Academic Press.

Lount Jr., R. B., Zhong, C-B., Sivanathan, N., & Murnighan, J. K. (2008). Getting off on the wrong foot: The timing of a breach and the restoration of trust. *Personality and Social Psychology Bulletin, 34,* 1601-1612.

Lowery, B. S., Hardin, C. D., & Sinclair, S. (2001). Social influence effects on automatic racial prejudice. *Journal of Personality and Social Psychology, 81,* 842-855.

Lucas, R. E., & Diener, E. (2008). Personality and subjective well-being. In O. P. John, R. W. Robins, & L. A. Pervin (Eds.), *Handbook of personality: Theory and research* (3rd ed., pp. 795-814). New York: Guilford Press.

Luce, R. D. (1959). *Individual choice behavior.* New York: Wiley.

Lyons, A., & Kashima, Y. (2003). How are stereotypes maintained through communication? The influence of stereotype sharedness. *Journal of Personality and Social Psychology, 85,* 989-1005.

Machiavelli, N. (2004). *The Prince.* London: Penguin Classics. (Originally published in 1513)

Macrae, C. N., & Bodenhausen, G. V. (2000). Social cognition: Thinking categorically about others. *Annual Review of Psychology, 51,* 93-120.

Main, M., Kaplan, N., & Cassidy, J. (1985). Security in infancy, childhood, and adulthood: A move to the level of representation. *Monographs for the Society for Research in Child Development, 50,* 66-104.

Malle, B. F. (2004). *How the mind explains behavior: Folk explanations, meaning, and social interaction.* Cambridge, MA: MIT Press.

Mandler, G. (1984). *Mind and body: The psychology of emotion and stress.* New York: Norton.

Mannetti, L., Pierro, A., Higgins, E. T., & Kruglanski, A. W. (2009). *Maintaining physical activity: How locomotion mode moderates the full attitude-intention-behavior relation.* Unpublished manuscript, University La Sapienza.

Mannix, E. (1997). *Federated Science Fund.* Dispute Resolution. Research Center, Kellogg School of Management.

March, J. G. (1994). *A primer on decision making: How decisions happen.* New York: Free Press.

Marks, G., & Miller, N. (1987). Ten years of research on the false consensus effect: an empirical and theoretical review. *Psychological Bulletin, 102,* 72–90.

Marks, R. W. (1951). The effect of probability, desirability, and "privilege" on the stated expectations of children. *Journal of Personality, 19,* 332–351.

Markus, H. (1977). Self-schemata and processing information about the self. *Journal of Personality and Social Psychology, 35,* 63–78.

Markus, H. (1980). The self in thought in memory. In D. M. Wegner & R. R. Vallacher (Eds.), *The self in social psychology* (pp. 102–130). New York: Oxford University Press.

Markus, H., & Kitayama, S. (1991). Culture and the self: Implications for cognition, emotion, and motivation. *Psychological Review, 98,* 224–253.

Markus, H. R., & Kitayama, S. (1998). The cultural psychology of personality. *Journal of Cross-Cultural Psychology, 29,* 63–87.

Marlowe, D., & Gergen, K. J. (1969). Personality and social interaction. In G. Lindzey & E. Aronson (Eds.), *The handbook of social psychology* (3rd ed., pp. 590–665). Reading, MA: Addison-Wesley.

Marsden, P. V. (1987). Core discussion networks of Americans. *American Sociological Review, 52,* 122–131.

Martijn, C., Tenbult, P., Merckelbach, H., Dreezens, E., & de Vries, N. K. (2002). Getting a grip on ourselves: Challenging expectancies about loss of energy after self-control. *Social Cognition, 20,* 441–460.

Martin, L. L. (1986). Set/reset: Use and disuse of concepts in impression formation. *Journal of Personality and Social Psychology, 51,* 493–504.

Martin, L. L., & Achee, J. W. (1992). Beyond accessibility: The role of processing objectives in judgment. In L. L. Martin & A. Tesser (Eds.), *The construction of social judgments* (pp. 195–216). Hillsdale, NJ: Erlbaum.

Masicampo, E. J., & Baumeister, R. F. (2008). Toward a physiology of dual-process reasoning and judgment: Lemonade, willpower, and effortful rule-based analysis. *Psychological Science, 19,* 255–260.

Maslow, A. H. (1943). A theory of human motivation. *Psychological Review, 50,* 370–396.

Mauro, R., Pierro, A., Mannetti, L., Higgins, E. T., & Kruglanski, A. W. (in press). The perfect mix: Regulatory complementarity and the speed-accuracy balance in group performance. *Psychological Science.*

Mayseless, O., & Kruglanski, A. W. (1987). What makes you so sure?: Effects of epistemic motivations on judgmental confidence. *Organizational Behavior and human decision processes, 39,* 162-183.

McClelland, D.C. (1951). *Personality.* New York: Sloane.

McClelland, D. C. (1961). *The achieving society.* Princeton, NJ: Van Nostrand.

McClelland, D. C. (1980). Motive dispositions. In L. Wheeler (Ed.), *Review of personality and social psychology* (Vol. 1, pp. 10–41). Beverly Hills, CA: Sage.

McClelland, D. C., & Atkinson, J. W. (1948). The projective expression of needs: I. The effect of different intensities of the hunger drive on perception. *Journal of Psychology, 25*, 205-232.

McClelland, D. C., Atkinson, J. W., Clark, R. A., & Lowell, E. L. (1953). *The achievement motive*. New York: Appleton-Century-Crofts.

McCrae, R. R. (2004). Human nature and culture: A trait perspective. *Journal of Research in Personality, 38*, 3–14.

McCrae, R. R., & Costa, P. T. (1987). Validation of the five-factor model of personality across instruments and observers. *Journal of Personality and Social Psychology, 52*, 81–90.

McCrae, R. R., & Terracciano, A. (2006). National character and personality. *Current Directions in Psychological Science, 15*, 156–161.

McDougall, W. (1914). *An introduction to social psychology* (8th ed.). Boston: Luce.

McGregor, I., Newby-Clark, I. R., & Zanna, M. P. (1999). "Remembering" dissonance: Simultaneous accessibility of inconsistent cognitive elements moderates epistemic discomfort. In E. Harmon-Jones & J. Mills (Ed.), *Cognitive dissonance: Progress on a pivotal theory in social psychology* (pp. 325–353). Washington, D. C.: American Psychological Association.

McGuire, W. J. (1966). Attitudes and opinions. *Annual Review of Psychology, 17*, 475–514.

McGuire, W. J., & Padawer-Singer, A. (1976). Trait salience in the spontaneous self-concept. *Journal of Personality and Social Psychology, 33* 743–754.

McMahon, K. (2002). *The fall of the god of money: Opium smoking in nineteenth-century China*. Maryland: Rowman & Littlefield.

McPherson, M., Smith-Lovin, L., & Brashears, M. E. (2006). Social isolation in America: Changes in core discussion networks over two decades. *American Sociological Review, 71*, 353–375.

Mead, G. H. (1934). *Mind, self, and society*. Chicago: University of Chicago Press.

Mellers, B. A., & McGraw, A. P. (2001). Anticipated emotions as guides to choice. *Current Directions in Psychological Science, 10*, 210–214.

Mendoza-Denton, R., & Hansen, N. (2007). Networks of meaning: Intergroup relations, cultural worldviews, and knowledge activation principles. *Social and Personality Psychology Compass, 1*, 68–83.

Merton, R. K. (1957). *Social theory and social structure*. Glencoe, IL: The Free Press.

Merton, R. K., & Kitt, A. S. (1952). Contributions to the theory of reference-group behavior. In G. E. Swanson, T. M. Newcomb, & E. L. Hartley (Eds.), *Readings in social psychology* (2nd ed., pp. 430–444). New York: Holt, Rinehart & Winston.

Metcalfe, J., & Mischel, W. (1999). A hot/cool-system analysis of delay of gratification: Dynamics of willpower. *Psychological Review, 106*, 3–19.

Meyer, D. E., Smith, J. E., & Wright, C. E. (1982). Models for the speed and accuracy of aimed movements. *Psychological Review, 89*, 449–482.

Meyer, J. P., Allen, N. J., & Smith, C. A. (1993). Commitment to organizations and occupations: Extension and test of a three-component conceptualization. *Journal of Applied Psychology, 78*, 538–551.

Mikulincer, M. (1998). Attachment working models and the senses of trust: An exploration of interaction goals and affect regulation. *Journal of Personality and Social
Psychology, 74*, 1209–1224.

Mikulincer, M., & Shaver, P.R. (2003). The attachment behavioral system in adulthood:
Activation, psychodynamics, and interpersonal processes. In M. P. Zanna (Ed.),
Advances in experimental social psychology (Vol. 35, pp. 53–152). San Diego, CA:
Academic Press.

Milgram, S. (1974). *Obedience to authority.* New York: Harper & Row.

Millar, M. G., Tesser, A. (1986). Effects of affective and cognitive focus on the attitude-
behavior relation. *Journal of Personality and Social Psychology, 51*, 270–276.

Miller, D. T., & Ross, M. (1975). Self-serving biases in the attribution of causality: Fact
or fiction? *Psychological Bulletin, 82*, 213–225.

Miller, D. T., Weinstein, S. M., & Karniol, R. (1978). Effects of age and self-verbalization
on children's ability to delay gratification. *Developmental Psychology, 14*, 569–570.

Miller, G. A., Galanter, E., & Pribram, K. H. (1960). *Plans and the structure of behavior.*
New York: Holt, Rinehart, & Winston.

Miller, J. G. (1984). Culture and the development of everyday social explanation. *Journal
of Personality and Social Psychology, 46*, 961–978.

Miller, N. E. (1944). Experimental studies of conflict. In J. McV. Hunt (Ed.), *Personality
and the behavior disorders* (Vol. 1, pp. 431–465). New York: Ronald Press.

Miller, N. E. (1959). Liberalization of basic S-R concepts: Extensions to conflict behav-
ior, motivation, and social learning. In S. Koch (Ed.), *Psychology: A study of a science.
Vol. 2: General systematic formulations, learning, and special processes* (pp.196–292).
New York: McGraw-Hill.

Miller, N. E. (1963). Some reflections on the law of effect produce a new alternative to
drive reduction. In M. R. Jones (Ed.), *Nebraska symposium on motivation, Vol. 11
(pp. 65-112).* Lincoln, Nebraska: Nebraska University Press.

Miller, P. J. E., & Rempel, J. K. (2004). Trust and partner-enhancing attributions in close
relationships. *Personality and Social Psychology Bulletin, 30*, 695–705.

Miller, S. M. (1979). Coping with impending stress: Physiological and cognitive
correlates of choice. *Psychophysiology, 16*, 572–581.

Mischel, H. N., & Mischel, W. (1983). The development of children's knowledge of
self-control strategies. *Child Development, 54*, 603–619.

Mischel, W. (1973). Toward a cognitive social learning reconceptualization of personality. *Psychological Review, 80*, 252–283.

Mischel, W. (1968). *Personality and assessment.* New York: Wiley.

Mischel, W. (1974). Processes in delay of gratification. In L. Berkowitz (Ed.), *Advances
in experimental social psychology* (Vol. 7, pp. 249–292). New York: Academic Press.

Mischel, W. (1996). From good intentions to willpower. In P. M. Gollwitzer &
J. A. Bargh (Eds.), *The psychology of action: Linking cognition and motivation to behavior* (pp. 197–218). New York: Guilford.

Mischel, W. (1999). *Introduction to personality* (6th ed.). New York: Holt, Rinehart &
Winston.

Mischel, W., Cantor, N., & Feldman, S. (1996). Principles of self-regulation: The nature
of willpower and self-control. In E. T. Higgins & A. W. Kruglanski (Eds.), *Social
psychology: Handbook of basic principles* (pp. 329–360). New York: Guilford.

Mischel, W., & Ebbesen, E. B. (1970). Attention in delay of gratification. *Journal of Personality and Social Psychology, 16*, 329–337.

Mischel, W., Ebbesen, E. B., & Zeiss, A. R. (1973). Selective attention to the self: Situational and dispositional determinants. *Journal of Personality and Social Psychology, 27,* 129–142.

Mischel, W., & Masters, J. C. (1966). Effects of probability of reward attainment on responses to frustration. *Journal of Personality and Social Psychology, 3*, 390–396.

Mischel, W., & Patterson, C. J. (1978). Effective plans for self-control in children. In W. A. Collins (Ed.), *Minnesota symposia on child psychology* (Vol. 11, pp. 199–230). Hillsdale, NJ: Erlbaum.

Mischel, W., & Shoda, Y. (1995). A cognitive-affective system theory of personality: Reconceptualizing situations, dispositions, dynamics, and invariance in personality structure. *Psychological Review, 102*, 246–268.

Mischel, W., & Shoda, Y. (1999). Integrating dispositions and processing dynamics within a unified theory of personality: The Cognitive Affective Personality System (CAPS). In L. A. Pervin & O. John (Eds.), *Handbook of personality: Theory and research* (pp. 197–218). New York: Guilford.

Mischel, W., Shoda, Y., & Rodriguez, M. L. (1989). Delay of gratification in children. *Science, 244,* 933–938.

Molden, D. C., & Dweck, C. S. (2006). Finding "meaning" In psychology: A lay theories approach to self-regulation, social perception, and social development. *American Psychologist, 61*, 192–203.

Molden, D. C., & Higgins, E. T. (2008). How preferences for eager versus vigilant judgment strategies affect self-serving conclusions. *Journal of Experimental Social Psychology, 44*, 1219–1228.

Monga, A., & Zhu, R. (2005). Buyers versus sellers: How they differ in their responses to framed outcomes. *Journal of Consumer Psychology, 15*, 325–333.

Monteith, M. J. (1993). Self-regulation of prejudiced responses: Implications for progress in prejudice reduction efforts. *Journal of Personality and Social Psychology, 65,* 469–485.

Monteith, M. J., Ashburn-Nardo, L., Voils, C. I., & Czopp, A. M. (2002). Putting the breaks on prejudice: On the development and operation of cues for control. *Journal of Personality and Social Psychology, 83*, 1029–1050.

Moretti, M. M., & Higgins, E. T. (1999a). Internal representations of others in self-regulation: A new look at a classic issue. *Social Cognition, 17*, 186–208.

Moretti, M. M., & Higgins, E. T. (1999b). Own versus other standpoints in self-regulation: Developmental antecedents and functional consequences. *Review of General Psychology, 3*, 188–223.

Morris, M. W., Menon, T., & Ames, D. R. (2001). Culturally conferred conceptions of agency: A key to social perception of persons, groups, and other actors. *Personality and Social Psychology Review, 5*, 169–182.

Morris, W., & Reilly, N. (1987). Toward the self-regulation of mood: Theory and research. *Motivation and Emotion, 11*, 215–249.

Moskowitz, G. B. (1993). Individual differences in social categorization: The influence of personal need for structure on spontaneous trait inferences. *Journal of Personality and Social Psychology, 65*, 132–142.

Moskowitz, G. B., Gollwitzer, P. M., Wasel, W., & Schaal, B. (1999). Preconscious control of stereotype activation through chronic egalitarian goals. *Journal of Personality and Social Psychology, 77,* 167–184.

Moskowitz, G. B., & Grant, H. (2009). *The psychology of goals.* New York: Guilford Press.

Mowrer, O. H. (1960). *Learning theory and behavior.* New York: John Wiley.

Murray, H. A. (1938). *Exploration in personality.* New York: Oxford University Press.

Neale, M. A., & Bazerman, M. H. (1992). Negotiator cognition and rationality: A behavioral decision theory perspective. *Organizational Behavior and Human Decision Processes, 51,* 157–175.

Neale, M. A., Huber, V. L., & Northcraft, G. B. (1987). The framing of negotiations: Contextual versus task frames. *Organizational Behavior and Human Decision Processes, 39,* 228–241.

Nelson, K. (2005). Emerging levels of consciousness in early human development. In H. S. Terrace & J. Metcalfe (Eds.), *The missing link in cognition: Origins of self-reflective consciousness* (pp. 116–141). Oxford: Oxford University Press.

Neuberg, S. L., & Fiske, S. T. (1987). Motivational influences on impression formation: Outcome dependency, accuracy-driven attention, and individuating processes. *Journal of Personality and Social Psychology, 53,* 431–444.

Neufeld, R. W. J., & Thomas, P. (1977). Effects of perceived efficacy of a prophylactic controlling mechanism on self-control under pain stimulation. *Canadian Journal of Behavioral Science, 9,* 224–232.

Neugarten, B. L., Havighurst, R. J., & Tobin, S. S. (1961). The measurement of life satisfaction. *Journal of Gerontology, 16,* 134–143.

Newcomb, T. M. (1961). *The acquaintance process.* New York: Holt, Rinehart, & Winston.

Newcomb, T. M. (1968). Introduction. In R. P. Abelson, E. Aronson, W. J. McGuire, T. M. Newcomb, M. J. Rosenberg, & P. H. Tannenbaum (Eds.), *Theories of cognitive consistency: A sourcebook* (pp. xv–xvii). Chicago: Rand McNally.

Nicholls, J. G. (1984). Achievement motivation: Conceptions of ability, subjective experience, task choice, and performance. *Psychological Review, 91,* 328–346.

Nisbett, R. E. (2003). *The geography of thought: How Asians and Westerners think differently . . . and why.* New York: Free Press.

Nisbett, R. E., & Ross, L. D. (1980). *Human inference: Strategies and shortcomings of informal judgment.* Century Series in Psychology. Englewood Cliffs, NJ: Prentice-Hall.

Nolen-Hoeksema, S. (2000). The role of rumination in depressive disorders and mixed anxiety/depressive symptoms. *Journal of Abnormal Psychology, 109,* 504–511.

Norem, J. K., & Cantor, N. (1986a). Anticipatory and post hoc cushioning strategies: Optimism and defensive pessimism in "risky" situations. *Cognitive Therapy and Research, 10,* 347–362.

Norem, J. K., & Cantor, N. (1986b). Defensive pessimism: Harnessing anxiety as motivation. *Journal of Personality and Social Psychology, 51,* 1208–1217.

Norem, J. K., & Illingworth, K. S. S. (1993). Strategy-dependent effects of reflecting on self and tasks: Some implications of optimism and defensive pessimism. *Journal of Personality and Social Psychology, 65,* 822–835.

Novemsky, N., Dhar, R., Schwarz, N., & Simonson, I. (in press). Preference fluency in consumer choice. *Journal of Marketing Research*.

Nozick, R. (1974). *Anarchy, state, and utopia*. New York: Basic Books.

Ochsner, K. N., & Gross, J. J. (2004). Thinking makes it so: A social cognitive neuroscience approach to emotion regulation. In R. F. Baumeister & K. D. Vohs (Eds.), *Handbook of self-regulation: Research, theory, and applications* (pp. 229–255). New York: Guilford Press.

Oettingen, G. (1996). Positive fantasy and motivation. In P. M. Gollwitzer & J. A. Bargh (Eds.), *The psychology of action: Linking cognition and motivation to behavior* (pp. 236–259). New York: Guilford.

Oettingen, G., & Mayer, D. (2002). The motivating function of thinking about the future: Expectations versus fantasies. *Journal of Personality and Social Psychology, 83*, 1198–1212.

Oettingen, G., Pak, H., & Schnetter, K. (2001). Self-regulation of goal setting: Turning free fantasies about the future into binding goals. *Journal of Personality and Social Psychology, 80*, 736–753.

Olds, J., & Milner, P. (1954). Positive reinforcement produced by electrical stimulation of septal area and other regions of rat brain. *Journal of Comparative and Physiological Psychology. 47*, 419–27.

Olson, M. A., & Fazio, R. H. (2004). Reducing the influence of extra-personal associations on the Implicit Association Test: Personalizing the IAT. *Journal of Personality and Social Psychology, 86*, 653–667.

Ortony, A., Clore, G. L., & Collins, A. (1988). *The cognitive structure of emotions*. New York: Cambridge University Press.

Orwell, G. (1949). *1984*. New York: Harcourt Brace Jovanovich.

Osgood, C. E., Suci, G. J., & Tannenbaum, P. H. (1957). *The measurement of meaning*. Urbana, IL: University of Illinois Press.

Osgood, C. E., & Tannenbaum, P. H. (1955). The principle of congruity in the prediction of attitude change. *Psychological Review, 62*, 42–55.

Ostroff, C. (2007). General methodological and design issues. In C. Ostroff & T. A. Judge (Eds.), *Perspectives on organizational fit* (pp. 352–356). Hillsdale, NJ: Erlbaum.

Ostrom, T. M. (1969). The relationship between the affective, behavioral and cognitive components of attitudes. *Journal of Experimental Social Psychology, 5*, 12–30.

Oxford English Dictionary, The Compact Edition, Volumes I & II (1971). Oxford: Oxford University Press.

Paine, J. W. (2009). *Follower engagement, commitment, and favor toward change: Examining the role of regulatory fit*. Unpublished doctoral dissertation, Columbia University.

Parkinson, B., & Totterdell, P. (1999). Classifying affect-regulation strategies. *Cognition and Emotion, 13*, 277–303.

Parkinson, B., Totterdell, P., Briner, R. B., & Reynolds, S. (1996). *Changing moods: The psychology of mood and mood regulation*. London: Longman.

Parsons, T. (1964). *Social structure and personality*. London: Free Press.

Pavot, W., Diener, E., & Fujita, F. (1990). Extraversion and happiness. *Personality and Individual Differences, 11*, 1299–1306.

Peabody, D. (1985). *National characteristics*. New York: Cambridge University Press.

Peake, P. K., Hebl, M., & Mischel, W. (2002). Strategic attention deployment for delay of gratification in working and waiting situations. *Developmental Psychology, 38,* 313–326.

Penley, J. A., Tomaka, J., & Wiebe, J. S. (2002). The association of coping to physical and psychological health outcomes: A meta-analytic review. *Journal of Behavioral Medicine, 25,* 551–603.

Pennebaker, J. W., Colder, M., & Sharp, L. K. (1990). Accelerating the coping process. *Journal of Personality and Social Psychology, 58,* 528–537.

Pennebaker, J. W., & Francis, M. E. (1996). Cognitive, emotional, and language processes in disclosure: Physical health and adjustment. *Cognition and Emotion, 10,* 601–626.

Pennebaker, J. W., Mayne, T. J., & Francis, M. E. (1997). Linguistic predictors of adaptive bereavement. *Journal of Personality and Social Psychology, 72,* 863–871.

Pennington, G. I., & Roese, N. J. (2003). Regulatory focus and temporal distance. *Journal of Experimental Social Psychology, 39,* 563–576.

Pepitone, A., McCauley, C., & Hammond, P. (1967). Change in attractiveness of forbidden toys as a function of severity of threat. *Journal of Experimental Social Psychology, 3,* 221–229.

Perky, C. W. (1910). An experimental study of imagination. *American Journal of Psychology, 21,* 422–452.

Perner, J., Ruffman, T., & Leekam, S. R. (1994). Theory of mind is contagious: You catch it from your sibs. *Child Development, 65,* 1228–1238.

Pervin, L. A. (Ed.) (1989). *Goal concepts in personality and social psychology.* Hillsdale, NJ: Erlbaum.

Pervin, L. A. (2001). A dynamic systems approach to personality. *European Psychologist, 6,* 172–176.

Peterson, C., & Seligman, M. E. P. (2004). *Character Strengths and Virtues.* Oxford: Oxford University Press.

Petty, R. E., & Wegener, D. T. (1998). Attitude change: Multiple roles for persuasion variables. In D. T. Gilbert, S. T. Fiske, & G. Lindzey (Eds.), *The handbook of social psychology* (4th ed., pp. 323–390). New York: McGraw Hill.

Pham, M., & Avnet, T. (2004). Ideals and oughts and the reliance on affect versus substance in persuasion. *Journal of Consumer Research, 30,* 503–518.

Piaget, J. (1951). *Play, dreams and imitation in childhood.* New York: Norton.

Piaget, J. (1952). *The origins of intelligence in children.* New York: International University Press.

Piaget, J. (1965). *The moral judgment of the child.* New York: Free Press (Original translation published 1932)

Piaget, J. (1970). Piaget's theory. In P. H. Mussen (Ed.), *Carmichael's manual of child psychology* (Vol. 1, 3rd ed., pp. 703–732). New York: Wiley.

Pierro, A., Cicero. L., & Higgins, E. T. (in press). Followers' satisfaction from working with group-prototypic leaders: Promotion focus as moderator. *Journal of Experimental Social Psychology.*

Pierro, A., Kruglanski, A. W., & Higgins, E. T. (2006). Progress takes work: Effects of the locomotion dimension on job involvement, effort investment, and task performance in organizations. *Journal of Applied Social Psychology, 36,* 1723–1743.

Pierro, A., Kruglanski, A. W., & Higgins, E. T. (2011). *How complementary regulatory modes in teams can enhance individual performance.* Unpublished manuscript, University of Rome 'La Sapienza'.

Pierro, A., Leder, S., Mannetti, L., Higgins, E. T., Kruglanski, A. W., & Aiello, A. (2008). Regulatory mode effects on counterfactual thinking and regret. *Journal of Experimental Social Psychology, 44,* 321–329.

Pierro, A., Presaghi, F., Higgins, E. T., & Kruglanski, A. W. (2009). Regulatory mode preferences for autonomy-supporting versus controlling instructional styles. *British Journal of Educational Psychology, 79,* 599-615.

Pittman, T. S., & D'Agostino, P. R. (1989). Motivation and cognition: Control deprivation and the nature of subsequent information processing. *Journal of Experimental Social Psychology, 25,* 465-480.

Pittman, T. S., & Pittman, N. L. (1980). Deprivation of control and the attribution process. *Journal of Personality and Social Psychology, 39,* 377-389.

Pittman, T. S., & Zeigler, K. R. (2007). Basic human needs. In A. W. Kruglanski & E. T. Higgins (Eds.), *Social psychology: Handbook of basic principles* (2nd ed., pp. 473–489). New York: Guilford.

Povinelli, D. J. (2000). *Folk physics for apes: The chimpanzee's theory of how the world works.* Oxford: Oxford University Press.

Powers, W. T. (1973) *Behavior: The control of perception.* Chicago: Aldine.

Plaks, J. E., & Higgins, E. T. (2000). The pragmatic use of stereotypes in teamwork: Motivational tuning to inferred partner/situation fit. *Journal of Personality and Social Psychology, 79,* 962–974.

Plessner, H., Unkelbach, C., Memmert, D., Baltes, A., & Kolb, A. (2009). Regulatory fit as a determinant of sport performance: How to succeed in a soccer penalty-shooting. *Psychology of Sport and Exercise, 10,* 108–115.

Powers, W. T. (1973). *Behavior: The control of perception.* Chicago: Aldine.

Putnam, R. D. (2000). *Bowling alone: The collapse and revival of American community.* New York: Simon and Schuster.

Pyszczynski, T., & Greenberg, J. (1987). Toward an integration of cognitive and motivational perspectives on social inference: A biased hypothesis testing model. In L. Berokowitz (Ed.) *Advances in experimental social psychology* (Vol. 20, pp. 297–340). New York: Academic Press.

Pyszczynski, T. A., Greenberg, J., & Solomon, S. (1997). Why do we need what we need?: A terror management perspective on the roots of human social motivation. *Psychological Inquiry, 8,* 1–20.

Redelmeier, D., & Kahneman, D. (1996). Patients' memories of painful medical treatments: Real-time and retrospective evaluations of two minimally invasive procedures. *Pain, 116,* 3–8.

Rescorla, R. A., & Solomon, R. L. (1967). Two-process learning theory: Relationships between Pavlovian conditioning and instrumental learning. *Psychological Review, 74,* 151–182.

Rescorla, R. A., & Wagner, A. R. (1972). A theory of Pavlovian conditioning: Variations in the effectiveness of reinforcement and nonreinforcement. In A. H. Black & W. F. Prokasy (Eds.), *Classical conditioning II: Current research and theory* (pp. 64–99). New York: Appleton-Century-Crofts.

Richards, J. M., & Gross, J. J. (2000). Emotion regulation and memory: The cognitive costs of keeping one's cool. *Journal of Personality and Social Psychology, 79,* 410–424.

Richeson, J. A., & Ambady, N. (2003). Effects of situational power on automatic racial prejudice. *Journal of Experimental Social Psychology, 39,* 177–183.

Robinson, M. D. (2004). Personality as performance: Categorization tendencies and their correlates. *Current Directions in Psychological Science, 13,* 127–129.

Robinson, M. D., Vargas, P. T., Tamir, M., & Solberg, E. C. (2004). Using and being used by categories: The case of negative evaluations and daily well-being. *Psychological Science, 15,* 521–526.

Robinson, T. E., & Berridge, K. C. (2003). Addiction. *Annual Review of Psychology, 54,* 25–53.

Roese, N. J. (1997). Counterfactual thinking. *Psychological Bulletin, 121,* 133–148.

Roese, N. J., Hur, T., & Pennington, G. L. (1999). Counterfactual thinking and regulatory focus: Implications for action versus inaction and sufficiency versus necessity. *Journal of Personality and Social Psychology, 77,* 1109–1120.

Roese, N. J., & Olson, J. M. (1993). The structure of counterfactual thought. *Personality and Social Psychology Bulletin, 19,* 312–319.

Roese, N. J., Pennington, G. L., Coleman, J., Janicki, M., & Kenrick, D. T. (2006). Sex differences in regret: All for love or some for lust? *Personality and Social Psychology Bulletin, 32,* 770–780.

Rogers, C. R. (1951). *Client-centered therapy: Its current practice, implications, and theory.* Boston: Houghton Mifflin.

Rogers, C. R. (1961). *On becoming a person.* Boston: Houghton Mifflin Company.

Rogers, R. W. (1975). A protection motivation theory of fear appeals and attitude change. *Journal of Psychology, 91,* 93–114.

Rokeach, M. (1973). *The nature of human values.* New York: Free Press.

Rokeach, M. (1979). Change and stability in American value systems, 1968–1971. In M. Rokeach (Ed.), *Understanding human values: Individual and societal.* New York: The Free Press.

Rokeach, M. (1980). Some unresolved issues in theories of beliefs, attitudes, and values. In H. E. Howe, Jr. & M. M. Page (Eds.), *1979 Nebraska symposium on motivation.* Lincoln: University of Nebraska Press.

Romero-Canyas, R., & Downey, G. (2005). Rejection sensitivity as a predictor of affective and behavioral responses to interpersonal stress: A defensive motivational system. In K. D. Williams, J. P. Forgas, & W. von Hippel (Eds.), *The social outcast: Ostracism, social exclusion, rejection, and bullying.* (pp. 131–154). New York: Psychology Press.

Rorschach, H. (1951). *Psychodiagnostics: a diagnostic test based on perception* (5th ed. rev.). Oxford, England: Grune and Stratton. (Original printing 1921)

Roseman, I. J. (1984). Cognitive determinants of emotion: A structural theory. *Review of Personality and Social Psychology, 5,* 11–36.

Roseman, I. J., Wiest, C., & Swartz, T. S. (1994). Phenomenology, behaviors, and goals differentiate discrete emotions. *Journal of Personality and Social Psychology, 67,* 206–221.

Rosenberg, M. (1979). *Conceiving the self.* Malabar, FL: Robert E. Krieger.

Rosenberg, M. J. (1956). Cognitive structure and attitudinal affect. *Journal of Abnormal and Social Psychology, 53,* 367–372.

Rosenberg, M. J., & Abelson, R. P. (1960). An analysis of cognitive balancing. In M. J. Rosenberg, C. I. Hovland, W. J. McGuire, R. P. Abelson, & J. W. Brehm (Eds.), *Attitude organization and change: An analysis of consistency among attitude components* (pp. 1–14). New Haven, CT: Yale University Press.

Rosenberg, M. J., & Hovland, C. I. (1960). Cognitive, affective, and behavioral components of attitudes. In M. J. Rosenberg, C. I. Hovland, W. J. McGuire, R. P. Abeison, & J. W. Brehm, *Attitude organization and change: An analysis of consistency among attitude components* (pp. 1–14). New Haven, CT: Yale University Press.

Ross, L. (1977). The intuitive psychologist and his shortcomings: Distortions in the attribution process. In L. Berkowitz (Ed.), *Advances in Experimental Social Psychology* (Vol. 10, pp. 173–220). New York: Academic Press.

Ross, L., Greene, D. & House, P. (1977). The "false consensus effect": An egocentric bias in social perception and attribution processes. *Journal of Experimental Social Psychology, 13,* 279–301.

Ross, L., & Ward, A. (1995). Psychological barriers to dispute resolution. In M. P. Zanna (Ed.), *Advances in experimental social psychology* (Vol. 27, pp. 255–304). San Diego, CA: Academic Press.

Ross, M. (1975). Salience of reward and intrinsic motivation. *Journal of Personality and Social Psychology, 32,* 245–254.

Ross, M., & Olson, J. M. (1981). An expectancy-attribution model of the effects of placebos. *Psychological Review, 88,* 408–437.

Ross, M., & Sicoly, F. (1979). Egocentric biases in availability and attribution. *Journal of Personality and Social Psychology, 37,* 322–336.

Rothbaum, F., Weisz, J. R., & Snyder, S. S. (1982). Changing the world and changing the self: A two-process model of perceived control. *Journal of Personality and Social Psychology, 42,* 5–37.

Rotter, J. B. (1954). *Social learning and clinical psychology.* Englewood Cliffs, NJ: Prentice-Hall.

Rotter, J. B. (1966). Generalized expectancies for internal versus external control of reinforcement. *Psychological Monographs, 80* (1, Whole No. 609).

Roysamb, E., Harris, J. R., Magnus, P., Vitterso, J., & Tambs, K. (2002). Subjective well-being: Sex-specific effects of genetic and environmental factors. *Personality and Individual Differences, 32,* 211–223.

Rozin, P. (2000). *Human food intake and choice: Biological, psychological and cultural perspectives.* Paper presented at the International Symposium: Food selection from genes to culture. Danone Institute. Paris, France.

Ruble, D. N. (1983). The development of social comparison processes and their role in achievement-related self-socialization. In E. T. Higgins, D. N. Ruble, & W. W. Hartup (Eds.), *Social cognition and social development: A socio-cultural perspective* (pp. 134–157). New York: Cambridge University Press.

Russell, J. A. (1980). A circumplex model of affect. *Journal of Personality and Social Psychology, 39,* 1161–1178.

Ryan, R. M., & Deci, E. L. (2001). On happiness and human potentials: A review of research on hedonic and eudaimonic well-being. *Annual Review of Psychology, 52*, 141–166.

Ryff, C. D. (2008). Challenges and opportunities at the interface of aging, personality, and well-being. In O. P. John, R. W. Robins, & L. A. Pervin (Eds.), *Handbook of personality: Theory and research* (3rd ed., pp. 399–418). New York: Guilford Press.

Salancik, G. R., & Conway, M. (1975). Attitude inferences from salient and relevant cognitive content about behavior. *Journal of Personality and Social Psychology, 32*, 829–840.

Salovey, P., Hsee, C. K., & Mayer, J. D. (1993). Emotional intelligence and the self-regulation of affect. In D. M. Wegner & J. W. Pennebaker (Eds.), *Handbook of mental control.* Century psychology series (pp. 258–277). Upper Saddle River, NJ: Prentice-Hall.

Sanderson, W. C., Rapee, R. M., & Barlow, D. H. (1989). The influence of an illusion of control on panic attacks induced via inhalation of 5.5% carbon-dioxide-enriched air. *Archives of General Psychiatry, 46*, 157–162.

Sandler, J. (1960). On the concept of the superego. *Psychoanalytic Study of the Child, 18*, 139–158.

Sanna, L. J. (1996). Defensive pessimism, optimism, and simulating alternatives: Some ups and downs of prefactual and counterfactual thinking. *Journal of Personality and Social Psychology, 71*, 1020–1036.

Sansone, C., & Harackiewicz, J. (1996). "I don't feel like it": The function of interest in self-regulation. In L. L. Martin & A. Tesser (Eds.), *Striving and feeling: Interactions among goals, affect, and self-regulation* (pp. 203–228). Mahwah, NJ: Erlbaum.

Sansone, C., & Thoman, D. B. (2005). Interest as the missing motivator in self-regulation. *European Psychologist, 10*, 175–186.

Sansone, C., Weir, C., Harpster, L., & Morgan, C. (1992). Once a boring task always a boring task? Interest as a self-regulatory mechanism. *Journal of Personality and Social Psychology, 63*, 379–390.

Sarbin, T. R. (1952). A preface to a psychological analysis of the self. *Psychological Review, 59*, 11–22.

Schachter, S., & Singer, J. E. (1962). Cognitive, social and physiological determinants of emotional state. *Psychological Review, 69*, 379–399.

Schafer, R. (1968). *Aspects of internalization.* New York: International Universities Press.

Schaufeli, W. B., Bakker, A. B., & Salanova, M. (2006). The measurement of work engagement with a short questionnaire: A cross-national study. *Educational and Psychological Measurement, 66*, 701–716.

Scherer, K. R. (1988). Criteria for emotion-antecedent appraisal: A review. In V. Hamilton, G. H. Bower, & N. H. Frijda (Eds.), *Cognitive perspectives on emotion and motivation* (pp. 89–126). Norwell, MA: Kluwer Academic.

Scherer, K. R., Walbott, H. G., & Summerfield, A. B. (1986). *Experiencing emotions: A cross-cultural study.* Cambridge: Cambridge University Press.

Schkade, D. A., & Kahneman, D. (1998). Does living in California make people happy? A focusing illusion in judgments of life satisfaction. *Psychological Science, 9*, 340–346.

Schlosberg, H. (1952). The description of facial expressions in terms of two dimensions. *Journal of Experimental Psychology, 44,* 229–237.

Scholer, A. A. (2009). *Motivated to change: Regulatory mode dynamics in goal commitment.* Unpublished doctoral dissertation, Columbia University.

Scholer, A. A., Grant, H., Baer, A., Bolger, N., & Higgins, E. T. (2009). *Coping style and regulatory fit: Emotional ups and downs in daily life.* Unpublished manuscript, Columbia University.

Scholer, A. A., & Higgins, E. T. (2008). Distinguishing levels of approach and avoidance: An analysis using regulatory focus theory. In A.J. Elliot (Ed.), *Handbook of approach and avoidance motivation* (pp. 489-503). Hillsdale, NJ: Lawrence Erlbaum.

Scholer, A. A., & Higgins, E. T. (2009). *Motivated to change: Regulatory mode dynamics in goal-setting.* Unpublished manuscript.

Scholer, A. A., & Higgins, E. T. (2010). Regulatory focus in a demanding world. In R. Hoyle (Ed.), *Handbook of personality and self-regulation* (pp. 291-314). Boston: Wiley-Blackwell.

Scholer, A. A., & Higgins, E. T. (2011). Promotion and prevention systems: Regulatory focus dynamics within self-regulatory hierarchies. In K. D. Vohs & R. F. Baumeister (Eds.), *Handbook of self-regulation: Research, theory, and applications* (2nd edition, pp. 143-161). New York: Guilford Press.

Scholer, A. A., & Higgins, E. T. (in press). Conflict and control at different levels of self-regulation. In R. Hassin & Y. Trope (Eds.), *Handbook of self-control.* New York: Guilford.

Scholer, A. A., Stroessner, S. J., & Higgins, E. T. (2008). Responding to negativity: How a risky tactic can serve a vigilant strategy. *Journal of Experimental Social Psychology, 44,* 767–774.

Scholer, A. A., Zou, X., Fujita, K., Stroessner, S. J., & Higgins, E. T. (in press). When risk-seeking becomes a motivational necessity. *Journal of Personality and Social Psychology, 99,* 215–231.

Schooler, J. W., Gerhard, D., & Loftus, E. F. (1986). Qualities of the unreal. *Journal of Experimental Psychology: Learning, Memory, and Cognition, 12,* 171–181.

Schunk, D. H. (1981). Modeling and attributional effects on children's achievement: A self-efficacy analysis. *Journal of Educational Psychology, 73,* 93–105.

Schwartz, S. H. (1992). Universals in the content and structure of values: Theoretical advances and empirical tests in 20 countries. In M. P. Zanna (Ed.), *Advances in experimental social psychology* (Vol. 25, pp. 1–65). New York: Academic Press.

Schwartz, S. H., & Bilsky, W. (1987). Toward a universal structure of human values. *Journal of Personality and Social Psychology, 53,* 550–562.

Schwarz, N. (1990). Feelings as information: Informational and motivational functions of affective states. In E. T. Higgins & R. M. Sorrentino (Eds.), *Handbook of motivation and cognition: Foundations of social behavior* (Vol. 2, pp. 527–561). New York: Guilford.

Schwarz, N., & Bohner, G. (2001). The construction of attitudes. In A. Tesser & N. Schwarz (Ed.), *Blackwell handbook of social psychology: Intraindividual processes* (pp. 436–457). Malden, MA: Blackwell.

Schwarz, N., & Clore, G. L. (1983). Mood, misattribution, and judgments of well-being: Informative and directive functions of affective states. *Journal of Personality and Social Psychology, 45,* 513–523.

Schwarz, N., & Clore, G. L. (1988). How do I feel about it? The informative function of affective states. In K. Fiedler & J. Forgas (Eds.), *Affect, cognition and social behavior* (pp. 44–62). Toronto: C. J. Hogrefe.

Seeman, T. E. (1996). Social ties and health: The benefits of social integration. *Annals of Epidemiology, 6*, 442–451.

Segal, S. J. (1970). Imagery and reality: Can they be distinguished? In W. Keup (Ed.), *Origin and mechanisms of hallucinations*. New York: Plenum Press.

Sehnert, S., Franks, B., & Higgins, E. T. (2009). *How scarcity situations can intensify negative reactions: The role of engagement*. Unpublished manuscript, Columbia University.

Seibt, B., & Förster, J. (2004). Stereotype threat and performance: How self-stereotypes influence processing by inducing regulatory foci. *Journal of Personality and Social Psychology, 87*, 38–56.

Seligman, C., Olson, J. M., & Zanna, M. P. (1996). *The psychology of values: The Ontario Symposium* (Vol. 8). Mahwah, NJ: Lawrence Erlbaum Associates.

Seligman, M. E. P. (1975). *Helplessness: On depression, development, and death*. San Francisco: Freeman.

Seligman, M. E. P. (1990). *Learned optimism*. New York: Knopf.

Seligman, M. E. P. (2002). *Authentic happiness: Using the new positive psychology to realize your potential for lasting fulfillment*. New York: Free Press.

Shah, J. (2003). The motivational looking glass: How significant others implicitly affect goal appraisals. *Journal of Personality and Social Psychology, 85*, 424–439.

Shah, J., & Higgins, E. T. (1997). Expectancy × value effects: Regulatory focus as a determinant of magnitude *and* direction. *Journal of Personality and Social Psychology, 73*, 447–458.

Shah, J., Higgins, E. T., & Friedman, R. (1998). Performance incentives and means: How regulatory focus influences goal attainment. *Journal of Personality and Social Psychology, 74*, 285–293.

Shah, J. Y., Friedman, R., & Kruglanski, A. W. (2002). Forgetting all else: On the antecedents and consequences of goal shielding. *Journal of Personality and Social Psychology, 83*, 1261–1280.

Shah, J. Y., & Kruglanski, A.W. (2000). Aspects of goal networks: Implications for self-regulation. In M. Boekaerts & P.R. Pintrich (Eds.), *Handbook of self-regulation* (pp. 85–110). San Diego: Academic Press.

Shah, J. Y., & Kruglanski, A.W. (2002). Priming against your will: How accessible alternatives affect goal pursuit. *Journal of Experimental Social Psychology, 83*, 368–383.

Shantz, C. U. (1983). Social cognition. In J. H. Flavell & E. M. Markman (Eds.), *Cognitive development*. Volume 3 in P. H. Mussen (Ed.), *Carmichael's manual of child psychology* (4th ed., pp. 495–555). New York: Wiley.

Shaver, P. (1976). Questions concerning fear of success and its conceptual relatives. *Sex Roles, 2*, 305–319.

Sheeran, P., Conner, M., & Norman, P. (2001). Can the theory of planned behavior explain patterns of health behavior change? *Health Psychology, 20*, 12–19.

Sheldon, K. M., & Elliot, A. J. (1999). Goal striving, need satisfaction, and longitudinal well-being: The self-concordance model. *Journal of Personality and Social Psychology, 76*, 482–497.

Sherif, M. (1935). A study of some social factors in perception. *Archives of Psychology*, No. 187.

Sherif, M. (1936). *The psychology of social norms.* New York: Harper & Brothers.

Sherif, M., & Hovland, C. I. (1961). *Social judgment: Assimilation and contrast effects in communication.* New Haven, CT: Yale University Press.

Sherman, S. J., Presson, C. C., Chassin, L., Rose J. S., & Koch, K. (2003). Implicit and explicit attitudes toward cigarette smoking: The effects of context and motivation. *Journal of Social and Clinical Psychology, 22*, 13–39.

Shoda, Y., Mischel, W., & Peake (1990). Predicting adolescent cognitive and self-regulatory competencies from preschool delay of gratification: Identifying diagnostic conditions. *Developmental Psychology, 26*, 978–986.

Shoda, Y., Mischel, W., & Wright, J. C. (1994). Intra-individual stability in the organization and patterning of behavior: Incorporating psychological situations into the idiographic analysis of personality. *Journal of Personality and Social Psychology, 67*, 674–687.

Showers, C. (1992). The motivational and emotional consequences of considering positive or negative possibilities for an upcoming event. *Journal of Personality and Social Psychology, 63*, 474–484.

Shweder, R. A. (1991). Rethinking culture and personality theory. In R. A. Shweder (Ed.), *Thinking through cultures: Expeditions in cultural psychology.* Cambridge, MA: Harvard University Press.

Shweder, R. A., & Bourne, L. (1984). Does the concept of the person vary cross-culturally? In R. A. Shweder & R. A. LeVine (Eds.), *Culture theory: Essays on mind, self, and emotion* (pp. 158–199). Cambridge, England: Cambridge University Press.

Shweder, R. A., & Sullivan, M. A. (1993). Cultural psychology: Who needs it? *Annual Review of Psychology, 44*, 497–523.

Simon, H. A. (1967). Motivational and emotional controls of cognition. *Psychological Review, 74*, 29–39.

Simpson, J. A. (2007). Foundations of interpersonal trust. In A. W. Kruglanski & E. T. Higgins (Eds.), *Social psychology: Handbook of basic principles* (2nd ed., pp. 587–607). New York: Guilford.

Skinner, B. F. (1953). *Science and human behavior.* New York: Macmillan.

Skinner, B. F. (1957). *Verbal behavior.* New York: Appleton.

Smith, A. (1994). *The wealth of nations.* New York: Random House. (Original work published in 1776)

Smith, A. (1997). *The theory of moral sentiments.* Washington, D. C.: Regnery Publishing. (Original work published in 1759)

Smith, C. A., & Ellsworth, P. C. (1985). Patterns of cognitive appraisal in emotion. *Journal of Personality and Social Psychology, 48*, 813–838.

Smith, E. R., & DeCoster, J. (2000). Dual-process models in social and cognitive psychology: Conceptual integration and links to underlying memory systems. *Personality and Social Psychology Review, 4*, 108–131.

Smith, M. B. (1947). The personal setting of public opinions: A study of attitudes toward Russia. *Public Opinion Quarterly, 11*, 507–523.

Smith, M. B., Bruner, J. S., & White, R. W. (1956). *Opinions and personality.* New York: Wiley.

Snyder, M. L., & Wicklund, R. A. (1981). Attribute ambiguity. In J. H. Harvey, W. Ickes, & R. F. Kidd (Eds.), *New directions in attribution research* (Vol. 3, pp. 199–225). Hillsdale, NJ: Lawrence Erlbaum Associates.

Snygg, D., & Combs, A. W. (1949). *Individual behavior*. New York: Harper & Row.

Sorrentino, R. M., & Higgins, E. T. (1986). Motivation and cognition: Warming up to synergism. In R. M. Sorrentino & E. T. Higgins (Eds.), *Handbook of motivation and cognition: Foundations of social behavior* (pp. 3–19). New York: Guilford.

Sorrentino, R. M., & Roney, C. J. R. (2000). *The uncertain mind: Individual differences in facing the unknown*. Philadelphia, PA: Psychology Press.

Sorrentino, R. M., & Short, J. C. (1986). Uncertainty orientation, motivation, and cognition. In R. M. Sorrentino & E. T. Higgins (Eds.), *Handbook of motivation and cognition: Foundations of social behavior* (Vol. 1, pp. 379–403). New York: Guilford Press.

Sorrentino, R. M., Short, J. C., & Raynor, J. O. (1984). Uncertainty orientation: Implications for affective and cognitive views of achievement behavior. *Journal of Personality and Social Psychology, 46*, 189–206.

Spence, K. W. (1958). A theory of emotionality based drive (D) and its relation to performance in simple learning situations. *American Psychologist, 13*, 131–141.

Spiegel, S., Grant-Pillow, H., & Higgins, E. T. (2004). How regulatory fit enhances motivational strength during goal pursuit. *European Journal of Social Psychology, 34*, 39–54.

Spinoza, B. de (1986). *Ethics and on the correction of the understanding* (A. Boyle, trans.). London: Dent. (Original publication, 1677).

Spiro, R. J. (1977). Remembering information from text: The state of the "schema" approach. In R. C. Anderson, R. J. Spiro, & W. E. Montague (Eds.), *Schooling and the acquisition of knowledge*. Hillsdale, NJ: Erlbaum.

Spruyt, H. (1994). *The sovereign state and its competitors*. Princeton, NJ: Princeton University Press.

Stasser, G., & Stewart, D. (1992). Discovery of hidden profiles by decision making groups: Solving a problem versus making a judgment. *Journal of Personality & Social Psychology, 63*, 426–434.

Steiner, I. D. (1972). *Group processes and productivity*. New York: Academic Press.

Stokes, J. P. (1985). The relation of social network and individual difference variables to loneliness. *Journal of Personality and Social Psychology, 48*, 981–990.

Storms, M. (1973). Videotape and the attribution process: Reversing actors and observers' points of view. *Journal of Personality and Social Psychology, 27*, 165–175.

Strack, F. (1992). The different routes to social judgments: Experiential versus informational strategies. In L. L. Martin & A. Tesser (Eds.), *The construction of social judgments* (pp. 249–275). Hillsdale, NJ: Erlbaum.

Strack, F., & Deutsch, R. (2004). Reflective and impulsive determinants of social behavior. *Personality and Social Psychology Review, 8*, 220–247.

Strauman, T. J. (1989). Self-discrepancies in clinical depression and social phobia: Cognitive structures that underlie emotional disorders? *Journal of Abnormal Psychology, 98*, 14–22.

Strauman, T. J., & Higgins, E. T. (1987). Automatic activation of self-discrepancies and emotional syndromes: When cognitive structures influence affect. *Journal of Personality and Social Psychology, 53*, 1004–1014.

Strauman, T. J., & Higgins, E. T. (1988). Self-discrepancies as predictors of vulnerability to distinct syndromes of chronic emotional distress. *Journal of Personality, 56,* 685–707.

Strauman, T. J., Vieth, A. Z., Merrill, K. A., Kolden, G. G., Woods, T. E., Klein, M. H., Papadakis, A. A., Schneider, K. L., & Kwapil, L. (2006). Self-system therapy as an intervention for self-regulatory dysfunction in depression: A randomized comparison with cognitive therapy. *Journal of Consulting and Clinical Psychology, 74,* 367–376.

Strube, M.J., Turner, C.W., Cerro, D., Stephens, J., & Hinchey, F. (1984). Interpersonal aggression and the Type A coronary-prone behavior pattern: A theoretical distinction and practical implications. *Journal of Personality and Social Psychology, 47,* 839–847.

Stryker, S., & Statham, A. (1985). Symbolic interaction and role theory. In G. Lindzey & E. Aronson (Eds.), *Handbook of social psychology* (Vol. I, pp. 311–378). New York: Random House.

Sullivan, H. S. (1953). *The interpersonal theory of psychiatry.* New York: Norton.

Suls, J., Martin, R., & Wheeler, L. (2002). Social comparison: Why, with whom, and with what effect. *Current Directions in Psychological Science, 11,* 159–163.

Swann, W. B., Jr. (1984). Quest for accuracy in person perception: A matter of pragmatics. *Psychological Review, 91,* 457–477.

Swann, W. B., Jr. (1987). Identity negotiation: Where two roads meet. *Journal of Personality and Social Psychology, 53,* 1038–1051.

Swann, W. B., Jr. (1990). To be adored or to be known? The interplay of self-enhancement and self-verification. In E. T. Higgins & R. M. Sorrentino (Eds.), *Handbook of motivation and cognition: Foundations of social behavior* (Vol. 2, pp. 408–448). New York: Guilford.

Swann, W. B., Hixon, J. G., Stein-Seroussi, A., & Gilbert, D. T. (1990). The fleeting gleam of praise: Cognitive processes underlying behavioral reactions to self-relevant feedback. *Journal of Personality and Social Psychology, 59,* 17–26.

Tajfel, H., & Turner, J. C. (1979). An integrative theory of intergroup conflict. In W. G. Austin & S. Worchel (Eds.), *The social psychology of intergroup relations* (pp. 33–47). Monterey, CA: Brooks/Cole.

Tangney, J. P., Baumeister, R. F., & Boone, A. L. (2004). High self-control predicts good adjustment, less pathology, better grades, and interpersonal success. *Journal of Personality, 72,* 271–322.

Tauer, J., & Harackiewicz, J. (1999). Winning isn't everything: Competition, achievement orientation, and intrinsic motivation. *Journal of Experimental Social Psychology, 35,* 209–238.

Taylor, A., & Higgins, E. T. (2002). *Regulatory mode and activity orientations.* Unpublished manuscript, Columbia University.

Taylor, S. E. (1991). *Positive illusions: Creative self-deception and the healthy mind.* New York: Basic Books.

Taylor, S. E., & Brown, J. D. (1988). Illusion and well-being: A social psychological perspective on mental health. *Psychological Bulletin, 103,* 193–210.

Teasdale, J. D. (1988). Cognitive vulnerability to persistent depression. *Cognition and Emotion, 2,* 247–274.

Terracciano, A., et al. (2005). National character does not reflect mean personality trait levels in 49 cultures. *Science, 310,* 96–100.

Terrace, H. S. (2005). Metacognition and the evolution of language. In H. S. Terrace & J. Metcalfe (Eds.), *The missing link in cognition: Origins of self-reflective consciousness* (pp. 84–115). Oxford: Oxford University Press.

Tesser, A. (1988). Toward a self-evaluation maintenance model of social behavior. In L. Berkowitz (Ed.), *Advances in experimental social psychology* (Vol. 21, pp. 181–227). San Diego, CA: Academic Press.

Tesser, A. (2000). On the confluence of self-esteem maintenance mechanisms. *Personality and Social Psychology Review, 4,* 290–299.

Tetlock, P. E. (1985). Accountability: A social check on the fundamental attribution error. *Social Psychology Quarterly, 48,* 227–236.

Tetlock, P. E., & Levi, A. (1982). Attribution bias: On the inconclusiveness of the cognition-motivation debate. *Journal of Experimental Social Psychology, 18,* 68–88.

Thaler, R. H. (1980). Toward a positive theory of consumer choice. *Journal of Economic Behavior and Organization, 1,* 39–60.

Thaler, R. H. (1985). Mental accounting and consumer choice. *Marketing Science, 4,* 199–214.

Thaler, R. H. (1999). Mental accounting matters. *Journal of Behavioral Decision Making, 12,* 183–206.

Thibaut, J. W., & Walker, L. (1975). *Procedural justice: A psychological analysis.* Hillsdale, NJ: Erlbaum.

Thomas, W. I., & Thomas, D. S. (1928). *The child in America.* New York: Knopf.

Thompson, E. P., Roman, R. J., Moskowitz, G. B., Chaiken, S., & Bargh, J. A. (1994). Accuracy motivation attenuates covert priming effects: The systematic reprocessing of social information. *Journal of Personality and Social Psychology, 66,* 474–489.

Thorndike, E. L. (1911). *Animal intelligence.* New York: Macmillan.

Thurstone, L. L. (1927). A law of comparative judgment. *Psychological Review, 34,* 273–286.

Tice, D. M., Bratlavsky, E., & Baumeister, R. F. (2001). Emotional distress regulation takes precedence over impulse control: If you feel bad, do it! *Journal of Personality and Social Psychology, 80,* 53–67.

Titchener, E. B. (1908). Attention as sensory clearness. In Lectures on the elementary psychology of feeling and attention (pp. 171–206). New York: Macmillan. (Reprinted in P. Bakan (Ed.) (1966). *Attention: An enduring problem in psychology.* Princeton, NJ: Van Nostrand.)

Titchener, E. B. (1910). *A text-book of psychology* (rev. ed.). New York: Macmillan.

Todorov, A., Goren, A., Trope, Y. (2007). Probability as a psychological distance: Construal and preferences. *Journal of Experimental Social Psychology, 43,* 473–482.

Tolman, E. C. (1932). *Purposive behavior in animals and men.* New York: Appleton-Century-Crofts.

Tolman, E. C. (1935). Psychology versus immediate experience, *Philosophical Science, 2,* 356–80.

Tolman, E. C. (1948). Cognitive maps in rats and men. *Psychological Review, 55,* 189–208.

Tolman, E. C. (1955). Principles of performance. *Psychological Review, 62,* 315–326.

Tolman, E. C., & Honzik, C. H. (1930). "Insight" in rats. University of California, *Publications in Psychology, 4,* 215–232.

Tomasello, M. (1999). *The cultural origins of human cognition.* Cambridge, MA: Harvard University Press.

Trawalter, S., & Richeson, J. A. (2006). Regulatory focus and executive function after interracial interactions. *Journal of Experimental Social Psychology, 42,* 406–412.

Triandis, H. C. (1989). The self and social behavior in differing cultural contexts. *Psychological Review, 93,* 506–520.

Triandis, H. C. (1996). The psychological measurement of cultural syndromes. *American Psychologist, 51,* 407–415.

Triandis, H. C., & Suh, E. M. (2002). Cultural influences on personality. *Annual Review of Psychology, 53,* 133–160.

Trivers, R. L. (1972). Parental investment and sexual selection. In B. Campbell (Ed.), *Sexual selection and the descent of man:1871–1971* (pp. 136–179). Chicago: Aldine.

Trope, Y. (1980). Self-assessment, self-enhancement and task preference. *Journal of Experimental Social Psychology, 16,* 116–129.

Trope, Y. (1986a). Identification and inferential processes in dispositional attribution. *Psychological Review, 93,* 239–257.

Trope, Y. (1986b). Self-enhancement and self-assessment in achievement behavior. In R.M. Sorrentino & E.T. Higgins (Eds.), *Handbook of motivation and cognition: Foundations of social behavior* (pp. 350–378). New York: Guilford Press.

Trope, Y., & Fishbach, A. (2000). Counteractive self-control in overcoming temptation. *Journal of Personality & Social Psychology, 79,* 493–506.

Trope, Y., & Higgins, E. T. (1993). The what, when, and how of dispositional inference: New answers and new questions. *Personality and Social Psychology Bulletin, 19,* 493–500.

Trope, Y., & Liberman, A. (1996). Social hypothesis testing: Cognitive and motivational mechanisms. In E. T. Higgins & A. W. Kruglanski (Eds.), *Social psychology: Handbook of basic principles* (pp. 239–270). New York: Guilford.

Trope, Y., & Liberman, N. (2003). Temporal construal. *Psychological Review, 110,* 403–421.

Tulving, E. (2005). Episodic memory and autonoesis. Uniquely human? In H. S. Terrace & J. Metcalfe (Eds.), *The missing link in cognition: Origins of self-reflective consciousness* (pp. 3–56). Oxford: Oxford University Press.

Turner, R. H. (1956). Role-taking, role standpoint, and reference-group behavior. *American Journal of Sociology, 61,* 316–328.

Tversky, A. (1972). Elimination by aspects: A theory of choice. *Psychological Review, 79,* 281–299.

Tversky, A., & Kahneman, D. (1974). Judgment under uncertainty: Heuristics and biases. *Science, 85,* 1124–1131.

Tykocinski, O. (1992). *A "pattern" approach to the tripartite model of attitudes.* Unpublished doctoral dissertation, New York University.

Tyler, T. R., & Blader, S. L. (2000). *Cooperation in groups: Procedural justice, social identity, and behavioral engagement.* Philadelphia: Taylor & Francis.

Tyler, T. R., & Blader, S. L. (2003). The group engagement model: Procedural justice, social identity, and cooperative behavior. *Personality and Social Psychology Review, 7,* 349–361.

Tyler, T. R., & Lind, E. A. (1992). A relational model of authority in groups. In M. P. Zanna (Ed.), *Advances in experimental social psychology* (Vol. 25, pp. 115–192). New York: Academic Press.

Tyler, T. R., & Smith, H. J. (1998). Social justice and social movements. In D. T. Gilbert, S. T. Fiske, S. T., & G. Lindzey (Eds.). *The handbook of social psychology* (4th ed., Vol. 2, pp. 595–629). New York: McGraw-Hill.

Uleman, J. S., Saribay, S. A., & Gonzalez, C. M. (2008). Spontaneous inferences, implicit impressions, and implicit theories. *Annual Review of Psychology*, 59, 329–360.

Vallacher, R. R., & Nowak, A. (2007). Dynamical social psychology: Finding order in the flow of human experience. In A. W. Kruglanski & E. T. Higgins (Eds.), *Social psychology: Handbook of basic principles* (2nd ed., pp. 734–758). New York: Guilford.

Van Dijk, D., & Kluger, A. N. (Sept 6, 2010). Task type as a moderator of positive/negative feedback effects on motivation and performance: A regulatory focus perspective. *Journal of Organizational Behavior*. [E-pub before print]

Van Poucke, D., & Buelens, M. (2002). Predicting the outcome of a two-party price negotiation: Contribution of reservation price, aspiration price and opening offer. *Journal of Economic Psychology, 23*, 67–76.

Vohs, K. D., & Baumeister, R. F. (2011). *Handbook of self-regulation: Research, theory, and applications*. New York: Guilford.

Vohs, K. D., Baumeister, R. F., Schmeichel, B. J., Twenge, J. M., Nelson, N. M., & Tice, D. M. (2008). Making choices impairs subsequent self-control: A limited resource account of decision making, self-regulation, and active initiative. *Journal of Personality and Social Psychology, 94*, 883–898.

Vroom, V. H. (1964). *Work and motivation*. New York: Wiley.

Wakslak, C. J., Trope, Y., Liberman, N., & Alony, R. (2006). Seeing the forest when entry is unlikely: Probability and the mental representation of events. *Journal of Experimental Psychology: General, 135*, 641–653.

Warren, R. E. (1972). Stimulus encoding and memory. *Journal of Experimental Psychology, 94*, 90–100.

Watson, D., Clark, L. A., & Tellegen, A. (1988). Development and validation of brief measures of positive and negative affect: The PANAS scales. *Journal of Personality and Social Psychology, 54*, 1063–1070.

Watson, D., & Tellegen, A. (1985). Toward a consensual structure of mood. *Psychological Bulletin, 98*, 219–235.

Weary, G., Elbin, S. D., & Hill, M. G. (1987). Attribution and social comparison processes in depression. *Journal of Personality and Social Psychology, 52*, 605–610.

Weber, M. (1971). *Max Weber: The interpretation of social reality* (J. E. T. Eldridge, Ed.). New York: Scribner's.

Webster, D. M. (1993). Motivated augmentation and reduction of the overattribution bias. *Journal of Personality and Social Psychology, 65*, 261–271.

Webster's Ninth New Collegiate Dictionary (1989). Springfield, MA: Merriam-Webster.

Wegener, D. T., & Petty, R. E. (1995). Flexible correction processes in social judgment: The role of naive theories in corrections for perceived bias. *Journal of Personality and Social Psychology, 68*, 36–51.

Wegner, D. M. (1989). *White bears and other unwanted thoughts*. New York: Viking/Penguin.

Wegner, D. M. (1994). Ironic processes of mental control. *Psychological Review, 101*, 34–52.

Wegner, D. M., Sparrow, B., & Winerman, L. (2004). Vicarious agency: Experiencing control over the movements of others. *Journal of Personality and Social Psychology, 86*, 838–848.

Wegner, D. M., & Wenzlaff, R. M. (1996). Mental control. In E. T. Higgins & A. W. Kruglanski (Eds.), *Social psychology: Handbook of basic principles* (pp. 466–492). New York: Guilford.

Weinberger, D. A., Schwartz, G. E., & Davidson, R. J. (1979). Low-anxious, high-anxious, and repressive coping styles: Psychometric patterns and behavioral and physiological responses to stress. *Journal of Abnormal Psychology, 88*, 369–380.

Weiner, B. (1972). *Theories of motivation: From mechanism to cognition.* Chicago: Rand McNally.

Weiner, B. (1985). An attributional theory of achievement motivation and emotion. *Psychological Review, 92*, 548–573.

Weiner, B., Frieze, I., Kukla, A., Reed, L., Rest, S., & Rosenbaum, R. M. (1971). Perceiving the causes of success and failure. In E. E. Jones, D. E. Kanouse, H. H. Kelley, R. E. Nisbett, S. Valins, & B. Weiner (Eds.), *Attribution: Perceiving the causes of behavior* (pp. 95–120). Morristown, NJ: General Learning Press.

Weinstein, T. A. R., Capitanio, J. P., & Gosling, S. D. (2008). Personality in animals. In O. P. John, R. W. Robins, & L. A. Pervin (Eds.), *Handbook of personality: Theory and research* (3rd ed., pp. 328–348). New York: Guilford Press.

Wellman, B., Carrington, P., & Hall, A. (1988). Networks as personal communities. In B. Wellman & D. Berkowitz (Eds.), *Social structure: A network approach.* New York: Cambridge University Press.

Wellman, H. M. (1990). *The child's theory of mind.* Cambridge, MA: MIT Press.

Wells, R. S., & Higgins, E. T. (1989). Inferring emotions from multiple cues: Revealing age-related differences in "how" without differences in "can." *Journal of Personality, 57*, 747–771.

Wells, W. D., Weinert, G., & Rubel, M. (1956). Conformity pressure and authoritarian personality. *Journal of Psychology: Interdisciplinary and Applied, 42*, 133–136.

Werner, H. (1957). *Comparative psychology of mental development.* New York: International Universities Press.

Wertheimer, M. (1923). Untersuchunger zur Lehre van der Gestalt: II. *Psychologische Forschung, 4*, 301–350.

White, R. W. (1959). Motivation reconsidered: The concept of competence. *Psychological Review, 66*, 297–333.

Wicklund, R. A. (1974). *Freedom and reactance.* New York: John Wiley & Sons.

Wicklund, R. A., & Brehm, J. W. (1976). *Perspectives on cognitive dissonance.* Hillsdale, NJ: Erlbaum.

Wicklund, R. A., & Gollwitzer, P. M. (1982). *Symbolic self-completion.* Hillsdale, NJ: Erlbaum.

Wiener, N. (1948). *Cybernetics: Control and communication in the animal and the machine.* Cambridge, MA: M.I.T. Press.

Williams, B. (1985). *Ethics and the limits of philosophy.* Cambridge, MA: Harvard University Press.

Williams, K., & Karau, S. (1991). Social loafing and social compensation: The effects of expectations of coworker performance. *Journal of Personality and Social Psychology, 61*, 570–581.

Williams, K., Karau, S., & Bourgeois, M. (1993). Working on collective tasks: Social loafing and social compensation. In M. A. Hogg & D. Abrams (Eds.), *Group motivation: Social psychological perspectives* (pp. 130–148). London: Harvester Wheatsheaf.

Williams, Jr., R. M. (1979). Change and stability in values and value systems: A sociological perspective. In M. Rokeach (Ed.), *Understanding human values: Individual and societal.* New York: The Free Press.

Williams, S. L. (1992). Perceived self-efficacy and phobic disability. In R. Schwarzer (Ed.), *Self-efficacy: Thought control of action* (pp. 149–176). Washington, D. C.: Hemisphere.

Wilson, T. D., & Gilbert, D. T. (2003). Affective forecasting. In M. P. Zanna (Ed.), *Advances in experimental social psychology* (Vol. 35, pp. 345–411). New York: Elsevier.

Wilson, T. D., Lisle, D., Schooler, J. W., Hodges, S. D., Klaaren, K. J., & LaFleur, S. J. (1993). Introspecting about reasons can reduce post-choice satisfaction. *Personality and Social Psychology Bulletin, 19*, 331–339.

Wilson, T. D., & Schooler, J. W. (1991). Thinking too much: Introspection can reduce the quality of preferences and decisions. *Journal of Personality and Social Psychology, 60*, 181–192.

Wilson, T. D., Wheatley, T. P., Meyers, J. M., Gilbert, D. T., & Axsom, D. (2000). Focalism: A source of durability bias in affective forecasting. *Journal of Personality and Social Psychology, 78*, 821–836.

Wilson, W. (1967). Correlates of avowed happiness. *Psychological Bulletin, 67*, 294–306.

Winkielman, P., & Cacioppo, J. T. (2001). Mind at ease puts a smile on the face: Psychophysiological evidence that processing facilitation elicits positive affect. *Journal of Personality and Social Psychology, 81*, 989–1000.

Witkin, H. A., Dyk, R. B., Faterson, H. F., Goodenough, D. R., & Karp, S. A. (1962). *Psychological Differentiation.* Potomac, MD: Erlbaum.

Witkin, H. A., & Goodenough, D. R. (1977). Field dependence and interpersonal behavior. *Psychological Bulletin, 84*, 661–689.

Witkin, H. A., Oltman, P. K., Raskin, E., & Karp, S. A. (1971). *A manual for the embedded figures test.* Palo Alto, CA: Consulting Psychologists Press.

Wood, J. V. (1989). Theory and research concerning social comparisons of personal attributes. *Psychological Bulletin, 106*, 231–248.

Woodworth, R. S. (1899). Accuracy of voluntary movements. *Psychological Review, 3*, 1–101.

Woodworth, R. S. (1918). *Dynamic psychology.* New York: Columbia University Press.

Woodworth, R. S. (1921). *Psychology: A study of mental life.* New York: Holt.

Woodworth, R. S. (1940). *Psychology* (4th ed.) New York: Henry Holt & Company.

Woodworth, R. S. (1958). *Dynamics of behavior.* New York: Holt.

Woodworth, R. S., & Schlosberg, H. (1954). *Experimental pscyhology* (rev. ed.). New York: Holt, Rinehart, & Winston.

Wright, H. F. (1937). *The influence of barriers upon strength of motivation.* Durham, NC: Duke University Press.

Wright, J. C., & Mischel, W. (1987). A conditional approach to dispositional constructs: The local predictability of social behavior. *Journal of Personality and Social Psychology* (Special Issue: Integrating personality and social psychology), *53*, 1159–1177.

Wright, R. A. (1996). Brehm's theory of motivation as a model of effort and cardiovascular response. In P. M. Gollwitzer & J. A. Bargh (Eds.), *The psychology of action: Linking cognition and motivation to behavior* (pp. 424–453). New York: Guilford.

Wright, R. A. (2008). Refining the prediction of effort: Brehm's distinction between potential motivation and motivation intensity. *Social and Personality Psychology Compass*, *2*, 682–701.

Wundt, W. (1999). *Outlines of psychology*. In R. H. Wozniak (Ed.), *Classics in Psychology, 1896: Vol 35, Outlines of Psychology*. Bristol, UK: Thoemmes Press (Original publication, 1896)

Wyer, R. S., Jr., & Gordon, S. E. (1984). The cognitive representation of social information. In R. S. Wyer, Jr. & T. K. Srull (Eds.), *Handbook of social cognition* (Vol. 2, pp. 73–150). Hillsdale, NJ: Erlbaum.

Yerkes, R. M., & Dodson, J. D. (1908). The relation of strength of stimulus to rapidity of habit-formation. *Journal of Comparative Neurology and Psychology*, *18*, 459–482.

Zajonc, R. B. (1968a). Attitudinal effects of mere exposure. *Journal of Personality and Social Psychology*, *9*, 1–27.

Zajonc, R. B. (1968b). Cognitive theories in social psychology. In G. Lindzey & E. Aronson (Eds.), *The handbook of social psychology* (Vol. 1, pp. 320–411). Reading, MA: Addison-Wesley.

Zanna, M. P., Lepper, M. R., & Abelson, R. P. (1973). Attentional mechanisms in children's devaluation of a forbidden activity in a forced-compliance situation. *Journal of Personality and Social Psychology*, *28*, 355–359.

Zanna, M. P., & Rempel, J. K. (1988). Attitudes: A new look at an old concept. In D. Bar-Tal & A. W. Kruglanski (Eds.), *The social psychology of knowledge* (pp. 315–334). Cambridge, England: Cambridge University Press.

Zeidner, M., & Endler, N. S. (1996). *Handbook of coping: Theory, research, applications*. Oxford, England: John Wiley & Sons.

Zeigarnik, B. (1938). On finished and unfinished tasks. In W. D. Ellis (Ed.), *A source book of Gestalt psychology* (pp. 300–314). New York: Harcourt, Brace, & World.

Zhang, S., Higgins, E. T., & Chen, G. Q. (2011). Managing others like you were managed: How prevention focus motivates copying interpersonal norms. *Journal of Personality and Social Psychology*, *100*, 647–663.

Zhou, R., & Pham, M. (2004). Promotion and prevention across mental accounts: When financial products dictate consumers' investment goals. *Journal of Consumer Research*, *31*, 125–135.

Zillmann, D., Johnson, R. C., & Day, K. D. (1974). Attribution of apparent arousal and proficiency of recovery from sympathetic activation affecting excitation transfer to aggressive behavior. *Journal of Experimental Social Psychology*, *10*, 503–515.

Zimmerman, C., & Bauer, R. A. (1956). The effect of an audience on what is remembered. *Public Opinion Quarterly*, *20*, 238–248.

Zou, X. (2009). *Social networks and subjective well-being: Regulatory fit between self-regulation and network structure*. Unpublished doctoral dissertation, Columbia University.

INDEX